BEYOND BOKHARA

Also available from Century

Mountains of the Gods *Ian Cameron*
Mountains of the Middle Kingdom *Galen Rowell*

BEYOND BOKHARA

The Life of William Moorcroft
Asian Explorer and Pioneer Veterinary Surgeon
1767–1825

GARRY ALDER

CENTURY PUBLISHING
LONDON

Copyright © Garry Alder 1985

First published in Great Britain in 1985
by Century Publishing Co. Ltd,
Portland House,
12–13 Greek St, London WIV 5LE

British Library Cataloguing in Publication Data

Alder, Garry
  Beyond Bokhara: the life of William Moorcroft,
  Asian explorer and pioneer veterinary surgeon,
  1767–1825.
  1. Moorcroft, William   2. Explorers—England
  —Biography   3. Explorers—Asia—Biography
  I. Title
  915′.043′0924   DS5.95

  ISBN 0 7126 0722 6

Photoset by Rowland Phototypesetting Ltd, Bury St Edmunds, Suffolk
Printed in Great Britain in 1985 by
Butler & Tanner Ltd, Frome, Somerset

Contents

List of Maps and Line Illustrations

Introduction

BIOGRAPHY FOR THE academic historian is a hazardous business. He who attempts it is liable to be dismissed by his sceptical peers as a member of what one has called 'the Ruritanian school of history, a pleasant region halfway between history proper and the historical novel'.[1] It is true that scholarly biographies of the great and the famous are still occasionally received with acclaim. But to attempt the life of an unknown man and, worse, a man about whom the evidence was often scanty or non-existent is professional folly. And to take more than twenty years over the task, however good the reasons, seems like folly compounded to the point of professional suicide. In these circumstances the author may perhaps be forgiven a personal word of explanation about the protracted gestation of this work.

Just why and how the Moorcroft story came to be so conspicuously neglected until comparatively recently is explained in the final chapter. The current revival of interest in him did not really begin until the 1950s when a senior veterinarian and historian, Jack Barber-Lomax, began gathering information for a Moorcroft life to be completed in retirement, but he was defeated by the sheer scale of the task and the pressure of his other commitments. I owe a very great debt indeed to Mr Barber-Lomax for so generously placing at my disposal the fruit of his researches over many years. In the late fifties another would-be biographer, Miss Rachel Gibb, was also at work on a popular life of Moorcroft. That project was cut short by her tragic death. It was at that moment that I fell heir to the task. I had first encountered Moorcroft a few years before while working on a study of India's northern frontiers. Like so many others I became intrigued by the little I knew, and the lot that nobody seemed to know, about him. In the years since then I have followed his trail both here and abroad. During that time I and others who fell under his spell have produced a sprinkling of lectures, articles, talks, chapters and even a radio programme about one aspect or another of his multi-faceted life. More recently, trekking parties in the Himalayas and beyond have followed parts of his route. Moreover, thanks to the recent initiative of the Veterinary History Society, the site of his practice in Oxford Street, London, is now marked with a memorial plaque. All this is as welcome as it is overdue. But it is scarcely enough. Plentiful as the scattered pebbles now are, they have not before been assembled into the solid cairn – that 'plain record' which he asked for[2] and so richly deserves.

The book's construction has not been easy. The attempt to get under the skin of a man across the centuries is always difficult. Biography, said Mark Twain, can only provide the clothes and buttons of a man, not the man himself.[3] But Moorcroft has presented some especial problems. First of all there is the immense scale of his journeys. The historian who follows his trail needs a stout pair of lungs as well as boots. In my attempts to pursue him along every permissible inch of the way (and sometimes just a little bit further) I have been arrested and detained in India, robbed in Afghanistan, buried in snow drifts in Iran, nearly murdered in Turkey and half frozen near the border of Tibet. Moorcroft, of course, would not have been surprised or very bothered at any of this. Infinitely more happened to him.

Then there is the man himself. He was active, often with distinction, in so many diverse fields and so far ahead of his contemporaries that his biographer often feels the need for a very large panel of experts to advise him. Then there are the sources. For the last six years of Moorcroft's life, the period of the great journey, there are more than 10,000 closely written pages of these, a vast and often nearly illegible sea in which a researcher can disappear for months at a time. This *embarras de richesses* is, or was, counterpointed by an almost total absence of primary information about the first forty years of his life. And for the years in between, although the scattered and very incomplete official record is adequate as a minimum, there is practically nothing to illumine his private and intimate world *entre les draps*. Even the written record that has survived is often less than helpful. Moorcroft, as he well knew and ruefully admitted, was at his worst on paper. His tangled, indigestible and long-limbed prose, painfully wrought from one heavily corrected draft to another, is often more of a barrier than a bridge to the vividly engaging man behind it. I have nowhere attempted to paper over the gaps, either with psycho- or pseudo-history and have asserted nothing that may not clearly be rested upon the surviving evidence. When occasionally I have found it necessary to pass from fact to speculation I have always made this clear. I have, as conscientiously and accurately as the evidence permits, delineated the clothes and buttons but I am only too well aware that the spirit of the man who wore them has often eluded me. It is at least partial consolation that Moorcroft's contemporaries and friends often felt the same way about him. They glimpsed but could not grasp, knew but seem rarely to have understood.

It was, I believe, Carlyle who asserted that it is as hard to write a good life as to live one. It can also take nearly as long. As if the inherent difficulties and delays were not great enough, I compounded them one nightmare winter day in Afghanistan by being robbed, not only of the completed manuscript of the book but also of most of the copious notes from which it had been written going back over more than fifteen years.

All this is not meant to suggest that the long pilgrimage in search of William Moorcroft has merely been one unhappy catalogue of difficulty, distance, delay, disaster and disappointment. On the contrary there have been magical occasions when the long intervening years have been brought close as if by a zoom lens and the elusive, half-seen man in the far distance has for a breathless moment seemed almost near enough to touch. I recall, for example, searching alone all one long golden day among the cool, purple caves high on the tawny cliffs above the huge figure of Buddha at Bamian in the Afghan Hindu Kush. Late in the afternoon, with patience and torch battery almost exhausted, suddenly there it was! Above a recess at the end of a large cave Moorcroft's unmistakable signature in charcoal, as sharp and as fresh as the moment when he had reached up and scratched it there, 150 years before to the very day. A magical moment. Or on another summer afternoon in the green and beautiful Mughal gardens of Shalimar just outside Lahore, discovering for the first time the little white pleasure pavilion in which Moorcroft lodged for a day or two in 1820 and described so minutely in his journal[4] that one could almost sense him at one's elbow in the shadows. Or again, this time in damp, midwinter London, unwrapping the lock of his wife's fine brown hair with its first hint of grey[5] just as he must have done when it and the news of her death near Paris finally caught up with him on the far side of the Himalayas. That lock of hair or the heavy thumbprint on a page of his journal made at about the same time[6] or the sharper, more deliberate impress of his oval signet-ring frozen into the wax at the foot of a commercial agreement[7] with a country no Briton had ever visited before – these small physical survivals from across the years and miles somehow bring one closer to the vanished physical presence of the man than do the mere strokes of his pen.

They are the nuggets which make up for all the tedious panning for the fine grains of the past. But there is another reward for the researcher as well. Like Moorcroft himself he encounters along the way the friendship, generosity, helpfulness and expertise of innumerable individuals who smooth his path and sometimes touch his heart. The research for this work has been long and so is the list of those who have helped to make it possible, so long indeed that an insultingly bare catalogue of the names of the more important of them is the only public acknowledgement I can offer in token of my gratitude. Mr J. W. Barber-Lomax I have already mentioned. He provided the veterinary expertise together with Professor L. P. Pugh and Lieutenant-Colonel John Hickman (Cambridge University); Ray Catton, Linda Warden, Professor F. R. Bell and Mrs M. Beryl Bailey (Royal Veterinary College); Professor D. L. Hughes and Dr J. R. Thomlinson (Liverpool University); Iain Pattison (Veterinary History Society); Professor M. Abdussalam (Institute of Veterinary Medicine, Berlin) and especially Miss Benita Horder (Royal College of Veterinary Surgeons). At the India Office Library and Records, where all Moorcroft research must start and finish, I received unnumbered kindnesses from the staff, many of whom I came over the years to regard as friends. In particular I must name the late Stanley Sutton and his successor, Joan Lancaster; Martin Moir; Richard Bingle; Tony Farrington; Valerie Phillips; Andrew Cook; Patricia Kattenhorn; Mildred Archer (and her late husband, W. G. 'Bill' Archer of the Victoria and Albert Museum). Unpublished Crown copyright material at the India Office and Patent Office is quoted by kind permission of the Controller of Her Majesty's Stationery Office. Others in this country to whom I am indebted for information and help are: Mayura Kanwar, Mrs C. Kelly (Royal Geographical Society), Jessie Dobson, John Hearsey, the late Brigadier Bill Kennett, John Keay, Richard Gibb, John Murray, Dr Stephen Pasmore, Ms A. Pope, Dr M. Waters, John Snelling, Dr Adam Stainton, A. Radcliffe-Smith (Royal Botanic Gardens, Kew), Colonel H. P. Croom-Johnson (Royal Green Jackets Trust), Robert Skelton (Victoria and Albert Museum), Major J. M. Tamplin (Ogilby Trust) and my mother. My sister, Gillian Clarkson, devoted hours to the improvement of my style and syntax; Sheila Dance and Chris Howitt to the maps; and 'Mac' Maclean and his team to the illustrations. In France Mme Girard-Madoux and Mme Saint-Dizier at the École Nationale Vétérinaire de Lyon and my friends in Paris, Jacques and Noreen Riols, were of great assistance as were, in Australia, Dr Julie Marshall, Ruth Schmedding of the National Library and Leal Squire-Wilson; in Turkey, Gay and Raoul de Pauligny; in Iran my former student Dr M. Reza Khajeh Dalooi and his family. In Afghanistan the hospitality and kindness of Mrs Pamela Drinkall (then at the British Embassy, Kabul), Max and Deborah Klimburg, Carla Grissman and Dick C. King was almost legendary. In Pakistan my old friend Sharif Farooq and the members of his family have never failed me in all the calls I have made upon them and Malik Muhammad Muzaffar, M. Ajmal Malik, Mr and Mrs Theo Phailbus, Peter Moss (then of the British Council, Lahore) and Drs Ronald and Molly Pont have all provided help. In Delhi the assistance of Mr M. M. Goswami (Ministry of External Affairs), Dr T. R. Sareen (National Archives of India) and the hospitality of Pamela and Norman Reynolds, coming as it did at a time of trouble, was invaluable. Professor and Mrs Parshotam Mehra and Dr C. L. Datta and their colleagues in the History Department at the Panjab University, Chandigarh provided me with friendship and a congenial home in which to work; Messrs R. L. Nanda and C. L. Sah Thulgaria generously made it possible for me to accompany the Naini Tal Mountaineering Club's 1974 assault on the Nanda Devi sanctuary; Dr Niranjan Shah (National Botanic Gardens, Lucknow) and ex-Lama Tsering Dorje, both of whom I met in the Himalayas at about that time, have shared with me then and since their extensive knowledge of the hills and Moorcroft's travels among them. My friends Christina Noble and Kranti Singh have been generous hosts and congenial travelling companions in the mountains and the latter was subsequently my guide to Pusa and its environs on the middle Ganges. More recently they have pioneered trekking parties of vets and others in and beyond the Himalayas 'in Moorcroft's footsteps'. I promised the members of one of the latest of these – Margaret, Sheila, Anne, Dorrie, Shelagh, Di, Anna, Rosie, Jadranka, Dinah, Mike, Bob, David, Kranti and Harry that I would acknowledge their companionship and patience during those Moorcroft sessions round the campfire under the stars – and I have now done so. In Calcutta, as doubtless Moorcroft did, I found the Asiatic Society's library in Park Street a haven in which to work and write and am grateful to the General Secretary and his staff. Indeed my debt to all the unsung people who staff the libraries, institutions and archives here and abroad in which I have found, or failed to find, Moorcroftiana is immense. Without them the writing of history would be almost impossible. Finally, I am glad to record my thanks to those bodies whose financial generosity made much of the research and travel possible: the Imperial Relations Trust, the British Academy, the Research Board of Reading University, the British Council and most of all the Wellcome Trust which made it possible for me to start all over again when everything had been lost.

Last, and most of all, I wish to thank my wife, who helped with the research, typed every word of the text, shared the driving overland to India, drew the vignettes and encouraged me in so many other ways to complete this work. Moorcroft, lover of nature and horses, was a man after her own heart. This book could not have been written without the two of them and to them both, along with my children, it is dedicated. For the inevitable errors, omissions and misjudgements I alone am responsible.

Garry Alder
University of Reading, 1985

1 LANCASHIRE CHILD, LIVERPOOL SURGEON,

1767–88

A FEW MILES east of Ormskirk in Lancashire the rounded outlines of Ashurst Beacon and Parbold Hill are plainly visible. Although only a few hundred feet above sea level, they command on a clear day an extensive view of the flat coastal plain of south-west Lancashire sandwiched between the Mersey in the south, the Ribble in the north and the open sea glinting away beyond Southport in the west. It is hard to believe, gazing over the ordered prosperity of this immensely fertile plain, that not so very long ago this was a desolate backwater of bog, peat moss and undrained moorland, broken on the higher ground by the dark loom of dense forest. So unattractive was it that the ancient British peoples, then the Romans and later still the Anglo-Saxon colonists coming across the Pennines from the east, all in turn passed it by. It was only inhabited, and then only thinly, when land-hungry Norse settlers from across the Irish Sea arrived on the barren sand-dunes and squat clay cliffs of its empty coast some time in the tenth century AD. Their names are there today, sown thickly across the map. Some of these Norse colonists made their settlements on the marshy shores of an extensive sea lake inshore of where Southport now stands, which later came to be called Martin Mere. According to the favoured tradition, it was one of the Norsemen called Orm who decided to remove his camp from the edge of this great stretch of water and settle instead 2 miles (3.2 kilometres) away across the moor on the lee side of the nearest hill, protected from the incessant west winds and on the drier sandstone soil of the ridge. The stockaded cluster of wooden huts and the little wooden chapel which later came to be built on that hill-top was soon being called Orm's church.

Eight hundred years later, by the middle of the eighteenth century, Ormskirk had grown into a compact market town, its narrow streets clustering round and below the fine early perpendicular church with its massive, squat, red sandstone tower standing shoulder to shoulder with all that was left of the adjacent spire. This structure, paying the price for its temerity in challenging the seaborne gales on this exposed hill-top, had crashed down in 1731. The little town was celebrated locally for its weekly market, its annual Easter fair and its gingerbread. It had very early established an easy ascendancy over the satellite villages which grew up on the drier ground on the moor round about.

Slowly, as year followed year, the axe and fire and hand-dug drain of man tamed the sterile disorder of much of the flat, surrounding countryside and sprinkled its black soil with small farms and scattered cottages. It was a long and very slow business. Neither Ormskirk nor Liverpool were thought worth a mention in the Domesday Book and the cursory treatment of the whole area in the survey is testimony to its emptiness and poverty. So it remained, a rural backwater with a thin population and a unique regional accent, cut off from the rest of the country without through roads of any significance and well to the west of the main north–south axis running up through Lancaster and Preston. Even Liverpool, only a tiny cluster of houses round its muddy 'pool' on the swirling tidal waters of the Mersey estuary, remained small and unimportant until about 1700. Both the coal seams which enriched and impoverished so much of Lancashire and the cotton industries centred on Manchester, left this part of the country largely untouched. The coastal plain round Ormskirk, although still divided by large and dangerous 'mosses' of undrained soil, remained predominantly a land of small farms and holdings of no more than about 50 acres (20 hectares) each.

Gradually, however, a few families consolidated their holdings into bigger estates of several hundred acres and built the 'halls' whose sites and names survive on the map today. Just east of Ormskirk was Lathom House, seat of the Stanleys, the Earls of Derby, and later of the Bootle family. East again on the slopes of Ashurst Beacon stood the home of the Ashursts. On the other side of Ormskirk, a few miles to the north-west towards Martin Mere, was Scarisbrick Hall, later the home of the Ecclestons. These and the other great families of the area, Royalists to a man and many of them Catholics, paid a heavy price for their loyalty to the king during the Civil War.[1] But when it was all over and another Charles Stuart was back on his throne in distant London, these families hastened into Ormskirk in September 1664 to record their pedigrees and coats of arms and justify their claims to be gentlemen before the king's Visitor. The Scarisbricks and Ecclestons were represented, as were the Ashursts, Bootles and the Stanleys of Lathom. So too were the Moorcrofts of Ormskirk.[2]

There had probably been Moorcrofts, that is those who dwelt on or owned an enclosed field on the moor, here from the very earliest settlements. There is clear evidence of their presence from 1200 onwards. By the time the first Ormskirk parish registers begin in the sixteenth century the Moorcrofts had spread all over the surrounding district in considerable numbers.[3] One Moorcroft has left his name on one of the ancient bells up in the Ormskirk tower, while below it and around it lie the bones of many others. Of course most of them were humble farmers or local tradesmen. The majority of the Moorcrofts married at Ormskirk in the eighteenth century were illiterate,[4] but those Ormskirk Moorcrofts who claimed in 1664 to be gentry would have been clearly distinguishable by their wealth and education from most of their humbler namesakes, even if they could claim no coat of arms. It was one of their descendants, Richard Moorcroft, grandfather of William, who in April 1741 married in Ormskirk church the heiress of another prominent local family, the Prescotts.[5] Richard and Dorothy Moorcroft settled first at Bispham, a mile or two north of Ashurst Hall, on land given to them by Henry Ashurst where they built themselves a house. They seem to have devoted themselves to managing their extensive lands and especially to dairy farming. For all the wealth of her family, his grandmother, Moorcroft recalled, was a practical woman who ran the dairy herself and kept it spotlessly clean. In 1747 Richard and Dorothy Moorcroft knew both catastrophe and consolation, both of which were to have important consequences for their future grandson. The great cattle plague of 1747 apparently wiped out the greater part of their dairy herd[6] but in the June of that same year they brought their little daughter, Ann, to be baptized in the fine, six-sided font at Ormskirk church.

Almost exactly twenty years later, on 25 June 1767, Ann was back, bringing her own first child to be baptized.[7] He was probably about a month old.[8] Ann Moorcroft, for she was still unmarried, chose for her son a name very popular among the Ormskirk Moorcrofts. She called him William. Although she could not have known it, Ann's illegitimate son was part of that astonishing population explosion which took place in Lancashire in the second half of the eighteenth century and which remains even today something of a mystery.[9] Certainly illegitimacy, as the Ormskirk registers attest with brazen frequency, was very common at the time. Fortunately for Ann and her bastard son they did not have to depend on local charity or the rigours of life on the current agricultural labourer's wage of 1s. 6d. (15p) a week,[10] for they lived with Richard Moorcroft. By that time he was living in or near Ormskirk itself and he was, of course, comfortably off. Quite apart from his own lands, those inherited through his wife were large enough when divided up later to serve 'as a competency to several families of respectability'.[11] There is evidence in the Lancashire Record Office of Richard Moorcroft's extensive landed interests and we know that even one of his tenants could be described as 'a large farmer'.[12] One of William Moorcroft's earliest childhood memories was of riding round Richard Moorcroft's estate, probably up in the saddle with his grandfather, fascinated by the humble oat porridge and 'hasty pudding' on which the servants of this tenant farmer seemed to subsist.[13]

We know almost nothing of William's boyhood years. He would have been sent off to school at about 7 or 8, perhaps to nearby Croston (where the schoolmaster later became one of his grandfather's executors). More probably he went either to the ancient grammar school just behind Ormskirk church where the Revd Naylor administered a heavy traditional diet of the classics, or to one of the private schools for the more well-to-do in nearby Church Street or Burscough Street. Later he certainly had a facility with Latin and Greek – and had neglected practical subjects like botany[14] – all of which suggests the traditionally narrow curriculum of the ancient grammar schools of the day. By today's standards, the school regime would have seemed hard, the working days long and the holidays few. Out of school William's life would have been framed by the ancient little market town, dominated by its fine old church where the Revd Knowles had been vicar for as long as most could remember. He would have grown familiar with Ormskirk's narrow, sloping streets, the

[3]

ancient houses with their jutting gables and jumbled roof lines, the bowed shop windows with the gleaming iridescence of their bull's-eye panes, the glazed half-doors and the steep, worn steps down into their dark interiors. There was the bustle of market day every Thursday, the old ducking stool still on the edge of the town field towards Aughton, the worn stocks and the horse-drawn fire engine with its leather hoses. There was the excitement of the annual Easter fair and, almost equally well known in the district, the legendary skill of Ormskirk's ratcatcher, Edmund Heathcote. These would have been some of the landmarks of the small and intimate rural world in which the young William Moorcroft grew to adolescence.[15] It was probably as good a prep-aration for adult life as any to be had in the kingdom. The warm west winds of the area usually kept the worst of the snow away, the air was good and the water excellent. Many of the local folk lived to a great age[16] and William Moorcroft himself in his middle years had the energy of a man half his age.

He was also very fortunate in the opportunities which his grandfather's wealth and friendships brought him. Richard Moorcroft was an educated man and he had a library of books and manuscripts which he later left to William. On one occasion he rebuked the lad with a Latin tag for writing his name on the wall of an ancient ruin.[17] One of Richard's friends and neighbours was Thomas Eccleston who came to live at Scarisbrick Hall on the north-west side of Ormskirk in 1778. Richard Moorcroft and Thomas Eccleston, rich in both capital and leisure, were very active in that movement of scientific farming and agricultural improvement which is such a marked feature of the late eighteenth century. Eccleston in particular was 'a great promoter of improvement in every kind of agriculture'.[18] His extensive and well-wooded estates witnessed such a series of experiments in horse- and cattle-breeding, in manures, in crops, machinery and drainage, that almost every year in the 1780s and 1790s he was able to claim in his notebook that he was 'the first ever in this county' to attempt them.[19] Even the king himself was aware of Eccleston's pioneering work.[20] The new Leeds and Liverpool canal ran for several miles through Eccleston's lands in its great sweep round the west and north side of the Ormskirk ridge and he designed and built at his own expense cuts from it to serve the needs of his own estate.[21] His most ambitious undertaking, however, was the attempt which he began in 1781 to drain Martin Mere, even then still covering 3600 acres (1456 hectares) of good soil. It was a big project requiring huge gates and banks to hold back the sea, over 100 miles (160 kilometres) of ditching and the deepening and widening of the ancient drain for 5 miles (8 kilometres) by armies of labourers working sometimes 20 feet (6 metres) below the surface.[22]

Eccleston seems to have treated the young William Moorcroft as a son and Moorcroft later referred to him as 'my more than father'.[23] Although Eccleston had sons of his own he seems to have formed a very close relationship with the young man and fostered in him that love for the land and its management which was already in his blood and which remained with him to the end of his days. William spent hours up at the old house at Scarisbrick listening while

Eccleston discussed his dreams for Martin Mere with the Duke of Bridge-water's canal engineer, John Gilbert. Moorcroft came to know him well.[24] Eccleston also introduced Moorcroft to the greatest stock-breeder of the age, Robert Bakewell. Later in the mid-1790s he was shown over Bakewell's Leicestershire estate by the great man himself shortly before he died.[25] A much more shadowy figure than Eccleston, although very important in the early world of the young William Moorcroft, was Eccleston's close friend Colonel Henry Aston. Aston seems to have been another wealthy and improving farmer on his lands across the Mersey in Cheshire. He was a stock-breeder and like Eccleston was in touch with Bakewell and known to the king. Moorcroft later described himself as Aston's 'protégé' and 'friend'.[26]

These three wealthy and civilized men – Thomas Eccleston, Henry Aston and Richard Moorcroft – seem to have done all that could be done to offset William's lack of an acknowledged father. They gave him affection, connections and probably 'considerable sums of money' as well. Those words come from Richard Moorcroft's will. His support of his grandson was as generous after his death as it had been during his lifetime[27] but his prime responsibility had to be to his surviving daughter Ann, especially when she married a not very prosperous junior civil servant called Henry Paine. In due course they had two children, William's half brother and sister.[28] Eccleston and Aston also had families of their own to provide for. Perhaps if William Moorcroft had had the more conventional beginnings which his family's position gave him a right to expect, the world would never have heard of him. He would have inherited the Moorcroft lands in and around Ormskirk, devoted himself to the practical problems of agriculture and improvement which always fascinated him, married the daughter of a local landed family and ended his days under one of the black, polished tablets in the floor of Ormskirk church. Since, however, William could look to no landed estate of his own – although later in his life he might have inherited one in England and one in India it seems[29] – then it was obviously important to give him a training for a career which would allow him to support himself in comfort.

One such career was surgery. At that time it was just shaking itself free from the old and harmful connection with the barber's trade and becoming a respectable profession in its own right, although the surgeon's role was still subordinate in public estimation to the sharply distinguished one of the physician. Once William Moorcroft had decided on surgery he could either attend the private school of an eminent surgeon like the great John Hunter down in London, or he could go to one of the university medical schools, which were mostly in Scotland, or he could apprentice himself to a practising surgeon at one of the larger hospitals.[30] The last of these alternatives almost suggested itself. Not very far to the south of Ormskirk, the infirmary at Liverpool had attracted a small group of gifted physicians and surgeons, one of the most influential of whom was an Ormskirk man, Dr Joseph Brandreth. Moreover, Eccleston was a financial supporter of the infirmary.[31] It was probably the influence of these two which secured for the young William Moorcroft one of the two available surgical apprenticeships with the Liverpool surgeon John

Lyon. So it was that some time in the early 1780s William Moorcroft finally left his country childhood behind him and set off on the 13-mile (20-kilometre) journey down the new turnpike road to Liverpool. We know tantalizingly little about him as he reached this milestone in his life. That he was intelligent and as well read and educated as he was well connected has already been mentioned. Physically slight and rather short, he was nevertheless strong, active and tough, extremely sharp-sighted, a good shot, a strong swimmer and a competent rider. He was also cleanshaven and right-handed. Anything beyond this is mere conjecture.[32]

Today Liverpool has spread its sooty tentacles across most of the once fair country between it and the rising ground at Aughton next door to Ormskirk.[33] In the early 1780s, however, it must have seemed very far away and strange. Some Ormskirk folk would never have visited it, nor in those days would there have been very much to visit. As late as 1700 Liverpool only housed about 5000 people in the clustered streets and houses behind the tidal 'pool' which served it as a harbour. Since then, however, its growth had been spectacular, doubling in size every twenty or thirty years until in the 1780s it had a population of about 40,000. By modern standards it was still, of course, tiny. You could walk all round it in a brisk hour and a half up on the open heath where the twenty-seven windmills turned, but after the market town cosiness of Ormskirk it would still have seemed very large indeed to William Moorcroft. Viewed from across the river it was dominated by the spires and towers of its many churches and in the foreground by the bulk of the Old Goree ware-houses. Away to the left towards the north was the enormous castle-like gaol, big enough to hold half of Liverpool it was said, and the new fort, bristling impressively but ineffectually with cannon, and standing as a constant reminder of the recent American war. Central to Liverpool's growth and prosperity were its bustling new docks crowded with shipping, their masts and spars soaring high above the neighbouring streets. Even critical visitors to Liverpool – 'this disgustful place' as one of them called it in 1780 – found the docks 'stupendously grand'.[34] Into them came the sugar, tobacco and raw cotton of the Atlantic trade; out of them went cotton goods, salt and coal and all the miscellaneous goods of the coastal trade. Perhaps the most profitable commodity of all to be carried in the Liverpool ships was never even seen on its broad quays. This was just as well for if the kindly Liverpudlians, taking a stroll on the stone quays and admiring the fine lines of some of these ships loading goods for the African Guinea Coast, had been able to see them a month or two later as they rolled across the Atlantic with their holds often sardine-packed with a cargo of black slaves for the American and West Indian markets, the outcry against the inhuman slave trade would have begun much earlier than it did. For the moment though this was Liverpool's boom time, the great decade of prosperity which began in 1783 and was sandwiched between the wars of the American and French revolutions. By the end of those ten years it had become, after London, the second port of the kingdom.

Behind the docks and quays jostled the bustling, narrow streets of the town. A few grand Georgian houses had gone up recently in Duke Street, Park Lane and Great George Street but most of the city's wealthy merchants and shippers – and doctors – still lived over their counting houses, offices and consulting rooms in narrower streets down near the docks. Liverpool was regarded in the 1780s as a healthy place although we would not have found it so. Drinking water was delivered by horse and cart, the old pool brook was an open sewer running down Whitechapel and Paradise Streets, and although the earlier practice of emptying the contents of privies into the streets was much less common, the street cleaners were still in the habit of piling the soil of houses and streets into huge middens for several days, much to the discomfort of the drunken or unwary who ventured into the ill-lit and mostly unpaved streets after dark. By day the air would also have been heavy with additional smells from the innumerable breweries, the salt and copper works and the oil factory on the windward side of the town where the whale carcasses were melted down. The tang of salt from the river or tar from the docks must have come as a welcome relief. Less welcome reminders of the sea were the roisterings of the sailors ashore. During the American war, when much of the lawful trade of the town had come to a standstill and many shippers turned privateer, Liverpool had gained an unsavoury reputation as a lawless place. For a time the town was placed under a tight curfew every night. The return of peace and prosperity brought some improvement but the sailors' taverns and brothels still flourished. In 1787, while Moorcroft was living in the town, the municipal authorities were forced to publish new regulations against 'excessive drinking, blasphemy, profane swearing and cursing, lewdness, profanation of the Lord's day, or other dissolute, immoral or disorderly practice'.[35] All in all Liverpool in Moorcroft's day must have been a scruffy, cheerful, vibrant and bustling place, chiefly dedicated to the making of money but, as even its admirers were forced to admit, rather short on culture and the arts.

For all their shortcomings the citizens of eighteenth-century Liverpool could be open-handed as well as open-hearted when a clear need existed. Chief monument to their generosity and humanitarianism – and there were several – was the Liverpool Infirmary, opened in 1749 and built and run by public subscription for those too poor to pay for medical treatment. It was a handsome, redbrick building erected upon what used to be known as Shaw's Brow, on the site of what is now Liverpool's great St George's Hall complex. Today this is in the heart of the city but when Moorcroft first arrived at the infirmary's gates he stood on the very edge of the town. From here one could look across the river into Cheshire towards Bidston Hill where the signal flags announced the arrival of the incoming ships some hours before they could reach the river and docks down below. Up here on breezy Shaw's Brow in the 1780s the buildings and streets fell away and the windmills, rope-walks and the open heath began. A contemporary described the infirmary as:

a neat brick building ornamented with stone. The principal building has three storeys consisting of large wards for the reception of the patients, and other necessary apartments. It is connected by handsome colonnades with two spacious wings, which form the sailors' hospital. Before the building is a large area enclosed with a handsome iron gate and rails, and behind is a useful garden walled round. On the top of each building is erected a turret, and in the middle of the pediment in front is a good clock.[36]

As if to remind the onlooker that this ordered exterior belied the realities of life inside, a four-line stanza over the gate began not very encouragingly,

> O ye whose Hours exempt from Sorrow flow,
> Behold the seat of Pain, Disease and Woe.[37]

So it was. Although enlightened by eighteenth-century standards the infirmary was very different from the ordered calm and antiseptic cleanliness of the modern hospital. Its surviving records[38] give a good idea of what it was like while Moorcroft was there. There were about 100 in-patients, including six of each sex with venereal disease. They were looked after by half a dozen female nurses under the matron, Mrs Layton, and in addition there were two porters, a cook, chambermaid, washerwoman and apothecary, besides the casual employees like Mr Mason who came in every day to shave the patients (for £4 a year) and the visiting clergy who held daily prayers in the board room. In addition to salaries, other items of expenditure included ale in large quantities, hog's lard, surgeon's tow, leeches, candles, 'gallypotts', trusses, wooden legs and, ominously, coffins. Rules similar to those in other hospitals of the time forbade smoking, gaming, illicit drinking and foul language among the in-patients. In 1788 the medical gentlemen, not for the first time, had to ask that the bed-linen should be changed fortnightly, feet washed weekly and the chamber pots scalded daily. Despite recent building alterations and frequent attention to the evil-smelling 'necessary-houses', the bad effects of overcrowding in the large wards were all too obvious and led to urgent representations from the 'gentlemen of the Faculty'. As one of them wrote,

> When such a number as from twenty to fifty persons, many of them afflicted with ulcers and other diseases which tend to aggravate the putrescency of the fluids, are constantly confined together in a room just large enough to hold their beds, there is no doubt but the consequences must be pernicious ... if a particular cause of contagion prevails, it is by their means communicated to greater numbers than it would otherwise be.[39]

Events confirmed this warning. In December 1787 for example, when the wards had been closed up for some days against the bitter weather, a contagious fever made its appearance in the infirmary and spread very rapidly indeed.[40]

Without antibiotics, inoculations or any kind of reliable painkillers the physicians were largely helpless in the face of contagion of this kind and were compelled to rely on the mainly traditional remedies of the mediaeval pharmacopoeia, extensive bleeding and palliatives like cold water washing to reduce high temperature. This latter treatment was pioneered at the infirmary and later used by Moorcroft in the treatment of lockjaw.[41] The eighteenth century has been well called 'the age of agony'[42] but undoubtedly the chief inflicters of

[8]

it, at a period when there were neither anaesthetics nor reliable antiseptics, were the knives, probes and saws of the eighteenth-century surgeon.

Human surgery was still in the Stone Age.[43] There had, of course, been small and unspectacular advances in technique and anatomical understanding in the eighteenth century, but until the surgeon could cut deep without regard either to the contorted agonies of his fully conscious patient or to the fatal consequences of post-operational sepsis, the scope for surgery was necessarily very limited. The staple of the surgeon's work was the removal of superficial tumours, amputation and lithotomy. Speed and deftness were the essential qualities of this sort of surgery. More daring and fundamental work, say on the brain or stomach, was normally only practised where there was no other hope or in serious accident and casualty cases. This was the grim trade to which William Moorcroft was now apprenticed.

It would be some time, of course, before he would be allowed to practise it on the living. His first task would be to acquire a theoretical knowledge of anatomy, reinforced by dissecting sessions with his master during which he would learn how to use the tools of his trade on the human corpse. Dissection could be a vilely unpleasant task in those days before the discovery of reliable preservatives. In the heat of summer the dissector often worked at great risk to his own health. To make things worse suitable corpses were usually in short supply and until the 1830s the Liverpool surgeons were often compelled to risk the law and resort to the graveyard body snatchers for an adequate supply. After dissection of the corpse came surgery on the living. Under the rules of the infirmary the surgeons were only permitted two apprentices at a time and these were allowed to assist at the operating table and learn by watching their masters at work. To us it would seem a grim and casual business. In the 1780s it was a rare surgeon who washed his hands or put on proper protective clothing before operating. The patient, perhaps 'relaxed' with gin, rum or a sedative potion, would usually be lying on a plain wooden table, often tied down to prevent a sudden and possibly disastrous movement. The dressers and apprentice surgeons stood round with swabs and instruments to hand, ready if necessary to replace the sawdust-filled trays under the table when they could no longer absorb any more blood.

Our knowledge of Moorcroft's experiences as a surgeon is very scanty. He assisted on several occasions with the amputation of hands shattered beyond repair by the explosion of cheap guns intended for export to Africa.[44] He also treated many cases of sailors returning from that continent with the unpleasant Guinea worm which had, patiently and gently, to be extracted inch by inch by winding it round a quill. Towards the end of his life Moorcroft recalled that a combination of clumsiness and nerves during his first two attempts broke the worm in each case but 'the serious consequences of this accident made me more cautious and more successful on subsequent attempts'.[45] This, of course, was relatively simple compared with the more testing internal surgery with which in due course he became familiar. On Saturday mornings the in-patients in the so-called 'cutting ward' were visited. On Mondays and Thursdays the surgeons and their apprentices were in attendance at the out-patients' clinic and on most mornings at least one surgeon was at the dispensary in Church Street where both in- and out-patients were seen. In addition there were the private patients on whose fees the Liverpool physicians and surgeons really depended for they received nothing at all for their work at the infirmary and indeed often gave it financial support themselves.

It is too easy for us to dismiss as crude the efforts of eighteenth-century medicine and surgery to relieve human suffering. Crude and ignorant much of it certainly was but the fact remains that the medical men at the Liverpool Infirmary in the 1780s were for their time remarkably gifted as anatomists and surgeons and certainly of a higher general education than most of their equivalents could claim today. The majority of them had studied in London or at one of the great continental medical schools and most could claim to be the pioneers of at least modest innovations in their chosen fields. The most distinguished of all was probably Dr James Currie, author of a much reprinted biography of Robert Burns and a tireless worker in many good causes including, to his great credit, the campaign to abolish the slave trade. This, of course, was a particularly delicate issue in Liverpool with so many ships and men in the trade as has been mentioned. Nevertheless many Liverpool doctors, including John Lyon (and Moorcroft himself) were whole-hearted abolitionists.[46] Moreover in their capacity as examiners of the surgeons required by law to be licenced for each slave ship, they insisted on high standards and their failure rate was high. These men – Brandreth, Park, Alanson and the rest – must have been a powerful influence on William Moorcroft.

Most important of all, however, was his master, Dr John Lyon.[47] He had been on the staff of the infirmary since 1768 after studying as a house-pupil of one of the most celebrated British surgeons of the previous generation, Percival Pott of St Bartholomew's in London. Lyon, unusually, had qualifications both as a surgeon and a physician. By the time Moorcroft knew him he had amassed both a large fortune and a correspondingly large family of twelve surviving children, all but one of them girls it seems. He was a sincere Christian and a warm and kind-hearted man, tireless in many local good causes as well as his private practice and his unpaid medical and committee work at the infirmary. Moorcroft came to believe that Lyon was considerably underestimated as a surgeon, probably because he was always too busy to commit his experience to a major work. He was certainly responsible for some valuable innovations in surgical technique, especially in amputation surgery.[48] Moorcroft gradually came to love this good man and his family in their modest home in Peters Lane not far from the Old Dock. The relationship between them was very close, even in the narrow legalistic sense. By an indenture legally enforceable between them, Lyon, in return for a substantial payment from Richard Moorcroft, would have contracted to initiate his pupil in 'the Art and Mystery of a Surgeon and Apothecary' and provide for him 'sufficient and enough of Meat, Drink and Lodging' in his own house, probably for five or even seven years. Moorcroft for his part would have bound himself to diligent study, obedience, the keeping of his master's secrets and abstinence from fornication, adultery, the haunting of taverns and ale-houses, unlawful gambling . . . and marriage.[49] It is clear, however, that what began as a legal relationship developed during the years they worked and lived together into a friendship based on mutual respect and affection.

Lyon was, in fact, so impressed by his young pupil that he suggested that he should widen his experience by further study in London and on the Continent. When he had completed that, Lyon intended to take him into his lucrative private practice on equal terms as a partner and resign to Moorcroft his position as surgeon at the infirmary. All he asked in return was Moorcroft's verbal promise that he would take on Lyon's only surviving son, John, as a pupil and train him as he had been trained by the boy's father. This impressively generous proposal is further evidence of Moorcroft's acceptability as a person and the first indication of his unusual gifts as a surgeon. Pre-anaesthetic surgery required outstanding manual dexterity combined with strong arms and hands to overcome the resistance of tensed muscles, a precise knowledge of anatomy, the ability to think and work swiftly and to keep calm while causing intense suffering to a fully conscious patient. Moorcroft must have mastered all these skills before September 1786 when Lyon's son died.[50] No wonder Richard Moorcroft was proud of his grandson, who was not yet 20.[51] His future as one of Liverpool's leading surgeons and medical men seemed assured.

However, as was to happen in William Moorcroft's life again and again, just when the future seemed most settled the unexpected was waiting to send him in an entirely new direction. That is certainly how Moorcroft liked it. In this case the unexpected came in the form of a pregnant Longhorn heifer which, on 20 October 1788, fell down in her field over at Standish Hall near Wigan and died shortly afterwards. Before the day was out two more animals were attacked and died within forty-eight hours.

Local and ancient remedies were immediately attempted by the cow-leech. The sick animals were bled copiously, their discharging nostrils were smeared with tar, and herbal packs of garlic and bearsfoot were inserted in the dewlaps. Thus men had hoped in vain to ward off cattle plague in all its variant and destructive forms for centuries. However, on this occasion the threatened animals were the temporary responsibility of a man whose own stocks had often been decimated by similar outbreaks and who always preferred to look to science and reason rather than to tradition in every branch of agriculture. That man was Thomas Eccleston.[52] It was almost certainly Eccleston who sent for help to his medical friends at Liverpool, Dr Brandreth and Dr John Lyon. Not surprisingly they sent Moorcroft, then near the end of his surgical apprenticeship, with a set of instructions to do what he could to save the remaining animals at Standish. If the outbreak spread all Lancashire's cattle might be endangered.

Moorcroft arrived at Standish in the last week of October together with one of the best-known farriers of the district, a Mr Wilson.[53] Finding one animal already close to death with a swollen neck and laboured breathing, Moorcroft, in typical fashion, immediately performed a tracheotomy and considerably eased the last hours of the doomed creature by opening its windpipe. He then examined the rest of the stricken animals noting carefully the clinical symptoms and progress of the disease and, most unusual in animal medicine of that period, recording the extremely high pulse rates of each. There was, in truth, little that could be done for them – either then or indeed until the relatively recent development of the sulphonamide and antibiotic drugs and of serum therapy. Whatever the disease was, and the symptoms may suggest something different from but just as devastating as the rinderpest of the earlier and later cattle plagues, the main thing was to prevent it from spreading. Moorcroft did what he could to save or relieve the animals and record their symptoms. Reluctantly he bled one animal, mainly to observe the state of the blood. He tried to relieve the swellings of neck and head by incision. He used the fever treatment developed by Brandreth and Currie of reducing the soaring body temperatures of the animals by dashing cold water over them. He administered, as directed by his instructions, the traditional draughts of 'large quantities of Peruvian bark, in port wine, or ale' and later, on the advice of somebody else, 'two drachms of emetic tartar, a scruple of calomel, and ten grains of powdered opium', followed later by a mixture of laudanum, camphor and strong ale. He also applied a painful, blistering ointment to the swollen parts. If asked why he would have replied in terms similar to those of a respected veterinary writer seventy years later – 'By producing superficial inflammation we may be enabled to remove a deeper seated one.'[54] Nonsense, of course, and for the animal very painful and counter-productive nonsense, but it represented unchallenged orthodoxy then and for many years to come. Perhaps the luckiest of the diseased animals at Standish was the one Moorcroft killed in order to give it a very thorough *post mortem* investigation and compare his findings with those of the dead animals in whom the disease had run its lethal forty-eight-hour course. We can imagine him in shirt sleeves kneeling in the grass over the opened corpse of the cow, stopping every now and again to wipe his hands and write some words in his notebook.

> The enlargement of the head and neck was owing to a collection of yellow transparent fluid in the cellular membrane, which coagulated on exposure to a gentle heat. . . . The lungs were in some part eroded, in others mortification had actually taken place; and on opening the chest, a quantity of putrid air rushed out.

It was not very pleasant and it might have been highly dangerous.

The happenings in that Lancashire field, unimportant though they might seem, were for Moorcroft an experience which altered the whole course of his life and by a curious chain of events had repercussions across the Himalayas and the desert uplands of Central Asia. Not, of course, that anything he did for the diseased animals at Standish made the slightest difference to their fate. The outbreak probably remained local and unknown only because of the very sensible and thorough efforts he made to isolate the diseased animals when alive and bury their corpses when dead. These were the twin pillars of his treatment as he recalled them over thirty years later when faced once more with cattle plague on a massive scale in the hills of northern India.[55] What the estate labourers thought when the young medical gentleman from Liverpool insisted that the corpses were buried 6 feet (2 metres) down is, perhaps fortunately, not recorded! Moorcroft knew that they had been lucky to escape a major local catastrophe.

This thought may have encouraged him to listen very carefully when Eccleston, and perhaps his grandfather or Colonel Aston, began to suggest to him a novel possibility, probably when he was on his way back to Liverpool early in November 1788. The three men had all suffered extensive livestock losses over the years. 'Could any reward,' asked Eccleston, 'be too great for a preventative or cure of that fatal disorder, of which so many thousands die annually in this kingdom?' They would, he argued, never get one as things were at present 'owing to the ignorance of cow-doctors in their disorders'. What was needed was a 'Veterinarian School'.

> In other countries they have already found the benefit of that useful institution. I am informed, at Copenhagen, a Royal Veterinarian School is established; and our wise political neighbours have two, viz. one at Paris, the other at Lyons. From several of my acquaintance in France, I am informed that horse-surgery and every other branch of farriery is much improved since their establishment.[56]

The situation was very different in England. Although human surgery was no longer left to the ignorant attentions of the barbers, animal surgery was still the preserve of the equally ignorant village farrier or cow-leech. What was required was a practical, educated person who loved and had grown up with animals and who had a thorough scientific and medical training to devote himself to the reform of animal medicine. Science had revolutionized agriculture in recent years – imagine its potential in animal medicine! Whether Moorcroft was fired at once with excitement or whether his approach to the great decision which transformed his life was more deliberate, we shall never know. Thirty-five years later, however, he recalled his feelings at this second great turning-point in his life:

> If I were to devote myself to the improvement of a degraded profession, closely connected with the interests of agriculture, I might render myself much more useful to the country, than by continuing in one already cultivated by men of the most splendid talents. [I was] convinced by their arguments, but opposed by other friends, and especially by my master.[57]

John Lyon must have been particularly upset to hear that his favourite pupil was thinking of abandoning the profession in which he seemed so gifted – and for one which most physicians and surgeons, indeed most people, regarded as inferior and degrading. Delabere Blaine, later a friend of Moorcroft's in London, told how his own family were 'indescribably shocked and disgusted' at his own decision to forsake human for animal medicine.[58] For Moorcroft it was precisely the challenge of attempting 'to rescue a branch of medicine from a state of debasement' as he put it,[59] which would have appealed to him so much. All his life was confirmation of his willingness – and wish – to go beyond the limits accepted by the rest of his contemporaries.

[13]

2 VETERINARY STUDENT, LONDON AND FRANCE,

1788–92

VETERINARY MEDICINE WAS certainly debased at the end of the eighteenth century,[1] even when every allowance is made for the exaggerations of those surgeons and physicians who criticized and mocked the farriers and cow-leeches. Most of these animal doctors were certainly ignorant and illiterate men who relied mainly on the traditional medicines, drenches and purges. Some of these were compounded deliberately from the bizarre substances of mediaeval pharmacy like goose grease, crab's eyes, lungs of fox, liver of eel and penis of tortoise or the more readily available human and animal urine and excrement. The treatments were equally barbarous. Wounds were often deliberately kept open by the introduction of foreign bodies and painful festering was encouraged in the belief that the more pus produced the better. Bleeding was part of every farrier's repertoire, often on such a scale that the animal collapsed from loss of blood. So too was blistering the skin with an ointment of corrosive sublimate or similar and cauterizing by applying flaming turpentine to a wound or plunging a red-hot iron into skin sores to seal or destroy them. The red-hot iron was also sometimes used as an aid to primitive surgery as, for example, when flatulence was treated by boring with the iron from the anus into the rectum. And so it goes on. Even shoeing horses was done with such savage use of the paring knife and buttress that lameness, sometimes permanent, was the result. As for the farriers' horse surgery,

> We shall see them daily sacrificing horses, by boldly mangling the organised parts of the body, without knowing anything of its structure. How many muscles, and tendons, divided cross-ways! veins opened! nerves destroyed! membranes torn! and essential organs more or less affected, by the ignorant boldness of these unskilful operators.[2]

It is very easy to pile up such contemporary criticism to illustrate the abysmal state of the veterinary art in the late eighteenth century, but the resulting picture is probably something of a caricature for it takes no account of the honest and skilful efforts of men like the farrier, James Clark of Edinburgh, or the handful of medical men who had already occasionally turned their attentions to the sufferings of domesticated animals. Nevertheless it was

[14]

enough of a virgin field to tempt William Moorcroft at the end of 1788. Veterinary medicine appealed to his countryman's love of animals and agriculture, his fascination for the unknown, his new skill as a surgeon and his already sensitive social conscience.

The opposition of many of his friends is also not surprising, particularly that of John Lyon to what Moorcroft conceded to be 'conduct bordering on ingratitude'.[3] It was probably Lyon who in the end suggested that they should submit the whole disagreement to the arbitration of the great John Hunter, the leading British surgeon of the day.[4] Whether Lyon knew Hunter personally is uncertain. They had both been pupils of Percival Pott and would certainly have had mutual friends since most of the Liverpool men had studied in London at some stage of their careers. Perhaps Lyon had already been in touch with him to arrange for Moorcroft to attend Hunter's lectures now that his Liverpool apprenticeship was almost over. At all events, some time between mid-November 1788 and the following mid-January, Moorcroft made the long coach journey down to London.

His interview with Hunter probably took place at Hunter's house in Leicester Square. There were certainly no airs about the great man, notwithstanding his massive reputation and genius. Plain speaking and plain dressing, the soft Lowland burr of his conversation often sprinkled with oaths but a courteous listener, he would have heard Moorcroft out. It seems that they talked for some time before Hunter gave his verdict. It was characteristically trenchant: 'If he were not advanced in years,' he [Hunter] said, 'he himself would on the following day begin to study the profession in question.[5] This declaration for Moorcroft was decisive. It is not surprising that Hunter should express it. A year or two later he was lending his very powerful support to the establishment of a veterinary college in London and, even if he had no hand in drafting its 1791 prospectus, that document certainly expressed his views and the sort of things he may have said to William Moorcroft.

> Veterinary practice should be second only to human medicine. The state of human medicine today is evidence of what awaits the cultivation of the veterinary art in Britain. It requires the sacrifice of as many years to become a skilful veterinarian, as to become a skilful physician: the acquisition of the science and the practice of each is a task sufficient to engage one man's life. . . . The nation requires a veterinary school in which the structure and diseases of animals can be scientifically taught.[6]

So it did, but in 1789 there was still no veterinary college in Britain. For a time at least it seems that Moorcroft and Thomas Eccleston hoped that one could be established in time for Moorcroft's studies. On 20 January 1789 Eccleston finished a long letter to the editor of the *Transactions of the London Society of Arts* with a postscript giving his young friend all the publicity he decently could.

> Mr. Moorcroft . . . is a young man of the greatest abilities, and has agreed to turn his thoughts from the practice of physic and surgery, entirely to that of farriery in every branch, provided he can meet with sufficient and certain encouragement in the

[15]

establishment of a Veterinarian School. If you can point out any method likely to raise a subscription for such a purpose, you will confer a singular favour on all in the farming line.[7]

In fact initiatives were afoot which resulted only two years afterwards in the establishment of the London (later Royal) Veterinary College. In the meantime there was no alternative for an Englishman who wished to have a formal veterinary training but to go to one of the continental veterinary schools. The Agricultural Society at Odiham in Hampshire, from whose initiatives the London college eventually sprang, had decided only the previous year to send two young men to study at the veterinary school in Paris.[8] Had they moved more quickly to implement this decision Moorcroft would not have been the first Englishman ever to receive a formal veterinary education.

1789 of course was no ordinary year. It witnessed the beginning of that violent and progressive upheaval in France which led in turn to revolution, civil war, terror and eventually to a continental war which convulsed Europe for a generation and helped shape the modern world. None of this of course was apparent at first. To most patriotic Englishmen the events in France in the summer of 1789 seemed welcome. After all the revolution had destroyed an unacceptable tyranny and given France a constitutional monarchy closer to the British model. In Liverpool, as elsewhere in Britain, the events of 1789, and their anniversary for two years afterwards were celebrated with illuminations. There would certainly have seemed no reason to change the plans which were being made by Eccleston and Richard Moorcroft, on Hunter's advice, to send William to one of France's two veterinary schools. That at Alfort near Paris was nearer and richer but the school at Lyons was older and was believed to offer a more practical training. Moreover it had built its reputation on its success with local cattle plagues.[9] For Richard Moorcroft, who was paying the bulk of the fees, that may have been reason enough for favouring Lyons. Besides Lyons was less likely to be disturbed by the continuing revolutionary upheavals than Alfort. The best time to enter the Lyons school was either at the beginning of April or in November when the summer and winter courses respectively began. It was eventually agreed that Moorcroft should enrol at Lyons early the following year in the spring of 1790.

In the meantime he returned to London, apparently at Hunter's suggestion. He attended Hunter's lectures and those of his surgeon son-in-law, Everard Home, and took whatever opportunities came along to broaden his veterinary experience. We know of one such case from the pen of Thomas Prosser, an elderly physician who had taken up veterinary medicine late in life and was soon to become assistant to the first head of the London veterinary college. Prosser had been called in to treat a valuable stallion with an inflamed testicle and a high fever. When it began to look as though surgery would be necessary he consulted Everard Home who promised to come with Moorcroft. Prosser does not name Moorcroft but describes him as '. . . an ingenious gentleman, who is now prosecuting his studies in London, with every advantage of a medical education; and who, after spending some time in the *Veterinarian*

Academy in *Paris*, intends returning to this country, to practise *farriery*'. It can be nobody else. In the end Moorcroft came to see the horse alone. He put Prosser right on the pulse rate of the healthy horse and treated the stallion with poultices, leeches and suspended dressings until the abscess burst.[10]

We know very little else about these brief few months in London in 1789. In October he lodged for a time at Russell Court, then a small group of houses and stables on the west side of St James's Street just north of Cleveland Row.[11] Some time later he moved a few hundred yards north into Half Moon Street off Piccadilly.[12] In November he was successfully elected to membership of the Society of Arts in the Adelphi. Moorcroft is described as 'surgeon' in the subscription book and probably most of his early connections in London were among the medical fraternity. His principal proposer for membership was the Chancery Lane surgeon William Houlston, doubtless a relative of the physician of the same name at the Liverpool Infirmary. The treasurer of the Society of Arts did not move quite fast enough and by the time he applied to Russell Court and then perhaps to Half Moon Street for Moorcroft's first 2-guinea subscription, his quarry was already out of London and far away. That subscription was never paid.

Exactly when Moorcroft left England is uncertain. He may have crossed over with Eccleston to Ostend soon after Christmas 1789 and visited Bruges and Brussels before entering France on his way to Lyons[13] but the Dover–Calais crossing, favoured by most English travellers of the time, is the more likely.[14] The 76 miles (121 kilometres) to Dover from London could be accomplished in one long day. Early next morning he would have been down in the harbour either taking the regular packet or bargaining with the master of one of the many sailing vessels designed to run passengers across the narrow sea. If the wind was kind and the tide right he could be landed safely on the quayside at Calais in less than four hours. If his luck was out the journey could take many hours and sometimes even days, ending perhaps with a long, wet trudge with the tide out and the city gates shut for the night. Most popular with English travellers at this time was M. Dessein's well-known inn but the visitor newly arrived on the quayside was usually besieged by waiters from many hostelries, all eager for his custom.

The first landing on foreign soil is always unforgettable. A much more seasoned traveller than Moorcroft wrote at this time of the 'sudden and universal change that surrounds him on landing at Calais. The scene, the people, the language, every object is new'.[15] Another contemporary author, Dr John Andrews, was careful to warn in one of his *Letters to a young Gentleman, on his setting out for France* against adopting a superior and condescending attitude to the novelties encountered there. In the very next letter, however, he admitted that everything seen on the road between Calais and Paris 'will afford a sensible Englishman powerful reasons for thanking Providence that he is one'.[16] Moorcroft came to share that view. He loved France but had a low view of the French and of the excesses which later disfigured their revolution.[17]

For all the heady upheavals of 1789, the visiting Englishman was in no real danger. In the early days, until the king's ill-judged and bungled flight from

Paris in 1792, France was labouring, in a remarkable spirit of national unity and enthusiasm to rebuild her institutions along lines congenial to most English observers. None the less it was, to use Moorcroft's own description, a 'tumultuous period'[18] and life for the English traveller would neither have been dull nor always comfortable. He might have his baggage rudely searched by scruffy citizen soldiery, be forced to pin a tricolour favour to his hat by an enthusiastic crowd, or be kept awake by demonstrations in the cobbled streets under his inn window. More sobering might be the glimpse from the coach of a blackened château consigned to the flames by its tenants.[19] France was certainly simmering in the years 1789 to 1792, but Moorcroft and every other Englishman who valued his freedom was safely back on the far side of that 'streight that separates England, so fortunately for her, from all the rest of the world'[20] before the moderate revolution slid into violent popular revolt, regicide, bloody civil strife, terror and finally global war.

Moorcroft arrived in Lyons at the beginning of March 1790. He may have taken the *bateau de poste* down the Saône from Chalons – he certainly knew the country in that direction[21] – or perhaps rumbled in across the beautiful country from the Monts d'Or. By either route one entered Lyons from the north along the road on the right bank of the Saône which squeezed between the wide quays along the swirling grey-green river and the craggy heights of the ancient hill of Fourvières. Gradually losing itself in the narrow, dark and crowded streets of the city, the coach then turned left and crossed one of the Saône bridges on to the narrow peninsula at the foot of hill Croix-Rousse, which separates the two southward-rushing rivers of Saône and Rhône.[22]

At this strategic river junction the proud, ancient and staunchly Catholic city, then as now second only to Paris, had stood since before Roman times. With their unerring eye for a key site the Romans had made it the provincial centre of their administration and the hub of a network of roads north of the Alps linking Switzerland and northern Italy, the Midi and Burgundy, the Massif Central and Dauphiné. Lyons never lost its dominance of southern France but rather had strengthened it in more recent times by developing into a great manufacturing, business and banking centre. Its products, above all its luxury silk goods, flowed out across its innumerable wharves and bridges in such quantity that in prosperous times they accounted for one quarter of all the nation's exports. Unfortunately the prosperous days were just a memory by the time Moorcroft arrived in Lyons and the silk trade was in deep decay. About a third of the workforce was dependent on public charity, some 20,000 or 30,000 'livid, fleshless spectres' according to one highly-coloured description.[23] The social and economic tensions in the city were certainly very acute and had exploded into strikes, violence and bloodshed in 1785 and 1789; they were to do so again in the years that followed. Bread was scarce and dear, housing short and poor, wages low and working conditions often abysmal. Even the municipality itself was on the edge of bankruptcy. The Suffolk squire, Arthur Young, arrived in Lyons at the end of 1789 a few months before Moorcroft. He commented sharply on the distress and stagnation he saw and confessed himself 'horribly disappointed' by Lyons itself, which he hardly even bothered to describe.[24] True, it was midwinter when the damp fogs rolling off the two rivers could mute the spectacular topography of even this unique and beautiful city. Under the azure blue of the southern summer sky, with the white- or ochre-washed walls of its tall houses slashed by long dark windows and peeling shutters and the shadowed, narrow streets far beneath, it could be magical. The most striking thing about eighteenth-century Lyons, even to somebody used to Liverpool's narrow streets, would have been the cramped and claustrophobic quality of its crowded site. It was hemmed in behind its crumbling but still massive walls, on the west by the Saône and the steep flanks of the ancient Roman hill of Fourvières; on the east by the Rhône and the administrative boundary that placed the marshes and low-lying land across the river in a different *département*; on the south by the newly reclaimed land at the junction of the two rivers; and on the north by the soaring hill of Croix-Rousse. From its steep sides the narrow, stepped and cobbled streets cascaded dizzily down into the dark and tangled centre of the city. Spectacular accidents with runaway handcarts were common. Cheated by nature and man of the chance to expand outwards, the ancient city had thrust itself upwards, the tiered and piled terraces of its often seven- or eight-storey houses pushing up out of the bare rock and lifting even some of the front doors to first-floor level. Here, in the shadowy interiors behind closed shutters or under bright awnings in summer, lived 120,000 people. Only the most wealthy of them were in the richer quarters, cut off from the strongly flavoured intimacy of the street by their high walls and dark cypress trees. Of course Lyons had its splendid *hôtel de ville*, its grand public buildings and windy open squares, monuments to an earlier period of prosperity, but these, often perched precariously on the steep gradients, were closely jostled by crowded streets and narrow alleyways. Lyons was unique, a sturdy, independent place, ever suspicious of upstart Paris and as much the natural centre of counter-revolution in the 1790s as it was of Resistance in the early 1940s.

The special flavour of this special city would have penetrated the conscious-ness of its latest English resident only slowly. Moorcroft's business was not in the city proper but eastwards beyond the river across the towered pont de la Guillotière into the low-lying and low-class *faubourg* of that name on the left bank of the Rhône. It was a mean place of carters' inns and pleasure gardens, notorious for its lawlessness and occasional violence. Through this seedy quarter ran the *grande route du Midi*, striding out eastwards across the flat, rich plain of Dauphiné as if it would run headlong into the distant, silver-purple line of mountains, Mont Blanc dominating them all. A few hundred yards down this road from the pont de la Guillotière and still within the built-up area, was the object of Moorcroft's long journey. Did his heart sink as he stopped for the first time outside this modest, two-storey building fronting the street, his eye perhaps taking in its two wings linked by a porter's lodge and a gateway to a gloomy passage which lead to a courtyard behind? It looked much the inn it once had been. The older inhabitants of Lyons would still remember the old *Logis de l'Abondance*, despite its name only a humble travellers' inn on the road to the east. Since January 1762 it had been the home of the oldest veterinary school in the modern world but, notwithstanding its seniority, it was always something of a poor relation to its richer and more favoured sister institution in the fine château at Alfort near Paris. Now in 1790, when Moorcroft arrived at its shabby door the Lyons school was in deep financial trouble. Even a cursory inspection of the establishment in its patently unsuitable building would have confirmed the fact.[25]

Perhaps the first thing Moorcroft would have noticed, if he stood at the entrance to the courtyard with his back to the street, was the smell from the dung heap, the stagnant pools of water and the open drain carrying the urine of its human and animal occupants. Behind him, in the right-hand corner of the yard were the porter's lodgings and, overlooking the street, the pharmacy. Above them both, up some narrow stairs, lived the school's dynamic director, Louis Bredin. It was he who almost single-handed was to hold the little institution together in the dark years to come when terror and siege threatened to destroy it utterly, but as Moorcroft looked at it in March 1790, a slow death by decay rather than by violent destruction would have seemed the most likely outcome. On the right of the courtyard was a series of low buildings: an isolation stable for diseased horses, a forge, horse-trough, gardener's room and a conservatory for the rather fine little botanical garden behind on the right. Directly in front was a small, open meadow with an avenue of trees on one side and to the left of the yard was the two-storey building within which most of Moorcroft's waking and sleeping hours in the next twelve months would be spent. On the ground floor furthest away was an airy stable for sick animals and nearer at hand an ill-lit dissecting room. One hopes the stench of the 'numerous putrefying corpses'[26] often found there was not too pervasive for it was through this room that the students had to pass to reach the plainly furnished refectory with its two scrubbed tables and long benches where meals were provided twice a day. Up a narrow staircase between these rooms and the stable, a door on the left opened on to the anatomy room, littered with stuffed specimens and prepared dissections palely preserved in jars. On the right, above the stable for sick horses, was the dormitory. It was an insanitary place, only 18 × 15 feet (5.4 × 4.5 metres), but crammed with nineteen beds and straw palliasses of assorted sizes. The latest student to arrive probably had to share a bed at first. The report of a commission of inquiry conducted while Moorcroft was actually there, commented disapprovingly on *'l'odeur qui sort des lits où plusieurs élèves couchent ensemble, ce qui est contraire aux bonnes moeurs et à l'ordre'*.[27] This room, airless in summer and fetid in winter, would have had all the unhealthy, cheery intimacy of the barrack-room and like the barrack-room it was the place where most off-duty time was spent. There, shutting out the badinage and the snores, Moorcroft would have done such lamplit reading or letter-writing as he could manage when the day's classes were over. Contemporary plans of the Lyons school make no reference to any wash-house – a sluicing under one of the two pumps in the yard was probably all that was available – nor to what Moorcroft's generation usually called a necessary house. But one there must have been though it was probably just like most other French lavatories of the time. Arthur Young described them with feeling as 'temples of abomination'.[28] It was all a far cry from the familiar comfort of John Lyon's home in Liverpool and if Moorcroft felt homesick at first it would not be very surprising.

In these humble and, by our standards, evilly insanitary buildings *Guillaume Moorcroft, 23 ans, de la Province de Lancastre* was entered on the register and spent most of the next twelve months of his life. On 8 March 1790 he was enrolled and duly paid his tuition, boarding, instrument and uniform fees for the next six months.[29] Originally, the course for the *brevet de privilégié en l'art vétérinaire* was a four-year one, both at Alfort and Lyons, but by 1790 the average stay at either place was not much more than one year. At Lyons all the courses were taught either by Louis Bredin the Director or by the Professor of Comparative Anatomy, Jacques-Marie Hénon, assisted by a demonstrator. During his twelve months at the school Moorcroft completed or covered four rather arbitrarily divided courses of study: anatomy, including a special study (from specimens) of bones and muscles in the summer course, and, in the winter, practical work on animal corpses with special attention to muscles and the stomach; the natural history course included the external appearance of domestic animals, hygiene, breeding principles, animal management and the use of fertilizers; the course in medicine involved a study of both chemistry and botany as well as practical work in the pharmacy; finally there was a pathology course which covered not only internal and external diseases but also their clinical and surgical treatment and the use of dressings and equipment.[30]

For Moorcroft one of the most interesting aspects of the work was Hénon's teaching and research into parasitic worms. On one occasion he and Moorcroft were in lively disagreement as to whether a substance Moorcroft had extracted from the foreleg of a mule was or was not a guinea worm. Moorcroft, calling on his experience at Liverpool Infirmary, was sure it was.[31] All in all the young Englishman seems to have done extremely well, notwithstanding the language difficulty. Louis Bredin could be a harsh critic when writing reports about his pupils, but he described Moorcroft as 'a model of work and application' and was especially pleased with the speed with which he mastered not only the French language but all aspects of veterinary medicine. 'Clever, intelligent and well educated: he knows a good deal for his age', was Bredin's considered judgement.[32] Of course Moorcroft had the immense advantage of his surgical training at Liverpool, and his genuine interest in the subject was never in doubt. He was different from some of the rather bemused country lads who found themselves at the school scarcely able to read or write.

Without the consolations of an interest in the work, life must have seemed very dreary to some of these pupils, for there was little else to do and the regime was a harsh one. Nobody was allowed out, except with the written permission of M. le directeur '*sous peine d'être arrêté et constitués prisonnier dans les prisons des Villes*', as the founder's regulations tersely put it.[33] Such harshness was not without justification. La Guillotière was a turbulent neighbourhood and the young veterinary students in their blue uniforms and copper buttons[34] must have been fair game for the roughs of the district. Certainly the history of the school had been punctuated by scuffles with the locals or with the forces of the

[21]

law. The year was broken up by no long holidays although every Thursday and Sunday as well as saints' days and festivals were free of classes. How they must have looked forward to those brief escapes. The taverns of the city were never very far away across the pont de la Guillotière and some no doubt sought the brief commercial pleasures of a shared bed in the inappropriately named rue des Vertus or the rue Confort.

In the warm summer days more appetizing and innocent game was to be had. At weekends many of the inhabitants of the old city, and especially the pretty silkworkers for whom the city was famed, repaired to the pleasure gardens of La Guillotière for a brief butterfly escape from the tedium and misery of their working lives. Moorcroft would have found a Sunday in La Guillotière very different from the strictly enforced sobriety of the Sabbath day in Liverpool. There was plenty of drunkenness – Lyons' third river, it was said, was the copious supply of cheap young Beaujolais coming down in the Saône barges – and although priests and parents would have drilled these young girls from childhood in the economic and moral value of their virginity, the warm air, the wine and the flirting would often have ended in sad little affairs, in which the girl was often left to carry the baby alone. We know of many such cases in the Lyons of this period, and at least one of the successful seducers was a fellow-student of Moorcroft's.[35]

In the light of what was soon to come it is hard to grudge these young people their brief hours of happiness. Before many months were out most of Moorcroft's fellow-students were drafted into the French army to help staunch the staggering losses of horses in the seemingly endless wars. Everyone left in the city was soon experiencing the horrors of siege, bombardment and starvation followed by mass murder, often carried out on the scrubby marshlands of Les Brotteaux just to the north of La Guillotière. Moorcroft left only just in time.

For him the end came on 7 March 1791, exactly one year after he had enrolled,[36] and on that day, albeit in a very modest way, he made history. He was the first Englishman ever to complete a period of formal veterinary training. What he did next is uncertain. It must have been at this time that he crossed the Mont Cenis pass into Italy.[37] He was certainly very much at home with its language and familiar with its art and culture.[38] We know also that he had friends in Switzerland near Geneva, a clean and ordered city after the earthy chaos of Lyons, and many years later he considered retiring to one of the farms dotted over the green hills around the lake.[39] His interest in agricultural techniques was very much in evidence at this time. He examined (and remembered) the way the walnut trees were grafted at Geneva and, on the Saône towards Mâcon, the espalier peach cultivation against the warm, south-facing walls.[40] It must have been a happy summer. Not until the beginning of September 1791 do we catch up with Moorcroft again, safely back home in the familiar little world round Ormskirk and no doubt regaling his grandfather and the others with tales of the Revolution. Adam Smith once grumpily complained that the young Englishman sent abroad to complete his education usually returned more conceited, unprincipled, dissipated and incapable of hard work than he could ever have become if he had stayed at home.[41] Dissipation we shall never know about. But lack of principle and work-shyness were never Moorcroft's hallmarks. On the contrary, he was soon very much at work, applying the new knowledge acquired under Professor Hénon in that southern city so far away. It happened like this. . . .[42]

One day in that September of 1791 he was called out to see a two-year-old Longhorn heifer, not unlike the one which had changed his life three years before. This animal, although otherwise in perfect health, had taken to rambling in a slow and almost continuous circular path round its meadow, its head held low and on one side. The local cow-leech would have called this condition the gid or the turnsick. In Lyons, *vertige* or *tournoiement* would be the word. Whatever you called it, the animal was under sentence of slow death from a developing tape-worm cyst on the brain unless what the veterinary dictionary of 1805 called 'a hazardous operation'[43] was attempted. At first Moorcroft seems to have hoped that there was a more benign explanation for the animal's behaviour, although her symptoms were classic enough. Only when there was nothing to lose did he decide to open the skull of the hapless creature. After she was cast on her left side and tightly secured Moorcroft opened up an oval hole in the skull by cutting two 1-inch (2.5-centimetre) discs of bone with the trephine or crown saw to gain access to the brain cavity. As luck would have it he was exactly in the right position. The surface of the brain immediately below the aperture yielded under his fingers as though there was fluid beneath it. He made a careful incision and was separating its edges with the handle of his scalpel when there was a dramatic development:

> I was struck with the appearance of a cyst, part of which protruded itself immediately with considerable force, through the bony opening, to the size of a hen's egg, when it burst, and gave issue to about three or four ounces [85–113 grams] of a thin colourless fluid. By laying hold of the torn edges, and drawing them gently from one side to the other, I detached the cyst from its connections.[44]

Moorcroft was able to look right into the clean cavity thus formed and, seeing no trace of the worms, all of which had come away with the capsule, was able to dress the wound and release the animal. It was with immense satisfaction that he watched her scramble to her feet and walk 'without appearing in the least disposed to turn or ramble'.[45] She ate a little that evening and when he came back next morning, she seemed to be completely cured. It was all very satisfying. Moorcroft's account of this classic case of *coenurus cerebralis* is not by any means the first on record as he readily admitted.[46] Nor could he claim a success denied to earlier practitioners for the animal had to be destroyed about two weeks after the operation. Sepsis was an almost inevitable consequence of the brain's exposure to the air and to Moorcroft's unsterilized instruments and hands. It remained a constant enemy to the deep and courageous surgery, in which Moorcroft came to excel, for all of his professional life and many more decades after that. Even so it was unfortunate that he was not able to give proper post-operative care to this animal, nor investigate her brain after death.

[23]

In fact he had done all that a modern surgeon would attempt and more. Early slaughter is still the usual treatment even today.

Five months passed before Moorcroft returned to Ormskirk, 'having some affairs which called me to the continent'.[47] Moorcroft seems to have persuaded his grandfather that it would be valuable for him to spend some time in Normandy examining the horse-breeding methods instituted years before by the great founder of the two French veterinary schools, Claude Bourgelat. He could scarcely have guessed that he would thereby learn some lessons which could one day be usefully applied in the low-lying lands on the faraway Ganges.

Moorcroft also argued that since the National Assembly was abolishing the royal studs and selling off much of their produce, there was an unprecedented opportunity to acquire superlative animals at bargain prices.[48] Thomas Eccleston was certainly interested, for he bought some thoroughbred Norman coach mares and horses and a marvellous stallion, 'the finest . . . ever seen in these parts'. For several years afterwards this animal was the heart of the substantial public and private breeding operation he carried on at Scarisbrick. He acquired in Normandy goats and rabbits too, as well as other horses. 'One I gave to Dr. Moorcroft'.[49] Perhaps Moorcroft was buying as his agent. At the beginning of November 1791 Moorcroft was certainly at the crowded *fête des morts* horse and cattle market at Bayeux. He spent the next few months of that very wet and muddy winter roaming through the length and breadth of Normandy, often putting up at farmhouses along the way, broadening his experience of horse-breeding and animal management (and of French food and wine), and, of course, indulging his apparently tireless love of travelling.[50] However, horses seem to have been the prime purpose of it all. His few months in London may already have convinced him that the best professional prospects lay not in the sort of rural cattle practice which his grandfather and Thomas Eccleston originally seem to have had in mind for him but rather in metropolitan practice, concentrating almost exclusively on the horses of the rich and well-to-do. At the end of February 1792 he was back in Ormskirk[51] and some time during the following month he returned south to his old lodgings in Half Moon Street off Piccadilly.[52] For the next 16 years London was his home.

3 PRIVATE PRACTICE AND THE VETERINARY COLLEGE,

1792–1800

THE LONDON OF 1792 was certainly a promising place in which to set up what was the country's first properly qualified veterinary horse practice. Its population had grown rapidly in the previous forty years from 675,000 to about 900,000. Much of the physical growth in this period was concentrated in the cornfields, pastures and marshy land to the north and south of the old Tyburn Way, now coming to be called the Oxford Street. Here, under the impressive leadership of the big landowners – Grosvenor, Portman, Berkeley, Manchester, Bedford and Portland – the fine streets, broad squares and elegant terraces which bear their names today, were pegged out and built. Into this new West End of London, increasingly the most fashionable part of the town, moved and lived most of the great and famous. London now stretched in an almost unbroken crescent from the handsome houses of Park Lane on the west, eastwards to the insanitary warrens and rookeries of Wapping and Rotherhithe. The unprecedented concentration of power, wealth and ability which it contained dominated the England of 1792 as never before. Commerce, government, fashion, taste, the arts and the sciences – in all of them London enjoyed an almost effortless superiority. It was probably the biggest, and certainly the richest, city in the world.[1]

Yet for all its size, it was still in many ways a country town. If Moorcroft, emerging from the shade of Half Moon Street, turned the corner into Piccadilly, he could stand before houses, the upper windows of which enjoyed across the river an open 'prospect of the beautiful hills of Surry'.[2] The West End of London was at that period literally the western end. The double wooden turnpike gates at the western end of Oxford Street, near where Marble Arch now stands, were still regarded as the western 'entrance to London'.[3] Where the brave new houses and streets ended the traditional country began. Beyond, to the north and west, the parks, fields and nursery gardens stretched away to the still rural villages of Paddington, Kensington, St Marylebone, St Pancras and Islington. The land round these villages and far beyond was increasingly devoted to supplying their huge and insatiable neighbour with vegetables, grain and milk. From further afield came the drovers and their herds of cattle, blocking the narrow streets round Smithfield Market. Much of London's milk came from cows within the town itself, often housed in tumbledown byres behind the high frontages of the terraced houses and shops.

Most striking of all was the immense number of horses. Robert Southey, writing at about this time, recorded his impressions of the western road into London like this:

> The number of travellers astonished me, horsemen, footmen, carriages of every description, waggons, carts, covered carts, stage coaches, chariots, chaises, gigs, buggies, curricles and phaetons, the sound of their wheels ploughing through the wet gravel was continuous and incessant as the roar of the waves on the sea beach.[4]

It requires a considerable effort of imagination to conceive the total dependence of Moorcroft's England on the horse.[5] It was not only a question of the myriad forms of road transport described by Southey. Agriculture, the army and sport all depended on the horse as well. The horse was as ubiquitous and essential to the life of his day as the petrol and diesel engine is to our own. 'In the entire history of man the horse was never more important than it was in the 18th century but never was it so ill-understood or so badly used.'[6]

In 1792 there were perhaps 150,000 horses in London alone, thronging the streets by day and, at night, mostly locked away in the often evil-smelling, airless stables which huddled behind almost every street. A considerable industry existed to serve the needs of the horse. There were carriage- and harness-makers, wheelwrights, veterinary druggists, livery, coaching and private stables, covered riding schools, sale-rooms and, of course, armies of hardworking and underpaid blacksmiths, driving their dehydrated bodies through the forge heat of a long working day with the help of a 'pretty free circulation of the porter pot'.[7] The disease potential, both for man and horse, of the fly-blown piles of dung, the standing pools of acrid urine in the back stable yards and the ill-washed wooden mangers and pails was immense. The London horse faced other hazards too. Sheer bad horsemanship, the failure to keep over to the left and the tendency of the gay and fashionable to whirl their carriages through the newly paved western streets of the metropolis 'with the most incredible velocity'[8], produced its daily crop of injured limbs and accidents in which animals were impaled on railings or the shafts of other carriages or entangled with the new iron lamp posts. Good horses were becoming harder to replace. London's growth and prosperity had pushed the price of almost every kind of quality animal in London up by 200 or 300 per cent in Moorcroft's short lifetime alone.[9] Fortunately, London was full of men who could still afford to buy them and could pay handsomely for the services of anyone able to provide them with a scientific veterinary or consultancy service. From every point of view the London of 1792 offered the young Lancashire surgeon, with his unique foreign veterinary training and his valuable connections, an enormous opportunity.

Unfortunately we know very little about his doings in 1792 and early 1793. At the end of March 1792 he sent off the detailed account of his surgery on the brain of the cow at Ormskirk the previous September, promising another which never materialized.[10] It was almost certainly later that same year, that he helped the itinerant Italian doctor, Eusebio Valli, with some of his electrical experiments on animals. Later, and it is further evidence of Moorcroft's facility with languages, he translated for Valli the results of these and other experiments from the Italian into a 390-page English edition which was published in 1793.[11]

The electric shocks produced by the electric eel and the torpedo fish had been interesting scientists for some years, and the broad similarity between them and other electrical phenomena was already recognized. An apparently exciting new direction to these studies of 'animal electricity' came in 1790, when the limbs of the dead frog on Luigi Galvani's dissecting table suddenly jumped at the same moment as an electrical discharge machine was operating in the room. Galvani's subsequent experiments convinced him and his fellow-countryman Valli, who repeated and extended them in 1791 and 1792, that the living tissue of animals could produce an electrical discharge in all respects similar to other electrical phenomena. Valli in particular sacrificed armies of frogs, lizards, larks, cats and dogs, to demonstrate in various ways the sometimes violent and often lifelike movements which could be induced in the muscles of dead and living creatures by completing electrical circuits through them with tinfoil and silver contacts. So convinced was Valli that he was on to something of revolutionary significance in the understanding and diagnosis of animal diseases, that he went on a grand tour of the major cities of northern Europe, demonstrating his experiments before surgeons and physiologists. It was probably while he was at St Thomas's Hospital, where Moorcroft had several friends, that he met the Englishman in 1792. 'My friend, Mr. Moorcroft, veterinarian surgeon', as Valli put it,[12] suggested that he might try similar experiments on a horse and duly obtained and dissected one for him. For an hour they worked together on the body of the dead animal, applying their silver contacts and certainly inducing some violent movements in the shoulder muscles. 'A shilling produced as much excitement as the spoon; and a guinea nearly as much as either.'[13] It does not sound very scientific. Nor does it ever seem to have occurred to either of them that, as Alessandro Volta was soon to demonstrate, the metal conductors and body liquids used in these experiments were what was producing the electricity, and not the nerves and muscles of the animal at all.

These were interesting diversions and Moorcroft was always fascinated by novelty, but his most urgent task was to build up a clientele and acquire suitable premises from which to practise as a veterinary surgeon. While he was still searching, his path for the first time crossed that of the infant London Veterinary College. As has already been mentioned, the Odiham Agricultural Society had decided back in 1788 to send two young men to study at the Alfort veterinary school near Paris. They never went and a group of the London-based members of the society decided to work instead for the establishment of a veterinary college in Britain. The story of how they did so has been well told elsewhere.[14] At the time there was obviously nobody in England qualified to take charge of the new institution. So in the spring of 1791, while Moorcroft was just coming to the end of his course at Lyons, the promoters of the new college chose as its first professor a former prize pupil of the Lyons school in its early days, a Frenchman usually known in England as Sainbel. Negotiations for the lease of a site in the fields close to St Pancras church were opened and there, in a makeshift building in January 1792, Sainbel began lecturing to just four pupils. There was trouble almost at once. Sainbel was a temperamental and pig-headed man and his thick, almost unintelligible French accent only added to his difficulties. There was an unpleasant row in which he was accused, correctly as it happens, of having lied about his qualifications and experience in France. On 9 May 1792 an investigating committee chaired by John Hunter confirmed Sainbel's suitability as college professor but rec-ommended that he be joined by a second professor as soon as the college buildings, then under construction, were completed. The matter of a second appointment was pressed again in committee in July 1792.[15]

This initiative may have more to do with Moorcroft than is apparent. One of Hunter's surgical pupils at this time was Joseph Adams. Writing of these events many years later he recalled that: 'Mr. Hunter would gladly have introduced a gentleman with whom he was well acquainted, and whom he knew to be docile: he was overruled.'[16] Adams's recollections of this period are sometimes extremely unreliable, but there is no reason to doubt the truth of this statement. The 'gentleman' referred to, although 'docile' is not an adjective that fits him very comfortably, was almost certainly the young William Moorcroft.[17] He was just back in London after his period of study at Lyons, he was already well known to John Hunter, he was the only English-man in the country with a formal veterinary training, and he was also at this time not yet established in regular practice. A year later, however, when the professorship at the college did unexpectedly fall vacant, things were rather different.

On 21 August 1793 Sainbel died suddenly from an illness which his doctor feared was bubonic plague but which was almost certainly glanders caught from the suppurating nostrils of a diseased horse. There was no doubt at all who should succeed him. 'All eyes,' recalled one of the college's ex-students, 'were directed towards Mr. Moorcroft, who was then in private practice.'[18] That, of course, was the difficulty. By the middle of 1793 – that unpropitious year when France murdered its monarchs and embarked on war with Britain – William Moorcroft had found the premises he was looking for. He had bought from William Vernon and Son the lease of 224 Oxford Street, London, on the north side and almost at the western end of the street, four doors beyond the corner with Orchard Street.

If Moorcroft had examined the property from across the road there would have been little except its 30-foot (9-metre) frontage to indicate why its rates should be more than eight times those of its narrower terraced neighbours.[19] On the face of it, it was the standard product of the time, the stock brick terraced house, in which nearly all of the inhabitants of Georgian London lived who were not either in fine mansions or hovels. What was unusual about this house, and it would have been the chief focus of Moorcroft's interest, was that instead of a front door opening on to the street there was a large covered archway big enough for a coach which passed under the house and gave access to the land at the back.[20] Here was a double range of stabling opening off two cobbled yards, running behind the next seven houses to the west, and providing covered accommodation for a considerable number of horses.[21] There was certainly the physical space here for the thriving horse practice Moorcroft hoped for. The annual outgoings were £23 6s. 8d. (£23.33) paid to the rate collector who called at the door at midsummer and Christmas, plus a rent to the landlord of perhaps £150 a year.[22] What the other capital costs of launching the new business would have been we can only guess. But Moorcroft's grandfather had backed him generously so far and must have been behind him now. Weighing all the pros and cons and doubtless taking a deep breath as he did so, Moorcroft put his signature to the lease some time in the first half of 1793. So it was that the business of 'Wm. Moorcroft, Veterinarian Surgeon and Hospital for Horses' as one of the contemporary trade directories put it,[23] came to London and the empty stables in the echoing yard under the arch behind 224 Oxford Street began to fill up.

The situation of the new business was perfect. The line of Oxford Street was an east–west communication which was in use before the Romans. By 1793 it was not only one of London's oldest streets but also 'for its length, width and strait direction . . . one of the finest streets in the metropolis'.[24] Its improvement had been very recent. Not many years before, and certainly in the memory of people still alive in 1793, it had been (as one of them recalled), 'a deep and hollow road, and full of sloughs: with here and there a ragged house, the lurking-place of cut throats'.[25] In those not so distant days when the piecemeal line of terrace houses and shops straggling westwards from St Giles had not reached very far, the street was unsafe at night and by day was often choked with herds of cattle and sheep coming in from the west on their way to Smithfield. However in 1753 London's first ring-road, the New Road (now Marylebone Road) in the fields to the north was opened and immediately relieved the congestion in Oxford Street, by offering a much more open approach to the City.[26] More recently, the ending of public hangings on the gigantic gallows at Tyburn, just a short distance to the west of Moorcroft's new house, also raised the tone of Oxford Street. The most dramatic improvement of all came with the building of the elegant streets and squares at the western end of the street. Most prestigious of all were Grosvenor and Portman Squares just round the corner, south and north, from Moorcroft's new house. Into them and those like them, attracted by the sense of space and light, the fine architecture, the salubrious air and the higher ground, moved what one contemporary called 'a considerable portion of the British peerage'.[27] Fortified with this new influx of wealth, the vestrymen of St Pancras, to whom Moorcroft's high rates were paid, were able to provide a standard of street-cleaning, night-watching, lamplighting and provision for the poor which, although laughable by modern standards, was exceptional at the time. Even the ruts and potholes of Oxford Street became a thing of the past. In the twenty years before Moorcroft moved in, the local authority gradually put in hand the paving of the whole of that unusually wide street with granite blocks, gutters, drains and kerbs to protect the increasingly elegant pedestrians on the level, stone paths.[28]

Small wonder that Oxford Street began to prosper. There were still many private houses, especially at the better western end where Moorcroft took up residence, but the transition to a trading street of better-class shops was already well under way by then and almost complete by the time he died. He could hardly have chosen a better place to launch London's first properly qualified veterinary practice. There was another advantage as well, which must have especially appealed to the countryman in him after the face-to-face narrowness of Half Moon Street. From the upper front windows of his new house he could easily see over the high wall into the green expanses of Hyde Park – 'the lungs of London' as Lord Chatham had called them.[29] From the back windows, the rolling hills of Highgate and Hampstead to the north would have been plainly visible.

It was on the Kentish Town turnpike running up towards those hills that the young veterinary college at St Pancras was now plunged into crisis when Sainbel died in August 1793. One of the college directors, William Sheldon, was quick to get in touch with Moorcroft.[30] Perhaps as a result Moorcroft wrote to the college secretary informing the committee: '. . . that in case they may conceive my services of any use towards obviating any inconveniences which might result from the present state of circumstances; they are wholly at their command, until such time as the vacancy be filled'.[31] This letter meant no more than it said. It was certainly not an oblique application for the vacant post. Moorcroft had only just taken over the Oxford Street premises, he had doubtless invested considerable capital in the venture and seems already to have been attracting a considerable business to it. The minutes of the college's medical committee, which met on 8 September, make it perfectly clear that a shortage of suitable British candidates was already extending the search abroad.

In sharp contrast to Moorcroft's lack of interest, was the determined candidacy of the young London surgeon, Edward Coleman, whose application was received by the college in mid-September. He had powerful backers – John Hunter himself before his own sudden death on 16 October 1793, and Henry Cline, the distinguished surgeon at St Thomas's Hospital, in whose house Coleman had lived for nearly two years as a medical student. There was only one problem. Apart from some small pieces of work on the eye of the horse and asphyxia in the cat and the dog, he was totally ignorant of veterinary medicine and surgery! It was probably the committee's doubts on this score which decided them to ask Coleman to approach the still-reluctant Moorcroft and work out with him some kind of scheme for a joint professorship.[32] The two men may already have been known to each other, since both had attended Hunter's lectures. In any case Moorcroft as an ex-surgeon had many connections with the London medical fraternity. Coleman was back before the college committee on 14 January 1794 for a preliminary discussion and he probably met Moorcroft on the morning of Tuesday, 4 February to put together the final version of their twelve-point proposals. These were laid before the committee at the Crown and Anchor tavern in the Strand later the same day. The committee failed to agree about them and they were still at loggerheads after another session the following Saturday. In the end they decided to remit the whole awkward question to a special sub-committee under the chairmanship of Lord Heathfield.

The main problem concerned clause 12 of the Moorcroft–Coleman scheme. This laid down that college subscribers would be charged an inclusive fee of one guinea for each horse sent there for treatment during three two-hour surgeries each week, when the professors would be in attendance for the purpose. It is perfectly clear from the early minute-books of the college that much of its financial support came from wealthy men who, in the absence of a reliable alternative, valued it chiefly as a means of getting sound veterinary treatment for their sick animals. Almost from the beginning, Sainbel had come under pressure to expand this side of the college's work at the expense of its teaching functions. Any scheme which would require the subscribers to pay something closer to the going rate for veterinary treatment, in addition to their annual subscriptions, was almost bound to cause violent objections. Besides, these two young, would-be professors were asking not only for a basic annual salary of 200 guineas (Sainbel had been paid £200), which would increase as the college grew, but they were also claiming, on good medical precedent, the lecture fees from the public and subscribers as well as course fees from the students themselves. In return for all this their commitment would be to give each year a course of lectures on the horse and 'occasionally' on other animals and four public lectures which the subscribers might attend without extra charge. It must have been Moorcroft who insisted in addition that the professors should not have to live in the college and that they would be free to continue in private practice.

The Coleman–Moorcroft scheme raised some awkward problems. It was obvious that the college, teetering on the very edge of bankruptcy, could not afford to antagonize its wealthy backers. Some of them were proving reluctant to pay their subscriptions punctually as it was. So on Monday, 10 February, once again at the Crown and Anchor, Lord Heathfield and his sub-committee tried to persuade Moorcroft and Coleman to drop their troublesome clause 12 altogether. When that proved unacceptable a new version was suggested with the quaint wording: 'the Professors shall give advice *gratis* to all horses belonging to Subscribers if sent on the hours of the days beforementioned'. Coleman was satisfied when to this was added a complicated scheme giving the professors a percentage on all medicines supplied to the college. He accepted at once. Moorcroft, still undecided, asked for a few more days to think about it and only notified the committee of his apparently unenthusiastic acceptance on 14 February. Three days later Moorcroft and Coleman were back at the Crown and Anchor once more for a 'very full and long examination' before a small committee of medical men. It is hard to believe that Moorcroft would have taken it very seriously, since none of his examiners had any real experience of veterinary medicine at all. Moreover Coleman's teacher and patron, Henry Cline, was in the chair and Moorcroft's sponsor for the Royal

Society of Arts five years earlier, William Houlston, was one of the examiners. In these circumstances the result was perhaps a foregone conclusion. Both men, the committee reported, 'possess great knowledge in the veterinary art and are qualified to teach and practise it with distinguished ability'. How they could have come to this conclusion about Coleman one can only wonder, but when the subscribers held their annual dinner a few weeks later, with the usual round of toasts and speeches, they must have thought that the worst of the problems besetting the young college were over at last with its two young professors now safely in harness and pulling together.

It was not so. The bombshell burst on 8 April when the committee, with Lord Heathfield in the chair, heard the secretary read a letter from Moorcroft, written a mere six weeks after his appointment 'stating his health to be such as to oblige him to offer his resignation of the situation he held in the College'.[33] More than forty years later Coleman recalled his reaction to this news:

> I could see no ill-health at all. He also pleaded interference with his duty to those by whom he was employed in private practice of considerable extent; but his time at the College had been clearly specified – two hours, three days in the week, and with little or no call upon him for attendance at uncertain hours. . . . I confess I felt myself rather ill-used.

Coleman was certainly in an awkward position, as he candidly confessed: 'I felt it would be presumptuous, perhaps dishonourable for me so little versed in veterinary matters, to superintend the interests and growth of the infant school.'[34] But presumptuous and dishonourable or not, he took his chance. He was still sole professor at the college when he died almost half a century later.

Just what caused Moorcroft to change his mind so quickly is as much a mystery today as Coleman claimed it was to him at the time. We can certainly discount ill health. Moorcroft enjoyed unusually good health as he often admitted, and there is no discernible slackening of his activity at this time. Indeed the reverse is true. His practice was growing rapidly and the pressure to take sick horses into residence, which was contrary to his agreement with the college, must have been overwhelming. Right from the start Moorcroft seems to have been reluctant to get closely involved with the college and his booming practice at Oxford Street provides reason enough. It is true, as Coleman said, that Moorcroft was only required to be up at St Pancras two hours, three days a week for consultation by subscribers with sick horses, but that was the least distracting part of the job. In addition he would have had to prepare and give public lectures as well as lecture courses to the students. Moreover, as joint head of the college he was bound to be drawn deeply into its administrative, financial and student problems. Only a month after his appointment, for example, the committee was calling for a development plan from its two professors.[35] The college certainly needed one. Its buildings were depressing, its constitution and situation unsuitable. The confusion following Sainbel's sudden death had doubtless made things worse, but even without it a combination of uncertain private philanthropy and amateurish (if not criminal) maladministration had brought the college to the very edge of bankruptcy in April 1794. Only a month after Moorcroft's resignation the committee was advertising a general meeting to discuss 'matters of most serious importance'[36] and for a time it was uncertain whether the young institution would survive at all. It is hard to believe that all of this played no part in Moorcroft's decision.

In addition some have conjectured that Moorcroft was appalled at his belated discovery of Coleman's ignorance of animal medicine, and at the realization that most of the work would fall on him if his reputation were not to suffer. This seems unlikely. Moorcroft after all, like Coleman, was trained as a surgeon and knew the limitations of human medicine as a training for veterinary work. Moreover, he may have come across Coleman earlier in the little metropolitan medical world of the day. They had certainly met on several occasions before their joint appointment at the college. It has also been suggested that the two men, both masterful, ambitious, and almost the same age, found it impossible to work together.[37] This is certainly a possibility which the later careers of both men renders plausible, but it was probably no more than a contributory factor in Moorcroft's decision. There is no hint of any public disagreement between them at the college, either at the time or subsequently. Coleman, although later critical in his lectures of some of Moorcroft's surgical techniques and theories on the contentious question of horseshoeing, always disagreed with his former colleague in a courteous and deferential manner, acknowledging 'the high sense I entertain of his talents and professional knowledge'.[38] This is in striking contrast to the rancour, animosity and vitriol which was such a feature of much of the polemical veterinary writing of the time. For his part Moorcroft was never drawn into a public dispute with Coleman over the horseshoe question and he later paid generous tribute to the professor's gifts as a public teacher.[39] It should also be remembered that Moorcroft's good relations with Lord Heathfield seem to have been unaffected by his resignation from the professorship. Their friendship ripened steadily in the years that followed, notwithstanding Heathfield's continuing and close involvement with Coleman and the affairs of the college.

The theory of Moorcroft and Coleman in open conflict does not seem to fit the evidence. Most of those who have supported it, contemporaries and veterinary historians alike, are precisely those who have had the highest view of Moorcroft and the lowest of Coleman. Coleman has had an almost universally bad press.[40] His initial ignorance of his subject, the low social status of most of his students, his failure to produce any written work of merit or originality, his seriously defective theories in some crucial aspects of veterinary practice, the training for which he dominated for so long – all this and much else is contrasted with what might have been if Moorcroft had remained at the college. To the later veterinary historian Sir Frederick Smith, a man of strong opinions and unqualified superlatives, Moorcroft was 'the most able man in the veterinary profession', Coleman 'the greatest enemy the profession has ever had in its higher ranks', and Moorcroft's resignation 'the greatest calamity the profession has ever experienced'.[41] For all their starkness, these were judgements which many in the profession at the time came to share.[42]

But the college's loss was certainly Moorcroft's gain, both personally and financially. He was perhaps temperamentally unfitted to be a good institution man, far too much the individualist, too restless and too catholic in his wide-ranging interests to work for long, without friction, within the narrow constraints set by committees and superintending boards. A later commentator who knew him by reputation, described him as 'a person ill-calculated to play second fiddle to any man, even supposing he could for any very long time content himself with equipollent sway'.[43] It is a fair judgement which all his later life confirmed. Moorcroft was happiest when he was master of his own destiny, free to set his own priorities and pursue his own interests. And in April 1794 those interests imperiously called for his full attention to what at 224 Oxford Street was rapidly becoming London's most prestigious and lucrative horse practice.

It is obvious that he could never have coped with such a rapid expansion without help. As the practice grew, so too did the numbers of those on his pay ledger. There would be the domestic servants in the house, a clerk or two to keep the accounts in the office, perhaps later an apothecary to look after the pharmacy. Moorcroft seems to have employed his own blacksmith with a forge and blacksmith's shop. He would certainly have needed ostlers, grooms and stable boys, clattering the buckets as they washed down the stable-yards or pitching the straw, and very soon more expert help on the veterinary side would be necessary too. We know that Moorcroft took on as a temporary assistant Samuel Bloxam, one of the four original students of the veterinary college until he was expelled in 1794. Bloxam lived in the house at Oxford Street for two years before returning to the college on Moorcroft's recommendation to complete his studies.[44] There were probably other young would-be veterinarians at work in the practice as apprentices later on. What Moorcroft needed above all, however, was a reliable and congenial right-hand man to whom much of the day-to-day routine of the practice could be safely left. He found such a man in John Field. They probably first met at the veterinary college, where Field was just coming to the end of his course at about the time Moorcroft resigned his brief professorship in the spring of 1794. Field was already so trusted by Moorcroft by August of that year, notwithstanding his initially low salary, that he was allowed to operate on a favourite horse belonging to the king. Moorcroft admitted him into formal partnership and a share of the profits in 1800. The association of Moorcroft and Field, almost exact contemporaries, seems to have been a success from the start. Many years later another veterinary surgeon, who knew them both, recalled that their partnership existed during the next eight years

> with uninterrupted harmony; and, in fact, the qualities of the partners were so balanced and so opposed, that, with well-constituted minds like theirs, good only could be the result. The scholastic education, and the tendency, yet a well-regulated one, to theoretical speculation in one [Moorcroft], was well balanced by the sterling anatomical knowledge and the straightforward practical course of the other; and they were friends as well as partners, and, in a manner, monopolized the greater part of the business of the west end of the metropolis.[45]

That business, of course, was exclusively concerned with horses and mostly with the best and most valuable animals in London. Even so, in that age of ignorance and disease, the range of problems which might face the two partners was vast. One of their friends and contemporaries was another ex-college student called Delabere Blaine. In a two-volume textbook first published in 1802, in the preparation of which he certainly consulted them, he has left us with a useful picture of the sort of problems which might face the horse practitioner at this time. The older and more colourful terminology of the farriers, which Moorcroft himself often used, was only just giving way to the duller descriptions of the scientific veterinarians. Blaine's euphonic list includes brain disorders like mad staggers, sleepy staggers and phrenzy fever; lung complaints known as the rot and rising of the lights; intestinal inflammation or red cholic; catarrh, thick and broken wind, dysentery, glanders and farcy, lock-jaw or stag evil, gripes, fret or gullion, worms, crib-biting, jaundice, bloody urine, pissing evil; stone in the kidney, bladder or intestine; dropsy, hydrophobia, wounds of various kinds, pole evil, fistulous withers, thrush, strangles, tumours malignant and benign, clap in the back sinews, fractures, windgalls, bog spavin, hernia; various diseases of the bones, eyes, feet and skin, as well as many abnormalities in the field of veterinary obstetrics. And much more besides. To help him cope with this array of problems, the horse veterinarian of the 1790s still had almost nothing (other than his superior education and training) beyond the traditional medicines, techniques and practice of the horse-leech and the farrier. Blaine's book admitted that 'the veterinary art is but yet in its infancy'. Some of the routine and experimental practices carried out in the name of medicine in those stables at 224 Oxford Street, would certainly have confirmed that. Sometimes horrific by modern standards, they can only fairly be judged by the knowledge of the time. By contemporary standards Moorcroft was an enlightened practitioner.

It is not a journey for the squeamish, but for those prepared to leave the reassuring daytime clatter of Oxford Street in the 1790s and penetrate under that echoing archway into the quiet yards and stables beyond, it is possible from scattered contemporary evidence to catch at least a glimpse of Moorcroft at work among his patients. Perhaps the best place to start is at the pharmacy with its glass and pewter measures; the pestles and mortars, tin funnels, brass scale and weights, and possibly a beam for the heavier substances; the rows of glass and stone bottles and jars containing a range of herbs, chemicals and substances, little changed for centuries and remaining in use until the development of sulphonamides and antibiotics which have so recently revolutionized the whole science of chemo-therapeutics. As was the practice at the time, Moorcroft had his own special and secret formulations, some of them in powder form to be reconstituted with liquids as diverse as malt spirits, brandy, vinegar, honey, molasses or nitrous acid. In 1795, for example, he put together for sale what he called 'horse chests', equine first-aid boxes containing what he considered to be the basic list of medicines for wounds and illnesses likely to be encountered by the horse in India.[46] These chests included ointment for wounds and powder for strains and lamenesses which, mixed with some of the liquids mentioned above, could also be used for wrung withers, bruised backs or bowel galls. There was a drying powder for suppurating sores, thrush mixture, blistering ointment, styptic tincture to stop bleeding, tincture for direct application to wounds, and then the 'balls' to be taken internally – the purging ball, the diuretic ball, the colic ball and the cordial or restorative ball. Just what these mysterious spherical pills contained we can only guess, but probably the traditional ingredients of homeopathic medicine still in wide use today.

We know that Moorcroft, like almost all of his contemporaries for at least another half century, prescribed drastic treatments at both ends of the body for even relatively mild conditions. To treat common gripes, for example, his advice was:

> dissolve one of the colic balls in a pint of warm water, and give by means of a horn. Wisp [wipe] the belly very well, and give a glyster [enema] made of two quarts of warm water, and half a pound of common salt, every half hour till the gripings go off. . . . Be particularly attentive to drench [force-feed] the animal with large quantities of thin warm gruel.

This apparently harsh regime was, however, only the second stage of the main assault on the complaint, which consisted of opening the jugular vein in the horse's neck and extracting 'from two to six, or even eight quarts, if the symptoms be very violent, and the horse strong'.[47] The horse certainly needed to be strong for Moorcroft recommended bleeding on this scale for a range of other conditions including swellings of the legs and inflammation of the eyes and body and he also favoured the use of leeches for the extraction of blood from areas around the affected part. If asked why, he would have replied in terms which represented medical and veterinary orthodoxy from at least the second millennium BC down to the second half of the nineteenth century. Bleeding, it was believed, vented the superfluous 'humours' in the blood from which all or most diseases came, or at least reduced the liquid pressures causing swelling and inflammation. However, Moorcroft did not practise blood-letting on the massive and harmful scale of his contemporaries who often took as many gallons as he took quarts until the pulse of the sick animal wavered or it fell senseless to the ground. Harmful as it was, however, blood-letting was at least relatively painless. Very different were the agonies caused by 'firing' or 'blistering'. We know that both these painful and traditional techniques were recommended by Moorcroft, although always in moderation. For skin ulcers he advised that 'it would be well to destroy them, by the application of a hot iron, care being taken that the burning do not extend too far'.[48] For severed blood vessels, 'endeavour to tie the bleeding ends with waxed threads, which should hang out of the wound; or the ends of the vessel may be touched with a hot iron'.[49]

Bleeding, purging, drenching and firing would have been routine treatments for many of the horses at 224 Oxford Street. Moorcroft would increasingly have left much of the routine work to others as the practice grew, concentrating when he could on the more interesting cases. Even so, he could never be sure of an uninterrupted night. John Field's son has left a vivid little picture of one such occasion which can probably stand for many more.[50] A valuable animal suffering from simple fractures in the pastern and metatarsal bones of the leg was under intensive care:

A man who sat up with him all night, about four o'clock in the morning, going into the stable to see him, observed the tail very low and on looking into the stall saw his hind foot turned up backwards. Mr. Moorcroft and my father were called up, and found that both metatarsal bones were fractured at the same time with the large pastern of the near fore leg, and that the horse having lain down, had made extraordinary exertion to get up again, by which the simple fissures in these bones had become converted into compound fractures.

The scene in the lantern-lit stable is easily imagined as the group of men, clothes hastily thrown over their nightshirts and casting long shadows on the walls, conversed in low voices as they examined the stricken and wide-eyed animal. There was little to be done. That horse, with the owner's permission, may well have been pole-axed or shot the next day and probably ended up, with the help of the block and tackle and the suspending frame, on Moorcroft's dissecting table.

It was the same with most of the other animals who died in unusual or mysterious circumstances. Moorcroft was always an indefatigable *post mortem* operator and even when aspects of the physical anatomy of the animal were still in dispute, there was much to be learned, particularly in cases of morbid anatomy or pathology. It could not have been a very pleasant occupation in those pre-formalin days before a cheap and satisfactory preservative was available. In summer, when the medical and veterinary schools abandoned practical anatomy until the autumn, the dissector must sometimes have risked his health to work on the rapidly decaying corpse. Moreover some horse diseases, and particularly the often loathsome and incurable glanders, were themselves highly dangerous to the careless or unlucky operator, as Sainbel had discovered to his cost. Moorcroft was well aware of this although Coleman was not. Moorcroft later claimed that he had developed a treatment for glanders which although 'difficult, tedious and expensive' was sometimes successful. Whatever it was, he subsequently abandoned it because of the dangers involved.[51]

Horse medicine could certainly be dangerous, but so too in those pre-anaesthetic days was horse surgery. The first decision was whether to restrain the animal in the standing position or in slings, or whether to hobble and cast him down. This in itself could be a hazardous business in an enclosed stable, both for horse and helpers alike, and required a high degree of teamwork by the men concerned. Carelessness at this stage could literally be fatal. On a Sunday morning in October 1802 one of Moorcroft's neighbours in Oxford Street, 'a noted and opulent dealer in horses', received a massive kick in the chest from a horse improperly secured for surgery and was dead before he landed on the other side of the yard.[52] The horse is a powerful animal and delicate or deep surgery with his body tensing with pain, even when properly tethered or cast

[37]

with grooms spreadeagled across him, could never have been easy. Beside his helpers, Moorcroft would have had at his disposal an arsenal of operating instruments – implements is perhaps a better word for some of them – like bullet forceps, silver male catheters, whalebone probes, choking probangs, spring eye specula, ebony-handled tenacula, pewter penis syringes (to take only some from a contemporary list).[53] But it was his skill with the knife and the boldness of his surgery that many of the young men who watched Moorcroft at work remembered most years later, when they themselves were in successful practice.[54] It confirms what we know from his time with John Lyon at Liverpool.

A glimpse of him at work comes from his own instructions for making an incision to relieve the eye of its aqueous fluid:

> This operation requires some steadiness and address in the execution. The horse should be cast; and when the head is properly secured, the operator should, with the fingers of the left hand . . . press upon the eye from the eye-pit, so as to steady it, which however is not easily effected. With his thumb he should raise the upper eyelid, whilst an assistant presses down the lower; then holding a lancet with its edges standing upwards and downwards, and consequently the flat part towards the eye, he should push it into the clear part, at the outer corner, just before the white part, and carry it horizontally forwards; taking care not to give any other direction to the instrument.[55]

That was only a relatively simple and minor operation. Deftness with the knife could in more unusual and pioneering surgery, on the nerves of the legs for example, have dramatic and disastrous consequences. In this case a wealthy client's horse

> with coffin-joint lameness being thrown and secured; the nerve on the outside of the fetlock bared by two strokes of a round-edged knife, was cut across with the crooked knife; the operation took a few seconds; but at the instant the nerve was divided the horse made a violent and sudden exertion to disengage himself; a crash, as if from within his body was heard by the bystanders, and my intelligent assistant felt the shock of internal fracture as he lay over the animal, and whispered in my ear, that the horse had broke his back. This, in fact, had happened, and the animal was destroyed.[56]

Moorcroft, unlike some of his contemporaries, was never afraid to admit his failures if he believed that they might save others from errror. We happen to know about another failure, also while attempting a rarely performed operation, from the pen of the often vitriolic veterinarian, Bracy Clark.[57] Moorcroft was one of the very few to win the old Quaker's praise, even affection, but Clark was very critical of what he regarded as a hazardous and unnecessary attempt by Moorcroft to remove the ovaries of a valuable carriage mare. Moorcroft it seems was not put off, even by an unsuccessful trial run on an old mare which he had purchased, like so many of his experimental animals, from the slaughterhouse. At all events the quality animal, like its humble predecessor, died.

So too, according to Clark,[58] did a horse which Moorcroft attempted to castrate using the ligature method once common in human medicine and which he may have learned at Lyons. By it the animal's spermatic chord was tightly constricted, often between two wooden cramps, until the testicle mortified and fell off. The dangers of extensive inflammation and severe pain in this method are obvious. Clark and several of the younger generation of veterinary surgeons advocated gelding with the knife and then searing with the hot iron, in preference to the ligature method favoured by Moorcroft at this time. The fearful risks of sepsis, hernia and haemorrhage, all with attendant agony for the horse, were perhaps slight in both methods compared with that favoured by the country gelders of 'opening the scrotum with a knife, and tearing out the testicles with their teeth'.[59] Much later even more excruciatingly painful and prolonged methods were being seriously advocated by some members of the veterinary profession, although Moorcroft himself later refined a quick and relatively painless technique which was very widely adopted by the army in India.[60] More interesting because more daring were Moorcroft's attempts to reduce inflammation or discharge in the brain or in the foot, by tying some of the arteries supplying blood to the affected part.[61]

One area of horse medicine in which Moorcroft particularly concentrated his 'ardour for research',[62] and in which he has a claim to be a successful pioneer was in the diagnosis and treatment of lameness.[63] He seems to have won himself a reputation in this field remarkably quickly. Less than three years after he opened his doors in Oxford Street, a published work was speaking of his 'abilities' and 'the reputation he so justly deserves' and looking forward to the day when he would publish the results of his research into the subject.[64] It is of course true that this preoccupation with lameness was itself another sign of the relatively immature state of veterinary medicine at the time, but it was a very sensible specialism for a man in a busy metropolitan practice. The bulk of his patients would be suffering, not from the vivid catalogue of diseases in Blaine's list, but from one or other of the many common and often painful forms of lameness. One contemporary veterinary surgeon estimated that as many as half the horses in Britain became useless before their time because of incurable lameness of one kind or another.[65] The problem was often complex. Diseases and disorders of the foot could have their origin in a multitude of causes – injury, faulty shoeing or even the sometimes abysmal standards of stable management then current. They might also be a symptom of some malfunction higher up the leg or even in the shoulder. The lame horse usually tried to relieve the pain by shifting his weight off the foot which often resulted in the contraction of the heels of that foot. At the same time the sound fetlock joint of the other leg, by carrying more of the weight, would itself soon become inflamed and the leg or foot or both would ultimately be damaged as well. Diagnosis in these circumstances and without X-rays was not easy.

Moorcroft began his investigations logically enough with the foot itself but frequently found, even after the contraction and other problems in the foot had been eradicated, that the lameness still persisted. The most that he achieved by this approach was the more or less certain knowledge in each particular case as to whether curing the contraction would end the lameness or not. *Post mortem* examination of the feet of some of the animals which he failed to cure, often revealed a curious erosion and breakdown of the surface of the small navicular bone and of the tendon where it passed close to that bone. This damage, navicular disease as it is now called, is irreversible. Moorcroft was already aware of it by 1794, well ahead of his contemporaries. Needless to say, his early attempts to cure it by external means – mechanical contrivances, poultices, chemical treatments, heating, cooling and the like – all came to nothing. He next tried the effect of reducing the blood flow to the foot by tying the arteries. He had noticed that diseased navicular joints often had more extensive and distended blood vessels than was usual in the healthy joint and hoped, by reducing the blood supply, to reduce the pressure and thus the inflammation. This too was a blind alley for he was once again tackling the symptoms rather than the cause. In many cases, as he frankly admitted, this approach only made things worse.

If reducing the blood supply *to* the foot achieved nothing, then why not reduce the pain sensations *from* the foot by cutting some of the nerves? Neurotomy was not altogether unknown either in human or animal surgery and had earlier been practised in France as a treatment for navicular disease.[66] Moorcroft may have learned of it there, or it may have been almost on impulse that he one day, in his own words, 'raised the outer nerve of the fetlock joint out of its bed by a bent probe, and cut it across with a pair of scissors'. This laconic description does less than justice to the problems he faced. With the horse lying on its side and tightly tethered, there was the preliminary shaving of the leg, followed by the cautious incision, taking care to avoid the vein and throbbing artery, and the exposure of the tough and distinctively white nerve, beautifully protected and hidden away behind them both. Then came the violent struggle as the nerve was cut. After stitching and dressing, the horse was freed and scrambled to its feet. A few cautious steps round the stable and, to Moorcroft's delight, the lameness was either greatly reduced or had disappeared completely. He was obviously on to something this time and repeated the experiment several times. Unfortunately the apparently miraculous cure was usually very shortlived, and it was often only a matter of weeks before the animals were brought back to Oxford Street as lame as ever. Investigation showed that in some cases the severed nerve had reunited but even when a small section was removed 'certain appearances in a substance occupying the space in between excited the suspicion that this new growth conveyed nervous influence'. Moorcroft's suspicions were correct although nobody at the time was fully aware of the extraordinary capacity of the sectioned nerve to repair itself. Quite apart from this problem however, it was plain that many of the animals operated upon were obtaining only partial relief from the pain which distressed them.

It was at this point that Moorcroft decided to attempt to isolate the brain from *all* sensations in the foot, by removing a section from both the outer and inner nerves using an instrument specially made for the purpose. It was a bold experiment, for the horse in question was valuable and the complex working of the nervous system was at that time only partially understood. Nerves, after all, carry instructions from the brain as well as sensations to it. Moorcroft was literally attempting the unknown, and the results for the mare chosen for this pioneer experiment may have been dire. He had already removed the nerve from one side of her leg but she had relapsed into lameness again. Now, in the presence of some very eminent men, he sectioned the other. The relief of all of them must have been palpable when 'the animal on rising from the bed, trotted bold and without lameness', only stumbling occasionally. In a few weeks her owner, Lord George Cavendish, was even galloping her without serious problems other than an occasional stumble. It must have seemed like a miracle cure after the crippling and painful lameness which had preceded it.

In fact strictly speaking it was not really a cure at all. The inflamed bone and tendon were as damaged as ever and the risks of further injury to them and the rest of the foot were enormously increased by the removal of all sensation. This was soon revealed when the same mare was brought back into London for Moorcroft's attention with a terrible wound to the neurotomized foot but not the slightest lameness. 'It appeared that the mare, in galloping over some broken glass bottles, had set her foot full upon the fragments of the bottom of one of them, which had cut its way through frog and tendon into the joint, and stuck fast in the part for some seconds, whilst the animal continued its course, apparently regardless of the injury.' As he examined this wound, without the mare showing the slightest trace of distress, Moorcroft must have reflected on the serious consequences which could follow a complete neurotomy of the foot, not to speak of the possibilities of deception by the unscrupulous. He seems to have taken some pains to keep the technique secret from all but a little group of trusted professional colleagues to whom he demonstrated it. Indeed so successful was he in restricting knowledge of it that, a few years later, Coleman's assistant at the veterinary college was able to claim the discovery of neurotomy as his own until Moorcroft's prior claim was demonstrated. Even then, some still doubted.[67] In responsible hands neurotomy could give an animal which otherwise was sentenced to a progressively painful and ultimately incapacitating lameness, years of useful and pain-free life. Some neurotomized horses were even hunted successfully. In that sense neurotomy deserves the 1836 description of it as 'a noble experiment . . . one of the most signal triumphs of our profession'.[68] Yet in the hands of the careless and unscrupulous, the most fearsome consequences ensued with a neglected animal 'stumping about, for it could hardly be called going, till his hoofs came off', as Bracy Clark put it later.[69] That is why in the end Moorcroft decided to give it up. The horror stories are still told today whenever neurotomy is mentioned as a treatment for navicular disease. But it is still almost all we have. In this matter, modern veterinary medicine, even after 180 years of progress and experiment, has moved very little beyond the point which Moorcroft reached at the end of the eighteenth century.[70]

4 Failure and Success – Horseshoes and the India Connection,

1796–1808

If neurotomy was Moorcroft's most dramatic success in the fight against lameness, his attempt to manufacture and market the ideal horseshoe was certainly his biggest failure.

That unsuitable shoes and ignorant shoeing were causing unnecessary lameness and pain to the horse was obvious.

> The 18th-century British shoe was a ponderous contraption that required some 15 to 18 nails. The foot was prepared for shoeing by cutting away the sole until it would 'spring under the pressure of the thumb, and the frog and bars removed until the blood began to ooze'. So anxious were farriers to avoid the frog pressure inherent in the natural design of the foot that the shoe, which was so broad as to cover the sole, was made concave on the sole surface, and convex upon the ground surface. It would be difficult to design a shoe better adapted to defeating the normal physiology of the foot.[1]

The feet of animals shod like this were, as one contemporary critic put it, like those of a cat in walnut shells.[2] Appalled by these absurdities and stimulated by a steadily increasing understanding of the complex anatomy of the horse's foot and leg, the more intelligent veterinary surgeons of the time embarked enthusiastically on the search for the ideal general-purpose horseshoe.

None was more persistent than William Moorcroft. By 1796, after much experiment, observation and dissection, he had convinced himself that the so-called 'seated' shoe was the one best designed to reduce the diseases and deformations caused by current shoeing practice. Lighter, narrower and thinner than the common shoe, it was also quite different in section. Its under surface was completely flat and so too was the upper outer surface where the crust of the hoof rested upon it. The inner angle of the upper surface was concave. This shoe was not Moorcroft's invention as he freely admitted.[3] He obtained it, as so much else, from the remarkably enlightened teaching of the great Scottish farrier of the previous generation, James Clark. Unfortunately the relatively complex shape of the seated shoe made it a craftsman's product. It was difficult to make and correspondingly expensive to buy. It could never be more than an unattainable ideal for the majority of horses unless its price could be reduced.[4] The means in those early days of the Industrial Revolution seemed obvious. As Moorcroft himself put it, '. . . the great advantages derived from introducing machinery in lieu of manual exertion, in many of the mechanical arts, naturally led me to consider of a mode of applying it to this purpose'.[5] Perhaps this is how he spent the £200 legacy from his grandfather's estate which came to him at about this time.[6] First, he experimented with the possibilities of pre-shaping the shoes by running the red-hot bars through etched metal rollers 'turned by a horse mill or other power' and pre-set to produce the right thickness and section. The bars were then cut and bent to shape on the anvil by the traditional means. Then, again in his own words, 'when the shoes have been so turned, I heat them again red-hot, and strike them between dies fixed in a common fly press (such as is used for coining money . . .'. The results of these modest experiments in die-stamping seemed very encouraging.

> The shoes . . . are more perfect in their shape, afford a truer and better support to the foot of the horse than the shoes in common use, and prevent many of the diseases incident to that part from the manner of manufacturing horses shoes now in common use.[7]

Early in 1796 Moorcroft decided to embark on the expensive and, at the time, rarely used process of obtaining a patent for his primitive invention.[8] On 16 April, after consulting his lawyer and riding round the town to at least five different government offices, doubtless disbursing handsome tips to speed things along as he went, he got it. It was worth waiting for – a splendidly packaged document on parchment, sealed with the Great Seal itself in yellow wax, 5 inches (127 millimetres) across and packed in a handsome wooden case, covered with leather and embossed in gold with the royal coat of arms. On 14 May, just inside the prescribed month, Moorcroft 'came before our Lord the King in His Chancery' and enrolled his patent.[9] In theory at least, he now had fourteen years in which to develop his invention free of imitation.

Things looked very hopeful. Doubtless Moorcroft fitted his shoes whenever opportunity offered to the horses which came and went at Oxford Street and to those of his friends who were prepared to trust him. One who did, enthusiastically it seems, was Lord Heathfield. He allowed one of his precious cavalry chargers to be shod with Moorcroft's dye-struck shoes and they lasted a triumphant twenty-eight months without significant damage either to the horse or to the shoes themselves.[10] 'I believe', wrote Moorcroft to a client in November 1797, 'that nothing more is wanted to have their superiority generally acknowledged than to procure for them a fair and extensive trial.'[11]

'Extensive' is certainly the word for Moorcroft's plans at this time. If these shoes were as good as they seemed, then the rudimentary methods of the 1796 patent and the limited production they made possible were just not enough to lower the price or raise the output. A great national revolution in shoeing technology needed something bigger and better. If power and simple machinery could improve the hand-made product to such an extent, then why not harness the full potential of mass-production by designing a machine which could complete the whole process with only the minimum of unskilled labour? This, of course, was a very big step into the unknown. Moorcroft was always fascinated by engines, but the production engineering problems involved in that age of still very limited machine technology were too formidable to yield to enthusiasm alone. Behind them lurked an even more intractable problem: the successful mass-production of cheap and serviceable horseshoes would have explosive social and economic consequences for the tight-knit and ultra-conservative world of the farriers.

Moorcroft seems to have resolved this difficulty, at least to his own satisfaction, with the comforting belief that a good, cheap, off-the-peg product would benefit the farriers as much as the public, by lowering their costs and improving their productivity.[12] That, to put it mildly, was optimistic, but Moorcroft *was* an optimist, an obstinate and persevering enthusiast for any scheme, whatever the odds stacked against it, if it seemed worthwhile and, above all, useful. By the end of 1797 he was far advanced with the plans for an ambitious project requiring, he calculated, an additional capital investment beyond his own resources of £2000.[13] As things turned out that was probably a very conservative estimate indeed, but it was still a very large sum to raise, particularly in 1797. The war with France was biting deep and there was no sign of an end to it. Money was short, the economy over-strained, and food prices soaring. Earlier in the year the Bank of England had suspended gold payments and later the first of several periodic invasion scares occurred which put London in turmoil. To make it all the more alarming the naval mutiny at the Nore for a few tense days cut off the movement of all merchant shipping up and down the London river. There could hardly have been a worse time to raise a large sum of capital for what was at best a highly speculative venture.

Moorcroft, after talking the whole matter over with his friends, managed it by 'applying to twenty gentlemen for the loan of £100 each, to be returned at the end of four years' at 5 per cent interest per annum.[14] Apparently undeterred, either by the mounting costs or by what he later called 'My anxiety in making a great variety of experiments'[15] or by the inevitable setbacks, the construction and modification of the great machine went slowly ahead. We do not know whether the work took place in specially converted accommodation at the back of Oxford Street or not but it seems unlikely. The machine in its final form stood on its great timber bed something like 26 feet (7.9 metres) in height and 18 feet (5.4 metres) long and would perhaps have weighed several tons.[16] It required a continuous and substantial power source, either literal horse-power from a horse-mill or its equivalent, perhaps from one of James Watt's recently-patented rotating steam engines or a water-mill. In addition, the production process called for a furnace to heat the iron bars red-hot. Moorcroft must have spent much of his time nursing this gleaming and unpredictable monster through setback after setback. The problems are plain from the patent specification. But at last the great machine was ready for a demonstration to its backers and on 3 May 1800 Moorcroft was granted his new patent for: 'A New, improved, and still more Expeditious Mode by the application of Machinery to my former Mode, of Making and Working Horse-Shoes'.

The next step was to publicise the new product. Moorcroft's sixty-page *Cursory Account of the Various Methods of Shoeing Horses* was deliberately written for the layman and contained no more anatomy than was absolutely necessary. It criticized, although in moderate terms, the other kinds of shoes currently available, including the thin-toed, thick-heeled variety being advocated by his former colleague at the veterinary college, Edward Coleman. Instead, Moorcroft argued the merits of the seated shoe and expressed the hope

> that at a period not far distant, I shall be enabled to offer to the public, better shoes than have usually been made, at a reasonable price. . . . With regard to the shoes made by my machinery, I rest my expectations of the public opinion, both to their form and other properties, on the result of public experience, being well assured, that the trial will be fair, and the verdict just.[17]

Just or not, the outcome must have been a shattering disappointment to Moorcroft. His little book was translated into German and some machine shoes were produced and used.[18] But the great machine was never able to go into the only kind of continuous production that would have justified 'the immense expence'[19] of its capital and development costs. Very soon it was silent, mute testimony to the wreck of its backers' hopes.

Moorcroft must often have wondered what exactly had gone wrong. Commercial failure was very common in those early years of mass-production machine technology. With high investment costs, novel design problems and rudimentary distribution networks this was perhaps inevitable. Even successful and revolutionary designs, like Arkwright's spinning frame, took five years to develop and cost £12,000 before it began to earn its inventor the first of the returns which eventually made him a millionaire and revolutionized the cotton industry.[20] For many reasons the application of invention to production was very slow, and never more so than when its adoption required a major change in the habits of a strongly entrenched, numerous and conservative labour-force, such as the farriers undoubtedly were.

Moorcroft, the practical countryman, had gained much of his early knowledge of animal medicine from the more intelligent farriers in Lancashire and, to his credit, he never stooped to the blanket abuse of them which marked the writings of so many of the new veterinarians.[21] Nevertheless the opposition of the farriers to the mass adoption of his machine-shoe was crucial. At least one farrier, John Lane, went into print. His pamphlet, with the revealing title *The Principles of English Farriery Vindicated*, was published in 1800 almost simultaneously with Moorcroft's book and patent. Without mentioning Moorcroft by name, Lane produced a very plausible critique of the whole concept of his machine-made pattern shoes:

> There is no pattern to go by but the foot. . . . When they come from the engine they will fit no foot; and if they would the pores of the iron being so open, they would have little wear, but bend to the foot. Every man knows, that unless a shoe is well-

hammered, when fitting, it will not wear well. Then how or where is the hammer to be applied without changing the form? The art of shoeing horses does not consist of making the shoes, but in fitting them properly to the foot, and safely nailing them on; as a man will, on an average, make three, while he can properly fit one. . . . However ingenious the construction of the engine will be, a practical farrier, that understands his profession, before he adopted it would reason thus: In the first place the iron must be drawn in a particular manner, which will cause nearly as much labour and expence, as to make the shoes; and the number of men, that are employed to prepare the iron for the engine, and to work it, can make many more shoes by hand, in less time, and much better than with the engine. . . . It is impossible to be done by such means.[22]

James Clark had earlier warned of the indomitable prejudice and opposition of the farriers to his seated shoe, without even giving it a fair trial. The prejudice was still around a century later.[23] The theoretical objections advanced by Lane were obviously not based on proper trials of the machine shoes, but they were, none the less, formidable.

The classic objection to the suitability of any single pattern was one which Moorcroft could have found in the writings of the very man whose views on shoeing he esteemed most highly of all, James Clark.[24] Even if, in principle, the seated shoe was suitable for hacks, hunters, cavalry, coach and carriage horses alike (and Clark certainly believed that), the considerable variety of size and shape required to be stocked in the busy forge would in itself constitute a formidable cost objection to the prefabricated shoe. Lane made the same point and the problem faces the retailer of off-the-peg human footwear today.

The need for 'hammer hardening' was another matter emphasized by Clark[25] but he was a farrier and Moorcroft had probably never shod a horse in his life.[26] It does seem clear from the wording of his patent specifications that he did not give sufficient attention to the metallurgical problems involved in machine manufacture, and he may have been misled in this matter by his experiences with the more limited prototype machine. The shoes which had served Lord Heathfield's charger so well, for example, were rolled and embossed by machine but were shaped and hammer-hardened on the anvil by the traditional methods.

The objections of the farriers to the machine-shoe might have been dis-counted or overcome in other ways if there had been unanimity among the wealthy horse-owners and contemporary veterinarians that the seated shoe was the most generally acceptable pattern to adopt. Unfortunately for Moor-croft there was no unanimity at all. No horse subject divided men more deeply than that of shoes and shoeing. Perhaps the most influential opponent of the seated shoe was Edward Coleman. He devoted nearly a quarter of the second volume of his only major veterinary work to an explicit criticism of it. He was polite but damning. He acknowledged Moorcroft's great abilities but added that: 'the more eminent Mr. Moorcroft's professional character, the more I feel it my duty to scrutinize those opinions . . . [which], although very plausible and ingenious, are nevertheless, in my humble judgement, founded in error'.[27] How much in error he made clear by arguing that Moorcroft's shoe would be better for the horse if nailed on upside down![28] Coleman's so-called 'college shoe', backed by his growing influence and prestige as the head of England's only veterinary college, was soon available at several London forges and, for a while at least, was a formidable competitor for the seated shoe. Several, who later admitted that Moorcroft had been right all the time, confessed that they had been led astray for years by Coleman's false teaching in this matter.[29] But Coleman was not the only one. Several powerful men in the profession, including some who had the highest regard for Moorcroft and spoke of him as a friend, were determinedly advocating their own favoured horseshoe designs and shoeing techniques.

The seated shoe, whether machine-made or not, obviously had almost no chance of widespread acceptance when the veterinary leaders of the horse world were divided and the farriers either implacably opposed or simply ignorant. The machine-made seated shoe was almost bound to fail – and in due course it did. In this, as in so much else, Moorcroft was far ahead of his time. His advocacy of the seated shoe, although contested at the time, was probably an important factor later on in bringing that pattern into general use in England by the mid-nineteenth century.[30] Most of the designs being advocated by his opponents have generally been rejected by posterity as impracticable or downright harmful, but the seated shoe is still used in special situations.[31] Moreover Moorcroft was right in his tenacious belief in the feasibility of a machine-made product. Once the production and metallurgical problems had been satisfactorily overcome, machine-made pattern horseshoes were widely and successfully used. They still are today.[32]

Other aspects of Moorcroft's horseshoe research were successfully taken up later too. One of the most interesting sections of Moorcroft's little book deals with the perennial problem of the horse which strikes and cuts one leg with the shoe of the other.[33] The problem had been puzzling him for at least five years before he went into print. In many cases he had been foiled in his attempts to eradicate the fault by adopting the then standard practice of building up the shoes on the inside so as to change the angle of the lower leg and throw the cutting foot outward. Being the man he was, he then decided to try precisely the opposite and, much to his surprise, it worked. Using carefully measured evidence from hoof-prints, he was able to demonstrate that an increase in the normal interval between the feet of up to 1½ inches (38 millimetres) could be achieved by raising shoes on the outside. This part of his book was frequently reprinted in the veterinary journals later on when all the rest had been forgotten.[34] In the 1850s Moorcroft's so-called 'twisted shoes' were said to be all the rage among the shoeing-smiths in the City of London.[35] The technique is still used on occasion today.

Posthumous success, however, is never much consolation to an inventor. By 1802, with his borrowed capital due for redemption and years of development work largely wasted, Moorcroft must have been heartily sick of the subject of horseshoes and horseshoe machinery. There is no evidence that any of his backers lost their money – he was always punctilious about repaying his creditors when taking risks with their money later in India – but he seems to have lost a great deal of his own, as much as £16,000 according to one estimate.[36] It is frequently asserted that the size of these losses eventually drove Moorcroft, like many a man before and since, to try and recoup his fortunes in India. The evidence does not support such a view. He was, after all, the senior partner of London's biggest and best veterinary practice. By 1798, only five years after he opened his doors at Oxford Street, he was already said to be worth £2000 a year and that was a fortune at the time.[37] Good horses remained in short supply and their price climbed ever higher as the war continued its apparently endless course.[38] The general economic depression might make the stock and other commodity markets slump but never that for horses. On the contrary, the evidence available suggests that Moorcroft's practice grew steadily more prosperous as each year succeeded the last. In either 1804 or 1805, with John Field's family growing fast, Moorcroft moved out of the Oxford Street house a few hundred yards to the west, beyond Tyburn, into number 9 St George's Row.[39] This was the name of an isolated double terrace of fourteen substantial houses on the north side of the Uxbridge (now the Bayswater) Road, backing on to St George's churchyard and the fields of Paddington village. The upper windows of these houses enjoyed superb views across Hyde Park towards the Surrey hills. From their size and position they were obviously the homes of gentlemen of means. Paul Sandby RA, the distinguished landscape artist and a great favourite of the royal family, was one of Moorcroft's new neighbours.[40] Two years after this, in 1806, the rateable value of the Oxford Street premises suddenly jumped by half and the rates paid almost doubled.[41] This suggests that some extra accommodation was acquired, perhaps the stabling which lay behind numbers 231 and 232 a few doors along the street. Either before or after this expansion, the practice is stated to have had accommodation for sixty-three animals in Oxford Street as well as several forges and a pharmacy.[42] In addition twenty or thirty more stables were acquired in the village of Hammersmith west of London.[43] None of this, nor much other evidence either, suggests that the horseshoe machine brought Moorcroft to the edge of bankruptcy. He was never 'a money-keeping man' as he later confessed[44] – it came easily and easily it went. Financial losses even on this scale never seem to have worried him very much and they certainly would not have driven him to India.

Nevertheless it is clear that he had invested and lost much more than mere money in the fiasco. At a critical stage in his career it had cost him precious time which could have been used in more directly useful veterinary investigations and publication. He never wrote the great authoritative work on lameness and diseases of the foot which his reputation at the time led people to expect. There is indeed a large and puzzling gap between his enormous contemporary and posthumous veterinary reputation and the fragmentary and perfunctory quality of his published work in this London period. Later on Moorcroft looked back on the missed opportunities of these years with regret.[45] We know that writing never came very easily to him and the demands of the practice must have been unremitting, even without the extra distraction of the horseshoe venture. All the same its failure was the first in a professional career which, until then, had been an unbroken chain of success. Whether it damaged his reputation seems doubtful, but it must have cost him, besides money and peace of mind, some of his self-esteem. Hints in his letters suggest that the memory of it still rankled years later.[46] Time was passing. He was already in his mid-thirties, a wiser if not yet a sadder man. The best years were slipping inexorably away, like the blood from one of those deep wounds he could cauterize and stitch so deftly. Only *this* was a flow which nothing could staunch.

Fortunately, in the wake of the horseshoe failure came a new professional interest. Indeed the year 1800 is something of a turning-point in Moorcroft's London life. In March he finished the horseshoe book. In the early summer he filed his patent for the great machine the book was designed to boost. In the autumn a new client came on to the account ledger at 224 Oxford Street – the Honourable United Company of Merchants of England trading to the East Indies.

At this time the East India Company, from behind the new classical façade of its modest building in Leadenhall Street, was presiding almost helplessly over those astonishing developments which were transforming it, in the sixty years after 1757, from a modestly successful chartered trading company into the ruler of a vast sub-continental empire in India. Moorcroft's informal connection with India went back to the very beginning of his London practice. He corresponded with a number of people there on the subject of horses and, in 1795 as a private, commercial venture, had produced for sale his first-aid chests designed expressly for the horse in India. The pitiful booklet he produced to go with it, of which he must have been heartily ashamed in later years, reveals an unsurprising ignorance of India's veterinary problems. In the book he appealed for more information and he certainly needed it. Significantly, his own awakening curiosity about the problems of horse-management in India in the 1790s, was being matched by that of the East India Company itself, and it was perhaps inevitable that, sooner or later, these converging interests would bring the company and London's leading horse-veterinary surgeon into a close and mutually beneficial business relationship.

The company's problem was this.[47] Cornwallis's second war against Mysore in 1790–2 had revealed a critical shortage of cavalry horses capable of carrying the 252-lb (115-kg) load of the dragoon and his equipment at speed over great distances in rough country. That war was won, although not easily, but in the years of peace that followed, the military balance of power in India continued to tilt against the company as rival native powers remodelled their armies on European lines. In this new situation an efficient and substantial cavalry arm was becoming essential. As the Mysore campaigns had shown, the company was not well-placed to fight a long war against a well-matched foe. It needed both the mobility and the shock-power which only a well-mounted cavalry and horse artillery could provide, and the capacity to drive deep into an enemy's territory and dictate peace there in a single campaign. The response to this need was a rapid augmentation of the native cavalry establishment of the Indian armies in the 1790s, masterminded by General John Floyd. Unfortunately almost no horses suitable for cavalry were bred in the company's territories at all. The military purchasing agents were forced to range further and further to the north in pursuit of a dwindling supply, as political upheavals in Afghanistan and elsewhere continued to erode the once-great northern horse trade. Even more serious, supplies from this source were liable to be cut off at a moment's notice by the Maratha powers across whose territories they came, just when they might be needed most.

To cope with this dangerous situation, government breeding-studs were established in Madras and Bengal in the 1790s, with the prime aim of producing an assured supply of suitable animals for military use. The results were disappointing, partly because parent-stock of the required height and bone was just not available in sufficient quantity. The only readily available pure-blood horse in India was the Arab, but for all its fleetness and beauty it was generally too slight to cross with the undersized country mares which were all that were available in quantity. The expert opinion available to the company in London, and that almost certainly included William Moorcroft's, suggested that the best solution would be to export to India good thoroughbred English stallions together with a supply of big, bony, halfbred English hunting mares to serve as a breeding-stock. That was easier said than done. The Napoleonic Wars were making enormous demands on the available supply of good animals and as the supply dwindled, so the price rose. Even when the right horses were found, enormous problems from weather, disease and French privateers, not to mention shipping such fragile and valuable cargo in a pitching East Indiaman on a six-month journey halfway round the world, still remained.

Yet the risks had to be faced if the breeding operations in India were to have any hopes of success. In London the driving-force behind the whole effort was one of the company's recently elected directors, Edward Parry. He, together with his old friend and fellow-director, Charles Grant, and men like Wilberforce and Henry Thornton, was one of the 'Saints', a member of the Clapham Sect, deeply involved in missionary work and Bible translation and the campaign against the slave trade. According to one of his colleagues Parry was 'a man who has infinite kindness in his character and mad only upon one subject – religion'.[48] Horses came a close second to religion. Parry, after service in Bengal as a younger man, had returned home to farm and during those thirteen years he had developed a special interest in horse-breeding. It was certainly a common passion for horses rather than for evangelical Christianity which would have brought Parry and Moorcroft into contact with each other, probably some time in the late 1790s. The earliest evidence of the connection comes from the records of the East India Company.[49]

In the autumn of 1800 Moorcroft was asked to use his extensive connections in the British horse world to find suitable animals for shipment to India as breeding stock. In February 1801, a stallion costing £420 was in the Oxford Street stables, the first of a steady stream of horses in the next half century to set out from that address down the road to Portsmouth and thence on the long and uncomfortable voyage to India. Soon Moorcroft was acting not only as the company's purchasing agent but as its equine shipping agent too, carefully calculating the daily ration of feed, medicine and bedding needed on the journey, arranging for it to be loaded at Gravesend and sometimes even finding the groom who took the horse to Portsmouth and travelled out with it to India. In those early days everything had to be worked out from scratch – the safest method of hoisting the animal aboard, for example, and the difficult question of where and how to keep him when he got there. In 1801 two brood mares were acquired and despatched and in October of that year the first bill – £185 14s. 7d. (£185.73) – to cover the keep of the animals was paid by the company to the credit of Moorcroft and Field, veterinary surgeons.[50]

Purchase on the home market for India's needs was a step in the right direction, but in Parry's view it was too costly and too uncertain to be relied upon alone. In March 1801 therefore, he urged that the company should lease a farm near London and start its own breeding operations there with a resident groom and 'under a Superintendent well-qualified who should visit them once a week and give every necessary direction'.[51] Things moved quickly after that.[52] A small 'committee for the improvement of the breed of horses in India' was set up to supervise the whole operation and search for a suitable farm. In the summer of 1802 the committee finally purchased the remaining fourteen years of the lease of a 130-acre (52-hectare) mixed farm at Padnalls, just north of the straggling village of Dagenham on the Romford turnpike which at that time crossed the gently sloping open country between the Thames marshes to the south and Hainault forest to the north.

Moorcroft, meanwhile, was still acting as consultant and purchasing agent to the whole project. He seems to have thrown himself into the work with his characteristic enthusiasm, ranging far and wide for bargains in an effort to avoid the increasingly exorbitant prices of the London market. On one occasion he went up to Billing beyond Northampton 'to see a colt belonging to Mr. Elwes which his state of health induced him to part with for 400 guineas but which he afterwards much regretted'. On other occasions he was at Petworth inspecting Lord Egremont's stud, at the annual summer sales at Newmarket, at the Horncastle Fair in Lincolnshire in the autumn of 1801 and, a year later, along with buyers from all over the country, he was in Cumberland for the great sale of the late Earl of Lonsdale's stock at Penrith.[53] He probably also attended the great horse fair at Howden in Yorkshire each Michaelmas when as many as 16,000 animals changed hands in ten days. Besides all this there were innumerable shorter journeys out of town to visit dealers who had advertised in the London newspapers and he frequently would have dropped in at the twice-weekly auctions at the Hyde Park Corner sale-ring of his friend Edmund Tattersall or lingered in the elegant dining-room to talk about horses with the other subscribers.[54] Moorcroft had a sharp eye for a bargain and the East India Company benefited greatly from his expertise. At first they were getting it on the cheap but eventually in April 1803 Moorcroft had to remind Parry that he was only charging for the keep of the animals and nothing for his own considerable time and expenses.[55] His letter prodded the committee into action. A week later he was formally appointed 'Superintendent of the Stud' at Padnalls on a backdated annual gratuity of £120 plus all expenses.[56]

The money was, no doubt, very useful in the wake of the horseshoe débâcle, but the company's work meant much more than income to Moorcroft. For years he had, as he put it,[57] 'repressed the indulgence of a fondness for agricultural pursuits' learned on the black soil of south-west Lancashire. Now he had both excuse and reason to get out of town at least once a week, to supervise the modest farming and breeding venture at Padnalls.[58] He must have looked forward to those weekly discussions with faithful Sam. Yull, the resident groom. There was building work to be done; new stabling to be designed and requisitioned; accounts and pedigree records to be kept up to date; crops to be harvested and the surplus sold; machines to be tried and recommended like that for bruising-corn or the 'dung picking-up machine' which caught his eye on a journey to Devon; trouble to sort out with one of the farm tenants in arrears with his rent; feedstuffs and vegetables to be found at reasonable prices in a period of wartime scarcity. Back in town there were reports to be written for the breeding committee and from time to time the need to ride down to Leadenhall Street, either to meet Parry or, more usually, James Coggan (who acted conveniently as secretary to both the stud and shipping committees). Years later, in another world on the other side of the Himalayas, Moorcroft characteristically remembered this faithful old company servant and sent him an Indian sword as a reminder of their brief but congenial working relationship.[59] In the spring of 1805 Moorcroft was buying bulls as well as horses for shipment to India. In 1807 he was investigating with the Portsmouth agent the loss of a valuable horse while loading and suggesting improved ways, using slings or wooden cradles, to prevent another such accident.

All this varied work must have been meat, drink and fresh air to Moorcroft and he seems to have done it very well. Parry was down at Padnalls on the last day of 1804 and next day recorded his pleasure at finding 'everything going on with so much success, regularity and good management' there.[60] In April 1807 the company paid Moorcroft an extra gratuity of £100 for 'his attention and the trouble and expenses he has incurred'.[61] Some years later Parry recalled to Warren Hastings his impressions of Moorcroft at this period.

> I had no doubt [of] his zeal in the pursuit [of horse-breeding], his surgical and his veterinary knowledge, his passion for horses. . . . I also knew he was fond of agriculture and the improvement of cattle generally, and having seen a good deal of his character I was sure whatever he undertook he would persevere in.[62]

It is the best and fairest summary we have of the public and professional man as his varied Oxford Street clients would have known him.

5 PRIVATE WORLD AND THE INDIA DECISION,

1792–1808

EVEN FOR THE indefatigable Moorcroft there was more to life than work. No picture of his London years would be complete without a glimpse into his more private, off-duty world.[1] That world, of course, was dominated by the French Revolution and the long years of international war which followed it. The two things acting together were posing unique and novel strains on late eighteenth-century Britain, and perhaps in London, with its astonishing concentration of extreme wealth and extreme poverty and its vulnerability to invasion, more than anywhere else in the kingdom. The 1790s were certainly a bad time to be poor – there was widespread unemployment, bankruptcy and soaring food prices, all made worse by a run of bad harvests and wet summers and the continuous dislocation of trade and industry caused by the long and exhausting war. In this situation, violent expressions of the hardship and misery being experienced at the lower end of the social scale were inevitable. The London newspapers of that time have frequent accounts of destructive mobs on the rampage and civil tumult of one kind or another.

More sinister, because more co-ordinated and articulate, were the activities of radical bodies like the London Corresponding Society. The Paris of 1789 onwards had shown just how explosive the mixture of working-class distress and articulate middle-class political opposition in a nation's capital could be. Arthur Young was not the only one who feared trouble in Britain. Indeed, in his view, the question of how far revolution would spread to the whole of Europe was the single most absorbing political question of the 1790s.[2] Moreover, once revolutionary France embarked on war, it was not just a question of spontaneous revolutionary combustion from within Britain, but of violent incursion from without as well.

The first great invasion scare to grip London, all the more easily because so much of the regular army was committed abroad, came in 1797–8. It was followed, more fiercely, by another when war was resumed after thirteen months of uneasy peace in the spring and summer of 1803. For the next two years Napoleon had an invasion force massed on the Channel coast near Boulogne, with London as its prime target. If the emperor had ever won naval command of the Channel for the few hours or days he needed, his 150,000 troops were to be rushed across for a swift landing in Thanet and were to be in the heart of the metropolis four days later. Their orders, at least according to the inflamed imagination and purple prose of one broadsheet writer of the time, were '*to murder all our Inhabitants bearing Arms in our Defence, violate the Wives and Daughters of our People, and plunder our Cities*'. To meet and repel this threat it was urged that all must join 'an ARMED HOST OF BRITISH FREEMEN, READY TO DIE IN OUR DEFENCE'.[3]

The speedy formation of a volunteer citizen army was an obvious response, not only to the danger of external invasion, but to that of domestic unrest too.[4] Spurred by patriotic excitement and propaganda, and encouraged by special legislation rushed through Parliament, almost every parish and town in the land had soon raised a local force. In London and the surrounding villages alone, more than 27,000 men were under arms and the squares and open spaces, even the graveyards, were pressed into service as parade grounds. For those like Moorcroft who lived near Hyde Park, the days were punctuated by the rattle of drums, shrill trumpet-calls, shouted commands and the sharper noise of pistol or musketry fire. Most of London's volunteer units were made up of foot soldiers, but for the wealthier citizens with fine horses in their stables at the western end of the town, there was the added possibility of volunteering in the more expensive and prestigious role of cavalry trooper. In February 1797 a handful of the gentlemen of Westminster met by agreement at the King's Arms tavern. They decided to form themselves into what they called the Westminster Volunteer Cavalry (WVC), and appealed to every horse-owning gentleman in the City of Westminster to come forward 'to protect his Life, Family and Property'.[5]

One of the earliest of Westminster's citizens to respond to this appeal was the architect George Saunders who lived at 252 Oxford Street. In no time at all he was playing a key role in the infant corps, negotiating on its behalf for the use of the Duke of Gloucester's riding house in Hyde Park, and using his professional skills to supervise the erection of additional accommodation nearby for the duke's displaced carriages and later of extensions to the riding house itself. Saunders was soon a pillar of the WVC, auditing its accounts and serving as its inspector with an *ex officio* place on its committee which he attended regularly for many years. Later he became treasurer of the corps.[6] As it happened Saunders lived just across the road from Moorcroft and was fast becoming one of his closest friends. Eventually, although not until after the renewed outbreak of war with France in 1803, Saunders persuaded his friend to join the WVC.

It is not known why Moorcroft resisted so long. As a genuine patriot and a man of property he had a vested interest in preserving the status quo. Moreover, he had had a close-up view of revolutionary France denied to all but a very few of his countrymen and the experience had left him with a not entirely favourable view of the French national character. Perhaps the horseshoe project was too all-absorbing and time-consuming to allow for the consider-able demands on his time (and his purse) which service in a volunteer cavalry regiment demanded. Perhaps he had too much of horse and cavalry problems in his daily work to want to spend his spare time with them too. Whatever his reasons Moorcroft seems to have held aloof from any volunteer soldiering until the spring of 1803 brought a greater risk of invasion than ever before.

It is said that not a Londoner in those tense months went to bed without first making sure that the huge warning bonfires on hills ringing the town were safely unlit. The War Department was hard at work on plans to ring south London with a line of defensive fortifications, gun positions were marked out and plans for evacuating the king and government were prepared in readiness. New legislation added powerful financial and other incentives to volunteer service and exemption from general enlistment in the army of reserve was offered to all volunteers who joined before mid-June 1803 and performed a minimum number of hours' training with their regiments. Personal pressures were at work too. On 2 June 1803 the committee of the WVC decided to circulate all its members with a series of resolutions 'in the present critical situation of the Kingdom, menaced with Invasion by a desperate and implacable Enemy'.[7] They pointed out among other things that it was the duty of every member of the corps to recruit new members. Saunders as a committee member was certainly in a good position to present the force of all this to Moorcroft. Besides, the corps needed a veterinary adviser and there was also the prospect of some modest business for the practice. Eventually Moorcroft was persuaded and on 23 July, along with twenty others, he was balloted for by the committee and duly elected.[8] Two days later Moorcroft rode over to the riding house to pay his subscription, take the oath of allegiance to king and country and sign the muster roll.[9] Very shortly afterwards Private William Moorcroft of 2nd Troop, Westminster Volunteer Cavalry would have received the three, newly printed, blue booklets setting out the regulations, bye-laws, uniforms and basic drills of his new corps.[10]

There were 252 names on the muster roll of the WVC at this time – three field officers, a chaplain, a surgeon and two trumpeters served the whole corps, and the remainder of the more junior officers and other ranks were divided into four cavalry troops.[11] None of them were expected to be mere names on the roll – 'paper men are not for these times' said one circular posted at the riding house.[12] Regular attendance at drills, field days and general musters was compulsory, both in summer and winter, with stiff fines for absence without prior permission. Leave had to be applied for in writing and, at the height of the invasion scares, no member was allowed to leave town without first leaving a written indication of where he could be reached at short notice. All members were required to make sure that their servants knew the special importance of any sealed letter with the WVC monogram on the back, and were to assemble at short notice in an emergency whenever required. Most of the civil disturbances, which in earlier years had frequently led the corps to turn out at the requisition of the local magistrates, were happily over but there were still inspections, reviews, state occasions and brigade manoeuvres to be attended as well as the more routine training sessions at the riding house. Membership of the WVC in these crisis years was a very heavy commitment indeed, both of time and money.[13] Having hesitated about joining for so long, Moorcroft, once in, seems to have thrown himself into civilian soldiering with his usual headlong enthusiasm.[14]

His first task would have been to visit the regimental tailor to kit himself out with the splendid but absurdly impractical, toy-soldier huzzar uniform of the day. This was a formidable undertaking in itself. In full dress he was required to appear on parade in white kid gloves and black neckband with his 'hair queued with ten inches of riband and rosette, and short sides'. On his head he wore the magnificent light dragoon peaked helmet 'with lining and pad, black bear skin crest, dark blue silk turban and bow, gold fringe tassels, gilt chains, bar, medallion (motto *non nobis sed Patriae*)',[15] the whole topped with a white feathery plume. The jacket was dark blue with gilt buttons and chain wings, scarlet collar and cuffs and trimmed with gold lace. His breeches were of soft white leather with pearl buttons, tucked inside long black leather boots with polished spurs. Across the shoulder on a white strap, he wore a cartouche box containing twelve rounds of ammunition and, at his side, a sabre hanging from a white sword belt. His dark blue cloaked great coat with scarlet edgings was carried at the saddle in a special dark blue case also edged with scarlet. For the horse he needed a pattern bridle, reins, headpiece, martingale, breast plate and a white collar. A leather pistol holster containing the regulation $5/8$-inch (15-millimetre) bore pistol and a shoe case, both with black bearskin tops, were carried each side of the special saddle with its hogskin seat, double skirts, black crupper, blue- and scarlet-striped girths and heavy polished stirrups. Of course the full splendour was mainly reserved for the big ceremonial occasions and for the twice-monthly Wednesday evening 'field days'. For the ordinary drill practices, a simpler undress uniform of plain blue jacket and pantaloons or overalls and half-boots was permitted.

Moorcroft, practised horseman though he was, had a great deal to learn, and would have spent a lot of time at the Hyde Park riding house under the eagle eye of the riding master and the regular sergeants, learning to control his horse using only his knees, while mastering the complex drill exercises. Arms drill on horseback was even more demanding. Loading the pistol required the cartridge to be bitten, the powder sprinkled on the pan and the ramrod used to ram the ball home before firing at the target. The mounted sword exercises were not much easier, many of them performed at the gallop and some while facing backwards 'looking directly over the horse's croup, with the sword arm over it in the rear cut' position. This exercise, advised one contemporary drill-book especially written for the volunteer cavalry man, should not be practised too often for it was seriously distressing to the horse.[16] The breathless civilian rider with aching muscles was probably distressed by it as well. But the purpose of all this was plain enough:

> To be able, with speed, to manoeuvre a number of horsemen into a well-dressed line; to throw that line at a wavering enemy with shattering rapidity; thus, in an instant, to smash all opposition, imposing irreversible disintegration, and, finally, to pursue with relentless vigour: these in the thinking of the majority of British cavalrymen, whether heavy or light, were the chief objects of all training. Preparation for the great and glorious moment of truth was everything.[17]

It certainly did not take Moorcroft and his horse very long to become certified as fit for field duty by the riding master and adjutant – far less than many of the new recruits needed. Before 7 a.m. on 14 September 1803 he rode over to Hyde Park for his first drill with his troop. The usual order at these two-hour sessions was half an hour of riding exercises under the orders of the quartermaster, followed by field manoeuvres taken by the senior officer present and ending with sword and pistol exercises.

There was a great deal of activity at the riding house that autumn and Moorcroft was on parade there at least twenty-five times before the end of the year. On 21 September the corps was reviewed in full marching order by Lieutenant-General the Earl of Harrington and, on 28 October, along with some of the other London volunteer corps, by King George himself.

It was very hard work, but there were lighter moments too – ill-trained horses refusing to come into line, officers causing utter confusion through faulty commands and 'great irregularities'[18] by the newer recruits on parade, who were both undrilled and improperly dressed. At one of Moorcroft's earliest drill-parades on 5 October 1803, one of the cornets used 'ungentle-manly and indecent' language to a superior officer and later two of the sergeants had also to be dismissed for drunkenness and bad language on parade.[19] Drunkenness at regimental dinners (and there was at least one each month) was, of course, a very different matter and if the amount of alcohol consumed at the first anniversary dinner set any kind of precedent, these must have been very hilarious occasions indeed.

Moorcroft seems to have fitted very easily into the masculine world of the corps. After only five months, he was elected to the committee in December 1803. In May 1804 he was one of the very few members who volunteered for what was quaintly called 'foreign duty', that is a ten-day period of field exercises out of town. As soon as he came off the general committee in December 1805, he was promptly elected to membership of a small committee of finance which did a great deal of work in the next two years to bring the corps' finances through a period of government cuts, presiding over some awkward redundancies among the full-time staff and rounding up many of the subscriptions and fines outstanding from previous years. In 1805 he served as unofficial surgeon to the corps when the regular surgeon was away. There were often minor personal accidents during the drills but he apparently did good work in more serious cases as well, perhaps a major sword or pistol wound. The December 1805 general meeting recorded a special vote of thanks to him for his services in this respect. Later he crops up again and again in the minute-book, seconding an officer for promotion or being elected to a small sub-committee to arrange a presentation of silver to his friend George Saunders.[20]

Committee work and routine administration were never one of his strong points, however, and he missed more committee meetings in the orderly-room than he attended. The 'disagreeable smell'[21] coming from the insanitary privy next door may have had something to do with that.

Yet his enthusiasm for the actual soldiering seems to have been unflagging.

He was present at nearly all the big occasions: the crowd control duties during big parades at Blackheath and Wimbledon Common; brigade exercises on Finchley Common; field manoeuvres before the king in Hyde Park on 9 May 1805, with an exhilarating charge at the gallop followed by the general salute and march past 'at about 50 paces from His Majesty'.[22] Early on the morning of 9 January 1806, with a black ribbon tied above his left elbow, Moorcroft assembled with the others at King's Mews, Charing Cross to prepare for the great state funeral of Lord Nelson, whose pickled body had been rushed home from Trafalgar for the occasion. A year and a half later he gathered again at the same place for the funeral of Charles James Fox.

By then – it was October 1806 – the great days of the volunteers were over. The last serious invasion scare in London came in August 1805 but thereafter the great battle at Trafalgar and Napoleon's growing preoccupations elsewhere, with increasing official parsimony as a result, soon led to a rapid run-down of the volunteer forces all over the country. Interestingly, Moorcroft's attendance record at drills and field days, although there were certainly fewer of these than in the crisis years of 1803–5, remained better than ever at a time when the WVC was shrinking to almost half its mid-1803 level. At Moorcroft's very last parade on 29 March 1808, only fifty-one members turned out, but it was Moorcroft's fifth appearance on parade that month alone.

In later years, in one tight corner after another on or beyond the Indian frontier, he found his military knowledge very useful and he must certainly have enjoyed the camaraderie of the parade-ground, buttressed by the convivial quarterly regimental dinners, with their endless and increasingly extrovert toasts. But he had no need of these things. His place in that small and brilliant London world was already secure. In 1798 a judge had divided the society of his day into 'noblemen, baronets, knights, esquires, gentlemen, yeomen, tradesmen and artificers'.[23] By that classification Moorcroft was a gentleman, and was often described as such. He was also an almost classic example of the way a man could move in a society far above his station, among 'the higher classes who patronised me so liberally', as he once put it.[24] Indeed one book actually cited Moorcroft by name as a prime example of the way respectable veterinary practice could achieve this.

> Such meritorious and humane occupation could not possibly injure the medical character of a gentleman in these enlightened times; on the contrary, it would be more probable to procure him connections of the most valuable sort, might be his passport and introduction to the families of sportsmen, and afford him the opportunity enjoyed by Swift's happy Parson, to 'Drink with the Squire –'.[25]

Moorcroft did rather better than that. His business and his expertise in an age when the horse was king gave him, through his friends, acquaintances and clients in London, access to the highest in the land. King George III and the Prince Regent were both his clients.[26] He was certainly a prime example of that process which was slowly making veterinary practice a respectable occupation for gentlemen. Indeed as the head of the first qualified horse practice in the country, he was also an important cause of the process.

Certainly the handful of other senior 'scientific' veterinarians of the day who knew him well – Edward Coleman, Bracy Clark, Delabere Blaine, William Youatt and, of course, John Field and his sons – all had the highest regard for him. There is in their later writings about him a degree of unanimity and respect for his skill and knowledge which is unique in that age of often rancorous controversy. Then there were the doctors and surgeons. As has been seen, some of Moorcroft's first contacts in London came from his earlier training as a surgeon at Liverpool. The doyen of them all was the great John Hunter. Through Hunter he would have met Hunter's brother-in-law, executor, plagiarist and successor at St George's Hospital – Everard Home. Years later, for old time's sake when Moorcroft was far away in remote Kashmir, Home (by then Sir Everard Home, Baronet and one of the country's leading surgeons) treated Moorcroft's little daughter, Anne, for a chest infection without charging a fee.[27] It was just as well for Home by then was very expensive and not renowned for his open-handedness either.

He treated Anne at the Oxford Street home of George Saunders. Saunders became one of Moorcroft's oldest and best friends in London. He was already established as a successful architect before Moorcroft came to Oxford Street and the two young men found wealthy clients and grew prosperous there together. Moorcroft was a frequent caller at the house and in the course of his visits became well known to Saunders's old nurse and housekeeper, Stedman. She, years later when Saunders was eminent as a writer, JP, Fellow of the Royal Society and Surveyor to the County of Middlesex, seems to have become nanny to Moorcroft's young daughter, whom she loved dearly.[28] Moorcroft eventually made Saunders both joint-executor of his will and a joint-guardian of his children. His trust was not misplaced.

While Moorcroft was in London one of Saunders's most prestigious commissions was to design for the trustees of the British Museum an extension to Montagu House, in which were later displayed many of the classical antiquities collected by the wealthy bachelor and art connoisseur, Charles Townely.[29] The Townely family came from the same part of Lancashire as Moorcroft. Eccleston knew them well and visited Charles whenever he came to London. It was probably he who introduced Moorcroft to Townely. Moorcroft was certainly familiar with Townely's house in Queen Anne's Gate, overlooking St James's Park, and its priceless collection of antiquities. Years later, lamenting his ignorance of the Bactrian and Buddhist relics he encountered on his travels, Moorcroft recalled his 'late friend' Townely and confessed to Saunders that all he knew of the fine arts 'in great measure was derived from the unrestricted entrée he was pleased to allow me to every part of his treasures and to his instructive conversation'.[80]

The useful arts were more in Moorcroft's line and one man with whom he probably discussed them eagerly was the great ex-governor-general of India, Warren Hastings. Hastings at that time was living just round the corner from Moorcroft in Park Lane. Their paths crossed at many points: horses and horse-breeding were a common passion; Hastings was an early subscriber to the veterinary college and, like Moorcroft, a member of the Society of Arts. At all events Moorcroft knew him well enough by 24 April 1795 to scribble him a warm personal note of congratulation on hearing the news that was all over London that day: Hastings had at last been acquitted of the impeachment charges which had been pursuing him ever since he had returned from India ten years earlier. In the note Moorcroft regretted that he had been too busy all day to come round and pay his respects in person.[31]

Another Anglo-Indian acquaintance and client was the father of Indian native cavalry, General Sir John Floyd. The horse casualties he experienced as a cavalry commander in the 1792–4 Mysore war and his subsequent conversations with Parry had much to do with the East India Company's decision to start breeding its own cavalry horses.[32] Now, as a colonel of dragoons in London, he was commenting knowledgeably to Moorcroft of the similar plight of the French, after the horse casualties of the 1792–4 campaigns had wiped out most of their breeding progress in the previous three reigns.[33] Much of the after-dinner talk at this time must have centred on the subject of cavalry horses, into which Moorcroft's work with the East India Company and his service with the Westminster Cavalry must have given him considerable insight. Even before this, he was already known to the doyen of all British authorities on the cavalry horse, the 10th Earl of Pembroke who died in 1794.[34] Closer to Moorcroft in age was his son George Augustus, the 11th earl and a vice-president of the veterinary college. In 1801 Moorcroft knew him well enough to obtain from him for Eccleston some acorns from his rare 'iron oak'.[35] Seventeen years later he sought from Pembroke something even more rare. In May 1818 he wrote to him from Bengal asking him to obtain through his Russian brother-in-law passports in case his projected journey to Bokhara should compel him to return to civilization by striking north into the immensities of Central Asia and Russia. The reply was both friendly and encouraging.[36]

The closest of all these aristocratic cavalry connections was undoubtedly Frances Augustus, the 2nd Lord Heathfield. One of the most active of the early backers of the veterinary college, he frequently took the chair at its committee meetings. His growing friendship with Moorcroft survived the latter's early resignation from the college, and Heathfield subsequently became one of the most loyal and generous backers of Moorcroft's horseshoe machine project. It has been surmised that Moorcroft supported Coleman's attempts in 1796 to get Heathfield to use his influence at court and Parliament in favour of the appointment of trained veterinary surgeons to cavalry regiments.[37] It is very likely. Gradually Heathfield became more friend than patron and later Moorcroft believed that he was probably closer to that shy man than almost anyone else. It was Heathfield who taught Moorcroft the prime importance of size and bone in a cavalry horse, a lesson which had an important bearing on his appointment to India and which was later vindicated by what happened at Waterloo.[38] In October 1804 Moorcroft travelled down to Devon to stay with Heathfield at his estate at Nutwell Court near Exeter, and came back not only with unforgettable memories of the jangling harnesses of West Country horses, but with some practical ideas for mechanizing the operations at Padnalls as well.[39]

Heathfield seems to have been his closest friend among the titled but he was not by any means the only one. The list of those he knew well[40] and/or corresponded with reads like an abbreviated *Burke's Peerage and Knightage*. It includes names like the Earls of Winchelsea, Egremont, Albemarle, Morton and Pembroke; Lords Angly, Somerville, Lyndoch, Lascelles, Harewood, Grosvenor, Hertford and Hastings; the Duke of Bedford to whom Moorcroft recommended a French stonemason to construct garden paths at Woburn;[41] Sir John Sinclair Coke, Sir John Sebright, Sir John Dashwood King, Sir Anthony Carlisle, Sir John Lade and Sir H. M. Vavasour. There were French aristocrats too. London was full of them during the revolutionary wars, and they were nearly all chronically short of money. One such was Charles André, Baron de Rouvron and his wife Elizabeth. Many years later, when fate brought these two across Moorcroft's path again in poignant circumstances, Saunders recalled that Moorcroft had come to believe that the baron was not altogether trustworthy.[42] Moorcroft apparently felt much the same way about lawyers, although he numbered some of the most eminent judges of the time among his acquaintances – men like Sir James Mansfield, Lord Ellenborough, Sir Vicary Gibbs and Sir Soulden Lawrence.

A catalogue of names like these – certainly a very incomplete one – gives only the faintest suggestion of the social world in which Moorcroft moved in his London years. Clumsy as he often is on paper, he must have been a lively and acceptable member of a society renowned for its wit and brilliance. He was never short of friends and everybody who knew him who has left a memory of him, has always done so in terms of affection and high regard. As the years slipped by, the nasal vowels of his south Lancashire accent, instantly recognizable to a man from those parts, doubtless became polished and rounded by the flow of what he later called 'the superfluities and enjoyments of life' and by contact with the 'great numbers of persons . . . who loaded me with civilities in the way of hospitality'.[43] But he repaid his social debts as well as incurring them, making good use of the knowledge of wine he had acquired in France and entertaining at *petits diners* in the first-floor dining-room of the house at St George's Row, or taking his guests to favourite places like the French Hotel in Leicester Square.[44] In many ways it was a good life.

Yet for reasons which mostly can only be guessed at, it was not enough. Perhaps the brilliant but highly artificial life palled as the years passed and he moved into his middle and late thirties. We know that he grew increasingly frustrated at his failure, or perhaps it was his inability, to get down on paper some of the fruits of his vast veterinary experience.[45] Writing never came very easily to him and it was lesser men, such as his friend Blaine or the Exeter veterinarian James White, who became the successful veterinary textbook authorities of the day, their works running into many real or (in the case of White) pretended editions.[46] Moorcroft's written output was certainly disappointingly thin when compared with his reputation. Both the *Horse Medicine*

Chest (1795) and the *Methods of Shoeing Horses* (1800) were no more than superficial practical treatises for the layman, both written primarily to boost sales of practical contributions to equine health. In a way that was precisely the problem. Moorcroft *was* a practical man, never happier than when grappling with practical problems, preferably outside the confines of the great city in which he lived. He once described himself as a 'merely practical agriculturalist'.[47] Moorcroft was not 'merely' anything, but deduct that word and you are left with a description of a central and crucial aspect of Moorcroft's life and interests.

Even before the East India Company consultancy gave him a reason, he was often travelling far and wide through the countryside in pursuance of his life-long interest in all aspects of agricultural improvement. He talked drainage and breeding with Bakewell at Dishley in Leicestershire, dairying techniques in Cumberland, viticulture and wine production with Sir Richard Worsley on the Isle of Wight and general estate management with Heathfield in Devon.[48] Once he had horses to buy for India and the Padnalls stud farm to run, he was never short of an excuse to escape from the routine of the busy Oxford Street practice. The ill-fated horseshoe venture and the demanding distractions of the Westminster Cavalry doubtless played the same role. Yet always there remained the bread and butter problems of the practice and these seem to have become more and more irksome to him as time went on. The editor of Moorcroft's published *Travels*, Horace Wilson, is infuriatingly oblique on this subject but the drift of his remarks is plain enough.

> The nature of the [veterinary] profession, . . . involved many occurrences unpleasant to a man of cultivated taste and warm temper, and amidst intercourse with persons of station and respectability, collision with individuals not always possessed of either. Mr. Moorcroft, therefore became disgusted with his occupation, although he speedily realised a handsome property by it.[49]

Disgust is a strong word, probably too strong. There was certainly one aspect of his veterinary work which he did come to loathe with feelings 'almost as disagreeable as the actual feeling of the Night Mare'.[50] His expert opinion as to the soundness of an animal was often sought by his clients before they either bought or sold, a necessary precaution at a time when the soaring cost of a good horse was tempting the unscrupulous to practise deception on a large and often very skilful scale. The contemporary pages of the *Sporting Magazine* describe some of the more outrageous of these cases with relish. Obviously the horse was the motor-car of his day in more ways than one! The trouble was that litigation frequently followed and the original dishonesty might then be compounded by perjury in court as well. It was often a mucky business as one of Moorcroft's contemporaries confirms:

> It is much to be lamented, that every horse cause brought before a Court savours more or less of this complexion . . . and it is not at all uncommon to have a body of evidence produced to swear a horse 'dead lame' on one side, and a much greater number to prove him PERFECTLY SOUND on the other . . . it is constantly seen in courts of law, to what a wonderful degree of villainy human depravity is extended.[51]

Moorcroft was not thick-skinned and he came to dread his own court appearances as expert witness. 'I suffered,' he said (and he was not a man to exaggerate his sufferings), 'more than can be conceived or was ever suspected.' His very last London court appearance, which he recalled clearly fifteen years later, was typical.

> A learned legal character was pleased to say that I came into court a prejudiced witness. I rose to request permission to reply when Sir James Mansfield (the Judge), observing my agitation, stated to the Court that the observation was wholly uncalled for, and unfounded, and justified my conduct in a manner which was abundantly satisfactory to my feelings as far as respected publicity.

Privately, Moorcroft was seething and as soon as he got home he dashed off a letter 'to the learned character who had indulged in this tirade'. He obtained at least a back-handed apology by being consulted later in another disputed case by the same man.[52]

Whether it was a fear of speaking in public, or a warm-tempered and sensitive dislike of the invidious position of any witness subject to expert and hostile questioning in court, or whether, quite simply, he scorned the wheeling and dealing involved in horse litigation is not clear. What was clear was that purchase consultancy was an almost inescapable part of his London practice and the resulting court appearances were bound to increase. Moorcroft's loathing of them seems to have had a quite disproportionate effect on his decision, when the chance came, to pull out of private practice in London altogether. It is also clear that he felt that he had achieved all that could be achieved in Oxford Street.[53]

There must have been more personal dissatisfactions at work too. Some time during this period – the London marriage registers are silent as to the date – Moorcroft seems to have got married. Mary Pateshall is a shadowy and elusive figure. Beyond her Northamptonshire name and her long, fine, brown hair tucked in a letter at the India Office[54] we know almost nothing about her or her relationship with William at this period. Even the evidence that they were married at all is tantalizingly ambiguous, as will be seen.[55] At all events the evidence suggests that their relationship was less than entirely happy and fulfilling. William was able to make the decision to start a new life without her on the other side of the world and it is possible that it was the failure of their relationship which helped to drive him abroad.[56] There was certainly never any question of divorce, as one historian came to believe.[57] Divorce was then practically unknown except by a ruinously expensive special Act of Parliament. The only other procedure available to the prosperous was annulment in the ecclesiastical courts on the grounds of adultery, cruelty or unnatural practices and they never took that drastic step, as we know from the court records.[58] In fact the bond between them proved remarkably enduring.[59] Mary used his name until her death and lived on in his house at St George's Row after he left England until at least 1811 or 1812.[60]

Later, when the long French wars were over and William far away, she went over to Paris and lived with the Baron and Baroness de Rouvron as Mme Moorcroft, widow. Perhaps she sickened of London without husband, children or close friends to fill her life. Equally it may have been the lack of children which helped to cast a shadow over their life together in London. Moorcroft was a warm-hearted man who loved children. It must sometimes have hurt to see the sons of his partner, John Field, growing up at Oxford Street and working alongside their father in the practice. These are all the bare facts that survive. Behind them is a mere hint, an echo of unhappiness faintly borne across the years, but it is no more than that and we can only guess at the truth.

One thing is clear. It must have been something very compelling indeed that inclined Moorcroft in 1807 to listen very carefully when Edward Parry, who by then had become chairman of the East India Company, put before him a possibility that turned his world upside down. Parry was delighted with Moorcroft's superintendence of the breeding operations at Padnalls and the quality of his direct purchases of animals for export to India. He was not so pleased about developments at the other end of that long journey.[61]

The Bengal stud had got off to a disastrous start in 1796, with most of the breeding mares proving to be either barren or unsuitable in other ways. The harassed superintendent, Major William Frazer, was not really responsible for this initial error, but he was believed at home to have made things worse by his excessive attachment to the Arab as the most suitable breeding stallion. Not only were most of his optimistic projections of future growth grossly falsified, but the animals produced by the stud tended to be far too slight for cavalry purposes. In 1805 after ten years' work and the expenditure of 10 lakhs (100,000) rupees, only forty-seven animals produced by the stud were considered fit for admission to the cavalry. This poor track record strengthened the scepticism with which the commander-in-chief in India, Lord Lake, had viewed the whole project from the beginning. In London it had spurred the more optimistic Parry to purchase Padnalls and employ Moorcroft in an effort to supply the horses of bone and size which both of them believed to be necessary in India. But the reports from Bengal continued to be thoroughly unsatisfactory.

It was all very frustrating for Parry and his committee. In London and at Padnalls everything seemed to be going along famously under Moorcroft's supervision, but the hopes attached to the fine animals travelling out to Bengal were being largely frustrated, apparently because of Frazer's erratic preference for undersized breeding-stock and

> his not possessing a knowledge of the anatomy of the horse, to judge of the different crosses which were likely to produce the points and powers required . . . It is also considered that a Superintendent of a breeding Stud should have a veterinary education . . . for many colts are spoiled when young for want of knowing how to treat the disorders they are liable to.

As the directors spelled out the inadequacies of their stud superintendent in Bengal,[62] they found themselves more and more describing the strengths of their stud superintendent in London. Horse-breeding for the Indian cavalry was beginning to seem too important an issue of national defence to be left to an amateur infantry major. On 8 April 1807 the court of directors informed India that, in their view, the breeding operation in Bengal

> may from the point it has reached soon be brought to perfection under the superintendence of a person who has by study and practice proved his veterinary knowledge and judgement in selecting horses and mares for breeding; and we therefore have it under consideration to send out a professional man who we think well qualified to carry the plan into effect without further loss of time.[63]

The man they described but failed to name was William Moorcroft.

Just how the bombshell suggestion that he should go to India was dropped into Moorcroft's familiar world in the early spring of 1807 is unknown. The disadvantages were very obvious. In his fortieth year Moorcroft would have to pull up his roots leaving his wife (?), friends, comfort and success in London's biggest veterinary practice. In only a few more years he could expect to have saved enough to buy a modest country estate to which he could devote his declining years and satisfy his frustrated love of farming and of country life. All this he would give up. And in exchange for what? An uncomfortable and tedious sea voyage which, if he cheated the perils of shipwreck and French privateers, might bring him six or seven months later to a remote stud farm on a muddy or dusty river bank in steamy up-country Bengal, with only a handful of his fellow-countrymen for company.

India, in those days of uncertain travel and unchecked disease, was a lottery in which a man gambled his hopes of a more speedy accumulation of wealth against the very short odds that his only reward would be a white headstone in the dust of some bleak little palm- or mango-shaded cemetery. Twenty years on, a veterinary surgeon explained why, even for those who survived, there was 'no inducement to go out to India, but on the contrary from the probability of remaining on foreign service for many years and being obliged to return home for recovery of health with broken constitution and habits totally unfitted for the vocation in England'.[64]

All this and more Moorcroft would have known very well from his many Anglo-Indian friends and correspondents. And yet, for some of the reasons already mentioned, his London life was not bringing him either the private satisfactions or the public benefits he had hoped for when he first embarked on it in the optimism of youth sixteen years before. Veterinary medicine was no longer the exciting virgin field it had been then. For all the warm sociability of his London life, Moorcroft was in some ways a loner, a man who preferred to pioneer in a field *en friche*, as he so often put it. That is why he took up veterinary medicine in the first place, why he was the first of his countrymen to study the subject abroad and why he brought his unique training and rare skills to London. Now, perhaps, he felt that it was time to move on, to face a new challenge in new surroundings while he still had the health to enjoy it.

He was blessed with what he once described as 'a constitution of great natural firmness'.[65] That was an understatement. He was as tough as they come. No wonder Coleman was so politely sceptical when Moorcroft resigned the joint professorship on health grounds. The only occasion in this whole London period when his customary good health is known to have been temporarily upset occurred back in 1795. Some time in that year he was thrown by a troublesome horse a considerable distance and landed heavily on his thigh. The pain was excruciating and a major fracture seemed certain but Moorcroft, when his many medical friends who called seemed unable to do anything for him, 'had recourse to an extraordinary application of camphor'. It worked in a few hours. The residual swelling he reduced by dressings soaked in spirits of wine and the efforts of one of his men who blew upon them 'with a pair of bellows'.[66] Apart from that, his health and figure seem to have survived remarkably unscathed the alcoholic battering of London life at this time, with its innumerable dinners and endless toasts.[67] Fears about his health certainly gave him few qualms when he considered the possibilities of a move to India.

Moorcroft seems to have been an optimist in whatever he attempted, be it making horseshoes or treating an apparently hopeless horse illness, and he was not always quite as alert to the difficulties and problems involved as he ought to have been. It seems to have been the same with the Indian post. Without enquiring too closely into the stormy relationship which existed between the stud superintendent and his political masters at Calcutta, he seems to have believed that in India he would have a free-ranging commission, much like that he had enjoyed in England under Parry's indulgent and approving eye, but on a vastly extended scale, to investigate and tackle the whole problem of India's horse-breeding and horse diseases which had interested him now for so many years.[68] In this, as it turned out, he was over-optimistic, but at least he had every excuse for believing that his position was to be a very senior one because of the very high salary that Parry began to mention as a possibility in those early discussions.

Many have followed Horace Wilson in believing that it was this salary which was Moorcroft's chief inducement to go to India – that he was going primarily to recoup a fortune lost at home.[69] Some of the reasons for doubting this have already been given. His long-term financial prospects at Oxford Street were excellent and the practice yielded him 'a large income'.[70] Like his junior partner, John Field, he too could have stayed on and made himself a wealthy man had he wished to do so. The Indian salary was high precisely because of the value and prestige of Moorcroft's London practice, as the East India Company directors freely conceded. The picture of the needy man tempted abroad by money is totally unconvincing. Moreover it does not match what we know of him from other evidence. Money by itself meant very little to him as the whole of his career bears witness – he spent it as freely as he earned it. If Moorcroft were ready at the age of 40 to consider a new life on the far side of the world, it could only have been because his old one no longer satisfied him and because he was tempted by the challenges which he believed the new would afford.

His friends, however, were horrified at the prospect and none more than one of the closest of them, Lord Heathfield. He bent his 'anxious endeavours' to the question of keeping his friend in England and made him 'munificent offers' to stay.[71] It seems that Heathfield was developing an ambitious plan for a national stud in the New Forest and was ready to urge the whole scheme on the Prince Regent and the government, if Moorcroft were willing to be its first superintendent.[72] Even this tempting and remunerative prospect failed to deflect Moorcroft once his mind was made up. It is another reason for discounting the poverty theory. Moorcroft must have indicated to Parry his provisional acceptance of the Indian post, should it become vacant, by early April 1807.

At that time the vacancy was only a possibility and perhaps Moorcroft did not take it very seriously at first. He soon had to do so, for the Bengal stud ran into a curious and perhaps ominous crisis, which might have given Moorcroft good grounds to pause had he known the full story.[73] It happened like this. A few days before Lord Lake retired as commander-in-chief and left India for good at the end of January 1807, he capped years of scepticism about the value of the Bengal stud by recommending that it should be abolished and the cavalry's requirements met in future by commissariat purchase in the open market. Opposition from such a source – and Lord Lake's military prestige was enormous – was more than an interim administration under a temporary governor-general could resist. On 19 February 1807 the governor-general's council in Calcutta accepted Lord Lake's recommendation. Major Frazer, the superintendent whose brain-child the stud had been since 1793, was dumb-founded, as was his loyal supporter on the Board of Superintendence at Calcutta, Thomas Graham. But their astonishment and anger was as nothing compared with that of Parry and his committee of influential directors when the mails arrived in Leadenhall Street with this news, early in September 1807. What surprised and puzzled them all was the fact that abolition seemed to fly in the face of a very favourable report on the Bengal stud by an inspecting committee of cavalry officers as recently as November 1806.

First to move in defence of the stud was Thomas Graham. In a masterly memorandum he demonstrated that Frazer had made solid progress, that the apparently large financial investment which had been made was much smaller than it appeared and that it was, in any case, at last beginning to show returns. So convincing were Graham's arguments, that the Indian authorities hastily changed their minds, even before their proposal for abolition reached London. It was just as well because Parry and his colleagues would certainly have overruled them on this matter. Graham spoke for them all when he argued the critical political and military importance of the Bengal breeding operation and its apparently hopeful prospects of meeting the cavalry's annual needs.

The opportunity to turn these hopes into realities arrived in the same mail as Graham's minute. Frazer it seemed had had enough and wished to return to Europe as soon as possible. In fact he had resigned in a rage after an unsavoury row with the Calcutta Board of Superintendence over a quite trivial issue, but it gave Parry and his colleagues the opportunity they had been waiting for. At the end of November, or early in the December, of 1807 Moorcroft was approached once more, this time to clinch the earlier negotiations for his appointment. With his acceptance duly confirmed, the powerful breeding committee met at Leadenhall Street on 4 and 11 March 1808, to thrash out their recommendations to the full court of directors. Despite the obstacles which had been encountered, they argued:

> with skilful and proper management . . . the Committee entertain no doubt that the produce of the Poosa Stud may in a few years be so diffused throughout the Company's Provinces . . . that the cavalry may be remounted without the necessity of having recourse to purchases by contract or otherwise in distant parts of India, which necessarily causes a great exportation of specie [coined money] from the Company's Provinces, a measure inconsistent with sound policy. . . . But to draw from the Bengal Institution all the advantages of which it appears capable, and to complete the chief object in view, the Committee are of opinion that a thorough knowledge of breeding cattle [i.e. horses] and veterinary practice are an essential qualification in the Superintendent of that establishment, therefore, as they are informed that Major Frazer, the present Superintendent, has signified his intention of coming home, they strongly recommend to the Court . . . that Mr. William Moorcroft, the gentleman who has so successfully established and matured the Company's Stud at home, be appointed Superintendent of the Stud and Veterinary Surgeon at Poosa in all its branches, and in consideration of the sacrifices he must necessarily make in this country, that his salary be fixed at Sicca Rupees 30,000 per annum, in full of all allowances whatever.[74]

This was an astonishingly generous proposal from a company which was at the time in dire financial straits after years of nearly continuous war. The 1801 census puts Moorcroft's tax-free 30,000 rupees, roughly £3000 a year, into perspective.[75] In Britain in 1801 only 200 families or individuals were in the same opulent £2500 to £4000 bracket as he. Even the 70,000 very rich people in the next category rarely had incomes of much more than half what Moorcroft was being offered. As for the company's servants in India, very few indeed would be earning more – only the governor-general, the commander-in-chief, the chief justice and a handful of others. No wonder Moorcroft's exceptional salary aroused such jealousy later on. If, for example, he had remained a surgeon and entered the company's civil employment in that capacity, he would have been paid no more than a basic £130 a year. Yet for all their notorious parsimony the full court of directors at Leadenhall Street accepted Moorcroft's proposed salary without significant opposition on 6 April 1808.[76] On that same day Moorcroft sat down to write his letter of resignation from the WVC.[77]

There remained less than four weeks to wind up his affairs and his life in London. His ship, the *Indus*, had almost completed her fitting-out at Deptford down the Thames, and was due to leave any day on the first leg of her journey round to Portsmouth where he would join her. Those next four weeks must have been frantic: there was the Oxford Street practice to value and assign to John Field; there were arrangements to be made at St George's Row for Mary and the servants; there would be possessions to dispose of, friends to grasp firmly by the hand, farewell dinners and speeches to be got through, much sadness and some tears; there were final arrangements to be made for his passage; clothes and equipment to buy; and a servant to be found willing to accompany him on the long sea voyage.

Whether he had time for a visit to see his friends and relations round Ormskirk we do not know. There were few of them left. Moorcroft's mother was married and was now bringing up her own family in Dublin. Thomas Eccleston usually got down to London from Scarisbrick once a year and, if the evidence of his visit in 1801 is anything to go by, saw a lot of Moorcroft while he was there.[78] He was staying in the Strand just before Christmas 1807 and in 1808 had entered the last year of his life.[79] Dr Lyon was still at the Liverpool Infirmary but only a year or two from that much postponed retirement.[80] Colonel Aston and Moorcroft's grandfather were both long since dead.

Some time in this last month Moorcroft spent £14 on veterinary instruments and £4 on experimental seeds for the Pusa farm, for both of which on 28 April he claimed reimbursement down at Leadenhall Street from his friend James Coggan.[81] The next day he was back there again, to sign the flowery contract which the company's lawyer had prepared for his signature. In it he undertook that he, 'his wife, children and family during his and their passage out' – did his eye flicker as he read that? – 'and his and their residence in the East Indies shall and will well and truly conform to and obey all such orders and directions as they shall from time to time receive'. So it went on. Reaching the end at last, he took the quill and signed with a flourish at the bottom.[82] It was probably his last official act in London for the East India Company.

Some time in the next day or two the coach would have carried him out across the Thames and rumbled away down the Portsmouth Road. Behind him the great city represented fifteen years of successful professional practice and probably the best years of his life. Ahead, across the rolling chalk downs, was the open sea and all the uncertainties of middle age and a new life across the world, far from every familiar landmark he had ever known.

Two months later the rate-collector made his usual midsummer call to the door under the archway at 224 Oxford Street, dipped his pen deep and with a broad stroke scratched out the name William Moorcroft from the record on which it had stood since 1793. Now John Field stood there alone.[83] Somehow the rasping finality of that thick ink line marks best the end of act one in the life of William Moorcroft.

6 Interlude – The Voyage to India,
MAY–NOVEMBER 1808

In the clear dawn of 15 April 1808 the company's ship *Indus* slipped her chain moorings at Deptford and moved down the peaceful London river on the first of the ebb towards Gravesend and the open sea.[1] It was the beginning of her third voyage to India. Ten days later she arrived off Portsmouth and rounded up a few cables from where nine other East Indiamen were gathering under the fifty guns of the man o'war, HMS *Leopard*, flying from her yard the flag of Rear-Admiral Berkeley. From that moment Captain George Weltden of the *Indus*, like all the others in the convoy, came under the orders of the admiral and would remain so until they reached the Cape,[2] for England was still at war. Ever since Trafalgar three years earlier, Napoleon had been feverishly rebuilding his battle fleet and news had recently been received that his squadrons in Rochefort and Toulon had both slipped the British blockade and vanished, perhaps into the grey-green emptiness of the Atlantic. The East Indiamen were far too valuable, and far too defenceless, to sail alone at times like these and were almost always escorted in convoy by the Royal Navy.

The *Indus* had been built on the Tyne in 1803 and chartered for six voyages to India by the Company in March 1804.[3] At 590 tons burthen, she was among the smallest of the East Indiamen of the day and may have looked it from a distance among her 800-ton sisters. But at close range she would have been impressive enough, from her apple-cheeked bows and the massive canted bowsprit, along the 120 feet (36.5 metres) of her swelling chequered sides, past the open gun-ports where the sixteen great cannon would have been visible, to her raised poop and ornate stern, rising almost sheer, 26 feet (6.2 metres) above the water.

Aboard there was still much to do in the short time that remained before the signal to weigh anchor was flown. The ship was trimmed and the ballast and cargo stowed, the sails were prepared and hung out to air on the fine, still days, the rigging was set up, the paint work freshened, the bilges pumped, the lower decks cleared and washed and the fresh water casks filled and stowed. Of the passengers there was normally no sign until the last possible moment. Most of those booked on the *Indus* did not arrive until Wednesday, 3 May, and among them was 'Wm. Moorcroft Esq., Superintendent H. C. Stud' and his servant,

John Phillips. By then the fleet had already moved down to St Helen's Roads off Bembridge. That fine English spring afternoon, as Moorcroft scaled the vertical ladder and stood on the sunlit upper deck of the *Indus* for the first time, the last thought in his head would have been that, one day, not only would he see that legendary river whose name he had read, elaborately painted and carved on the ship's side, but explore almost to its remotest source beyond the Himalayas.

Already something like 160 persons were aboard. In addition to the crew of eighty, there were fifty lascar seamen returning to India to man the homecoming fleets and some twenty-seven passengers. This was an exceptionally high number, even for a larger vessel than the *Indus*, and, unfortunately for them, the ship was not really designed to carry any passengers at all. Most of them would be housed either in the after end of the poop or in the roundhouse immediately below it, the more important or wealthier of them in cabins with access to one of the great stern windows. If Moorcroft were lucky, or senior, enough to be high in the poop, he would be saved the airlessness, the smells, the creaking of the rudder post and, in foul weather when the deadlights were up, the darkness – all of which were characteristic of the roundhouse cabins. In return for his drier and more airy situation, however, he would have to put up with a much more violent rolling motion, as well as the constant noises on the poop deck above of the farmyard animals and the crew working the mizzen sails. In truth it was a choice of evils and few passengers aboard an Indiaman really enjoyed the experience except during the, usually brief, intervals of kindly weather.

The horrors to come must have been hard to imagine on that fine Wednesday afternoon when Moorcroft clambered aboard. John Phillips would probably have already prepared his tiny cabin for him. If John knew the ropes, he would have swung his master's cot fore and aft rather than across the ship, lashed the table, chair and chests firmly to the deck against the weather to come, and hung up high the precious canvas bags containing the seeds with which his master intended to experiment if he ever got to Pusa.[4] Whether Moorcroft slept that first night is debatable and, even if he did, the poultry, cattle and goats just above his head would have woken him early the next morning as the first grey light shaped the ships all wet with dew out of the darkness. Captain Weltden had already been rowed across to the *Leopard* for his final orders and everybody knew that the fleet sailed next day on the afternoon tide. For Moorcroft and the other passengers, that Thursday at anchor was the last full day to get to know each other and the routine of the ship before she sailed.

The more important passengers of course took all their meals at a long table with the officers just forward of the roundhouse in the cuddy with its windows opening on to the quarterdeck. Breakfast was usually at 8 a.m., a light meal from which the two ladies, Miss Sophia Eade and Mrs Hannah Skipp, would probably absent themselves. Dinner was at 2 p.m. – a ceremonious affair for which all at the captain's table dressed and at which George Weltden himself presided in his blue coat with its black velvet facings and gold buttons. If

Weltden's two Portuguese cooks knew their business and the weather was kind, there would be three main courses, dessert and coffee, washed down with an ample choice of wines. There would be fresh meat as long as the animals on the poop survived, fine curries, pies, puddings and tarts. On a bad ship, on the other hand, even in the relative peace of St Helen's Roads on a spring afternoon with no seas breaking aboard to put out the galley fires, it would be watery soup, murky jellies, underdone meat and stodgy pastry. Weltden's log is silent about such things but one nobleman who had sailed with him a few years earlier believed him to be unsurpassed in 'abilities, information, manners, or good nature'.[5] Such a man was unlikely to fail his passengers in the catering arrangements at the captain's table. After dinner the ladies would withdraw, the cloth would be removed, the bottle would circulate two or three times more among the men and the party would then break up about 3.30 p.m. probably for an afternoon doze on the quarterdeck if the weather were fine. Tea of bread and butter was served at 6 p.m. at the end of the dog watch; bread, cheese and soup was at 9 p.m. Then early to bed for all except the watch on deck. Every cabin lamp had to be blacked out by 10 p.m. in wartime.

Everyone would be up betimes on the morning of Friday, 6 May, infected by the excitement and bustle on deck, as the crew cleared the ship for sea. Just after noon George Weltden, sitting alone in his cabin on the starboard side of the ship, put down his pen, closed his harbour log and began a new page. There would be no leisurely dinner that day. Weltden or his mate would be watching the signal pennants flying from the *Leopard*, the last departing guests would be scrambling down into the waiting boats and the last messages flung across the widening gaps. There would be many tears. They all knew that very few who left for India ever returned. Just before 3.30 p.m. the signal to weigh went up. As the *Indus* began to move against the tide the waiting boats gradually slipped astern, the cheering became fainter and, heeling a little, the eleven great ships shook out their canvas in the southerly breeze and began to move in procession towards the open sea. Half a year, and half a world away, was India.

When supper was called that first evening, Culver Cliff could just be seen in the dusk a few miles to the north-west. The sea was calm but if Moorcroft were awake in the darkness he would have heard the watch change twice and, at 2 a.m., the shouted farewells as the pilot clambered down and the pilot cutter dropped astern. Next day at four in the afternoon, in poor visibility, the *Leopard* signalled the fleet into close convoy and they proceeded slowly down Channel together a few miles offshore during the rest of that Saturday. Later as the wind freshened and backed round to the south-west the *Indus* probably gave her passengers their first taste of things to come, as sheets were hardened and the swell came rolling in from the west against the ebb tide. Certainly Weltden, like the captain of every other Indiaman, took no chances with the weather. That evening, some time before dusk and the Portland Bill light was lit, he took in his royals and topgallants and made all snug for the night. It was a practice repeated nearly every evening for the rest of the voyage.

There were no premiums for a first arrival in the Indian market and the golden days of the clipper ship, pressed down under a cloud of canvas, were still to come. The East India Company was secure in its trade monopoly and the safety of the ship was paramount. So long as Weltden got his private investment of hams, spirits, pickles and cheese to Calcutta by the start of the cold season when entertaining began early in November, that was all that mattered to him. So it is that practically every page of his log is scattered with references to reefing and sail shortening, whenever the weather looked in the slightest degree ominous. It was the main reason why the voyage took so long. When the company's trade monopoly was partially breached a few years later, these same stout ships when pressed could almost halve the voyage time. Even so, the *Indus* must have pitched and rolled most of her passengers into private torments in their dark cabins, that first Saturday night at sea. In due course Moorcroft would show that he could take acute physical discomfort better than most, but even his place at that long dining-table was probably empty on occasions over the next few days, until he got used to the motion in what Weltden described laconically as 'fresh winds'.

Next day was Sunday – their first at sea and a fine one. Normally, if the weather permitted, divine service was held on deck with the passengers in their finery, the crew neat and scrubbed and Weltden in full uniform. The company did not leave the piety of its captains to chance. Weltden would have in one of the drawers of his desk the reminder that 'the Court have resolved to mulct you in the sum of two guineas, for every omission of mentioning the performance of divine service, or assigning satisfactory reasons for the non-performance thereof every Sunday'.[6] In fact on this voyage, the *Indus* was at sea on twenty-one Sundays and Weltden only managed to hold a service on ten of them. He was, with an eye to his 2 guineas, understandably punctilious about recording his reasons – sails had to be changed, or rigging repaired, or the ship was rolling too much, or the wind was too boisterous, or the rain was too heavy or the weather too cold. Curiously enough, the only time he risked the loss of his 2 guineas by failing to give a reason, was on this first Sunday of the voyage, but that was doubtless because he was busy mustering the whole ship's company on deck and making out his quarter bill, in which every man, woman and child aboard was assigned a place in case of action. There was also the regular and important Sunday chore of counting the fresh water supplies still left in the casks down below.

On this Sunday Portland Bill was clearly visible away to the north-east and for the remainder of that week Moorcroft would have watched the familiar landmarks slipping by for ever, and learned 'to accommodate his movement to the motion of the vessel'.[7] On Monday morning they were close in-shore, in clear view of the lovely country between Start Point and Prawle, not far from where Lord Heathfield had his estate. That evening they were off Plymouth, with the light from the twenty-four tallow candles at the top of Smeaton's tower on the lonely Eddystone Rock clearly visible. Progress was very slow. Thursday, 12 May was grey and foggy with the *Leopard* firing a gun every half an hour to keep the convoy together. Just about noon the fog lifted and there was a glimpse of Lizard Point off the bow, low to the north-west. Then the curtain of sea fog closed in again. The dim shape of that craggy headland would have been the last of England Moorcroft ever saw.

And now they were fairly at sea as the *Indus* thudded her gleaming bluff bows into the green swell rolling in from the south-west, kicking up the spray and trampling out her white wake behind her as she staggered south and west into the wide Atlantic. Despite the boredom and the discomfort, there was great beauty in the changing patterns of sky and water for those with eyes to see: the moonlit nights with the silvered sails arched against the velvet sky and the phosphorescence dripping under the bow; the bright days when the ship ghosted on a burnished sea with all her sails hanging limp, or romped the white spray high over the lee rail. Moorcroft rarely recorded scenic beauty: the mechanics of the ship and her equipment would have interested him more. There would be the pleasure of conversation with the more congenial of his fellow-passengers, probably talking horses to the cavalry officers or medicine with the ship's surgeon. There was ample time to read and dream, and perhaps to get his adroit tongue around the intricacies of Bengali. Traditionally it was the ordinary soldiers who fared worst on these long journeys, with apparently little to do but grumble and quarrel, doze and play cards – and get drunk.

Even for them there were occasional diversions. There were anxious hours on 13 May when the rest of the fleet was, for a time, out of sight. However much Weltden might chafe under the orders of Admiral Berkeley, the *Leopard*'s guns were a welcome insurance against confinement in a French prison and in those May days the fleet was in dangerous waters. It must have been a relief when they were all together again. Only two days later they sighted a strange sail in the south-west. The *Leopard*, flying a signal to the rest to shorten sail, wheeled off with her canvas spread to investigate. Aboard the *Indus* Weltden would have been on the quarterdeck, his glass on the stranger, the drum would be beating for quarters, the guns run out, the crew and passengers mustering, small arms and cutlasses being issued to all who could use them, and the women going below with the surgeon to prepare for casualties. It was for moments like this that they practised action stations every Saturday and Wednesday at sea and exercised the guns. Luckily the stranger answered the *Leopard*'s coded signals correctly. They exchanged news, which would have been passed quickly round the fleet, and the convoy resumed station and pressed on south-westwards into the open Atlantic. Several times during the next few weeks the call 'sail ho' rang down from the rigging – always with much the same results.

There were other diversions too, pleasant and unpleasant, to provide conversation for the passengers. One Saturday morning one of the crew was caught 'selling his clothes for his liquor and selling his own liquor for money'. This curious double transaction is not explained in Weltden's laconic log, but since both clothes and liquor were provided by the company, their sale was punishable. All hands were mustered and the hapless wretch was stripped and given twelve lashes at the gangway. Floggings were rare aboard an Indiaman. More common was the loss of a man overboard and once in the water there was little hope for him. A ship like the *Indus* could not quickly be hove-to, it took time to lower a boat and it was never easy to spot a head in the water, even in daylight. So it was on the morning of 20 May in only a moderate wind, when one of the boys fell overboard from the rigging. He was lost to sight among the waves almost as soon as he hit the water. There was even less chance for the man who went overboard at night as did another of the crew some weeks later.

Moorcroft never forgot these incidents. Years later while travelling in the Himalayas he speculated about the possibility of saving lives by having inflated animal skins 'so hung to some part of a ship at sea as to be in constant readiness to be let down on the instant it should be known that a person had fallen overboard'.[8] This very modern idea might have been a considerable improvement on the cumbrous lifebuoys in use at the time.

A happier experience for the passengers came on the frequent windless days when, if there was not too much sea running, the ships drifted close together and put down their boats to exchange passengers for dinner. New faces, new conversation and perhaps the attentions of a different cook, must have been very welcome. It was during one of these exchanges that Moorcroft met a young assistant surgeon named Horace Wilson on his way out to Calcutta.[9] Thirty years later Wilson, back in London and by then renowned as an oriental scholar, edited and published Moorcroft's *Travels*, the only substantial work with Moorcroft's name on it that ever appeared in print.

As the last week of May, their third at sea, drew to its end everyone must have looked forward to their first landfall. Their progress so far had been extremely slow and some days earlier the *Leopard* had signalled that they were to make for Madeira to replenish the precious water supplies. This was wonderful news but not only because of the water. Madeira meant above all things relatively cheap supplies of its wine, then at the height of fashion and normally very expensive. It also meant fresh vegetables, a break from the incessant noises and smells and movement of a ship at sea, and the latest news of the war in Europe. There were also, it was said, dark and beautiful girls on the island and a ball was usually held for the passengers and officers of visiting ships . During the afternoon of Sunday, 29 May, the dark smudge of land was sighted low on the horizon and, by midnight, Madeira itself was plainly visible in the bright moonlight, under the shadows of the great volcanic peaks of Pico Ruivo and her sisters. Moorcroft was probably on deck with the other passengers late that lovely evening, leaning on the rail watching the silver moon-track and the darker shape of the land, as the *Indus* and the other ships worked slowly in to Funchal roads opposite the old town. They anchored at eleven the next morning and immediately after lunch the passengers and the empty water butts went ashore.

The streets of Funchal, squeezed between the stuccoed walls of the houses, were narrow and dirty, but the next three days must have been a delight. The weather was kind and the British merchants on the island were renowned for their hospitality to their visiting fellow-countrymen. Moreover, the island was of great beauty with its craggy mountains, tumbling ravines and precipitous, basalt cliffs falling away sheer into the sea, its vineyards and white country houses, and its tropical fruits in rich profusion. Only the stringent measures to prevent the fleet from being taken by surprise at night were reminders of the harsh realities of the war in Europe.[10] It was probably this full watch, maintained through the hours of darkness, which foiled the plan of the bosun's mate and the quartermaster of the *Indus* to take the jollyboat and desert to the island. Perhaps they were making for 'the disorderly houses in the neighbourhood of the beach and the pernicious liquors vended thereabouts', described in one contemporary account.[11] At all events, they were put in irons and received eighteen lashes each for their pains as soon as the fleet was at sea again.

On the last day of May, Admiral Berkeley called all the captains of his convoy aboard his ship and announced that the fleet would sail the following evening. Right on time at 5.30, the signal to weigh went up. Within a few minutes, all of the ships were moving slowly out to sea in the gentle evening breeze, the passengers at the rails and perhaps some of their new friends out in small boats to wave them God speed on the next leg of their journey. Next evening, the island was but a smudge on the empty horizon.

Almost at once they picked up the north-east trade wind, as every navigator's manual said they should. There followed nearly two weeks of perfect sailing weather, day after sunny day of blue seas with the white wake streaming out behind, porpoises, albacores and flying fish playing round them, and nights with the windsong never dying in the rigging. Weltden, greatly daring, even left his topsails up all night on occasions, as his ship steered south-west, rolling off 2 degrees of latitude each day. This sort of weather, although good for morale, could put the ship under great strain and the log records that she was steering heavily and had to be pumped out every few days.

The wind and the fine weather left them on 15 June, as the old hands knew it must, sooner or later. They were still 11 degrees short of the Equator and now had to cross the region known as the Variables, an area of calms, heavy rains and sudden vicious squalls of thunder and lightning, which sits astride the midsummer Equator in the Atlantic. It was a trying time for everybody. One minute, as in the early hours of 18 June, the crew might be struggling to tame the tattered remnants of the topsails blown out in a screaming squall, and a few hours later watching helplessly as two of the ships rolled closer and closer together in the still air, until at last they had to be towed apart by straining muscles in the rowing boats.

Weltden, by luck or judgement, soon found a drastic solution to that problem. On the evening of 21 June, perhaps fearing another squall, he reefed the ship right down. He was probably over-cautious this time for at dawn next day the rest of the fleet was discovered hull down, far to the south. For the rest of that sultry day, with the sails hanging idle in the light airs, Weltden tried to manoeuvre his ship closer to the others and all that night the *Indus* burned flares. Next morning, when Moorcroft came up on deck, he would have found the full circle of the horizon completely empty for the first time. It was not unknown for the master of an East Indiaman, chafing perhaps under the tactless orders of a younger naval captain or the need to go at the pace of the slowest, to give the convoy the slip in the darkness and trust to luck about meeting the French. Weltden had done it himself on a previous occasion[12] and may have done so again this time. For the passengers there would be no more social visits to the other ships and for the lonely look-out, arching high above the rolling deck, more need than ever to keep his eyes peeled. It was probably some consolation therefore when, two days later and still well short of the Line, they unexpectedly picked up the south-east trade wind they were seeking.

One can picture the *Indus* after frustrating days spent drifting under grey skies in flat calms, at last rolling up the blue waters of the South Atlantic, all a-sparkle in the sunshine. On the sunny morning of Tuesday, 28 June, Father Neptune came aboard and administered the rough ceremony of ducking and shaving all those, like Moorcroft, who were crossing the Equator for the first time. Now, safely clear of the Equator, Weltden would steer south across the wind, it mattering little that he was being pushed far out westward towards the coast of Brazil. Years of bitter experience in these waters had shown that a few hundred or even a thousand extra miles here were nothing, compared with the advantage of getting as soon as possible into the roaring forties. Once in those stormy latitudes the westerly gales would, if necessary, blow a ship halfway round the world into the China Sea. So, alone through that July of 1808, the *Indus* rushed southwards, the spray often breaking high over the quarterdeck.

The only diversion in the whole of this long month came at tea-time on 4 July, when a strange sail was seen under the clouds in the south-east and closing fast. The *Indus* was cleared for action and by 6 p.m. the two ships were only 4 miles apart, each preserving its anonymity and waiting for some signal of identification from the other. One can only assume the stranger was a neutral ship, probably American, for the log makes no further reference to her. It is a pity that Weltden did not sometimes let his pen take him beyond the minimal and laconic catalogue of winds, courses, sail changes, work on the ship, noon sights, weather and distance run.

As July 1808 ran out its last few cloudy days, a new bustle aboard the *Indus* would have indicated that a landfall was imminent. The harbour gear was brought up on deck and the anchors bent on in readiness. At dawn on Tuesday, 2 August, the line of something more solid than cloud was clearly visible about 36 miles away in the north-east and that evening the masts of the ships at anchor in Simon's Bay, Cape Town, could be plainly seen. The bay was too strewn with submerged rocks to risk a night approach, and it was not until noon the next day that the *Indus* dropped anchor close to the *Leopard*. Immediately after dinner, Weltden would have rowed over to pay his respects to the admiral and explain how he broke convoy. Moorcroft and the other passengers went ashore.

The Cape settlement had only recently been captured from the Dutch and had little of the exotic Portuguese charm of Madeira. Simon's Town had nothing to offer the visitor beyond fresh fruit and vegetables, drinkable water, a hospital, a barracks and about 100 houses. Cape Town, at the head of the neighbouring Table Bay, was much more spacious and it was there perhaps that Moorcroft took rooms with one of the well-to-do Dutch families, and exulted in the plain delights of fresh food, clean sheets, a stable bed and ample hot water. When rested, he probably embarked on the fairly limited tourist round of the day, which included a visit to the citadel and the official residence of the governor, set in its gardens above the town, a trip to the menagerie on the lower slopes of Table Mountain, and a climb to the top of Table Mountain itself. Unlike most tourists, he also made a close study of the viticulture being practised at the Cape and came away with a supply of seeds of the Muscadet and Constantia grapes which, in due course, he grew in large quantities on the banks of the Ganges.[13] The weather was very unsettled during most of the *Indus*'s seven-day stay at the Cape. On two days it blew an unseasonable south-east gale straight into Simon's Bay, which must have given Weltden and the other captains, watching their straining anchor cables, an anxious time.

The *Indus* sailed again on the morning of Thursday, 11 August, alone this time, and almost at once ran into the stormy weather so characteristic of the Cape latitudes. The strong winds, squally rain and thunderstorms stayed with them for the rest of that month as they steered due east along the 37th parallel. There was no possibility of divine service on the Sundays in this month, for the ship was pitching and rolling unmercifully and the seas breaking heavily on the decks. Even the laconic Weltden was persuaded to use the word 'gales', although it was the only occasion he did so on this voyage. The captain of the *Harriet*, which left Portsmouth in the same fleet as the *Indus* and was now a few days ahead of her, was far less reserved. His log is liberally scattered with references to gales, both before and after passing the Cape.[14] One can only imagine the misery of most of the passengers at this time, faced with the empty choice of either swinging in their cots in their darkened and stuffy cabins, perhaps with their belongings awash on the floor, or struggling to keep their feet in the hammering wind on the heaving decks. However, notwithstanding the heavy wind and rainstorms, the torn sails and the gear carried away, they were making good progress. At last, on 5 September, due south of Cape Comorin, Weltden turned his ship north to escape the clutch of the westerlies and seek again the more kindly south-east trades. Almost at once the sun came out. On Sunday, 11 September, under a warm sun, Weltden was able to take service on deck for the first time in seven weeks. The worst of their torment was over.

So they ran north before the trade wind through the rest of that September, passing very close to the eastern shore of Ceylon but failing to get a sight of it. At last, just after tea on Thursday, 29 September, the leadsman with a shout got a touch at 50 fathoms and by sunset they could plainly see land away to the north-west. If Moorcroft was up on deck early next morning, and there would not have been much sleep to be had below, he could easily pick out the tall flagpole, rigged like a ship's mast and still in its old position next to Fort St George on the water's edge at Madras. Despite seven weeks without a sight of land, Weltden's navigation was faultless. Some of the ships they could see rolling at anchor in the Madras Roads were last seen in the South Atlantic three months before. The best bower anchor rumbled down at ten in the morning and, as soon as the ship was made snug, Weltden and the passengers went ashore in the flimsy native boats which alone could cross the surf on to the sandy beach. Luckily the wind was light that day and nobody was pitched into the curling breakers to take his chance with the sharks. Some time just after noon on the last day of September 1808 William Moorcroft set his foot on the glistening sands of the Coromandel Coast.

The *Indus* spent two weeks at Madras putting her cargo ashore, restocking with food and water, loading a consignment of hemp for Calcutta and carrying out repairs after her buffeting in the Indian Ocean. For Moorcroft it would have been a jovial round of visits and entertaining, and his first taste of the heavy drinking which characterized the English society of Madras and Calcutta. He may even have been quite glad to get to sea again. Weltden certainly would have been. The Madras roadsteads were an unhealthy place for ships at the best of times, rolling and pitching 2 miles offshore in the heavy swell. The only relatively safe time was during the south-west monsoon, which in most years blows in the Indian Ocean from April to October. Well, it was already October, Sunday, 16 October, when the *Indus* stood away out to sea again. It would not have escaped Weltden's notice that this was the very day when all insurance on ships along the Coromandel Coast ended for three months. As both he and the underwriters knew, during this period the monsoon usually breaks up in a series of gales. If a ship bound from Madras to Calcutta up the Bay of Bengal were unlucky enough to miss the last of the favourable south-west monsoon, a journey of six or seven days could become a dreary battle against contrary winds lasting as many weeks.

But the *Indus* was lucky and, in 1808, there remained enough strength in the south-west wind to take them about 75 pleasant miles a day on the direct route up the bay. It was an uneventful trip apart from three days when they had a disabled ship in tow. Not that a French attack could be discounted even here, for French privateers were still very active and only the previous season had captured twenty British ships between Madras and Calcutta.

There were other hazards besides the French as they approached the mouth of the Hooghly River. The delta, then as now, was a navigator's nightmare, a low-lying area of silting shoals, awkward currents and shifting sands, where a ship might be sounding in less than 10 fathoms without land in sight at all. It is not surprising that on the squally afternoon of 26 September when the *Indus* got into soundings, Weltden prudently shortened sail to arrest his ship's headlong dash into danger in the shoaling water. For the rest of that evening she and a naval frigate bound in the same direction, slipped along together under shortened sail, sounding as they went, until it was too dark to see and then anchoring for the night. There would have been little sleep to be had that night because the members of the night watch were busy getting the topmast rigging down. At first light they were off again and Weltden must have been very relieved when, in only 9 fathoms of water, the pilot schooner was sighted romping towards them. When the pilot came aboard Weltden's official responsibilities were over and at noon that day he closed his sea log. For him the journey was virtually over. Moorcroft can hardly have shared his captain's feelings, for his impatient eyes still had no sight of land.

Probably the first he saw of it, later that day, would have been no more than a low-lying sandbank somewhere near Saugor Point. Calcutta was still 100 dreary miles (160 kilometres) away up the river and the *Indus*, unlike the bigger ships, was going all the way. The next few days must have seemed endless – a dreary postscript to an already interminable journey. The ship could usually only sail with reduced rig on the swirling flood tide, probably with half a dozen native rowing boats alongside, the slim brown bodies of the oarsmen straining in their efforts to keep her off the shoals. As soon as the tide turned she had to anchor in the narrowing channel for six hours. There would be little to see – a few native boats out from Kedgeree or Fulta hawking fresh fruit and vegetables, and otherwise just miles of low, muddy shores fringed with jungle, with perhaps a cluster of huts here and there and an occasional alligator in the water or on the bank. After dark the night sounds of the tiger-infested jungle might bring the passengers to the rail, braving the mosquitoes. Calcutta on the last day of October must have seemed almost as far away as ever.

In those days, the river at this point hid the city almost until the last moment, although the scattering of splendid white houses on the river bank, with their wide porticoes and green shutters must have been a welcome reassurance of approaching civilization. And yet next morning if Moorcroft were up in the first light of dawn, and he probably was, he could have feasted his eyes on what many at the time believed to be the finest city landscape in the world.[15] For they were anchored in Garden Reach, Calcutta. The river at this point was about twice as wide as the Thames in London, with fine gardens running down to the water's edge. Behind, facing the water in an irregular line and bright in the clear air, were the recently built, magnificent villas and palaces of the well-to-do and, a few hundred yards upstream, the ivory splendour of the new Government House. The crowded native town with its tangle of mat and thatch huts and narrow lanes – the real India – was out of sight just to the north.

Soon after noon in bright sunlight the little *Indus* slid up the river under the grey walls of mighty Fort William, giving and receiving a nine-gun salute as she passed, and finally dropped her anchor into the muddy river bed opposite the main ghat or landing place. It was the first day of November 1808 and the *Indus* was 177 days, almost half a year, out from Portsmouth. Even so it was a good journey with average weather. Moorcroft had had his usual luck. Soon after the *Indus* left for home in January 1809, leaking fast and throwing her guns overboard in mountainous seas, she came within an ace of sinking somewhere off Mauritius. A few months later when nearly home on the same voyage, she sprang a leak in the Channel and nearly sank again. But that is another story and it did not concern William Moorcroft. Probably some time later on that afternoon of 1 November 1808, when work had already begun on getting the sails off, he would have thanked George Weltden, and climbing down into a waiting boat with his servant and baggage, would have been rowed ashore.

The interlude was over and the second more extraordinary act of his life about to begin. He was 41.

7 DISILLUSIONMENT – CALCUTTA AND PUSA,
NOVEMBER–DECEMBER 1808

THE ANIMATED SCENE which must have faced Moorcroft as he came up the wide steps from the boat at Chandpal Ghat was lightheartedly described by another British arrival a few years later. It would not have been very different on that November afternoon in 1808.

> I landed amidst a crowd and bobbery to which even the Tower-stairs, or the piers of Boulogne and Calais . . . can hardly furnish a parallel. Many women and children, sipping, dipping, and dabbing, like ducklings in a shower; females bearing pots or jars on their heads, and children, resembling little black monkeys, astride on their hips; bhisties, or water-carriers, filling their bags from the turbid tide, well-seasoned with coconut husks, defunct brahmins, dead dogs, etc; puckalls, or bullocks, bearing huge skins of the same *pure* element; palankeen bearers, gabbling (to me) unintelligible abuse, in eager competition, pushing into the very river, and banging their portable boxes one against the other in their struggle to secure fares among the frequent arrivals from the shipping; baboos, parroquet-venders, chattah-bearers, sailors, lascars, and adjutant birds – Europe and Asia commingled in heterogeneous but pleasant confusion.[1]

If Moorcroft could have disentangled himself from the confusion on the ghat he could have looked away across the wide, grassy *maidan* to his left towards Lord Wellesley's splendid new Government House and the other public buildings in Esplanade Row. Before him, more distant still, beyond the massive grey walls of Fort William, were the fine white Palladian houses of the wealthier European inhabitants, strung out along Chowringhee and beyond. The lifestyle of these British exiles has been fixed for ever in the pages of William Hickey's *Memoirs* – the extravagance and luxury, the armies of servants, the prodigious eating and drinking, the astonishing parties – and the presence of swift and sudden death.[2]

But things were already, slowly, changing. Hickey had left for a well-earned retirement in England six months before Moorcroft arrived. The old buccaneering, get-rich-quick days of greed and extortion in Bengal were over, and a more sober society and administration were slowly taking their place, although, as yet, there was none of the rigid and harmful exclusiveness which turned the Victorian sahibs into yet another separate caste. Despite half-hearted official discrimination against the children of mixed parentage, relationships with Indian or half-caste mistresses were common and European wives still something of a rarity. Calcutta was a uniquely cosmopolitan city in which the wealthy and literate Bengali families – the Debs, Tagores and the rest – mixed easily in European society. Out of this cultural fusion there came at this time the brief flowering of that intellectual movement which scholars have called the Bengal Renaissance. Luckily a few outstanding Europeans, unlike Hickey and his friends, preferring books to the bottle, devoted themselves to the study of Indian language, literature and history with quite remarkable results.[3] The most visible and enduring symbol of this movement in 1808 was the newly completed building of the Asiatic Society of Bengal, still there today in Chowringhee at the top of Park Street. Moorcroft's visits to Calcutta were necessarily infrequent but, in due course, he became a member of the Asiatic Society and made many friends in the 'city of palaces'. After six months spent cooped up aboard the little *Indus*, he must have found Calcutta a refreshing and congenial place.

It would have been hard to believe that the proud, modern city was a very recent creation. Any local inhabitant only a little older than Moorcroft could have recalled the malarial swamp and jungle which had hemmed in the little British trading settlement, with its tiny fort and minuscule garrison, on the river bank where these proud buildings and busy waterways now stood, and would have grown up with stories of the easy capture and sack of the place by the Nawab of Bengal. That was in 1756, only twelve years before Moorcroft was born, and it was the beginning of a crowded half century which transformed the map of India and converted the East India Company into a great territorial power.

In 1700 the Mughal emperor's writ ran nearly 2000 miles (3200 kilometres) from the Hindu Kush down past Madras almost to the southern tip of India. The tiny European trading settlements, dotted along the coast and up the Hooghly, were quite insignificant. But Aurangzeb, who died in 1707, was really the last emperor to exercise imperial sway over this great area in the old legendary style. Within an astonishingly short time the great sub-continental empire was reduced, by an almost classic mixture of greed, incompetence, treachery and violence, to a few hundred miles of territory round Delhi. Predatory monarchs from beyond the mountains to the north made whirlwind raids into India and sacked Delhi several times over. Within the sub-continent itself, one imperial satrap after another asserted his independence and carved out a kingdom for himself. In the south there were the Muslim rulers of Mysore and Hyderabad. North of them were 'the mountain rats of the Deccan' as Aurangzeb had called them, the tough and wiry Maratha peasants, pushing their power right across India from sea to sea and harrying not only their Hindu brethren, the Rajput chiefs of the north-western deserts, but the Nawab of Bengal and the Sikhs of the distant Punjab as well.

In this swirling tide of anarchy and war, it was impossible for the European trading companies to maintain their former nature and neutrality. Besides, a new and decisive factor from the 1740s onwards was the introduction into India of that great worldwide Anglo-French struggle which continued at intervals until 1815. The costs, and the possibilities, of the unprecedentedly large military and naval forces which were required in this struggle, and the need for allies and revenues to sustain them, soon made a dramatic impact on the fluid conditions of late eighteenth-century India. Within a generation of that humiliating occupation of Calcutta in 1756, the East India Company found itself master of the whole of Bengal and Bihar as far north as Allahabad, with Oude a protected buffer state just beyond. Further south it acquired greatly extended territories down the Coromandel Coast towards Madras and round that settlement.

At that stage, in the 1780s, the company was still just another of the successor states to the Mughal inheritance and that is how its directors in Leadenhall Street wished to keep it, but Lord Wellesley, who arrived in India as governor-general a decade before Moorcroft, had a very different and much more consciously imperialistic vision of the future. Significantly enough he was one of Moorcroft's heroes.[4] In eight whirlwind years, by an unscrupulous combination of military and diplomatic force, he brought about a political and territorial revolution in India. In the south, Mysore was smashed, Hyderabad reduced and Madras linked with Calcutta by a continuous swathe of territory all the way up the long Coromandel Coast. In the north-west, Oude was surrounded and beyond it Maratha territory between the Ganges and Jumna was annexed. The British north-western limit moved on another 500 miles (800 kilometres) beyond Delhi to the southern limits of the nascent Sikh kingdom of Ranjit Singh in the Punjab.

Even so, the Indian sub-continent in 1808 when Moorcroft arrived was by no means wholly or securely British. The rough question mark which the company's territories now formed on the map, hung over their future too. Wellesley's headlong career of expansion had faltered dangerously in the torrid summer of 1805, when two of the principal Maratha chiefs had combined to oppose him. They remained weakened but not crushed, biding their time for another strike across the long exposed western frontier of the British territories in Bengal and beyond. In the north-west the formidable genius of Ranjit Singh and his European-trained army was pushing out the frontiers of the Sikh kingdom in all directions, and in the north, scarcely noticed as yet, another race of formidable fighting men, the Gurkhas of Nepal, were extending their own authority towards the north-west step by step with that of the company for 600 miles (960 kilometres) along the edge of the plain and in the hills and mountains beyond. Little wonder that the fear of a great Hindu combination between these three, falling like a tidal wave on the dangerously extended British lands in the north and sweeping them back to the sea, should come to preoccupy the governor-general during Moorcroft's later years in India. For, notwithstanding the reassuring wealth and stability of Calcutta and the vast sweep of territory which it now controlled, European influence in the *mofussil*, the up-country districts outside the capital, was spread very thinly indeed as Moorcroft would soon discover. All-weather roads were practically non-existent and, until the metalled Grand Trunk Road reached Delhi in 1850, that frontier outpost was three months' ordinary travelling time away from Calcutta. The Ganges remained the main highway to the civil and military stations strung out along its length. They were like tiny white islands in the engulfing green and brown ocean of the endless Ganges plain. In a civil station, beside the soldiers, there might be a judge, collector, surgeon, postmaster and registrar, with perhaps a handful of indigo planters, running their waterside estates and primitive factories from handsome white villas, in stark contrast to the mud homes of those they employed and exploited. 'A handful of scattered strangers' was how a later governor-general described his countrymen in India.[5]

Beyond the thin formal lines of houses, thatched bungalows or parade-grounds which marked the British presence, was the real India – the India of the village and the field. Here millions were locked season by season in the great circle of birth and death, seedtime and harvest, their lives dominated by the arching sun, the melting snows in the unseen Himalayas, the great rivers and the mysterious annual rhythms of the rain-bearing winds from the great southern oceans. The alluvial plain of the sacred Ganges – from the river's first tempestuous rush out of the hills into the plains at Hardwar, far away at the very northern limit of British rule, all the way down to its steamy delta south of Calcutta – is as flat as a lake, with scarcely a hill to break the wide horizons. The river, a broad and shining ribbon of light, flows through the endless panorama of field and crop and village, broken only by the clumps of mango and tamarind or the deep shadows beneath some ancient peepul or banyan tree, or the occasional ancient city, mouldering temple or fort. The untold millions who thronged and tilled this ancient land followed, in their complex village societies, a way of life which had scarcely changed in a thousand years.

By November when Moorcroft arrived, the rains in northern India are over and it is mercifully cool and dry again, after the steamy heat and heavy rains of high summer. This is the best time. The air is clear, the nights cool, the rivers full and the world all green and gold. In the fields the autumn crop of Indian corn, millet or rice is gathered and ploughing and sowing for the spring harvest follows at once. That crop grows to maturity as the year turns and the sun grows gradually hotter, parching the earth and slowly burning the great plain from a sparkling green to dusty brown. Only when the spring crop is safely gathered does the Indian peasant leave the dry soil and seek the shade for a short respite from the mind- and body-sapping heat of the wheeling sun in April and May. As the great monsoon clouds build up, all wait for that first dramatic cloudburst which soon, miraculously, turns the tired soil black, fills the empty river beds again and launches a new midsummer cycle of ploughing and sowing and exuberant growth. Engulfed in the broad rhythms of this ancient land, the next ten years of Moorcroft's crowded life were spent.

One morning in the first four days of November 1808 – it would certainly have been in the morning for in the cool season all work for the day was over in British Calcutta by 1.30 p.m. – he presented himself at the spacious house, down near the river, occupied by the stud Board of Superintendence. The news of Moorcroft's appointment had only preceded him by three months and the part-time, unpaid members of the board, nearly all of them professional soldiers, must have been very curious to meet this civilian who, although subject to their joint authority, was earning far more than any of them. For his part, he only knew of the board 'as a medium of communication with the Government and as a check upon expenditure'.[6] One of the first of the many nasty shocks he experienced during the coming weeks was the discovery, when browsing through the voluminous records of the board, that it had uncomfortably extensive powers to interfere with, and overrule, the plans of the superintendent. In England, Moorcroft's relations with the stud committee, chaired by a well-wisher like Edward Parry and prepared to let him get on with his job without interruption, had been entirely harmonious. In the volumes before him he found alarming evidence of interference and friction between board and superintendent. He later summarized what he saw there of Frazer's difficulties.

> Unforeseen difficulties produced embarrassments, which were met by a change of measures. In further progress further embarrassments arose. Change followed change with such rapidity, that the Board of Superintendence, not fully comprehending their objects, lost confidence in the Superintendent, who felt himself in turn but ill requited for his activity, integrity, and zeal. Discussions and altercations impeded the course of public business. A support, neither wholly granted nor wholly withheld, paralysed the powers of the Superintendent, and converted devotedness and energy into apathy and disgust.[7]

This was a not inaccurate picture of the previous five years. The fact was that the board *was* general superintendent of the stud and clashes with whoever held that title were well-nigh inevitable. Still, Moorcroft consoled himself, Frazer had enjoyed none of Moorcroft's advantages, least of all the powerful personal support of the court of directors at home. Surely they would never have appointed him at such a salary if they had intended him to be confined by an interfering committee of amateurs whose knowledge of horse-breeding and animal medicine was minimal compared with his own? Most of them were not even cavalry officers.[8] He was right – for a time.

On one of those early November mornings the governor-general, Lord Minto, called Moorcroft and the board to Government House for a full discussion of stud affairs and all of them promised the new superintendent their fullest co-operation and support.[9] They were as good as their word. In the first five years of his superintendence Moorcroft was largely untroubled by the hostility and interference which, in recent years, had destroyed his predecessor's peace of mind. He was allowed, as one later critic put it with some exaggeration, at the express request of the governor-general 'to do everything and anything he liked'.[10] And he was grateful for it. Later under a different governor-general and board it was a very different story. Then Moorcroft ran into storms more fierce than anything experienced by the outgoing superintendent.

Frazer, still at Pusa, was becoming increasingly anxious to get down to Calcutta as soon as possible, to catch the ship booked to take him to England early in January.[11] A personal handover of such a complex and geographically extensive responsibility as the breeding operations centred on Pusa, was obviously desirable, but there was little time left. Frazer's original suggestion had been to hand over to his successor in the presence of the committee of cavalry officers which made its annual inspection of stud animals for the cavalry each October,[12] but it was already too late for that. Eventually, in mid-November, when the Calcutta preliminaries were over, Moorcroft was ordered up-country with 'all practicable expedition' by the quickest means of travel then available, and the postmaster-general required to 'have bearers laid on the old road to convey Mr. Moorcroft by dawk [dak] from the Presidency to Patna'.[13] And so, some time towards the end of the month, probably in the cool of the evening with Calcutta's enormous population of crows and kites flapping slowly home across the golden sky, and the blue smoke of a thousand cooking fires from the Indian end of the town adding their peculiar fragrance to the swift Indian twilight, Moorcroft would have climbed into the creaking contraption that would be his home, day and night, for 300 jolting miles (480 kilometres).

Travelling dak in a palanquin could be an unnerving experience and despite its relative comfort and speed (a steady 4 m.p.h. (6.4 k.p.h.)) few Englishmen seem to have enjoyed it. One who did not was Lieutenant Richard Burton.

> After a day or two, you will hesitate which to hate most, your bearers' monotonous, melancholy, grunting, groaning chaunt, when fresh, or their jolting, jerking, shambling, staggering gait, when tired. In a perpetual state of low fever you cannot eat, drink, or sleep; your mouth burns, your head throbs, your back aches, and your temper borders on the ferocious.[14]

Every 8 miles (12.8 kilometres) or so, the four weary, slender, brown men handed over their burden to a fresher team. Besides this there would be other innumerable interruptions – for food and drink, for calls of nature, to hand out endless small coins to buy oil for the lamp or pay the ferrymen to carry them across the small rivers lying across their way. Then Moorcroft would probably stump up and down to restore the circulation to his cramped limbs. Then on again, hour after hour and day after day, slowly moving north-west across the great plain towards Patna. In those days Patna was a long, narrow and very turbulent town on the right bank of the Ganges with many substantial houses and an unusually large number of European inhabitants, most of them engaged in the company's opium trade.[15] Here Moorcroft would part company with his conveyance of the previous week and in due course take a boat across the wide river, and up the green and winding Great Gandak tributary the short distance to Hajipur. He arrived there on 30 November, the day a worried Frazer was expecting him at Pusa.[16] He still had another 40 miles (64

[87]

kilometres) to go. At last on 2 December 1808, exactly seven months after he had started out across the Thames, Moorcroft reached Pusa and grasped the hand of the man he had come to replace.

The next two days – for that is all that Frazer could spare – must have been frantic. First of all there were the introductions: to Lieutenant Wyatt, whose appointment as assistant superintendent ended as soon as Moorcroft arrived; to James Gibb, the civilian veterinary surgeon from the London college; and to some of the key Indian workers on the estate. There would be long hours in the saddle or on foot spent checking endless inventories of live and dead stock and inspecting animals and buildings. Not only was there the extensive estate at Pusa itself to see, but there were all the stud animals quartered in the stables and yards of the local farmers and breeders for miles around. It was an impossible task to accomplish in two days. The annual cavalry committee needed well over a week to do the job and they were already familiar with Bengal's customs and language. Moorcroft later reckoned that it took him five years to serve his apprenticeship at the stud.[17] At the end of those two crowded days in December 1808 he must have been dizzy with the unfamiliar kaleido-scope which had passed before him. About the only instantly familiar things – for Moorcroft had a wonderful eye and memory for a horse – would be the relative handful of animals he had purchased in England or reared at Padnalls, and which had made the long journey before him from those distant stables behind London's Oxford Street. One imagines Moorcroft and Frazer, deep in earnest conversation, with Wyatt and Gibb riding or walking in attendance and joining in from time to time. Frazer would be doing most of the talking, explaining the intricacies of the fourteen-year-old institution he had created almost single-handed. The two men would have made an interesting contrast. One, the soldier, sallow from a long career under the Indian sun which had shattered his health and undermined his early zest for the stud, anxious to be off and yet also pathetically concerned to justify his creation to his successor. Frazer had gained his knowledge of horses and horse-medicine in the hard school of trial and error, but he was deeply knowledgeable about every aspect of the stud and the language and customs of the local farmers. The other man, the civilian, perhaps a year or two younger and still tanned from his long sea voyage, was the most highly qualified English veterinarian of his day, with an encyclopaedic knowledge of horse medicine and horse-breeding, but utterly ignorant of the ways of India and of the difficult charge which, in a few hours, would become his sole responsibility. Moorcroft did not conceal his doubts about what he saw[18] but he seems to have got on good terms with his host, as with most of the men in his life. Indeed Frazer said that he would happily have stayed on to help, if his passage home had not already been booked.[19] He should at least have delayed. The stout East Indiaman waiting peacefully for him in the Hooghly River carried him, not to a peaceful retirement in the green fields of England, but to a violent death in the boiling sea during a great gale off Mauritius only a month or two later.

At last, on the evening of 4 December 1808, and perhaps alone for almost the first time since he arrived at Pusa, Moorcroft sat down to draft an official letter to the secretary of the board, the first of thousands over the next decade. It began:

> Sir, I have the honour of reporting to you, for the information of the Board of Superintendence, that Major Frazer has, this day, formally transferred to me the charge of the whole of the Honourable Company's Stud dead stock at Poosa and its dependencies, along with the sum of Sicca Rupees 22,526 1 anna 7½ pies [about £2800] of which the principal part is in cash and bank notes.

It ended with an appeal which, behind the sober official wording, has almost a hint of panic about it.

> The short time I have been here has enabled me to take, as yet, only a cursory and limited view of the details of the present system, but as far as it has gone, it has clearly convinced me, that if I were to be deprived, at this moment of the assistance of Lieutenant Wyatt, the interests of the Honourable Company might be materially injured by the circumstances to which, my want of acquaintance with the language and customs of the natives would necessarily expose me. Thus situated, I feel it is absolutely incumbent on me to request that the Board will be pleased to lay before His Excellency, the Governor General in Council my opinion of the great necessity there exists for delaying Lieutenant Wyatt's removal.[20]

That Moorcroft should feel overwhelmed after his first two whirlwind days at Pusa is scarcely surprising. For leaving aside the stud animals which were stationed mainly to the west over an area as big as the southern counties of England, the 5000-acre (2023-hectare) estate at Pusa alone constituted a substantial empire. It made the modest 130 acres (52.6 hectares) at Padnalls seem very small beer indeed.

The heart of the Pusa estate, then as now, was on the right bank of the Burhi Gandak River, its wedge-shaped grounds hemmed in by the elbow of the river on two sides.[21] There was also more land for cultivation on the other side of the river. Some of the ground on the very edge of the river was under water for half the year and more was liable to inundation when the Burhi Gandak and its many brothers were striving, in the spring, to carry off the snow-melt of the great Himalayan range to the north, or at the height of the summer rains. Pusa had more rainfall than Ormskirk, and practically all of it fell in two months of the year. In Moorcroft's time, the whole of the gently sloping alluvial plain between the northern mountains and the Ganges was badly drained and damp, with many *jheels* or low-spots of standing, stagnant water throughout the year, although he noticed a significant improvement in this respect during the decade he was there.[22] The area round Pusa, Tirhut as it is called, was immensely green and fertile. Today it is perhaps the most intensively farmed and densely populated area in the whole of India. Frazer had chosen it deliberately for the fertility of its soil, its ability to produce abundant feed for horses and the excellence of its water. But in addition it was well placed for water-borne communication with Calcutta downstream and, important

[89]

strategic target that it was, relatively secure from a scything Maratha raid from the east.[23]

In the prime position at Pusa was the two-storey house of the superintendent, standing on a dry rise overlooking the main landing-place and with 'a commanding view of an extensive reach of the river both to the East and to the West'.[24] It was a substantial building, 100 feet (39.6 metres) long and 76 feet (23 metres) wide with ten major rooms, two bathrooms and deep verandahs running along its long sides at right angles to the river. Nearby were the offices and some of the stables, built of limed, sun-dried brick and thatched, like almost all of the many buildings on the estate. Besides the ranges of stabling there was a granary, a lumber-house, carriage-house, larder, dairy, bake-house, workshops and furnaces to heat the huge cauldrons for preparing animal food and provide heat to the medicated steam bath for the sick horses. There was an infirmary and horse-hospital, a saddlery, store-rooms and kennels, a smithy, a cook-room, a treasury, a gaol to house the estate's convict labour-force, houses for the assistants and more humble accommodation for many of the other folk who worked on the estate. There was a veritable army of them – clerks, grooms, herdsmen, stable-boys and grass-cutters, night watch-men, carpenters, an Indian doctor, a blacksmith, a riding master, invalid soldiers to exercise the horses, and several hundred convicts with an armed guard to work the lands and build paths and roads. There was even '1 person at 4 Rupees and 3 others at 3 Rs. each per month for striking the hour' to encourage 'regularity among the servants in their hours of attendance'.[25] The 1300 humans at Pusa were matched by roughly the same number of horses. There was an experimental nursery for young trees, an orchard and fields of experimental grasses – all that was left of Frazer's earlier enthusiastic experiments in scientific farming with the assistance of an agricultural expert and the latest modern machinery imported from Europe. On the face of it, the Pusa estate was just the sort of challenge to satisfy in Moorcroft all the frustrated love of the land and improving zeal he had first learned in Lancashire, all those long summers ago.

Or rather, it should have been. In fact the overwhelming mood it created in him in those early days was one of deep gloom. He had of course expected to find room for improvement – after all the company directors in Leadenhall Street had long ago lost their earlier confidence in Frazer. But what Moorcroft was not prepared to find was the evidence of apathy and neglect, ill-judged economy, mismanagement and gross error which he detected there. The latest reports available in London, when he made his decision to go to India, had spoken in the very highest terms of the stud's 'valuable breeding stock of first rate stallions and excellent mares'.[26] As far as he could see, the great majority of them were utterly unsuitable for the purpose. He brought with him the highest standards of contemporary European horse and farm management and, by those standards, nearly everything at Pusa seemed impossibly bad.

Perhaps his most fundamental doubt concerned the site itself. Green and fertile it certainly was. But the amount of standing water and the shallow marshes choked with decomposing plants worried him greatly both as a source of unhealthy air (what he would have called 'miasma') and as a breeding-ground for insects and other dangerous pests. The fact that the second rather than the first was the major cause of disease was not yet fully understood, but whatever the cause, Pusa's health record had not been very good. Frazer was utterly misleading on this point. He called Pusa the 'Montpelier of India', the healthiest place in the whole sub-continent. Moorcroft's concern was not really diverted by the bland assurances of his predecessor, and with good reason as it turned out.[27] But leaving aside speculations about the healthiness or otherwise of the Pusa site, it was glaringly obvious to Moorcroft that the health of the horses was also being jeopardized by gross mismanagement. To his eye the stables were dilapidated, dark, airless and overcrowded. The treatment of the young stock, both by stud employees and by the local breeders, seemed to be causing 'serious and permanent mischief'.[28] In his view the foals were being born at the wrong time of the year, with consequent ill-health and a quite unnecessarily high death-rate; they were being handled too young; and they were being allowed to run at liberty in large pastures too early, with consequent damage to the action of their legs.[29]

It was not only the horses that showed signs of neglect and mismanagement. Frazer left Moorcroft with numerous outstanding debts to the stud, going back many years. Moreover his rudimentary accounts were all kept in Bengali, with no proper means of keeping a check on the very large sums of money which passed through the stud books.[30] Moorcroft found too that at least a quarter of the convicts retained to work the lands were useless 'from great age, weakness, leprosy and other causes'.[31] The results were all too visible. Much of the land set aside for crops was choked with weeds and jungle-grass, poorly drained and unproductive. Moreover much potentially valuable land on and near the river bank had never been put under the plough but remained undrained and often under water. To Moorcroft this was more than bad management and a health risk.[32] He was seriously uneasy that the supply of available animal feed round Pusa was so precarious that a bad season might result in acute scarcity if not downright famine. There seemed to be far too many horses on and around the Pusa estate and the serious overcrowding threatened not only the food supply, but also an outbreak of epidemic disease on a catastrophic scale.[33] To make a bad situation worse, some 360 horses from the discontinued stud down in distant Madras were slowly making their way northwards to swell the stock at Pusa.[34]

All these symptoms of Frazer's declining health and zest in recent years, though surprising and disappointing to the new superintendent, would not by themselves have seemed beyond remedy. Indeed they offered ample scope for his considerable energies. Moorcroft was never the man to shirk a challenge – the very opposite is true – but what alarmed him above everything else was the clear evidence, which his sharp, professional eye detected, of a puzzling and rapid degeneracy in the last three generations of stud produce. The size, form, bone and action of the animals were all visibly deteriorating.[35] Many of the young animals were weak in the loins – the condition known as *kumri* – and their action varied from scarcely detectable faults to what he later called 'irregular movements and absolute palsy'.[36] Frazer was either blinded by familiarity with the low and declining standards, or he no longer cared. But Moorcroft was not exaggerating. His very first inspecting committee composed of five cavalry officers spent nine days in and around Pusa in October 1809. Its report was damning in its criticisms of Frazer's animals and errors. Of the entire stock it rated over half the animals as 'bad' and recommended that more than a third of all of them should be disposed of as quickly as possible.[37]

Even the optimistic Moorcroft was perplexed and discouraged by all this, as he later confessed.[38] One imagines him sleepless in the still warm nights, plagued by the attention of the mosquitoes, probably lonely and homesick and perhaps with his bowels afire, like most newcomers to India. Or, on another kind of night, lying awake listening to the dramatic fortissimo of a nor'wester beating against the verandah and wondering whether he and the whole house with him might be blown into the river. That was not idle speculation either. The superintendent's once proud house was now almost the most dilapidated building on the whole estate. Quite apart from the ravages of white ants in the rafters, an earth tremor, five months before Moorcroft arrived, had weakened the structure alarmingly.

> There is not a single room in the house the wall of which is not cracked from top to bottom in several places independent of the clefts over almost every one of the windows and doors, and of the chazms in the cornice and surbase – and . . . every floor of the upper story has cracked and partially separated from its connection with the surrounding wall in almost the whole of its circumference. Every room has an obvious dip towards the center, and the vibration produced by a hasty foot is very considerable.[39]

His house, Moorcroft might have reflected, was a symbol for the whole stud venture at Pusa in its neglected awfulness. For this he had renounced security, friends, comfort and one of the world's great cities, only to find at the end of his six-month journey, not the invigorating rural challenge he had expected, but a range of problems so mountainous that for a while he thought seriously of abandoning the task altogether. Why not return to England, perhaps to take charge of a national stud in the cool and green New Forest, while his health and reputation were still unimpaired? Stables were his life but these were Augean ones, he reflected grimly.[40] Surrender must have been very tempting, but the mood and the doubts passed. He was a natural fighter, both obstinate and tenacious, and always disinclined to accept defeat in anything. His pride was involved and so was the confidence and trust of Parry and the others in Leadenhall Street. He *would* stay and see the job through.

But what then should his policy be? As with his house, so it was with Frazer's breeding operations. It was hard to know whether to repair or whether to demolish and make a fresh start. All Moorcroft's instincts told him that he would never produce a sound cavalry remount from the motley collection of animals he found on the stud books. That had been Frazer's error. Moorcroft now knew in his heart that the apparently startling decision in 1807 to abolish the stud was really the sound one.[41] Ideally he should dispose of every unsuitable animal, and that meant the bulk of them, and start again with new, hand-picked breeding stock. In 1815 Parry, disappointed in his hopes of rapid progress, blamed Moorcroft bitterly for not doing just that,[42] but really such a course was hardly practical in 1808. The stud, after all, represented too huge an investment to be written off, and large numbers of unsuitable animals could not be unloaded onto the market quickly without knocking the bottom out of it. Besides, the stud was enmeshed in contractual obligations to hundreds of local breeders, which could not be broken either easily or quickly. In any case, notwithstanding the loyal support of both Lord Minto and the board, there was inevitable restlessness in Calcutta whenever Moorcroft began to propose radical alterations to his predecessor's schemes too quickly.[43] After all, Frazer had learned the game over many years. Any newcomer, ignorant of the customs and language of the neighbourhood, who thought he knew better was liable to rush into even more serious error. Cautious rebuilding seemed on all grounds the best way to proceed, as Moorcroft had anticipated even before he arrived at the stud.[44] He decided on a plan. He would examine each of the various departments of the stud in detail, starting with the simplest. He would make immediate recommendations to correct the grosser abuses and errors he found, but defer a major change until he had mastered every part of the stud operations and until his growing local knowledge was sufficient to give him the insight and authority he would need to embark on root and branch reform.[45] Given all the circumstances it was probably the best way to proceed. Perhaps only then, in the hour before dawn, Moorcroft may have turned over and slept.

8 REFORMS AT PUSA,

1809-10

THE STUD ESTABLISHMENT which Frazer bequeathed to Moorcroft was divided into three branches known respectively as the *nisfi, zamindari* and home or stable departments.[1] From the very beginning Frazer had realized that he would never achieve the general improvement in the quality of the horses in the British territories (which was one of the original aims of the stud), let alone keep pace with the soaring demand for cavalry horses (which was the other aim), unless he extended the breeding operations far beyond the newly erected bamboo fences at Pusa. In 1798, after some disappointing failures, he had at last set up a workable system by which stud stallions were loaned to selected local breeders. For a fixed fee, the stallions were to cover up to fifty mares annually of at least the standard cavalry height, belonging to the local *zamindars* (literally, landholders). The best of the produce from this so-called *zamindari* scheme was bought by the superintendent and kept at Pusa until it was ready for transfer. The colts were normally destined for direct admission to the cavalry and the fillies usually went on to the breeding registers in another department.

By the time Moorcroft arrived, Frazer had extended his *zamindari* scheme over such a wide area that proper supervision was all but impossible. From this stemmed most of the problems which beset the *zamindari* branch from the very beginning. First, Frazer found it frustratingly difficult to get hold of the best of the young produce. Most of it either disappeared into the hands of foreign dealers and left the company's territories altogether or found its way into the cavalry after being bought on the open market by the cavalry purchasing agent, at a much higher price than Frazer was authorized to pay. Inadequate supervision meant that the *zamindari* stallions were often shamefully neglected by the breeders to whom they were entrusted. Aware of this, Frazer used as stallions many animals of poor quality, later summarized as 'cast horses from the cavalry, horses gratuitously presented by individuals, worn out horses from the Stable [i.e. Home] Stud and cheap purchases'.[2] Moorcroft had his first close look at some *zamindari* stallions a week after his arrival at Pusa. Three of them were too ill to travel. Moorcroft was horrified by the rest. Twenty of them he proposed to geld or sell at once because of 'disease, old age and such defects in conformation as experience has shown to be unfit for the endurance of fatigue'.[3] The remaining fifteen he only kept with the greatest reluctance because there was nothing better available.

If horses, even of this doubtful quality, had been put to standard-height mares as was required by the contract then the resulting offspring might have been just adequate for cavalry purposes. In due course however, Moorcroft realized not only that there had been widespread and systematic falsification of the stud records, but other animals had even been substituted for stud-bred ones.[4] A close examination of the whole *zamindari* department area by area dominated much of Moorcroft's second year at the stud. The results were often startling. In the autumn of 1810 for example, after riding round the Pusa district meeting the breeders, inspecting their animals and examining the breeding registers, Moorcroft estimated that as few as 20 per cent of the mares put to the *zamindari* stallions in that season were of the required height and many of those were either too old, too diseased or too misshapen.[5] Some were so awful, 'their forelegs diverging from each other like a half opened pair of compasses' as he put it,[6] that he had to laugh. No wonder the *zamindari* offspring were so consistently poor and no wonder that Frazer was so often compelled to buy sub-standard colts. Moorcroft's first inspecting committee was damning in its criticisms after looking at 133 animals purchased when young by Frazer for admission to the cavalry. 'Not one single animal amongst the whole of these, is now or ever could have been fit for this purpose, or ever held forth a probability of becoming of any use to the Service.' It was, they concluded, 'a gross misapplication of publick money'.[7]

The truth is that the *zamindari* branch in Frazer's time was so seriously neglected that it had become a kind of Cinderella, never allowed a proper chance to achieve its potential.

Moorcroft, on the contrary, brought to Pusa the view which prevailed in Leadenhall Street: that the *zamindari* scheme under proper supervision and management was the most likely of all to meet the needs of the cavalry.[8] Moorcroft had seen a similar scheme working very successfully in Normandy before the French Revolution swept it away, and everything he saw in those early years at Pusa convinced him that it could work there too.[9] After all, despite all the neglect and shortcomings, the *zamindari* branch had managed to produce some remarkably fine colts.[10]

First he divided the breeding districts into two, each the responsibility of a resident assistant superintendent, with a sufficient junior staff to supervise the breeding operations properly.[11] Lieutenant Wyatt's pending transfer from the stud was finally rescinded and he was given charge of the upper district between Hajipur and Ghazipur further up the Ganges. The lower district round Pusa was put in the hands of a new assistant, Lieutenant William Dickson. Once Moorcroft could be sure that the *zamindari* branch was closely supervised, he was then able to entrust stud stallions of a much higher quality than previously to the local breeders. He called in all the unsuitable animals and gradually replaced them with better stock from wherever he could obtain it, even including some of the stallions being sent out from England. The

breeders were encouraged to co-operate by more generous financial allowances and especially by an ingenious incentive scheme, which gave them
proportionately greater return the more foals they sold back to the stud.[12]
Another improvement was a new system which pre-empted the travelling
horse-dealers, by purchasing the colts at a younger age and giving them
improved housing and management at Pusa. By these means Moorcroft was
able to get hold of far more of the best colts which previously, through Frazer's
neglect and the avarice and poverty of the breeders, had gone to foreign dealers
for export. The unsuitable colts he resolutely refused to buy, despite what he
called 'clamorous representations on all sides'.[13] At the end of each breeding
season the stallions were called back to Pusa instead of being left with the
breeders during the rains, when they were most liable to neglect. All these
measures, Moorcroft concluded after a two-month tour of the upper districts in
early 1810 with Wyatt, gave grounds for believing that the *zamindari* branch
'with due encouragement may be expected in the course of a few years to
furnish a considerable and progressively increasing body of horses for the use
of the Army'.[14]

Moorcroft had far less confidence in the *nisfi* branch, which had received
most of Frazer's encouragement and attention since 1799. He had pioneered it
then as a means of overcoming three of the chief weaknesses of the *zamindari*
system – the poor quality of the local mares, the difficulty in getting hold of the
best of the colts for the cavalry, and the problem of what to do with the fillies.
Under the *nisfi* scheme stud mares were placed with the local breeders, who
were paid 1 rupee each a month for their keep, and who were required to put
them to a stud stallion at Pusa once a year. The stud guaranteed to purchase
the resulting foal when a year old at an independent valuation, half (*nisf* in
Arabic) going to the breeder and the other half being set aside to meet the costs
of the system. Moorcroft admired both the theoretical ingenuity of the scheme
and Frazer's persistence and diplomatic skill in persuading the suspicious
local farmers to co-operate in it, but he certainly did not share Frazer's
simplistic view that the *nisfi* system had only to be extended to achieve all the
aims of the stud.[15] On the contrary, he could see serious and fundamental
objections to it, as he told Frazer in December 1808. His doubts were
confirmed when he had more time to examine the system in detail after Frazer
had left.

The *nisfi* branch and the home stud absorbed most of Moorcroft's time and
attention in that first year. He soon discovered that Frazer had not only
launched the scheme with unsuitable mares but had continued to draft into it
animals which were too small or were sub-standard in other ways.[16] One of
Moorcroft's first proposals was to sell off most of the *zamindari* fillies which
Frazer had recently purchased as breeding mares for the extension of the *nisfi*
scheme. Moreover he soon found that most of the existing *nisfi* mares were not
of the standard size, as recorded in the falsified stud breeding registers, but, on
the contrary, were often seriously undersized. Since the height of the female
parent, in horses as in humans, appears to be one of the key factors in
determining the height of the male offspring, it is scarcely surprising that

Frazer's *nisfi* scheme usually failed to produce sufficient animals big enough for the cavalry. After some determined research in the registers Moorcroft found that in seven years there were only 162 of them from over 2000 mares! And things seemed to be getting worse:

> a comparison of the oldest fillies with their dams shewed that the first generation was scarcely as good as might have been expected, and the subsequent successive progeny by the dwindling of size, diminution of substance, degradation of form and debility of action too forcibly indicated a degeneracy both continued and rapid.[17]

The trouble was that under the *nisfi* contract, and unlike that in the *zamindari* branch, the stud was obliged to purchase *all* of the young stock, whatever its quality or sex. Thus one of its great theoretical advantages, the security of the produce, turned out in practice to be one of its biggest disadvantages. Moreover, it encouraged the breeders to be extremely careless in their management of the stud mares and foals entrusted to them. The 1 rupee a month offered for the mares' upkeep was so marginal that few of the wealthier and better-educated farmers were interested and only the poorest men of the lowest castes were persuaded to participate. They, through ignorance, poverty or a shortage of forage, neglected their charges so that the incidence of still-births and fatal casualties among the young stock was excessive. After dissecting a number of these little creatures, Moorcroft soon convinced himself that most of them had died from the 'want of a sufficient quantity of milk, induced in all probability by the mothers not having an adequate supply of green and succulent food'.[18] Their impoverished keepers, it seems, were often using the miserable allowance to prevent their own children from suffering the same fate as their horses. So here again the cheapness of the *nisfi* scheme, which was another of its theoretical advantages, turned out in practice to be a major disadvantage.

Moorcroft wisely decided to proceed cautiously. The *nisfi* scheme was too complex to master quickly and the real causes of its disappointing results were not altogether clear. In particular Moorcroft wanted to test by experiment whether it was poor breeding-stock or poor management, heredity or environment, that was chiefly to blame. He was puzzled by the fact that successive inspecting committees, on the basis of more local experience than he could yet muster, had praised the *nisfi* branch in very unqualified terms, and he wanted time to test its cost and performance against that of the other two breeding departments. So to begin with he tackled only the most glaring abuses. All the unsuitable mares scattered round the district were gradually weeded out and the unsuitable fillies were given away.[19] More generous financial terms were introduced and, as in the case of his *zamindari* reforms, financial incentives were offered to encourage higher standards of management.[20] The control of the breeders was tightened up and lazy or incompetent ones were warned, fined or relieved of their responsibilities. Changes in the breeding timetable were introduced, so as to ensure that the foals were not born in the dangerous hot weather as previously. When valiant efforts to improve the breeders' management of the young stock proved largely unavailing, Moorcroft concluded that the only solution was to move the foals to Pusa just as soon as they were weaned and rear them under his own supervision.[21]

He arrived at this decision reluctantly knowing that there were already more animals on and around the Pusa estate than was prudent. He would have preferred to concentrate all the available resources at Pusa on the third division of Frazer's stud, the home or stable branch. In Moorcroft's view this was the heart and soul of the whole breeding operation and the one on which all future progress ultimately depended.[22] The home branch was intended to produce, not cavalry horses, but the future breeding-stock from which those horses would come. Its fillies would become *nisfi* mares and its colts, in time, would be the stallions of the *nisfi* and *zamindari* departments. Frazer, Moorcroft believed, had reduced and neglected the home department, stripping it of its better animals, either to bolster the other departments or to raise revenue by their sale to individuals in the open market. Once again Moorcroft was highly critical of Frazer's selection of breeding-stock and his apparent carelessness or ignorance in the selection of crosses. One marked and inconvenient feature of the home stud in Frazer's time was that over two-thirds of its produce were female. Long before he ever dreamed that he would come to India himself, Moorcroft knew, from his discussions with Parry, that Frazer was felt to be making poor use of the big and bony half-bred English horses that were being sent out to him, preferring blood to size in his parent stock and favouring unduly the purer but slighter Arab stallion.[23] Moorcroft hoped to change all that in due course, but before any major expansion of the home stud was possible he had to quieten his growing doubts about the healthiness of the Pusa site.[24] Until he had removed all the other obvious causes of decline and disease there – the overcrowding, mismanagement, poor stabling and precarious food supplies – even that step was not possible.

Once he had made up his mind to stay, Moorcroft threw himself into the immense task with all his characteristic drive and enthusiasm. The frustrated agricultural improver in him was given full rein at last and he now attempted on the middle Ganges what an accident of birth had denied him on the black loam of his native Lancashire. Even he, diffident as he often was about his own doings, admitted that his 'experiments in rural affairs [were] on a tolerably large scale'.[25] His official letters to the board, or such of them as have survived, give a vivid picture of his daily preoccupations in these whirlwind reforming early years when, as he put it, his 'zeal well nigh outran the bounds of discretion'.[26] Moorcroft was often extraordinarily long-winded but it was the magnitude of the task, as much as his verbosity, which explains the torrent of words he poured on Calcutta in the next few years, literally doubling both the board's correspondence and its hard-pressed office staff.[27]

Moorcroft's very first letter, written on the day he took over the stud and already quoted, plunged straight in with a request for a substantially increased military guard for the Pusa treasury, in view of the large sums of cash held there and the size of his 200-strong convict labour force, a quarter of whom were robbers 'of determined and daring character'.[28] Later he sought to treble the number of convicts on the estate and when that source of labour seemed insufficient, tried to persuade invalid soldiers to settle at Pusa and work the land.[29] Making the most of this greatly enlarged labour-force and calling on all he had learned as a young man from Thomas Eccleston and others, he embarked on an ambitious programme of clearing, embanking, draining and manuring so as to raise his crop yields and bring additional areas under cultivation, both on the Pusa side and across the river.[30] A large number of wells were sunk to serve the drier parts of the estate[31] and he also persuaded the board to purchase for stud use Frazer's private estate and stabling at Hajipur.[32] As if all that was not enough, he even began to dream of a great canal scheme to irrigate the whole vast area between the Ganges and the mountains.[33]

He initiated a new round of experiments with forage crops and supervised with special care the planting of the oat seeds that he had brought from London. And thereby, in a small way, he made history. Many argued that oats simply would not grow in such low latitudes. Moorcroft, who had grown up with oats in Lancashire, thought he knew better, especially when his sharp eye spotted a type of wild oat growing on one of the low islands in the middle of the Ganges not far from Pusa.[34] He was right. Frazer seems to have been the first to introduce the domesticated oat (*Avena sativa*) into India but Moorcroft was the first to grow it successfully there on a large scale.[35] When he left the stud ten years later over 3000 acres (1214 hectares) round Pusa were under successful oat cultivation. Moorcroft later attributed most of the striking improvement in the general health of the Pusa horses to its beneficial influence.[36] However, even oats could not survive drought and in the bad seasons of 1815–16, and again three years later, nearly all the crops failed disastrously. It was against such an eventuality that he contracted for grain supplies with the local farmers on a new, more secure and cheaper basis than before, by paying in advance.[37] The new system justified itself at once, for his first three years at the stud were all seasons of unusually low rainfall and rising food prices. Another important contribution to the problem was the spacious granary he designed and built in 1809, which the inspecting committee of that year regarded as 'remarkably good'.[38]

Much of Moorcroft's time and attention had to be devoted to the buildings in view of their generally dilapidated state on his arrival.[39] Highest priority of all was the stabling. Unlike Frazer's, Moorcroft's new stables were light, airy and small, with only twenty horses in each and with their own small paddock attached. He also sunk wells to serve them, not entirely trusting the water of the Burhi Gandak for drinking.[40] The committees of 1809 and 1810 were full of praise for these new stables,[41] but Moorcroft did not confine his building improvements to them. The gaol too was made cleaner, more airy and more spacious for the hundreds of convicts when they returned from a day in the fields. Later he built a village on a raised mound just outside the stud perimeter fence for some of the Indian labourers working on the estate, with a specially built bazaar in purpose-built buildings to serve them.[42] In order to encourage some sort of departmental pride, he proposed that the stud workers should all wear a specially designed badge, engraved in the Roman, Arabic and Devanagari scripts and that the stud should have its own seal.[43] In 1809 he proposed a covered riding school so that the young stock could be examined, broken-in and schooled in all weathers, and later recruited European grooms for the task.[44]

Nor did he neglect the health of the animals although he had far less time for this than he would have liked. The hospital was enlarged and improved and Moorcroft, with Gibb proving a very valuable right-hand man, was as active as ever as a *post mortem* operator, ceaselessly speculating about the often unfamiliar diseases which faced him and pursuing, whenever he could, his longstanding interests in the causes and treatment of lameness and shoeing methods.[45] His old fascination for machinery was evident too. In May 1810, for example, he requisitioned from England a cattle mill powered by a 4 hp steam engine similar to the one he had found so useful at Padnalls. Later other cumbrous agricultural machinery was ordered from England and laboriously towed 500 miles (800 kilometres) up the river by coolies. The steam engine was eventually housed together with quantitites of grain in Moorcroft's increasingly dilapidated house on the river bank.[46] He first recommended the need for new accommodation in December 1808 but it is typical of the man that he was too busy to get round to the matter again for another nine months.[47]

For much of the time of course he was never at Pusa to use it. His responsibilities extended over an area as big as the south of England and were tending to increase all the time. Moorcroft was never happy to be in one place too long and all his working life had been spent grasping opportunities to get out and about and feed his restless mind with new sights and sounds. His little convoy of servants and baggage must have become a familiar sight in Tirhut, as he rode round in all weathers inspecting the horses, checking the registers and meeting and discussing their common problems with the Indian farmers and breeders. He acted as surgeon and doctor to the people too, not only the stud employees and their families but 'throughout the Lower Districts'.[48] In those days leprosy was rife along the middle Ganges and Moorcroft often examined as many as twenty cases in a single day.[49] Malnutrition was another frequent cause of disease and deformity. He later recalled that he had often seen 'the inhabitants of villages turn out the whole of their sick to be inspected. . . . Amongst these the proportion of diseased children, from infants at the breast to those of age twelve or fourteen, with enlarged bellies and wasted limbs was vastly greater than in villages of equal populousness in Europe.'[50] All this must have been exhausting as well as rewarding. Moorcroft later claimed that he had worn out three sets of tents on stud business and it is easy to believe.[51] He also wore out assistants. Lieutenant Dickson, who only had one of the districts to worry about, later claimed that his job required 'a greater degree of personal toil and exertion' than any in India.[52] Moorcroft himself seems to have been tireless in meeting the stud's punishing demands in these early years of furious activity and reform.

The year 1810 can stand for them all. Between the end of January and the end of March he was touring in the upper district with Wyatt, examining the *zamindari* breeding arrangements in detail.[53] He returned briefly to Pusa to deal with the accumulating business there and then, in the second week of April, was off again in the steamy heat, when no European ever travelled unless it was unavoidable. This time he went north towards the Nepalese border to examine it as a potential horse-breeding area and, if possible, to make arrangements with the Nepalese civil governor of Janakpur for a supply of sal timber to complete his building projects at Pusa. It is perhaps just as well that he was overtaken by a breathless messenger and recalled to Pusa, for Janakpur was in the terai, that dank and swampy strip of sal, bamboo and elephant grass along the northern edge of the plain. The terai, a big-game hunter's paradise in the cold season, was a lethally dangerous place from April until October when one bite from the myriad malarial mosquitoes could bring sickness, fever, raging madness and death in a few hours. Perhaps cheating disease himself, Moorcroft hastened back to Pusa to deal with an outbreak of disease among the animals which was all the more burdensome because Gibb was away on sick leave. Having sorted that crisis out, and it kept him busy until almost the end of May, he set out on tour to inspect the lower district *zamindari* horses, and returned during the night of 30 June for a muster of *nisfi* mares the next day. In the second week of August – and by now the rains had started – he was off again to the upper district to select breeders to take *nisfi* mares on his improved plan and working, when time permitted, on his long report about the lower district.[54] He returned to Pusa towards the end of September, but hardly for a rest, for he encountered there an unpleasant little row which involved all three of his assistants. At the bottom of it all was Lieutenant Dickson.[55]

He, it seems, had been a nuisance almost from the moment he arrived at Pusa, grumbling about his salary and what he regarded as the unduly restricted nature of his duties. He had been nominated by the governor-general over Moorcroft's head and this may help to explain why so much of his animus was directed at Moorcroft personally. Dickson seems to have resented both the superintendent's high salary and his civilian status. He also disliked Moorcroft's 'mode of behaviour [which] was such as seemed to me better suited to a groom than to a gentleman'. By that no doubt, he meant the superintendent's willingness to roll up his sleeves and work alongside his men. Moorcroft, in his turn, found Dickson's work faulty and disliked his tendency to make 'comments which required much forbearance on my part'. Forbearance was never in plentiful supply among the isolated European population in India, particularly in the hot weather, and if the impertinent and tactless letters of Dickson on the files are anything to go by, Moorcroft, who was a warm-blooded man himself, would have required the patience of a saint to forbear with his troublesome assistant. He only managed it as long as he did out of respect for the governor-general, but by the autumn of 1809 he and Dickson were no longer on speaking terms after a heated argument.

Now, on 27 September 1810, Moorcroft was furious to discover that his explicit order not to geld any more horses had been disobeyed and he called Gibb and Dickson to his house for an explanation. Dickson was found to have ordered the operation and what happened next is vividly described in Moorcroft's own account.

> The conversation was here interrupted by Lieutenant Dickson rising suddenly from his chair, wishing me a good morning, and saying that he would not stay to subject himself to be lectured by me or by any man else for two hundred rupees a month. I observed that I had no intention of lecturing but wished to have an explanation of a circumstance which was in direct opposition to the instructions I had given him – Lieutenant Dickson then said he would not have any further conversation with me but that if I had anything more to say, I might write. I observed that there did not appear to me any necessity for writing as we were then together and I had many more matters to notice, he refused to stay any longer, I followed to state that I wished him to take charge during my absence for a few days, but he precipitately left the room while I was speaking.[56]

The upshot of this affair was that Dickson, after failing to put in an appearance when the committee of inspection was at Pusa the following month, claiming that he had Moorcroft's permission and that in any case his pregnant wife was in labour, eventually submitted his resignation and returned seething to his regiment. Had he not done so he would certainly have been dismissed. Although he had been nominated by Lord Minto, the governor-general went out of his way to support Moorcroft in the whole affair. Later Moorcroft, who was warm of heart as well as of temper, recommended that the empty house Dickson had built for himself at Pusa should be purchased by the stud to save the man from financial loss. Eventually it became the superintendent's house.[57]

Two days after his stormy interview with Dickson, Moorcroft was 40 miles (64 kilometres) away at Hajipur on stud business.[58] He was back at Pusa at the beginning of October 1810 and at the end of the month received the annual visit of the inspecting committee, conducting it on its rounds in the Pusa estate and neighbourhood and then moving up with it to Hajipur for the great six-day horse fair held there each November.[59] This had been launched in 1801 largely on the initiative of the then president of the board, Thomas Graham.[60] The encouragement of the government and the amenities of its excellent site, near the confluence of the Great Gandak with the Ganges opposite Patna, enabled it to prosper. By 1808 it was said that over 13,000 animals were gathering there in the mango groves, attracting dealers from all over the north of India.[61] Moorcroft evidently enjoyed these occasions, so similar and yet so different from the Michaelmas fair at Howden in Yorkshire, the Newmarket sales or the *fête des morts* at Bayeux in Normandy. They were always vivid occasions, all colour and noise and animated bustle, attracting not only distant horse-traders but jugglers, pedlars and entertainers of every kind. At the Hajipur fair the tent of the superintendent was always a centre of activity. He had strings of unwanted stud horses for sale and, with the deep purse of John Company to draw on, he was in the market for suitable young stock, or older horses for direct admission to the cavalry. Moorcroft's first Hajipur fair in November 1809 had been something of a disappointment in this respect and he was not very successful in either his purchases or sales.[62] Moreover, he was handicapped by having to transact his business through Dickson as interpreter and of course they had a violent quarrel into the bargain.[63] That is the last evidence during the remainder of his life at the stud that he had difficulty in making himself understood. The gift for languages which he had shown in Europe must have come to his aid in India too.[64]

By the end of that hyperactive year of 1810 Moorcroft had been in India two years, and his understanding and knowledge of the stud's complex affairs and the novel local environment in which it operated had grown enormously. The minor gaffes which marked the early months of his service, and his heavy dependence on Lieutenant Wyatt's expertise, were now things of the past. Even so there is a praiseworthy diffidence and caution about Moorcroft's pronouncements on stud matters, which are in striking contrast to the headlong and misleading optimism of his predecessor. In October 1810, for example, he was confessing his need for more knowledge of the habits of the breeders in the upper district before introducing major changes there.[65] The committee of cavalry officers, who later that same month spent several days in Moorcroft's company, formed a rather different opinion of the stud superintendent.

> His arrangements for breeding, feeding and managing horses appear to the Committee to be extremely judicious – his knowledge is as conspicuous in the minute details of the several branches as it is extensive in comprehending the general interests of this important establishment, and his zeal and attention to the arduous duties with which he has been charged seems unremitted and indefatigable. The errors and difficulties with which Mr. Moorcroft has had to contend will no doubt be finally surmounted by his steadiness and perseverance.[66]

It was an opinion repeated over and over again by the board and the governor-general in these early years and must have given Edward Parry, scanning the incoming despatches in faraway Leadenhall Street, much satisfaction.

Nevertheless, as Moorcroft was uncomfortably aware, this is precisely how Frazer had begun his superintendence. The same high hopes in high places, the same high praise, the same frenetic activity, the same mounting expenditure – and the same lack of real progress in meeting the annual needs of the cavalry. It is true that in these early years it was the fruit of Frazer's, not Moorcroft's, breeding operations that were being admitted but the figures were certainly dismal. In 1809 the stud was only able to provide 89 animals for direct admission from its own stock, with another 103 purchased at the 1809 Hajipur fair. In that year the cavalry requirement was 838.[67] In 1810 only 73 came from the stud leaving a shortfall of 320.[68] The next year was no better.

Unfortunately while the stud's production of suitable animals remained obstinately static or falling, the cavalry's needs were rising fast. In the first fifteen years of the stud the Bengal cavalry establishment increased twelve-fold.[69] When Moorcroft arrived in 1808 the possibility of a Napoleonic invasion of India was stimulating a demand for even more. Although that threat died away as quickly as it came,[70] there remained the ever-present danger of Maratha and Pindari attack to put the highest premium on the tactical mobility which the cavalry arm provided. The horse-breeding operations over which Moorcroft presided were a crucial part of military defence in India and failure would not be tolerated for long. He was uneasily aware from small incidents, mere catspaws on the calm surface of his relations with the board, that he could not count on fair weather in that quarter indefinitely. He also knew that, for all the body-sapping energy he was expending on the unwieldy institution which Frazer had bequeathed him, he was simply not achieving the decisive breakthrough that was necessary if the stud's supply were ever to meet the cavalry's annual demand.

The more Moorcroft reflected on the situation, the more convinced he became that two fundamental problems underlay the lack of dramatic progress, both of them in existence before he arrived. The first concerned the healthiness of the Pusa site itself. Moorcroft's doubts about its suitability as a centre for horse-breeding on a large scale had grown with the experience of every passing year, notwithstanding Frazer's breezy assurances to the contrary. At first he had been inclined to blame bad management for the tendency to *bursati* sores, strangles and the *kumri* weakness in the back and loins which he had noticed in the Pusa stock when he first arrived, but these conditions all persisted despite everything he could do. So too, although fortunately only periodically, did the outbreak of more serious disease. In 1809 a mysterious infection killed many of the foals at Pusa.[71] In April 1810, as has been mentioned, Moorcroft had to hurry back to deal with a much more serious epidemic which struck at young and old of both sexes indiscriminately and was particularly serious in its destruction of the valuable older English stallions.[72] For a time Moorcroft even began to fear for 'the very existence of the stud'.[73] He became convinced that the situation of Pusa was at the bottom of it. In particular, using contemporary miasmic theories of disease, he blamed the east wind which blew at the time of the epidemic, loaded as it was 'with noxious air collected from a long line of shallow marshes abounding with shell fish, insects and plants in a state of rapid decomposition'. Could it be, he began to wonder

> that the weakness of action in the hind parts of animals bred at Poosah and its vicinity, the casualties etc amongst colts dropped immediately after the cold season, and the greater disposition to strangles of a more serious kind during the cold season depend upon the action of the same cause or train of causes? And if so does this cause obtain in a greater degree at Poosah and in the lower district than in the upper district and in other places?

He did not know – 'my acquantaince with the Honourable Company's territories and with the varieties of horses produced in them and in Asia generally is very scanty' – but even his two-month tour with Wyatt as far as Ghazipur early in 1810 suggested that the higher and drier soils of that district away from the river, might be more healthy for breeding on a large scale than

Pusa. Might there not be areas more suitable still in those 'other places' he had mentioned?

The second of the fundamental obstacles to rapid progress, and it was perhaps a direct consequence of the first, was that the stud breeding-stock and its offspring in and around Pusa was, and remained, generally far too small and slight for cavalry purposes. The only way to break the vicious circle of genetic transmission was to find, and introduce on a large scale, bigger and bonier parent stock.

> The Cutch mares and several of those brought from the western and north western parts of Asia which have fallen under my notice are of such a size and frame as to prove abundantly that the countries which produced them are capable of producing horses very fit for the use of the army. On this account, it appears to me desirable to know how far the production of the Hon'ble Company's provinces nearest to the countries in question hold out a fair promise of being favourable to the breeding of horses.

It was all very tentative but if he were right – if both the heredity and the environment of the animals round Pusa were holding back progress – then a reconnaissance to test the possibilities elsewhere was imperative.

On 24 September 1810 he completed ninety-nine paragraphs of a letter to the board which expanded these arguments, and laid down a specific four-point programme for a suggested tour up-country, once the Hajipur fair was out of the way and everything settled for the coming cold season at Pusa.[74] First he proposed to visit the reputedly very successful stud of the Nawab Vizier of Oude at Lucknow. Then he would proceed to Rohilkhand, 150 miles (240 kilometres) further on and once the home of a famous breed of horses, to see whether a new *zamindari* branch could be established there. Third, he would visit the ancient horse fair at Hardwar to buy stallions for the *zamindari* branch and some big, bony mares and learn as much as he could of the once legendary horses coming from the more remote parts of north-west Asia. Finally, on his return he would visit as many cavalry regiments as possible in the western provinces, 'to form a precise idea of the kind of animal which experience shall have shewn to be the best adopted to the several Services in this country'. All this, Moorcroft innocently believed, could be done in four months. His superiors in Calcutta probably knew better but their ungrudging approval of all his proposals was given at the end of October and the resident at Lucknow was ordered to make all the necessary arrangements with the Nawab Vizier.[75] Thus it was that the name of the superintendent of the company's horse-breeding stud at Pusa entered the secret files of its external affairs branch, the so-called Political Department, for the very first time.

It certainly was not the last.

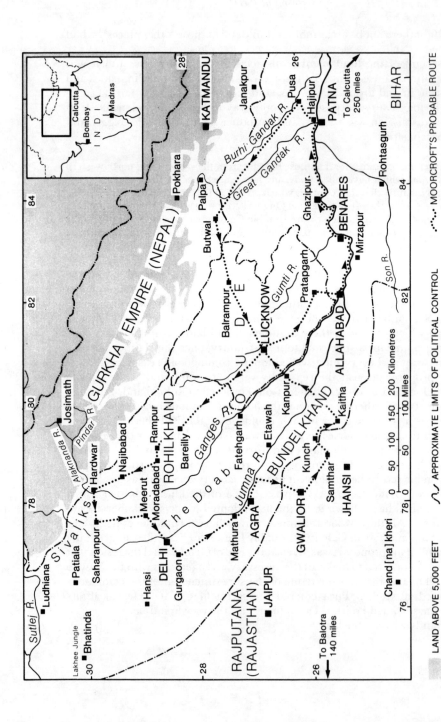

1. THE FIRST JOURNEY, 1811

LAND ABOVE 5,000 FEET

APPROXIMATE LIMITS OF POLITICAL CONTROL

MOORCROFT'S PROBABLE ROUTE

GURKHA EMPIRE (NEPAL)

KATMANDU

Janakpur

Pusa

Hajipur

PATNA

To Calcutta
250 miles

BIHAR

Burhi Gandak R.

Great Gandak R.

Rohtasgurh

Pokhara

Palpa

Butwal

Balrampur

Ghazipur

BENARES

Mirzapur

Son R.

Gumti R.

LUCKNOW

Pratapgarh

ALLAHABAD

U D E

O

Josimath

Alaknanda R.

Pindar R.

S i v a l i k s

Ludhiana

Patiala

Hardwar

Najibabad

Rampur

ROHILKHAND

Meerut

Moradabad

Bareilly

Ganges R.

T h e   D o a b

Saharanpur

Hansi

DELHI

Gurgaon

Mathura

Jumna R.

Fatehgarh

Etawah

Kanpur

Kaitha

BUNDELKHAND

Kunch

Samthar

AGRA

GWALIOR

JHANSI

RAJPUTANA
(RAJASTHAN)

JAIPUR

Lakhee Jungle

Bhatinda

Sutlej R.

Chand[na]kheri

To Balotra
140 miles

0   50   100   150   200 Kilometres

0   50   100   Miles

Calcutta

Bombay

Madras

I N D I A

9 THE FIRST JOURNEY,

1811

MOORCROFT'S JOURNEY TO the north-west in 1811 is quite crucial to an understanding of his later career in India but it is scarcely even mentioned in any published work.[1] Even the route he took can only be reconstructed with some difficulty.[2] Yet the journey marks an important stage in the transition of William Moorcroft from an outstanding veterinarian and horse-breeder to a pioneering explorer. In some ways given the nature of the man and of India, the development was almost inevitable. After all, even his part-time consultancy at Padnalls and his interest in agricultural improvement had led him on journeys all over England and part of Europe. Now, after only two years in India, his scientific training, his natural restlessness and the wide range of his interests already meant that the Bengal breeding operation was being approached far more broadly than either Frazer or the board could ever have imagined. Moorcroft believed that a big problem required an encyclopaedic solution. Looking back on this 1811 journey three years afterwards Moorcroft listed the principal matters he had wished to investigate:

> The history and inspection of breeds of horses supposed indigenous or admixed with foreign blood; in the plains and in the mountains; within the British provinces and in the Nepal and Marhatta borders; the diseases of horses, frequency, causes and the treatment followed by the natives; the vegetables used in feeding horses and their effects; topography as affecting the health of the horse and its security; present composition of the cavalry; comparison betwixt horses formerly and those now admitted, as to form, constitution, etc, collecting opinions of officers as to the kinds found to have been most suitable to the service; as to the effects of castration, etc, formed some of the principal objects of this journey.[3]

What Moorcroft did not say, nor perhaps even knew, was that there was in him a growing wanderlust to be satisfied as well. His imagination may have been fired by the stories he heard from the north-western horse-traders – swarthy, bearded men like Kipling's Mahbub Ali, squatting round the fire outside his tent at the Hajipur fair;[4] or perhaps, over dinner in the big houses of his friends along the river bank at Patna, from some of the Europeans passing down the Ganges from the distant north-west. Moorcroft was not the first, and certainly not the last, of his race to be drawn to those ancient cities and marvellous lands, unrolling mile after mile across that gigantic, chequered and crowded plain towards the distant silver-purple mountains which hem it in so dramatically on the north and north-west.

Of course the journey he planned, in its official version at least, did not take him beyond the shadowy limit of the company's territories or those under its protection. Nor in any sense was it an exploration, although the principal survey of these territories had been completed only three years before and the available maps were extremely rudimentary. Even so, in those early days of British rule it would have been challenging enough for most men. Beyond Allahabad, Moorcroft would be on lands conquered or acquired by the company only in the last few years. Much of it still bore the scars of the half century of war, rapine and maladministration which had ravaged the once peaceful heartland of the Mughal empire. The walled villages and mud forts, the desolate lands and the choked irrigation ditches all told their own tale of the recent troubles. Outside the new military stations or the old court centres like Delhi, the work of pacification had scarcely begun and the revenue officer often needed a company of sepoys to help him enforce his tax demands. In these turbulent lands no traveller with any sense would journey alone, or make his camp at night outside the reassuring walls of an old serai or fort. Apart from the ancient network of dirt tracks linking village with village, roads were practically non-existent. The fragility of the British grip on this great corridor of land was emphasized by the still-dangerous enemies surrounding it on three sides. Undeterred by any of this, Moorcroft excitedly began his preparations in the November and December of 1810.

Truth to tell he did not prepare very expertly. For his personal transport he bought a mare from Lieutenant Wyatt which proved to be very stiff and lame in the cool dawns but which soon settled into an easy gait and carried him all the way.[5] His baggage, including the watches, telescopes and shawls he bought for presents and for barter,[6] travelled in creaking carts which often got into trouble on the narrow or muddy tracks. He would have done better with camels or pack-ponies.[7] He had too much baggage and the escort of sepoys, which was changed at each military station he came to, was often not big enough. Moreover, having made no adequate arrangements to draw cash at the principal treasuries as he went along, Moorcroft often found himself in remote places short of funds and outrunning both his salary and his credit.[8] On this journey, as on all the others he made in the company's service, he never received a single rupee for his own travelling expenses and sank much of his substantial salary into his journeys without complaint or regret. To be on the move was reward enough.

Moorcroft spent Christmas 1810 at Pusa. He was probably very relieved indeed to receive Dickson's resignation on Christmas Eve as well as a written promise of future good conduct from Wyatt.[9] Life together at Pusa in the wake of their row must have been uncomfortable for all of them. The journey finally began on or just after, 7 January 1811.

Instead of passing up the Ganges westwards, Moorcroft struck off north across the lush plain of Tirhut towards the terai and the green hills which marked the limit both of the plain and of the company's possessions. His rather surprising destination was the decaying old town of Butwal, now just inside the Nepalese border on the road to Pokhara, but in 1811 the centre of a fertile district claimed both by the company and by the encroaching Gurkhas, pushing down their revenue collectors and soldiers from the northern hills. Three years after Moorcroft's visit, in the spring of 1814, the company enforced its claim to the Butwal district by planting police posts there and it was the murder of eighteen of these policemen by Gurkha troops shortly afterwards which launched the Nepal war.[10] Moorcroft's visit had no connection whatsoever with these developments. He had noticed at the recent Hajipur fair that some good horses had apparently come from a horse fair held at Butwal each January and had immediately opened a correspondence with Amar Singh Thapa, the ferocious old general in charge of the Gurkha troops on that border.[11] It was this man's hawkishness, and his personal influence as the uncle of Nepal's prime minister, which did much to precipitate the Anglo-Nepalese war three years later. Not surprisingly, he received Moorcroft's overtures with the deepest suspicion at first, but Moorcroft seems to have met him in or near Butwal and done all any Englishman could to charm the old man. The horse fair was a disappointment for no animals at all arrived while Moorcroft was there. He did hear that horses of quality were bred twenty days' travel further into the mountains of Nepal but decided, in view of the palpable mistrust of his host, to pursue that quest at some more opportune moment. The Gurkha was at least persuaded to promise safe conduct to any stud officer who came to purchase horses at Butwal in the future and he did press on Moorcroft the only horse available, a small and miserable creature which was later disposed of at Bareilly. In 1812 Moorcroft, 'to prove that it was intended to resume the business with him respecting horses at a convenient opportunity', sent him a double-barrelled gun.[12] It turned out to be a good investment for Amar Thapa lent his influence to secure Moorcroft's release from detention in Nepal later that year.[13] Moorcroft was not blind to the risks of his first dabble in trans-frontier politics. His report took care to anticipate criticism that he might be encouraging cavalry-horse-breeding in Nepal to the company's disadvantage. The Gurkha hill men, he asserted, 'are never likely to use horses offensively in the Company's territories'. From the glimpse he had of their oppression and misgovernment, he sincerely hoped not.

Disappointed in his hope for horses, Moorcroft returned across the terai to the great plain, now heating up day by day as the sun wheeled his ancient course between the wide horizons. At Balrampur in Oude, the site of a small horse fair, Moorcroft took up again his enquiries into the horse-breeding activities of the Gurkhas across the mountains to the north. He also, and perhaps for the first time on his travels beyond the vicinity of the stud, smoothed his way by using his medical knowledge to treat the young son of the local chief. On then, south and west, to Lucknow, the capital of Oude, which he reached some time in February. Moorcroft, like nearly all of the British travellers who passed through Lucknow at this period, would have lodged in style in the spacious British residency, set in its peaceful gardens of roses, oleanders and hibiscus and framed with mango and cypress trees, close beside the south bank of the Gumti River.[14]

Oude was a classic example of the ensnaring pitfalls of the so-called subsidiary alliance system. Inside one generation its hereditary rulers, having wrested their independence from the failing Mughal power at Delhi, were reduced by the British to the status of client kings, almost surrounded by British territory and placed very much under the thumb of the imperious British resident, Colonel Baillie. He had a fund of good stories about the court of the Nawab Vizier. Saadat Ali was only on the throne at all because the British had intervened to remove his brother in 1798. He was really the last of the strong Muslim rulers of Oude, by reputation a tight-fisted man, but prodigal in the sumptuousness of his dress and entertainments, and in the scale of his building projects. Although the narrow streets and bazaars of Lucknow were as filthy as ever, 'stinking like an Abyssinian's armpits' according to a poet from rival Delhi,[15] Saadat Ali and his predecessors had enriched the city with some fine palaces, mosques, bazaars and gardens. These did not of course rival the incomparable marble splendours of Mughal Delhi and Agra but were, and still are, impressive. The court style of the nawabs was splendid too. For the English visitors of this period it was the nearest thing to the *Arabian Nights* they had ever seen – elephant fights, veiled dancing girls from the harem, fine carpets, sumptuous rooms full of gold and precious stones, elaborate firework displays and costly illuminations. Lucknow in this period was the Babylon of India, a harlot of a city but also an important centre of Urdu scholarship and Muslim culture. Rather incongruously, Saadat Ali had acquired a veneer of European habits during his long exile as a British pensioner and was inclined to entertain his English guest *à l'Anglais*. Or so he thought. On one occasion splendid Staffordshire chamber pots were found on the banqueting table masquerading as milk jugs.

Sadly one can only guess at Moorcroft's experiences in Saadat Ali's palaces or at the residency. We know that the weather was very hot and dry during his stay – perhaps the nawab gave his travel-stained visitor the exquisite refreshment of his *hammam* or Turkish bath. Perhaps some of Moorcroft's other bodily needs were catered for too. At another sumptuous oriental court some years later it was averred of Moorcroft that 'his principal occupation was making love'.[16] Saadat Ali, corpulent, with grey hair and missing teeth was nearing the end of his life. He was probably as happy in the company of his animals as of his wives. He owned 700 elephants, together with a collection of enormous, gilded two-storey carriages which they pulled on ceremonial occasions. He also had an impressive menagerie in which Moorcroft may well have had his first meeting with the rare shawl-wool goat of Tibet. If so it was a more significant encounter than he could have realized at the time. But it was horses he had really come to see and here he and his royal host certainly shared a common passion. They probably spent several hours together in the great stables as some of the 1500 animals were brought out, examined and discussed. Moorcroft knew that the nawab had supplied a considerable number of horses to the

British cavalry during Lord Lake's campaign of 1803. He was also well aware that some of the better horses he had seen at Hajipur had come from Lucknow. He was certainly impressed with the lack of disease in the stables as compared with Pusa (although he saw some evidence of glanders) but was disappointed to find that his host favoured pure-blood and slighter animals. If Moorcroft's official report is anything to go by, the most striking thing of all in the nawab's stables was the dramatic effect in the dry air of static electricity on the manes and tails of the horses. The two men seem to have played like schoolboys, touching off sparks with the tips of their fingers and making scraps of paper jump. It is also somehow typical, both of Moorcroft and Saadat Ali, that the one filled the other with enthusiasm for the benefits of a giant steam pump from England which could lift water from the Gumti to irrigate the royal parks, cool the palaces and work the fountains in the palace gardens and streets of the newer city. Not only that, the practical Moorcroft pointed out, but pumped water would also be useful to put out accidental fires in the city. A complete gentleman was Moorcroft's impression of his congenial host.[17]

Tearing himself away at last from these various delights, Moorcroft turned his little convoy north-west towards Rohilkhand. The populous town of Bareilly and the small, semi-independent state of Rampur beyond were his principal objectives. Rohilkhand was, as its name indicates, the land of the Rohillas, those tall, athletic and handsome people who had come from Afghanistan a century earlier. Their turbulent land was part of that great crescent of territory which Wellesley had recently stripped from the Nawab Vizier to pay for his augmented British defence force. Before Mughal decline and Maratha raids destroyed its prosperity Rohilkhand was once a flourishing horse-breeding centre. Moorcroft believed it could be again. Indeed, he was so impressed by the dryness of its sandy soil and the freedom from disease which he noticed in the horses he encountered, that he rated it the best natural area for horse-breeding he had yet seen in India and earmarked two particularly ideal locations for the new stud depot he hoped to establish. Here many of the surplus animals now at Pusa could be housed and it could also serve as a receiving station for north-western horses purchased at the Hardwar horse fair.

Rampur seemed the most active centre of the horse trade in Rohilkhand. It was from the Rampur dealers that Moorcroft picked up the best twenty horses he secured on this trip, their quality all the more impressive because traditionally the best of the northern horses were always taken down into the Maratha country for disposal to the chiefs there. The Rampur dealers assured him that they would be willing to divert many more quality animals to Hardwar, if sure of a sale there. Moorcroft must have felt that at last he was among men who really knew their horseflesh. His enthusiasm for the 'cadence, precision and brilliancy of effect' resulting from the schooling of their horses brought him as near to poetry as his plodding official reports ever came.

Interesting as all this must have been, however, it was time to move on again across that vast plain in which all his life in India had so far been spent. From the dreary walled town of Moradabad it is possible, in the clear air after the rains, to see to the north that breathtaking northern rampart of snow peaks, cloud-high beyond the piled outer ridges of wooded hills. But this was late March and the dust-laden air, as the sun grilled the plains russet brown, would probably have denied Moorcroft any sight of the hills and high peaks which bring the Gangetic plain to such a startling termination, until he was almost upon them. The escape from some of the furnace heat of the plains when he finally reached Hardwar must have been an immense relief.

Most English visitors were captivated by Hardwar. There the young Ganges, crystal clear and very cold after its torrential 180-mile (288-kilometre) journey through the mountains from the glacial ice-cave of its birth, rushes out from the green hills that rise behind the town. To its riverside temples and ghats, pilgrims and traders flocked from all over India to join there the holy men – strange, half-naked creatures daubed with mud and paint and crying for alms. It was also in the verdant meadows beside the river and in its bed that the annual *mela* (fair) was held each April. The scene there has often been described.

> The Kabool people bring down strings of horses, dried fruits, assafoetida, and other drugs; the Punjaubees bring camels, horses and cloths; the Hurreeanas bring bullocks, cows, and horses; elephants come from Goruckpoor . . . and there are many thousands of braziers' shops, with the brass and copper pots piled up in bright shining columns. The shawl merchants come from Cashmere and Amritsir; the Jeypoor merchants bring coral beads and jewelry, besides turbans of chintz and cloths; . . . the Dooaub sends soft sugar, sugar-candy, cotton cloths . . . from Benares come silks . . .; besides indigo, all the dyeing drugs almost come down from the mountains. The number of confectioners' shops is very great; and the pedlars make a most glittering appearance with their . . . tinsel, beads, tin and pewter ornaments.[18]

Wandering through this moving kaleidoscope of animal and human life Moorcroft was particularly fascinated by the horses from places far away to the north and west, the golden deserts of Rajputana, the Punjab, the bare brown hills of Afghanistan and beyond even to Persia and Turkistan; fascinated too by the wisdom of Sikh, Rajput and Pathan horse-dealers, weatherbeaten men with wind-etched faces and knowing eyes wrinkled against the glare and dust of the long roads they travelled. He probed, questioned and haggled, perhaps in the traditional way of the trade, by finger pressure with the hands under a cloth to cheat the curiosity of inquisitive onlookers. At the end of it all he had not only acquired a string of fine bony mares and colts, but also a much more accurate idea of the north-western breeding grounds and the seasonal channels of the ancient northern horse trade as well. He also knew exactly where he wished his next journey to be.

But first he had to finish this one. It was April and his four months' leave had expired already. If he were to be back in time even for the Hajipur fair in October, and to see all the other things he hoped to see, it was time to face again the heat of the high-summer plains. There was no time, as he had hoped, to strike north to visit the cavalry regiment at distant Ludhiana on the Sutlej, the most northern limit of the British territories. With that single exception he visited every other cavalry regiment in the field command of the western provinces – at Saharanpur, Meerut, Gurgaon, Mathura, Kaitha, Kanpur and Pratapgarh. The hospitality of these far-flung outposts was legendary and Moorcroft acknowledged it in his official report. In return for his accommodation and the generous mess dinners, Moorcroft examined the animals, advised on health problems and general stable management, demonstrated his new castration technique and dispensed the fruits of his lifetime study of lameness. He noticed sadly that the horses received most recently from Pusa were nowhere near as good as many of the older animals and he quizzed his hosts carefully about the qualities they needed in a cavalry horse. It is possible to capture the flavour of these earnest discussions at the scattered, up-country cavalry stations from just one surviving letter.[19] In it Moorcroft recapitulated for Colonel MacGregor at Meerut his detailed, and very sound, suggestions for dealing with that most deadly and unpleasant of horse diseases, glanders. He also thanked MacGregor and his brother officers for what he called 'the flattering attention they were pleased to give certain operations and professional suggestions' he had given to them.

Moorcroft's peripatetic veterinary tour was pleasantly interrupted by a visit to Delhi.[20] Notwithstanding that Delhi was reckoned to be the hottest posting in British India and this the hottest time of the year, Moorcroft enjoyed his meeting with the little band of Englishmen who were, by a combination of guile, persuasion and force, beginning the huge task of bringing order and peace to that lawless territory. He may have had an audience with the Mughal emperor Akbar II, resplendent with sonorous titles and long white beard but ruler of an empire which went little further than the massive walls of his great red fortress-palace beside the Jumna. Here too Moorcroft would have met for the first time the new resident, Charles Metcalfe. Still only 26, he was already tipped for the highest positions the company's service could offer. Moorcroft remembered him as playful, charming and good-natured and the two men in due course became firm friends.[21] At Agra, like every visitor before and since, Moorcroft surely marvelled at the exquisite marble beauty of the Taj, in those days visible to the traveller from afar, floating above a wasteland of decaying gardens and ruined mosques.[22] Whether its ethereal beauty under a bright moon clutched even the practical and down to earth Moorcroft by the throat is impossible to tell. His report does not even mention it.

Although it formed no part of his original four-point programme – and might not have been allowed if it had – soon after leaving Agra Moorcroft turned south on a detour into the dangerous borderland known as Bundelkhand, the land of the Bundelas. Here the wide Ganges plain broke up into jungles infested with wild animals amid the rocky hills and ravines which are the first outriders of the great heartland plateau of central India. This was Maratha country and dominating that corner of it was the immense camp of Daulat Rao Sindia in the plain near the towering Gwalior outcrop. That corpulent and insolent chief had already tried his French-trained forces against the British in 1803 and was tempted to do so again a few years later. He proved a generous host to Moorcroft, exercising his riding and bodyguard horses in the dusty plain for his visitor's benefit. Moorcroft remembered his enormous emeralds[23] but was not impressed with his horses. The fleetness and endurance of the Maratha horses was legendary but he was disappointed at their slightness and generally poor quality. There seemed no hope of getting breeding-stock from this turbulent neighbourhood.

What Moorcroft did get in abundance was information, pumping his Maratha hosts and every chief or itinerant horse-merchant he met for news about the horse fairs of Rajputana and the Punjab, whence the few animals of real quality seem to have come. One of his most valuable informants at Gwalior turned out to be a Rampur horse-dealer called Ahmad Ali Khan. From a lifetime of experience on the road hawking northern horses round the Deccan, he was able to explain to Moorcroft the once strong ebb and flow of the great northern horse trade. He recalled how, as little as fifteen years ago, Afghan merchants went north to buy horses at Bokhara. For the first time the name of that legendary desert city far away beyond the wrinkled mountains of Afghanistan and the fabled Oxus River appears in Moorcroft's official correspondence. The Afghan horse-dealers, with their strings of fine Persian or Turki horses from Bokhara, used to come down into India and cross the Indus in November, buying where they could along the way and selling their animals as far down as Kanpur or Lucknow. But that was before war and anarchy in Afghanistan and northern India disrupted the traffic. Even so according to Moorcroft's informants, there were still fine animals to be had in Rajputana and in what was then called the Lakhee Jungle, a fertile district some 100 miles (160 kilometres) west of Patiala on the edge of the great desert in the neighbourhood of Bhatinda. Much of this confirmed or amplified what he had learned at Hardwar and Rampur.

Additional confirmation came in the form of the few very fine horses from these areas which he saw and admired in the stables of the various local chiefs of Bundelkhand. The difficulty was to get hold of any of them. Delicacy and expediency forbade him to ask if they were for sale. The result would have been either the offer of the horse as a gift or for sale at an outrageously high price. Both would be embarrassing. Only at the court of the raja of the little state of Samthar did Moorcroft stumble upon the proper way to resolve the dilemma. This, he wrote, 'consists in offering by way of present an assortment of such articles as from their novelty and utility may be highly gratifying to the receiver, and excite a desire of making a suitable return'. The raja of Samthar, in exchange for 'a very large telescope', gave Moorcroft a large stallion of such quality that he enthused about him for several paragraphs of his report. Unfortunately he sent this prize ahead of him back to Pusa and the animal, for reasons never discovered, died suddenly on the journey.

It was now mid-June and the great monsoon clouds would be hunching up in the south-east preparing their annual respite from the choking dust and the vibrant glare of the summer sun, but also threatening to make travel on muddy tracks with heavy carts a wet and wearisome business. Moorcroft hurried on.

He was at Kunch near Samthar on 20 June and he would have visited the cavalry regiment at Kaitha soon afterwards. On 29 June he was at Kanpur, already the biggest military station in the north-west but with little else there yet except a bazaar and a huddle of mud houses.[24] In July he returned to the more civilized delights of Lucknow and Baillie's residency. In early August he reached Akbar's lofty fort at Allahabad, dominating as it still does the holy meeting-place of the crystal clear Jumna and the already brown Ganges. From this point the monsoon-augmented waters of the two great rivers would have afforded a much more rapid and restful means of transport to lower Bengal than plodding through the mud in the steamy heat of the rains. On 8 August Moorcroft dashed off a letter to the board from Allahabad requesting permission to come down to Calcutta as soon as he had inspected everything at Pusa, so that he could report in person on the experiences of his seven months on the road.[25] That day or the next, with the baggage and perhaps the horses loaded aboard a fleet of small wooden river boats, the last and most rapid stage of the journey would have begun.

River travel was never entirely uneventful at this time of the year. The violent storms of wind and rain often scattered the ramshackle boats or threatened to capsize them in the fast-flowing current on one of the many swirling mud banks. When the beating wind and rain were stilled, swarms of flying insects joined the ceaseless croaking of frogs or the jackals' howling at night to torment the traveller. But the washed and limpid riverscapes after the rainstorms were full of beauty and interest too, and the innumerable contemporary accounts of this journey record them faithfully: the sinister stillness of the half-submerged alligators or perhaps the playful attentions of a dolphin; the rainbow-scattering plumage of the darting birds; the decaying Hindu temples among the trees; the little clusters of white figures on the passing bank, attending the funeral pyre of a relative or consigning the half-charred remains to the sacred river; the graceful, colourfully attired women, beating clothes or fetching water.

On 11 August Moorcroft was at Mirzapur,[26] the chief cotton town on the river with its handsome but somehow alien European houses extending along the banks of the river for several miles. A day or two later he would have been sliding past the marvellous curving panorama of Benares. Most visitors, then as now, were enchanted by the colourful spectacle of the pilgrims thronging its stepped ghats from early dawn, the fine carvings of its yellow and red stone temples, the ceaseless tinkle of bells or the deeper note of conch horns, and by the busy skyline of domes and pagodas, their gilded tridents glittering in the sun. Further downstream, Moorcroft disembarked at Ghazipur to inspect the *zamindari* breeding operations in that neighbourhood. He found them still lamentably short of animals of any size but with some encouraging signs of progress and a general healthiness in the area which made even Hajipur, never mind Pusa, seem far less suitable for horse-breeding on a large scale. Before embarking again, Moorcroft also noted with interest that the big cavalry depot at Ghazipur, with stable accommodation for over 700 animals, was now standing empty. On again they slid down the great river until at last the familiar lines of houses on the right bank of the river gave warning that Patna was almost in sight, with Hajipur only a short distance away but hidden by the lush curves of the Great Gandak River. Moorcroft probably spent a little time with Wyatt at Hajipur and he certainly saw plenty to reinforce his concern at the disappointingly poor results of the *zamindari* operations in that neighbourhood. At last, on 26 August 1811, he reached Pusa.

He had been away nearly eight months, twice as long as he had expected. In that time his views about India, about its horse-breeding and perhaps about the pattern of his own future life were transformed. The next few depressing days at Pusa confirmed the change. He spent two days looking very carefully at all the animals which had arrived in his absence from the abandoned stud at Madras and noticed again the same alarming degeneration in three generations that had appalled him when he first saw Frazer's animals three years before.[27] He then inspected the animals at Pusa, and the *nisfi* mares and their foals with the breeders in the district round about. Gibb had done as well as any man could during his absence.[28] The obstacles, as Moorcroft could now see clearly, were inherent and probably insuperable. In the first place, Tirhut was too damp and too unhealthy. Frazer had been wrong. It was time for the company to cut its losses and transfer its breeding-operations lock, stock and barrel to drier and healthier locations further west. Along with Frazer's site, Moorcroft was also ready to throw out his cherished *nisfi* system. Gibb had done his best but all the old problems remained and seemed, if anything, to be getting worse. Neither the animals nor the Tirhut breeders were capable of producing the horses the cavalry needed.

A change of location, however, would not by itself be enough. In 1811, as in every year since 1794, the basic problem was the lack of size in the breeding-stock and particularly in the brood mares. Moorcroft now knew from personal observation that the Ganges plain, from its swampy delta right up to the Sutlej River beyond Delhi, could not provide animals of the size and quantity the stud needed. He was properly cautious about hearsay information from over-enthusiastic or self-interested traders, but he had both purchased and seen horses which confirmed that big bony animals could still be had, despite the alarming decline in the old northern horse trade. They were obtainable, it seemed, in the breeding districts situated on a great arc of territory lying just to the north and west of the furthest limits of his own recent journey.

Moorcroft knew exactly what he had to do. He must visit these distant breeding-grounds in Rajputana and the Punjab in order 'to become acquainted with the resources of these countries as to horses generally; to purchase stallions, colts, fillies or mares and to encourage the breeders to send their young stock annually to Hardwar, and to other fairs in British territory, where a steady demand from the stud for suitable animals would be assured. Unfortunately – or fortunately – such a tour over so vast a distance would not only take him into turbulent and unsettled areas beyond the fragile limit of the company's possessions, but would also remove him from Pusa for many months, just when the radical changes he favoured would have to be introduced. No wonder Moorcroft wanted to get down to Calcutta to argue his case before the board in person. He always achieved more in an hour of conversation than in months of correspondence. By mid-September he was back on the river again and on the evening of the 22nd, almost three years after his first and previous visit, he returned to the civilized delights of the presidency capital.

We know something of his doings in the next few weeks. He had two audiences with the commander-in-chief and, at his request, inspected the horses of the governor-general's mounted bodyguard.[29] He visited one of the repositories in which were kept and sold the imported so-called 'Arab' horses, so popular at that time as carriage and riding horses in fashionable Calcutta. Moorcroft was withering in his scorn of the 'contemptible' animals he found there. Wealthy Calcutta could indulge its 'Arabomania' if it wished, but the flood of these small, inferior animals from the Persian Gulf was helping to kill the northern horse trade and that was serious. Moorcroft wanted the import of small horses to be discouraged by stiff import duties, which would have the additional advantage of helping him to unload on the market the large numbers of undersized animals he wished to discard from the stud stocks. Most of his working hours in Calcutta would have been spent at the board, endeavouring to sell to its members his difficult double programme of extensive reforms to the stud together with a lengthy absence from it. There is not much doubt which of these was uppermost in his mind. By 3 October he was already engaged in the enjoyable task of planning his next journey.[30]

Much less pleasant would have been the painful writing of his report on the last. It was, even for him, a wordy and disordered document – 309 rambling paragraphs, sprinkled with innumerable footnotes, digressions and inessentials. Moorcroft was not very happy with it and it is easy to see why.[31] His head seems to have been so crammed with new information and ideas, that he was quite unable to decide what to leave out. The resulting hotch-potch gives only the most confused picture of his recent journey, although this served as a useful smokescreen to obscure the awkward fact that he had been away twice as long as expected and twice entered hostile, or at least foreign, territory. Nearly as confused is the analysis of his enquiries over many a camp-fire or supper table into the pattern of the old northern horse trade and the reasons for its current decline. Very clear indeed however were Moorcroft's brisk proposals for the reform of the stud. The *nisfi* system should be abolished. It had been given a two-year trial against the home stud and been found wanting. *Zamindari* breeding should be discontinued, both round Pusa and Hajipur. The two estates should be retained as depots for the stallions and brood mares, but the young stock should be transferred before the usual onset of disease in their second year, to a new and more healthy depot in the vacant cavalry stables at Ghazipur. There a newly recruited European riding master and European staff should train the foals until they were ready for transfer at four years old. The existing *zamindari* breeding system round Ghazipur should be extended and improved. At the very end of the report came Moorcroft's proposal for his new tour.

He was back at Pusa early in November, fearful that he had not put up a clear enough case for a new journey up-country, when the eagerly awaited despatches arrived. This is what he read.

> The comprehensive view which Mr. Moorcroft has taken of the subject of horse-breeding in the Company's territories and the adjacent countries has proved highly satisfactory to His Excellency in Council and is very creditable to that gentleman's talents. The proposition of the Superintendent to undertake another journey for the purpose of visiting the Lakhee Jungle, the Rajpoot States, the Punjab and the fair at Chand Kerie or Balotra and other places where the breeding of horses is carried on to a considerable extent and with great success and where several general fairs are annually held, for the purpose of obtaining horses and mares of a description well calculated for parent stock, has met with the entire approbation and sanction of Government and the Resident at Delhi will be desired thro' the Political Department to request Rajah Sahib Sing of Puteealah to furnish Mr. Moorcroft with letters of recommendation to the principal natives of the neighbouring districts to which his influence may extend.

Every one of Moorcroft's proposals for changes at the stud were also approved.[32]

This is the official version. The truth certainly but, one wonders, is it the whole truth? The stud superintendent, now in his mid-forties had just completed a punishing journey of over 1500 miles (2400 kilometres) through some of the hottest parts of India and during the hottest months of the year. For most Englishmen of his age that journey, even performed in much more comfortable conditions and season, would have been enough. Yet here was Moorcroft, just back after eight months away, not only immediately proposing another long journey and anticipating 'a great length of time before I shall return', but already speculating about the 'possibility of my being obliged to make other journies' after that.[33] Was all this travel strictly enjoined by the urgent problems facing him at Pusa, as the board and governor-general in council were still prepared to believe? Or was this restless, endlessly curious man beginning to seek a partial escape from routine administration into the exhilarating freedom of the open road? Was travelling beginning to be more important for him than arriving? The answer to these questions must probably be yes.

It is true that the official case for a reconnaissance to the distant breeding-grounds of the north-west looked sound enough, as Moorcroft presented it. But his previous life suggests that an even stronger imperative than new breeding-stock may have been his own persistent inner drive to escape from the confines of routine and orthodoxy. It was there when he forsook human for animal medicine; there again when he went to France at the height of the Revolution; there too when he neglected his practice for horseshoes or volunteer soldiering or for long journeys round Britain in search of agricultural improvement or breeding-stock for the East India Company. It was there in middle age when he decided to build a new career in India. Now it was there again, as he justified, and prepared for, his second long journey to the north-west. Yet not even he could have imagined that this time he was going where no European had ever been before.

10 RETURN TO THE NORTH-WEST,
JANUARY–MAY 1812

MOORCROFT BEGAN HIS preparations for his second journey in late September
1811 almost as soon as he reached Calcutta and some considerable time before
he had official permission to go. He was a man in a hurry. There were major
and far-reaching changes at the stud to set in train before he could leave.
Moreover, the spring horse fairs of the great northern deserts, and the breeding
districts round Bhatinda even further north, had to be reached before the
searing heat of early summer. Moorcroft made none of the amateur traveller's
mistakes this time. He now knew the logistics of the open road and there is a
directness and professionalism about his requisitions quite different from that
of the previous year. Indeed one of his requests appeared to the governor-
general in council rather too professional. Maps? That was reasonable enough,
although there was little enough available to give him, but surveying instruments, compasses and a cumbersome iron and brass perambulator to measure
distances were all firmly vetoed. They would arouse legitimate suspicions in
the foreign territories Moorcroft intended to visit and would also prove a major
encumbrance.

If these curious requisitions from their stud superintendent aroused any
suspicions in Calcutta there is no hint of them in the official correspondence.[1]
After all he could argue justifiably that route surveys were badly needed to
confirm or modify existing information and fill the still-yawning gaps on the
few reliable maps of the north-western provinces that existed. So they were,
but he would have quite enough difficulties to contend with in the turbulent
lands he planned to visit, without jeopardizing both his timetable and his
safety unnecessarily. What he lightheartedly called 'the chance of accident'[2]
was far greater than he realized. The political files of the distant British
outposts he proposed to visit reveal very vividly the groundswell of lawlessness
and violence which remained after the stormy years of anarchy and war. This
was the case even in the newly-acquired British territories. Beyond them,
predatory banditti preyed on passing traffic and the hapless villagers almost at
will.

Moorcroft intended to travel light; light, that is, compared with the previous
year when his convoy of lumbering carts had delayed him immeasurably. This

time he hoped to use carts only for the transport of his baggage to the nearest point where it could be loaded on to the commissariat carriage animals which the commander-in-chief had promised him.[3] In the deserts Moorcroft intended to use camels. To keep his cash down to safe limits, elaborate arrangements were made for him to draw bullion (and part of his salary) at the company treasuries as he passed.[4] Even so, he was bound to find himself once again at the head of a small army. He would be carrying the 10,000 rupees' worth of European articles purchased for him by the board in Calcutta[5] in the hope that they could be used in the same sort of gentlemanly and productive way as the telescope which had extracted a fine stallion from the raja of Samthar. As these barter goods and the company's gold rupees in his baggage dwindled so, it was hoped, his string of horses would grow.

Not only was Moorcroft expected to purchase breeding-stock for the stud, but the commander-in-chief had asked him to purchase for direct admission to the cavalry as well, so desperate was the shortage of suitable animals in 1811.[6] It is not, therefore, very surprising that a substantial armed escort was required for the caravan, nor that the up-country British outposts were called upon to obtain introductions and safe conducts from the powerful chiefs whose lands it would cross. Anyone who has organized even a simple overland expedition will marvel that Moorcroft was able at the same time to despatch a steady stream of detailed recommendations for reform at the stud. He was at the Hajipur fair early in November 1811, still writing busily, and even on Boxing Day 1811 the torrent of ink continued to flow.[7] Long after the journey had begun, letters about stud business still drifted in to the board – from Benares, from Agra and from places even further to the west.

When Moorcroft finally set out is not clear. It was certainly very much later than he intended. He was still at Hajipur selecting horses for the governor-general's bodyguard on 9 January 1812[8], but a fortnight later he was 200 miles (320 kilometres) away, at Benares.[9] By early March, he was across the British frontier, deep in discussion with Richard Strachey, the resident at Daulat Rao Sindia's vast, tented town near Gwalior. Dick Strachey had taken over from Metcalfe in April 1811, just two months before Moorcroft's previous visit.[10] They may have met then, but it was on this occasion that Strachey's information became so decisive an influence on Moorcroft's future plans. Strachey was as inquisitive and active a traveller as Moorcroft himself, but he was also far more experienced. He had been to Persia with John Malcolm in 1800 and acted as secretary to Mountstuart Elphinstone's diplomatic and fact-finding mission to the Afghans eight years later. He was one of the very few Englishmen who could talk from first-hand knowledge of the great northern desert which he had crossed in 1808 on the way to Peshawar and he had also gathered much hearsay information of the lands still further to the north and west. Elphinstone's mission had been expressly told to discover as much as possible about horses and there is much on the subject, even in the sumptuous account of the journey which was eventually published in 1815.[11]

The gist of Strachey's advice to Moorcroft in March 1812 is clear. He believed that the chances of obtaining quality horses at the Rajputana horse fairs were slender. Years of continuing oppression, anarchy and warfare in the area had almost destroyed the horse-breeding, and the horse trade it nourished, of former and happier times. So it proved. Much of the information about the allegedly flourishing Rajasthani horse fairs which Moorcroft had gathered from the dealers the previous year was, he later discovered, pure fabrication, designed only to inflate the value of the strings of inferior horses they had for sale. He later discovered, for example, that the once great fair at Chand[na]kheri, not much more than 150 miles (240 kilometres) from Gwalior and one of the prime targets of his present mission, had not in fact been held at all for several years! Strachey's rather depressing information led to a simple conclusion. Only if what Moorcroft called 'new lines of operations' could be opened up, would he secure the quality breeding-stock the stud so desperately needed.

Here Strachey's information was more encouraging. The big Turki and Turcoman horses obtainable in northern Afghanistan and along the Oxus really were as good as Ahmad Ali Khan of Rampur had claimed in 1811. Not only that, but it seemed that there was 'nothing particularly formidable', either from natural or man-made difficulties, in the way of getting a string of them safely back to India.[12] With his head stuffed full of dreams of golden Bokhara and the fascinating web of ancient caravan trails across the mountains and deserts of Afghanistan, Moorcroft left Strachey and pressed on up-country to enjoy again the warm hospitality of his fellow-countrymen at the shabby Delhi residency. To judge from the chaffing and affectionate letters that passed between Charles Metcalfe, the resident, and Moorcroft at this time[13], they not only became friends but Metcalfe also lent his enthusiastic assistance to Moorcroft's hungry search for more information about the lands beyond the Khyber. The teeming Delhi bazaars were scoured for anyone who had been there and one man, a merchant who had traded to Bokhara, proved especially useful. We have only Moorcroft's word for it, of course, but this man apparently agreed with all the other informants that the long route to Bokhara was easy and safe, at least for large caravans. Not only that, but the northern horses on sale in the Bokhara market were big, bony and plentiful. Quite simply, Bokhara was 'the greatest horse market in the world'.[14]

From that moment the urge to get there dominated Moorcroft's thoughts and plans – thirteen years later it killed him. The more accessible breeding areas just beyond the immediate British frontier – Rajputana, the Lakhee Jungle, the Punjab – all of which were the official destinations of his present journey – now seemed comparatively uninviting. Every bit of information obtained in Delhi only confirmed Strachey's jaundiced views of them. Even if they were still able to produce a few good horses, they were never likely to meet the longer term needs of the stud so long as they remained exposed to the locust sweep of Maratha, Sikh, Pindari and Pathan irregular cavalry.

Bokhara seemed, or could be made to seem, almost the only hope. But a journey to that remote and fabled city across unknown lands, where no Englishman had been since the Tudors, was not something that even the cavalier Moorcroft dare attempt without prior official approval. It seems to have been Metcalfe who suggested that he should first send an intelligent and trustworthy Muslim emissary to spy out the land and test the feasibility of the journey, and it was Metcalfe, 'with every manly wish to co-operate', who made available exactly the right man for the task.[15]

Saiyyid (or Mir) Izzat-Allah was working as a confidential Persian interpreter and secretary on Metcalfe's staff at Delhi. Strachey also knew him well for he had distinguished himself on Elphinstone's mission to Peshawar in 1808. Moorcroft was certainly impressed by the way this charming man set about the task of seeking information in the Delhi bazaars 'with spirit and judgement, possessing penetration and good sense with a considerable share of address and prepossessing appearance and manners'. He was courageous too for, notwithstanding the hazards and the distance, he jumped at the chance to visit the city from which his forefathers had come sixty years earlier. Moorcroft briefed him thoroughly. His task, as Moorcroft summarized it, was 'to trace the western dealers to the countries wherein they purchased their horses, to ascertain where the best kind were to be met with, their prices, numbers, the difficulties, dangers and expenses of the road, with all such other information as might have any bearing on the subject'. As if that was not enough, he was to travel to Bokhara not by the direct route across Afghanistan, but in a great arc across some of the most forbidding mountain and desert terrain in the world, by way of Kashmir, Ladakh, the Karakoram, Chinese Turkestan and the Pamirs. They were all virtually unknown to Europe. No wonder Moorcroft augmented the mir's official allowances with a hundred rupees a month from his own pocket 'by way of encouragement'.[16]

He needed it, for he was running a considerable risk, quite apart from the extraordinary perils of the road. For one thing the mysterious and sensitive bazaar network of Muslim Asia would not overlook the fact that this man, the friend and servant of Feringi (Europeans), had already been on a political mission to the previous ruler of Afghanistan.[17] Moreover he would be carrying letters from Moorcroft to some of the rulers of the lands through which he passed which might well have compromised him with others along the road. Moorcroft was uneasy about this and not only on Izzat-Allah's behalf. He later confessed to the board that he had been guilty of what he called 'many irregularities' in 1812[18], and this was certainly one of them. The letters themselves were harmless enough – florid and complimentary effusions in the fulsome diplomatic style of the day and probably composed by the saiyyid himself[19] – but there were good and obvious reasons why government servants, even those employed in the Political Department, should not feel themselves free to open a private correspondence with foreign rulers without permission. The down-to-earth files of the board in Calcutta had certainly never before carried such exotic letters as that from Moorcroft to Mahmud Shah, ruler of Kabul. It began, 'Anointing the eye of hope with the sacred dust of the foot of Majesty' and went on with the brazen avowal that Moorcroft 'passes his nights and days in prayer for the prosperity of His Majesty's Government'. It is doubtful if he ever passed a single night in prayer for anyone, but literal truth was never very important in this sort of correspondence. The letter to the bloodthirsty bigot who ruled at Bokhara, for example, began with the prescription, 'To the Commander of the Faithful, the Imaum of the Moslems, the Asylum of mankind, the Succourer of high and low, the shadow of the Almighty, the Viceregent of God, may his favour to all be perpetual'.

Buried in a long letter to the board, giving cover to these documents and dated 25 April 1812, Moorcroft at last came out into the open, although with almost studied casualness, about his all-consuming Bokhara dream. Mir Izzat-Allah's prime task there, wrote Moorcroft, would be to obtain 'permission for me to visit the city for the purpose of purchasing a considerable body of animals if they suit my purpose'. He added the hope that the board would not object to Izzat-Allah's mission. It would not really have made any difference if it had for Moorcroft's letter was not received in distant Calcutta for another two months. Five days before it was even written and several weeks after the scheme was hatched at the Delhi residency, Mir Izzat-Allah, with all his preparations completed, had set out into the unknown.[20] Moorcroft thought the mir would be away six months but his capacity for underestimating absences and difficulties was becoming almost chronic. In fact Izzat-Allah, surviving both illness and imprisonment, was not back until the end of the following year. His Persian journal, full of new information about lands and places almost unknown to geographical science, was an immediate success. It was translated into the major European languages and published in English on at least three separate occasions.[21]

Not surprisingly it also increased Moorcroft's consuming desire to follow the same circuitous route to Bokhara at the very first opportunity. The wish is evident even in the deliberately measured phrases of Moorcroft's official letter of 25 April 1812. Indeed, there is a clear hint in that letter that if Izzat-Allah could report favourably within about five months as Moorcroft hoped – and his private and official correspondence both confess his 'anxiety' on this score[22] – then he would like to set off direct for Bokhara without returning all the weary and familiar miles to the presidency first. In Calcutta, where this astonishing letter was solemnly considered in council on 6 July 1812, immediate steps were taken to prevent him from doing any such thing. Only after careful consideration of Izzat-Allah's conclusions 'relative to the degree of personal risk attending the journey, the resources of the country in horses fit for the purposes of Government, and the practicability of conveying them from so remote a quarter through barbarous and little known countries would . . . the expediency of Mr. Moorcroft's proceeding in person to Bokhara be considered'. In case that was not crystal clear they added, 'It is of course understood that Mr. Moorcroft will not enter on the journey without a previous communication with Government.'[23] They were beginning to realize the sort of man they were dealing with. In fact when those words were drafted their subject had already disappeared on another dangerous journey in an entirely different direction. Incredible as it must have seemed at the time, he was already in Tibet. He had crossed hostile Gurkha territory and penetrated the mightiest mountain range in the world, in disguise and without prior permission of any sort from anyone!

It happened like this. After despatching Izzat-Allah on his long journey to Bokhara, he had come up from Delhi to Hardwar at the beginning of April in time for its thronging annual *mela*. Moorcroft had high hopes that the contacts he had made with the traders the previous year would bring to the fair considerable quantities of fine, big animals from the breeding districts further west. Sure enough many of the Sikh dealers brought horses from the Lakhee Jungle. But their quality was so poor that Moorcroft rejected most of them, merely purchasing, rather unenthusiastically, fourteen colts for the stud and three undersized animals as a private favour for Richard Strachey.[24] The good horses, as usual, were somewhere else. Most of those intended for him, he was furious to discover, had been snapped up along the road by his old friends the Rampur dealers and by agents from Bundelkhand or the Deccan and spirited away across the company's western borders. From the stud point of view, his journey so far had been utterly abortive.

In April he was, or pretended to be, puzzled as to what he should do next. All his evidence suggested that Rajasthan was too unsettled to be worth visiting and the health hazards of entering the Lakhee Jungle area in the hot weather seemed to rule that out for at least another three months. As for the Punjab, although Ranjit Singh had given his approval for a visit, it seemed prudent to defer it until the results of Izzat-Allah's reconnaissance were known 'lest that Chief should think that something more than horses were in view'.[25] Moorcroft, although he did not say so, was already hoping that he could examine the Punjab on his way to Bokhara later on, and so to some extent he did, although not for another ten years. In the spring of 1812 the only remaining possibility – of course it never occurred to him to do nothing and ride the heat out quietly at Hardwar – was to look north. 'A period of nearly if not fully three months must elapse before I can begin my business in the Lakhee Jungle,' he wrote, 'and I do not see how I can apply this interval to better account for the public service than by endeavouring to penetrate to the confines of Tartary.'[26] It is hard to know whether Moorcroft was unintentionally, or deliberately, using such a casual phrase. For what he was talking about was a pioneer crossing of perhaps the greatest natural physical obstacle in the world outside the polar ice-cap.

The Himalayas have dominated India's culture as they have dominated its landscape since that awesome collision of two drifting continents 45 million years ago first began to heave them up from the bed of the primaeval ocean.[27] Perhaps Moorcroft fell under their spell as he was carried up-country for the first time in the cold weather of 1808 when, on a clear dawn, he would have glimpsed that breathtaking thread of silver high in the sky 150 miles (240 kilometres) away across the plain. At Pusa, the Burhi Gandak which flowed smoothly round the estate and past his windows had its tempestuous birth unseen in the eternal ice and snowfields of some of the biggest giants of all, not so many miles away to the north. Now, heading towards Hardwar once again in the spring of 1812, he may have had again an occasional revelation of the skyward sweep of that chilling and spectacular northern horizon; much as another Englishman had seen it from the same direction three years before.

> The grey mist of the dawn was deepened in our front by the shadows of the mountains of Kemaon, over which arose the sun in magnificent splendour, spreading a broad stream of light that gave a delightful effect to the varieties of the surrounding scenery. Directly before us, at the distance of thirty or forty miles [48 or 64 kilometres], was a range of hills, rich in verdure, and covered to their summits with stately forests of saul, sissoo, and fir-trees; while far beyond, towered high above the clouds the gigantic Himalaya mountains, their heads crowned with eternal snow, and glittering with the effulgence of the solar beams playing on the immense glaciers of those unexplored regions.[28]

They were very much unexplored. Some still believed that the spectacular plume of snow which can often be seen streaming from the highest peaks was smoke from slumbering volcanoes, and no one had as yet more than a suspicion that these were indeed the highest mountains in the world. The estimations based on triangulation from the plains seemed to give figures so impossibly high that many felt that the calculations must be seriously in error. In fact they were sometimes too low.

In the last week of April 1812 Moorcroft was at Saharanpur trying to arrest another outbreak of disease among the horses of the native cavalry regiment stationed there and struggling to find words to explain away what was his latest and most daring trans-frontier foray. From Saharanpur on a clear day a distinct gap in the distant snowy range is visible. On the right is Nanda Devi and its great outer ring of satellite peaks nearly 3 miles (4.8 kilometres) clear above the floor of the plain. On the left is Kamet and the great peaks above Kedarnath and Gangotri. In the gap between them, although nobody properly understood it at the time, lies the thunderous gorge of the Alaknanda, one of the two major sources of the Ganges, cutting right through the main axial range from the northern side. Four years earlier in 1808, two British officers, Webb and Raper, and a young Anglo-Indian soldier of fortune called Hyder Hearsey, had forced their way some distance up that gorge during an attempt to penetrate to the source of the sacred Ganges and solve the tantalizing mystery of its true origins.[29] According to lamaistic legend the Ganges (and the Indus, Sutlej and Brahmaputra) all rose in Lake Manasarowar, far beyond the Himalayas up on the high Tibetan plateau under the silver peak of Mount Kailas where goddess Siva dwells. Such an inherently implausible explanation for four of the world's mightiest rivers was no longer accepted by scientific geographers in Europe at the beginning of the nineteenth century but disproving it was another matter altogether. Webb, Raper and Hearsey, following the lesser of the two principal Ganges feeders almost to its source in that wilderness of glacier and snow, were more or less able to establish that the Ganges at least could not possibly flow out of the lofty sacred lake of Tibet. The hydrography of the other great rivers remained as confused and puzzling as ever.

Moorcroft learned all this from Captain Hyder Hearsey himself. This astonishing man, the illegitimate half-caste son of a British infantry officer, had spent almost half of his colourful twenty-nine years serving as a mercenary soldier, first for the nawab of Oude, then the Marathas, then the Irish military adventurer George Thomas, and finally the British. In the course of all this he had had a string of adventures which read like pure and implausible fiction. Hearsey had settled down, if that is the phrase, near Bareilly on an estate which he acquired by grant, from the Mughal emperor himself, at the time of his marriage to a princess of the former ruling house of Cambay. It was probably at Bareilly that Moorcroft met him on his way to Hardwar in the spring of 1812.

That Hearsey was shrewd, brave and tough is obvious from his career,[30] but he was not altogether popular with the Calcutta authorities. After joining Webb's mission to the source of the Ganges just for the devil of it, he was accused, perhaps falsely, of pirating the official map of the expedition when Webb was ill and sending it home as his own work.[31] In 1812 he again fell foul of the British authorities, this time for levying excessive tolls on goods passing through his estates and for raising a private army to drive the Gurkhas out of the fertile valley or *dun* of Dehra, part of which he claimed by right of purchase from its impecunious former ruler. Hearsey was obviously finding the new *pax Britannica* in these border districts rather restricting. In a sense the same was beginning to be true of Moorcroft. Both men had a buccaneering streak and one suspects that Moorcroft would instantly have recognized a fellow-spirit in this charming rogue. 'Very ingenious but uneducated' was how the commander-in-chief's wife summed him up.[32] Moorcroft came to see the man's qualities rather more generously, crediting him with 'courage, spirit of enterprise, acquaintance with the language, manners and habits of the natives of Hindoostan and its borders, decisiveness of character and fertility of resource'. Just the man in fact for 'prosecuting difficult geographical enquiries, or others'.[33]

The geographical and especially the 'other' enquiries which Moorcroft was beginning to plan in April 1812 were certainly 'difficult' and no one knew that better than Hyder Hearsey. In 1808 Webb's party had had both official British backing and the approval of the Gurkha authorities, across whose territories in the hills of Kumaon and Garhwal they had to pass. Even so they had managed to penetrate between the plains and the high Tibetan tableland to the north only with considerable difficulty, had reached the source of merely the more accessible of the two principal Ganges feeders and had had some awkward moments with the Gurkhas on their return. Now Moorcroft was coolly proposing not only to push up the unknown gorge of the main tributary where no European had ever been before to its source but also to cross the watershed on to the Tibetan plateau and all this without the prior permission of any authority, British, Nepalese or Tibetan! As he jested to Metcalfe,[34] and it was truer than he knew, 'I am more likely to be caught by than to catch either a Gorkhah or a Tatar.' That both would oppose his journey was a foregone conclusion. The only way to escape their vigilance, he convinced himself, was to make a dash for it, bearded, in disguise and along a pilgrim route of sorts. Even if the disguise failed, there was at least a chance that, because no Europeans had done it before, no precautions to stop them would have been taken. It was precisely this aspect of the scheme, as he was well aware, which would cause such dismay in Calcutta when the authorities there eventually heard of it three months later. He knew they too would have stopped him if they could. In order to make quite sure that they could not, he delayed telling them anything about it until the very last possible moment,[35] several weeks after the journey was first decided upon and only a few days before it actually commenced.

Even discounting the formidable political difficulties, there were immense physical hazards too: the rocks and landslips of the thunderous and unforgiving Dauli River gorge; the thin, dry air on the high passes above the watershed; the wind like a whetted knife on the lofty Tibetan plateau; the huge extremes of day and night temperatures – all these and more were enough to tax a young man in his late twenties like Hearsey let alone one, even an unusually tough one, on the wrong side of 45. Moorcroft flattered himself before he went that his spartan and wandering life in the last year and a half had made him pretty fit, as no doubt it had, but this time, as he discovered, he was pushing himself to the very limit of his endurance. He suffered miseries from repeated illness of one kind or another before he emerged triumphant into the plains again at a peak of physical fitness 'consequent upon hard work and spare diet'[36], such as he had never known before in India.

None the less the question remains, why did he go at all? It is always difficult to disentangle reason from excuse in Moorcroft's official explanations and they are really the only evidence we have. That the shawl-wool goat of Tibet was somewhere at the bottom of it is beyond doubt.[37] Whether he had first heard of this elusive creature from Warren Hastings in Park Lane or seen a specimen in John Hunter's menagerie at Earl's Court or more recently in that of Saadat Ali at Lucknow is unknown. During the long and harsh Tibetan winter the shawl goat, like the mountain sheep of those upland pastures, produces for its own protection next to the skin, a fleece of particular fineness and softness which it sheds each summer. For centuries traders from Ladakh had toiled over the high, empty plains in the thin air every summer to purchase, by custom and treaty-right, this precious wool, carrying it back to Leh in Ladakh, whence it was taken down to Kashmir for making up into expensive, exquisite and gossamer-fine Kashmir shawls. Long before Moorcroft came to India, especially during the time of his old London acquaintance Warren Hastings, the East India Company with its sharp nose for a potentially lucrative trade had shown a keen interest in this, as well as in the other traditional commodities of the trans-Himalayan trade beyond the northern borders of Bengal. Could not English woollen goods, Sheffield cutlery and Indian grain be exchanged for shawl wool, as well as for gold dust and borax? Having tried and failed to breach the very fiercely guarded shawl-wool monopoly of the Ladakhi and Kashmiri merchants, by diverting some of the wool trade into British territories, the company then tried to obtain some of the Tibetan goats themselves in order to test the feasibility of producing the wool commercially in Britain. If the experiment had succeeded the benefits would in theory have been substantial.

Moorcroft, who pursued this vision more zealously than anyone else, later tried to explain it to his sceptical colleagues at the board. The goats, he argued, would represent

> a new species of stock [in Britain] that within the course of a few years may cause lands of a nature at present ungrateful, to yield a produce not inferior in value, as far as fleece is concerned to that raised on the highest priced lands of Lincoln or Leicestershire. By so doing they will not only be instrumental in benefiting the cause of agriculture but assisting also in furnishing to those classes of the poor too young or too old or too infirm or too delicate for outdoor labour or a means of earning an honest livelihood, *at their own houses*, by separating the fine wool of the goat from the hair. . . . When possessed of this material in abundance to what extent the manufacture of shawl goods may be carried by British capital, ingenuity and enterprize it is not easy to foresee.[38]

Even to Kashmir, he told Metcalfe,[39] the shawl trade was worth 2,300,000 rupees a year. What might it be worth to Britain?

It was a marvellous dream and it is not hard to see why the search for this golden fleece awoke such a surprising enthusiasm in William Moorcroft. It somehow fused his veterinary interest in scientific breeding and his youthful love of agricultural improvement, together with his patriotism and a ready compassion for the downtrodden and the oppressed. There is an additional, almost mystical element at the back of it too, which is easier to detect than describe. Moorcroft it seems was fascinated by the ancient seasonal mechanisms and patterns of the traditional overland trade of Asia – those thin lines, from a distance like scratches across the bare hillsides and empty deserts, along which the patient pack animals, the strings of horses or the swaying camel caravans have crossed and recrossed the empty spaces for centuries. The loving way Moorcroft researched and built up a picture of the ancient northern horse trade was one example of this fascination. His obsession with the shawl-wool trade, which makes his writings a prime source for those interested in its history, was another.

Before Moorcroft turned his enthusiasm to the subject, earlier British attempts to obtain supplies of the shawl-wool goat had not been at all successful. The immense barrier of hill and mountain which divided the Ganges plain from the elevated breeding-grounds of the goats was, of course, one reason for that. So too was deliberate obstruction by those who had everything to lose if the traditional, trans-Himalayan outlets of the trade running westward to Ladakh and Kashmir were jeopardized by direct British initiatives from the south. John Gilman, the civil surgeon at Bareilly for many years, had acquired a considerable body of information about the trade across the mountains to the north and he made several attempts through native agents to obtain some shawl goats. He only ever managed to secure some male animals and even they appeared by crude surgery to have been deliberately rendered incapable of breeding. Lieutenant-Colonel Robert Colebrooke, the late surveyor-general of India, had a similar experience with the two female goats he obtained. The Board of Agriculture in London continued at intervals to exhort the East India Company to greater efforts (and they in turn their men on the spot), bɑt still without any real success.[40]

Until, that is, William Moorcroft on his way up-country in the spring of 1812 was shown at Etawah the latest of these exhortations, a despatch from London dated 10 October 1810.[41] Shortly afterwards, at Meerut, he met John Gilman.[42] They probably reminisced about St Bartholomew's Hospital, London, where Gilman had trained and Moorcroft more recently had many acquaintances, but they also talked about the mysteries of the shawl trade. Gilman not only gave Moorcroft some of his precious samples of the wool itself but also sent a man on ahead of him to get further information at the Hardwar fair.[43] The subject came up again soon afterwards in conversation with Hearsey at Bareilly and it was he who gave Moorcroft an introduction to the old Kumaoni brahmin called variously Pandit Harbalam or Hurbullubh. The pandit had visited Tibet in his younger days and had proved his worth as a resourceful guide on Webb's expedition to the source of the Ganges in 1808.[44] The meeting with this shrewd and wiry old hill-man at Hardwar was decisive. Not only did he give Moorcroft authentic information about the Tibetan shawl goat's breeding-grounds, he offered to take him there. Moorcroft was not the man to hesitate very long over a chance like that and by 8 April 1812 his mind was made up.

The old pandit had provided the information and the means but he also unintentionally provided the excuse. The phrasing of an unbuttoned letter which Moorcroft wrote to Metcalfe at this time is very significant: 'In endeavouring to find out the country of the shawl wool bearing animal I have met with intelligence of horses'.[45] Moorcroft did not rate the old pandit's eye for a horse very high but his positive and surprising assertion that large numbers of them were bred 'on tracts of table land still more to the north' beyond the mountains was just what Moorcroft needed. It reinforced the similar echoes of trans-Himalayan horses which he had picked up in his conversations with Warren Hastings back in London and more recently with Amar Singh Thapa at Butwal, with the raja of Balrampur and with the nawab vizier of Oude in 1811. None of the information amounted to much but it was just enough to legitimize the company's stud superintendent's cool proposal to risk his neck in the high Himalayas. 'With respect to horses', he wrote to the board on 25 April – and his tongue was surely in his cheek – 'were I to leave such a clue as I now hold unfollowed I really should consider myself as shrinking from my duty.'[46] Later, when this same curious sense of duty had involved his government in a full-blooded international incident, Moorcroft deemed it prudent to pretend that horses were 'the primary object' of his journey to Tibet.[47] They emphatically were not. Even his official letter of 25 April 1812 to the board positively bubbles with enthuasiasm about the shawl goat while the horse figures in it scarcely at all. Moorcroft later regretted this imprudent and excited letter. It was, he confessed to the board, 'less forcible and less perspicacious than I could have wished, and some objects of secondary importance occupied too much of the fore ground'.[48] They certainly did.

Apart from the shawl-wool goat, there were what Moorcroft called[49] 'many incentives' besides for the journey, not all of which could be admitted in an official letter. Exploration and the chance to unravel the puzzling hydrography of the trans-Himalayan rivers came into it, although this was certainly not the prime aim as some have thought.[50] Horses were part of it too. So also was the call of the high passes and of that other Buddhist world beyond them. Add to that a sheer zest for adventure – and self-esteem.

> After mature reflection, I found that however much various considerations of prudence might justify me in not undertaking the enterprize, and however much its prosecution might expose me to danger, both of person and character, I should sink in my own estimation if through apprehension for my personal safety, I should leave undetermined, points of so much public moment and so intimately connected with my public engagements.[51]

Only the final phrase of that long sentence is suspect. It is doubtful whether even Moorcroft at the time, let alone the distant observer a century and a half later, could really disentangle his true motives and set them in order of importance. Perhaps it is enough to say that in 1812 he was presented with a unique opportunity, and he seized it with all his characteristic energy, curiosity and enthuasiasm.

Once the decision was made, probably at Hardwar in the first week of April 1812 and certainly by the 8th, all was bustle. There was no time to lose. Moorcroft had to be back in the plains in three months if he were to salvage any of the original aims of his present journey and still have time to spend in the Lakhee Jungle before either returning south to Pusa or, as he much preferred, setting his face towards the north and Bokhara. The summer sun which was already browning the plains beyond the town was also at work on the snows choking the unseen river gorges and high inner passes away beyond the hills to the north. In a few more weeks the passes would be open for the brief chilly months of summer before the first autumn snowfalls once again locked the high Tibetan plateau into another long winter. Moorcroft sent the disappointing string of horses purchased at the Hardwar fair, together with some of the servants, to his friend Captain Skinner at the fort of Hansi north-west of Delhi. The transport animals probably went to nearby Saharanpur, whence Moorcroft followed at the end of the month on a hurried visit to advise on a serious outbreak of glanders in the cavalry stables there. Those servants who were least able or least reliable (and most plainsmen had a deep and superstitious dread of the mountains) were packed off thankfully to spend the hot summer in Delhi. Their wages, together with most of the unused barter goods and surplus cash were consigned to the care of the ever-willing Charles Metcalfe at the residency there.[52] Moorcroft kept about 2000 rupees in gold coins, which were strapped in special belts round the waists of his most trusty servants. A modest trading caravan consisting of 'an assortment of glass beads of various colours, a few of indifferent coral, three spying-glasses, some articles of Hurdwaree ornaments for women, a little Europe cloth, nutmegs, cloves, Guzzerat cardamum and black pepper' was made up in bundles designed for the backs of hill-porters.[53]

In all these preparations Moorcroft must have leaned very heavily on the advice of the old pandit and Hyder Hearsey himself. Just when the latter became 'desirous of partaking the perils of the way', as Moorcroft quaintly put it,[54] is not clear. He may have been in from the very beginning. If so, then he and Moorcroft concerted their correspondence with the governor-general's agent, so that Hearsey's application for permission to go was also delayed until it was too late to stop him. In fact, as it turned out, Sir Edward Colebrooke was so misled by Moorcroft's talk about shawl wool goats and trans-Himalayan horses that he thought that the government would want the mission to be given every assistance and cheerfully assented to Hearsey's crossing the Gurkha frontier.[55] Only when the expedition had set out did he receive a rebuke for not stopping what the government considered 'a project too replete with danger to be productive of advantage to the public service'.[56] It was precisely because of these dangers that Moorcroft welcomed Hearsey's collaboration. He was a good man in a tight corner. Moreover he brought to the expedition not only his own formidable talents and local knowledge, but also the valuable services of his faithful and tough Afghan retainer, Ghulam Hyder Khan. Fifteen years later this same indestructible man, by then with a bullet in his head, faithfully followed Moorcroft to the bitter end of his long pilgrimage to Bokhara and was almost the only one of the party to return to India alive.[57]

The collaboration of Hearsey and Ghulam Hyder in the venture had only one serious and obvious disadvantage – both men had already been involved in several armed skirmishes with the Gurkhas across the border and were only too well known. For both of them as for Moorcroft himself disguise seemed essential. The choice almost suggested itself. Their route lay for much of the way along the punishing but well-beaten pilgrim tracks to the mountain shrines along the young Ganges. Some hardy pilgrims even forced their weary way beyond the mountains to the sacred lake in Tibet which they believed gave it birth. As *gosains*, Hindu trading pilgrims, they should attract little attention and perhaps even gain some useful reverence and help from the hill-folk amongst whom they passed. Hearsey was soon exulting, although prematurely as it turned out, that beneath his white cotton robes, beads, red turban and sash and with the help of his new beard and the effects of the summer sun he was, as the Hindu pilgrim Hargiri, 'exempt from all fear of discovery'.[58] The fair-skinned Moorcroft *alias* Mayapoori was another matter altogether.[59] The more credulous and naïve of the hill-villagers were certainly deceived by this unusual holy man and physician, but in fact he must have been outrageously unconvincing, especially when the mountain winds had cut his raw and peeling face to shreds. Hearsey could scarcely keep a straight face as the simple villagers touched his friend's feet and begged his blessing.

Mr. Moorcroft . . . casts a most ludicrous appearance, a large patch of lamp black round each eye and his face and neck first stained with the juice of walnuts, then smeared with the ashes of burnt cow dung, with a gravity of countenance highly edifying has an irresistible effect on the eyes of his beholders who take him for sanctity itself.[60]

The suspicious Gurkha rulers of Kumaon and Garhwal, however, were not to be so easily fooled.

It was probably to minimize the risks that the travellers decided not to cross the border at once by taking the more usual pilgrim route along the river behind Hardwar where they were all much too well known. Instead, to reduce their transit across Nepalese territory to the minimum, they would strike eastwards in the safety of the plains under the sharp southern scarp of the Siwaliks, before turning north into the hills. At the end of April Moorcroft came posting back from Saharanpur, probably meeting Hearsey at Najibabad early in May where they made their last purchases for the journey. The party assembled, fifty-four people in all (including the porters) and a flock of goats, at a small village near Chilkia. In those days before the railway came to nearby Ramnagar, this was the main market of exchange between the plains and the hills in this direction. It was also very much a place to be avoided by those anxious to escape detection.

In the cool of the early morning on Saturday, 9 May the tents were struck and the caravan moved slowly off on foot into the green hills a few miles to the west of Ramnagar.[61] The last letters had by then been sealed and despatched, including that to the board which Moorcroft had finished on 25 April. Its last (and one hundred and seventy-sixth!) paragraph read as follows:

I am fully aware of this being an undertaking that promises danger and privation, but of the former using all prudent preparations, I must incur the risk, and my mode of life for sometime past in a degree has prepared me for the latter, I remain, Sir, etc., William Moorcroft.[62]

That was virtually the last that the Calcutta authorities heard of their highly paid superintendent of stud until smuggled word arrived across the border six months later that he and his party were prisoners of the Gurkhas. What happened in those intervening months during the summer and autumn of 1812, while Napoleon's grand army was on its way to destruction in the frozen wastes of Russia, has won a secure place in the annals of trans-Himalayan exploration.[63]

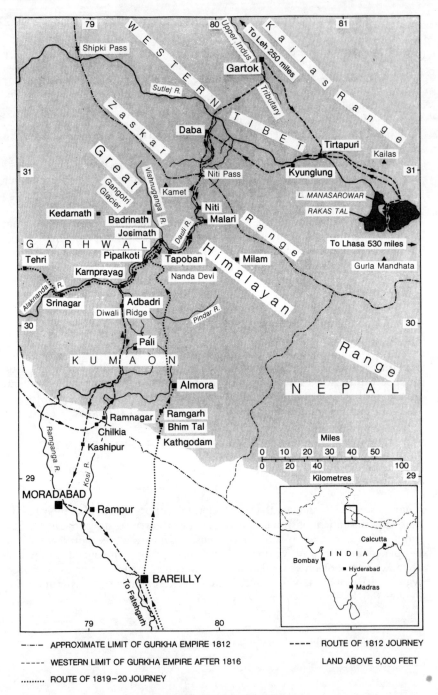

2. THE 1812 JOURNEY
(AND START OF THE GREAT JOURNEY, 1819–20)

APPROXIMATE LIMIT OF GURKHA EMPIRE 1812

WESTERN LIMIT OF GURKHA EMPIRE AFTER 1816

ROUTE OF 1819–20 JOURNEY

ROUTE OF 1812 JOURNEY

LAND ABOVE 5,000 FEET

11 JOURNEY TO TIBET,

MAY–AUGUST 1812

THE FIRST PART of the journey, for which the only surviving evidence is Hearsey's manuscript notebook,[1] lay across the magnificent sea of tumbling, tree-clad Kumaoni hills. They are indeed hills by comparison with the snow giants across the wide horizon beyond, although even the valley floors are more than twice as high as the tallest English mountains to the north of Moorcroft's native Lancashire. The nearest thing to paradise for an Englishman, especially if he has just been toiling in the furnace-heat of the plains of India, must be this purple-green hill-country in springtime. The sparkling streams and the deeper roar of the great river, the all-pervasive perfume of the pine, fir and cedar forests marching up to the sharp skyline; the sturdy, handsome hill-people with their flat faces, ready smiles and wonderful teeth; the stone and timber houses and the tiny terraced fields and alpine meadows of the perching villages high above the valley floor; the rhododendrons and wild flowers – all these things are pure delight.

Unfortunately Moorcroft was in no state to appreciate them at first. On the third day out, as they toiled up to the narrow ridge which divides the Kosi from the Ramganga river basins, he was attacked with the first of the violent diarrhoea and shivering which for a time denied him proper rest at night and made him wretchedly weak during the day. That first disturbed night, and he was up for much of it, he was probably very grateful that the porters had built up fires to discourage the prowling leopards from getting in among the tethered goats, for it was very cold and very windy. Hearsey was tough, but his admiration for the way his older companion kept going was unbounded. Two days later, on 13 May, he noted:

Mr. Moorcroft felt himself very weak and proceeded very slowly, nothing but an extraordinary firmness of character and resolution of mind in the condition he was in could have carried him on, the way tho' pretty good required the attention of the eye at almost every step even to the person in health and spirits, this plainly shows how much control the mind has over the body and what benefits accrue to the person possessed of that advantage going thro' the vicissitudes of human life in a very active sphere.

[135]

Next day, well up the beautiful, open valley of the Ramganga, they ran into what looked like their first crisis. The old pandit, who had pushed on ahead of the main party, came hurrying back with the news that a small Gurkha force was waiting for them at a ford a short distance ahead. This proved to be a false alarm but it is clear from Hearsey's journal that they were very much on the alert for trouble during these May days. On one occasion, Hearsey, at the rear of the long line of porters and animals, had to cover up his compass and notebook hastily when he was surprised by the inquisitive priest of one of the many dark little temples past which their road lay and in each of which they made their pilgrim offerings to the resident deity. Later, parties of pilgrims heading south interrupted Hearsey again but this time he managed to keep his route survey going by making discreet and minuscule notes on his fingernails. Beside him Harkh Dev, the old pandit's nephew, kept the running tally of his measured 24-inch (0.6-metre) paces every step of the way, transferring his figures at intervals either to the notebook which Hearsey kept tucked in the folds of his robes or to Hearsey's fingernails. It was crude but it worked. When the journey was over Hearsey produced an elegant map, the distances and bearings of which have proved in the light of later surveys to be remarkably accurate.

Moorcroft was usually somewhere up ahead with the old pandit, often shielding his sharp eyes in the bright sunshine the better to observe some detail which caught his eye in those immense vistas. For the first time we catch a close-up glimpse of Moorcroft the traveller. He must have been the strangest *gosain* ever seen on that ancient pilgrim road. Chasing butterflies, stalking lizards, pouncing on wild flowers and herbs and popping them in his bag, examining the fossils and rock strata and cursing that his disguise allowed him no pockets, dissecting with interest any unusual insect, animal or reptile which came his way and endlessly, endlessly questioning.

Yet he was not too engrossed to notice the accumulating evidence of Gurkha oppression and misrule in these once happy valleys. Hearsey felt the same. He could even see a marked deterioration since his journey across the same hills only four years earlier.

> From the various scenes of misery I have been an eye witness of and the change that has visibly taken place in the population and cultivation of this once happy country it promises soon to be a jungle. The cause of humanity calls for the aid of the British Government to interfere, ere these remaining fields are covered with nettles and forest and the remaining inhabitants be driven to the last resort of their hapless countrymen!!!

Both men came to hate the Gurkhas on this trip with an almost murderous intensity but there was little they could do, other than pour vitriol into their journals and give a helping hand to the unfortunate victims whenever they came across them.

Early in the morning of Sunday, 16 May, a week after they set out, they reached the summit of the steep ridge which, crowned with forts, shuts in the Ramganga valley to the north and marks the ancient frontier between Kumaon and Garhwal. The view of peaks, ranges and tree-clad hills in all directions, from the low 7000-foot (2132-metre) saddle across this ridge, is beautiful, although painful swellings from the bite of a particularly vicious fly which attacked them all must have robbed the scene of some of its enchantment. From here the track descends steeply through the trees, past Adbadri with its ruined temples, into the valley of the Pindar, foaming down from its exquisite glacier source. 'Delightful road and romantick to an extreme,' commented Hearsey on 18 May. The Kumaoni hill-porters stumbling under their loads saw it rather differently. Early the next morning when they were ready to start at 5 a.m. as usual the porters refused to go on, 'wishing to enhance their value' as Hearsey thought. It was 'at least two hours before the rascals would come to a sense of their duty. I found it necessary to use some policy with them,' he added grimly. The 'policy', whatever it was, worked but only for a time. Later that day they reached the junction of the Pindar with the Alaknanda at Karnprayag, one of the eight Hindu holy places of pilgrimage and at this time a mere huddle of houses round the shrine with the soaring hills all round, gloomy with forest to the skyline.

From this point they were back on the main pilgrim track coming up from Hardwar and familiar to Hearsey and the pandit from their journey in 1808. The pathway struggled along the very edge of the roaring, tumbling river or crossed it and its tributary streams by narrow, rickety timber *sangas*, mere spars flung across the torrent. In some places a recent landslip had carried the old track into the river and necessitated a new, crumbling pathway, sometimes only inches wide, higher up the mountain. Although the nights were cold and the dawns cool with the valleys still deep purple, once the sun flooded the colour back and warmed the rocks, the temperature soon climbed at midday into the nineties and added to the party's problems. It must have been a relief when on occasions the hills fell back and allowed the path to leave the noisy river altogether. Then they crossed tiny open valleys and fields, the lighter green of their spring cultivation contrasting with the darkness of the great trees higher up and offering a chance of a partridge or two for the cooking pot. But it was all too much for the porters, who evidently preferred the gentler terrain of their native Kumaon.

On the night of 24 May just outside Josimath, a great hullabaloo awoke Moorcroft and Hearsey. They took the noise to be the signal for the not altogether unexpected departure of the porters. Finding the men still in camp, they held a short midnight conference to make some contingency plans before again going back to their separate tents, pulling the heavy blankets round them and dropping again into the deep sleep of the hill-traveller. The porters, however, did not. Some time later that night and well before sunrise they slipped away into the darkness heading south down the tumbling Alaknanda for home. It was, conceded Hearsey 'an awkward predicament'. If the carriers in their flight spread word about these would-be holy men, a detachment of Gurkha soldiers might soon be on their tail. There was obviously nothing to be gained by lingering at Josimath, high on its ridge above the river junction. The problem of course was how to leave it.

In those days, as today, most pilgrims struck off to the north up the magnificent narrow gorge of the Vishnuganga towards Badrinath. Looking down and back from Josimath, Hearsey could have seen very plainly the track up which he had passed with Webb, Raper and the old pandit in 1808. This time the route lay more to the east, up the other main feeder of the Alaknanda. 'Along the banks of the Dauli', Raper had written then, 'is one of the high roads leading' to Tibet.[2] High it certainly was but it was not a road in any strict sense of that word at all. Nevertheless for all its ruggedness, the cheery Mongol-featured Bhotia traders each summer shepherded their flocks of sheep and goats along it, carrying grain upwards across the Niti pass into Tibet and bringing down salt, saffron, borax, gold dust and coarse woollens. Today a world obsessed with frontiers and security has closed that ancient trade and, although the new military road pushes on up the Dauli for some miles more beyond Josimath, that high and breezy place still feels very much at the edge of the inhabited world. In 1812, during the brief and busy summer months, it would not have been the easiest place to procure porters at short notice for the rugged journey up the Dauli River to Niti.

Hearsey discovered this on 25 May when he met Bhowanni Singh, the revenue farmer of this part of Garhwal, 'an ugly looking fellow with a goitered neck, dressed rather curiously'. It cost the best part of the day, much haggling, some awkward questions and 87 rupees, before the agreements were finally signed for the conveyance of all the baggage safely to Niti. Bhowanni Singh was as ugly as he looked. Moorcroft and Hearsey discovered later that most of the people who eventually arrived to shoulder the loads were poor village women, pressganged into service without payment of any kind. When, a few days later, two of these unfortunates fell into the river and were drowned Moorcroft, tender-hearted as ever, was deeply upset. But whatever his methods, Bhowanni Singh's influence proved sufficient to get their baggage safely up to Niti.

They set off from Josimath at 8.45 the following morning. So far as is known they were the first Europeans ever to take that road. Up to the almost deserted village of Tapoban, under the soaring forested slopes on the right and the towering precipices on the left, the track, as today's road, followed the left bank of the Dauli through a wild but still relatively open valley of great beauty. The two holy men seemed to be enjoying themselves in the cool air. One of them was fascinated by the tadpoles in a warm spring. The younger man, more practical and less curious, had the spring cleared of pebbles and took a bath there by the roadside.

Beyond Tapoban, which they left on 29 May after some further haggling over exorbitant customs demands, the Dauli gorge becomes a more serious proposition altogether. From there to Niti by the modern jeep road is only 36 miles (57.6 kilometres). It took Moorcroft and Hearsey eight of the most exhausting days either of them had ever experienced. Although they did not realize it they were in fact penetrating the main range of the greatest mountains in the world. Locked in that precipitous gorge, with its walls soaring thousands of feet above on either side, they were so absorbed in the struggle for balance and breath above the murderous current, that they caught scarcely a glimpse of the great snow peaks, Kamet and Nanda Devi and the others not far away, lifting their serene white heads nearly 5 miles (8 kilometres) clear into the thin blue air.

From the hunched shoulders of these giants even the line of the Dauli gorge is untraceable in that heaving wilderness of rock and snow. Far down below in the shadows of its thunderous gorge the two unusual holy men and their straggling party were inching their way upwards at the end of May 1812 across the rockfalls and the avalanches, fighting those heart-pounding little private battles for survival which every modern rock climber knows, but without either his equipment or his skills. At one moment on the 29th Moorcroft was edging his way across a nearly vertical rock face

> on which, irregularities for the toe to hang upon, were at a most inconvenient distance. My left foot having slipped off one of them, I lay for a few seconds upon the poise, but a snatch at a clump of grass, which on being seized, luckily did not give way, and a sudden spring, brought me to a comparatively safe spot, with the loss of some skin from my knees and elbows, and some rents in my trowsers and sleeves.

There were amusing moments too of course. Although they had already paid a consolidated sum for transit dues on their baggage and had a receipt written on birch-bark to prove it, this did not prevent further demands being made upon them. They had another 'scuffle', as Hearsey calls it, on this day. One old fellow was so obstreperous that Hearsey 'insisted upon his relieving a carrier from his load, which he actually took part of the way up the hill; and then skipping from under the load slid down a face of rock, and though old, skipped away from point to point of a rough road with the agility of a deer'.

The agility of a deer was something they all needed two days later when the ascending track seemed to come to an end at what Hearsey called, quite simply, 'the most tremendous place I ever saw or dreamt of'. When he finally made it safely again to the bed of the river he wrote, 'Thank God safe over. I was obliged to take off shoes and stockings!!' Moorcroft, who was also barefoot on occasions, was persuaded by the old pandit and the daunting sight of the carriers apparently stuck on a high ledge overhanging the abyss to attempt a longer but apparently easier detour still higher up. It availed him nothing. He too was soon clinging to tufts of grass and creeping along on hands and knees to prevent himself from sliding away on the scree into the river far below.

After a welcome respite passing through a gloomy forest of immense pines and cedars, 'of which many would have been large enough for main-masts of first rates' noted Moorcroft practical as ever, the path again became so dangerous that even the old pandit momentarily lost his nerve. Moorcroft realized why when he reached the place:

> an angular piece of rock having slipped out of the ledge or cornice on which we were walking; and a piece of stone, which just, and only just, rested with both ends on the

opposite edges of the gap, shewed a precipice of a depth sufficient to alarm the anxiety. . . . From the fatigue of this detour, I was so enfeebled as to be under the necessity of halting five or six times in ascending a steep mountain, and obliged to creep on my hands and knees for a great distance, not having sufficient confidence in my legs. My knees tottered, and I was frequently attacked with such a violent pain in the right knee, as for a second or two almost deprived me of the use of the limb.

It probably saved his life. For, creeping along on all fours on the very edge of the precipice, he suddenly glimpsed through a crack the vast emptiness beneath him, just as he was about to trust his weight to a loose rock which would almost certainly have taken him arching into eternity.

His relief when he eventually tottered down to Hearsey and most of the others waiting beside 'a cool stream of excellent water' can be imagined. Hearsey, who had taken the easier and certainly shorter route shared those feelings. 'Should it ever be at my option to return by this route', he wrote, 'I would swim the river five times to avoid it; the water is chilling cold, still I would suffer that in preference to going back by the road.' Neither of them would easily forget the last day of May 1812. And all this, they reflected bitterly, for want of one or two simple tree bridges to take the path across the torrent away from the landslips and sheer rock walls on to the easier side. It was another item in their mounting tally of hatred for the Gurkhas – 'the present government does nothing to ameliorate the state of the country or to increase the happiness of its subjects'. For Moorcroft, not to be an active improver and not to ease the lot of ordinary people were two of the greatest crimes possible.

The road became very much easier from this point and the river, although still a torrent, gradually dwindled in size and violence. Each day the unmelted beds of snow moved closer, the trees thinned and shrank, and the nights grew colder. They were in a sense passing back through the natural year as they climbed upwards, and the state of the flowers and crops in the tiny terraced fields of the scattered villages confirmed it. Moreover the great snow peaks to the south of them were beginning to look distinctly lower.

Strictly speaking they had already passed through the Great Himalayan main range and, pushing up over the 11,000-foot (3351-metre) contour, were now embarked on the ascent towards the ridge of the subsidiary Zaskar range to the north. It is not in the least surprising that, locked as they were in the chaos of that rocky wilderness, they should fail to appreciate the astonishing fact that rivers like the Dauli actually carved their way through the huge range from sources on its north side. Their own experience on the ground and visible evidence of the watershed suggested rather that the summit of the main range was still ahead of them. That is certainly how Hearsey showed it on his map.[3] His misleadingly slender 'Himachal Mountains covered with perpetual snow' ran roughly from north-east to south-west through the line of the Niti pass. Modern maps show the main range 30 miles (48 kilometres) further south.

On 1 June 1812 however, both Moorcroft and Hearsey were so thankful to be alive that they would not have worried unduly about such academic problems. Indeed Moorcroft actually permitted himself one of his rare, and it must be admitted not very lively, pieces of descriptive writing about the 'wild' and 'most imposingly majestic' scenery of snow peak and river gorge through which they were passing. Hearsey for his part was writing about natural beauty of another kind. Two of the female porters 'decidedly were handsome, much credit must be allowed to their chastity, as offers were made very liberally to persons in their situation, which either want of language or management on our part prevented having the desired effect'. The holy man, Hargiri, was still very much bound to the wheel of life. When they all reached Niti without further adventures on 4 June, he launched a new assault on the virtue of some of the overworked village women there, again with a total lack of success. It was all very frustrating.

Niti proved a frustrating place for Moorcroft and Hearsey in more ways than that. Here agreement for the porterage of their baggage ran out. At first it did not look as if they would make another very easily. When they had their first meeting with the suspicious old headman of the village late on the afternoon of the 5th, he did not mince matters. Pilgrims, he said, did not usually come this way and they never came armed and with so much baggage. Rumour had it that they were either Europeans or Gurkhas in disguise, come with hostile designs on Tibet. Appropriate measures, he hinted, had already been taken by the Tibetans beyond the pass. Indeed later they heard 'of large bodies of troops having been detached to all the passes . . . to prevent the entrance of any white people, or persons wearing white clothes [!], into the country'. Things did not look hopeful. It was finally agreed that, if the results of a letter despatched across the pass to the nearest Tibetan authorities at Daba proved favourable, then help with carriage would be forthcoming. Hearsey did not believe a word of this. It was all a plot

> to derive as much benefit from us as they possibly could, by retarding our advance . . . to oblige us to come to their terms with regard of carrying our baggage forwards. . . . I never met with such a mean cunning low race, void of faith and cowards to an extreme. . . . I saw very plain thro' their low policy.

He was probably right.

For the moment there seemed to be nothing for it but to settle down and wait at Niti for the ten days or so before a reply could be received from across the frontier. Moorcroft and Hearsey did their best to ensure that this would be favourable by surreptitiously giving the two Tibetan messengers a generous *douceur* to help them on their way, as well as tantalizing glimpses of the goods they would have for sale if allowed to proceed. They also set to work to create the most favourable impression possible among the Niti villagers themselves. They carefully swallowed their convictions and deferred to village arbitration in a dispute between one of Moorcroft's servants and a villager. They sought the goodwill of the womenfolk with some of the little trinkets from the Hardwar fair and Hearsey at least tried for something more than goodwill, notwithstanding the more obvious obstacles to amorous dalliance.

Their cleanliness is not very great either in dress or person; they smoke tobacco, drink spirits and have no reserve, they are great beggars; but tho' tempted very much would not swerve from their duty to their husbands.

It was probably just as well for a successful seduction even by a devout pilgrim would have done their cause no good at all. Nor probably their health. One can see why the amoral Hearsey needed to carry medicine for 'the venereal complaint'. Instead of risking these dangers he and Moorcroft were able to earn positive gratitude from these unadventurous villagers by organizing a torchlit, nocturnal foray in successful pursuit of armed robbers who had stolen some of the villagers' sheep and goats. Every line of Hargiri's loving and excited account of this episode betrays his own yearning to abandon his disguise as a man of peace and join the fun.

Instead he busied himself with his sketch-pad. Niti, with its cluster of two-storey houses huddling out of the bitter winds on its mountain ledge 11,500 feet (3503 metres) above the sea looks pretty enough in his delicate watercolour.[4] Later travellers certainly tended to portray these alpine villages as the epitome of rustic simplicity, free from the cares and distractions of modern life. Moorcroft and Hearsey's enforced stay at Niti in the bare early springtime gave them a truer picture. The houses, they found 'exceedingly filthy within . . . swarming with vermin' and the inhabitants correspondingly unhealthy; there was little enough to eat except enormously expensive grain and the occasional stringy goat. Their attempts to bag game in the thin air on the precipitous slopes above the village proved remarkably unsuccessful and they found the contrast between the freezing nights and the heat of the day during the few hours when the sun was above the hills extremely trying. At least, Moorcroft consoled himself, the water was excellent. And the nights were sublime. In the thin, clear air and utter darkness of the high hills the stars burn with astonishing intensity. In the daytime Moorcroft was busy recording the temperature, speculating about the weather, measuring the diurnal rise and fall of the river down below the village, collecting botanical specimens, marvelling at the geological riches of the rock strata and much else besides.

All this curious detective work seems not to have jeopardized their slowly improving relations with the local villagers. Two days after the Tibetan envoys had left for Daba, the villagers sent off a messenger of their own to vouch for the good behaviour and *bona fides* of the pilgrim visitors and their party. Moorcroft watched this man go without a great deal of confidence in the outcome 'for in attempting to ride upon a bullock, he with difficulty mounted in consequence of being very drunk, and fell off four times before he was able to reach the top of the mountain'.

The long-awaited reply from Daba arrived on 13 June. Unfortunately, or rather fortunately as it turned out, neither the Tibetan messengers who brought it nor the villagers of Niti nor, presumably, Moorcroft's Tibetan interpreter, Birbul, could make head or tale of it. Solemn councils were held both at Niti and at the villages lower down, at which the leading men debated what they should do. The Tibetan messengers argued strongly that the pilgrims and their swollen caravan should be turned back. The headmen hesitated, torn between respect and even affection for the pilgrims, greed for their money, and fear of the consequences if they earned some of it by helping them. Moorcroft and Hearsey, meanwhile, began to make ostentatious plans for falling back down the Dauli valley to the village of Malari, where the headman seemed to be more co-operative and there was a chance of forcing a passage across the Zaskar range in another direction.

Perhaps it was this bluff that finally broke the deadlock. As it happened Amer Singh, the son of the Niti headman, had good reasons of his own for fleeing the country. He eventually decided to turn necessity into advantage by offering the travellers not only help with carriage to Daba, but also to stand surety there for their good behaviour while they were in Tibet. 'As we were sick of halting we struck a bargain with Amer Singh', wrote Hearsey. In the darkness, while the village slept and the river thundered below in its dark gorge, the old pandit went to the father and son in the smoky lamplit room and made them affirm their part of the bargain on oath. Even then it took another week of haggling and procrastination, further payments from their dwindling supply of rupees and the sacrifice of a precious bottle of brandy before they were free to go.

They moved off after their unwelcome twenty-day sojourn at Niti just before noon on the morning of 24 June, with Hearsey and Moorcroft for the first time in their lives perched rather self-consciously on yaks. It was something of a triumphal procession. Hearsey, with mingled pleasure and regret, could not help observing that

> most of the women of the village had assembled to bid us adieu and waved their hands as we passed. I returned their compliments and was much pleased at this mark of attention, but the men altho' I have been in all most every part of India, I never met with such a low, mean, lying race of beings; they are cowards to an extreme.

His bitterness is understandable for he wrote those words no more than a mile above the village. That is as far as they got before the porters once again left them in the lurch, this time apparently for a feast in memory of one of the late villagers. At least, Moorcroft consoled himself, they were in a much better position here than in the camp outside the village, to defend themselves if treachery was afoot. Not that they were really in much danger even if it were. Hearsey reckoned with a touch of wistfulness that with his ten servants he could cope with the men of all of the last three villages they had passed and make off with all their flocks and herds into the bargain. But there was no need. There really was a revelry and its incapacitating effects were such that on the third morning after it had started, there still being no signs of movement from the village, Hearsey sent down one of the servants to see what was happening. The answer was, nothing. 'All the inhabitants [were] fast asleep from the effects of intoxication. Men, women and children lying in one promiscuous heap upon the floor.' Not surprisingly there was no movement that day either.

Moorcroft, restless as ever, spent these waiting days prowling high in the

adjacent mountains in search of game and botanical specimens. He climbed
three hours the first day and five hours the second, forcing his body on in the
icy, thin air and exulting in the fact that on the wrong side of 45 he could still
outpace all but one of the others. He must have been at well over 15,000 feet
(5470 metres), and the view of the up-thrusting phalanx of cloud-capped
peaks and glaciers of the great range to the south is sublime, but he was
given a sharp reminder that he too was a mere mortal in that abode of the
gods.

> On turning my back to the wind, [I] felt a sudden fulness in my head accompanied
> by giddiness; and fearing apoplexy, I threw myself on the ground with precipitation.
> After a short time the gasping for breath became less frequent, the action of the head
> was less violent, and I quitted the turf; but although I walked as leisurely as possible,
> I was twice again attacked with the same symptoms. . . . Although not particularly
> aware of any remarkable degree of heat or of cold, yet I found my hands neck and
> face very red, and the skin sore, and blood had burst from my lips.

For the next few days, although inexpressibly weary, he often found himself
fighting for breath, even at rest in his tent and on the edge of sleep. It was a
classic case of altitude sickness and if the party had not been delayed so long at
Niti, the symptoms would have been even more severe, perhaps dangerously
so. Although among the Bhotia traders the Niti pass was always regarded as
one of the easiest approaches into Tibet – everything is relative, of course, and
it is certainly not the highest – it has a bad reputation for altitude sickness.[5]
Moorcroft was only the first of many Europeans to suffer in the same way in
that lofty neighbourhood and Indian soldiers from the plains still suffer there
today. Even the yaks are often affected.

At last on Sunday, 28 June, three and a half weeks after their first arrival at
Niti and seven weeks since they had left the sweltering plains, they set out on
the first of the three short but exhausting marches to the summit of the pass.
Moorcroft and Hearsey travelled the easy way, on the backs of two of the
sure-footed yaks. Even so they were feeling very much under the weather in the
thin air and so were the twenty-five servants, panting along in private misery.
Up and up they went, beyond the last of the great river's snow-choked feeder
streams, beyond the last of the stunted trees, crossing beds of melting snow,
climbing high above the jagged chaos of alpine rock and mountain torrent into
the bleaker emptiness of the great Tibetan plateau.

The summit of the pass was fortunately in sunshine and without its usual
gale when they arrived there about noon on the last day of June 1812. Like so
many of the high passes the summit of the Niti is something of an anti-climax.
Just an empty, windswept saddle marked only by its cairn of stones and the
tattered prayer flags fluttering forlornly in the keen wind. Yet it marks the
watershed and the great geographical, cultural and historical divide between
the teeming monsoon land of Hind down below and the harsh, mysterious
Buddhist world of high Tibet. Even the usually boisterous Hearsey, gasping
for air, seems to have been subdued by it all – 'awfull' and 'dreadful' are the
words he used to describe the scene. Fortunately there was no Tibetan force
waiting on that windy saddle to contest the way as Amer Singh had feared. It

was just as well. Moorcroft believed that 'the height of this pass is so great and long, that a very small body of resolute men on the top might defend it almost against a large army, merely by rolling down stones', but no one was there. They made their offerings to the guardian spirits of that lonely place and plodded on thankfully. Soon they found themselves beside a stream which was flowing to the north-east. Moorcroft was quite correct in his surmise, although it is a highly improbable one, that these sluggish snow streams were some of the feeders of the mighty Sutlej and would journey nearly 2000 river miles (3200 kilometres) before losing themselves in the warm, brown waters of the Arabian Sea on the far side of the great sub-continent.

Later, in chilly misery as the ice-wind tugged at their tents all night, they probably wished that they too were back in those burning northern plains. It was their first real taste of the knife-edged Tibetan wind, which usually rises in mid-afternoon as the sun declines and soon cuts through the woollen layers, giving, as Moorcroft put it, 'the sensation of sinking into the flesh'.[6] They were all feeling too fragile to cope with it. Hearsey wrote:

> Mr. Moorcroft and self and most all our servants complain of headaches. Mr. Moorcroft took away near 16 ounces [.45 litres] of blood from his left arm. I took some black salt and aniseed. The wind was so very cold that a person could not stir out after sunset.

At this encampment they met two Tibetans with a flock of sheep and goats laden with salt on their way to Niti. On Amer Singh's advice they either persuaded, bribed or forced these men to return with them to Daba so that no adverse rumours should arrive there before them. Hearsey, suspicious as ever, was convinced it was just another trick by the Niti men 'to fleece us of our money', and so indeed it might have been.

They were off at 5.30 the next morning and when they reached the ridge of a secondary pass, they were intrigued by the prayers and veneration which the two Tibetan traders directed to the snow-tipped peak of Mount Kailas, visible far away to the east across the treeless, broken plateau. Moorcroft settled down with a line at one of the rivers and caught a substantial fish off which he and Hearsey dined. Later that afternoon their hunter, who had so far been conspicuously unsuccessful, at last came in with a small wild sheep. The deprived Hearsey voted it 'the finest flavoured flesh I have ever tasted'. It is somehow exactly what one is coming to expect that Moorcroft should have dissected the four-part stomach of the animal and found there a tapeworm. Things were looking up. Even the wind seemed less cold and there was no more talk of altitude sickness.

Next day they came across the first of the flocks of sheep and goats which dot the Tibetan plateau in summer as the snows melt and the young spring growth comes thrusting up again out of the stony soil. Both Moorcroft and Hearsey seem to have been especially intrigued by the first Tibetan woman they had ever seen – a cheery, dirty, gap-toothed soul, wife of one of the goatherds, who must have been very patient with the two holy men from Hind who seemed so fascinated by every detail of her dress and jewellery. The resulting word-portrait is instantly recognizable as is much else that they describe in Tibet to anyone who visits Ladakh or Tibet today. The most astonishing and somehow reassuring discovery Moorcroft made that day was that 'the art of making black puddings' seemed as familiar to the men of Niti as it was to those round London's Smithfield market.

Very early the next morning on 3 July they were in sight of Daba. It was a weird place, clinging to the jumbled side and bottom of a ravine with its soft, eroded rocks contorted into curious shapes and caverns. At about 8 a.m. they passed through its gate and pitched their tents beside the first cultivated land they had seen since leaving Niti over a week before. Amer Singh hastened to pay his respects to the chief men of the place and, it seems, received a stinging welcome for bringing the party on in defiance of express orders. Despite Hearsey's perennial suspicions, Amer Singh was true to his word. He not only spoke up for them but offered to stand surety for their good behaviour as long as they remained in Tibet. After a good deal of debate, it was finally agreed that the visitors could remain where they were, free to trade, until permission to proceed had been received from the higher authorities at Gartok.

Next morning Hearsey and Moorcroft with the old pandit and a few of the senior servants, preceded by their ceremonial presents of cloth, sugar and spices on a brass plate, went to the little stone house which served as the administrative headquarters. 'Filthy enough, stench abominable', noted Hearsey. There, in a low room crowded with curious people, they had their first audience with the three men who represented civil and priestly authority in those remote Tibetan borderlands. Both Moorcroft and Hearsey committed the interesting details of that novel meeting to paper as soon as they were back in their tents and both accounts have been published in part. The interview went very well, despite the still very evident suspicions of the Tibetans that these two men, especially perhaps the older one with his curiously red and peeling face, were either Nepalis or Europeans in disguise. None the less the letter which was drawn up with much ceremonial and sent off to Gartok was, so far as they could understand it from Amer Singh's translation, eminently satisfactory. It said

> That the former report sent by the people with regard to our being Europeans was incorrect; . . . that we were peaceable goseins come on pilgrimage to Mansurwur and that we were altogether 25 men, the arms we had were for the protection of some property we had brought for sale; that as much delay had ensued to us from misrepresentations that had taken place . . . he requested to have a speedy answer . . . as we had been put to much unnecessary expense. He likewise informed the Gortope Chief that the 7 sheeanahs [Amer Singh and his party from Niti] had given a written agreement to him, with a very heavy fine in case we should cause any disturbances hereafter and had become surety for our good conduct.

What Hearsey does not describe was a curious little incident which, he simply noted, 'has given rise to a set of reflections of the greatest possible utility to the British Government in India all caused by the sight of a dog!!!!!'

It all began when two small European dogs, a pug and a terrier, caught sight of Moorcroft in that crowded room. According to his later account[7] they

> suddenly rushed towards me, fondled, caressed me, frisked, jumped, barked and appeared as much rejoiced at seeing me as if they had recognised in me an old and favoured acquaintance. After their first demonstrations of joy were somewhat subsided they appeared desirous of showing their accomplishments by sitting up on their haunches and pushing forwards their forelegs . . . as is sometimes taught to those animals in imitation of presenting firearms. . . . They were said to have been brought by Ooroos.

Russians! Moorcroft could scarcely believe his ears. He had been surprised enough to learn in Delhi a few months earlier that the Russians were trading as far south as Bokhara,[8] but the discovery that the allies of the malevolent Napoleon (as Moorcroft wrongly believed) should be filtering round on the relatively easy north side of the Himalayas and visiting not only Chinese Turkestan but Ladakh and Tibet as well, seemed very sinister indeed. Those two little dogs so innocently betraying their European origins (and his too although this does not seem to have occurred to him) were, he believed, the tip of a very alarming iceberg. 'I have little doubt', Moorcroft later wrote to Metcalfe, 'that Buonaparte has received important information respecting the condition of countries never pressed by the foot of an Englishman though within 34 days journey of the Company's Provinces.'[9] To all the other tasks of his mission was now added the urgent need to discover as much as possible about what seemed like a breathtaking political development.

For the next few days the pilgrims once again had to compose themselves in patience to await the result of the appeal to Gartok. They spent the time seeing the sights of the curious little town and, as they had at Niti, winning the goodwill of the more important of its inhabitants. The women and children as usual were easy. Moorcroft had noticed the wife of one of the headmen, 'a young woman of pleasing face . . . with a pretty child in her arms', at the first audience on 4 July. Later that day she and her sister came to the tents with their husbands to look over the trading goods and fell in love with a ring which 'of course' she was given. Moorcroft was always susceptible to a pretty face. The children preferred the sweet biscuits, sugar candy and gingerbread. Next day Moorcroft 'sent for his medicine chest and gave them some peppermint upon sugar with which they were highly delighted as also with the smelling salts'.

On Sunday, 5 July, leaving their shoes at the door, they went with Amer Singh and the old pandit to the large and well-kept monastery which dominated the town. In the inner sanctuary 'on opening the great doors, we were struck with the magnificence and arrangement of the objects before us, the first impression struck was the likeness to the Roman Catholic'. Anyone who has seen the colourful and cluttered profusion of the dark Buddhist *gompas* (monasteries) with their strange imagery, both rich and tawdry at the same time, knows exactly what Hearsey meant. He seems to have been particularly impressed by all he saw and his description of the visit is a detailed one.

Moorcroft was delighted when one of the monks, 'a laughing ugly fellow', took them up to a small verandah and showed them a few coils of unpicked shawl wool for which they struck an immediate bargain. It was the only wool he was able to purchase in Daba, for a stern injunction had been issued from Gartok confining all sales to accredited Ladakhi traders, apparently as a result of the purchases made on behalf of John Gilman a year or two before. Their subsequent audience with the old head lama was, however, a great success, particularly after Hearsey, when the conversation flagged, made the brainwave suggestion that Moorcroft should present to the old man the beads from his neck. It broke the ice and a touching friendship across the cultural and language barriers seems to have sprung up between the real and the pretended holy man in the next few days. Later, when Moorcroft came to take leave of this old man, he found 'something particularly affecting in his manner and utterance, and I could not help bending over his outstretched hand with emotion'.

They left Daba soon after daybreak on 12 July, not for the great lakes across the plateau to the south-east as planned but north and east, escorted by two Tibetan horsemen, across the western extension of the Kailas range to Gartok. If they were to be back in India inside the three months promised to Calcutta, they should already have been heading south. It is doubtful if Moorcroft even gave it a thought. He pretended reluctance at this enforced detour so far off their intended route to the great lakes and persuaded the Daba authorities to provide carriage. In reality he was delighted, for Gartok was the great summer trade mart of western Tibet and there, if anywhere, he should be able to obtain not only shawl wool but news of the mysterious Ooroos who came there to trade (and spy?) each summer.

The 50-mile (80-kilometre) journey to Gartok by what the Tibetans called the lower road they did in five easy marches. Usually they left camp in the chilly and often frosty dawns and made camp about midday when the summer sun had pushed the temperature in the tents sometimes well over 90°F (32°C), and before the afternoon wind came cutting in from the south-west, plummeting the temperature as the sun went down and driving them all once again under the heavy blankets for the night. It was the pattern of their weather and their travelling during the whole of their stay in Tibet. There was little scenic variety. When they passed a couple of poplar trees, the first and only ones they saw in Tibet, Hearsey carefully marked them as a principal feature on his empty map while Moorcroft lay happily beneath one of them listening to the goldfinches singing. The scenery may have been unremarkable but the rich and sometimes novel fish, animal and bird life of the great plateau fascinated both men and provided some welcome variety in their sparse diet as well.

They forded the young Sutlej, already 80 yards (73 metres) wide and running very strongly to the north-west, without accident on the first day out from Daba and then had to climb to cross the watershed into the broad, open valley of the upper Indus in which Gartok stands. The peaks of this ridge are all about 20,000 feet (7293 metres) high and snow-covered but because of the great height of the surrounding plains present no serious obstacle to traffic in midsummer. The sure-footed yaks made light of the snow and ice beds on the ridge which gives separate birth to those two great rivers, the Indus and the Sutlej, which later join forces in the Indian plains and together make their way across to that opposite sea.

Moorcroft seems to have been his usual indefatigable and nosey self, poking about for fossils, dissecting the wild hares, examining with a keen professional eye through the telescope the small wild horses glimpsed from time to time in the middle distance, and very much else besides. On 16 July they shared a camp-site with a party of friendly Tibetans. This not only provided an opportunity to have a closer look at their horses and the way they shod them, but enabled Moorcroft to examine the simple medical instruments of a doctor who was in the party. He had 'an eye cleanser, 3 lancets and a fleam. Mr. Moorcroft took out the whole of them to examine and the owner showed no hesitation whatever'. In general both he and Hearsey found these simple, friendly people much more attractive than their avaricious counterparts on the Indian side of the Niti-la, but not, it seems, the women. Even Hearsey, deprived as he was, seems to have remained untempted.

> They have little or no cleanliness in the whole of their habits, seldom or ever wash either their hands or face, or even their bodies. Their clothes are seldom changed and are greasy and filthy to an extreme. The extreme cold of the climate prevents fleas and they have many body lice about them. In their hair they are very particular, the dressing and plaiting of which entirely belongs to the department of the women. Of their beauty, cleanliness and appearance I can say very little in their favor but altogether I never saw in my life so many ugly faces.

'They have few children,' he added in an eloquent non-sequitur.

Several hours before they reached it on 17 July, the black-tented township, which is Gartok in summertime, came into sight in the clear air far away across its broad, grassy plain 'covered by prodigious bodies of sheep, goats and yaks'. Hearsey estimated that there were about 2000 people there. As the Tibetan horsemen from Daba led them to their camping place beside the stream, many of these people

> assembled round us out of curiosity. The countenances were perfectly Tatar, several of the most savage appearances; others had copied the Chinese, altogether a most curious groupe; as it was natural we should be objects of curiosity, we allowed them to examine every thing about us, they were civil but wished to know what the things were, to this we could make no answer but by signs.

Their curiosity was matched by that of the garpon or governor, a powerful man whose jurisdiction covered the whole of western Tibet and its summer caravan trade with the lands to the north, east and west. But for all his power and wealth and the great deference with which he was treated, his audience-hall (to which Moorcroft and Hearsey were summoned as soon as the tents were up) was only a shabby, low hut made of turves. It was almost the only permanent building in the whole of Gartok.

The first interview in this room was a long one. Whether it was their successful lying, or the representations from Daba, 'or the weight of our presents' as Moorcroft cynically put it, the garpon seemed quickly satisfied that they were the genuine trading pilgrims they claimed to be. Thereafter most of the discussion was about trade. On 18 July the pilgrims laid out for him their wares for inspection – the double-barrelled shotgun, the telescopes, the cutlery and scissors, the pearls, the scarlet, green and yellow broadcloth. After a great deal of prolonged haggling a price was settled with the garpon for the red and green cloth.

Almost as soon as they returned to the tents, Moorcroft and Hearsey were approached by the servant of a Kashmiri Muslim called Ahmad Khan, the chief agent of the ruler of Ladakh for the summer purchase of the shawl wool. Moorcroft and Hearsey seem deliberately to have kept this man at a distance and did not meet him personally until their last day at Gartok. Nevertheless he provided much valuable information, not only about the shawl-wool trade to Kashmir but also about Russian commercial penetration north of the Himalayas. He confirmed in considerable detail that the Ooroos had not only reached the desert towns of Chinese Turkestan, but had visited Gartok and recently even Kashmir, and were suspected of being in some cases more emissaries than merchants. Later this flow of information dried up suddenly but fortunately Ahmad Khan's innocent servant, 'untutored by his master', continued to supply compromising intelligence.[10] Moorcroft suspected the garpon but it is more likely that Ahmad Khan's sudden caution, if it existed at all other than in Moorcroft's overheated imagination, arose when he got wind of Moorcroft's interest in purchasing shawl wool. This of course threatened the jealously guarded Ladakhi and Kashmiri monopoly on which the agent's livelihood depended. Moorcroft preferred more complicated explanations. There is an engaging cloak-and-dagger innocence and zest in his purposeful hunt for clues concerning the Great Game at Gartok – a game he believed with a prize no less than 'the promised plunder of India and the addition of its immense territory to the Russian Empire'. Even Hearsey's engagingly uninhibited journal becomes suddenly secretive at this point. So did the garpon. When Moorcroft noticed more of the small and apparently European dogs beside him and remarked with studied casualness that a certain nation called Ooroos had a similar breed, 'an air of reserve and circumspection immediately covered his countenance' and the subject was swiftly changed. Moorcroft of course was undeceived by what he called the garpon's 'overstrained ignorance' of the subject. Where did the red leather of his boots come from or that blue linen cloth worn by two of his horsemen or the lettering engraved on that sword-blade? All were Russian. Even the garpon's evident anxiety to hurry the travellers on their way seemed sinister. He *said* he was anxious that they should get back across the Himalayas before winter closed the passes, but to Moorcroft it was just as likely that he wanted to get them away before the Russians arrived at Gartok.

Not that any of the party wanted to linger in that empty spot longer than was necessary. There was only one more piece of secret business to transact. The garpon was persuaded, partly no doubt by more oil of peppermint essence on sugar and the other little gifts with which Moorcroft softened him up, but most of all by the hope of a lucrative future trade with Hindustan, to offer his Indian visitor both shawl wool and horses. Hearsey contemptuously called the latter 'only overgrown Tattoos' and Moorcroft firmly declined to buy any because they were too small for anything except mounted rifles or light cavalry. Later, in many lyrical paragraphs in a report to the board, he described their sure-footedness, strength and resistance to cold. There was certainly not much else concerning horses to report. Between the British frontier and Tibet they had only seen one miserable specimen. But Moorcroft of course was trying to justify not only his present journey but the one after that. He went on to remind the board of the significant fact that all the information he had gleaned in Tibet about large horses to the far north provided important corroboration of all he had learned at Delhi. All the evidence agreed. Bokhara was the great horse Mecca and the best way to reach it was by way of Ladakh and Yarkand, the route Mir Izzat-Allah was exploring at that very moment.[11]

This interesting information and much else besides came from Ahmad Khan whose tent Hearsey and, later, Moorcroft visited on their last day at Gartok. The Kashmiri may not have realized, when he solemnly explained how the Ladakhi monopoly of the shawl-wool trade was enforced on sentence of death by the garpon, that his physician guest had already done a deal that very day with the garpon to breach that monopoly. Ahmad Khan, they later discovered, was very tough with any non-Ladakhi trader he caught in possession of even a small quantity of the wool. Of course Moorcroft had to pay through the nose for his prize – 'gross roguery' he called it. The garpon took pains to explain the extent of the favour he was granting, reminding Moorcroft that 'there was an order of government inflicting the loss of his head on any man that should sell this wool to any other person'. He was not far wrong. Later he was carried off in irons to Lhasa and imprisoned there for three years for his disobedience.[12]

The garpon also claimed that it was fear for his head which made him insist that, after their pilgrimage to Manasarowar, the travellers must return by the same route they had come, across the Niti pass. When he heard this Hearsey was cast into gloom. It has, he wrote, 'much damped the pleasure of our future trip'. By that route not only were there the nightmare hazards of the Dauli gorge to contend with, but the Gurkhas would almost certainly be waiting for them too. They had hoped to explore new ground in Tibet much further to the west before recrossing the Zaskar range by or near the Shipki pass.[13] It may well have been the old pandit's enquiries about the feasibility of the route in that direction which had aroused suspicions of their intentions in the first place.

Moorcroft's journal gives a good idea of the anxious discussions which must have taken place in his tent that evening. The old pandit was all for ignoring the garpon's orders, but there were many objections to that course. It would jeopardize the new trade connections which Moorcroft was so anxious to establish and it would probably have serious consequences for Amer Singh

[151]

and the Niti headmen who were still standing surety for their good behaviour at Daba. Another suggestion was to cross the Niti Pass and then try to find a route to the east between the two ranges, but that would have been quite impossible without re-entering Tibet. In the end it was decided to go for Hearsey's plan. His suggestion was to return down the Dauli gorge at least as far as Tapoban. Then, leaving the animals in the care of the servants, they could make a dash on foot by a different route across the snowy range, somewhere in the awful shadow of the Nanda Devi and her sisters, in the hope of reaching the plains before they could be stopped. It seemed the least objectionable of a series of unattractive alternatives, but, whatever the outcome, it was time to move on. Their business at Gartok had detained them a week, their funds were dwindling and the hard night frosts were a constant reminder that winter in those high altitudes was now not very far away.

They left on 23 July, heading south-east towards the great lakes. This was a route already trodden, although Moorcroft and Hearsey could not have known it then, by the astonishing Jesuit missionaries Freyre and Desideri a century earlier.[14] Once you are used to the thin air, it is not a difficult journey in summer. Apart from the gentle climb to the 16,200 foot (4936 metres) watershed between the headwaters of the Indus and Sutlej, they had mostly only to cross the treeless plain, its immense distances dwarfed by the clarity of the air under the pale sky. There was no shelter from wind or rain up here. To their left the plateau ran out at the foot of the Kailas range, dominated more and more dramatically as they travelled eastwards by its great broad-shouldered, angular, snow-capped namesake peak. On the right, further away at first, the plain ran out at the ridge of the Zaskar range. Behind it, mostly hidden at this time of the year in the swirling monsoon clouds and subdued by the great height of the plateau, were the giants of the Himalayas. Not that the journey from Gartok to the lakes was uneventful. They were on the Tibetan equivalent of a main road. Hearsey called it 'a thoroughfare'.[15] Modern maps label it 'the Ladakh Lhasa Trade Route'. Day after day they passed the caravans and encampments of the traders and herdsmen passing to and from Gartok. Indeed they had to send some of their own servants back there to sort out an unpleasant misunderstanding about the sheep, goats and yaks which Moorcroft had purchased from the garpon in exchange for the broadcloth, and to complain of the behaviour of the two Tibetan horsemen who were accompanying them to the lakes.

While they halted, Moorcroft put the delay to good use by boring the noses of their yaks in the Tibetan manner so that they could be tethered. 'This operation was easily performed by Mr. Moorcroft,' noted Hearsey. Next evening, a wet and windy one, Moorcroft was treating himself with an emetic 'which had the desired effect and he voided a great quantity of bile, [although] the fever still remains'. He was very unwell all next day, alternatively shivering and sweating between bouts of violent sickness. Hearsey watched his friend anxiously all day and through the night, carefully cataloguing his course of medicines – '10 grains of Calomel, 3 of James's Fever Powder and 2 of Dr. Robinson's Brown Pills'. Moorcroft was well enough to move on again the following day, although he must have found the crossing of the icy, swift-running and rapidly rising stream of the young Indus in a freezing wind intensely miserable. Some of the servants and animals were benighted on the near bank and those that did get across had to have brandy or the ever-useful peppermint essence on sugar forced between their chattering teeth to revive them. It was short commons next evening too – some thin soup, a cup of boiled yak's milk and tea was the sum of it. However they made up for it the following day with grouse stew and hare cutlets, garnished with a huge mushroom Moorcroft had found along the way. It must have been a very welcome repast for they had more river troubles that day, twice fording the swollen snow-melt waters of the young Sutlej. Hearsey confessed himself 'very cold and very much fatigued'. Moorcroft who was still very weak seems to have been twice deposited by his over-lively yak either on the ground or in the freezing water. There must have been many moments when he asked himself what on earth he was doing at all, wandering about on this cheerless, inhospitable plateau.

One answer to that question came next day, 30 July 1812. It was a historic date, they believed, because it 'may be reckoned as the root of a traffick with this country which may be highly beneficial to the Hon'ble Company and of which we have the credit and satisfaction of being the founders'. The words are Hearsey's but the sentiments are Moorcroft's. Hearsey marked the occasion with a delightful watercolour. It shows two Tibetan horsemen following Hearsey and Moorcroft with the yaks laden with the shawl wool which Moorcroft had purchased from the garpon. No other figures are depicted although some wild horses and Mount Kailas are added in the background for good measure.[16] In reality they were not alone and the curiosity of the other merchants at their camp-site that evening made things rather awkward. Hearsey believed that he had 'entirely allayed all suspicions' by a cleverly chosen lie. Yet it could well have been one of these shrewd-eyed men whose information ensured that this first consignment of shawl wool direct from Gartok to India was also the last.

Fortunately Moorcroft and Hearsey's satisfaction was unclouded by any glimpses into the future. If they contemplated the future of the trade at all it was with an engaging optimism about its beneficial effects, spreading out-wards from this day and remote spot even to the shoulders of beautiful women in the *salons* of distant Europe. And if the government were too blinkered to see the possibilities of the shawl-wool trade and shawl manufacture, then the go-ahead Hearsey at least knew what to do:

> it would be a certain and ample fortune to a company who would establish the commerce. Seven people advancing about 20,000 Rs. each would in about 5 years entirely beat Cashmere and supply not only India but Europe with this elegant article of wear, far superior in texture, the fashion of the borders and in colour.

It was an exciting prospect.

A century later the great Swedish explorer, Sven Hedin, was so impressed by the geographical results of Moorcroft's Tibetan journey and his evident awareness of the complex hydrographical problems waiting to be solved at the great lakes, now only a day or two away to the east, that he believed that Moorcroft's purchase of the shawl wool was only 'to hide and mask his real intentions'.[17] On the contrary, the pursuit of this golden fleece added immeasurably to his difficulties and dangers and attracted much unwelcome attention which he could well have avoided if exploration and discovery had been his prime motivation. They clearly were not, although Moorcroft was of course determined to take full advantage of what he believed would be the first European sighting of the lakes. Even a recurrence of the fever which had been troubling him ever since they left Gartok failed to stop him. It struck again on 1 August. The following day he travelled 'with much difficulty very unwell'. He was not much better on the 3rd and on the 4th was so bad that they had to halt for a day while he recovered his strength. Next day they reached the northern shore of Lake Manasarowar. This astonishing expanse of water in that empty wilderness at 15,000 feet (4570 metres), mirrors only the occasional eagle or migrating geese, the pale sky and the snow peaks of Kailas and Gurla Mandhata that stand silent sentinel beside it. For at least four millennia the lake and its guardian peaks have been one of the world's most mysterious and inaccessible places, sacred to men of all the great Asian faiths.[18] Even today it is to the Hindu the source of the holy Ganges, no matter what the geographers may say. Some of Mahatma Gandhi's ashes were consigned to its waters on 8 August 1948 to prove the point. All of the handful of Europeans who have seen it have been impressed, whether by its serene emerald stillness or, as Moorcroft and Hearsey saw it during their brief stay, ridged by the biting wind and pounding its shallow, grey-green surf on the rocky shore.

Moorcroft set out on the chilly morning of 5 August 1812 with two of the servants, his fishing rod, gun and telescope and only a cup of tea under his belt, for his historic reconnaissance along the western shore of the lake. The clarity of the air seems to have deceived him into believing that he would have time for some sport along the way although he was still far from well. He was not looking his best either, with 'a weather-beaten face, half stripped of its natural covering by the joint action of a hot sun and cold wind, blistered lips, a long bushy beard, and mustachios . . . with a gait not of the firmest'. But he knew exactly what he was looking for. He was already sure beyond reasonable doubt that not a drop of Ganges water could come from this side of the Zaskar range (he called it the Himalaya). His experiences in the gorge of the Dauli, and that was only one of the tributaries of the great river, had convinced him that Webb's 1808 conclusion was the right one. There was more than sufficient water pouring off from those immense glaciers and snow-fields, let alone from the annual monsoon rain clouds, to account for the Ganges without seeking a Tibetan lake source and a fabled tunnel through the range to the 'cow's mouth' at Gangotri in accordance with Hindu tradition.

The source of the Sutlej, however, still remained an open question. The old pandit, when he was last at Manasarowar sixteen years before, had seen and crossed a stream running strongly westward from the lake towards its sister, Rakas Tal (or Rawan Rudd, as they called it), a few miles to the west.

Everything they had learned confirmed that from that lake in turn flowed the main branch of the Sutlej. It only remained then to authenticate the pandit's sighting of a connecting stream to settle the question once and for all. As the day wore on Moorcroft stumbled on through the soft sand on the shore or clambered unsteadily over the high rocks which occasionally fringe the lake. Gasping for breath in the thin air, parched with thirst and frequently forced to lie on his back to relieve the violent pain in his limbs, he became more and more mystified. At about four in the afternoon with the sun now sinking fast, he was still only about halfway along the western side of the lake. For all his weakness, he had covered something like 14 miles (22.4 kilometres) in six hours. But he had seen not a glimpse of the pandit's stream. From a vantage point he swept the whole of the western and southern shores, bright in the late afternoon sunshine, with his telescope and sent one of the servants on to examine the one place that was obscured. The result was always the same. Nothing. The lake had no outlet to the west or south nor any sign of one.

And yet at about noon Moorcroft, normally so hawk-eyed, must have crossed the dry bed of the old pandit's stream. Not only did he not see it, but he convinced himself at first from other evidence that the Manasarowar could never overflow on the west side and that the old pandit's stream must have come from the mountains, not the lake. Puzzled and weary, he turned for home. Seven 'very distressing' hours later he returned in the darkness to the camp, 'benumbed with cold and completely overcome with fatigue' after his 28-mile (44.8-kilometre) hike. It would have been a considerable achievement at that altitude even for a young, fit and properly breakfasted man. Six miles (9.6 kilometres) had been more than enough for Hearsey when he set off about half an hour after Moorcroft that morning. Now at nearly midnight over a steaming cup of tea, Moorcroft shared his conclusions with Hearsey. A further exhausting exploration by Harkh Dev right round to the south side of the lake next day merely confirmed them. Manasarowar, in Hearsey's phrase, seemed to be 'perfectly insulated'. It had no outlet, at least not on its northern, western or southern sides.

Later visitors to the lake, faced with a strong and easily visible west-going stream linking the two lakes just as the old pandit saw it in 1796, expended a great deal of implausible ingenuity to explain how the normally observant Moorcroft (and, it should have been added, three of his most intelligent servants) came to overlook the obvious.[19] In 1907 Sven Hedin reached the lake and once again the connecting stream had again disappeared. At last Moorcroft was vindicated. Hedin's explanation was so simple that one wonders why it was not considered seriously before.

Moorcroft saw no channel in 1812, because there was none. . . . But in spite of Moorcroft's and Harballabh's experiences being diametrically opposite, both were right. In 1796 there was an effluent which had dried up in 1812. The same phenomenon was reiterated 35 years later . . . and it has again been reiterated, as I shall show hereafter. This periodicity, which may have been going on for thousands of years, and which has nothing to do with the general desiccation of postglacial time, depends simply on the monsoon.[20]

In fact this is not really very different from the conclusion that Moorcroft and Hearsey reached themselves.

On making further enquiries with regard to this subject it appears that what old Hurbullub the Pundit mentioned with regard of a river issuing from this lake into Rawun Rudd, it took place about 16 years ago; since which time or near 8 years since it has dried up and the bed risen considerably above the highest level of the lake.

Unfortunately the extract from Moorcroft's journal which Colebrooke published in 1816 is not expressed as clearly as this, although Colebrooke himself correctly guessed the periodicty of the flow out of the lake. One wonders why it needed another century of argument before the puzzle could be finally resolved, for all the essential clues were noticed and recorded by Moorcroft on those two chilly days at the beginning of August 1812.

Hearsey was fond of carving his name on things. He had even brought a special engraving tool for the job. Now after breakfast on the morning of Saturday, 8 August, exactly three months after they had set out from the plains, he set up by the lake a stone with his and Moorcroft's name carved on it. Then, doubtless shivering in the strong wind, he took his last dip in its icy waters. Moorcroft, who was again very unwell that day, did not. At 11 a.m. they turned away and began the long homeward march. As the last of the muffled figures passed one by one out of sight over the ridge, only the cold camp-fire ashes and the alien lines and circles of that silent carved stone were left as witness to their intrusion into this strange, high and desolate place.

12 Prisoner of the Gurkhas and Release,

AUGUST–DECEMBER 1812

THE FOLLOWING NIGHT, 9 August 1812, the wind thundered round the huddled tents and animals and by the morning the world was white under 2 inches (5 centimetres) of snow. It reminded Hearsey, who had spent his childhood there, of England in December. Would that it were, he probably thought. Moorcroft, wafer-thin and feverish again, must have contemplated the monochrome scene and its implications with even more gloom than his young and healthy friend. Hearsey spoke for both when he wrote:

> This morning scene induces us to be anxious to quit the country with all expedition as should the snows on the Hymalia be heavy, we shall be locked out of Hindostan completely, a thing we do not desire for we have had specimens enough of the extremes of variety to which this climate is subject even in the course of one day.[1]

It is possible that they were being deliberately misled. It was an unusual year indeed that completely closed the Niti route to yaks before mid-December, although other animals had to cross the pass well before then to be safe. Of course it was not only the weather that was worrying them. Awkward rumours were circulating both above and below the passes that they were 'Europeans or the servants of Europeans', and it was said that the Gurkhas had already taken revenge on the people of Niti for helping them on their way.

Moorcroft's illness, and the inclement weather, unfortunately prevented him from making the close examination of the hydrography of Rakas Tal that he had intended, and this too threw quite unnecessary doubt on his observations at Manasarowar. Hearsey's map of the second lake was based only on what he could see from a distance. He not only got its shape and size very wrong but also misunderstood the alignment of the main Sutlej feeder. This was already a substantial stream running strongly to the west-north-west and they journeyed along its broken valley for the next few days. On 13 August they returned to Tirtapuri *gompa*, squatting on its craggy limestone ridge, with the mud-brick houses huddled round it and its weird hot-springs nearby. The intention was to collect the wool and animals they had left there a fortnight earlier and press on, but next day Moorcroft was again too ill to proceed, although early in the frosty morning he tried the effects of a hot bath in the springs.

Two days later at Kyunglung, another typically stacked monastery village, he was inspecting with keen interest the remarkable steamy sulphur-spring caverns there. Lamenting his amateur's ignorance of the geological riches on display, he at least felt sure that there was clear evidence of 'an antiquity that baffles research and would afford food for sceptics' (presumably of the apparently recent Creation described in Genesis). Five years later, a reviewer of Moorcroft's cautious words would have none of this. 'Had Mr. Moorcroft known nothing (and he does not seem to know much) of geology, or known more, his own faith would not have been staggered, nor would he have discovered any "food for sceptics".'[2] It is a pity that this anonymous armchair explorer did not tell his readers why. No wonder Moorcroft later felt ill-used by the critics. Not all of his reflections in the caverns at Kyunglung were upon the infinite past. He was reminded of the *grotto del cani* near Naples and, perhaps even more wistfully, of the spa waters of Harrogate just across the Pennines from Ormskirk. To Hearsey, with fewer European cultural roots to draw upon, the water simply tasted 'like rotten eggs', although that evening he was moved by 'the scene by moonlight of the surrounding white rocks lovely and soft beyond description'.

It was as well that Moorcroft began to feel better about then, because, from this point almost to Daba, the route across the broken edge of the Sutlej valley proved much more difficult than they had anticipated. The agility and durability of their heavily laden yaks was a never-failing cause for astonishment. On 21 August, two of these great, shaggy creatures were nudged by their baggage off the edge of a narrow path and fell 30 or 40 feet (9 or 12 metres) into a ravine without injury. The descents they deliberately made were nearly·as alarming – 14 feet (4.2 metres) on one occasion and on others, with Moorcroft and Hearsey on their backs, they flung their great bodies without hesitation down 5-foot (1.5-metre) drops. 'Not very agreeable', wrote Hearsey and certainly not a pastime for a feverish passenger.

Nor was game-shooting at that altitude. At last, however, Moorcroft began to feel better. On the 18th he was out bagging hares and three days later his marksmanship proved far better than Hearsey's when they went together after game-birds for the pot. It was tiring work. 'The greatest difficulty the sportsman here suffers' wrote Hearsey, 'is in climbing, the want of breath which is very distressing for if he goes out of a common walk he is obliged to blow and sigh dreadfully.'

The little caravan returned to Daba late in the afternoon of 22 August, dispensing biscuits and raisins to the grubby, rosy-faced children who turned out to give them an enthusiastic welcome. It was good to be back in the weird little vertical town for a few days' rest before facing again the bleak saddle of the Niti-la and the precipitous horrors of the Dauli gorge down below. That first evening back in Daba, to the accompaniment of the unforgettable rasping bass of the long horns, with the conch trumpets and cymbals, of the two Buddhist monasteries, they were called out of the tent by the old pandit to witness an extraordinary total eclipse of the moon. According to Hearsey, 'the surface was covered only with a thin red shade which appeared spotted but the moon could not send any rays of light thro' it'. Two hours later, doubtless to the great relief of some of those superstitious Daba folk, the untrammelled moon once again shone serenely down out of a still and cloudless sky, on the little town and the huddled tents of its alien intruders.

The next few days were pleasant. There were visits to make and presents to be exchanged, most enjoyably to the humble old head lama whom they regarded as the most 'enlightened' man they had met in Tibet. There were trade goods to be disposed of and gold-dust, saffron, shawl goats and provisions to buy. They found further evidence of the apparently sinister combination of Russian trader and French manufacture in this remote corner of Asia – some coarse cloth even had stamped upon it the impudent words '*drap très fin*'. The Ladakhi trader who peddled this stuff said that the Russians who brought it took well over two months to bring goods from their own country, via Yarkand and the Karakoram, to Ladakh. All the more reason to wonder what they are playing at, thought Moorcroft. More friendly in its implications was a visit they had at this time from two young Bhotia brothers from the village of Milam on the Indian side of the watershed north-east of Nanda Devi. Deb and Bhir Singh brought greetings and the offer of a loan from their father. He, clearly unconvinced that they were the peace-loving pilgrims they pretended to be, sent offers of help in a great uprising againt the Gurkha oppressors if the need should arise. Years later, after the British had replaced the Nepalis as masters of the hill-states of Kumaon and Garhwal, the sons of these two Singh brothers became extremely successful members of that elite corps of anonymous native explorers, which the British used to penetrate the wall of ignorance which persisted along the closed Himalayan borderland. The written testimonials which Moorcroft gave to Deb and Bhir Singh on 25 August 1812 near Daba were still being lovingly unfolded, and their fading ink shown to British mountaineers and officials, at least three-quarters of a century later.[3] They were not by any means the only written relics of Moorcroft's journeys to turn up years later along India's wild borderland.

Some writers have believed that Deb and Bhir Singh helped Moorcroft and Hearsey's party to escape Tibetan detention at Daba.[4] However, far from wishing to detain them, the Tibetan authorities were very anxious indeed to be rid of them. On the 24th they summoned the old pandit and told him bluntly that as his masters were Feringhi, they could not be allowed ever to return to Tibet. The spirited old Kumaoni replied, with equal bluntness, 'that they well knew . . . that they had it not in their power to prevent our visiting the country whenever we pleased. That whether we should do so or not depended upon the order of our superiors.' No wonder that, when Moorcroft and Hearsey declined to leave next day, a rather clumsy and ineffectual attempt was made to force them by denying their yaks access to pasturage outside the town gate. The misunderstanding was easily resolved. Moorcroft and Hearsey, for reasons which had more to do with the weather on the pass and Gurkha movements beyond it, were as anxious to be on their way as their Tibetan hosts were to be rid of them. With the preparations and farewells at last complete, they set out for the pass on the morning of 26 August.

It was slow going for the animals were still weak and some had to be abandoned. The route was familiar enough but the year had turned in the two dry months since they had last passed that way and the contrasts were great. Summer was already gone and the hard night frosts, the brown grass, the stunted plants already in seed, and the bitter wind all spoke of a harsher season soon to close this land once again to access from the south. They reached the empty saddle of the pass on the afternoon of 29 August. The 'most piercingly cold' wind tugged at the pocket handkerchief which Hearsey hoisted on a stick 'fastened very strong' and snatched away the sound of the seven musket shots he offered to the guardian gods of the gusty ridge. Ahead and down below, the mountains were wrapped in swirling monsoon cloud. This deprived them of a breathtaking view down into the distant plains but at least it also obscured the unnerving fact that from that high vantage point there is no visible route for anything but an eagle across the tumbling chaos of rock, snow-field and glacier heaped up across the near horizon. But the gods of the pass were kind that day. Moorcroft survived without injury what might have been a very dangerous charge by a deranged yak on the narrow path when they were just short of the summit; and only when they were safely across did it begin to snow heavily.

Now the horrors of the Dauli gorge awaited them. As soon as they descended to the river, they noticed at once that even at that height and so near its snow and glacier sources, it had already become an angry, milk-coloured torrent, deep enough to wet a yak's shoulder and strong enough to give him no quarter if he missed his footing. Anxiety for the precious bales of shawl wool on the yaks and the recklessness of the shawl goats gave Moorcroft a thousand torments over the next few days. On 1 September he wrote:

> The road was almost as bad as possible. Indeed it is scarcely in the power of imagination to suppose, that such a surface could be trodden by men and cattle, without their being precipitated into the Dauli, which rolled a tremendous current at the foot of the slope, over which the path ran (if that could be with any propriety called such a name, when effaced in many places by recent slips, and in others by blocks of stones, for nearly a quarter of a mile [0.4 kilometres] together). This was a march of disaster. The yaks, in inclining their bodies towards the mountain to prevent their slipping into the river, struck their loads against portions of rock, and tore the packages. At every hundred yards [91 metres], there was a cry of something being wrong . . . the yaks . . . found no more effectual way of escaping from these annoyances, than by running down the almost perpendicular face of the rock and dashing into the cold stream. Sometimes by the slipping of the soil they fell into the water with some violence, and after cooling themselves, to my great mortification, generally lost their loads in climbing over stones to regain the road.

There were compensations too. Every downward step brought them nearer to the world of men, of trees, of warmth and of the rich, high-altitude vegetation – the flowers, the abundant soft fruit, the ripe crops ready for the sickle, the great trees, the wild life – which remind every European who comes into these hills of home. As one of them put it, 'No European who has ever experienced the horrors of a Tibetan climate, who knows the wretchedness of a barometric pressure of fifteen or sixteen inches [38 or 40 centimetres], and has convinced himself how little of the sublime and beautiful these elevated regions can show him, will willingly cross the Himalaya a second time.'[5] This later anonymous writer certainly spoke for Moorcroft and Hearsey. They were both astonished and delighted at the transformation since they had passed up the valley in the bleak muddiness of early spring. Now the lower villages and valleys were ablaze with autumn colours and in places were hardly recognizable. It was probably then that Moorcroft first began to consider the possibility of eventual retirement to these hills.

There were more immediate realities to prepare for first. As the beauty and civilization increased, so too did the danger from the Gurkhas. There seemed no point in persevering with their disguises any longer for the whole of Garhwal and western Tibet seemed to know that they were Feringhi. Hearsey was startled to discover that Bhowanni Sing's brother even knew his name. And someone else who had met him in 1808, although not recognizing him behind his beard, knew his voice at once. The information of the more credulous was less exact. According to common report relayed to Hearsey 'we had stolen the Philosopher's Stone and 3 lacs of rupees from the Company's wife, who had made application for us to be seized and sent back'. They had a good laugh over that but there was a sting in its tail. The possibility of being seized and sent back was becoming very real. It was with considerable relief that they learned, as they descended to Niti on 3 September and the village children came out to lead them in, that there were no Gurkha troops waiting for them there.

There were, however, the familiar delays over the question of porterage. 'Patience was our only remedy', wrote Hearsey. He used some of the time to put the guns in good order; Moorcroft took the opportunity to construct a long letter to the secretary of the Political Department in Calcutta, spelling out all the astonishing evidence of Russian commercial activity on the other side of the Himalaya and the horrifying political and military implications which could underlie it.[6] They decided to leave Moorcroft's surviving yaks – eight cows and four calves of each sex – at Niti until the cold weather in the plains. The rest, on hire from Daba, were returned across the pass and their loads broken down into bundles small enough for a porter. Unfortunately, negotiations on the question of who should carry them and at what cost were getting nowhere. By a supreme irony the deadlock was broken by the arrival of a small detachment of Gurkha troops, ostensibly on a revenue-collecting visit but also, rather ominously, with orders to see their baggage safely down to Josimath. If Moorcroft and Hearsey smelt a rat, their diaries betray no evidence of it. They were probably only too relieved to have escaped from the skilful procrastinations of the Niti headman in only five days. It had taken twenty-five coming up.

They set off down the valley just after midday on 8 September and soon were at grips once more with the familiar hazards of the Dauli gorge. In some places the humans were forced to pass on hands and knees and in others even the shawl goats refused to go on. There were the inevitable – and, for Moorcroft, heartbreaking – animal losses, sometimes by falling or drowning in the torrent, sometimes by poison from something eaten along the way. He always did what he could for them: 'One [animal] very badly underwent the operation of letting out the wind from the large bag by a puncture, it gave her ease.' Hearsey seems to have been a very interested observer of his friend's surgical and *post mortem* techniques. When another goat died and was opened up Moorcroft patiently explained how 'its death was caused by a blow upon the loins with a stone which had materially injured the rib and fractured the inside of the kidney, the bleeding from whence had filled the bladder and the blood had got clotted and unable to pass through the neck of the urethra'. There were plenty of human patients for Moorcroft along the way as well – local people, the Nepalese soldiers and civilian representatives, even himself. It could not always have been very pleasant. Hearsey on one occasion found even sitting with two of Moorcroft's patients something of a trial, for 'here the body lice and fleas are so prevalent and the generality of the people have such large stocks of them in their dirty woollen cloaths, that they seldom go without leaving some of the family behind'. Later, when they reached the monsoon fever zone, all the servants were solemnly purged to keep them from fevers. 'It had pretty good effect,' remarked Hearsey, with evident if ambiguous satisfaction.

Once they were clear of the worst of the Dauli gorge, and it seems to have been far less alarming to them than when they went up, there were plenty more pleasant diversions to pass the time. Hearsey was kept busy sketching the botanical specimens which the unwearying Moorcroft kept bringing in from the steep forested slopes and fields high above the road. Moorcroft seems to have been consistently the better shot of the two but both men were out, whenever they saw the opportunity, to augment their sparse diet. On one occasion they lay in wait all night, with the guns primed and camp-fires banked up, for a man-eating leopard to make an attempt on the goats, but the dawn came without a sign of it. Hearsey found the bears something of a disappointment too. They were, he grumbled on one occasion, 'very timid and evinced no spirit whatsoever but ran about as cowardly as sheep'. Perhaps this was sour grapes for he could not even bag one of them in the whole of a long day, but there were always other diversions.

> Coming home and ascending to the huts where the Gorkheas were encamped saw a beautiful girl with one of the finest necks, shoulders and breasts I have ever seen, she belongs to the Detachment. Mr. Moorcroft saw another a very fine girl sitting down near one of the huts, these are the spoils of Kumaon and Gurhwal fallen to the share of the soldiery on their invasion of the country.

The Gurkha soldiers were never very far from their thoughts, as each day's march brought them closer to the more accessible hill-country below Josimath. It was hard to escape the feeling that the noose was slowly tightening round them. Both Bhowanni Sing and his brother had been punished for their help to the travellers on their way up and were already in hiding. A bigger

Nepalese force was waiting for them beyond Josimath and, although its attitude was outwardly courteous, Moorcroft and Hearsey began to suspect that they were being deliberately delayed and restricted in their movements. Moreover the number of troops about them seemed to be growing all the time. On 1 October Hearsey counted forty-six of them and, from that day onwards, he and Moorcroft always marched with their guns loaded, on constant watch for treachery. The Gurkhas seemed uneasy too and with good reason in Hearsey's opinion:

> I have no doubt that they fear their subjects will revolt and of which they have shown every inclination. An event which should it take place they have not force sufficient in the country to oppose them and the few troops they have would all be sacrificed ere they could get assistance. . . . The arms they have are miserable indeed and the poor wretches are in a miserable state from want of pay, provisions and cloathes.

Two years later Hearsey discovered, and it nearly cost him his life, that he had considerably underestimated the tenacity of the Gurkha grip on Kumaon and Garhwal. The Nepal war soon revealed just how formidable those natural fighters could be in their own hills. Open conflict was still two years away but relations along the long southern border of Nepal were already very tense by the end of 1812, notwithstanding the stiffly courteous letters still passing between the two governments. Indeed rumours that war had already begun were persistent enough to cause Moorcroft and Hearsey some concern. They had no wish to be interned or held hostage.

It is not really surprising in these circumstances that alarm bells had rung at Katmandu, when it was eventually reported that a large armed party led by two Englishmen in disguise had crossed the frontier without permission in May or early June.[7] Several of these reports linked Moorcroft and Hearsey's visit with local disaffection, but even if that were untrue, the Nepalis could be forgiven for believing that the visit was at least a reconnaissance. It could hardly be a pilgrimage. The leader of the party was a senior government official in the Military Department and the other was an active soldier who had already surveyed the hills with an official party three years before and since then had been making a considerable nuisance of himself in what the raja of Nepal termed 'various disputes on the frontier'.[8]

The Gurkhas were right to fear the consequences of the visit. Moorcroft and Hearsey's private journals are ample evidence of a developing hatred for the Gurkhas and all their works. Not only that but both men were unashamedly anxious that British rule should replace them. Thus Hearsey on 10 October:

> In 1808 the country was flourishing to what it is now, on every side desolation stares you in the face; the lands that were cultivated now forming into a Jungul, from whence arises the sickness so prevalent among the remaining inhabitants, fevers and agues. . . . Such is the miserable lot of these once happy people. This is all owing to the wretched Govt. under which they are now groaning. No one to hear them and the British Govt. did it know its own interests, even in the course of humanity ought to

free them from this most horrible state of slavery they are subjects too [*sic*]. What are Spice Islands to England when put in the scale with the utility, the resources, the benefits and the good name to be derived, by freeing these people, giving them their Rajahs, a code by new laws and . . . the Christian religion. . . . I believe I may without exaggeration state that not only the navy of Great Britain may be furnished with every material requisite, but . . . all Europe. To India this country is as a wall, which if in the possession of an European enemy would insure to them the conquest of the whole of the flat land. The climate is more suitable to Europeans, the race of people bred here much hardier than those of India and a hardy race of soldiery could be formed from the natives.

This is worth quoting at length for it is, apart from the omission of the trans-Himalaya trade, the classic British case for the later annexation of Kumaon and Garhwal. Equally, every word of it justified the Gurkhas' suspicions and their determination to stop these fake pilgrims, in order to discover exactly what it was they were playing at.

Some kind of showdown was therefore almost inevitable, for Moorcroft and Hearsey were determined to resist arrest, even with loaded guns if necessary. There is a great deal of hair-splitting in Moorcroft's emphatic insistence later that he had not behaved aggressively. From the Nepalese point of view the whole mission was a piece of aggression, and the refusal to stop when officially ordered to do so was further evidence of that fact. As the noose tightened, Moorcroft and Hearsey had a clear choice. They could leave the animals and most of the baggage and try to make a dash for the British frontier, travelling light and across country. Hearsey was still inclined to favour this course but Moorcroft, understandably, would not hear of abandoning the precious shawl-wool goats they had expended such time and effort to obtain. In that case, the only other possibility was to force their way onwards by bluff and threats towards the plains so that, if eventually they were overwhelmed, the news of it would more speedily reach the ears of the British authorities across the frontier. On 6 October at Pipalkoti on the Alaknanda, they sent off letters in duplicate by different routes for forwarding to Moradabad. In his letter to Metcalfe at Delhi, and the others were probably similar, Moorcroft simply announced their safe return from Tibet and their hope to be back on British territory in three weeks 'in case of meeting with no obstruction'.[9]

The first overt attempt at such obstruction, albeit a very civilized one, came three days later on the evening of 9 October, just after the crossing of the Pindar River by the swaying rope bridge at Karnprayag. Bandu Thapa, the local Nepalese governor at Pali, was waiting for them with a predictable catechism – why had they gone to Tibet, why in disguise, why without permission? He admitted that his orders from Katmandu were to detain them until those questions were satisfactorily answered. Indeed he tried to persuade them to halt until he could consult his colleagues. Needless to say, Moorcroft would have none of this. 'Had we have shown the least irresolution, I am certain we should have been detained for at least 15 days', wrote Hearsey. On the surface, it was all very amicable. Bandu Thapa embraced his visitors when they met; they in return gave him a present and Moorcroft prescribed some pills for the governor's rheumaticky knees. But the hint of menace was there and the number of soldiers around them seemed to grow by the day.

In the circumstances it was, to say the least, rather imprudent of Moorcroft and Hearsey to take different routes to Adbadri three days later. The only hint of disagreement between the two of them on the whole journey comes with Hearsey's exasperated entry in his diary that evening: 'I do not know what could induce Mr. M's going and which I suspect will be the cause of his detention.' The answer was that Moorcroft wished to take a different route in order 'to avoid some narrow paths, thro' very high grass in low grounds in which our progress might have been arrested without a favourable opportunity for employing resistance'.[10] In fact Hearsey and the remnant of the party were ordered to stop that day by a party of soldiers on orders from Katmandu.

> In reply I told them I was no servant or subject of theirs, but a traveller on the high road. One scoundrel . . . was very impertinent and said I should not go on – at which I gave the signal to my men to charge my firearms and then told them whoever dared to oppose my progress by force should be a dead man. . . . I proceeded onward and left them fuming and foaming and putting flints to their musquets.

Hearsey went to bed that night after a scanty supper with five guns beside him and a guard on watch, wondering anxiously what had happened to his friend who had set out just after midnight that morning to go his separate way. He learned the full story when Moorcroft came in about noon next day. He too had been ordered to stop by one of the Gurkha officers who, in Moorcroft's words,

> placed himself in a menacing position striking his musket violently against the ground. I snatched my gun from my servant, cocked it, and stopped with the intention of shooting him if he advanced a single step towards me.

It worked – temporarily. Reunited again and with the last of the carriers deserting them, Moorcroft and Hearsey pressed on at speed carrying what baggage they could and shadowed constantly by the Gurkha troops. On the 14th they crossed the tiger-infested Diwali ridge into Kumaon. The British frontier was then only 50 miles (80 kilometres) away and everything suggested that the showdown would come the next day.

Moorcroft was off with the goats in the frosty dawn so early that the Gurkhas were apparently taken unawares and had to hurry after him. Twice that day he refused to stop when challenged. The second occasion was particularly tense.

> A body of *sipahis* [soldiers] ran before to gain a narrow part, which confined the path. One went through the goats; I followed to push him from amongst them, and found about twenty men had formed a line upon the path. The man I had pursued, probably exasperated by being obliged to run in the sight of his countrymen, put himself in a menacing position on the path. I retired a few paces, dropped on one knee, in order to get a steady and low aim . . . the person who appeared so resolute, threw down his musket and presented his neck also. I ordered the soldiers to quit the path, and they drew up on the side for me to pass.

As if this indomitable man had not had enough excitement for one day that evening he 'performed an operation on one of the Gorkeeahs who had a caries [decay] of the breast bone and took out 2 pieces'. Hearsey, meanwhile, was embroiled in further abortive negotiations with one of the Gurkha leaders, 'an ugly son of a b——h of a Bramin', to whom once more he made it plain that they had no intention of halting until they reached Pali, where they had promised Bandu Thapa that they would wait for two days.

This clearly was not enough. Whether the Gurkhas feared that their visitors would break their word, or felt that Pali was much too near the British border, or simply needed more time to consult their masters at Almora or Katmandu, one can only guess. It must by now have been very plain to the soldiers that, as long as Hearsey and Moorcroft were prepared to use their guns and they were not, probably on orders, then the two men were likely to go on evading arrest indefinitely. Even if the troops were free to resort to arms it would not have done either side much good. Hearsey tried to discourage any attack by painting the likely consequences in very strong colours:

> We should certainly kill 20 or 30 of them and be killed ourselves, by which they would gain very little but be the cause of our Govt. revenging our death; and the loss of their bread and the lives of many thousands of their countrymen.

The only remaining possibility for the Nepalis was to attempt to overwhelm them by sheer weight of numbers before they could use their arms, and this is precisely what happened on the morning of 16 October.

It was foggy and still, 'the trees as if commisserating [*sic*] our situation from their leaves were dropping big drops', noted Hearsey rather inexpertly. His prose was not very elegant even at the best of times, and this was definitely *not* the best of times. They were up early, but the Gurkhas were ahead of them, filtering something like 100 men in among their disorganized camp. Moorcroft was sitting on a stone with his gun in one hand and his breakfast in the other, when he saw that they were being rapidly surrounded.

> I called to my companion to prepare and sprung into the path, desiring the soldiers to stand clear. The main body opened a little, and I independently advanced with too much impetuosity. A man or two advanced, and I shoved them back. My gun had in an instant as many hands upon it as could find room to touch it, but they could not wrest it from me. . . . [At last] one man got upon my neck and stuck his knees into my loins, endeavouring to strangle me with my handkerchief, whilst another fastened a rope round my left leg and pulled it backwards from under me. Supported only by one leg and almost fainting from the hand round my neck, I lost my hold on the gun, and was instantly thrown to the ground. Here I was dragged about by the legs until my arms were pinioned.[11]

Hearsey, who was cleaning his teeth at the time, neither heard Moorcroft's shout nor saw this struggle. The first warning of danger he had was when he saw about sixteen Gurkha soldiers attempting to overpower the servant who had charge of his guns.

I came to his assistance and was surrounded in an instant by 7 or 8 men; 2 or 3 I dislodged with my fists and got hold of the double-barrelled gun – in attempting to wrest it from them a fellow seized me round the throat and 3 others round the wrists; others by my legs and I was obliged to let go and was carried away. The first object I beheld was a drawn sword and a cluster round as I supposed the body of Mr. M. who I concluded they had killed. This idea made me prepare for my own death and I looked for the means of dying revenged. My attention was attracted to the kookuree of one of my guards and I was preparing to make a last effort to seize it when I was delighted to see Mr. M. alive bound hand and foot.

Hearsey was furious. 'Villains', 'cowards', 'treacherous scoundrels', 'barbarians', 'wretches', 'cowardly shitten rascals', 'cussed deceitful race' – the epithets pepper the page of his fuming journal that day, together with a little drawing to show how their arms were for some time lashed behind them.[12] Hearsey ended on a more philosophical note:

> Thus ended this eventful day – a day we shall not easily forget. If the traveller has his pleasures yet let no one doubt the dangers and difficulties he has to encounter – if we ever escape this force it will be ever hereafter a day of thanksgiving to the *Great Preserver*. These are no common incidents. Oh Humanity, Humanity where hast thou fled? Return once more to this unfortunate country as an Avenger. The first day's imprisonment is passed.

There were sixteen more ahead of them. Detention, though, is a better word than imprisonment, for they were not even confined to their tents under the dripping mulberry trees but allowed the freedom of the camp.[13] It was the servants who suffered most, being both fettered and ill-treated at first. Moorcroft and Hearsey were so loosely guarded that, on one occasion, they managed to slip outside the stockade that was built to contain them and reconnoitre the surrounding country for about an hour before they were missed. What they saw did not look very hopeful. If the Gurkhas did not get them, the bears and tigers probably would. They saw plenty of evidence of both even in camp, but in any case there was no immediate need for flight, because it soon became clear that they were not going to be murdered as they had genuinely feared at first.[14] Their captors indeed soon became courtesy itself, while they awaited orders from Almora and Katmandu. Moorcroft and Hearsey did their best to hurry things along. Moorcroft had, in his usual open-hearted way, taken on as goatherd a bearded fakir near the Niti pass. This man – they code named him Ambrose de Lamela – now repaid that kindness by slipping away in disguise with letters from Moorcroft and Hearsey concealed in the lining of his ragged clothing. Moorcroft's letters are now in Edinburgh. It is typical of the man that his chief fear was for the safety of the old pandit and his nephew and he instructed that a monthly income should be paid from his estate to the families of both if they were all killed.[15]

When the fakir's absence was discovered a great hue and cry was raised by the Gurkhas. Moorcroft and Hearsey and some of the servants who were in on the secret pretended to abuse him as an ingrate who had deserted them in their hour of need. But he did not fail them, and the news he carried to the British authorities across the border set off a widening circle of correspondence which eventually led to a direct appeal from the governor-general in Calcutta to the raja of Nepal.[16] Of course none of this was known to Moorcroft and Hearsey until much later. They, counting the days and hoping for the best, made other less successful efforts to smuggle news out. Hearsey, rather unreasonably in the circumstances, waxed highly indignant at 'the low cunning and duplicity of these scoundrels' when he discovered that the guards were on the watch to intercept these efforts. It was all very irksome. We cannot even 'proceed to the necessary without one or two men following our footsteps', he grumbled.

There was nothing for it but to settle down as patiently as they could while the night frosts transformed the hills and forests from summer green to autumn gold almost before their eyes. Hearsey busied himself protracting his route survey into a book as a preliminary to drawing his large-scale route map. Moorcroft had more medical work than he could cope with. At first he preferred to employ his medicines and his surgical skill for the benefit of the local people, at least until the servants were released from their fetters. One farmer's son was tapped of 10 pints (5.6 litres) of dropsical fluid from his navel and in return his father slipped away with more duplicate letters under the very noses of the Gurkhas who were watching. An old woman, blinded by a massive cataract, had it

> extracted with much care and little pain . . . as soon as the membrane was displaced she said she beheld the light. Another subject was a young woman with an extensive caries of the jawbone – a piece of old bone was clasped by new ones on each side similar to a man in a coffin. Below was a sinuous ulcer occasioned by the caries.

There is something very touching about these scenes, and they were repeated endlessly during Moorcroft's life in India, whenever this tough but compassionate little man saw an opportunity to ease the pain and distress of simple village people. The soldiers, more than half of whom were suffering from venereal disease, were not neglected for long either. They, in return, seem to have done what they could to make life as pleasant as possible for their two captives, although Hearsey, still seething, was not inclined to be grateful. For instance, some of the Gurkhas spent three days like small boys trying to dam and reroute the Ramganga, so as to provide some good fishing for their two captives. They failed, as later they failed to capture a bear, armed only with their kukris. 'The fish were too sly to be caught and the bear too fierce to be taken by such stupid animals as a detachment of Gorkeah soldiery,' commented Hearsey sourly.

At last, early on the morning of the seventeenth day of their captivity, news arrived from Bim Sah, the governor of Almora, that they were to be released, their arms restored and coolies provided to carry their baggage to the frontier. It was 1 November. Later that day the hill-servants who had been taken off to Almora arrived back in camp. Only the two pandits remained behind in captivity, but they were apparently being well treated. In the afternoon with some of the soldiers as beaters, Moorcroft and Hearsey celebrated their freedom by going out in search of game and succeeded in killing an old male bear of such size that four men could not even lift him from the ground. Next morning they marched down the valley, writing letters as they went to report the favourable turn of events.

The relief, when two of these letters reached Calcutta some time in the last week of November, was immense.[17] Private congratulations from their friends and well-wishers poured in from every side.[18] Neither man, still embittered by his arrest and the oppression he had witnessed, was inclined to give the Gurkhas much credit for his release. Moorcroft's theory was simple: the soldiers had bungled it by leaving the attack far too late which was the main reason why they eventually had to be disavowed by the Nepalese government. A more impartial reading of the evidence suggests that this was unjust. Both Moorcroft and Hearsey drew frequent and indignant contrasts between their own experiences and that of Nepalis in the company's territories, able to go about their business as they pleased. The two cases were not really comparable. Kumaon and Garhwal were for Nepal highly sensitive frontier zones, thinly held by Gurkha troops and seething with disaffection. The unauthorized presence there of armed foreigners travelling in disguise was bound to cause alarm. In many ways Moorcroft and Hearsey deserved all they got. They were fortunate not to get very much more.

Their feelings can be well imagined as they descended the last of the hills into the safety of the broad plain, and pushed on for Kashipur. They arrived there on 12 November and the only disappointment was not to find the old pandit and Harkh Dev waiting for them. Moorcroft immediately sent off yet another letter to Bim Sah, although in fact the two men had already been released by then. Whether Moorcroft had a personal opportunity to thank these two faithful servants is unknown, but it was not the last time they would travel the hills together.

Moorcroft was at Moradabad on 17 November and a week later with Colebrooke at Fatehgarh, from which he wrote a warm letter of thanks to the governor-general.[19] On 1 December he was almost at Lucknow. To Metcalfe in Delhi he sent instructions for his servants who had been waiting there for nearly six months and confessed his anxiety for news of Izzat-Allah somewhere on the road to Bokhara.[20] On 20 December he was at Ghazipur, inspecting the empty cavalry cantonment prior to its takeover by the stud as he had recommended and meeting the recently arrived riding master, his colleague and later friend, Antoine de l'Étang. Did Moorcroft's heart sink as the accumulated routine of the stud reached out to engulf him? The floor of the Ghazipur stables, Moorcroft recommended to the board, 'would be much improved by being dug up and its surface coated with elephant dung'.[21] He must have sighed. The great and extraordinary adventure was well and truly over.

Just what had it all amounted to? From the stud point of view not very much, as Moorcroft cheerfully admitted. There were horses on the other side of the

Himalayas, droves of them and with remarkable qualities – but certainly not for cavalry-horse-breeding.[22] Instead of the great 'benefit from the indefatigable efforts of Mr. Moorcroft to open new sources for supplying an improved parent stock' which the government had expected,[23] 'the fruits of this expedition, as far as they were connected with the stud was [*sic*] confined to the acquisition of one solitary female ass' recalled a member of the board later.[24] It was scarcely an exaggeration. Moorcroft's private summary of the results of the journey did not mention horses at all.[25]

The members of the board felt much the same about the other major animal 'fruits' of the expedition, especially the shawl-wool goats. Their disquiet on this score can be traced back to the indiscreet letter Moorcroft dashed off to them on 25 April from Saharanpur.[26] So far as the board was concerned, woolly mammoths would have done just as well. Goats were none of its business, nor his either. By the time Moorcroft came to compose the official explanation of his journey in January 1813, he had realized his error. There is not a single reference to the shawl-wool goat beyond an apologetic reference to 'objects of secondary importance' which had 'occupied too much of the foreground' of his earlier letter.[27] It was too late. From this time Moorcroft's reputation as a chaser of shadows hung round his neck like an albatross. Worse, there was a not entirely unjustified feeling that he was a man prepared to bend the rules when it suited him. This latest journey had confirmed what the previous one had already demonstrated – that he tended to act first and seek permission afterwards, and that his estimates of the likely duration of his absence were, to put it mildly, somewhat misleading. Once could be forgiven as carelessness; twice looked more like habit.

The official rebuke from the governor-general,[28] Lord Minto, was not as harsh as it might have been but its drift was clear enough.

> If time had admitted of your receiving a communication from Govt. previous to your departure upon that expedition [to Tibet] there is no doubt that the assent of His Lordship in Council would have been withheld. . . . 1st The extreme personal hazard to which it must expose you. . . . 2dly The strong political objections to a measure so likely to give umbrage and excite suspicion as the passage of an English gentleman high in the service and confidence of this Govt. without permission, but especially clandestinely and in disguise through the Nepaul country. 3dly Because it was from the beginning believed to be impossible that the plan could be accomplished in the time allotted. . . . 4thly Because . . . the deviation appeared greater than was quite consistent with the proper and regular purposes of your Superintendence; and indeed several of the objects of pursuit in this enterprize, altho' by no means unimportant or uninteresting in themselves . . . appear nevertheless, somewhat too foreign to the particular nature of your charge.

None the less, concluded the letter, the confidence of the government in you remained unimpaired. That reassurance was probably put in to meet a fear which Moorcroft had frankly confessed to Lord Minto in private earlier,[29] but unfortunately it was just not true. Moorcroft had not only put his person at risk in 1812 but his public reputation as well. Among the members of the board at least, just as Moorcroft feared, there was never again the old trust and readiness to give his proposals their unreserved backing.

The same change from unqualified confidence to profound mistrust can be seen in the letters of Moorcroft's old well-wisher and patron, Edward Parry. An agricultural improver himself, he was at first delighted when he heard of Moorcroft's initiative in carrying out the directors' orders regarding shawl goats. As he explained to another country squire who knew Moorcroft and had once pioneered the Tibetan connection, the great Warren Hastings,

> Mr. Moorcroft's arduous, energetic and successful journey into Chinese Tartary has received the most unqualified approbation of the Bengal Government, his letter to me has been read by every Director and numbers out of the Court, great praise is bestowed upon his disinterestedness, and courage which determined him to undertake so perilous an enterprise solely for public advantage.

That was written in February 1814.[30] Less than eighteen months later, as will be seen, Parry was grumbling to Moorcroft that his letters were 'full of extraneous matter – such as goats, shawl wool etc which never can answer' and accusing him of shameful neglect of the true interests of the stud.[31] For much of this he later apologized, but it indicates the kind of information beginning to filter through to him from Calcutta.

Parry's bitterness was undoubtedly aggravated by the utter failure of the attempt to domesticate, in Britain, some of the precious shawl goats which Moorcroft brought safely out of Tibet. They were despatched home at intervals from 1813 onwards, not without difficulty and much to the irritation of the board which had to act as shipping agent. Those goats that survived the journey were sent to the Scottish estates of the Duke of Atholl, one of the 'enthusiastic practical farmers, men of fortune' that Parry told Hastings he was looking for. On the face of it the results seemed to suggest that Scotland was not cold enough, and perhaps not high or dry enough either, to induce the growth of the fine shawl wool. The animals languished. By October 1815 no male had survived in England more than a month and only seven females were still alive. In any case the wool proved to be of very little value. Later experiments all ended in the same way. It seemed clear that the change of environment was simply too great. That is not how Moorcroft saw it. He was withering in his anger at the neglect and mismanagement which is evident even in the published account of what happened.[32] He had kept the goats without illness through a monsoon season on the middle Ganges and he remained convinced that they could produce commercial quantities of shawl wool outside Tibet if properly looked after.[33] He was absolutely right, although it has taken nearly a century and a half to prove it. Recent experiments, notably in Australia where a shawl-wool industry is developing rapidly, have confirmed his view that heredity and not environment is what determines whether the fine shawl wool is produced or not. To Moorcroft's contemporaries, however, the shawl goat results of his journey looked as abortive as the horse results. It was much the same story, although a very much briefer one, with the sixteen hapless yaks that Moorcroft left behind at Niti. They all died through ill-management, ill-luck or worse, long before they even reached the plains.[34] In terms of livestock – whether horses, goats or yaks – the 1812 journey appeared to be a remarkably consistent failure.

Moreover, the shawl wool which Moorcroft purchased at considerable cost was later found to be dirty, the wrong colour and almost impossible to separate from the coarser wool entangled with it.[35] An ancient and complex industry did not yield its secrets as easily as he at first imagined. Yet it was on this journey that Moorcroft began that patient accumulation of information about every aspect of the shawl trade and manufacture which, by the early 1820s, made him its greatest Western authority and his writings the single most important source of information about its modern history.[36] In addition his collections of dried plants and flowers produced many specimens unknown to Western science and there is still a considerable number of species carrying his name in the classification lists of Himalayan flora, some collected on this journey.[37] His chief botanical interest, however, was always in the 'applied' as opposed to the 'pure' side of the subject, as his journals testify. Anything of practical benefit to man fascinated him above everything else. Almost as soon as he returned from this journey he was planning a follow-up by one of his trustworthy servants and using his new contacts across the border to obtain seeds or samples of rhubarb, saffron, the large pines and cedars, the 'paper tree', hemp, upland rice, pomegranate, quince, walnut and much else besides.[38]

But then Moorcroft made everything his concern and Hearsey, although lacking his friend's education and intellect, seems to have come out of the same mould. That is why their journey proved such a valuable source of information about Kumaon and Garhwal and their trans-Himalayan connections. Indeed, in the light of the Anglo-Nepalese war only two years away, it proved to be an extremely timely piece of reconnaissance, for little was known about these areas before their visit. Their knowledge of trade patterns, routes, topography and natural resources, easily became the raw material of important strategic and political decisions. Moreover, Moorcroft seems to have made a deliberate effort to maintain his contacts across the border. The Tibetan authorities at Daba and Gartok, Amar Singh Thapa at Palpa, Bim Sah at Almora and even the raja of Nepal at Katmandu were all among his correspondents.[39] Most of them were the recipients of his gifts as well. Some investigators, puzzled by all this and intrigued by the frequency with which his name and opinions appear in the files of the Political and Secret Departments of the Indian government, have turned effect into cause and Moorcroft into an undercover agent. Looked at in this way, his 1812 journey was a planned reconnaissance, perhaps to assess the Chinese and Tibetan reaction to a British attack on Nepal.[40] There is not a shred of solid evidence for such a view, but a man who travels with his eyes open where none of his countrymen have been before is bound to accumulate facts of political or military significance in the event of war in those lands. Moorcroft admitted that the Gurkhas were right to be highly suspicious as things turned out.[41] There can be little doubt that his and Hearsey's evidence of Gurkha unpopularity, oppression and military weakness in Kumaon and Garhwal, and their belief in the economic potential of both districts, played a significant part in Lord Hastings' war strategy and his decision to annex them at the end of it.[42]

The thoughts of the governor-general were already turning in this direction shortly after his first meeting with Moorcroft in the summer of 1814. In early December of that year, as he gazed out morning after morning from Moradabad at that gleaming northern snowline high above the plain, he reflected that, although

> this immense barrier would seem sufficient to limit the concerns of India; yet at this moment I am speculating on the trade which may be carried on beyond it, should the present war with the Gorkhas leave us in possession of Kemaoon. From that province there are valleys between the hills which afford passage of not much difficulty, and greatly frequented into Tartary. The holding of Kemaoon would give to us the exclusive purchase of the shawl wool, to be paid for in cutlery, broad-cloth and grain.[43]

Moorcroft peeps out from almost every line. This is not to argue that the 1814 Nepal war was undertaken out of greed for the trans-Himalayan trade or indeed for Kumaon and Garhwal; there were other more urgent political and strategic imperatives involved.[44] But the opportunity to take the hill territories was seized avidly when it came – for the various reasons spelled out by Lord Hastings and, not least, as a means to compete with the Russian trade which Moorcroft had discovered on the plateau beyond.[45]

Unfortunately, most of the dreams, which Moorcroft dreamed above all others, of a rich trans-Himalayan eldorado remained mere dreams. Ironically enough, his own unauthorized journey was partly responsible. The alarm he caused ensured that he would have few successors. The Tibetans and their Chinese masters were even more acutely suspicious than they had been before of any attempts at European penetration from the other side of the Himalayas. With the evidence before them of the way the trading East India Company had acquired a huge territorial empire, who can blame them? Moorcroft's garpon of Gartok was imprisoned for three years and all known to have helped the visitors in any way were fined.[46] In the years that followed, one British traveller after another was courteously but firmly turned back at the summits of the passes. All this put a premium on Moorcroft's information about western Tibet, but it effectively destroyed his hopes, and those of his successors, for a great trade through the Himalayas with that hidden land. Finally, when Lord Curzon decided to open Tibet by force at the beginning of the twentieth century, he did it to counter just those Russian intrigues which Moorcroft thought he had discovered at the beginning of the nineteenth.

To Moorcroft this was the most important result of his journey. At the very first opportunity on the Indian side of the Niti pass, he despatched a secret letter to Calcutta summarizing his discoveries and their significance.[47] He wrote in the belief, already outdated by another swift revolution in European affairs, that Napoleon and Tsar Alexander of Russia were still plotting that joint Franco-Russian attack on India which they had discussed in 1807. In 1808, the year Moorcroft came to India, the Indian government had responded to this threat with a series of diplomatic counter-measures in the north-west of India and in Persia and made contingent military plans for action there as well.[48] In 1812 Moorcroft believed that his discoveries required a radical rethinking of that defensive strategy. 'In the plans of defence against an European Army invading India I have understood that the British forces would take post on the left bank of the [middle] Indus, but if a Galli-Russian Army were to follow the route of the Russian traders to Yaarkund this position would be of no use as the station would be turned without a contest and the river be passed in a place little more than knee deep.' Once across the river and the outer ring of mountains, the invaders could either refit in Kashmir at leisure, or move freely eastwards behind the Himalayas on the Tibetan plateau and choose their sally-ports for irruption into the Ganges plain almost at will.[49]

These breathtaking possibilities seemed far less absurd to the men of Napoleon's generation than they do to us, with our hindsight knowledge of his flawed genius and the immense topographical and logistic difficulties involved. Moorcroft was too close to see clearly. He had lived most of his adult years in the shadow of the revolutionary wars, and his loathing and fear of Napoleon was perhaps all the greater for having seen some of the first effects of the revolution in France at first-hand. Now, like most men with a new *idée fixe*, he found it easy to rationalize changing circumstances to fit it. Thus, as soon as he returned to the plains and learned that Napoleon's army was on the march into Russia, he began to play with the 'monstrous . . . supposition of the present warfare between the French and the Russians being concerted to ask a scheme for invading Hindoostan'! Even supposing it were genuine war,

> if for instance the usual good fortune of Buonaparte should attend him in Russia the simple fact of having an army so much nearer Hindoostan than at any former period might induce him to think it a more favourable opportunity for pushing on part of it in conjunction with the troops of the fallen Emperor than at a later period.[50]

The possibility was taken seriously in London, but in Calcutta the governor-general and his council remained politely sceptical.[51] Even Moorcroft could scarcely sustain his alarm when Napoleon withdrew from Russia with a shattered army and the emperor of Russia became a valued ally in the great coalition which in 1815 destroyed Napoleon for ever.[52]

Curiously enough, it was in that year that there was a brief flicker of interest in Moorcroft's discovery of Russian intrigues in Kashmir, when it was learned in London that Ranjit Singh's army had attacked Kashmir in 1814.[53] His conquest was in fact postponed for a few more years, but so long as both Ranjit Singh and the Russians remained British allies, any alarm seemed premature and Moorcroft's intelligence was quietly shelved. All the same he remained unrepentantly suspicious of Russia's activities beyond India's borders and, within ten years of his death, a new generation of British administrators and soldiers came to share those suspicions and build new policies upon them. In this as in so much else Moorcroft was ahead of his time. He was one of the earliest players of the Great Game before most of his countrymen even knew it existed.[54]

None the less the most enduringly significant aspect of the 1812 journey was as a pioneer piece of exploration, and this perhaps was the one Moorcroft valued least. He had a quite remarkable incapacity for self-advertisement, as his veterinary career in London has already illustrated. This may have been partly due to the difficulty he always found in writing fluently, but in this case it also owed something to a very proper feeling that his information belonged primarily to the government. Instead of rushing into print, as most men who believed that they were the first Europeans to cross the Himalayas and visit the mysterious great lakes of Tibet would have done, he simply used his rough journal to write an abbreviated account of the journey intended for presentation to the government. Or so he said. The account which, he claimed, cost 'half of the nights of three months' was rather mysteriously stolen in 1813.[55] Thereafter he appears to have done nothing more about it, despite the nagging of his friends.[56]

Eventually the influential president of the Asiatic Society of Bengal, of which Moorcroft had recently become a member, persuaded him to hand over his rough journal so that an abridged version could be produced for publication by somebody else. Horace Wilson, Moorcroft's acquaintance of the voyage out and now secretary of the society, may have done the actual editing although the article appeared under the name of the president, Henry Colebrooke, when it eventually appeared in 1816.[57] It was inevitably a scissors-and-paste job, put together from an unpolished journal which was never intended for publication and was mostly written by Moorcroft in his tent at night, when he was dog-tired or ill after an exhausting day on the road. For this reason, the editor's well-intentioned insistence on using Moorcroft's exact words and merely cutting bits out was not entirely satisfactory. Nor was the failure to let Moorcroft see and correct the final version.

The article certainly attracted what Moorcroft called 'the ridicule and lash of the critic'[58] and some of the ill-informed and ill-natured criticism seems to have upset him a great deal. His misleading statement that Harkh Dev 'was directed to stride the whole of the road at paces equal to 4 feet [1.2 metres] each' was particularly unfortunate. The reviewers all fell about with laughter, imagining the hapless pandit trying to maintain this crotch-splitting and unnatural gait on the near vertical sides of the Dauli gorge. The misunderstanding persists even today.[59] The true explanation was very simple. Moorcroft later provided it – but of course too late and privately.

The length of a single ordinary stride of Harkh Dev Pundit . . . was measured and found to average two feet [0.6 metres] but as he represented that in his former journeys he had been accustomed to count by his right foot alone and as he apprehended that a change in his plan would lead him into mistakes he was ordered to pursue his usual method. He counted therefore by the double pace of four feet

[175]

calling this only one pace . . . had Mr. Colebrooke when he entertained doubts of the accuracy of the mode adopted intimated his suspicion of mistake the obscureness would speedily have been removed.[60]

Unfortunately the misunderstanding which resulted was more than just funny for it cast quite unmerited doubts on the accuracy of the map which Hearsey constructed on the basis of the pandit's paces and his own compass bearings. Considering the nature of the terrain and the fact that he was not equipped to do a proper route survey, Hearsey's map, for all the innocence of its execution, is impressively accurate in its general scale and configuration. In due course the new information it contained was embodied in the 4 miles to the inch (6.4 kilometres to 2.5 centimetres) Survey Atlas of India.[61] Later travellers were also full of praise for the unadorned accuracy of Moorcroft's typographical and general observations.[62]

Even so there remained, and remains, some confusion about what exactly it was that the exploration had achieved. Moorcroft and Hearsey were certainly not the first Europeans to reach the great lakes and see Mount Kailas. As has been mentioned, the remarkable Jesuit missionaries had forestalled them by a century and more although their accounts in 1812 were largely unknown. Moorcroft and Hearsey were, however, the first Europeans to explore the Dauli branch of the Ganges, and were thereby able to confirm Webb's speculative 1808 conclusion that the river had no sources in the Tibetan lakes. They repeated Webb's erroneous belief that the Niti summit marked the main Himalayan ridge and its erroneous corollary that the Ganges rose south of the main ridge.[63] Anyone who has penetrated that extraordinary maze of rock, river gorge and snow peak can easily understand the error, for it matches self-evident, commonsense observation on the ground. The highly implausible fact that the rivers rise north of the main range (indeed were there before it existed) and that the Niti-la is on the summit of a more northern, subsidiary range is a later, theoretical refinement, which does not really alter their essential conclusion: whether main range or subsidiary, the Niti saddle marks the true water-parting at this point and no Ganges water crosses it.

Moorcroft and Hearsey correctly identified the river flowing past Gartok as the young Indus and that at Tirtapuri as the young Sutlej. Moreover they were entirely right in believing that the Brahmaputra did not flow eastwards out of Manasarowar and, in 1812 at least, that the Sutlej did not flow from it westwards. And they provided all the evidence required for an accurate guess that it had done so in the past and could do so again. Moorcroft's illness certainly seems to have blunted his perceptions at Manasarowar, and it prevented him from examining Rakas Tal at all, except from a distance. The resulting errors in Hearsey's map have already been mentioned. These, and the puzzling fact that Moorcroft's observations on the lack of a Manasarowar outflow into Rakas Tal did not match what others found, subsequently led to an undervaluing by later geographers of his contribution to the century-long debate about the true hydrographical origins of the Sutlej.[64] It was not until Sven Hedin, probably the greatest of all the explorers of high Asia, reached and examined the lakes in 1907 that Moorcroft's 'excellent and conscientious' observations were given their real due. Hedin thought this was quite simply 'one of the most brilliant chapters in the history of exploration round the lakes and the sources of the great rivers . . . by this journey one of the most important geographical and hydrographical problems of Tibet and India was, at any rate, solved in a preliminary way'.[65]

Whatever the wider significance of the 1812 journey, it was a crucial turning-point for Moorcroft himself. Notwithstanding the ill-health, the miseries, the difficulties and the dangers, his determination to risk them all again and penetrate to Bokhara was now total. He was not one of those uncomfortable men who exult in hardship and are only fulfilled by danger. On the contrary, he was often unashamedly frightened and keenly miserable, but to him those things were of little account. They were simply the unavoidable means towards ends which to him were becoming all-consuming. To most others these ends were merely quixotic, irrelevant or unobtainable. It is at this time that the label 'enthusiast' begins to be attached to him. The word has changed its meaning. Those who used it to describe Moorcroft were suggesting disapproval – they meant that he was fanatical, infatuated or worse. It is not really surprising. In mid-November 1812, newly released from captivity, at the end of a journey which had damaged his health and threatened his life, he was blandly assuring his friend Charles Metcalfe at Delhi that, although he would 'probably be under the necessity of going to the Stud if not of visiting Calcutta . . . it will only be *reculer pour mieux sauter* and I shall speedily return' to embark on the long road to Bokhara.[66]

He was wrong. His fretting colleagues on the board would see to that. More than seven precious years passed before he did return and in every one of them he urged and begged to be allowed to go. The 1812 journey was then something of a personal tragedy for Moorcroft. It both gave him the Bokhara obsession and set in motion powerful forces to prevent or delay his satisfaction of it. And there was so little time. By all normal standards of the day, he was already too old for the rigours of trans-frontier travel and exploration in some of the wildest political and geographical terrain in the world. For all his vaunted fitness at the end of this journey, he must have been uncomfortably aware of the contrast between his own recurrent illnesses and the younger Hearsey's continuous rude health. The spirit in him burned more fiercely than ever but, as the years closed in, his body could serve it less and less. He was given a sharp intimation of this in January 1813 just after his return to Pusa. Something – he called it rheumatism – deprived him for a time of the use of his limbs and rendered him unable either to ride, or scarcely even to walk, without severe pain.[67]

Although the 1812 journey held a hint of personal tragedy for Moorcroft and threw a long shadow over his remaining years at the stud, it was also a deeply fulfilling experience. Indeed, one begins to feel that he was only truly himself when out on the open road and free from cramping routine. The vintage traveller of the last great journey was already fully formed in 1812: the tireless interest in everything he saw; the generous expenditure of time and skill on the relief of suffering; the simple pleasure in the variety of men and things encountered along the way; the endlessly busy, enquiring mind; the occasional intuitive flash of insight across the language and culture barriers dividing East and West, ancient and modern.

Nothing reveals a man's qualities and strips him of all pretence quicker than travel in the world's wild places. One who responded to Moorcroft, who dedicated his map to him and was proud to call himself his 'companion and friend', was that other extraordinary man, Hyder Hearsey.[68] The friendship between them, forged in the shared difficulties and delights of their arduous trans-Himalayan journey survived as long as they did. In a curiously touching way it still survives. Hearsey in due course named his beloved eldest son William Moorcroft Hearsey. In 1982, more than a century and a half later, a Hearsey still proudly bore that name. Moorcroft would have rejoiced at that unexpected memorial to their epic journey together in 1812.

13 FRUSTRATION AT THE STUD,

1813–14

RETURNING TO PUSA at Christmas 1812, Moorcroft went not to Frazer's dilapidated house, which was now a granary, but to the more modest building which Lieutenant Dickson had originally built for his own use and which was now the superintendent's lodge.[1] No doubt the usual army of personal servants presented themselves to minister to Moorcroft's needs after the great journey. There may have been a more personal and intimate welcome for him as well. Just exactly when Purree Khanum, the apparently beautiful young Indian girl,[2] entered Moorcroft's life is uncertain, but it was probably at about this time. He came to care for her very deeply indeed[3] and in due course she produced for him two children. All this was a timely blessing. Moorcroft was going to need all the domestic happiness and fulfilment he could find during his seven remaining and intensely frustrating years at the stud.

The most urgent task awaiting him was spelled out in a short but pithy letter from the governor-general in council to the board. It compared, or rather it contrasted, Mr Moorcroft's authorized journey north-westwards to the Punjab and Rajasthan with his unauthorized foray north-eastwards into Nepal and Tibet. And it asked, with exquisite but ominous politeness, that Mr Moorcroft be required to explain the difference as soon as possible.[4]

He did so, obviously with immense labour and care, signing the 100 or so long paragraphs on 13 January 1813.[5] It is one of the best official papers he ever wrote. In it he sought to justify, not only the Tibetan journey, but the whole of his first four years at the stud, and upon that basis to explain his aspirations for the future. He began with a magisterial two-part survey of the stud and of the northern horse trade based on his own observations and enquiries and on the information gathered for him by the various agents he had sent into the north-western breeding-grounds. His conclusion from all this was clear and stark.

Taking in consideration the diminished numbers and degraded quality of horses raised within Hindoostan; observing the general inferiority of the horses admitted in the cavalry within the latter years, to those of former times; examining the history of the Government Stud; viewing its present state; calculating its future powers by the employment of means within command; and contemplating the possibility of accidents; I cannot but see an imperious necessity for taking speedy and vigorous measures to oppose the further diminution of horse resources before the day of positive scarcity shall arrive.

If an adequate cavalry remount was impossible to attain in peacetime, what would be the problem in wartime, perhaps with a glanders' epidemic thrown in as well? 'What has happened to a Regiment in cantonments, may befall an army of cavalry in the field.' The shape of the argument – and Moorcroft's strokes are very deft indeed – begins to emerge. A desperate problem justified unorthodox and radical solutions, even if this meant pursuing them on the far side of the Himalayas in disguise and without permission. Moorcroft admitted 'the unexampled irregularity' of all this. He could scarcely do otherwise. Moreover, he made no bones about the fact that from the stud point of view the mission was a total failure. Still, he implied, negative evidence was still evidence. It was now clear that the best remaining chance of obtaining the suitable breeding-stock which the stud urgently required lay along the road to Bokhara by way of Yarkand.

Until Izzat-Allah returned from those distant cities in person to confirm this, Moorcroft suggested (and his reluctance is almost tangible) that he had better stay at the stud for the coming year. One can almost hear the spluttering sounds which would have emanated from the board when those words were read at Calcutta a week or two later. Meanwhile, as an interim measure, Moorcroft suggested that Lieutenant Wyatt should make the long journey to western India to obtain a supply of big Kathiawar stallions from Cutch and Gujarat. This would have the additional advantage that it might restore Wyatt's health, shattered by the demands of the stud while Moorcroft was away. The board, forwarding all this to the governor-general, unanimously endorsed this proposal. It was, it added, far preferable to Moorcroft's Bokhara scheme 'as the supplies procured in this way would not be so liable to be stopped in war when they are most wanted'.[6]

Behind this objection lay a very much bigger one. Back in 1811 when some of the soldiers on the Board of Superintendence had been called away on the expedition to Java, a civilian employee of the company called William Trant had been appointed to the board. He was soon both its president and its most dominating personality. By his own admission his chief qualification for the job was only 'some fondness for horses' and a desire to learn[7], but he soon took the lead in a determined assault by the board on Moorcroft's management and the independence he had previously enjoyed. One of the earliest straws in this new wind from Calcutta was visible in March 1812 while Moorcroft was away. He had asked before he left for extra veterinary help at Pusa, a request which until then would have gone through on the nod. Not so this time. It was rejected and on the (for Moorcroft) ominous grounds that 'Mr. Moorcroft will probably not be much absent from Poosah after he shall return from his tour'.[8] The words were among the first on the stud files to be written by William Trant, and they were written at the very time Moorcroft was at Gwalior and

Delhi heaping up the evidence to light his consuming passion for the Bokhara journey.

The shape of the future conflict was thus already visible by 1813. To the members of the board Moorcroft's prime duty, and the only justification for his extraordinary (they would have said scandalous) salary, was a close personal supervision of the breeding and rearing operations in and around Pusa. His task and theirs was to produce cavalry horses. He was not employed to chase shadowy speculations over the hills and far away, in the distant deserts of Central Asia. If he were not confined to the stud, then someone with a tenth of his knowledge (and salary?) would do just as well. 'I may know how the two or three horses in my stable should be treated, but if I never go near it my horses will not be bettered for all my knowledge,' as one of them put it later.[9] Failing to share or even understand his dreams, the board tended to dismiss them as idle or irrelevant.

For Moorcroft, on the other hand, a wide-angled examination of horse-breeding and disease was as central to his task as the imperative need to secure new parent-stock. He did not believe that Parry and the other directors had recruited him on a high salary merely to run a breeding-stud on the middle Ganges, particularly once he had convinced himself that the means available there were inadequate. There was, of course, much more to it than that. Moorcroft's two journeys had rolled back even his wide horizons to encompass new lands and cultures, new sights and scenes, new politics and geography, botany and history, geology and meteorology, trans-frontier trade and imperial security. Horse-breeding was now only one strand in a broader and more brightly coloured weave. The man who returned to Pusa at the end of 1812 was not the man who had left it. Not only had his total commitment to the details of its absorbing and demanding problems gone for ever, but he now believed he saw those problems with a new clarity and perspective. He was right, but those who stayed in Calcutta could never share that vision. Moorcroft, thin-skinned and obstinate at the same time, was not the man to suffer opposition without a fight. So conflict between him and the board was next to inevitable.

Developments at the stud while he was away also helped to bring a collision closer. Gibb and Wyatt, at Pusa and Hajipur respectively, had completed the withdrawal of the *nisfi* mares, selling some, putting others in the home stud and supplying yet others at low cost to the *zamindari* contractors. Unfortunately, however, the new riding master at Ghazipur, de l'Étang, had not yet taken any of the young stock for training. Both Pusa and Hajipur were therefore overcrowded with unsuitable animals when the cavalry committee made its inspection in November 1812, while Moorcroft was hastening back down the Ganges. Without the benefit of his explanations, its report[10] roundly condemned many of the animals it examined. The committee was also critical of Moorcroft's predilection for gelding, being 'perfectly assured that this operation injures the figure and courage of the animal'. That, of course, was a perennial subject of dispute among cavalrymen and it went rumbling on for at least another half century.[11] Most ominous of all, the committee could only find eighty-three colts suitable for admission to the cavalry. It was all very reminiscent of the sort of treatment Frazer had been getting at the end of his superintendence.

So too was the gruff and unqualified response of the Bengal commander-in-chief, old Sir George Nugent. As soon as the committee's adverse report reached his desk early in February 1813 he announced his intention of visiting the stud to see for himself and promptly anticipated the outcome by endorsing the committee's remarks about gelding and their strictures on the unsuitable animals at Pusa and Hajipur. He could not, he said, 'perceive one single object of public utility . . . by retaining animals . . . in a breeding institution for the purposes of which they are declared to be totally unfit'. Finally, he urged the board to purchase Arabs and other breeding-stock in the Calcutta markets.[12]

This uncomfortable dossier did not catch up with Moorcroft, who had gone up to his ruined bungalow at Hajipur in early February, until late in March 1813. He was understandably (and outspokenly) furious and still seething over it six months later.[13] He scoffed at the competence of any *ad hoc* committee to form reliable views about 2000 animals, a complex and scattered breeding operation, fifty-seven major buildings and two widely scattered breeding-establishments all in the course of three days, and he resented the slur on his own competence which the criticisms of the committee implied. 'Former testimonies of Government being satisfied with my conduct along with the favourable evidence of three previous Committees, have all been put to hazard.'[14] He was not the man to accept that without protest. In a series of forthright and lengthy letters, backed by all his accumulated experience, he criticized the remarks of the committee and the commander-in-chief point by point.

With no immediate likelihood of suitable breeding-stock what else could he do but attempt selective breeding with inferior animals? The attractively simple proposal to sweep away all the inferior animals when there was no prospect of replacing them would have been 'a species of insanity'[15] (not the term usually used to describe the views of the senior soldier in Bengal). In any case, the suggestion that he, William Moorcroft, was unfit to weed out the inferior horses, unless assisted by yet another committee, was insulting. Arab stallions were not the answer. It was bone not blood that was needed. Even if the Calcutta markets were able to provide animals of sufficient size (which they were not) the board was certainly not competent to know what was required. Purchase must always remain under the superintendent's exclusive control. As for gelding, Moorcroft conceded that in this matter the commander-in-chief's decision was final but he nevertheless rehearsed all the arguments in its favour, supported by the sentiments of many cavalry officers whom he had talked to on his travels.[16]

It is clear, with hindsight, that this whole episode was merely the preliminary skirmish before the bigger battles to come. It seems, from the record, that Moorcroft's 'clear and able' reports were well received by the board and the governor-general in council[17] – and in ominous silence by Sir George Nugent. The superintendent returned from Hajipur to Pusa in April to receive Sir

George's promised – or was it threatened? – visit but this was cancelled at the very last minute.[18] That was a pity, for Moorcroft was always a much more effective ambassador in person than on paper. In May, with daytime temperatures soaring to a sticky 130°F (54°C) and ugly clouds of flies everywhere, there was a serious outbreak of *bursati* sores among the sweating animals both at Pusa and Hajipur. At Hajipur alone the outbreak left eighty of them incurably blemished.[19] In June and July Moorcroft was back there again, this time struggling to sort out an elaborate network of forgeries in the stock sales accounts.[20] In September he was pleading, in private letters to the outgoing governor-general[21], that another committee of inspection be convened, this time composed so far as possible of men who had examined the stud in the year Moorcroft had arrived. Only then, he believed, would his management be vindicated and the ill-informed criticisms of the recent committee revealed for what they were. This was not just the wish of a sensitive man to justify his achievements. He was already beginning to consider a radical reform of the whole breeding operation and needed his authority and reputation unimpaired to push it through. In early November, with the heat and the rains mercifully out of the way for another year, his tent under the mango groves at the Hajipur fair was the usual centre of activity as he sought, with considerable difficulty this time, to pick up adequate animals at reasonable prices for direct admission to the cavalry.[22] In December he was up at Benares to hand over to the army authorities such animals as he had been able to obtain.

Those are the bare bones of Moorcroft's first year back at the stud so far as the surviving official record goes. That record is, in fact, unusually silent about the day-to-day detail of his life at this period and the silence conveys an impression of calm and inaction which is at odds with everything we know about his tireless activity and insatiable curiosity. For three months of that year of 1813, for example, he was under canvas out and about in the breeding-districts. No doubt he was also busy with his peripatetic medical practice and vaccinating for smallpox when his intermittent supplies of serum permitted. Besides, his knowledge of horses always brought him a great deal of extra work. He seems to have run an informal consultancy service on all the various problems associated with the animal, conducting an extensive correspondence with his more distant enquirers, purchasing animals for his friends or their friends, and dealing with requests to buy, exchange or examine animals belonging to private individuals. Nor was it only horses. He was breeding bulls, mules and cattle at Pusa as well and, as in Lancashire, occasionally facing the baffling problems associated with a periodic outbreak of cattle plague. He had a library of the major works on the subject and indeed maintained his interest in it to such an extent that, when moves were afoot later to found an agricultural society at Calcutta, responsibility for its domestic cattle section was planned for him.[23] Another important animal preoccupation in 1813 was nursing the precious Tibetan shawl-wool goats through their first hot and rainy season in the plains prior to shipment to England.[24]

Then there were all the other associated agricultural activities on the extensive Pusa estate. He was pushing on his multifarious fodder crop experiments – especially with oats, lucerne and potatoes – and in 1813 was requisitioning more seed strains and bruising mills from the Cape and from England.[25] There was a double and urgent purpose to all this. Moorcroft was anxious to rid himself of the dangerous dependency on locally grown crops, particularly doab grass, which had to be purchased on the open market and was seriously liable to be diminished or cut off in times of scarcity. Moreover, pursuing careful lines of enquiry he had first developed back in Europe, he was becoming convinced that the excessive quantity of sodium carbonate ingested with the traditional grass feedstuffs was itself a potent contributory factor in the debilitating *kumri* and *bursati* outbreaks, which were causing such havoc at Pusa and Hajipur. He devoted a great deal of time to painstaking *post mortem* investigations of both diseases and, while failing to find a cure, as he candidly admitted, his clinical notes confirm that his conclusions in some particulars were far ahead of his time. In the case of *kumri* he was particularly interested in the great increase of spinal fluid which he found in his *post mortem* subjects. Whether he pioneered the technique of draining some of this fluid from the living animal by intrathecal puncture in the atlanto-axial space is uncertain, but he was certainly being given the credit for it more than a century later.[26] Moorcroft's extensive but scattered notes on the equine diseases he encountered at Pusa and Hajipur would repay close investigation by a veterinary expert.[27]

That, however, was only a tiny part of his all-consuming search for improvement at the studs which scarcely figures in the official record at all. In the Pusa orchard, for instance, he was experimenting to find the best apple strains for a lowland Indian climate (at a time when apples were virtually unknown there) and comparing the yields of standard trees against espalier cultivation. In his highly productive vineyard, he struggled to match the flavour and size of the parent strains he had seen growing at the Cape. Later he experimented with different varieties of cotton and encouraged his neighbours to do the same in the hope of expanding the local spinning and weaving industry. He investigated leather tanning and obtained details of a French technique which he passed to the government. He recruited a skilled native ironsmith in the hope of discovering a new method of making sword-blades.[28] He continued to acquire additional botanical specimens from the Himalayas for his friends and twice sent a man to Nepal to obtain more seeds of a plant from which paper was made in the hills and upon which he believed a flourishing Indian and British industry might be founded.[29] Again, for much the same reason, he studied the architecture of a Mughal temple near Hajipur and the enamel-like decorations on temples near Ghazipur with immense care, not as an art or social historian but as part of his constant search for innovations or techniques which might be pressed into service to relieve poverty in India or at home.[30] He wrote extensively for the Calcutta journals, particularly on animal diseases, and he carried on an active correspondence with like-minded individuals in India and Europe.

There must have been some leisure too. He seems to have had many friends, both Indian and European, in Patna.[31] No doubt the fine cheeses, the madeira, the port and the porter which his friend John Palmer was supplying to him from the incoming ships at Calcutta, occasionally provided a convivial and noisy evening in the superintendent's house at Pusa, or at his recently repaired bungalow at Hajipur.

It was the high cost of that repair and of Moorcroft's other extensive building operations at Pusa and Hajipur in 1813 – including new stables and wells, a new mill-house and exercise yards and a specially designed boat for landing and carrying horses – which seems finally to have brought the board to the point of summoning Moorcroft down to Calcutta in January 1814. There were, it claimed, matters 'requiring grave consideration'.[32]

By then the first real storm had broken. In November 1813 Sir George Nugent returned once more to the attack. He had probably been holding his fire until Lord Minto, Moorcroft's staunch supporter, was safely on the boat home. The new governor-general, like Nugent a soldier, at first fell in obediently behind his commander-in-chief. Indeed Lord Hastings and his council made use of Nugent's exact words in their sweeping denunciation of the stud and its management.[33]

> The little progress which has been made since the Establishment of the Institution towards the objects in view, has rendered it in the opinion of Government absolutely necessary that a *radical* change should take place in the system hitherto pursued. Both the formation and management of the Stud have been evidently on erroneous principles, the greater part of the mares being of such description as to be incapable of producing stock fit for the remount of the cavalry.

That being so they insisted the deficient horses be weeded out by an *ad hoc* committee, to include William Trant, who was going to be travelling on business in the vicinity of the stud, early in 1814. He was by this time president of the board and neither he nor the other members were in any mood to defend Moorcroft from the serious charges which had been laid against his management. On the contrary, the board had already officially conceded that the stud had achieved 'very little success'.[34] That admission was made on almost the same day that Nugent launched his latest attack. It is hard to believe that it was entirely a coincidence.

Two months later, in January 1814, while Moorcroft was still hurrying down the river from Benares and Pusa, the board had completed the 1813 stud accounts and was even less inclined to support Moorcroft than before. His recent building programme, it argued, had pushed the annual deficit up to its highest level ever. The greatly enhanced expenditure which had occurred since his arrival had not made any difference whatsoever to the only statistics that really mattered, the number of horses transferred into the cavalry. In 1812–13 it amounted to a derisory 147 and that was exactly the number transferred by Frazer in 1807–8 at the time of Moorcroft's arrival. The board's hostility towards Moorcroft's new buildings, his accounting procedures, and indeed his management generally, is painfully evident from almost every line of this document.[35] Without even waiting for either his arrival or his views, the

board forwarded to the governor-general, with their full support, a recommendation from Trant that the breeding operations at Pusa (which he had
not even visited) should be abandoned as soon as possible and new *zamindari*
breeding circles set up further west at Meerut, Bareilly and Moorshedabad.[36]
Trant actually told poor de l'Étang, the recently appointed riding master at
Hajipur, that he should look for a new job while the going was good and he
thereupon briefly entered the service of the Nawab Vizier at Lucknow.[37] It was
plain that this time the beleaguered Moorcroft was fighting his corner
practically alone, apart, of course, from the loyal support of his friends in
Calcutta, like the Palmers.

In the event he did it superbly well. He had been working on a radical plan
for reorganization at the stud for many months.[38] Now he brought those plans
and a spirited defence of all he had done together into a major work entitled
Observations on the Breeding of Horses[39] which he completed at Calcutta in March
1814. It was a minor classic. The government printed it at the time and
reprinted it forty years later when the studs were again in crisis. It was never
published but almost all who came across it have acclaimed it as a *tour de force*.
In print it runs to fifty-five closely set pages and is written in a very effective
staccato style much closer to that of Dickens's Mr Jingle than its author's usual
tangled sentences. Moorcroft provided a magisterial survey of the history of
the stud and the rationale behind his own work there, but he also looked much
further: at the history of Indian breeding and the Asian horse trade; at the
immense constraints on horse-breeding resulting from India's geography,
history, climate, society and culture; and at the consequently rapid decline in
the quality of successive generations of animals. All the evidence showed, he
concluded, 'the right method of managing horse-breeding never yet to have
been adopted. It indicates the necessity of taking better measures, or . . .
quitting the pursuit. It is conclusive against the mode, but not against the
object. Through a different mode the object may be attained.' It was skilfully
done. He disarmed those who attacked the stud by agreeing with them.

So what 'different mode' of stud management did he suggest? Inevitably he
returned to his old theme. Without adequate parent-stock the project was
doomed. His Bokhara excursion was a *sine qua non*. He estimated that 500
brood mares and 100 stallions were required and that he could be employed in
no better way than going in search of them. Then,

> After Parent Stock shall have been procured, the next step will be through it to
> connect the interest of the farmer with the benefit of the State. . . . It has been shown
> that the Home Stud is too expensive, and does not extend the practice of breeding.
> That the Nisfee branch extends, but does not improve the race, and that the
> Zumeendaree branch, though it extends, is insecure, and subject to be checked.

A new system was required which would give the advantages of each branch
without its disadvantages. The essence of the new system would be breeding
by Indians, but rearing by the state.

What he proposed was a system he had been experimenting with ever since
his return from Tibet. It should, he argued, be extended over a great swathe of

territory from Patna up the Ganges as far as Hardwar. Wherever the local mares were inadequate, government mares as well as *zamindari* stallions should be distributed to the native breeders under contract, in the ratio of twenty-five mares to one stallion. They would be closely supervised. The government would have the option of purchasing all suitable offspring, when twelve months old, at scale prices determined according to quality. The colts would be kept in training-depots till old enough for the cavalry and the fillies would make up new breeding circles. Despite doubts about the healthiness of Pusa and Hajipur, the prohibitive cost of acquiring and developing new depots made it unavoidable that both places should be kept as training-depots for the colts until they were 2 years old. Ghazipur would take them at 2 and train them either for the cavalry or for the market. Finally, Moorcroft suggested that, before extensive breeding was attempted in the remoter parts of the upper provinces, an experimental colony of horse-breeders should be set up on government lands in Hariana, north-west of Delhi. He, of course, should visit the area as soon as possible and report.

While Moorcroft was down in Calcutta, assembling all this information into what amounted to a small book, Trant was outflanking him at Pusa and Hajipur. He seems to have made little effort to conceal his criticisms of Moorcroft in front of the assistants,[40] and was certainly outspokenly critical of him in his reports. His high praise for de l'Étang and Gibb was in eloquent contrast. Trant was emphatic that all unsuitable animals should be cleared from Pusa and Hajipur at once, whether Moorcroft was there to superintend the operation or not, and before long he was also recommending that both Pusa and Hajipur should be sold off as quickly as possible.[41] By the time Moorcroft submitted his *Observations* to the other members of the board, they had already committed themselves to Trant's recommendations. They were willing to endorse Moorcroft's broad strategy of extending breeding on a revised circle system westwards, but they differed sharply from him, both about the speed of the disposal of the unsuitable animals and, even more, over the question of abandoning Pusa and Hajipur.[42] Moorcroft would certainly have resisted hasty disposal of the two estates. Indeed when he had left Pusa a few months before, the stock was so healthy that he was inclined to think that the disease problem there had been finally resolved. He was wrong. In mid-April 1814 news arrived in Calcutta of an extensive outbreak of disease both at Pusa and Hajipur. Moorcroft was shaken into a reluctant change of opinion which he put on record on 15 April. He had what seems to have been an aimiable dinner with his antagonist, Sir George Nugent, and then, tearing himself away from the congenial society of his Calcutta friends, hurried back up the river to Pusa.[43]

The reaction of one of these friends, John Palmer, who was head of Calcutta's most successful agency house, provides a revealing postscript to Moorcroft's few months in Calcutta. He wrote:

We are not insensible of the pleasure derived from your society though I find all opinion that you were coquetish in dispensing it so rarely. I do assure you that for several days after you were gone, the complaint was pretty general of a blank being left in our great parties.[44]

Moorcroft was going to need the support of friends like the Palmers. His war at the stud was only just beginning.

As soon as he was back at Pusa, coping with unprecedented losses among the young stock both there and in the surrounding districts, he admitted again that his faith was shaken in the whole idea of keeping a home stud going at Pusa and Hajipur.[45] His opponents did not let him forget that admission. A week or two after his return, Trant and the *ad hoc* committee assembled at Pusa to weed out the unsuitable animals. No doubt much to Trant's discomfiture, the committee's report was an almost unqualified vindication of Moorcroft's management, just as he had predicted. It spoke in the highest terms of the great improvements since he had come to the stud and of the wisdom of his proposals for the future.[46] Trant refused to let Moorcroft even see a copy of this (for him) embarrassing document, despite an explicit order to the contrary by the governor-general the previous year.[47] No wonder! For while Moorcroft had been hurrying back from Calcutta a few weeks earlier, he would have been passed in the other direction by a very long and frank letter from Trant to the board.[48] It endorsed the broad strategy outlined in Moorcroft's *Observations* and conceded that his zeal, talents and exertions were worthy but. . . . It was a big 'but' which took Trant, as he admitted, on to ground of 'a delicate nature'. Moorcroft, he hinted, was unsuitable for the task facing the stud. Next time the superintendent should not be a man from outside who was totally ignorant of the languages and customs of India. As for Moorcroft's 'researches in foreign countries' and his repeated proposal to go and seek parent-stock in the far north, Trant reminded the board that many of his 'speculations' have already proved 'impracticable'. 'I admire the intrepidity and honest zeal which prompted Mr. Moorcroft to such an undertaking,' he added. 'But even if danger were out of the case I do not think that the interests of our Institution would be best promoted by it.'

In the middle monsoon months of 1814, there followed an ominous silence from Calcutta while the bureaucratic machine (itself running far from smoothly because of rankling personal animosities resulting from the appointment of the new governor-general) ponderously digested this mountain of incompatible judgements and recommendations concerning the stud. Moorcroft, being himself, did not sit on his verandah waiting for the outcome. Despite the heat and the rain he was out and about, ranging over the breeding-districts, buying colts and opening negotiations with the breeders and company officials further up the river and south of it, in case his recommended extensions of a modified *zamindari* scheme in that direction were approved. He had every reason to suppose they would be, since Trant himself had encouraged him to embark on this work. Tangled and lengthy memoranda, reporting his activities and detailed proposals, came pouring into the board. They included the renewed suggestion that he should, with Mir Izzat-Allah, make a curving reconnaissance north-west of Delhi into Hariana and the edge of the Rajasthan desert, returning by way of Bareilly and Lucknow and buying every suitable horse he came across along the way.[49]

In the middle of August 1814, probably at Patna, Moorcroft waited on the new governor-general who was making his first tour up-country. It was Trant who seems to have suggested that Moorcroft should see the blunt, heavy-jowled old soldier, both to review affairs at the stud and to seek Lord Hastings' formal permission to make the Hariana journey. Moorcroft seems to have charmed him as nearly every other man he ever met. The two men certainly had much in common – a love of practical agriculture, dynamic energy and a steely determination to assert British interests wherever it seemed possible to do so.[50] And that included parts of Nepal. Very much on Hastings' mind at this time was his impending war with that country in the wake of the Gurkha atrocities at Butwal. The man he was talking to knew Butwal and the geography of some of the Nepalese possessions in the hills of Kumaon and Garhwal from personal experience, had investigated the trans-Himalayan shawl trade and had very strong ideas of his own about the desirability of replacing Gurkha oppression in those hills with British rule. That these ideas rubbed off on Lord Hastings is, as has been seen, beyond argument. The two men must also have talked about Moorcroft's Bokhara dream because, a few weeks later when Hastings reached Benares, he received from Moorcroft a request for permission to reply to the friendly letters he had just received from the chiefs of Kabul and Balkh beyond the Hindu Kush offering him safe conducts through their territories. Yes, was the reply. The more immediate foray into Hariana and Rajasthan was also approved.[51]

Moorcroft must have thought that things were looking up when he received this letter on 7 September. A day or two later, a rather different future was sketched for him in a brutally short letter from Calcutta. It said quite baldly that it would be unwise for him to plan any journey to the north-west since the authorities were contemplating the complete abolition of the existing studs![52] Moorcroft must have doubted the evidence of his eyes, but it was all too true.

On 25 August, probably less than a week after Moorcroft had his encouraging meeting with Lord Hastings, Trant and his three colleagues on the board had recommended to the government, with a huge dossier of supporting documents, that all attempts to breed or rear horses in the existing stud depots, even on Moorcroft's modified plan, should be abandoned. Health considerations apart, the cost was unjustifiable when adequate supplies could still be obtained by importation. Citing Adam Smith's well-known example of grapes grown in Scotland which were good but more costly than foreign alternatives, they argued that the 100 colts recently supplied to the cavalry by the stud were 'somewhat in the predicament of wine made in Scotland'. Just how costly the stud horses were was explained by Trant in an apparently damning minute, based on what must have been considerable research in the board's archives. In all the years since the foundation of the stud, he calculated, the 1296 stud horses supplied to the cavalry had cost 1 million rupees more than the realizable assets which were then available, and that took no account of the cost of Moorcroft's latest rash of proposals. Trant calculated, with considerable exaggeration, that these would amount to another 3 lakhs (300,000) rupees a year. It was time, in his and the board's view, to stop throwing good money after bad. Pusa and Hajipur should be summarily disposed of, Ghazipur retained as a cavalry-training depot only, and some simple, modi-fied *zamindari* scheme, by which local breeders should have the use of government stallions in return for a fair price for the resulting foals, should be introduced further west.

Two of the three ordinary members of the board at least had the grace to record generous praise for Moorcroft's efforts and abilities.[53] Trant did not. On the contrary, he laid much of the blame for what had happened at Moorcroft's door and then damned him further with the barbed excuse that 'of course [he] laboured under great disadvantages from his ignorance of the language, the manners and customs of this country, the nature of the climate and the peculiar diseases of horses, therefore it is not surprising that his course of practice exhibits a degree of changeableness'! As for Moorcroft's latest plans to visit Hariana, never mind Bokhara, Trant confessed that he did not 'wish Mr. Moorcroft to go very far from home in the present state of our Establishment'.[54]

It is much easier for us to see what had happened than it would have been for Moorcroft at the time. In the first place, the long years of peace since Lord Wellesley's time had so much diminished the cavalry's remount needs that they were now 'inconsiderable'.[55] Second, the unremitting pressure from London for financial retrenchment in India had coincided with the soaring costs at the stud which inevitably accompanied Moorcroft's whirlwind re-forming and innovatory activity there. And third, there was the devastating effect of widespread disease among the stud animals in 1814. Together, these developments all converged to raise again the question which had been asked of the breeding operation in Frazer's day: was it all worth it? Trant's researches had made him well aware of the earlier crisis and he used that knowledge with telling effect now. Not only did he recall Lord Lake's attempt to abolish the stud in 1807, but he re-examined the apparently cogent arguments of Thomas Graham which had saved it. The board made good use of Graham's ringing prophecy that the stud would fulfil all its objects in five more years. That, it noted drily, had been written seven and a half years ago.[56] The more recent optimism of the latest committee of inspection could be discounted in exactly the same way. The stud records were strewn with optimistic forecasts by inspecting committees.

There is no doubt that the blow was much more powerful and better aimed than in Frazer's day. Its timing was well-nigh perfect. This time there was nobody of Graham's ability to fight for the stud from within the board. Indeed, the members seem to have been united in their determination to destroy it in its present form. Moreover the council, to whom their sweeping recommen-dations were sent, was, in the absence of Hastings up-country, under the chairmanship of Sir George Nugent. He, as commander-in-chief, had already made his own position clear and he ran true to form now. 'I consider,' he minuted, '. . . the Company's Stud in this country, on the footing it has hitherto stood as not only an useless expense but founded on an erroneous principle. The sooner it is abolished the better. . . .' The other two council members present, Seton and Edmonstone, broadly agreed with him as usual. Shortly before Christmas 1814, therefore, the enormous dossier on 'this highly interesting and important subject' was posted off up-country to Lord Hastings with a strong recommendation for abolition.[57] At the same time, and quite unknown to Moorcroft, many of these highly critical papers were sent home officially for the eye of the company directors in London.[58]

Moorcroft of course was, by now, well aware that a major assault was being mounted on his work and reputation, but he was not sent any of the board's statements, and papers were withheld from him even when he asked to see them. Not surprisingly he became convinced that he was the victim of a conspiracy by the board to keep him in the dark and prevent his own views reaching the ears of government. Trant, he believed, had deliberately misled him, for he had encouraged him to seek the governor-general's approval for his schemes at the very time when he must have been preparing to sabotage them. Moorcroft was outraged. He fired off an understandable, but very ill-advised, private letter to Trant which more or less accused him of naked duplicity.[59] Palmer was horrified when he heard of it and, ever the peacemaker, hastened to soothe his friend's ruffled feelings as tactfully as he could:

> A mind so ardent as yours, does I see sometimes fly into extremes and a possible event engenders an extravagant conclusion. I cannot suspect that the Stud will be suddenly broke up or that you shall ever become an useless pensioner.

Moorcroft, for all his pugnacity, was not so sure. Indeed he even began sounding Palmer as to the possibility of buying a partnership in the Palmer agency house. John Palmer, who knew Moorcroft better than he knew himself, was quick to scotch such a notion. The work, he reminded Moorcroft, involved much 'hateful' poring over ledgers and 'a capacity for continued sedentary labour'. That was not Moorcroft at all. A much more suitable occupation for him, in Palmer's opinion, would have been managing a string of indigo plantations or developing a great caravan trade with the far north-west, but he was sure that none of this would be necessary. Sit tight and put your trust in Lord Hastings was the gist of his advice.[60]

Fortunately that was all the easier to do because, just at that time, some absorbing distractions from stud worries were suddenly provided by the outbreak of the war with Nepal, just across the border to the north of Pusa.[61] To Moorcroft it was something of a godsend.

14 WAR IN NEPAL AND VICTORY
AT THE STUD,
OCTOBER 1814–MAY 1819

THE COLD WEATHER months of late 1814 and early 1815, spent mostly at Hajipur, were an uncomfortable limbo period for Moorcroft, as he waited for decisions about the future of the stud – his own future – which never came. The silence in Calcutta was deafening. Moorcroft could not even get authority from the board, sometimes after three requests, to carry out pressing and routine stud business, such as distributing stud animals to the breeders, or purchasing *zamindari* colts in the districts before the itinerant horse-dealers pre-empted him and spirited the best of the young animals away across the borders before the Hajipur fair even took place. Finally, pleading stark necessity, he set out without authority on a dash westwards up the Ganges in late October 1814, buying colts on government credit as far as Benares.[1] Then he posted *dak* back to Hajipur, which he reached on the night of 19 November, just in time for some important meetings.

Those meetings concerned the war with the Gurkhas. Just before Lord Hastings had set out on his tour up the Ganges in early June 1814, he had received news of the murder of company policemen on the Nepal border at Butwal. This deliberate outrage made war with Nepal almost unavoidable, once the monsoon was over. Later at about the time he reached Patna in late August 1814 and had his meeting with Moorcroft, Hastings received a thoroughly unsatisfactory reply from the raja at Katmandu. Separate military columns were hastily assembled on the east of the plains for a simultaneous, four-pronged drive into the hills, and a frenetic search for maps, routes and information was launched to guide them in what was virtually unknown terrain. In all this Moorcroft, like his friend Hearsey, had a crucial part to play. Not only was he one of the very few Englishmen to have penetrated the hills of Nepal, but he had deliberately maintained his medical, botanical, commercial and intelligence contacts across the terai ever since. Lord Hastings must have impressed on him the urgency of the situation, for their meeting was followed by a flurry of activity by Moorcroft which he reported in a busy spate of letters, posted off after the governor-general as he proceeded slowly on up the river.[2]

Moorcroft's usual boyish enthusiasm for any novel adventure outside the routine of everyday business was clearly reinforced, on this occasion, by his loathing for the misrule of the Gurkhas in Kumaon and Garhwal, and his hopes for the increased trade and improvement of the region which would follow their ejection. He recruited informants from among his servants and passing horse-traders, wandering fakirs, local indigo planters and well-connected Nepali exiles living near the frontier; he despatched his servants in all directions on confidential missions; and he began to compile a dossier of routes and sketch-maps to aid the invading armies. Central to all this intelligence-gathering was a Kashmiri merchant from Patna called Ahmad Ali. Moorcroft had already enlisted this man's trading connections with Katmandu, in an attempt to introduce vaccination across the Himalayas, as he had promised to do on his 1812 journey. Now he had several highly secret meetings alone with Ahmad Ali, watching him carefully for any betraying gesture or suggestion that he was lying. It was vital to guard against treachery, for a false guide could lead an army into a time-wasting cul-de-sac in those everlasting green hills or, worse, into an annihilating ambush. Moreover, the Gurkhas had an evil reputation for personal reprisals, which could have been a powerful lever on a man like Ahmad Ali whose livelihood was earned from trade with Nepal and who lived close to its borders. Moorcroft seems to have torn himself away from all this with the greatest reluctance when he made his horse-purchasing dash through the districts to Benares late in October. Now he took it up again with enthusiasm, as soon as he got back to Hajipur on 19 November.

In early December he received an exciting letter from Major-General Bennet Marley, who was leading the column which was to strike from Dinapur direct towards Katmandu. Marley, whose hesitant conduct in this campaign was to lead to swift disgrace and obscurity, was very anxious about the deficiencies of his column and the difficulties of the tasks it had to perform. His request to Moorcroft was simple. Would he, as quickly as possible, raise a force of irregular cavalry to act as auxiliaries to the main column? 'My answer of course was immediately affirmative.'[3] Of course. Moorcroft threw himself into part-time soldiering with the same sort of enthusiasm he had shown in the Westminster Volunteers fifteen years before.[4] He chose sixty mares from the stock at Pusa and offered 8 rupees a month to any willing to join him. Dipping deep into his own pocket he placed orders for lances and saddlery, borrowed police pistols till more suitable replacements could be found, and pressed the craftsmen on the Hajipur estate into service to make cartouche boxes, uniforms and boots. Later he offered to raise a corps of pikemen, and recruited the help of the raja of nearby Bhojpur to raise 400 infantrymen as well. On 10 March 1815, the very day that he had arranged to muster and review this little private army, orders arrived that all but the mounted troops were to be disbanded and paid off. Moorcroft's cavalry subsequently performed very useful service in support of Colonel Gregory's sweep to clear the Gurkhas from the borderlands to the north of Patna.

Moorcroft did not go with them. Probably the only thing that stopped him was the continuing uncertainty hanging over the stud. For him, war with the Gurkhas was not the only war to be fought early in 1815. That in defence of the stud was all the more unnerving for being at this time largely a silent war. Eventually, smarting under a burning sense of injustice at the 'grievous attacks' on his reputation,[5] which he claimed were undermining his health, and, deeply concerned at the ill-consequences of continued delay, he went on the offensive in January and February. The blistering letters which he then fired off to the board were, commented Trant, written 'under the violent influence of passion'.[6] They certainly were. The board found them 'very objectionable' and the supreme council read with 'great displeasure the offensive and insubordinate tone and style of Mr. Moorcroft's remarks. . . . The asperity of sarcasm and the levity of humour can never correctly find a place in public correspondence'.[7] Even Moorcroft's well-wishers were appalled. Palmer gently chided him for correspondence that was 'more pithy than prudently measured . . . more perfectly right, than cunningly discreet'.[8] It is all true – but for once Moorcroft's official letters make splendid reading.[9]

On the very first day of 1815, he had tried to bring matters to a head by seeking authority to press on with all the plans he had proposed earlier. When he heard that Trant had recently proposed closing down Hajipur and transferring its stock to Ghazipur, he commented acidly:

> The President has lately recommended the abolition of the Stud. The President now recommends provisions for its continuance. With great deference I beg permission to observe that provisions devised for the benefit of the Stud by the very persons who have just devoted the Stud itself to destruction assume a dubious character and constitute an anomaly almost without parallel in modern economics.

The rest of the board were also in his sights, and particularly their claim to know better than he what sort of animals were required for stud-breeding. On 20 January he was calling them (not very obliquely) 'those hypocrites in horse affairs, who admiring a particular kind of horse for their own use, recommend it also for military service', when they had not even seen the mares of the districts nor given the stud more than the most cursory inspection.

Obviously Moorcroft had almost had enough. In January he was talking about going overland to Europe to pick up the low-priced, disabled animals which should be available in the wake of the Napoleonic wars. In February he offered to resign if someone more suitable were available. Finally on 20 February he recapitulated the events of the past few months as he saw them. He was clearly still very angry indeed, but in his efforts to hold himself in check, slipped once again into the pithy, staccato style of the *Observations*. And very effective it is. Practically every sentence is a paragraph and every paragraph an accusation. It merits quotation at length.

> *Alone*, I advocate the cause of the Stud against a board deputed to watch over its interests but who aim at its destruction. . . . I have wished to draw the attention of the Board to points they may have overlooked. My observations have been laid on the shelf.
> I am called to severe account for transactions to which I have not been privy.
> I have been exposed by the Board to the reproof of the Government for taking a

responsibility imposed on me by the conduct of the Board themselves. I ask for information. It is withheld. I send facts and evidence. They are suppressed.

The measures I propose are shorn of their merit for want of proper agents to execute them.

I see the affairs of the Stud, and through them the public interest, exposed to injury and by every exertion in my power I strive to avert it. I see the young stock of the District, raised at much public expense, carried off as a remount to the reputed enemies of the State. I see private adventurers enriched by selling the District colts and fillies.

I make representations to the Board but they are disregarded. . . .

The Board think that the Stud will fail under any measures.

I think that the Stud will succeed through measures of vigour.

The competency in one party must be questioned.

One must be wrong.

But there Moorcroft himself was wrong. It was hardly his fault. He was so reprehensibly starved of information about what was being planned at Calcutta, that he genuinely believed that all government breeding operations were to be abandoned. They were not. The board certainly wished to abandon Pusa and Hajipur, but in all other matters were really not very far from the position which Moorcroft had advocated in his *Observations* the previous year. Many of the apparent disagreements were more the result of misunderstandings, personal antipathies and the 300 miles (480 kilometres) which separated Pusa from the presidency capital, than of genuine differences. To the uninvolved observer – and Lord Hastings, physically removed from both Pusa and Calcutta, was certainly that – the broad, strategic, common ground between Moorcroft and the board must have seemed very much greater than the tactical differences which divided them. Despite the intense preoccupations which must have burdened him in the wake of the first unsuccessful winter campaigns against Nepal, his arbitral judgement on the future of the stud in mid-March 1815, took its stand firmly on that middle ground.[10] It is significant, however, that in nearly all the disputed fringe matters he supported Moorcroft against the board.

Pusa and Hajipur were to be closed and the horses either sold, or drafted into the new breeding-circles which would be established further up the river along the lines suggested by Moorcroft in the *Observations*. The yearling colts (although not the fillies) would be trained for the cavalry at Ghazipur and an experimental breeding-stud would be set up in Hariana, mainly to produce stud stallions. These were to be the broad outlines of future development and within them Moorcroft and the board together were to hammer out an agreed set of detailed proposals for Lord Hastings' final approval. Nothing was said about any Moorcroftian initiatives further north-west along the road to Bokhara.

It took another fourteen months of lengthy (and not always polite) correspondence as well as face-to-face discussion at Calcutta, before the final decisions about the future of the stud were approved in May 1816. By then the differences still remaining between Moorcroft and the board had been narrowed essentially to two. First, Moorcroft had become convinced by the new healthiness of the animals at Pusa and Hajipur, and his successful and extensive oat cultivation at both places, that his hasty agreement to their closure the previous year had been wrong from every point of view. Now, instead of the hasty run-down which the board favoured, he wanted both places to be retained, at least until the new breeding-circles further west were properly established. Moorcroft had already seen enough evidence that *bursati* and *kumri* were not confined to the area round Pusa, to suggest great caution before all the investment in the older depots was written off and vast new expense incurred further up-river. Second, he was convinced that one assistant could not properly supervise both the new breeding-circles and the new depots that would serve them, as the board believed. He wanted two men in each place – and an extra man at Pusa and at Hajipur as well.[11]

Despite these smouldering disagreements Moorcroft must have felt, in the summer and autumn of 1815, that things were at last beginning to look up. It was some time in that same summer that Purree Khanum became pregnant.

Then, on the afternoon of 16 September, the long-awaited flotilla bringing Lord Hastings back down the Ganges to Calcutta, turned aside up the Great Gandak River and anchored opposite Hajipur. 'The scenery was beautiful,' Hastings noted. 'The width of the river, and its turnings, gave our anchorage the appearance of being in a large lake.' Moorcroft would have been waiting to welcome him on the landing-stage and to act as his guide and host during the visits of inspection to the stud which he made during the next three days. That first evening Moorcroft entertained the governor-general and his party together with a large number of his friends from Patna, to dinner. Next morning soon after dawn Hastings was ashore once again with Moorcroft, watching a large number of the 2-year-old colts and fillies led past. The old soldier was very favourably impressed by all he saw and by the potential of Moorcroft's new modified *zamindari* circles. Through them, he thought, there was a good prospect 'of securing a remount of horses sufficiently strong for the cavalry, so as not to be left to precarious dependence on neighbouring countries which at best rarely send to us horses of adequate bone'.[12]

That of course was the original *raison d'être* of the breeding operations, and it remained Moorcroft's best guarantee of continuing employment at the stud for as long as he wanted it. The years of peace in India were over and, once again, the demand for cavalry horses was beginning to outstrip the supply. In the very month that Hastings was writing those words in his diary, seventy-one horses, out of 111 purchased on the open market by military commissariat agents for a cavalry regiment at Agra, were rejected as unfit for service.[13] Just a month or two later, the commander-in-chief was recording his concern at the dearth of suitable animals.[14]

Exactly the same view was taken in London, when Calcutta's unchallenged condemnation of Moorcroft's work arrived in Leadenhall Street and abolition was in the air once more. The military secretary at East India House put the problem best of all on 7 February 1816:

The Court of Directors will perhaps be of opinion that nothing short of an almost physical impossibility of ultimate success could justify the rulers of probably the second Empire in the world, estimated by its population, in abandoning a project upon which the safety of that population may, and probably will, at no distant period, entirely depend.[15]

The writer was thinking chiefly of defence against enemies beyond the north-west frontier. But war nearer at home against the Pindaris and Marathas, who were both masters of irregular cavalry and rapid movement, was looking more and more likely in 1816. It came less than a year later.

All in all, Moorcroft must have been feeling much more cheerful after the successful visit of Lord Hastings. There could hardly be another attack on his work and reputation by a hostile board and council acting in combination once the governor-general was back in Calcutta.

Besides, Moorcroft had other claims on the governor-general's goodwill. During Lord Hastings' last morning ashore at Hajipur Moorcroft slipped into the hand of John Adam, secretary of the Political and Secret Department, a letter in Persian from Ahmad Ali who had been so valuable an informant the previous year. Moorcroft suggested, as a reward for the Kashmiri's loyalty and as compensation for the heavy losses he had sustained as a result of the Nepal war, that he should be used secretly by the government to explore the feasibility of opening up trade links with Lhasa. Hastings accepted the proposal with surprising alacrity, appointing Moorcroft to supervise the whole 'adventure' in view of 'the attention which you have given to this subject and the general knowledge you have acquired of the commerce of Tibet and the adjoining countries, combined . . . with your zeal and public spirit'.[16]

There was more good news in September and October 1815. In September, Moorcroft at last received the permission he had been seeking for months, to follow the governor-general down to Calcutta after the fair, to discuss the remaining details about the stud's future with the board face to face.[17] In October Colonel Fagan, the longest-serving member of the board, visited Pusa for the first time in seven years and was so impressed by the health of the animals and everything else he saw there, that he apologized to Moorcroft for the board's attack on his work and agreed to support Moorcroft's opposition to any over-hasty disposal of the estate and its livestock. Fagan even seems to have been won over to the Bokhara scheme.[18] Shortly afterwards came the marvellous news that Trant was resigning from the board and would be replaced as president by the now well-disposed Colonel Fagan.[19] Moorcroft completed his work at the Hajipur fair for another year and, leaving Purree Khanum to face the wearisome final months of her pregnancy without him, set off down the river with twenty-eight horses for the Calcutta market in early November.

He was clearly feeling very much more confident. On 13 November 1815 he revived the Bokhara scheme once more. The extended new *zamindari* scheme, he argued, required a major infusion of new parent-stock. Mir Izzat-Allah had reported conclusively that suitable animals were readily obtainable along the distant River Oxus, in quantity and at the right price. Once the new system was established, therefore, Moorcroft proposed that he should go and buy them.

> Under a conviction that in no other way can my services be more useful to the . . . object of my mission . . . I wish to employ the few years of activity I may possess as usefully as possible. . . . I ask no increase in allowances, I am anxious that the Government should receive value for those I already possess and which I fear has not hitherto been thought to have been the case.[20]

Again on 29 November, shortly before he reached Calcutta, he produced more detailed arguments to justify the Bokhara journey and on the same day Fagan supported him at the board. Two of the others, however, emphatically did not.[21] Not all his troubles in that quarter were over just yet.

However his much looked forward to five months in Calcutta began promisingly enough. On 1 December Moorcroft was in the Calcutta sale ring watching as Mr Edwards called the bids for the stud horses he had brought down with him. Moorcroft must have been hard put to keep a smile off his face. Just as he had anticipated, the very high prices fetched made a nonsense of the sort of crude *per capita* valuation which Trant had used to attack the economic credibility of the whole stud operation.[22]

A few days later the governor-general in council ruled in some of the matters still in dispute between Moorcroft and the board. The decision to dispose of Pusa and Hajipur was deferred once again, but Moorcroft certainly lost his battle over the number of assistants to supervise the new breeding-circles. Only two were to be appointed to supervise the new *zamindari* districts instead of the four he wanted, and none at all were allowed for Hajipur and Ghazipur.[23] To add insult to injury, Moorcroft learned that one of the new assistants was to be that same Captain William Dickson who had caused him such trouble six or seven years before.[24] The other, Captain John Hunter, was to cause him even more. The next blow came on 5 February with the resignation from the board of Colonel Fagan, claiming that he differed fundamentally from the rest of his board colleagues about the future shape of the stud.[25] Whether it was that news, or because of what happened at a long board meeting which Moorcroft attended on 9 February 1816, is not clear, but a few days later he too seemed ready to resign.

> Adverting to what has happened during one half of the period of my residing in India, to what is gradually developing, and to what it most probably will lead, if His Excellency the Governor-General in Council should think that the little ability I may possess likely to be useful in any other branch of the Service, I would receive the change with sentiments of the most profound gratitude.[26]

It was remarks like this which later led to the belief among some of his colleagues, a belief Moorcroft firmly denied, that he was trying to carve out a niche for himself in the political service. He was certainly still pursuing dreams of trans-Himalayan trade and adventure at this time. On 17 February he wrote to the Political and Secret Department with further suggestions about the Lhasa scheme. Five days later he was broaching an entirely different proposal, by which a fakir in his service should be sent with gifts to Moorcroft's Tibetan friends at Daba and Gartok and obtain from them the Tibetan books and alphabets which were being sought by the remarkable Baptist missionaries and scholars, Carey and Marshman, before going on to the forbidden city of Lhasa.[27] It is not hard to see why one of Moorcroft's would-be biographers believed that he was a secret agent and spymaster. He was not but he often behaved like one.

On the same day he was locked again in another marathon meeting with the board. The whole vexed question of the disposal of Pusa and Hajipur and the purchase and building of elaborate new depots in the districts was under discussion once more. Moorcroft, of course, was becoming more and more determinedly opposed to both. He urged again the value and healthiness of the older depots, the cost and risks of building new ones elsewhere and the sheer impossibility that one assistant could give proper supervision both to a depot and to an extensive breeding-district round it. The board opposed Moorcroft at every point, reminding him of his earlier (and shortlived) belief in April 1814, in the wake of unprecedented but equally shortlived epidemic disease at Pusa and Hajipur, that both would have to go. He seems to have left the meeting seething, although the board later claimed to believe that he was in full agreement with all that it was proposing.[28]

What finally brought him to explosion point once more, at the end of February, was the arrival of a personal letter from his former friend and well-wisher in London, Edward Parry. It makes scorching reading even today. 'Dear Sir' was almost the only polite sentiment in the whole letter and its effects on Moorcroft can be easily imagined. Barely eighteen months earlier Parry had been full of praise for Moorcroft, optimistic for the stud and pleased at the successful purchase of the Tibetan shawl goats. Now he wrote with frustrated self-pity because of what he regarded as Moorcroft's neglect of all his efforts to acquire horses in England, and anger at what (on the one-sided evidence he had received from Calcutta) he regarded as Moorcroft's neglect and maladministration. All in all, he wrote, it is 'a very deplorable picture. . . . I always thought you set out upon a wrong system . . . your letters are full of extraneous matter – such as goats, shawl wool etc which never can answer . . . great blame must attach to you in the failure of the late plan'. And so it went on.[29]

Moorcroft was appalled, as much at the extent of Parry's bitter misconceptions as at the treachery of the board which had created them. His reputation in London had been destroyed. Indeed it seems that Parry only prevented the other East India directors from sending a crushing official rebuke, with the greatest difficulty. Moorcroft first sought the advice of council members like Seton and Edmonstone and obtained from them permission to send home in the official bag, a lengthy private letter to Parry attempting to set the record straight.[30] That was sensible. Much less so, although understandable enough in the circumstances, was the bitter and reckless official letter which he unleashed on the members of the board. He blamed it and its late president, William Trant, for all the failures and delays in the past, and for their attempt to sabotage the future by the over-hasty disposal of Pusa and Hajipur and the inadequate provision of assistants to supervise the new breeding-districts. He even urged, once again, the Bokhara journey and the urgent need for new parent stock, although surely without any hope of a sympathetic hearing. Indeed it is very hard to imagine what Moorcroft hoped to achieve by such a letter except the release of his own pent-up frustration and anger. All he got for his pains was even more personal criticism from the board.

> Mr. Moorcroft's frequent failures warrant the supposition that he was inadequate on his first arrival. . . . The Board has every reason to hope that his future labours will be more successful, provided he is kept steady in their pursuit . . . and not allowed to waste his time in . . . wild and romantick excursions to the banks of the Amoo and the plains of Chinese Tartary or in a fanciful overland trip through Vienna to Paris for the purpose of importing . . . the rejected and reduced horses of the French and Austrian cavalry.[31]

He asked for it. In due course there also followed an inevitable letter from the governor-general in council condemning Moorcroft's 'improper . . . disrespectful and totally indefensible' language. We shall never know whether it was carelessness by one of the copy clerks or a desire to see justice done which led to the word 'indefensible' being rendered as 'indispensable' in the copies sent home to London![32] It did not make much difference of course. On 31 May 1816, the governor-general resolved every remaining disputed issue in the board's favour against the views of the stud superintendent.[33]

By then Moorcroft was back in Hajipur, travelling *dak* ostensibly on the grounds of public necessity, but doubtless with another pressing reason for haste as well. And at Hajipur, on the verandah of the thatched bungalow constructed of stout tar trees which he had built there at his own expense,[34] he at last met his first child. By April 1816 she was already three months old. He called her Anne, perhaps after her paternal grandmother in faraway Dublin.

That must have been about the best thing that happened to him in the troubled year of 1816 as the peevish, tetchy, lengthy letters began to pass between him and the board once more. It criticized his accounts, insisted on an early closure of the Hajipur estate, returned letters to him when he did not stick to the point and flatly disagreed with his suggestions for a document (which all agreed was necessary) to define and delimit the respective roles and powers of board and superintendent.[35] In September another irritable letter from Parry reached Moorcroft with the news that the directors were all 'angry with him . . . for deviating so widely from the instructions laid down . . . and running after goat's wool etc etc. *Horse breeding* . . . has thereby suffered so materially that almost the whole of your time appears to have been nearly wasted.'[36] On top of all this Moorcroft had to be away from his young family and on the move as never before. He reckoned that in the twelve months after his return from Calcutta he spent no more than a fortnight at any one time under a solid roof. The main reason of course was to choose suitable sites for the two new breeding-depots. He then had to negotiate for their purchase or acquisition, put in hand the necessary building operations and set up all the arrangements with the breeders in the new breeding-circles around them. Before and during the Hajipur fair in October 1816 he was also buying young stock from the older districts as usual. Another important new requirement was to find suitable land for oat cultivation to supply the new circles and depots in place of the Hajipur and, eventually presumably, the Pusa estates. It was that need which in late April and May 1817 took Moorcroft on a long journey south of the Ganges with the local collector to look at government land in the Shahabad district.[37] And one day he found himself on the summit of the stupendous fortified mound of Rohtasgurh, 23 miles (36.8 kilometres) in circumference, which heaves itself up nearly 700 vertical feet (213 metres) above the baking plain of Bihar and overlooks the Son River about 80 miles (128 kilometres) south-east of Benares.

There, no doubt breathless after the precipitous scramble up the decaying and overgrown road which climbs the cliffs to the airy summit, he found decayed palaces and religious buildings, half buried in an encroaching forest of mango and tamarind, choked canals and lakes, and dried-up ponds and fountains. More to the point he found a rich soil, all the materials needed for enclosures and buildings and a readily available labour-force in the villagers and herdsmen who lived on the mountain-top. All this land was in the ownership of the government, available to the stud at a peppercorn rent for at least five years. The only apparent snag was that it had an evil reputation for unhealthiness, but Moorcroft was convinced that clearance and proper drainage would soon take care of that. His mind must have raced. Here was a challenge to delight any agricultural improver. Up here, without encroaching neighbours, he could pasture and feed immense numbers of animals, conduct his experiments into disease and grow enough fodder crops to supply the needs of the new circle depots. From the bottom of the mountain these could be conveyed to the new depots down the Son and up the Ganges by water.[38] Besides, now that Captains Hunter and Dickson were in post in the new depots and districts, his continuous presence there was no longer required. Pusa was under threat and Moorcroft's first real home at Hajipur was now already sold up. Some of the empty apartments in the royal palace of Sher Shah with spectacular views out across the vast plain to the north and east would make a (literally) royal home for Purree Khanum and little Anne. For him too. The punishing nomadic regime of the last few years was beginning to sap even his superhuman energy and health. He sometimes used to refer to his long expeditions of 1811 and 1812 as his first and second journeys, but the truth is that his life at the stud was one continuous journey, punctuated by only brief periods in one place. Now, in the spring of 1817, after a bout of recurrent high fever and a curious nervous insomnia, Moorcroft for once seems to have been tempted by the prospect of settling down. All in all Rohtasgurh must have seemed irresistible.

On 18 May 1817 he composed an enthusiastic letter to the board urging the advantages to be gained by his experimental residence on the top of the great mound. And when they replied with chilly disapproval he pestered them again to such good effect that at last he won a very reluctant assent.[39]

Not that he waited for it of course. He set to work at once, with all the zestful enthusiasm which is one of his most endearing characteristics, to create some sort of habitable dwelling on the summit before the hunching monsoon clouds engulfed it and blotted out those immense vistas. Soon oxen were labouring up the steep flanks of the hill bringing ploughs and seeds. Labourers were hired and some of Moorcroft's apprehensive servants and staff were enticed to live and work there with generous supplies of tobacco, sugar and grain. A European overseer was appointed. Those slumbering, decaying lands and overgrown buildings were soon echoing to the crash of falling timber, the hum of voices, the grunt and creak as wooden ox-ploughs turned the soil. The water began to flow once again in the irrigation channels and reservoirs and in no time at all several hundred acres of oats, grasses and other experimental fodder crops were pushing up out of the fertile soil. Later still came stud horses for experiments on various aspects of disease and diet. Moorcroft even had one of the cumbrous boilers for steaming animal feed dragged across country and up on to the hill-top.[40]

For much of this activity he could only plan and rely upon the work of others. The stud (not to speak of his young daughter) required his presence in Hajipur through the monsoon midsummer months of 1817 as he wound up the estate and disposed of its animals.

His relations with the board remained as frosty as ever. He was just preparing to make his annual appearance at the autumn Hajipur fair, when he was startled to receive a directive limiting his purchases there to animals for direct cavalry admission or for military training at Ghazipur. The yearling produce of the district breeding-circles, however good, he was forbidden to touch. The board's laudable intention was to prevent Moorcroft from outbidding the stud assistants in the districts by paying higher prices for the animals at the fair. But, as Moorcroft pointed out, once the animals had been brought to the fair they would be entirely lost if he did not buy them because the foreign horse-dealers would. Never nicely scrupulous if he believed a vital national interest was at stake, he took advantage of the tiniest ambiguity in the wording of the board's directive to ignore it altogether. He purchased the young stock just as he had always done.[41]

A more serious row blew up at about this time as well.[42] For years, since well before Moorcroft's time, there had been simmering disagreement between board and superintendent about the use of the few thoroughbred animals on the stud registers. The board was always anxious that pure-blood horses should not be widely crossed with half-breeds, not least because it always wanted to raise funds, and the prestige of the stud, by selling some quality bloodstock each year at the Calcutta autumn sales. Moorcroft, on the other hand, regarded the needs of the Calcutta turf and its fine carriages as something of a distraction from his essential task of breeding animals of sufficient bone and size to meet the needs of the cavalry. To that end, he had no compunction at all about diluting his blood strains by judicious crosses with half-breed animals. In the autumn of 1817 the whole issue came to a head when Moorcroft – probably deliberately – sent down animals of such coarseness to Calcutta that the board members hurried to the breeding-registers for an explanation. Their outrage, when they discovered what Moorcroft had been doing with their precious thoroughbreds, can easily be imagined.

They were even more peeved when the autumn mails brought from London the first detailed official reaction to their pessimistic and anti-Moorcroft reports sent home nearly three years before. The view in London was far less critical of the superintendent, and far more hostile to their own views, than they could have expected, not least in this very matter of blood versus bone in breeding for the cavalry. The board's position in this matter was vulnerable, as Moorcroft well knew. If the immensely experienced stud superintendent were not to have full discretion in the choice of breeding crosses, then it was hard to justify his existence at all. Not only did the directors in London take that view, but they also ruled in Moorcroft's favour in the highly contentious matter of keeping a home stud going on the Pusa estate.[43] His long and detailed private letter to Parry had obviously found its mark. The board, of course, simply reiterated its views more defiantly than ever: Pusa was unsuitable; Moorcroft's experiments when he first arrived were unsatisfactory; a home stud was unnecessary. It added, not entirely logically, that it needed a substantial supply of stallions from England, 'a measure which has become more urgently necessary owing to the Superintendent having without consent of the board thrown away the full Blood mares on inferior horses and given the full blood horses to common country mares'.[44]

The despatch from London gave Moorcroft his first opportunity to put his case before the directors officially, and he did not let the opportunity pass. He admitted that he did not know what allegations had been made to London about him, but he spelled out at great length his own problems and aims from the very beginning.[45] It was his most bitter attack yet on the devastating and underhand attacks of the board and of its late president in particular. He was as personal as Trant had been about him. Admitting the 'indelicacy' of such allusions, he hinted darkly that Trant's behaviour and irrational prejudice was the consequence of some unnamed 'previous circumstances in that Gentleman's life . . . for which no blame can attach to him'.

And so 1817, the year of Moorcroft's fiftieth birthday, came to an unhappy end. He, as usual, was on the move and pugnacious as ever. In early December he was at Patna, on Boxing Day at Muzaffarpur, on New Year's Eve at Jalnaggur. He was re-examining these areas where the earliest district breeding had taken place, to confirm his belief that their new dryness and healthiness in recent years justified the retention of Pusa as a depot.[46] That extensive estate, about which he had once briefly despaired, was assuming an almost symbolic importance to him. Later he admitted[47] that he must at this time have 'appeared somewhat contumacious by the obstinacy with which I have adhered to my opinion'. The board would not have accepted the 'somewhat'.

Early in February 1818, at Pusa, he defended that place once again, in a fighting letter which began briskly, 'As far as the Board have permitted me to become acquainted with their ideas for improving the Stud, I am induced to consider them unfitted to circumstances, either existing or prospective . . . specious . . . contrary to the public interest'. He went on at great length, amassing arguments for the retention of Pusa and asking explicitly that these views should be laid before the governor-general in council. They were not. He also requested that, if his arguments did not induce the board to give Pusa a fair trial, then he should be allowed to visit Calcutta and appear before the supreme council to state his case under interrogation and on oath if necessary. The request was ignored.[48]

Moorcroft was certainly obstinate. So was the acting-president of the board and, since Trant's departure, Moorcroft's most outspoken and bitter critic, Henry Wood. In March 1818, he came up-country to sort out some still-unresolved inconsistencies in the stud accounts and inspect the progress that was being made in expanding the new depots and running down the old ones.[49] Moorcroft had a predictably chilly and unhelpful meeting with him at Pusa. Wood was full of praise for Gibb's work there, but he still insisted on its early disposal. He declined Moorcroft's invitation to visit Rohtasgurh, queried some of the expenditures incurred there and curtly told him to withdraw at once the below-standard stud horses he had taken there for experimental purposes. Wood believed that Moorcroft's Rohtasgurh enthusiasm was not merely irrelevant, it actually jeopardized the new plans at the stud.

> I am of opinion that the Superintendent should devote his whole time and attention to the duties which have devolved upon him, without speculating on any new plan. I consider his residence should be as centrical as possible . . . and that instead of corresponding with his Assistants he should communicate with them personally . . . and at all times be in the vicinity of the Depots to afford his aid and assistance when required.[50]

This view Wood reiterated over and over again in his pointedly enthusiastic reports on the progress being made by Moorcroft's assistants in the new depots.[51] To which Moorcroft might have replied that such success was clear proof that his constant attendance was *not* required.

One reason perhaps why he did not so reply was a very serious accident he had just at this time in April 1818. We only know of it at all from Palmer's anxious letter[52] which talks of 'disappointments and misfortunes', 'excruciating pain' from broken bones and dislocations and 'unskilful or unlucky efforts' to repair them by native doctors. Palmer added, revealingly,

> Do make somebody drop me a line to say that bones are socketed and fractures reduced: for the impending trial as to the former is really appalling to me. I know you are a little of a coxcomb in stoicism and have brought yourself to live with smiles in agony of body as mind. . . . My women [his wife and daughters], who really love you Moorcroft, were sadly affected by your accident and have repeated many kind enquiries since: they offer their condolence and good wishes.

Moorcroft was on the move again in June but there was more bad luck to come. While he was out in the breeding-districts, multiple disasters struck at Rohtasgurh. Many of the workmen deserted for higher pay in the army which passed across the plain nearby, work on the estate slowed down and the English manager went sick and resigned. Then cholera broke out in the plain at the foot of the hill. When many of Moorcroft's personal servants fled in terror, some of them were also struck down by the disease. By the time Moorcroft arrived, his horses were in deplorable condition and most of his other promising agricultural experiments in ruins.[53]

In view of all this, it is not perhaps surprising that, in July 1818, Moorcroft resurrected his earlier proposal to return to England to buy parent-stock for the stud. It was about his only proposal that year which received the board's support. It probably hoped to see the back of him for good. Fortunately the governor-general in council anticipated serious objections in London and Moorcroft was privately advised to drop the idea. It was just as well. When Parry got wind of the scheme he was hostile in the extreme.[54] Later in 1818 Moorcroft seems to have been seriously considering making his home in a specially converted boat on the river, to facilitate his movements between the various depots up and down the river.[55] It was an unsettling time.

There was another painful and very personal problem looming for him by mid-1818 as well. The child Anne was already 2½ years old – a wild, handsome, athletic little tomboy.[56] She was spending all her time with her mother and the Indian servants and, because her father was away for so much of the time, could scarcely speak a word of English. If she were to be brought up as her father's daughter, it was already time to think of sending (or taking) her back to Europe for her education. Fortunately Purree Khanum was pregnant again, so the blow of parting would be softened for her. If Moorcroft himself were not allowed to take his daughter to Europe then he would send her. But to whom?

Not a single letter between Moorcroft and his wife (if that is what she was) has survived and their relationship remains impenetrable. By this time Mary was living with the Baron and Baroness de Rouvron just outside Paris. She and Moorcroft were obviously keeping in close touch by letter and the survival of a strong bond between them across the world is clear. He was sending her a regular remittance and, in his will the following year, set up a generous trust for her in the event of his death.[57] She in turn earmarked 'fifty pounds to William Moorcroft . . . for a ring' in the event of her own death. Perhaps the most telling pointer to the enduring bond between them is the fact that he could consider entrusting his beloved little daughter to her and that she, childless and with the first hint of grey in her long brown hair,[58] was willing to take responsibility for his illegitimate half-caste child.

As soon as Moorcroft's plan to return to Europe himself was overruled, he immediately made enquiries at the end of 1818 of his friends in Calcutta for a suitable French ship and a nanny to take Anne on the long journey across the oceans to Mary.[59] Then, in October 1818 at Hajipur, Purree Khanum was safely delivered of a little boy named Richard – 'very, very little . . . who can't walk with his skin quite red' as his sister recalled later.[60] For Moorcroft, the birth of a son must have been almost the only bright spot in a year which ended, as it had begun, with more bitter wrangling with the board over its steely determination to close down the operations at Pusa, and its continued public criticism of his 'slackness and procrastination . . . in carrying into effect the Board's instructions'.[61]

As soon as he had sorted out a particularly unsavoury financial scandal at Hunter's depot, which came as the culmination of much other trouble with that hot-tempered and rash young man,[62] Moorcroft returned to Hajipur towards the end of the year to collect Anne. Then, in late December or early January, (without even bothering to consult the board it seems) he set out with his lively little companion, on their first, and last, long journey together down to Calcutta. Their object was the French ship *La Caroline*, then loading in the Hugli River for Le Havre. Moorcroft must have felt in turmoil on 3 February 1819 as the diminutive little figure with her young nurse beside her slipped out of his life down the broad river on the first of the ebb-tide that day and he returned, like the tormented father in the Thackeray story, to climb alone and unseeing up those worn river-stairs.[63]

Fortunately there were plenty of friends and distractions in Calcutta to console him. There was the now much-loved Palmer household. There was Walter Nisbet, secretary of the Board of Trade, at Chowringhee.[64] There was the remarkable Rammohun Roy whose keen mind was wrestling with the problem of reconciling Western learning with India's ancient cultural and religious traditions.[65] There was James Robinson up at the Insane Hospital, with whom Moorcroft often discussed the nature of baffling diseases like elephantiasis.[66] All these and many more were his friends. Moreover, he was always in great demand to advise on the purchase or health of the horses of the Europeans in Calcutta.[67] In addition, he had for some years been a member of the trailblazing Asiatic Society of Bengal. A few days after Anne had left, he was at the handsome building at the top of Park Street to present to the society's growing (and now priceless) collection of Asiatic antiquities and curiosities, a stuffed specimen of an ant-eater and a Sanskrit inscription he had recorded at Rohtasgurh.[68]

Just what his personal relations with the members of the board were, we can only guess. Fortunately Wood, his most implacable enemy, was still up-country although reporting enthusiastically on almost everything Moorcroft's assistants were doing and, whenever he got the chance, critically about Moorcroft.[69] He was still at it four years later. By then, however, he was an isolated figure on the board and there were already signs of this in early 1819.[70] In that new year, things at last began to go Moorcroft's way. In the first place, unusual winter frosts in 1818–19, followed by freakishly dry weather, all but wiped out the winter crop over much of Bihar, but Moorcroft's ample acreage of oats at Pusa largely survived. It was a clear vindication, not only of all his arguments for the retention of Pusa, but also of his fodder crop experiments at Rohtasgurh. He soon had 100 bullocks and twenty-five ploughs hard at work up there and in due course the board was only too glad to eat its words and avail itself of his offer of nearly 2000 tonnes of Rohtasgurh hay.[71] Even at the pre-dearth rate, that would have cost them more than 150,000 rupees on the open market. The shortage of fodder confirmed Moorcroft's judgement in another important matter too. As the oat component in the feed of the animals at the new depots dwindled in the wake of the dearth, there were outbreaks of exactly the same diseases as had afflicted Pusa and Hajipur earlier.[72] It was, of course, a triumphant confirmation of Moorcroft's belief that oats were a powerful preventive against these diseases. He believed that the reduction of disease, by 90 per cent during his superintendence, was his greatest achievement at the stud. Oat cultivation certainly remained critical to the success of the breeding operation long after he had left.

The 1819 crisis also powerfully confirmed all he had been saying about the foolishness of disposing of Pusa before extended trials in the new depots. As he had been arguing for some time, there was nothing intrinsically unhealthy about Pusa at all nor, it now seemed, intrinsically healthy about the new breeding-districts further up the river. Yet another vindication of his foresight came in 1819. Ever since he had first outlined the new breeding plan in 1814, he had insisted that one assistant would not be able to cope, both with running a depot and supervising an extensive breeding-circle. The board and government had disagreed but Moorcroft was absolutely right. The board was soon pressing for urgent permission to recruit the extra European assistant at each depot, which he had urged all along.[73] One way or another, Moorcroft in 1819 must have been feeling much more satisfied about the way things were going at the studs.

By then there were encouraging signs that the new circle system which Moorcroft had first detailed in his *Observations* five years before was at last beginning to succeed. One could perhaps discount Wood's enthusiastic reports from up-country, board pronouncements, even appreciative comment in the public press: all that had been heard before. Entirely new were the solid statistics of falling unit costs and the startling rises in the quality and quantity of the cavalry admissions from 1819 onwards.[74] For a little while the Bengal breeding-studs came close to realizing the high hopes held out for them from the very beginning. Indeed Moorcroft's period at the stud was later looked back on by his baffled and disappointed successors as an unattainable golden age and the credit was always given to him.[75] The board would have disagreed, but one thing it and he could whole-heartedly agree on in 1819 was the acceptance of Wood's recommendation that the new system should be extended still further to the north-west, into Rohilkhand and the lands west of Delhi.[76]

But the final stud triumph of 1819 was Moorcroft's alone and it was a double one, which must have been immensely sweet to him after the seven long years of opposition and frustration since his return from Tibet. First, there arrived early in April 1819 a despatch, written in London the previous October, reaffirming Moorcroft's sole right to purchase horses for breeding, and reducing the salaries of all the senior European stud employees except him.[77] And that was not all. By the spring of 1819 the directors in London had belatedly become convinced that the board rather than Moorcroft, as they had at first been led to believe, was chiefly to blame for the earlier failures. Handsome private apologies to Moorcroft from Parry and the others were accompanied by a sizzling official censure of the board, worded in the strongest terms.[78] When it reached Calcutta in the autumn of 1819, Wood was sent into another paroxysm of buck-passing, but this time it availed him nothing[79] and he resigned soon afterwards.

Parry's personal letter to Moorcroft in February was critical of two things only – his intemperate language in official correspondence and his 'roving spirit'. Two months later Parry wrote again to reinforce the latter point. We have, he wrote, at last a chance to provide for all our cavalry needs 'at no very distant period. . . . I hope you will not allow any other pursuit to take off your thoughts from this main object'.[80] By a supreme irony that admonition, addressed to Moorcroft at Calcutta, was forwarded after him to Pusa . . . then to Fatehgarh far up the Ganges . . . then to Almora on its forested ridge far into the pine-scented foothills of the Himalayas . . . and then onwards again along the rugged trail towards Tibet.

That was Moorcroft's second and greatest triumph of 1819. Against all the odds, when he must have felt that the dream had gone for ever, he finally secured the permission he had been seeking since 1812 – to go on full salary, in search of horses, to that ancient and fabled oasis city in the heart of the Central Asian deserts, across 2000 dangerous and virtually unknown miles (3200 kilometres) of mountain and desert: to Bokhara the Noble.

15 THE GREAT JOURNEY BEGINS
AND IS CHECKED,

1819

ON OR ABOUT 14 May 1819 Moorcroft received in Calcutta an official letter signed by his old friend, Charles Metcalfe. It began:

Sir,

His Excellency the Governor-General in Council is pleased to grant you leave to proceed towards the North Western parts of Asia, for the purpose of there procuring, by commercial intercourse, horses to improve the breed within the British Provinces or for military use.[1]

There was no need to read any further. That one sentence gave him the permission he had been seeking through the board, year in year out, since 1812. Had he not got it he would in the end probably have gone anyway, resigning his post and travelling privately. He would, he assured Parry later, even have disguised himself 'as a Fakeer rather than have quitted the design'.[2] One can almost believe it. Moorcroft was deadly serious and he was not a quitter. Once he had convinced himself that a course of action was right he pursued it to the end *'avec obstination moutonière bien dirigée'*, to use his own phrase.[3]

Even so to have obtained official backing was something of a triumph. Needless to say he did not obtain it from the board. That body appears not even to have been consulted. 'I carried my views in the end thro' the Political Dep[artmen]t,' Moorcroft told Parry later.[4] Luckily, one of his principal allies in the 1812 adventure, and his long-time friend, Charles Metcalfe, was now in charge of that department, with a ready access to the ear of the governor-general. Lord Hastings himself was also personally well-disposed to Moorcroft and had a 'strong interest' in the Bokhara project. Not only did he promise to provide an escort of Gurkha troops, but was apparently willing to give the scheme much more overt official backing than that, although his council colleagues later persuaded him to be more cautious.[5] Lord Hastings was in the chair at the Asiatic Society on the evening Moorcroft made his presentations to the collection. That very day – 12 February 1819 – Moorcroft had submitted his first long memorandum in favour of the Bokhara journey through the Political Department. The response must have been encouraging for he wrote further amplifying memoranda in March and April, urging Metcalfe privately all the while of the need for a speedy decision. Moorcroft's brief little formal request for permission to buy horses 'in any part of Asia', dated 6 May and submitted through Metcalfe, has all the feel of a formality. It was doubtless all very unorthodox, but it worked.[6]

One is still left with the question why. What was it that led a man of 52 to embark on a journey across some of the most difficult political and geographical terrain in the world? Certainly it was not the bliss of ignorance. Izzat-Allah's earlier journey had made it clear that there would be risk, hardship and danger. Moreover, as Moorcroft knew and lamented, the political situation in Afghanistan was far less favourable than it had been a few years before, when he had received friendly letters of welcome from the rulers at Kabul and Balkh.[7] Afghanistan south of the Hindu Kush was sliding into civil war once more after the blinding and murder of the regime's strong man, Fath Khan, in 1818. Shortly afterwards the precarious balance of power north of the mountains was also destroyed, by the death of the powerful and apparently friendly chief of Balkh. This, in Moorcroft's words, 'produced a chasm in that line of road which will not be readily filled'.[8] It was in fact filled, by the sinister and unscrupulous Murad Beg of Kunduz further east. Moorcroft did not know all of this in early 1819, but he knew enough to realize that his journey was likely to be dangerous in the extreme.

So the question stands. Why did he want to go? Part of the answer has already been given. The same imperatives which in 1812 took him into unexplored Tibet, were still tormenting him even more strongly seven years later. Horses certainly. There is no need to doubt the sincerity of Moorcroft's firm conviction, that the stud urgently needed parent-stock of size and strength to offset the rapid degeneration which so alarmed him. He was convinced, particularly now that the new breeding-circles under his assistants were so plainly prospering, that the opening up of the legendary horse markets of Central Asia would be the most effective way available to achieve the original objects of his appointment to the stud.[9]

There was much more to it than horses. Shawl goats and the shawl trade were there too. Moorcroft was as keen as ever on both. As has been said, he believed that the failure in Scotland to rear and breed from the goats he brought from Tibet in 1812, was the result of careless management; but even if the goats themselves were not available to British industry, their fine wool could be. Since 1812 one of Moorcroft's abiding ambitions had been to unravel the secrets of the ancient craft of shawl weaving and, by harnessing British technology to that knowledge, capture for Britain the lucrative shawl markets of Europe.[10]

Even that was only part of a wider dream and enterprise which Moorcroft and his associates code-named 'the Himalaya concern'.[11] This was no less than an attempt to test the feasibility of capturing the apparently limitless trade of inner Asia for British woollen, cotton and industrial goods. Needless to say, Moorcroft did not declare such an aim too openly in his official correspondence at first. More prudently, he argued that the best and safest way of paying for the horses he hoped to buy along the Oxus would be not by bills or bullion but by barter. As he put it to Metcalfe at the end of 1819,[12]

> It may be urged that the extension of British commerce was not within the scope of my mission, and that as much time as such extension may occupy is so much abstracted from its direct and special object. I will freely admit the first part of the position, but not the last, as the countries in which it is proposed to procure horses are not accessible to an European, except as a needy adventurer or as a merchant. The former . . . is absolutely useless . . . whilst the latter may subserve the general interests of commerce, and [is] the only mode by which horses are profitably procurable. Hence it follows, I presume, that the time employed in prosecuting that form of intercourse through which alone horses are profitably obtainable, is legitimately employed in promoting the special objects of my mission.

He had the candour to admit his 'satisfaction in finding these two objects so blended'.[13]

Satisfaction is hardly the right word. Moorcroft was positively enraptured at the possibilities. Not only would the potential profits go far to write off all the investment in the Bengal stud, but the beneficial effects would be felt in Britain as well. The opportunities waiting in Asia, Moorcroft believed, whether in markets and raw materials or ancient production and agricultural techniques unknown to Europe, were sufficient to lift Britain out of her post-war depression and bring blessings to millions, both there and in Asia itself.[14] It was a magnificent dream fusing his love of improvement, his genuine humanitarianism and his uncomplicated patriotism. The Bokhara journey, then, was among other things an extended exercise in market research and Moorcroft himself travelled, to use his own phrase, as 'a kind of commercial tourist'.[15] The great caravan, the loving and detailed description of the novelties he found, and the crates and bundles of samples he sent back are inexplicable otherwise.

There was yet another motive too. Moorcroft's discoveries in Tibet in 1812 had convinced him that the Russians were already embarked on their own bid for commercial hegemony in Asia and to some extent he was right.[16] He suspected that there was much more to this than the desire for trade. Behind commerce, he feared, lay vast political and military designs which, if not met and checked, could threaten Britain's whole position in Asia. Moorcroft was nearly always ahead of his contemporaries, and not least in his undoubted Russophobia. It had lain dormant in him during the years of Anglo-Russian cooperation since the 1812 journey, but it was fully formed and soon brought to vigorous wakefulness again by what he found – or believed he found – on this new odyssey beyond the frontiers.[17] Britain, he was sure, could win this battle for supremacy in middle Asia by pushing her trade. She had the industrial muscle, the entrepreneurial skills and the lower costs to do it, but the effort had to be made consistently and in good time.

The promotion of the public good and the national interest was always very important to Moorcroft. Looking back on his career later, he thought he could explain its development entirely in those terms as a consistent life principle.[18] At a superficial level this is probably true, but more significant, and much less obvious to Moorcroft himself, were the other tangled personal motives and longings at work. It is plain that his frustrating experiences at the stud since 1812 had destroyed his pleasure in the job and he soon made up his mind never to return to it once the great journey was over. That apart, there was always the deeper need in him for challenge, for novelty and for diversion from numbing routine. Plain during his earlier life in Britain, if anything it grew stronger as he got older at Pusa. This deeply restless man could only indulge his tireless and consuming curiosity about the endless diversity of life all around him by a matching, multifaceted diversity within his own life. John Palmer was almost certainly wrong in his suspicion that his friend deliberately courted privation and hardship 'as the seasoning' in his life.[19] He merely accepted them as the price for doing what he most longed to do. In a poignant letter to his old Oxford Street friend, George Saunders, Moorcroft confessed in 1822 that, for the first time in his life, he was truly fulfilled. The Bokhara journey, he said was 'by far the best act of my life and the only time with the passing of which I am well satisfied notwithstanding the privations and inconveniences and anxieties it constantly presents'.[20] In May 1919 that journey was at last within his grasp.

Anyone who has planned an expedition into the wilds will have some idea of how those hot, early summer days in Calcutta would have raced by in a flurry of lengthening lists and accumulating gear. There were other distractions too. Moorcroft was still deeply involved in stud affairs and at the end of April he had to go into print to defend his prior claim to neurotomy as a treatment for equine lameness.[21] But the great journey must have absorbed most of his energies. In size, his party was more like a small army which was expected to be away for at least two years[22] and which, for some of that time, would need to be entirely self-sufficient. At the heart of it all was the great caravan of English cottons, woollen broadcloths, chintz, cutlery, hardware and ironmongery provided, as an act of friendship and at their own cost and risk, by the two Calcutta business houses of John Palmer and James MacKillop. Its total value was the (at the time) immense sum of £4000,[23] and everything else about the expedition was on the same generous scale.[24] Moorcroft did not intend to rough it more than he could help. His blue accommodation tent, 9 feet (2.7 metres) square and with high walls was fitted up with Mirzapuri carpets, folding tables and chairs, a substantial library of well over 100 reference books and his precious, portable, mahogany writing desk. The smaller sleeping tent would have been dominated by Moorcroft's pride and joy, his splendid folding brass bedstead. This, when unpacked from its leather case and fully assembled with its chintz hangings and mosquito netting and with the colourful bedside rugs beside it, must have been a heartening sight at the end of a long day in the saddle or on foot. So too the 'portable necessary-house' usually set up nearby for the principals of the party. Needless to say the rigours of the journey, which in the end took not two years from start to finish, but six years merely to reach the halfway point, made sad inroads into these splendid equipages.

There is evidence of very much more: medicines for the portable chest; catheters and other surgical instruments; leather hernia trusses; weapons, ammunition and cartouche boxes; surveying equipment, compasses, spy-glasses, thermometers and barometer tubes; stationery; personal supplies of sugar, chocolate and brandy; a comprehensive collection of fishing lines and flies; a vast array of presents including kaleidoscopes, silver and plated articles like tea-pots, soup tureens and sugar basins, telescopes, watches, cut-glass chandeliers, pistols, scissors and penknives. All this was only a minute fraction of the thousand and one items that had to be listed, obtained, checked and then crated for transport. Later, new and sometimes bizarre requests came back to Palmer out of the blue, such as when Moorcroft asked his friend to obtain a pipe organ and gifts suitable for the harem of the ruler of Himalayan Kulu.[25]

All in all, Moorcroft conceded, the result was a 'somewhat numerous and bulky' collection of bales, boxes and tin trunks. Even when much depleted it still weighed nearly 8 tonnes.[26] To move it required a small army in itself. At one stage, six elephants and forty camels were used; at another, sixty porters, fourteen horses, four mules and a number of bullocks; at yet another, 300 porters.[27] In addition there were personal servants, grasscutters, grooms, a baker, a draughtsman and two botanical collectors. Moorcroft had about fifty souls in all permanently on his payroll, and all had to be fed, clothed and paid.[28] Despite substantially enhanced rates of pay, it was not always easy to get or keep them. It proved utterly impossible to find a blacksmith who would go with them and some of Moorcroft's oldest, but plains-bred, servants deserted soon after the journey began, rather than face the horrors of the mountains.[29]

The animals proved more faithful. Moorcroft deliberately took both horses and mules to test the feasibility of his chosen routes for horse transport, watching them closely for lameness and trying to assess the best means of shoeing them for the varying terrain they had to cross.[30] Then there were the dogs. Moorcroft always had dogs at his heels and wrote affectionately of them in his journal. Most loved of all was Missy, the English spaniel bitch who always hunted with him and whose death in the Khyber reduced him to tears. Later he acquired fierce Tibetan sheep dogs in Ladakh and in Kabul a pointer, called Sheena, and a setter.[31] There were others too.

This huge army of assorted animal and human livestock and the great mountain of baggage represented not only a logistical problem of daunting proportions but also a cash problem. Company bullion was only useful to them until they reached the hills. Thereafter Moorcroft had to depend on about 6000 rupees' worth of drilled and strung pearls as currency for everyday use. Beyond that, he planned to draw on British frontier officers or Indian bankers as he needed, against his bank account with John Palmer down in Calcutta.

For his principal lieutenant, responsible for the route survey, the mapping, sketching, and other geographical enquiries, the daily temperature, latitude and altitude readings and command of the escort, Moorcroft chose the youngest son of an old friend from his Westminster Volunteer Cavalry days who more recently had become his lawyer in Calcutta. George Trebeck, tall and slim and only 19 when they set out, was a romantic who proved to be the perfect foil to the practical, down-to-earth Moorcroft. They became as devoted to one another as father and son. Moorcroft nursed the younger man when he was seriously ill and cheered him when he was depressed. Trebeck in turn became imbued with Moorcroft's ideas and hopes and defended him stoutly when his reputation came under renewed attack during their absence. Moorcroft never regretted his choice of Trebeck and spoke highly of him to the very end. How one historian could turn this faithful young Englishman into a suspiciously unreliable German is a mystery.[32] Moorcroft was equally pleased with his medical assistant and compounder, a young and cheerful Anglo-Indian assistant apothecary from Dinapur Hospital called George Guthrie.[33]

The principal Indians of the party also justified their selection. Doyen of them all, of course, was Mir Izzat-Allah. Now in his forties he was the expedition's Persian secretary, diplomatist and translator. His son and brother came too. Moorcroft had the highest regard for the silver-tongued Izzat-Allah, saving only a tendency on occasions to give the clever rather than the prudent answer during his crucial verbal fencing with some of the powerful chiefs they encountered along the way.[34] Izzat-Allah was not the only member of the 1812 venture to sign on again. Moorcroft had hoped to persuade Hearsey to join him but, failing that, took instead his faithful old retainer, Ghulam Hyder Khan. Since their 1812 Tibetan journey together, the old warrior had acquired a Gurkha bullet in his head and was sometimes inclined to be forgetful, but otherwise seems to have been as tough, resourceful and indestructible as ever. He was almost the only one among the lot of them to return to India alive.[35] Another member of the 1812 party was Moorcroft's much trusted personal servant, Hafiz Muhammad Fazl, whose position on the new journey was second only to that of Izzat-Allah himself. Hafiz had already travelled right across Afghanistan and the Hindu Kush, carrying letters from Moorcroft to Balkh where he had been given a very friendly reception by its chief. Even those two useful hill-men, the old Pandit Harbalam and his nephew Harkh Dev, were on Moorcroft's payroll for a time in the winter of 1819 as the party passed through Kumaon and Garhwal.[36]

All these men, with one notable exception who will be mentioned later,[37] seem to have worked extremely well together – a real band of brothers, as Moorcroft fondly described them on one occasion. The credit for that, of course, was mainly his. It says a great deal for Moorcroft's qualities as leader and as a man, that so many of the 1812 party were willing once again to face the unknown with him and remain united when the hard times came.

The fact that so many of these men were government servants raises an important question. Was this an official mission or not? There is no straightforward answer. Right from the very start, there was an ambiguity about the whole project which reflects both its unorthodox origins and its mixed objectives. The official purpose of the mission, as defined in Moorcroft's leave of absence, was entirely confined to horses and his substantial salary as stud superintendent continued to be paid through the Military Department as usual. Moorcroft was given no formal political functions whatsoever and was roundly rebuked when he began to exercise them. Yet permission for the journey, and correspondence about its details, was so completely in the hands of the Political Department that the board claimed that they had never had official notification of it at all.

Moorcroft himself was always adamant that the journey was undertaken strictly for public purposes and that all his reports and findings were the property of the government. He was, after all, a senior government servant on full salary; his mountainous caravan was carried to the limit of British territory by commissariat transport animals at public expense and free of customs duties; his medicines and surgical equipment were supplied from public stores and many of the presents, which had originally been purchased at public expense for the 1812 journey, were now formally released to him once again. Guthrie, Izzat-Allah and Hafiz were all public servants on full pay, as indeed were the fourteen Gurkha soldiers who made up the escort. Moreover, carefully stowed somewhere in his baggage, Moorcroft carried documents in English, Russian, Persian and Chinese bearing the great seal of the company and stating that he was indeed its servant, travelling in search of horses.[38]

In all these ways the mission was an official one. Yet the official element in it was strictly and deliberately limited. As Moorcroft tried to explain to one understandably puzzled British official on the frontier, 'though a public servant proceeding with the sanction of the Government upon an enterprise that has public advantage for its object, I am neither accredited by the Government for the purposes specially in view nor for any other'.[39] When he tried to get Lord Hastings to write an official letter of introduction to the emir of Bokhara, he was turned down flat. Metcalfe had to remind him bluntly 'that it was never intended to accredit you or vest you with a public character', however much that would improve his prospects.[40] The reason is not hard to understand and it clearly worried the government from the very beginning. Moorcroft had already got into one serious scrape beyond the frontier and his reputation for discretion was as low as the risks of his enterprise were high. He was going far beyond the reach of the company's long arm where, if he ran into trouble, he would have to be entirely on his own. As Metcalfe explained in the letter quoted above, the government dare not be more heavily involved in his mission than it already was for, if trouble came, it 'would be committed – unpleasantly and contrary to its design'. Moorcroft's position in that respect was somewhat analogous to that of a government secret agent. Some historians, Russian, Indian and British, have assumed this is precisely what he was.[41] Not so. The abundant evidence means exactly what it says and no more. The fact that later he exploited the ambiguity of his position and ventured into areas much more appropriate to a political agent than to a stud superintendent, does not alter the case.

Moorcroft's original plan, early in 1819,[42] was to make first for Leh, the capital of Ladakh, situated due east of Kashmir beyond the Himalayas on the upper reaches of the Indus River. Leh seemed to be not only the best place to tap the shawl wool coming down from Tibet and divert it into British territory, but also the best springboard from which to launch an assault on the markets of Central Asia to the north and west. Moorcroft also wanted to complete some unfinished hydrographical enquiries concerning the course of the upper Indus. He believed, although with excessive optimism as it turned out, that he could repeat what he had done in 1812, that is to say, appear on the summit of the Niti and by a judicious mixture of bluff, bribery and bloody-mindedness, push his way past the jovial and unaggressive Tibetans into Tibet. This time, however, he would go west following the Lhasa–Leh caravan trail to Ladakh.

Once there and with British trade securely established, there were three alternatives. He could either follow the ancient caravan trail across the Karakoram north-eastwards to Chinese Turkestan before approaching Bokhara from the east across the Pamirs as Izzat-Allah had done. That was his preferred plan. Alternatively, he could turn north-westwards and penetrate to Bokhara by way of Gilgit, Chitral, and the Upper Oxus. Both routes were totally unexplored by Europeans. Only as a very third best would he risk Sikh opposition and Muslim fanaticism by descending from Ladakh via Kashmir into the Punjab, and then penetrating to Bokhara across Afghanistan, by way of Peshawar and Kabul. Moorcroft's first and probably more feasible intention in early 1819 was to push on himself across the Niti-la, crossing in June or July and travelling lightly laden with presents only. If all went well, he expected to reach Leh inside three months and then would move on, leaving the commercial goods to make their ponderous way up to the British frontier and await further instructions from him, in the light of the situation he found beyond the mountains. He did not really expect to get the goods across those mountains until the following year.

Several developments sabotaged these tentative plans almost as soon as they were made. As has been said, Moorcroft's formal permission to leave Calcutta was delayed until May (he had originally hoped to be at Almora in the hills by then). In that month, as the official record shows, he was still up to his neck in stud problems.[43] One of his minor triumphs, a characteristic one, was to plead successfully that his assistant, Lieutenant Hunter, who was facing dismissal from the stud for gross misconduct, should be given just one more chance. On 30 May Moorcroft was down in Charles Trebeck's office putting his signature to his will.[44] It is a long and complex document, pulling together the strands of the passing years. The three important women in his life – his mother (Ann Paine), now very frail in Dublin,[45] Mary in Paris, and Purree Khanum at Hajipur – were each provided with an income from three capital trusts. On their deaths the trusts were to be settled equally on the children, Anne and Richard, and used for their education. Moorcroft hoped that Richard would become a doctor or surgeon. In the event of their deaths the residue was to go to Moorcroft's stepbrother and sister in Dublin or be used to found a medical college in India.

He was still delayed in Calcutta in June. By mid-July he was tidying up his affairs at Pusa before moving on to Hajipur for the painful parting from Purree Khanum and young Richard.[46] There, on the first day of August, Moorcroft opened his account book and brought the servants who were accompanying him on to the payroll.[47] Even then he was still writing at length to the board on stud business, although that may well have been his last day with his family. Three days later he was gone for ever.

He did not, as it happened, go very far. At Patna, he was dismayed to find not only that many of the goods had not yet come up the river from Calcutta, but that the flotilla of boats that had been ordered to take them upstream to

Fatehgarh was also missing. This was all the more serious because Moorcroft had modified his original plan. He was now hoping to get not only himself, but his immense baggage train across the Niti pass before the winter snows closed it for six months at the end of the year.[48] By this new schedule he was already a month late and the delays at Patna cost the best part of another. But at last the journey, tracking painfully up the swollen river, began. They were still below Benares on 4 September and not at Kanpur till about the 19th. There, Thomas Keene, another young man from Trebeck's office who was employed to act as Moorcroft's forwarding agent, met them and accompanied them on the last of the river journey up to Fatehgarh, where a warehouse for the storage of goods in transit had been hired. Keene was still there forwarding goods until well into 1820 and, it seems, he inadvertently caused still further delays by disobeying Moorcroft's instructions.[49] The general impression of haste, confusion and ill-preparedness comes over strongly from the fragments of correspondence that have survived. Even basic items like cups and coffee-pots were still missing when they reached the hills.[50] To make a bad situation worse, the rains went on exceptionally late into the autumn in that year.

The precise dates of the party's movements from this point until the end of the year are almost impossible to determine from the contradictory evidence available. The first objective after leaving the river was Bareilly, where Izzat-Allah, Ghulam Hyder Khan and Hyder Hearsey were waiting to greet them. Moorcroft hoped that his old travelling companion could be persuaded to join them on this expedition. Hearsey, shaking his head at the immense cavalcade winding on to his estates, was convinced that his friend was approaching Bokhara entirely the wrong way. Instead of trying to cross the mightiest conglomeration of mountains in the world, he urged that they should instead go to the Gulf by sea, cross Persia by well-beaten roads to Meshed and then approach Bokhara across the desert from the west. There was a sharp disagreement and Hearsey in the end declined to join them although, then and later, he gave them all the assistance in his power.[51]

It was the end of October before the caravan left Bareilly and crossed the last of the plain to Kathgodam, where today the railway runs out abruptly against the steep, green outer face of the hills.[52] From this point it is hard climbing nearly all the way through the sombre, pine-scented trees, up past Bhim Tal, its beautiful lake cradled in green hills. One breathless day beyond Ramgarh, following the path round a rocky shoulder, they would suddenly have had their first real glimpse of the snow giants spread out spectacularly across the eastern horizon. In the foreground Almora is visible, perched on its high forested ridge and behind it 'the immense snowy range of mountains lift up their heads . . . to the skies'.[53] It is a view to lift the spirits – or sink them. The more pessimistic would have noticed in the keen wind that the flanks of the mountains were already gleaming ominously far down with the first snows of winter.[54] Among the servants who bolted as soon as they reached Almora was the excellent cook Moorcroft had hired for the journey. 'My table has since frequently exhibited a fare that would not have seduced an English day-labourer,' he lamented later.[55]

At Almora Moorcroft was soon in earnest conversation with the British warden of those marches, Geoffrey Traill, the commissioner for the affairs of Kumaon. The two men had been corresponding for months and seem to have taken to each other at once. Traill, despite the lateness of the season, was ready with porters to push the party on to Josimath, and assured his visitor that essential bridging and road work in the Dauli gorge made the journey up to Niti much easier than when he had attempted it with Hearsey in 1812. At Moorcroft's request, Traill had also summoned to Almora the man whose yaks, influence and knowledge seemed to offer the best chance of getting the party safely across the Niti-la at this eleventh hour.[56] Deb Singh, 'farmer, forager and trader', was one of the two brothers who had appeared out of the blue at Daba in August 1812 and offered what Moorcroft called 'more facilities than it was prudent to accept' to get his party out of Tibet quickly.[57] Now Deb Singh was needed to get them in again. It must all have looked quite encouraging. The Niti route is usually uncomfortable after October, but most years anyone prepared to push his way through deep snow up to the saddle girths of the yaks, could get across till December.[58] Deb Singh offered his services as guide and promised fifty yaks at Josimath to carry the baggage. Despite the mysterious and inflated rumours of Moorcroft's caravan that had been circulating in these hills for months, he seemed to think that any Tibetan guards waiting for them on the icy summit would long since have withdrawn into winter quarters. 'Once through the pass they would certainly not have the power of stopping you,' Traill assured Moorcroft.[59]

Leaving the unburdened commissariat elephants and camels to make their slow way back to the plains Traill's porters bent their backs to the loads and set out single-file up the gloomy and rugged river-valley behind Almora towards Josimath. It was about 23 November 1819 and almost at once things began to go wrong. On 27 November, although it was months before the news caught up with them, Mary Moorcroft died in far away Paris after a short illness, very soon after poor little bewildered Anne reached her. Perhaps Moorcroft had a premonition for he wrote to Mary that very week.[60] But there were worries nearer at hand as well. Three days out from Almora, George Trebeck was suddenly struck down with a soaring fever and wild delirium. It was cholera. For fourteen anxious hours Moorcroft thought he would lose his young friend. Even after the first crisis was over Trebeck was so ill for the next ten days that he had to be carried all the way to Josimath in a litter.[61]

If Moorcroft treated Trebeck as he later treated one of the servants for cholera, it is scarcely surprising! Moorcroft was convinced that a drastic treatment was the only hope when the pulse was failing. After dosing with laudanum, he soaked balls of cotton in turpentine and burned them on his patient's back and navel. 'He roared from the pain of the burning which lasted about a minute but the pain in the intestines ceased and his pulse rose,' Moorcroft noted. Four men were then set to work to put his limbs in violent motion, his body was massaged and his feet placed in hot water. 'I have not lost a single patient when this practice was resorted to early,' Moorcroft wrote.[62] One can only conclude that his patients must have been too busy to spare the time for dying. At any rate they survived and so did Trebeck.

Some of the horses and mules were less fortunate. As soon as the long caravan descended into the precipitous basin of the Alaknanda River just beyond Pipalkoti, the numbing track shrank to only a few inches wide in places. Neither the animals themselves nor the servants were yet familiar with the hazards of this frowning, angular, vertical terrain. In quick succession one of the Arabs and one of the mules went tumbling to their deaths down the steep slope into the river ½ mile (0.8 kilometres) below.[63] That left only eight horses and mules. Perhaps the doubters, who said that none would ever get to Ladakh alive, were right. Ghulam Hyder Khan was also nearly a casualty at this time. He and Moorcroft had gone out at the request of some villagers near Pipalkoti to bag a black bear that had been raiding the fields. Moorcroft's shot only winged the creature who, maddened with pain, went for Ghulam Hyder Khan who was down below him in the bed of a watercourse. Luckily the old warrior had armed himself with Trebeck's sword and as the bear rushed at him he had, as he told the story, 'the presence of mind to cut him in two pieces'.[64] Did all these things seem like ill-omens? Perhaps in retrospect, for when the caravan finally straggled into Josimath high on its lonely ridge above the empty terraced fields and the river junction 1500 feet (457 metres) below, there was no sign of Deb or the yaks. The brewing snow-clouds to the north and all the other evidence suggested that the Niti-la was already closed for the winter. There was nothing for it but to settle down at that sombre spot and wait.

In a friendly letter to Traill, Moorcroft wrote 'that a band of opera dancers would have relieved our ennui but none seem to dare the speculation'.[65] Any boredom in the party was certainly not shared by its leader. Notwithstanding the tedious food, he was as restless and hyperactive as ever. Urgent letters flowed out from his little portable desk across the tree-girt ridges to Almora, and beyond to the plains, with requests for things left behind or overlooked. Lord Hastings's refusal to write a letter of introduction to the gloomy and unpredictable ruler at Bokhara, the one important chief on the journey who had not sent a letter of welcome, inspired not only a renewed personal plea to the governor-general[66], but also a long and revealing valedictory letter to Metcalfe.[67] Wilson quoted it at length and almost verbatim in his introduction to the *Travels*. Moorcroft confessed his disappointment but defiantly reasserted his confidence in what he was doing despite the 'diminished probability of success. . . .'

> If I fall, my country will set a due value on my motives and at least allow me a claim to disinterested perseverance. But to turn back would be voluntarily to invite the indications of scorn and to load me with feelings which would hurry me to the grave. If I fail, I shall lose my time, my property, perchance my reputation and probably my situation. . . . I must push the adventure to its end.

And so he did. Hafiz was despatched to Fatehgarh to bring up the goods that had arrived in the warehouse under young Keene's supervision since their departure.[68] There was trouble with the servants to sort out. Unlike many of his countrymen in India, Moorcroft resorted to corporal punishment of his servants on only three occasions in ten years, and even then only after a quasi-judicial hearing. This was one of those occasions, 'on the fact being proved that one of my servants had endeavoured to take a [married] lady's lost favors without settling the preliminary of her consent'.[69]

There was also much work still to be done on the equipment. The account book suggests a fever of activity which must have given a considerable boost to the local economy at Josimath. Tailors, blacksmiths and leatherworkers were all set to work making or repairing tents and tent pegs, stitching heavy-weather clothing for the shivering servants and retinning the copper cooking pots.[70]

While all this was going on Moorcroft seems to have penetrated up the Alaknanda as far as the sacred temple at Badrinath. What is more, he persuaded the temple brahmins to lend him four copper inscriptions from the temple walls to send down to Calcutta for translation.[71] It is further evidence, and there is plenty, of the astonishing power of this dynamic little man from the other side of the world to inspire trust, across the gulfs of language and culture, among the people of inner Asia.

One means of achieving the same end lay in the use of his medical and surgical skill. It was during this waiting period at Josimath that Moorcroft, for the first time on this journey, attempted to restore the sight of a man blind with formidable cataracts. It was a difficult case and Moorcroft was unsuccessful.[72] Yet, from this small beginning, there quickly blossomed what became a major feature of Moorcroft's odyssey for the next four and a half years. He refined his cataract technique as he went along and eventually, with Guthrie's help, seems to have achieved a remarkably high and permanent success rate, considering the lack of adequate hygiene or post-operative care. Moorcroft's achievements in this field have been noted but never studied in detail, although there are scattered among his papers detailed clinical notes and case histories and much other incidental evidence of how he went about it. He was never a man to turn his back on human suffering, but his medical work had other advantages as he soon came to realize.[73] In particular it helped to allay the absurd but dangerous rumours that rippled out ahead of his advancing cara-van and, acting as a kind of life insurance, guaranteed him a friendly welcome in wild places where the reception might otherwise have been very different.

For much of this waiting period Moorcroft was out on the snow slopes or trekking through the great forests about Josimath, in search of game to relieve their dreary diet. He was also falling in love again with that marvellous land of soaring, pine-scented forests, rich upland pastures, mist-curtained river gorges and tough, smiling hill-people,[74] all set against the eternal backcloth of 'mountains stupendously high and whether barren or bare or cloathed with forests or with snow always displayed features most majestic and sublime'.[75] Moorcroft rarely wrote of scenic beauty like this, but even more beautiful to the pioneer and the scientific agricultural improver in him were the rich natural resources of this area – the game and wildlife, the untapped timber potential of the great forests, the fish in the tumbling rivers, the potential of the fertile soil and ample water for cultivation of all kinds. Gradually, as these things do, a shadowy idea going back to 1812 slowly took shape and hardened into a resolve. When the great Bokhara journey was over, he would resign from government service and retire here. The wheel was turning full circle. What might have filled his life from the very beginning near the minuscule hill from which Ormskirk surveys its fertile plain, would occupy its end on these grander hills somewhere between Karnprayag and the Tibetan frontier.

The more he thought about it the more attractive it seemed. His work at the stud would either be crowned with a massive infusion of blood-stock brought triumphantly back from the banks of the Oxus, or he would fail and be sacked. Either way, he would have given what he could and it would be time to hand over to younger and fitter men. He could no longer afford retirement among old friends on the green slopes above Geneva or on some modest country estate in England, as he had previously intended. Much of his savings since coming to India had been lost by a defaulting agent, and the cost of his ceaseless travel on stud duties, together with the enormous expense of the present expedition, had consumed much of the rest. What he would be able to afford, even with a liberal allowance for the education in England of Richard and Anne, would be 'a cottage and a farm in the mountains of Himachal'.[76] Besides, his spartan and wandering life in India had thoroughly spoiled his taste for the material comfort and affluence of high society life in Europe and had kept him fit. He believed an active retirement would continue to do so. 'A life of incessant occupation and labour may preserve a constitution of great natural firmness for some few years longer,' as he put it.[77] Above all, Moorcroft believed that he could in this way be 'more actively useful in the decline of life than I could be in any other situation'.[78] Utility was always a prime yardstick for Moorcroft and it loomed very large indeed in the retirement dream he sketched for himself in loving detail over the ensuing months in his journals, letters and requisitions. It was partly a kind of hobby and partly a distraction from the preoccupying cares of the open road, but all men reveal a little of themselves in their retirement dreams and Moorcroft was no exception. Besides, he dreamed with unusual precision.[79]

At the heart of it all was the modest, grey stone, two-storey house under its heavy tiled roof – 'more of a cottage than a mansion' – tucked into the steep hillside out of the valley winds. Inside 'the whole of the fittings etc to harmonize on the principle of neatness rather approaching that of the Quaker than running into shewiness'. In the living-room behind the heavy, plate-glass windows, a great log fire would burn in the grate, with a roast on its iron turning-spit if guests were expected. The brass door furniture, the heavy curtain rings, the mirrors, the silver candlesticks and the cut glass of the sideboard, would all shine in the firelight when the spring roller blinds were down and heavy chintz curtains pulled on cold winter evenings. The general impression would be spacious and light, from the plain, distempered walls to the heavy, waxed oak furniture made locally and the polished oaken floor with its colourful Mirzapuri rugs, and the brightly coloured local weaves thrown across the comfortable armchairs or sofas.

One imagines the table laid for dinner with its blue water glasses, its neat and simple Wedgwood dinner service, the heavy silver cutlery, the cut-glass decanters, salt-cellars and pickle-jars all gleaming under the glass hanging lamp suspended on its pulleys from the ceiling: or Moorcroft working by the soft light of the copper night lamps at his library table, the heavy inkstand to hand, the quill from the portable writing case scratching busily, perhaps a book from the library shelves raised on the bookstand before him, and the plain eight-day table clock chiming the quarters through the silent house. Upstairs, off the lamplit landing, would be the bedrooms with their plain, oaken bedsteads and fresh linen, silver candlesticks, light chintz curtains, the tortoiseshell comb brushes and the plain swing mirror on the oaken chests, and sheepskin rugs on the polished floors. No doubt, from the bedroom windows there would, under the moon, be spectacular views across the shadowed valley to the silvered snow giants beyond.

Moorcroft intended this comfortable farmhouse home to be the nerve-centre of a farming enterprise of considerable scale and complexity. At one end would be a small conservatory and, back and front, a large walled nursery garden with beehives. Not far away would be the farm buildings: a dairy with churns and cheese-making equipment for experimental dairy production from yaks, goats, buffalo and sheep, as well as cows; a granary; a piggery; stables; a cow-house for 100 animals; a salting-house for curing the bacon and pickled pork; a shed housing the 6 hp threshing and winnowing machine driven by a waterwheel in one of the streams rushing down the hillside; and storage buildings for the ploughs, drills, hoes, billhooks, sheep shears, the distillation plant and steaming apparatus, and the scaring nets for trapping the hares, bears and hogs which would threaten the crops. Beyond the orchard, above and below the house on the hillside, would be the terraced fields, banked with stone walls and divided by an intricate network of stone irrigation channels, supporting a range of experimental crops from pease, hardy cabbage, potatoes, hybrid beetroots and carrots to oats, yellow lucerne, rape, chicory, sainfoine and burnet. Away on the high summer pastures would be vast flocks of sheep, specially bred from merino rams, and shawl goats guarded by fierce Tibetan sheep-dogs and by shepherds with guns and blue lights at night. In the pastures nearer the house would be the experimental yak crosses and the half-wild Tibetan horses.

All this and more was not merely the wishful thinking of a frustrated agricultural improver. Moorcroft was deadly serious. The letters and long lists were intended to be the basis for orders when the time should come but, more than that, his retirement farming enterprise was not intended for himself alone. Very little of Moorcroft's ceaseless activity was. He was quite right to see the public good as one of the continuities in his working life. For Britain he hoped to be the means 'of providing materials for British industry, of improving the constitution of British sheep, of importing new varieties of animals which may be useful to agriculture in Britain'. As for the Himalayas, 'it is my object to improve the condition of the native inhabitants of the hills, to introduce new settlers and to found a system of polity comprehending agriculture and branches of manufacture and commerce based upon well directed industry and an ameliorated state of the mind through a religious and moral education of the children'. He had helped to rid the hills of Gurkha oppression, now he hoped, with government backing, to open them up with roads, and carve canals from the Ganges to the edge of the plain, which could carry away both the produce of the hills and goods from beyond the mountains. Settlers would be encouraged with grants of land, money, seed, tools and 'a liberal market for new commodities' and Moorcroft's farm would provide the research, the training in new techniques, and the technical know-how. It was a magnificent dream. Moorcroft was always ranging far into the future beyond his contemporaries. There is nothing even remotely comparable with the breadth of this vision for the future of the hill-states, until the post-independence development plans of our own day.

In December 1820 most of this was no more than a twinkle in Moorcroft's eye, as he filled the short winter days with activity and waited as patiently as he could for the arrival of Deb Singh at Josimath. There was just one Tibetan visitor from the north, a man sent from Gartok to report on whether Moorcroft had an army with him. The pass was obviously still open. The Tibetan recognized him at once, despite the absence of the beard and the lampblack he had worn seven years before. Moorcroft took advantage of the visit to pass friendly messages and gifts back across the range.[80] Christmas day – with plenty of snow – came and went. The seasonal rejoicings of Trebeck, Guthrie and Moorcroft must have been rather muted. At last, after dark on Boxing Day, Deb arrived from Niti, pretending to be both anxious and ready to proceed. In fact he was neither. In the cold light of the next morning, measuring with his eye Moorcroft's mountainous baggage and swollen caval-cade against his insufficient and miserably out-of-condition yaks, he declared the task was impossible. They were, he said, a fortnight too late.

For one mad moment Moorcroft considered reverting to his original plan and, with Izzat-Allah, Ghulam Hyder Khan and three or four of the servants, making a dash across the pass to Tibet and Leh, leaving the caravan to follow in the spring. He decided against it when the guides flatly refused to risk their lives on the pass.[81] The alternatives were nearly as bleak. They could wait at that desolate spot at the very edge of the habitable world, riding out the long winter until the pass was clear once more. Moorcroft considered that option briefly in the optimistic belief that three months would have been enough. It could well have been six.[82] Perhaps it was that possibility that finally drove him to the only alternative – of turning back and avoiding Tibet altogether, by a circuitous route north-westwards across the hills and valleys along the edge of the plains, before turning north again to approach Ladakh direct. Apart from the expense and delay of such a journey, the biggest snag was that it would take them across the outer limits of the formidable Sikh ruler of Lahore, Raja Ranjit Singh. They might just slip through without delays. It was a risk that would have to be taken. Moorcroft had been considering this possibility for some time. Now he wasted no more time.[83]

Within a day or two of Deb's arrival, the first of the party was on the march again with 160 porters, back down the magnificent river gorge of the Alak-nanda towards Pipalkoti.

It is at this point, at the beginning of January 1820, that Horace Wilson's two-volume paraphrase of Moorcroft's daily journal begins.

16 An Encounter with Ranjit Singh,

JANUARY–JUNE 1820

Two DAYS' MARCH from Josimath down the rugged Alaknanda valley, they came once again to Pipalkoti.[1] There a woman came to Moorcroft complaining that she had been made outcaste on a false charge of adultery with one of Moorcroft's servants. Most men in a hurry would have dismissed this as a hard-luck story and pressed on. Not Moorcroft. Smelling injustice, he halted his party for several days and summoned the elders from Josimath so as to lay before them the strong evidence of collusion among the witnesses, including the woman's husband. Eventually the elders were persuaded to put the woman's virtue to the test by plunging her arm into boiling oil to retrieve a stone. Whether Guthrie and Moorcroft gave justice a nudge, by concocting some low-boiling-point liquid for the ordeal, is not recorded. At all events the woman passed the test triumphantly. Moorcroft had a personal problem of his own while they were at Pipalkoti 'from a hurt in my leg which seemed as if it would have proved of the most serious nature'.[2] He did not say what it was, and he never referred to it again.

Once past Karnprayag, still following the tumbling Alaknanda, they were, for Moorcroft, on new ground. Another precious horse fell into the river and was hurried away to a swift death in the white water, but every day's march reduced that risk, taking them away from the savage vertical scenery of Josimath into a rounder, greener world of soft hills and fertile, lush valleys. Moorcroft felt strangely bereft. He rejoiced to see the tomtit and the wagtail again as a reminder of England, but they were poor compensation for the mountain eagle and the 'majestic and sublime' mountains they had just left. The truth was that he had lost his heart to that magnificent landscape round Josimath.

In due course the straggling caravan reached Srinagar, the once-important capital of ancient Garhwal. By 1820 it was a dreary place, much reduced by earthquakes, by Gurkha oppression and by the occasional violence of the river Alaknanda, on whose left bank it stands. Moorcroft halted there for nearly a month, taking advantage of Traill's generous offer of the use of his bungalows and gardens.[3] One reason for the delay was an unpleasant row with one of the Europeans of the party.[4] Moorcroft, always very aware of his own ignorance of the natural sciences, had signed on as geologist a man called Alexander Laidlaw, who had joined them at Josimath. He was prickly and unsociable from the very start, keeping himself very much to himself and confining himself to monosyllables whenever he could. Moorcroft seems to have done his best with Laidlaw, lending him some of his books and treating him considerately in other ways, but what Moorcroft was not able to stomach were Laidlaw's 'sudden gusts of passion' and his 'intemperate treatment of the natives'. Ghulam Hyder Khan, more bluntly, called it cruelty.[5] Such behaviour, of course, was personally offensive to Moorcroft but, more than that, it could be highly dangerous in 'countries in which even slight indiscretions might compromise our liberties or our lives and endanger the success of the enterprise'. On 22 January, Moorcroft summoned Laidlaw and, in Trebeck's presence at an hour-long meeting, told him that he dare not risk his presence with the party any longer. The geologist retired to his quarters seething with anger and later began pacing up and down in front of Moorcroft's tent in a state of great agitation. It looked as though he were spoiling for a fight. Moorcroft therefore wrote to him just once more saying that he would, reluctantly, give him the satisfaction of a duel provided that it was done formally with seconds present. Moorcroft said he would wait one more week at Srinagar, until the beginning of February, for Laidlaw to make up his mind. Fortunately, the geologist made no further move and, when at last the great caravan moved off, to their great relief he remained where he was. That was 4 February 1820. They never saw him again, but it took another three years for Moorcroft to get his books back.[6]

Needless to say, he did not waste his time during this extended halt at Srinagar. Wilson's version does not convey any idea of the care with which Moorcroft examined the old royal palace on the river bank. His detailed notes are an important though neglected record which is all the more valuable because the ancient building was finally engulfed by the river seventy years later. Other things on the river bank intrigued Moorcroft too. The techniques of the fishermen and particularly the delicate line they used seemed to have such potential for British textile and hose manufacture that he ordered two cartloads of the wild creeper used in its manufacture to be collected and sent on after him. And at Tehri, two days' march further on, he had the whole manufacturing process demonstrated before his tent. In due course detailed notes and samples were on their way to Calcutta. Other things caught his eyes and passed his time at Srinagar – the gold-panning, the local trade, harrowing stories of Gurkha oppression before the Nepal war, the state of the horses' feet, the anatomy of some local wild animals. As ever, his curiosity was tireless. His crowded days were matched only by the crowded pages he produced when the long day was over. Nine-tenths of Moorcroft's surviving papers from this last period of his life consist of detailed observations and free-ranging speculations on a truly staggering variety of topics. The hurrying pen seems only to have come to a halt when frost or scorching sun checked the flow of the ink or the weary writer at last fell asleep over the page.

The whole party must have been glad to get away from Srinagar. It was not

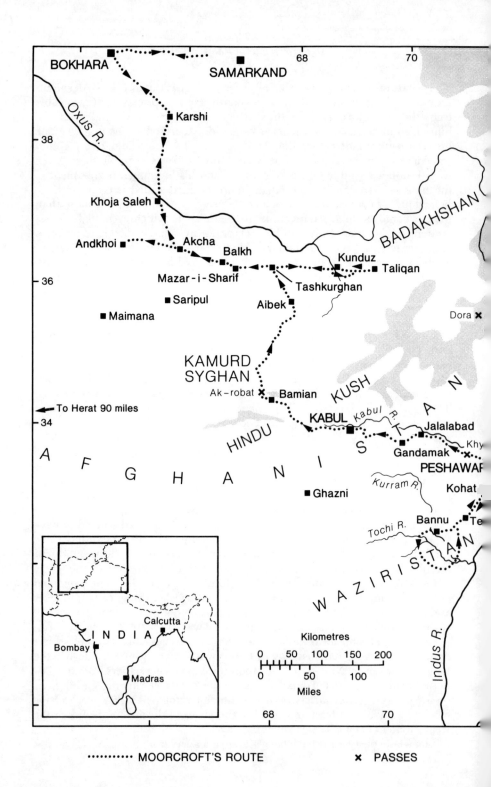

BOKHARA

SAMARKAND

68

70

Oxus R.

Karshi

38

BADAKHSHAN

Khoja Saleh

Andkhoi

Akcha

Balkh

Kunduz

Mazar-i-Sharif

Tashkurghan

Taliqan

36

Saripul

Aibek

Dora ✕

Maimana

KAMURD
SYGHAN

KUSH

Ak-robat ✕

Bamian

To Herat 90 miles

34

KABUL

Kabul R.

Jalalabad

Khy

HINDU

Gandamak ✕

A   F   G   H   A   N   I   S   T   A   N

PESHAWAR

Ghazni

Kurram R.

Kohat

Bannu

Te

Tochi R.

Calcutta

I N D I A

Bombay

WAZIRISTAN

Madras

Kilometres

Indus R.

0   50   100   150   200

0   50   100

Miles

68

70

·········· MOORCROFT'S ROUTE   ✕   PASSES

3. THE GRE

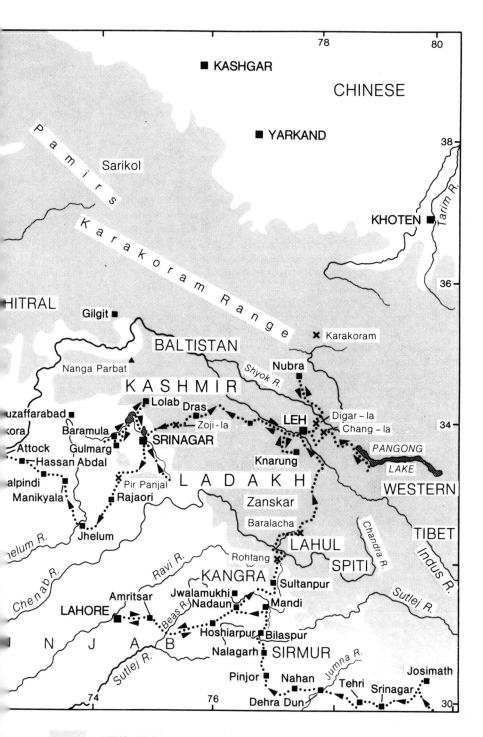

LAND ABOVE 13,000 FEET

JRNEY, 1820–25

a place to linger in, hemmed between its fickle river and the bare hills and often stiflingly hot in its engulfing mango groves. In 1820, as now, the old pilgrim road down to Hardwar crossed on to the right bank of the Alaknanda below Srinagar. Once safely across, Moorcroft and his party turned north-west away from the river and struck out across an increasingly fertile landscape of terraced fields, the winter wheat and mustard already showing above the ground. It was on this march towards Tehri on 5 February that Trebeck, 'my young friend whose industry kept pace with his zeal', finally abandoned the cumbrous, angular fathom measurer which he and the servants had been swinging like a huge pair of dividers ever since they left Almora. From now on Trebeck measured his distances by paces. That first day there were 15,916 of them in five and a half hours of marching to go into his notebook.

At Tehri, on its little plain hemmed in by hills, lived the son of the last ruler of independent Garhwal before the Gurkhas overran it. He was now chief of so-called Tehri Garhwal, the half restored to him after the Nepal war by the British. Sudarshan Sah, then in his thirties, was the first of many local rulers whom Moorcroft encountered on this journey. They had of course a great loathing of Gurkha misrule in common, but Moorcroft thought he had found in Sudarshan Sah a fellow-improver as well. He lingered at Tehri for nearly a week, preaching to his host the exciting potential of mulberry and silkworm cultivation, promising to obtain suitable eggs for him from British India and investigating the possibilities for tea and saffron growing. How typical of Moorcroft that he should advise Sudarshan Sah not to go in for the mineral development of his little kingdom, because mining was much less healthy for his subjects than working in the fresh air!

Moorcroft made his own direct contribution to the health of Tehri by opening his surgery. Four successful cataract operations and the removal of an unsightly growth from the eyelid of the chief's guru were among his tally there. Moorcroft always much preferred to operate when he could stay at least a few days to supervise the post-operative treatment. It seems that his reputation as a miracle healer was already beginning to run ahead of him for, a few days later, a partially-sighted wretch arrived all the way from Hardwar to seek treatment. His faith in Moorcroft was not misplaced. When the great caravan stopped again at the end of February, the man's sight was fully restored.

They left Tehri on 12 February and pushed on at their usual rate of five or six hours' marching a day. The road passed through hamlets and well-watered, cultivated valleys or, climbing higher on to the wooded hillsides, opened fine vistas of distant forts perched on top of a sea of green hills, with the marching clouds rolling sunshine and shadow across it all. This is almost the best time of the year in the Himalayan foothills and nothing very much has changed in the century and a half since Moorcroft's cavalcade passed that way.

Some things, however, are different. Today, for example, one would not encounter, as Izzat-Allah did on 14 February 1820, a pack of wolves in the very act of pulling down a large deer. The mir and his fellow-Muslims were chiefly interested in the supply of venison that was offered. Moorcroft on the other hand, was more concerned to get the complete corpse to his tent in order to sketch and measure it before undertaking a clinical dissection. After four men in relays had staggered along with the dead beast in great heat for 2 miles (3.2 kilometres), Moorcroft at last conceded victory to the cooking-pot and kept for science only its head, skin and hind leg. Even so, he covered pages of his journal with dissection notes and speculations before the dogs claimed their share of the prize and carried it off in the night.

Nor was that quite the end of the affair. It so delayed Moorcroft and those of the party with him, that they didn't catch up with the tents and the food before dark. With storm clouds gathering, they were driven to seek shelter for the night in a none too fragrant herdsman's hut. When at last the heavens opened in a crescendo of thunder and lightning, Moorcroft recalled,

> the rain poured through the flat roof and mixing with the dung of the cattle on the floor drenched and somewhat annoyed us . . . especially as soon our fires were put out by the wet. I called to Meer Izzut Oolla that as yet we had no earthquakes to complete our mishaps by overwhelming us with stones. He had scarcely uttered a grateful exclamation in reply when our attention was attracted by a grinding, grumbling and confused noise which I recognised as the precursor of an avalanche and for a short time the rushing and crashing and bounding of stones was most appalling.

They missed death that night by 50 yards (45.7 metres). No wonder Moorcroft's friends thought him mad. He on the contrary, bedraggled and stinking with what he wryly called 'the mist of the night', seems almost to have enjoyed it.

By now they were only a short march from Dehra Dun, that elevated and fertile valley sandwiched between the gentle inward slopes of the Siwaliks and bounded at each end by the Jumna and Ganges Rivers. The Dun had been the scene of some hard-fought battles during the recent Nepal war and was only just beginning to thrive again, after half a century of neglect and oppression. Hyder Hearsey claimed (in vain) that he was the legitimate owner of this valley.[7] Moorcroft could see why, as he stood in that marvellous springtime of 1820, looking down from the Nala Pani ridge on its beauty and mouth-watering potential. Needless to say, he dreamed his improver's dream of the day when the Dun would be a happy valley once more, the encroaching forest cleared and the fields re-established. For two or three days the whole party was housed in the cantonments just built at Dehra for the newly formed Sirmur infantry battalion. It was the last time Moorcroft ever enjoyed the hospitality of a British mess.

They left on 18 February and with the weather steadily warming up pushed on north-westwards just inside the first line of hills. On their right was the towering wooded scarp of the next great ridge on which the future British hill-stations would be perched. They crossed the Jumna by ferry boat, entered the raj of Sirmur and halted for a few days at its airy capital. Nahan was a handsome little town of stone houses and temples straggling along the edge of the plateau. With the air clear after the winter rains, it would have offered marvellous views across the nearer hills to the plains of northern India. As usual when they halted, Moorcroft's cataract needles were busy.

While they were at Nahan he was irritated to receive a letter from the British officer at the new cantonment at Sabathu in the hills to the north of them, complaining about reports that one of Moorcroft's Muslim servants – could it have been Ghulam Hyder Khan? – had been empressing men and animals to carry their baggage. What is more, the incident had been reported to Sir David Ochterlony, Metcalfe's successor at the Delhi residency.[8] Whatever the truth of the matter, the huffy correspondence which followed seems to have encouraged in the prickly Sir David a growing irritation at the reverberations of Moorcroft's slow, semi-official perambulation across the north-western limits of his territory. It had very unfortunate consequences later on.

They departed from Nahan on 1 March. Next day Hafiz caught up with them after his long journey from Josimath to the plains, bearing the missing goods and much welcome mail.[9] On 3 March the uncle of the raja of Sirmur, a fierce-looking man with a reputation to match, visited Moorcroft's tent seeking relief for the chronic arthritis which affected his thigh after a musket wound. Next day Moorcroft encountered something even more aggressive than Krishna Singh of Sirmur.

Moorcroft, as he often did, had wandered on ahead of the main party. Hot and tired, he had thrown himself down in the welcome shade of a peepul tree and was so busy writing that he did not see the mischievous small boy who crept up close and hurled some accurate stones into the nests of wild bees hanging in the tree not far above Moorcroft's head. The results were dramatic. An angry bee, reconnoitring to and fro at head height, suddenly made a dive and fastened on Moorcroft's left eyelid. He had scarcely pulled it off when several more attacked his face. It was not very often that Moorcroft ran away from anything, but now he rushed out from under the tree, swatting ineffectively with his sheets of paper, and dived through a thick hedge with the bees in hot pursuit. With the help of a villager, Moorcroft was given refuge under a blanket and sat half-suffocated in the smoke of a straw fire for more than an hour. When he was at last able to venture out without further attacks, he found a scene of utter confusion. It was alarming, but also irresistibly funny. Men and animals were flying in all directions – the latter often still loaded and plunging and kicking wildly, the men lying on the ground and batting helplessly at the bees with flailing arms and legs. The neighbouring town was in an uproar too. It took the rest of the day to restore some sort of order and round up the scattered caravan.

Very few men after such a day would have settled down, as Moorcroft did that evening, to two tricky cataract operations that set him thinking of ways to refine his technique. He then covered pages of his journal reflecting on the significance of the day. Why do bees go for dark colours? Why do they attack the face? What battles in history have been won and lost by the intervention of bees? It would have been very late that evening before the lamp in Moorcroft's tent went out. And it was very early next morning that they all stole away – just in case the bees (or the small boy) decided to have some more fun at their expense.

The next destination was the Mughal gardens at Pinjor, then on the new military road wriggling up into the hills to the cantonment at Sabathu. Today it is a popular tourist halt for buses on the way from Chandigarh to Simla. Moorcroft was intrigued by the ancient ruined Hindu monuments round about, (including a carved pillar filled with 'pairs of dancers' in postures which 'in other countries decency would have covered with a veil'). But he was enraptured by the neglected but still magnificent Mughal pleasure gardens, which he described in detail. What a place for an experimental botanical garden! The company should buy it from the raja of Patiala and pioneer fruit strains for the benefit of the local farmers. Moorcroft's journal fairly bulges with the possibilities and he still remembered them some years later.[10] He was also perhaps the first to see the potential of these hills for apple cultivation which today is such an important part of their agricultural economy.

A day or so later at Nalagarh, high on its bluff on the outermost edge of the hills, they unloaded the baggage from bullocks on to hill-porters and turned north into the hills. Three months had elapsed since leaving Josimath, but they were back on course for Ladakh once more. As they climbed higher across the forested ridges, they could look back and glimpse the magnificent Sutlej, meandering across the great summer plain of northern India. Soon they could glimpse the same young river ahead of them, carving its way down from the remote sources near Manasarowar, which Moorcroft had seen eight years before. On 12 March he came to its banks at the little town of Bilaspur.

In those days the swollen Sutlej hurrying past the town was about 50 yards (45.7 metres) wide in springtime. Today Moorcroft's Bilaspur has disappeared under the waters of the magnificent, placid lake of Govind Sagar, still spreading back into the valleys behind the gigantic Bhakra dam, which now arrests the river's headlong dash to the plains lower down. In Moorcroft's day, and for another quarter of a century afterwards, the Sutlej marked the northern limit of British territory and also represented a formidable physical obstacle to movement. Moorcroft as usual was busy. He had eighteen cataract patients during their two or three days at Bilaspur, eleven of them in a single day. Fortunately the local raja (whose stud of rather indifferent Lakhee Jungle horses Moorcroft inspected) declined surgery, for his case was a tricky one.[11] Moorcroft was also busy at his writing desk, to judge from the letters which have survived.[12] To the British officer at Sabathu there was the latest in the continuing saga of the allegedly empressed coolies. To Sir David Ochterlony at Delhi, notwithstanding that officer's unhelpful refusal to forward Moorcroft's letter to Ranjit Singh, whose hill territories they were about to enter, Moorcroft composed a friendly and diplomatic letter. The great and sensitive Ochterlony was too powerful a figure to antagonize and his good offices might be badly needed later on. Then there were the easier letters to his friends. To Palmer on 15 March, Moorcroft was in cheerful mood. He was delighted with young George and Izzat-Allah, his eye surgery was improving all the time, nobody in the party had died, and the road to Kulu was open.

Next day they crossed the Sutlej and left British soil for ever. To judge from his journal Moorcroft scarcely noticed this milestone.[13] He was absorbed in the spectacle before him. Thirty-one watermen, each astride an obscenely inflated buffalo skin, conveyed the whole immense party and its baggage across the swiftly running and icy river in about one and a half hours. Think of the value of such skins to save a man overboard at sea or to move an army rapidly across rivers! His journal is crammed with the possibilities.[14] Trebeck, usually the more romantic of the two, later rather punctured this dream by pointing out that, if the passage was disputed, 'a few shot holes would rather inconvenience the passengers'.[15]

That they were on territory new to Europeans and that their chances of slipping across Ranjit Singh's territories without fuss were slight, were both underlined when the leaders of the caravan reached the small raj of Sukhet two days later. Moorcroft's scruffy little escort of fourteen Gurkhas had, it seemed, been swollen by rumour into a force of nearly as many thousands, and the people had fled, 'crying that the Feringhees were coming to pillage'. Later that evening, however, curiosity about the first white men they had ever seen overcame their fear of the evil eye and, with growing confidence, they crowded round the tents to watch. Moorcroft, anxious to scotch the dangerous rumours, let these simple folk stay until a dust storm drove them away. Next morning he demonstrated his goodwill by three cataract operations. He must have been feeling tired for the night was not a peaceful one. They were disturbed by the mournful, flesh-tingling chorus of a pack of hyenas close to the tents. Later a single cannon shot booming out from the fort had the Gurkhas ready to fire in return, had Moorcroft not called out sharply from his tent in the darkness to prevent them.

Sukhet, in its open valley ringed with hills is, like Dehra Dun, a halfway house, sharing the rich monsoon vegetation of the plains but within sight of the great hills. From Sukhet, above the fruit trees in blossom, they could see the dramatic snowy ridge of the Dhaula Dhar sweeping down from the north-west and curving away to the east in front of them. It looks its very best in springtime and Moorcroft must have felt once again that lift of the heart at the hint of the cooler air and marvellous scenery ahead of them. A few more days should see them well into the deeper valleys running out from the main range.

That dream was shattered next day almost as soon as they entered Mandi, the next little sister-state to the north. A ragamuffin group of the raja's soldiery was drawn up across their path, their bows and arrows ready to fire and the musket matches alight. Their orders were peremptory. Moorcroft must either show his pass from Ranjit Singh or remain where he was. The raja, full of goodwill on his own account, confessed that he dare not let them proceed without permission, for fear of the wrath of his Sikh overlords, particularly since some of them were in the neighbourhood collecting revenue. It was all very frustrating. From a temple perched on a hill-top near Mandi one can gaze up the Kulu valley and plainly see the serrated peaks of the main snow ridge behind. Beyond that lies Ladakh.

If Moorcroft were tempted to make a dash for it he soon abandoned the idea. His letters and presents to Lahore may never have reached Ranjit Singh and, if the inflated rumours of his party were as great in the capital as they were in the hills, then his passage without permission would have caused an immense diplomatic storm, if nothing worse. On the other hand, if Ranjit refused transit permission, then the mission was virtually at an end.[16] It was a disquieting time but fortunately there were lighter moments even then. The armourer of the raja proved himself a lively and amusing raconteur, explaining with appropriate gestures the local custom of providing one slave girl to every fifty men of the garrison of the fort. 'Decency,' wrote Moorcroft, 'forbids me to detail the particulars recited to me by this very facetious old man.'

Moorcroft soon made up his mind. Guthrie, Hafiz, the bulk of the party and the goods, all in the charge of 'my young friend' Trebeck, would remain at Mandi under the protection of the raja. Moorcroft himself, taking Izzat-Allah, Ghulam Hyder and a handful of the servants, would hasten down to Lahore to seek permission in person from Ranjit Singh. It was a course of action not entirely without risk, for it would divide the party. He would be placed in Ranjit's not entirely scrupulous power and the vulnerability of the rest of the party left behind in Mandi would be greatly increased. That airless, crowded little town on the Beas river junction, hemmed in with the heat-reflecting bare hills is very picturesque, but is not high or open enough to be the ideal place to face the three hottest months of the year. In fact, as humidity, temperature and tempers all rose together, Trebeck's nerves began to fray and towards the end of his enforced exile at Mandi, Moorcroft was having to write encouraging letters to keep his spirits up. To make things worse, cholera struck the party. Moreover, the local Sikh commander was first obstructive and later so threatening, that Trebeck began to fear open violence.[17]

The risks were plain, but Moorcroft calculated that they were worth taking. All his life he had won more by personal charm than he ever had by his clumsy letters. Besides, he was probably curious to see Mughal Lahore and meet Ranjit, the living legend, who had carved himself an independent kingdom in the Punjab second only in power to that of the British themselves. Above all, Moorcroft had a plan by which he hoped to turn that wily chief into an active partner of 'the Himalaya concern'. Mixing blarney and commercial blackmail in more or less equal portions, Moorcroft intended to remind Ranjit that Britain now had direct access to the shawl wool of Tibet from its own territories. Since its power looms would soon compete with Ranjit's own expensive Kashmir product, his best chance of offsetting the consequent and inevitable decline in his revenue would be to benefit from the opening of Central Asia to British merchandise. Moorcroft hoped to win in the Punjab, not only favourable transit duties and safe conducts for British goods, but even perhaps a modest market for British goods, 'with patterns of which I am well provided'. Ever the optimist, Moorcroft set out with his little party for Lahore on 23 March.

They came first to Nadaun on the left bank of the Beas, the ancient capital of the now much reduced raj of Kangra. Its chief, Sansar Chand, was at his summer palace further up the river, but his greetings by letter were friendly and Moorcroft promised to visit him on his return. Since Ranjit Singh was not expected back in Lahore for a few more days, Moorcroft turned aside to visit the little Hindu temple and place of pilgrimage at Jwalamukhi. It was, and is, regarded as a place of special sanctity because of the flames of natural gas which issue from the ground inside the temple. Moorcroft was not impressed. He found the inside of the temple so suffocatingly claustrophobic that he was forced to beat a hasty retreat. The outside was nearly as bad – 'most disgustingly offensive and displayed the total absence of ordered decency'. Of the priests, beggars and cows, he found the last the most attractive of the three. The whole place cried out for improvement. Moorcroft as usual thought he could give nature a scientific nudge and proposed piping the natural gas inside the temple to an artificial lotus flower. Lest this suggestion should attract criticism as pandering to ignorant superstition, he added a very revealing personal confession.

> On this head I satisfy my own conscience by the persuasion that the religion or devotion of the Hindoo however obscured by mystic symbols or by circumstantial ceremonies is directed to the 'great first cause least understood' Jehovah, Jove or "Lord". Gratitude at least is due from me to that tolerant principle which has forbore all resentment whilst I have pushed enquiry so far as would perhaps have shewn me the road to martyrdom had it been conducted with equal freedom or indiscretion in some of the more polished countries of Europe professing a more enlightened faith.

Moorcroft's Christianity was more akin to the tolerant, easy-going Anglicanism of the mid-eighteenth century than the born-again zeal of the post-Wesleyan evangelical movement, with its inescapable loathing of the errors and gross idolatry of Hinduism. Moorcroft was forward-looking in so many ways but in this he was more like the men of an earlier generation – more in the mould of his former London acquaintance, Warren Hastings, than of Edward Parry and his fellow-'saints'. His undeniable pride in the superior blessings of Western civilization, scientific improvement and the Christian faith, never led him, as it did many of the insensitive and utilitarian Victorians who came later, into dismissive contempt for the older and more subtle cultures of India.[18] On the contrary, he took all things and all men on their merits without prejudice, certain that there was something to be learned from all.

The point was nicely illustrated even while he was still at Jwalamukhi on 28 March 1820. At considerable trouble and expense, he borrowed from the local confectioners two big iron cauldrons, in which he boiled off the water from a local salt spring which had a high reputation for curing both goitre and skin complaints. Moorcroft was sceptical but, being the man he was, he determined to put the matter to the test. Some of the residual salts he sent down to the Medical Board at Calcutta for analysis and kept the rest for his own experiments. In his now familiar style, his mind went racing off into the future, his pen scratching busily for page after page, meeting and solving problems of bottling, distributing, marketing, exporting and preventing the adulteration of the salts, and dreaming of the great boost to the needy local economy that would follow. The curious temple brahmins, perhaps hoping for sweetmeats, must have been very mystified, but then so were many of Moorcroft's British contemporaries, content to live in their own time and not hustle the future as he was wont to do.

He was back at Nadaun next day and, on 30 March, set off with his little party along the old caravan road from the hills, down to Amritsar and Lahore in the teeming northern plains. Almost as soon as they crossed Raja Sansar Chand's western border on 1 April, they were surrounded by a scruffy but threatening Sikh force, but soon released on the orders of the local revenue farmer, Magar Mull. He was 'a well-informed and facetious old man' who laughed heartily at the abounding rumours of the fifty warriors said to be contained in each of their magic trunks. The Sikh authorities at the next stopping place, however, were genuinely alarmed. The whole party was halted in the weavers' town of Hoshiarpur for the rest of April, while Izzat-Allah posted off ahead of them, first to the local governor and then on to Lahore, to obtain permission for them to proceed.

It was a very trying time indeed. Moorcroft was compelled to erect his tent on the baking roof of a flyblown dosshouse for beggars and downwind of a watercourse, 'in which the female part of the population of Hoshiarpoor daily made offerings to Cloacina [spoof goddess of the sewer] not a little repugnant to European notions of what is due to female decorum. The stench and heat were extreme'. So extreme, quite the worst Moorcroft had ever experienced, that he reckoned that, had the nights not brought some respite, and had he not cut out all meals but breakfast and lived simply on liquids, he would have succumbed. As it was, he became so light-headed that he completely forgot which month or day it was, and so confused Wilson that he believed that the stay at Hoshiarpur was twice as long as it was.[19]

Needless to say, Moorcroft did not lie about sweltering in his tent. He prepared some immensely detailed notes on the mechanisms of the cotton trade and the manufactures of the town, which must have been based on extensive enquiries in the bazaar. He devoted about four hours each day to a free clinic, at which he provided surgery and medicine to long queues of miserable wretches. There was a man with a hideously deforming hydrocephalus, a woman with a cancerous tongue, and some forty cataract cases requiring surgery. Moorcroft, refining his technique all the time, covered pages of his notebook with his clinical observations, difficulties and successes. He concluded,

No eye has suppurated nor has any pupil been obliterated or materially deformed. The iris has in no instance been perforated during the operation or torn from any part of its circumference. . . . I operated sometimes in the open air without shade, sometimes in an open shed, or under a tree or in a veranda or in my tent and my patients in some instances came twice a day in the sun whilst in others they absented themselves for two or three days yet altogether I was by no means dissatisfied with the general result.

For all the purgatory of that fetid month at Hoshiarpur, that hint of satisfaction in a job well done must have been a mighty consolation to him. Doubtless too, many of his patients in that unlovely town had their own reasons to bless the unlikely chain of events which brought and kept the little Feringi *hakim* in their midst in April 1820. However Hoshiapur is one of the places in which one of Moorcroft's certificates testifying to good treatment will not be found. He refused point-blank to provide one for the local governor.

In camp at sunset on 29 April, with Hoshiarpur one day's march behind him, Moorcroft breathed deeply and gratefully the first fresh air round his tent for a month. The heat was as great as ever and the account book records expenditure on devices to keep them cool.[20] Indeed, the next day Moorcroft had such a blinding headache from the heat and glare that they travelled most of the rest of the way, across the (in those days) largely uncultivated country of the north Punjab plain, before the sun was up and rested during the day. Moorcroft was obviously feeling the delayed effects of his enforced stay at Hoshiarpur. Most unusually for him, he was obliged to travel much of the way in a litter. Nearly every day as they approached Lahore brought some fresh mark of attention from Ranjit Singh or his chiefs along the way – a large escort, trays of sweetmeats, ice, and more comfortable accommodation. On 5 May Moorcroft, who had been examining the horses of the Sikh escort with considerable interest, stopped to look over one of Ranjit Singh's breeding-studs. He was not very impressed, either with the animals or their management, particularly when the grooms of one stallion said they dare not take him from his stall because 'he would be very troublesome if . . . a mare was not given to him *as he never left his stand except for* that purpose'. So much for healthy exercise.

Next morning about nine, after another early start, they reached the great and once glorious Mughal garden of Shalimar, on the western outskirts of Lahore. The crude little whitewashed and once water-cooled pavilion in which Moorcroft stayed[21] still stands there today, and the cool chamber in which he slept now houses bottled drinks for the modern Pakistani tourists. Very few of them notice the only public memorial to Moorcroft ever erected in Asia, a tiny marble plaque in English commemorating this visit in 1820 and erected high on the pavilion wall by some later, unknown admirer, after the British had become masters of the Punjab.[22] Moorcroft would have been pleased by the plaque, but delighted at the replacement of Sikh authority. He gradually came to reserve for their oppression and misrule the kind of loathing which he and Hearsey had earlier felt for that of the Gurkhas. He did not, however, have anything to complain of in the generosity of his welcome by Raja Ranjit Singh.

Next morning, he was invited by the raja's trusted doctor and minister, Aziz ud Din, to transfer his quarters to a more splendid pavilion which was then standing on the banks of the Ravi near the fort. It has now been engulfed by the waters of the river and is fast disappearing. That evening he was visited once again by the intelligent and handsome Aziz ud Din, eldest of three brothers who were all high in Ranjit's favour.[23] Moorcroft came to like them all and enjoyed their urbane conversation, but it was with the physician, Aziz, that he had most in common. It was this man who, on the evening of 8 May, arrived to conduct Moorcroft to his first audience with the raja. Together on horseback, with Izzat Allah close at hand to interpret the Punjabi dialect, they would have crossed the terraced gardens past the marvellous Badshahi mosque, with its tall sandstone minarets and bulbous domes of gleaming white marble, and then passed through the massive sandstone gateway of the fort opposite.

The Sikhs were never able to match the splendour of the Mughals in their heyday, but Ranjit had certainly done his best to impress his English visitor on this occasion. He rose from his golden chair and directed Moorcroft to a silver one, set about 15 feet (4.5 metres) away on a sheet of gold tissue. Between them, on a carpet, sat a double row of his court officials, all splendidly bearded, robed and turbaned. Moorcroft was by now no stranger to Eastern court ceremonial but he must have been especially curious to meet this powerful and successful ruler about whom their mutual friend, Charles Metcalfe, would often have talked. Ghulam Hyder Khan was an interested eye-witness too.

> The rajah is about five foot seven or eight inches [1.7 metres] high, stout, but not fat; has a long beard, which from age is white and black; has an oval formed face, common nose, face very much speckled with the small-pox, and has lost his left eye . . . he seems active and intelligent . . . his voice was soft and pleasing to the ear.[24]

This first meeting was, of course, mainly ceremonial and devoted largely to civilities and the exchange of presents. Ranjit seemed pleased with the brace of double- and treble-barrelled pistols and, even more, with the exquisitely engineered six-pounder mini-cannon which they had heaved all the way up from Fatehgarh. Although unlettered, he was highly intelligent and almost as curious about everything as Moorcroft himself. The questions came, as they always did from Ranjit, thick and fast. Soon the two men were in animated conversation about their common passion, horses. In no time, fifty of Ranjit's priceless animals from all over Asia were paraded, richly caparisoned, on a flooded pavement just below where they sat. It was a good start.

Early next morning Moorcroft was back again to see the horses exercized. He sat under an awning in a garden with his host, and marvelled at the perfect schooling of another fifty splendid animals. In four days Moorcroft saw something like 200 of Ranjit's finest horses. Encouraged by the chief's growing cordiality, Moorcroft spent some time at his desk on 9 May drafting a commercial agreement by which British merchandise would be admitted to the Punjab at a 2 per cent *ad valorem* transit duty and gave it to Aziz to lay before his master. Next day it was the turn of Ranjit's army to show its paces in manoeuvres on the plain outside the city while, on an adjacent rooftop, Ranjit chattered animatedly to Moorcroft about his campaigns. Two days later there was musketry and gunnery exercise, this time in the Shalimar gardens. The men's aim seemed as poor as the guns. Five soldiers were injured firing the cannon and two more had hands shattered by bursting musket barrels.

Ranjit's chief preoccupation, it seemed, was with his own health, although it took some time before he had enough confidence in his visitor to go to the heart of the matter. At last, on 10 May, he got as far as confessing to Moorcroft that he still had all his old desire for strong liquor 'but from which he felt not the gratification experienced in former times'. What he was really referring to was the decline in his ability to gratify his sexual appetite, although this was still only hinted at behind a smokescreen of dyspepsia and irregular bowel action. It was a delicate business, made all the more trying for Moorcroft by 'a thousand impertinent suggestions and hints of advice' from the court quacks.[25] At last Moorcroft was permitted to give the chief a thorough medical examination. There seemed nothing organically wrong, so Moorcroft sensibly prescribed a brisk course of abstemiousness, hard work and no worry, with some aloetic pills as a placebo. Privately Moorcroft thought Ranjit was a hypochondriac. He was also realistic enough to realize that the chief would take little notice of his recommendations and that the pills would probably be forced down the neck of some hapless courtier, just in case.

Still, the private consultation was a singular mark of trust and so too was Ranjit's permission to roam at will through the crowded, colourful streets and bazaars of the city. He even provided an elephant from which to do it. From this high vantage point Moorcroft had a splendid view of the town whores sitting and saluting him at their first-floor windows. In a section of his journal which Wilson did *not* use he wrote:

> In general they are well dressed, have a profusion of ornaments, have good complexions but I am sure none that would have been considered beautiful when compared with women of this class in Europe, although the manners of the former have in them nothing offensive to decency.

Ranjit would have understood Moorcroft's obvious interest in the subject. He would not have been quite so understanding if he had known with what care his guest was noting the capability of the city and fort to defend itself against 'any European force'. Moorcroft was a bit uneasy about the ethics of all this since Ranjit was a British ally and he his guest. It is, he told Metcalfe, 'altogether more allied to a modification of espionage than is perfectly agreeable to my feelings'.[26] Moorcroft's journals of this period are full of shrewd insights into the strengths and weaknesses of Ranjit's kingdom and remarkably accurate in their forecast of what would follow Ranjit's death, including the eventual British annexation.[27]

He was treading on very thin ice indeed. Behind the veneer of colour, polish and Ranjit's 'increasing familiarity at each successful audience'[28], was a darker reality of tortured and maimed political prisoners, appalling diseases, misgovernment, intrigue and oppression. Moorcroft was quite sure that some of the men who came breathing treachery against Ranjit were sent to test him. Others appeared more genuine. One wretch, who had been tortured by hot bricks and then blinded by the smoke from wet straw, came seeking medical help as also did the incarcerated ex-rulers of Multan. On another occasion, Moorcroft believed his intentions concerning the shawl trade were being tested when he was offered, at an absurdly low price, a precious shawl pattern book and he decided to pretend to be uninterested. The compromising information still flowed in, however, much of it from an eminent shawl broker who consulted Moorcroft for 'a most formidable disease'.[29] In due course, the shawl-weave samples this man supplied were smuggled out of Kashmir and were soon on their way to Calcutta.[30] Other men were helped simply because their need was desperate. One dying man brought to Moorcroft

> owes his recovery to means, which have been condemned as cruel because they have been banished from the polished practice of medicine as applied to man in Europe. *Nullius addictus jurare [in verba] magestri* [owning no master] I frequently travel out of the beaten road in desperate cases and do not find my conscience the heavier.[31]

He did not elucidate.

In Moorcroft's view, of course, the basic trouble was that Ranjit Singh, for all his charm and urbanity, was not an improver. He was far 'more interested in increasing the extent of his dominions than in improving their produce or in augmenting the comforts of his subjects'. When Moorcroft judged the moment opportune, and notwithstanding the risk, he made what he called[32] 'some strong reflections direct to him upon his oppression and tyranny'. The Punjab, Moorcroft realized, with its abundant water resources and fine climate, could be one of the richest corners of Asia. It would also, he hoped, be a great highway of British commerce passing up the broad rivers and into the heart of Asia. That dream Moorcroft shared with Ranjit himself but not, needless to say, his associated hope and belief that one day these rich resources would all be British. 'This idea may be censured as ambitious, extravagant and improbable,' he wrote to Parry,[33] 'but however it may be scouted at present "to this conclusion you must come at last".' He was right.

So those busy days at Lahore at the beginning of May 1820 slipped away. It may have been at some time during this period that one of Ranjit's court artists painted the only portrait of Moorcroft known to have survived.[34] The final audience of leave with the raja took place on 13 May. Ranjit had already very firmly consigned what Moorcroft called his 'waking dream',[35] the opening of the Punjab to British trade, to the tomorrow which never comes. Moorcroft, equally firmly, signalled his determination to keep it on the agenda by telling Ranjit, at this final audience, that he had sent a report about the whole matter to the resident at Delhi.[36] Ranjit kept his counsel. Just what Sir David Ochterlony thought about this 'irregularity' (Moorcroft's word) can be guessed by what came later, but, for the moment, Moorcroft had every reason to be satisfied. He had the passports he needed, the road to Ladakh by way of Kulu was open and, if all else failed, he had Ranjit's permission to leave Ladakh by way of Kashmir. On 15 May he crossed the Ravi to inspect the Emperor Jahangir's 'most surprisingly grand' multi-coloured marble mausoleum, then turned east and hastened off across the plain towards Amritsar.

At Amritsar there was a five-day delay while Moorcroft recruited more servants. At least that was the ostensible reason. In those days there was in the town a substantial colony of impoverished and exiled Kashmiri shawl weavers. They proved to be a rich source of information and Moorcroft even wondered to Metcalfe whether some of them might not be tempted to Britain to launch the industry there. He also set a wool picker to work and watched closely to see why his own attempts in 1812 to separate the fine shawl wool from the rest had gone so disastrously wrong. In due course, pages and pages of information on this and other more political subjects were on their way to Metcalfe at the Secret Department in Calcutta.[37] While in Amritsar, Moorcroft also received the disquieting news of the death of the chief of Balkh, on whom he had been counting for safe conducts north of the Hindu Kush. He retired to his portable desk and soon three letters were on their way northwards. One was to Muhammad Azim Khan, the Afghan chief at Peshawar, reminding him of the offers of help made by his late brother, and two similar ones were sent to the new rulers in the vicinity of Balkh. All accounts suggested that Afghanistan was sliding into fratricidal civil war – dangerous pirate waters in which his fat and ponderous merchant caravan would be very vulnerable indeed. Moorcroft was more anxious than ever to push on across the Himalayas to Ladakh as quickly as possible, in the hope that he could then cross the Karakoram to the north and avoid Afghanistan altogether.

Problems nearer at hand soon cut short long-range plans of this kind. While Moorcroft was halting at Amritsar between 17 and 22 May, the first of a flurry of letters from Ranjit Singh arrived[38], announcing the serious illness of his son and asking Moorcroft to prescribe something for him. If this was a hint, Moorcroft ignored it and pushed on as fast as he could. But on 29 May, he received from Ranjit a letter too peremptory to be ignored. He must return to Lahore at once. It was a black moment. Moorcroft ordered the rest of his small party to join Trebeck and push on as fast as they could to Kulu, before the now imminent monsoon rains launched their violence against them. He, meanwhile, almost alone and full of foreboding, turned back towards Lahore.

It was clear as soon as he was in session with Aziz that the stories about Ranjit's son were largely fictitious.[39] Ranjit himself was the one who wanted Moorcroft's medical services – or magic spells. Apparently the intermittent feverish ague, and the alternative bouts of shivering, sweating and vomiting which he was suffering, were being attributed to an evil spell conjured up by Moorcroft before he left Lahore. Moorcroft flatly refused to diagnose without seeing the patient but, for one reason or another, was not allowed to do so until 2 June, when Ranjit seemed somewhat better. It was a delicate situation. Moorcroft felt pretty sure from the symptoms that Ranjit would recover completely in a few days. If he were right, then he could win substantial benefits from the chief by appearing to be the cause of his recovery: but if he were wrong, and Ranjit died under his treatment, the consequences could be dire indeed. Moorcroft decided to play for safety and keep himself in the background but it is clear that he was uneasily aware, in those suffocatingly hot June days, that the net might be closing round him. Ranjit had an unsavoury reputation for keeping his visitors under duress, while plying them with every mark of attention. He provided Moorcroft with elephants, bearers, bullocks and the house of a royal prince to live in, but one expedient after another made the promised departure endlessly deferred. Even when he did get away at last, on one of Ranjit's elephants on the evening of 8 June, something rather odd and sinister happened. 'In the middle of the night I was dexterously turned out of the road by the guide and was in full march back to Lahour when the rising of the moon discovered the detour and the mistake.'[40]

Was it a mistake? Moorcroft thought not. He therefore contrived to give his mounted escort the slip and reached Amritsar by late morning on 9 June, after a circuitous, fifteen-hour nightmare journey in the heat of the sun. Feverish, sleepless and with a blinding headache, Moorcroft now received a return for his own generous treatment of the sick among the Kashmiri weavers some days before. One of them patiently fanned him and relaxed the taut muscles in his back and neck with skilful massage until, with the Englishman at last in a deep and restful sleep, he stole silently away. It was not the first, and certainly not the last, occasion on which Moorcroft's patients tried to repay in the only way they could, the great debt they felt they owed him. That evening, greatly refreshed, he was at work once more on three advanced cholera victims. He bled one and placed on the stomach of another 'little balls of cotton dipped in camphor and set on fire'. This time he was unsuccessful and one of the three died, but the father of one who recovered was so grateful that he helped to smuggle Moorcroft out of the town in the early hours of 10 June, after the gates were shut for the night, so that he could get well ahead of any pursuers.

Seven hours later Moorcroft, and his handful of servants and elephants, reached the less-frequented Beas ferry near Vairowal, well to the south of the main trunk road, and crossed over in the evening. Then, turning north-west and travelling all night, they staggered into Hoshiarpur at eleven next morning, glad to see even that unattractive town once more. For all his haste and exhaustion, Moorcroft lingered a whole day at Hoshiarpur to examine some of his cataract patients, while the servants and elephants rested. In two cases the opaque lens had risen again and blindness had returned, but two others had entirely clear eyes and another had unexpected vision in one eye although the other was still inflamed. Moorcroft was reasonably satisfied with this 50 per cent success rate, considering the appalling conditions.

On 13 June he at last entered the first of the hills on the very edge of Ranjit's territory and caught up with the remainder of his party, who themselves had been delayed. Even then, or so Moorcroft believed, Ranjit had not quite finished with them. At an exorbitant rate of interest, Moorcroft had raised 2000 rupees in Amritsar to meet their travelling expenses on the road to Kulu. During the night the bag in Izzat-Allah's tent was stealthily cut open and two-thirds of the contents spirited away into the darkness.[41]

Three days later the heavens opened. In the next month Moorcroft experienced more rain every day than he had ever known before. It was the last straw, and his simmering anger against Ranjit Singh, exploded.

> I have been compelled to waste many thousands of rupees, have lost four months of time, am plunged into all the difficulties necessarily attending a passage through a most difficult country in the midst of the rains, have had much property injured and been exposed to the risk of losing the season for passing the mountains.[42]

He and Ranjit Singh had not quite finished with each other yet but, for the moment at least, the situation was about to improve.

17 KANGRA, KULU, LAHUL AND ARRIVAL IN LADAKH,

JUNE–SEPTEMBER 1820

THE THUNDEROUSLY HEAVY monsoon rains, which began on 16 June 1820 while they were somewhere in the hills just to the east of Nadaun,[1] were certainly one reason why they gratefully accepted the invitation of the Kotoch raja of Kangra, Sansar Chand, to stay at his court.[2] Another was the genuine warmth of the welcome. When Moorcroft had passed through Kangra on his way down to Lahore three months before, he had been startled to receive two letters from the 'Captain Commanding' Sansar Chand's army and signed James O'Brien.[3] It was hardly a local name. This Irishman, a deserter from the British cavalry and temporarily sober between heavy drinking bouts, was the first to welcome Moorcroft to Kangra. He led him to the River Beas where 500 men of Sansar Chand's colourful, toytown army were waiting, drums beating, to escort him across the river to the Alampur gardens where Sansar Chand spent the summer. There they lined up, while Moorcroft solemnly rode down the avenue between them to where his tent had been pitched in a pleasant garden under the mango trees beside the Beas, about ½ mile (0.8 kilometres) from Sansar Chand's summer palace. That evening Moorcroft had his first meeting with that tall and still handsome, hawk-nosed and dark-skinned Rajput chief.

Raja Sansar Chand of Kangra had once, before the rise of the Gurkhas on one side and Ranjit Singh on the other, extended his sway over all that glorious hill-country between the Indus and the Sutlej. Even now, despite his shrunken fortunes and thickening waistline, he still maintained a court in considerable state, although the really great days when his harem at Nadaun gave that place a legendary reputation for the pleasures of the flesh, were over for good. Even so, the superlative banquets he provided for Moorcroft and his party in the modest little summer palace at Alampur (the ruins and gardens of which are still impressive today), must have been very memorable. Sansar Chand had not lost his taste for handsome dancing-girls and it would have been surprising if he had not offered his principal guests their traditional services. Certainly, the sharp-eyed and gossipy Ghulam Hyder Khan noticed that Moorcroft later sent a piece of fine cloth 'to his favourite dancing-woman, named Jumalo'.[4] She must have been an exceptional woman, for in the closing months of Sansar

1 Indian portrait, said to be of Moorcroft, 1820

II Ormskirk in Moorcroft's time

III John Hunter

IV Liverpool in 1797 (the
Infirmary is to the right of
the central windmill)

V Edward Coleman

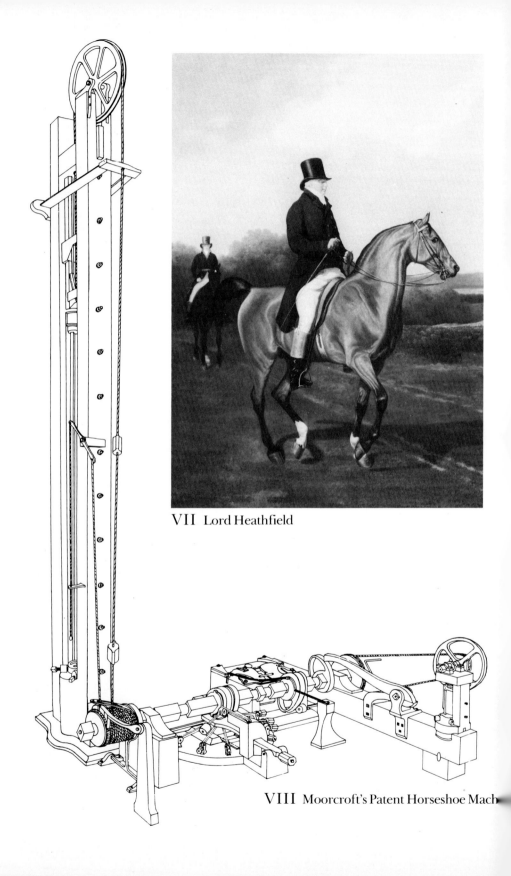

VII Lord Heathfield

VIII Moorcroft's Patent Horseshoe Mach

IX Afghan and Persian Horse Merchants

X The Hajipur Fair

XI Lord Minto,
    Indian Governor-General 1808-13

XII Lord Hastings,
     Indian Governor-General 1813-22

XIII Horace Wilson

XIV The Abbé Huc

XV, XVI Pavilion and plaque in the
Shalimar Gardens, Lahore

IN THIS PAVILION, BUILT BY RANJIT SINGH,
THE FAMOUS TRAVELLER
WILLIAM MOORCROFT
STAYED DURING HIS VISIT TO THE COURT OF THE
MAHARAJA IN MAY 1820, ON HIS WAY TO
TURKISTAN WHERE HE DIED IN 1825.

XVII Lithograph from Trebeck's drawing of Leh, Ladakh

XVIII Hearsey's painting of Moorcroft (extreme left) and himself in Tibet, 1812

Chand's life three years later, he is said to have spent most of his time in her company. The ruins of some of her houses at Nadaun and her name are still remembered even today.[5] If she were already Sansar Chand's favourite by the time of Moorcroft's visit then, of course, Ghulam Hyder Khan's remark is rather less salacious than appears at first sight.

But, dancing-girls or not, after the threatening friendship of Ranjit Singh and the heat and rain of the recent journey, one can see why Moorcroft was in no hurry to depart from Kangra. There was, as always, much more to his six-week stay at Sansar Chand's court than the mere fleshpots to be found there. For one thing he and the raja, both much the same age, seem to have become firm friends. Moorcroft believed that, if Sansar Chand had been suitably educated, 'he would have been a character probably superior to any Asiatic that has appeared since Shah Jehan'.[6] Moorcroft set about repairing that omission by preaching to his host all manner of schemes to develop the natural resources of his kingdom. He even persuaded Sansar Chand to agree to take on the Anglo-Indian engineer and Calcutta shipbuilder, James Kyd, as his development manager on a 25 per cent commission on profit basis. Minerals, silk, rhubarb, cotton, timber, honey, paper, coffee, opium, vegetables – they were all possible foreign currency earners in Moorcroft's opinion.[7] To provide for the future, Moorcroft wanted to send Sansar Chand's grandsons down to Calcutta for an enlightened education under 'the fatherly care of my friend Ram Mohun Raie', the man still regarded by many today as the intellectual father of modern India. Letters and men were despatched by Moorcroft out of Kangra in all directions, to obtain improving advice, seeds and technical know-how. In his spare time he investigated and recorded local alphabets for the Asiatic Society as well.[8] Sansar Chand's impressions of his dynamic and extraordinary visitor have unfortunately not survived, but they were clearly favourable. He soon moved Moorcroft out of his dripping tent and into one of his bungalows in the palace gardens[9] and there, almost every morning, he came down to enjoy an hour or two of congenial conversation with his visitor.

Those conversations were not by any means confined to improvement. The raja was a lover of music, a fine chess player and, above all, a very distinguished patron of the arts. The practical Moorcroft did not entirely approve of the hours spent on the first two, but he was entranced by Sansar Chand's 'immense collection of coloured drawings of Hindu mythology'.[10] They were, he concluded, greatly underestimated in Western art circles. How right he was! His description of this great collection before it was broken up, was the first Western record of Pahari hill-painting and, according to its greatest Western historian, provides 'crucial' early evidence for what is now recognized as one of the glories of Indian art.[11] Sansar Chad very generously allowed Moorcroft the pick from his collection, but the white ants and the mishaps of the road ensured that most of those delicate treasures would never survive to grace the walls of that dream house on the mountain-side near Josimath.[12] It was possibly one of Sansar Chand's court painters who executed, during this stay, the portrait sketch of Moorcroft which has already been referred to.[13]

Moorcroft's original plan was to leave Alampur about a week after his first arrival, but disquieting news from the main party not far away at Mandi on 20 and 22 June delayed his departure. Ranjit Singh had not quite finished with them yet, it seemed. Trebeck, very low in spirits, wrote to say that he believed that he and the great caravan were virtual prisoners. Moorcroft immediately despatched letters, of complaint to Ranjit at Lahore, and of encouragement to his young companion higher up the river,[14] and decided to stay where he was until the situation was clearer. The delay had interesting consequences.[15]

On 29 June Sansar Chand's younger brother, the popular and gallant Fateh Chand, 'a stout man about fifty-four', consulted Moorcroft. The prince was in great distress with a violent pain in his right side and severe bleeding from ruptured piles. Moorcroft was mystified and asked to examine him thoroughly, but two days later he learned that Fateh Chand had been taken seriously ill. Moorcroft hurried to his bedside and found him unconscious, breathing as though apoplectic, and tossing about violently. Beside his couch a naked fakir and the court physicians were trying to exorcize the evil spirit which they believed had taken possession of him.

By next morning the prince, with his pulse scarcely detectable, had been given up for dead and Sansar Chand was willing to let Moorcroft loose on him, even if Fateh Chand would lose his high caste in the process. Moorcroft had nothing to lose. Without much hope of success, he set to work on the prince that same night. The phrase is an appropriate one, as a very frank set of clinical notes reveals. Moorcroft seems to have suspected cholera. That dangerous and highly infectious disease was certainly raging in a neighbouring village and Moorcroft naturally resorted to his well-tried and violent methods of assault upon it. He first bled his royal patient 'until the pulse began to fail and flutter'. Then, using a home-made enema apparatus consisting of a bamboo tube and the large intestine of a goat, 'a quantity of oil of turpentine and of sesamum [was] injected into the rectum'. Moorcroft kept this up for nearly two hours without significant result so he then tried to purge the hapless man by medicine given orally. Next, he burned oiled cotton on Fateh Chand's stomach to prevent the usual violent and often fatal stomach spasms. So it went on practically all through the night of 2 July, although luckily the prince was too far gone to know much about the horrors of that night. Next morning, when he miraculously regained consciousness, Moorcroft gave him warm baths in a huge cauldron and then, when he was feeling stronger, surgically repaired his damaged rectum. Fateh Chand after one more major relapse on 5 July, which required more drastic rectal surgery, was soon convalescing. The astonishment and delight of Fateh Chand's family (including, understandably, his wives who would otherwise have been immolated on his funeral pyre) was immense.

So too was their generosity to the royal doctor. Sansar Chad offered him an estate of many miles' extent wherever he wished it to be. Later Moorcroft was quite ready to take up the offer and retire to the beautiful Kangra valley, if his favoured Kumaon scheme fell through. Fateh Chand conferred on Moorcroft perhaps an even more remarkable honour. In the words of the astonished

Ghulam Hyder Khan, this high-caste Rajput prince 'exchanged the turban off his head for Mr. Moorcroft's [peaked] hat, which he put on (the greatest mark of attention he could pay him), and called him brother'.[16] It was literally true. By that simple but solemn act the commoner from Ormskirk became by adoption a member of the ancient ruling house of Kotoch with a pedigree, so Moorcroft believed, older than the invasion of Alexander the Great. The Bourbons were upstarts by comparison he told his friend Saunders.[17] Moorcroft had nothing comparable to give to his royal brothers in return and could only write to Palmer asking for a goodly collection of presents to be sent for the women of the harem and for Sansar Chand himself. His shopping list was a nice mixture of the artistic and the useful – cloth of various kinds, two telescopes, a gold watch, a pipe organ, a box of clothes for Sansar Chand's son, a collection of seeds, a dripstone and silkworm eggs with full instructions.[18] He also, needless to say, gave Sansar Chand a generous testimonial to his good treatment.[19]

By mid-July it was time to face the rigours of the road once more. Fateh Chand's remarkable recovery had coincided with the welcome news that the ugly deadlock at Mandi was at last broken and that Trebeck was preparing to put the great caravan in motion once more. There were sad farewells at Alampur on the morning of 22 July. Moorcroft was loaded with presents, a dress of honour and so much food specially cooked by the ladies of the harem that it kept him going for more than a week. Sansar Chand also provided provisions, an armed escort, and porters for the party. There were even three hardy shepherds ('my clansmen', as Moorcroft fondly called them) to act as mail-runners so that he could keep in close touch with Kangra all the way to Ladakh. The rain was still pouring down, as they set off eastwards along the old caravan trail which leads into the sea of wooded hills and up towards the Dulchi pass.

It was a miserable business despite the short marches. The rain made cooking practically impossible and soaked the bedding and baggage. They sheltered where they could, often on the floors and verandahs of shepherds' huts and usually tormented by fleas, bugs and rats. Even the little hillside streams had become torrents, often dangerous to cross. As they slithered in the mud over stones, their softened feet became badly blistered and their shoes stretched and were perpetually wet. 'Our gilt is all besmircht by painful marching in the rainy field' Moorcroft wrote to Metcalfe,[20] misquoting from Shakespeare's *Henry V*. His sense of humour seems to have survived all the same, as his journal bears witness. He described how on one occasion he tried in vain to sleep inside his leaky tent under an umbrella. On another he noted that they took shelter with the wives of some absent buffalo herdsmen 'who have the character of being liberal with their favours' but who proved disappointingly 'respectful and modest'. One lady who was neither was involved two days after this in a very noisy and entertaining public altercation with her husband. 'I pitied the woman' Moorcroft wrote, 'though I little doubted of her delinquency as I had seen her exhibit at a window views of coquetry which indicated a disposition not to allow her charms to bloom unseen.' Even the endless rain did not dampen his appreciation of the 'pretty features and well-turned limbs' of the handsome hill-women along the way.

What it did do, however, was deny him any proper appreciation of the magnificent forested hill scenery through which they were passing, as they trudged damply towards the sharp ridge of the Dulchi pass into Kulu. Only once did the weather relent. It did so dramatically just after they had passed the Dulchi ridge on 1 August 1820, and were beginning the long afternoon descent down the valley towards Bajaura. Suddenly the clouds rolled back and the first sunshine for days flooded down into the valley directly below them. It is a spectacular view. Even Moorcroft was inspired to some rare, descriptive writing. The scene, he wrote, was

> delightful to look upon. Vast slopes of grass studded with clumps of cypress cedar and fir go off from the summit in various lines. . . . The bottom of the valleys glitter in the sun with ribbands of water. The mountains near at hand thrusting their green peaks into the sky sometimes are wholly visible clear and defined and at others are hidden . . . by dense clouds or mists. . . . In the clear part of the atmosphere the snowy mountains seem to form an insuperable barrier to our progress. The surface of the ground is literally enamelled with small asters, anemones and great varieties of the sterile strawberry as scarlet, crimson, white and yellow. . . . Vast flocks of white goats tended by women depasture the summits of the lower hills and every patch of table land gives a site to a village surrounded by cultivated lands now in their richest livery.

They were back in the sort of landscape Moorcroft had fallen in love with round Josimath – the world of snug stone and timber houses, rhododendrons, rich terraced fields below the dark forests, cool air heavy with pine, thunderous mountain torrents, and, high above all, the ethereal snow peaks and glaciers thrusting up into the empty sky. Today only the nomadic shepherds and parties of trekkers come into Kulu by this beautiful ancient route.

That evening, after a very long march, they halted at Bajaura beside the Beas. Moorcroft was not too weary to examine its ancient stone temple and describe it in his journal, just as it is today.[21] Next morning they set out up the main Kulu valley and, some hours later, came to Sultanpur, the valley's capital and in those days its principal town. There 'I found Mr. Trebeck in good health and spirits and the rest of my party well,' recorded Moorcroft thankfully. There was much rejoicing and much to tell that first evening in their camp-site beside the noisy, grey-green Beas, just below the little town.

Moorcroft's joy must have been cut short for, soon afterwards, he received an express letter forwarded by Palmer and hurried on to him by Sansar Chand.[22] It brought news, in Moorcroft's words, of 'the decease of a most valued friend in France and I was engaged one day in giving directions for the education of my daughter entrusted to the care of the female whose decease was reported'. In this tantalizingly cryptic way, Moorcroft recorded the death of the elusive Mary Moorcroft in Paris on 27 November 1819. Perhaps it is possible to explain the curious wording by a natural reticence to commit to paper personal matters which might be read by someone else. Yet why did

Palmer also refer to her in a letter to Moorcroft as 'your friend'.[23] Later he even pretended he had forgotten who or where she was.[24] Why did Saunders, in his most personal and private letters to Moorcroft, persistently call her 'our late friend' or construct even more cryptic phrases to avoid naming or describing her?[25] Why did the Baroness de Rouvron, announcing the news to Moorcroft, also use the term 'friend' and make a point of explaining to Moorcroft that Mary had lived and was buried as Mrs Moorcroft? What were 'the details most distressing to me' which, she said, would have to be mentioned if she were to attempt in law to prove that Mary was Moorcroft's wife?[26] Why did the baroness lie and describe Mary to the notary as Moorcroft's widow?[27] Why indeed did Moorcroft use in his will what was the unusual form 'Mary Pateshall otherwise Mary Moorcroft'?[28] And why does no registry evidence survive to confirm that he and Mary were married? If the answer to the last question is because they never were married, then much of the mystery disappears, but then a new question requires an answer. Why did they never marry? The surviving evidence is silent in the face of these questions. Unfortunately, the letter, which Moorcroft says he spent all day writing to Saunders on 9 August, has not, it seems, survived.

The problem with regard to young Anne must have been very worrying for Moorcroft. He had never liked or entirely trusted the Baron and Baroness de Rouvron when he knew them during their exile in London. Indeed it looked from Saunders' letter as though they were not only trying to secure the whole of Mary's estate (including Moorcroft's regular remittances to it), but seeking to keep Anne in France with them as well. Fortunately Saunders had remembered Moorcroft's earlier instructions that, if anything happened to Mary, the child was to be sent to London and educated at Mrs Palmer's school for young ladies at Blackheath and he lost no time in pressing the de Rouvrons to release the child.[29] Even as Moorcroft wrote she was already safely in Oxford Street, bringing light and delight to Saunders and his faithful old housekeeper, Stedman.[30] There was really nothing more that Moorcroft could do, except leave the whole matter in the hands of his old friend. He simply spelled out in great detail his wishes for Anne's education and his longing for further news of her progress.

There were of course plenty of other pressing matters to attend to during their eight-day stay at Sultanpur. In all 160 porters had to be recruited and a large stock of provisions purchased for the next stage of the journey.[31] There was the friendly and helpful *de facto* ruler, Wazir Sobha Ram, to repay with presents and a certificate confirming the good treatment they were receiving.[32] More urgent still was the subject of a long letter to Ochterlony.[33] Soon after leaving Kangra, Moorcroft had noticed a number of cattle carcasses floating in a back eddy of the Beas. Since then it had become clear that cattle plague was raging all along the right bank of the river in the hills and that it was making heavy inroads into the sheep and goat population as well. Moorcroft performed some *post mortems* but without learning very much. Now, in a massive letter, he alerted Ochterlony to the danger and suggested closing the frontier along the Sutlej to all cattle movements. In this and other letters he also bombarded the Delhi resident with information about frontier trade, enlisted his help in the forwarding of packages, samples and mail, asked him to honour drafts for the purchase of samples for government use and much else besides. Metcalfe would have coped with all this for friendship's sake, but the irascible Ochterlony was apparently becoming more and more exasperated at this tiresome and disturbing whirlwind on his frontier. His anger eventually reached flashpoint, although not just yet. There were, of course, many other letters to write, including one to Metcalfe.[34]

Then there was the health of the party to attend to. The incessant rains had brought much intermittent fever and diarrhoea among the servants and Izzat-Allah had been quite seriously ill on the journey across the hills from Kangra. Moorcroft also did at least one cataract operation while they were at Sultanpur, on a poor little deaf, blind and nearly dumb boy, which appeared to be completely successful. The plentiful symptoms of unhealthiness, especially goitre and leprosy, which Moorcroft noticed among the people of the district, made him even more anxious to be on his way up the valley as soon as possible.

They left Sultanpur at last on 10 August 1820, the swollen Beas on their right never far away. Two of the ponies were such a nuisance on that first march that Moorcroft gelded them next day, an act of such impiety according to the locals that the rain fell all night and half the next day. He was amused to notice, however, that as 'one of our accusers was observed slyly to carry off the offending parts which had been left on the ground . . . to his house it was presumed that he meant to expiate the offence with a broil'. Moorcroft's journal is full of wry observations like this and Wilson's paraphrase would have been rather more entertaining if he had included some of them. They camped near the then tiny hamlet of Manali and Moorcroft and Trebeck, like many modern tourists today, crossed over to the left bank of the river and climbed to examine the hot sulphur springs flowing from the hillside at Vashisht.

They moved on again on 14 August, up the old caravan road which is still visible on the hillsides beyond the right bank of the river towards that towering Solang ridge which shuts in the Kulu valley on the north. At each step the valley closes in, the villages and cultivation becomes scanty, and the stony track zigzags up and up through the trees, across the high pastures and out at last on to the bare rock high above. Up there, the busy river has become a mute grey ribbon of light far below and, in the enveloping silence of the cooler air, one becomes aware of new and lesser noises – the wind keening in the sparse grass, the clop of hooves on rock, the sudden clatter of a tumbling stone and the rhythmic pumping of one's own pulse. On 16 August they were halfway up to the summit of the ridge and already above the puffy, white clouds drifting over the immense, green valley below them. For the first time for weeks there was the promise of a dry night. The worst of the monsoon is usually over in Kulu by the middle of August and they had reached its outermost limit. The great heaped rain clouds were rarely able to penetrate across the serrated rock ridge which reared up close above them.

The empty saddle of the Rohtang is not, by Himalayan standards, a high pass although many have died on it, even in summer, in the demonic snowstorms which can strike almost out of nowhere. It is, however, one of the great natural divides in the world. *Kulanthapitha*, the end of the living world, was the ancient name for the Kulu valley[35], although it fits the pass itself better. As Moorcroft stood there on the southern rim of the saddle on 17 August 1820, he could look back down the Beas into the lush, forested, inhabited and cultivated valley up which they had just come. Half a mile (0.8 kilometres) beyond, on the other rim, the empty Buddhist world of Tibet begins. It is a humbling prospect – an austere and empty moonscape of orange, brown and purple rock with not a tree, house or field visible in the deep Chandra valley at one's feet. Beyond and above, a vast amphitheatre of bare rock, snow peak and glacier is piled, ridge upon ridge, to the pale sky. Moorcroft had crossed a divide like this once before, at Niti in 1812. Perhaps that is why his journal says so little about the scenery. Trebeck, however, was astonished at the contrast between 'the sublime scenery of the Himmaleh' and the appalling 'desolation and ruin [which] seem to reign over the wide expanse before him and the long succession of winter clad peak, barren cliff and sandy valley or defile would seem to proclaim the almost total extinction of animal and vegetable life'.[36]

Trebeck measured the height of the pass with his long barometer tube and got it almost exactly right at 13,300 feet (4053 metres). Moorcroft, meanwhile, was examining the little shrine above the spring trickling from the rocks and deciding, also correctly, that this was the true source of the mighty Beas River. Like most travellers, they added their stones to the lonely cairn that stands sentinel beside the track at the top of the saddle and then passed on thankfully over the edge. Even the long arm of the malevolent Ranjit Singh could not, they believed, reach them now.

At the very bottom of their precipitous descent down the zigzag path into the valley of Lahul, they could see, on the far side of the river, the first of the small and scattered villages lying along the empty valley. A jumble of flat-roofed, mud-rendered houses; the dung-cakes and harvested crops out to dry on the roofs for the long winter months ahead; the little fields of ripened wheat and barley; the sacred *mani* walls and Buddhist prayer flags fluttering forlornly in the wind; and of course, the cheery, flat-featured Lahulis – all were quite different from the Hinduized hill-people on the Indian side of the pass. To reach them, however, Moorcroft's party had first to cross the thunderous River Chandra. Although the porters and people could, with their hearts in their mouths, just manage the swaying *jhula* of birch twigs which spanned the foaming torrent, the horses manifestly could not.

The first attempt next morning to swim Guthrie's pony across, supported by a halter and ropes spanning the river, ended in disaster. Shouted orders were lost in the roar of the plunging water, the frightened animal lost its footing on the smooth rocks and was dragged to its death in front of their eyes. It was a tense moment. All along the sceptics had said that they could never get the baggage and animals to Ladakh by this route. Winter was coming and there was simply no other possibility open to them. Moorcroft went hurrying off downstream to reconnoitre a better crossing-place but, while he was away, the animals were safely crossed over higher up with the expert help of some shepherds from Kangra. The local people pretended to be astonished. 'They exclaimed that if this river could not stop the Feringhees they had no other barrier.'[37] With three high passes still to cross and the ever-present hazard of landslip and other mishaps to contend with, that judgement must have seemed to Moorcroft somewhat premature.

Yet he had grounds for cautious optimism too. The great flocks of sheep and goats coming down the valley from the high summer pastures, and the long caravans of laden pack-ponies, were proof enough that the route, one of the great and ancient commercial high roads of Asia, was still open. Indeed almost the best time to travel in those high, empty valleys is at this season, after the worst heat and glare of midsummer is over. Then again they were amply provisioned, excessively so as it turned out. Above all, Moorcroft felt instantly at home among the smiling and friendly Lahulis, with their dazzling teeth and heavy woollen clothes, so like their distant relatives whom he had met eight years before at Daba or Gartok. There was little chance of treachery or violence from these peaceful folk. Even the breathlessness and the unpleasant altitude headaches must have seemed familiar. Yet the danger of accident was never far away, as they were forcibly reminded only a day or two later. Guthrie had just finished compounding some powerful red purgative pills and put them outside his tent to dry when they were found and eaten by one of the Arab horses who usually wandered round the camp in search of titbits after dinner. Despite all Moorcroft's efforts to save him, he died in the night. 'This loss was heavy,' he wrote, 'as the animal was particularly active and I depended upon him for riding down wild horses and asses in the steppes of Tartary,' but, he consoled himself, this was all part of the trial. 'I was willing to expose the horses to all disadvantages in order that I might more decidedly appreciate the influence of the climate and journey upon them in reference to future experiments.'

Those 'future experiments' were never very far from his mind. As his journal shows, he was observing the route very carefully indeed, just in case the condition of Afghanistan should compel him to return to India with his string of fine horses from Bokhara by this route. The caravans of little pack-ponies coming down from Ladakh with goods from places even further afield, intrigued him for the same reason. So too the tall, graceful women of the carriers, striding along beside them, all a-jangle with jewellery. They were, wrote Moorcroft 'extremely curious and inquisitive'. If the highly detailed commentary, in his journal, on their dress, jewellery and implements is anything to go by, so was he. It was not, however, idle curiosity. 'These matters may be thought of a trifling nature but I apprehend a large [caravan?] of them sold at a low rate by a person deputed for the purpose . . . would give the women a taste for European articles.' Moorcroft's journal and his correspondence throughout this long journey provide innumerable examples of his careful and detailed attention to the possibilities of future markets for suitable, and sometimes purpose-made, British goods.[38]

So, as one sunlit day followed another in that late August and early

September of 1820, they pushed on north-westwards down the Chandra valley, mere specks in that immense, empty landscape. At Tandi, where the Bhaga River from the north-east joins the Chandra, the Kulu porters were paid off and the goods transferred to seventy ponies and some 500 goats and sheep.[39] Somewhere out in front of this cavalcade would be the diminutive figure of Moorcroft, peaked cap pulled low over his eyes against the glare from the rocks, dressed in the same clothes he had worn for the past two months, sitting easily astride his saddle-mule, Dapple, and whistling up the dogs from time to time. Trebeck, tall and thin, would as usual be prowling about, taking cross-bearings and checking his angles with compass and sextant, his note-book jostling with figures, usually within hailing distance of the man carefully counting his paces along the track down below.

At Darcha, on the valley floor but almost 11,000 feet (3351 metres) above sea level, they came to the last village in Lahul. Moorcroft was mesmerized by the immense forces at work as a mountain not far from the little village slowly subsided into the valley.

This is almost the finest scene I ever witnessed it varies after every fall some of which are accompanied by noises like the discharges of heavy artillery the pealing of thunder or the rattling of musketry. I regret that I cannot do justice to the effect but independently of want of powers and of time I am annoyed at this moment by clouds of small flies endeavouring to enter my eyes, nose and mouth while I am sitting under the shade of a cypress.

The flies are still there and so are the now silent results of the great landslip. The cypress tree has gone.

That tree must have been almost the last they saw for many days, as they panted on up the track in the thin, chilly air, with scarcely another living thing to break the immense silence, other than the rapidly dwindling river itself. On the night of 4 September the water in the brass pots outside the tents froze hard, much to the astonishment of the men from the plains. They had certainly run a remarkable gamut of weather and temperature in the past three months. 'In June I was almost broiled at Lahour, in July and August drenched on the Himaleh and in September shiver amidst the snows of Tartary,' wrote Moorcroft. It was 18°F (−8°C) in the tents next night,[40] just to add to the misery of altitude sickness and the feverish insomnia which often goes with it. 'My face almost stripped of skin and my lips are shrivelled and cracked. Most of our people were too much tired to be able to cook and went to bed dinnerless,' noted Moorcroft.

On 5 September they reached the summit of the Baralacha-la. Moorcroft was astonished to find from his barometric calculations that they were practically at the height of Mont Blanc, Europe's highest mountain. In fact they were already 250 feet (76.1 metres) higher than that, although there is certainly no sense of height on the Baralacha pass and nothing much in the way of a view to justify the immense labour of getting there – just a ragged, swampy, uneven, broad-backed ridge, with many bleak, snow-covered peaks piled up on every side. Moorcroft of course went scrambling up as high as the thin air and his pumping heart would allow, in a vain search for a better view. He thought he saw a better way. 'The suggestion may be thought whimsical and its realisation impractical but I apprehend no accurate map of the Himaleh can be found except observations from below be corrected by others from above.'[41] How right he was, except that planes and satellites have been used rather than the hot-air balloons which he had in mind. Needless to say, Moorcroft was not talking only about geographical accuracy. The precision would above all be *useful*. An 'aerostatic apparatus' (as he called it in his journal) would 'in one week more benefit the inhabitants of, and facilitate the operations of, commerce than twenty of the most scientific operations proceeding upon terra firma.'

They rested for a day to refresh the men and animals beside the silent Yunam lake, just below the Baralacha summit. Then they plodded on, making long marches through the desolate, fractured valleys, devoid of tree, village or vegetation, and over two more high passes. The intermittent sleet and snow and the cutting wind suggested that winter might be closing in early. At last, on the morning of 17 September, they came to the first village in Ladakh and the first settled human habitation they had seen in a fortnight. It was not much of a place in itself (although Moorcroft was quick to notice the hardy barley growing in the minuscule fields and made a mental note to send samples down to his friend Dr Wallich at the Calcutta Botanical Gardens and to Eccleston's son for trial on Martin Mere). It was what this little settlement symbolized that mattered. Seeing three red-robed Buddhist monks hastening anxiously away from them in the fields, Moorcroft hurried after them. 'I saluted them and repeated the phrase "Oom ma nie put me hoon" which I knew would excite their attention.' The mispronunciation of such a sacred phrase probably did, but no offence was taken. The oldest of the three hesitantly extended to Moorcroft a wrinkled hand containing some ears of corn. That simple greeting from the first settled Ladakhis they encountered must have given Moorcroft great satisfaction. The Himalayas were behind them. They had been on the road almost exactly a year, but they had arrived.

That afternoon they camped outside Gya, the first Ladakhi town of any size on this road, with its twenty or so houses and six or eight precious poplar trees. They were advised to go no further until permission was received from Ladakh, but most of the party were feeling so frail after the long marches and short commons of the past fortnight, that it must have been a welcome respite. That evening they were unexpectedly visited by a Muslim official called Abdul Latif. It soon emerged that he was a pupil of a celebrated Muslim holy man in exile in Ladakh called Khoja Shah Nias, whom Izzat-Allah had met and become friendly with in Yarkand in 1812. The fortunate connection proved, then and later, to be of inestimable value. Abdul Latif was readily persuaded that they were bona fide traders and promised to go with Izzat-Allah next day to plead their case before the man they called Khaga Tanzin. Khaga Tanzin was brother-in-law of the chief minister of Ladakh and an important figure. It seems that he had come especially to meet them, in order to judge their intentions.

Just what the Ladakhis were afraid of became clear next morning from their searching questioning of Izzat-Allah. As usual, exaggerated rumours had run on ahead of them. The rulers of this cloistered kingdom at the crossroads of the trans-montane caravan routes, were naturally anxious at this novel intrusion, particularly by the representatives of a race which, they knew, had spread its power all over the Indian plains under the guise of commerce and now lapped the hill-regions to the south. Izzat-Allah's silver tongue, Abdul Latif's cogent support, testimonial letters from Raja Sansar Chand and Wazir Sobha Ram, and some well-chosen presents from Moorcroft seem together to have done the trick. Khaga Tanzin pronounced himself satisfied. He would write favourably to Leh and, the following morning, would receive Moorcroft's ceremonial visit.

As Moorcroft rode into the little town next day, the women on the rooftops 'huddled behind each other [and] peeped with diffidence as it were by stealth'. At the entrance to the courtyard, he noticed 'two low and stout woolly-haired dogs with heads much resembling those of bears'. It was a curious echo of the dogs which had figured in his first interview with the Tibetans at Daba eight years before. Indeed much must have reminded him of that occasion, including of course the ceremonial tea-drinking. Moorcroft privately wished he had been able to stomach another cup of the greasy buttered tea 'like weak broth', if only to have a closer look at the marvellously gilded copper tea-pot from which it came. Every detail of that room and its occupants found its way into the pages of his journal just as in 1812. This, however, was a much easier interview. There was no embarrassing disguise to maintain or lies to tell, and the people were all smiles from the start. Once again it looked as though the very scale and absurdity of the rumours about them had worked to their advantage. Later, a return visit by Khaga Tanzin and his entourage to their tents, lubricated by more presents and some alcohol, proved equally successful. Next day, 20 September, they all set out for the capital, confident that the necessary permission would soon be given.

Ladakh is perhaps the highest inhabited land in the world. Most of it is empty – a weird, tawny moonscape of jagged mountain peaks and narrow, crumbling, waterless valleys under the pale sky and the high fluffy clouds. The fantastically contorted rock formations to be seen everywhere in Ladakh were a never-failing source of amazement to Moorcroft. He even lamented the absence of the tiresome geologist, Laidlaw, who ought at least to have been able to offer some explanations of the rich geological mysteries all round them. Only where there is water and soil can there be habitation and colour and it is all the more magical by contrast with the awesome desolation all round. Geographically and culturally, Moorcroft was back in Tibet. There were the same stacked, flat-roofed towns clustering round the skirts of the great vertical *gompas* or monasteries; the same lines of delicate poplar trees, now lovely with autumn foliage; the same smiling people busy in the little fields by the water courses, gathering or winnowing the last of the golden crops, with the bullocks treading the grain to the accompaniment of those haunting, wordless working-tunes which can still be heard all over Ladakh today. The only thing that marred their pleasure at being back in the world of men was a growing doubt about their reception at Leh. Izzat-Allah was quickly downcast, first by reports that they would have to avoid the capital altogether because of smallpox fears and then by the unnerving silence that followed. Moorcroft, more optimistic and striving to keep up the spirits of his party after their long journey, argued that the Ladakhi authorities would never have allowed their great caravan to come so close to the capital if they had really intended to stop them.

He was right as they learned a few days later. Indeed this was precisely one of the arguments which had already been used on their behalf by the influential Khoja Shah Nias. On 21 September, they unexpectedly encountered this amiable and learned old man in a tent set up for the purpose on an island in the young Indus at Sheh, not far from the capital. They were most warmly welcomed. The khoja was a descendant both of the Mughal emperors and more recently the hereditary rulers of Tashkent and he had been wealthy and influential in Kashmir before Sikh oppression drove him into exile in Ladakh. Even in Buddhist Ladakh he was a figure of considerable power and even more so in Muslim Yarkand, beyond the Karakoram to the north. In both places he loyally backed Moorcroft's claims against those, like the Kashmiri merchants, who wished to keep him out. In return, Moorcroft won for this civilized and generous man a small pension from the Indian government and the promise of restitution from Ranjit Singh. Shah Nias was, Moorcroft came to believe, the most complete gentleman he had ever met in the Muslim world.[42] Later, the two of them planned to travel on to Bokhara together.

At last, late in the afternoon on 24 September Moorcroft and his party arrived at the line of *chortens* (Buddhist shrines) outside Leh. They are plainly visible in the foreground of Trebeck's drawing of the capital[43] and are still there today. As the cavalcade passed in among the houses, 'the streets and walls of Leh were lined and covered with crowds of men, women and children to witness the entry of the Feringees into the city'. Moorcroft studied the sea of faces with keen interest – the smiling Ladakhis, the high bonnets and more mongoloid features of traders from across the high Karakoram to the north, and the suspicious Kashmiri merchants from the south, 'remarkable for their Jewish countenances, their dirty woollen clothes and large muslin turbans'. Moorcroft believed that he and Trebeck were the first Europeans ever to reach this commercial crossroads. The Ladakhis thought so too.[44] In fact those astonishing Jesuit missionaries, who had preceded Moorcroft to Lake Manasarowar in 1812, had beaten him to Leh as well, as he later disbelievingly discovered.[45] He and Trebeck were certainly the first Europeans to reach Leh for over a century and they were the first ever to attempt the journey from the south – and with an immense trading caravan to boot.

By any standards it was a formidable achievement and Moorcroft was right to be pleased. Apart from the man and boy carried off by cholera at Mandi while he was away, he had lost neither a member of the party nor any significant item of merchandise during a full year of arduous travel along and across the greatest mountain range in the world.[46] He and Trebeck had discovered much new political and geographical information and corrected some of the errors concerning the sources of the Punjab rivers. The losses among the horses and the mules had been severe, but the experiment had triumphantly vindicated Moorcroft's belief that the route was feasible for horses at least as far as Leh. It was therefore available as a channel for the conveyance of goods to and from the markets of Central Asia, if Moorcroft's preferred route by Josimath, Niti and western Tibet proved in the end impossible.[47] Whatever might happen in the future, he told Parry,[48] and

> if instead of the success anticipated I find a grave, my countrymen may reasonably conclude from what I have already done that perseverance in attempts to open a commercial intercourse with the northwestern and central parts of Asia will finally prove successful.

Moorcroft had no intention of finding a grave just yet. On the contrary, despite the rigours of the journey and his advancing years, he had never felt better. As he put it in a long and revealing letter to Palmer some time later,[49]

> excellent health founded on a strong and unimpaired constitution gives no indication of decay in any part of the fabric. . . . I am reckless of the superfluities of life. He who can make a hearty meal daily and for months on turnips or alternate them with Tartar tea and dry unleavened cakes may dispense with the *petits diners* of polished society, and whoever in a reeking hut extended on the floor surrounded by men and cattle as his inmates, his saddle cloth for his bed and saddle for his pillow can enjoy undisturbed repose may think the eider mattrass or festooned canopy not essential to his slumbers. Nothing teaches practical philosophy like a journey similar to that I have undertaken or calls forth more imperiously the resources of the mind or powers of the body.

'It teaches,' he told Parry, 'such lessons as books or study cannot impart.'[50]

The feeling of achievement and self-fulfilment is unmistakable, but it was only the end of the beginning. Moorcroft now had to recruit Ladakh into his great scheme of opening the heart of Asia to British commerce. It would not, he knew, be easy. Formidable opposition from the vested interests involved – the Tibetans, the Kashmiri merchants and Ranjit Singh himself – was virtually certain. He expected that. What he did not anticipate, however, was opposition from two entirely different directions. But long or short, his stay in Ladakh was not likely to be uneventful. With Moorcroft nothing ever was.

18 Triumph in Ladakh,

SEPTEMBER 1820–AUGUST 1821

THE CHIEF MINISTER of Ladakh,[1] Khalun Tsiva Tandu as Moorcroft called him,[2] had set aside a spacious house for their use, with a walled courtyard on two sides big enough for the animals and the bales of merchandise. The mud walls and stout timber gates had the additional advantage of protecting them from the crowds who gathered outside the house or tried to catch a glimpse of them from the neighbouring rooftops. To men used to 'long residence in tents so injured by the weather as to give entrance to every blast as well as to every smart shower of rain', the house must have seemed like a palace. Now, wrote Moorcroft in his journal, 'we rested comfortably without hearing the rush of torrents or the crash of avalanches'. He would not have been quite so content if he had known that they were going to spend the next *two* winters at Leh. Nor indeed if he had realized just how numbingly cold those winters could be.

Every single night, from the time of their arrival till the following May, there were hard night frosts. Just before Christmas, the temperature plummeted in Moorcroft's room to 16°F (−9°C) and more than once caused him to drop the pen from his frozen fingers.[3] Outside there were sometimes 15° of frost. No wonder the account books reveal considerable expenditure on fuel and timber to shutter the glassless windows.[4] Snow was not such a problem, rarely falling more than 4 inches (10 centimetres) deep in the town and often clearing before the next snowfall, although on the high passes it was a very different story.

Leh is usually cut off from the outside world before the end of November, and sometimes earlier. It was obviously important for Moorcroft not to delay the Lahuli carriers from starting out on their long journey back across the high passes. On 27 September, after all the baggage had been weighed and assessed for customs by the Ladakhi authorities, he paid off these men generously. The galling fact that the grain they and the animals had carried could have been purchased much more cheaply in Leh when they arrived he merely noted phlegmatically. Only his three shepherd kinsmen from Kangra were held back to carry any urgent messages later on.

Two days after their arrival at Leh, Mir Izzat-Allah had his first uncomfortable audience with the khalun. This toothless but shrewd 60-year-old wielded most of the effective power in Ladakh on behalf of the raja. Profound suspicion was evident in practically every question he asked. It was not till 1 October that Moorcroft was allowed to proceed to the khalun's audience chamber, riding together with Trebeck and the mir through the crowds of sightseers, behind the royal messenger. The interview seems to have gone well enough, except when Moorcroft rather rashly tried to inspire the khalun with his own enthusiasm for Jenner's vaccine against smallpox. The form and the ritualized tea-drinking on these occasions was already becoming familiar. So was the smell of too many unwashed bodies packed into the low-roofed room and the 'other odours which in a numerous assemblage of persons not delicate in their food sometimes derange the olfactory nerve and discompose the features'. It was presumably not entirely a coincidence that he shortly afterwards sent over to the khalun some *eau de cologne*, French perfume and Indian attar of roses.

More meetings (and more presents) followed, each apparently more friend-ly than the last, but there were no decisions. The weather-cock khalun was being blown this way and that. On the one hand were the warnings of his Tibetan and Balti neighbours, together with what Moorcroft described as 'a phalanx of Kashmeeree traders whose foresights of foreign competition in a lucrative commerce was sharpened by their fears [and who] in judicious array waged a steady and active opposition against our views'. On the other, were the friendly representations of Khoja Shah Nias, Khaga Tanzin and the persuasive tongues of Izzat-Allah and Moorcroft himself. It seems to have been a real cliffhanger. Moorcroft wrote nothing in his diary for a fortnight after 11 October, 'in the hope of having to insert the accomplishment of some commercial arrangement with the authorities of this country'. That was certainly over-optimistic.

The khalun continued to hesitate but at last, after an anxious state council, asked the mir on 21 October to state his master's wishes. Moorcroft had already primed him with the answer:

First. Free liberty to trade with Ladakh and through it to other countries.
    Secondly. That in consideration of the great distances when British property was brought there should be some remission of duties upon it.
    Thirdly. That a house should be hired in Leh to be occupied as a British factory.
    Fourthly. That the good offices of the Kaloon were required to be exerted with the authorities at Gardokh to open the Neetee Ghat [pass] to British commerce.

The first three points were readily accepted but the khalun was understand-ably uneasy about the fourth, without prior discussion with the neighbouring Tibetan authorities at Gartok. One wonders just how closely the Tibetans there linked all this with the pseudo-pilgrim who had visited them eight years before. At all events they rejected the suggestion out of hand a few weeks later. Moorcroft kept up the pressure. 'Without using a shadow of menace I represented the fixed resolution of the British merchants to establish a commercial intercourse with Toorkistan' and their ability to do so, with or without Ladakh. Presumably, equally free of menace and certainly equally without authority, he hinted that the British could, if they chose, embargo the

Tibetan grain trade and virtually starve Tibet into submission![5] Moorcroft was never too nice about means, if he was convinced that the ends would bring blessings, although he confessed his uneasy conscience to his journal. It made no difference. Indeed, it was becoming clear that, since the khalun was now talking of appealing to Lhasa over the heads of the Tibetan regional authorities at Gartok, Moorcroft would have to settle down and ride out the winter in Leh, if he was to secure his cherished commercial engagement.

Further delay was in some ways most unwelcome, but it did solve a number of pressing problems. In the first place, it was dangerously late in the year to navigate the unwieldy caravan across the Karakoram, along what is perhaps one of the most difficult and hazardous caravan trails in the world. Even comparatively recently, it was said to be strewn with the bleached bones of the men and pack-animals who never arrived.[6] Besides, only one small caravan from Yarkand had reached Leh in 1820 and the Yarkand market was said to be depressed because of sporadic Muslim disturbances. It did not sound like the best time for an Englishman to appear before the Chinese authorities at Yarkand, unannounced and without permission. Moorcroft did briefly consider taking the mir with him and making a dash for it across the Karakoram pass, leaving Trebeck to bring the caravan over in the spring. Later he wished he had, but at the time it looked altogether too risky.

> Were I to visit Yarkund without invitation, perhaps the Joong [Chinese Governor] out of an excess of zeal, might introduce me to the Sovereign of the Celestial Empire at Peking instead of permitting me to pursue my route and intention towards paying my *devoirs* to the Commander of the Faithful at Bokhara, a mutation of plan not altogether convenient in my present circumstances.[7]

Financially, those 'present circumstances' were very embarrassed indeed and that was another good reason for staying put in Ladakh for the winter. The outgoings required to move, feed and pay his small army of more than forty men were so heavy, and the major dislocation of his plans caused by the closure of the Niti-la in late 1819 and the intervention of Ranjit Singh in the summer of 1820 so severe, that he was practically at the end, both of his cash and his credit. He had expected to be in Leh early enough to send back for all those goods left behind at Fatehgarh, which were intended for sale along the way and at Leh. Now they were on the far side of the Himalayas with the passes closing and with no banking facilities available at Leh from which cash could be raised.

On 5 December, dangerously late in the season, the faithful Hafiz was despatched to the plains by way of Kashmir and the Punjab carrying urgent letters to Palmer at Calcutta, Keene at Fatehgarh and Sir David Ochterlony at Delhi.[8] His task was to return in the spring, as soon as the passes were open, with the missing caravan goods, urgent supplies of books, medicines and smallpox vaccine and, most desperately needed of all, the 20,000 rupees of credit which Moorcroft asked Ochterlony to make available to him, against a draft on his own account with Palmer in Calcutta. Moorcroft knew he had several months to wait before he would see Hafiz again, but, ever the optimist, he thought that it might be possible to move on again in March 1821, if Hafiz were not delayed by robbers, by Ranjit's machinations or by the perils of the road.[9] The one thing he could not have expected was that the most intractable obstruction, both to moving the goods and obtaining the cash, would come from the prickly Sir David Ochterlony himself.

So winter shut in the little community at Leh, and snow and frost choked the runnels of its labyrinthine streets and alleyways. Wilson summarized Moorcroft's life that winter in a single sentence which barely hints at the darting activity of the man.[10] Moorcroft himself later captured the flavour of it best in two telling countryman's metaphors. 'The multiplicity of subjects that force themselves on my mind from their novelty,' he told Saunders, is 'like too much game before a greyhound. . . . I am obliged to pounce upon my subjects like a hawk on its quarry.'[11] And pounce he did.

First of all, he lost no time in opening his medical practice. He soon noticed that there was a striking absence of the worm and the leprous conditions which were so common south of the Himalayas. Could it be, he wondered, that large-scale tea-drinking had something to do with it? In no time at all he was anticipating the future once more, by outlining the possibilities and the experiments needed for a great, indigenous tea industry in the Himalayan hills. Tea, he correctly believed, might become in India the drink of the people, as China tea had in England.[12] Whatever may have been the medicinal qualities of tea, he still had more patients in Leh than he could cope with, including those with the usual ophthalmic surgical, apoplectic, and rheumatic conditions. There was also one severe case of inflammation of the liver which yielded to – or was bludgeoned into submission by – one of Moorcroft's grim but unspecified 'active treatments'. By the end of that first winter, Moorcroft reckoned that, of the 'many' patients referred to him as incurable by the local doctors, he had lost only two.[13] Soon the reputation of the little *Goba-Feling-pa* (as he rendered the Ladakhi for 'head of Europe-living men') was spreading across the Karakoram even to Yarkand, as well as to the surrounding countries. Moorcroft once hoped that it would even outlive him in the folklore of Ladakh.[14]

In this he was disappointed but it might have been different if he had been allowed to achieve his dream and end the smallpox scourge beyond the Himalayas. He had been trying to introduce vaccination there ever since his 1812 visit to Tibet and, as has been mentioned, raised the subject unsuccessfully at his very first meeting with the suspicious khalun. By the end of that first winter in Leh, however, he was so known and trusted, and had trained sufficient vaccinators, that he could have succeeded if he had been able to secure sufficient quantities of active vaccine before he left Ladakh. He tried and tried, almost to his last day there, but one batch after another proved to be heartbreakingly inert at the end of its long journey from the plains.[15]

Apart from this honourable failure, Moorcroft was well pleased with his medical work in Ladakh. Not that it did very much to offset the alarming depletion of his cash reserves. 'My medical fees,' he remarked to Metcalfe, 'rather amuse than enrich me.' One can see why from a delightful word-picture Moorcroft later painted of himself at the end of a summer morning's surgery, somewhere outside the capital.

> Seated on a carpet under the shade of a large apricot tree I was surrounded not merely by a crowd of patients but by a fortress of which the inner walls were formed by piles of wheaten cakes, lumps of yak butter, dishes and bags of roasted barley wheat and heaps of onions whilst the outworks consisted of wooden bowls filled with milk, dahee [curds], large teapots of buttered tea and flagons of Chang or some barley beer with here and there a sheep tied to a stone. My servants fared sumptuously from my labours and were enabled to spread a liberal board for our numerous visitors.[16]

For Moorcroft himself, there was a very evident satisfaction in bringing what relief he could to the suffering and it shines out of nearly all his journal entries on the subject.

As usual, however, there were more advantages than mere satisfaction to be had from his medical work. He found, for example, that treating the very Kashmiri merchants who were intriguing against him slowly brought about a very marked change in their attitude towards him. Again, medicine gave him access to some of the important men in the Ladakhi political and religious establishment. The *lompa*, or mayor of Leh, was successfully treated and later Moorcroft taught him the rudiments of animal physiology by dissection, thereby winning a valuable ally against Kashmiri intrigues. There were others too – the octogenarian imam of the mosque at Leh who became a close friend; the head lama of Zanskar, who became one of Moorcroft's surgical and vaccination pupils; and his 'friend' the *banka* or master of horse at the royal palace.[17] Eventually even Raja Tuntuk Namgial himself, to whom Moorcroft was at first deliberately denied access, consulted him about his health and he was also allowed to meet the young heir-apparent. That was a high honour, but most astonishing of all perhaps, Moorcroft won the sequestered but influential rani as an ally, by tempting presents of cloth, coral and gold earrings. Later Moorcroft sold pearls to her at 'a diminished price, *well understood* fixed without violation of delicacy on her part or too great sacrifice on mine . . . we soon felt the value of this arrangement'.[18] The combination of Moorcroft's charm, presents and scientific attainments proved as effective in Ladakh, as elsewhere in Asia, in winning confidence and bridging the gulfs of language and culture.

It also took him inside the homes, palaces and great monasteries of his patients, and that provided him with ample opportunity, of which he took full advantage, to note in often minute detail the details of their architecture and furnishings. He was particularly intrigued by the neat and sanitary arrangements made by the Ladakhis for the disposal of what he would have called night-soil, and for its subsequent use as a valuable manuring agent in the fields. Leh, he wrote in amazement, had more and better necessary-houses than any town in Europe and he contrasted them with the filthy, haphazard and wasteful methods in use, then and now, on the edge of Indian villages. The attention he devoted to the subject is astonishing, and who but Moorcroft would have drafted an elaborate and lengthy set of model regulations for the disposal of night-soil in India and its controlled use as a manuring agent in the fields?[19]

Not everything he found in a Ladakhi house was a model of its kind. Nor, of course, did he confine his medicine and his social relations to the great and the rich. His journals of this period are scattered with references to nights spent as the guest of peasants or humble farmers. He was appalled at the acrid smoke from the yak-dung fires which filled every Ladakhi living-room in winter and he often insisted that the fire be put out, or lay on the floor to clear his streaming eyes, before he could treat some of his sick patients. All for want of a chimney! He soon had a detailed specification for a demountable model of a farmhouse range and chimney on its way to George Saunders in Oxford Street. We shall immortalize you beyond the Himalayas by calling it a Saunders, he told his friend. Moorcroft also lobbied the khalun and tried to turn him into the patron of the chimney.[20] He laboured in vain. It was the later Moravian missionaries to Ladakh and Lahul who won the gratitude of the people by introducing the stove and chimney, which now make the long winters there bearable, and removed for ever the smoke or sub-zero inconvenience of a hole in the ceiling. But Moorcroft certainly tried.

Cynics might say, were it not for all the evidence from the rest of Moorcroft's life, that it was precisely the cold of the Ladakhi winter that drove him into hyperactivity. There was nothing else to do. Certainly there was not much diversion to be had from female companionship. Trebeck thought the women mostly ugly and none too clean.[21] Moorcroft had not lost his eye for a pretty girl, still occasionally noting that he had met one,[22] and it is quite plain, from hints in his letters to his friends, that he was missing them badly. As he told Palmer, 'The want of female society is perhaps one of the greatest privations experienced by a traveller.'[23] Few male travellers would disagree with him. That arch-humbug Victor Jacquemont, the emancipated French visitor to Ranjit Singh's court ten years later, wrote that whereas his own 'virtue is the subject of universal admiration, M. Moorcroft did not set a like example of European continence here. His principal occupation was making love, and if his friends are surprised that his travels were so unproductive, they may ascribe it to this cause.'[24]

There is not a shred of evidence to substantiate this picture of Moorcroft as a kind of itinerant satyr, and there is very much to deny it. Besides, the idea that his travels were 'unproductive' is laughable, even if it were not a judgement made by such a conspicuously unproductive traveller as the languid, silver-tongued Jacquemont. All one can say is that if, against all the other evidence, Jacquemont was right (and his other statements about Moorcroft do not exactly inspire confidence), then Moorcroft's abundant daytime energy in middle age is even more remarkable than it appears at first sight.

During that first twelve months in Leh, in letters alone, he produced almost as much material 'as would fill a moderately thick quarto volume closely printed and when my despatches shall have been received their voluminous appearance may cause a perusal of them to be postponed *sine die*'.[25] Before he left Calcutta, he had agreed with Metcalfe that he would send information about 'what in this journey might seem worthy to be brought under the notice of the Government'.[26] In Moorcroft's eyes, that was practically everything. The words spilled out, when freezing fingers or rheumaticky shoulder would allow, in such astonishing profusion, that he actually began to index his own despatches. An essay on the shawl goat peters out after seven and a half pages, but a footnote on snowfall uncoils into a lengthy discourse on weather, rocks and erosion for another thirty-six closely written pages.[27] A letter to Metcalfe, about Ladakh's political importance, fleshes out even the most insubstantial speculation, until the letter has swollen to an obese and closely written seventy-four pages.[28] Moorcroft's justification for letters, despatches and memoranda, the like of which the dazed copywriters in Calcutta had probably never seen before, was simple and unchallengeable. He was the first Englishman ever to visit these areas, much of what he encountered was of paramount importance to his country and the ever-present risk of accident or worse was such that it was prudent to report at once, warts and all, rather than 'through an ill-timed scrupulousness that it should be wholly lost'.[29]

And so he did. The range and detail of topics touched on is so voluminous that even a long list must omit more than it includes.[30] He was an interested recorder of the dark, colourful temple ceremonies in the great monasteries and the annual dance dramas with their huge gongs, conch-shell horns and grotesque masks. He examined the great libraries of illuminated manuscripts and longed to discover their secrets. He cautiously prospected for coal and iron as minerals likely to improve Ladakh's standard of living. He observed in immense detail, as the year turned, the techniques and yields of Ladakh's fruit, vegetable and crop husbandry and wrote at particular length about novelties like the little-known purgative drug, rhubarb.[31] Rare or novel seed strains were packaged up and sent down to the Calcutta Botanical Gardens or to his landed friends at home, together with animal skins, coins, specimens of calligraphy and alphabets addressed to the Asiatic Society.[32] Twice daily, detailed weather and temperature observations were recorded. Plague-struck cattle were dissected in search of cause or cure. Detailed market research was carried out and a stream of samples, designs, colours, dimensions and drawings flowed back to Calcutta and England, to assist British manufacturers in producing goods exactly tailored to the market.[33] Old interests like paper-making and, more discreetly, the shawl trade were investigated. By the end of that first winter, Moorcroft was already persuaded that, if Britain was to get direct access to the wool, she must not do it in Tibet, for that would dislocate the ancient trade by way of Ladakh and cause untold distress there and among the already wretched weavers of Kashmir. New sources of supply further north on the Pamirs would have to be tapped and developed by Britain, he now believed.

One can see, in this important readjustment of his ideas, the double-sided aspect of all his investigations. On the one hand there was Moorcroft the patriotic son of Britain, concerned about post-war depression at home and anxious to boost its economy by the opening-up of Asiatic markets. This was not merely economic imperialism. There was also Moorcroft the benefactor, anxious to create a fruitful, two-way trade which would raise living standards in Asia. These twin strands were almost inextricable in all his enquiries and reports. His journey was becoming a crusade, and when, in due course, he first sensed and then learned of official lack of interest in, or active disapproval of, his activities, the note of obstinate defiance which is one of the hallmarks of the crusader became more and more pronounced.

Despite all this activity, he managed to find a little time for himself. In the November of that first winter in Leh Moorcroft settled down to turn his retirement dream into a detailed shopping list of all the items he believed he would need to import from Europe, including two merino rams from Lord Somerville.[34] His family too was very much on his mind, especially little Anne and her schooling in faraway London.[35] The hint of private sadness is always there, like an elusive shadow hovering on the very edge of the field of vision, sensed but never seen. It must be so. A dynamic spirit like Moorcroft's, which is driven to explore both space and knowledge, is bound thereby to deny itself the static blessings of home and hearth. That was the price and he chose to pay it, but it was not without pain.

So the long Ladakhi winter of 1820–1 passed and the sun, climbing a little higher in the pale sky each day, began once more to warm the thin air of that serene, high and empty land. As the snow-melt swelled the rivers, there also poured down out of Ladakh the pent-up flood of paper which represented Moorcroft's winter activity and which he released on the sinewy backs of his three shepherd kinsmen from Kangra, as soon as the passes to the south were open in May.

They carried triumphant news. Negotiations about Moorcroft's prized commercial engagement had languished during the winter, although the behind-the-scenes battle for supremacy over the counsels of the khalun and the raja raged as fiercely as ever. The Tibetan and Kashmiri merchants, wrote Moorcroft, 'have presented an opposition so obstinately and unceasingly alert as to call forth the utmost exertions of patient counteraction on my part. Narration of particulars would be intricate, tedious and useless. *L'affaire est faite.*'[36] It was, and Moorcroft won. After some tense last-minute negotiations, at which unacceptable conditions were first made and then withdrawn, Moorcroft worked far into the night on a final draft for signature before anyone could change his mind yet again.[37] On 4 May 1821, at a little ceremony formally witnessed by Trebeck and Izzat-Allah, Moorcroft pressed his oval signet into the warm wax and sealed the engagement 'on the part of the British merchants of Calcutta'.[38]

The final document represented a considerable departure from the conditions originally proposed by Moorcroft the previous October, but he believed that he had won an even better bargain. So indeed he had – for British goods coming to Leh by any route but that from Gartok. In return for certain limitations on the size of armed escorts accompanying the caravans and on access to Tibet from Leh, the Ladakhis engaged to open their country to

British merchants and remit one quarter of the usual customs duties levied. The approach to Leh via Gartok was, however, expressly prohibited. Hitherto Moorcroft had always regarded this as critical, because it would have allowed British goods to reach Leh without crossing Ranjit Singh's territories. Long discussions at Leh, however, made it plain that the Tibetans would never agree to it and, since Moorcroft had revised his opinion about tapping the shawl-wool trade in Tibet, it was not so necessary anyway. Moreover, he was still hopeful that routes could be found from British territory direct to Ladakh by way of Spiti and Lahul which would be beyond the furthermost reach of Ranjit Singh. The engagement said nothing about a British commercial agent at Leh although in due course Moorcroft appointed one. It says much for the progress he believed he had made in allaying the Kashmiris' suspicions, as well as the need to keep their goodwill, that he appointed the principal Kashmiri merchant in Leh to be Britain's first commercial agent there, selling British goods on commission.

Moorcroft confessed to the Indian government that, strictly speaking, he had no authority to negotiate on behalf of anybody except the merchant houses of Palmer and MacKillop. He had studiously kept the British government out of the document itself but, he argued unanswerably, there was nothing to be gained by not extending the commercial advantages to *all* British goods coming from India. All the more because, he believed, the long-term advantages could be immense. Ladakh itself would offer only a limited market for British manufactured goods but its role as emporium and depot was the important thing. It stood at the heart of a network of traditional caravan trails radiating outward to every part of Central Asia, from the Caspian to the Pacific. Along these lines would go British goods, British influence and all the blessings of science and modern technology. As a result, he told Calcutta, 'a field so vast has been opened to British manufactures that it would appear bordering on hyperbole were I to attempt to speak otherwise than very guardedly of its probable extent'.

It was, in Moorcroft's eyes, not merely a commercial field but also a political, and even a strategic, one. He, it will be remembered, had attached the most alarming implications to the Russian commercial activity he had stumbled upon at Daba and Gartok in 1812. Much had happened since then which seemed to confirm his worst fears. During that first winter at Leh, he began to compile a dossier of information about this apparently sinister Russian activity in areas so remote from the Russian frontier and on the very doorstep of the rich British territories in the plains below the passes.

All Moorcroft's reawakened fears and anticipations during that winter became focused on the person of a single Russian agent, the mysterious Agha Mehdi.[39] This remarkable man, Mekhti Rafailov as he is known to Russian historians, had first penetrated across the Karakoram into Ladakh and Kashmir in 1808. He did so on instructions from the Russian Foreign Ministry and in the guise of a merchant from Yarkand. Along this route subsequently came Russian and European goods which were exchanged mainly for Kashmir shawls. Agha Mehdi himself returned several times, narrowly missing an encounter with Moorcroft in 1812, extending his and the Russians' knowledge of the area and earning civil rank and title for his efforts. One of the first fruits of the confidence, which Moorcroft created in the Ladakh authorities in late 1820, was the sight of a letter from the Tsar to the raja of Ladakh, which Agha Mehdi had brought some six years before.[40] Then, soon afterwards, came the electrifying news that Agha Mehdi was on his way once more. At the end of November 1820, if Moorcroft's calculations were correct, he could not be much more than about two weeks' march away on the far side of the Karakoram pass.

Moorcroft awaited what he called[41] this 'doughty opponent' with a mixture of anxiety and characteristically genuine relish.

> This man's life has been made up of a rapid succession of extraordinary incidents and after the many anecdotes of him recited to me both by his friends and by his enemies I am at loss how to class him except generally as a man endowed with natural talents of a surprising cast. Had he lived a few years longer he might have produced scenes in Asia that would have astonished some of the Cabinets in Europe. . . . I have detected traits of an expansion of view seldom indeed entertained. . . .

Most of that was just as true of Moorcroft himself. Their missions too were not very dissimilar in purpose. One can see here the mixture of rivalry and respect which was such a typical feature of many of the later encounters of British and Russian emissaries on the borderlands of their empires in Asia.

To Moorcroft's mingled relief and regret, what would have been a historic first meeting of this kind was forestalled by Agha Mehdi's violent death near the lonely summit of the Karakoram pass. His substantial caravan did not straggle into Leh until mid-April 1821 and among the curious crowd watching in the street was doubtless a short, middle-aged Englishman from Lancashire. It did not take him very long to get a sight of the official letter Agha Mehdi was carrying to Ranjit Singh but, suspiciously, there appeared to be no other papers.[42] Even so, the caravan itself with its enormous emeralds and rubies and its comprehensive range of cloth samples and dyestuffs was startling enough.[43] It looked as though the Russians were trying as hard as Moorcroft himself to gain access to the secrets of the Kashmiri shawl weavers. Indeed, it transpired that one of Agha Mehdi's tasks, rather like that of Moorcroft in 1812, was to get hold of some shawl goats for experimental breeding in Russia. Very much in the later traditions of the Great Game, Moorcroft tried to thwart the dishonesty of Agha Mehdi's double-crossing assistant and ensured that the official letters (once he had carefully noted their contents, of course) reached their destinations. It is somehow typical of Moorcroft that he should also have taken steps to ensure that Agha Mehdi's little orphaned son was properly provided for and educated.

Behind the personalities, Moorcroft was convinced, there lay policies of the utmost seriousness. Why should the cabinet of Imperial Russia be devoting so much treasure and effort to the cultivation of political and trading connections with kingdoms so remote from its own frontiers? It could hardly be because of the trade alone. What Moorcroft called[44] 'a monstrous plan of aggrandize-ment' revealing 'a grasp of ambition most gigantic' seemed to be taking shape under the guise of trade. The underlying aim seemed to be to open up an entirely new and unexpected approach to Hindustan from the north by way of the ancient caravan trails across (or round) the Karakoram to Leh, and onwards from there into Kashmir and the Punjab. Where caravans and pack-animals could go armies could follow, especially armies of irregular horsemen of the kind Central Asia had known since the days of the Huns and Genghiz Khan. Moorcroft was the first to rediscover that armies of this kind had, in the past, reached Ladakh from the north. In one case they had come by a mysterious, but apparently much easier, route from Khoten further east, which halved the journey from Yarkand to Leh and opened up an easy, direct approach, not only to the plateau of western Tibet but to the plains opposite Delhi. Moorcroft thought he had stumbled upon part of this secret route by accident in 1812. Later in 1821 he made it his business to explore the Ladakh end of it near the Pangong Lake.[45] He was convinced that the omniscient Agha Mehdi had already discovered this short-cut and reported it in detail to his paymasters at St Petersburg.

Moorcroft rarely let the facts speak for themselves. In 1821 and 1822 he speculated at prodigious length, for the enlightenment of his masters at Calcutta about the way things could develop.[46] He reminded them that the shaky military grip of the Chinese on their remote western provinces was compounded by the simmering hostility of their Muslim subjects there. Moorcroft's intelligence suggested that the Muslims were ready to rise up in support of any invader who would help rid them of the hated Chinese yoke. It looked as though that invader was going to be Russia. Agha Mehdi, it seemed, had intended to take back to Russia as honoured guests, not only representa-tives of Ranjit Singh and the ruler of Ladakh, but also of the former Muslim rulers of Chinese Turkestan. Moorcroft conceded in his ponderous way that this

> demonstration of magnanimity may be disinterested but directions to Agha Mehdee to whisper in confidence to Moosulmans of respectability in Chinese Toorkistan the generous intentions of H[is] I[mperial] M[ajesty] create a surmise of it being designed *en coup de théâtre* to generate an impression favorable to the accomplishment of ulterior projects in which the agency of a numerous Moosulman population is desirable.

Even without Muslim help, a mere 60,000 Russian troops poured into the Tarim basin by the easy routes from Kokand would be sufficient to overwhelm the mediaeval Chinese garrisons in Kashgar and Yarkand. Thence, there would be nothing to stop them entering Ladakh, either across the Karakoram pass or by the apparently easier routes to the east. Conversely, the Russians might first attack Ladakh by an uncontested approach across the Pamirs direct from Kokand by way of Sarikol (whose chief was in open rebellion against the Chinese), and then invade Chinese Turkestan from there. It was Moorcroft's intention to examine both the suitability of the Pamirs line 'for the march of large bodies of troops' on his way back from Bokhara, and the feasibility of the British and Russian approaches to Chinese Turkestan on the way there.[47]

Once Chinese Turkestan became a Russian province, any of several dire consequences might follow. If Russia went east, then Moorcroft did not even rule out the possibility that the whole of China might be conquered. After all, had not Clive boasted that with five good regiments he could conquer China and pay off the national debt? For Russia it was 'by no means impossible'. The consequences if China's resources and trade became Russia's or if European technology became China's, would be immeasurable. The annihilation of Britain's tea trade alone would be catastrophic. Moorcroft summarized the cost as 'two millions of pounds annually to the Exchequer, the comforts of the whole population of Great Britain to whom tea is now become a necessity of life, the employment of an immense capital and the subsistence of thousands'.[48]

These breathtaking speculations about the ally of Waterloo, which Moorcroft began to assemble for the benefit of Calcutta in the winter of 1820–1, were liberally sprinkled with disclaimers about his unsuitability and their indelicacy. He was very much aware that he had neither authority nor qualifications to comment on political or military matters in this way. As always, he argued that if he did not do it, who would? Moreover, he was so fearful that his unofficial capacity and reputation as an enthusiast might lead his warnings to be ignored or dismissed, that he laboured all the harder to persuade the sceptics. As a result, these enormously long-winded, disordered and defiant despatches came rolling in to the incredulous political department at Calcutta, almost to the very end.

March 1821 was Moorcroft's original target date for his departure from Ladakh. It came and went without any news of Hafiz or the vital goods, medicines and cash he was sent to obtain. Moorcroft even began to fear that, if no news came soon, he might eventually be forced to sell off his caravan at a huge loss in Ladakh, simply to meet his immediate necessities, and retire ignominiously to the plains with his mission in ruins. Later he recalled that he carried at this time 'a load of anxiety that for a period was oppressive beyond expression'. The 'days were racked with anxiety, my nights passed in sleeplessness'.[49] In April, July and again October 1821 more requests to Sir David Ochterlony to honour his drafts (now totalling nearly 20,000 rupees) were anxiously posted off into the blue.[50]

Money, however, was only part of the problem. Moorcroft was becoming uneasily aware that he had already been away from the stud nearly two years and that his masters would be becoming restless at what they would regard as unnecessary delays to, and distraction from, the business of securing horses at Bokhara.[51] Nor was he far wrong. In June 1821 the board, still resisting pressure from London to cut its salary bill, provocatively suggested to the supreme council that as 'Mr. Moorcroft has been employed beyond the Bengal Provinces since the year 1819 on duties and pursuits unknown to the Board and as far as their information goes unconnected with the Stud Institution . . .

we beg respectfully to submit whether his salary ought not to be charged to the Department under which he is at present employed, and the Stud relieved for the time of this heavy item of expence.'[52] This initiative was smothered in mid-1821, but it was bound to surface again. Nor is it to be wondered at. Moorcroft had certainly wandered very far from horses and the needs of the stud. Indeed the subject only occurred in his correspondence sporadically and, it would seem, perfunctorily. Ladakh, like Tibet, is not the most obvious place to find quality horseflesh.

In addition to these acute problems, Moorcroft in the summer of 1821 still had no certain news from the Chinese authorities at Yarkand. Almost as soon as he had reached Leh the previous autumn, he had despatched letters including one from Khoja Shah Nias, requesting permission to traverse the country as a trader *en route* to Bokhara. Unknown to him, however, Agha Mehdi had successfully prevailed upon the Chinese to refuse that permission and he was carrying their replies to that effect when he died on the Karakoram. Moorcroft believed that the long silence was caused by Muslim insurrection on the western borders. Whatever the reason, the letters never arrived. All Moorcroft could do while he waited was to accumulate information on the route to Yarkand, woo the Yarkandi merchants in Leh by prescribing for their ailments, and put in hand an experiment to determine whether the Karakoram could be crossed by laden camels. In case Chinese Turkestan should in the end be denied him, he did what he could to keep open the alternative options of skirting that land to the west, either across the Pamirs or through Badakhshan. Local informants with knowledge of the routes across the mountains in that direction were sought, letters were despatched to some of the chiefs along the way and suitable presents for them were sorted and stockpiled.[53]

It was probably the growing possibility that they would in the end have to move on by one of these unknown and hazardous routes, as well as the need to minimize quarrelling and keep everyone fit and busy, that persuaded Moorcroft and 'Corporal' George Trebeck, with the help of the two Gurkha NCOs, to begin exercizing the escort. The ten remaining Gurkha troops were augmented by the mir, his son, George Guthrie, eight of the Afghan and Indian servants and a Persian haji as 'volunteers'. Moorcroft later kitted out this little corps in smart and colourful new uniforms which sound remarkably reminiscent of those of the Westminster Volunteer Cavalry. He cheekily requested some extra matchlocks and bayonets from Ranjit Singh, set men to work on the faulty equipment, increased the pay of the regular soldiers from his own pocket and tried hard to get them replaced by fresh men from the garrison at Subathu. Then he set to work to drill his little army into an efficient fighting force. He had a tiny cavalry arm of eight men, and an artillery wing capable of assembling its two tiny one-pounder mountain guns and bringing them into action at a moment's notice. At first the gap-toothed and cheery Ladakhis, peering through the gates of the compound or over the wall, were highly amused at all this activity and the little boys with willow wands on their shoulders began to mimic the English commands whenever they encountered

Moorcroft in the streets. But eventually, or so Moorcroft believed, 'the changes and combinations were executed with precision and rapidity' at the sound of the bugle so well, that surprise and respect replaced amusement.[54] That little force was the first modern army ever seen in Ladakh.

By the early summer of 1821 Moorcroft was a familiar figure in Leh, respected for his medical work by the people and trusted by the Ladakh authorities, particularly once the commercial engagement was safely signed and sealed. Apparently it was the influential rani who secured for Moorcroft permission to visit the hot springs at Nubra beyond the Ladakh range in the far north of the country.[55] Ostensibly the trip was for the sake of his rheumaticky shoulder, but Moorcroft was probably far more concerned to examine the route used by the caravans in summer on the way to or from Yarkand.

When he left Leh in late May 1821 the young crops were already showing in the fields, but when he attempted the high crossing of the main Ladakh range which divides the basins of the Indus and Shyok Rivers, he ran into such heavy snow and sub-zero temperatures that he was obliged to send the rest of his party back. He, however, waited with one servant at the foot of the Digar-la in a small tent 'very indifferently supplied with food, and without any fuel'. It must have done wonders for that rheumatism! Moorcroft reckoned that he had 'never met with a mountain so difficult to scale'. Coming back across this 18,000-foot (5484-metre) pass three weeks later, the snow on the south face had almost gone but the ice was such that 'although my shoes were shod with new and sharp nails I could not keep my footing and wore out my trowsers by another mode of travelling'.[56] The horses had the same trouble. 'An Arab horse of mine, having missed his footing, slid down a sheet of ice for some distance, and recovered himself only by a vigorous effort, just on the brink of a precipice several hundred feet high.' No wonder the later British gazeteer rated this pass 'very difficult . . . yaks should be used'.[57]

Once across the pass, Moorcroft enjoyed himself hugely in the isolated villages of those empty, open, upland valleys, rimmed with snow peaks. He held his clinics where he could and was warmly received and generously entertained in return. He was also, of course, making notes of all he encountered as busily as ever. The hot springs at Nubra, flowing into a crude enclosure open to the keening wind, proved something of a disappointment. Moorcroft visited them one chilly evening to take his obligatory 'cure' but, 'although I had secured my clothes by placing large stones upon them, they were quickly sent after me into the bath by a violent gust of wind from the mountains'. Fortunately a warm and hospitable house belonging to Khaga Tanzin was nearby. Moorcroft escaped pneumonia, although what this experience did for his rheumatism is not recorded. At the end of the second week of June he turned back for Leh and arrived in the town late on 21 June. As it turned out, this trip was the nearest he ever got to Yarkand.

During his absence Trebeck and Izzat-Allah had been pushing on with an important negotiation with the khalun which Moorcroft had launched some months earlier.[58] Almost as soon as he reached Leh in the autumn of 1820, he had been astonished to find, as he put it, that '*Ladakh is tributary to Dihlee!*'.[59]

What Moorcroft had discovered was that documents existed at Leh which confirmed that Ladakh had once offered allegiance to the Mughal emperors. He saw the implications at once. Since Britain by right of conquest had fallen heir to Mughal rights, she had a claim to Ladakh. In the spring of 1821, Moorcroft began to suggest to the Ladakh authorities that they should broach the possibility of publicly affirming their dependence on Britain. From their point of view this had two great advantages. It would deflect any hostile British designs which might be lurking behind Moorcroft's visit. More important, it would protect them from the more imminent danger from the ambition and growing assertiveness of Ranjit Singh. That chief had recently conquered Kashmir, just across the mountains to the north-west. Indeed it was a curt demand for tribute from Ranjit which hustled the khalun and raja into making a direct request for British protection while Moorcroft was away on his Nubra trip.[60] By the time he got back to Leh on 21 June the mir and Trebeck had already drafted a formal document for signature. Its very existence was a personal triumph of no small kind for Moorcroft. It was the most impressive example yet of his almost uncanny knack of inspiring the confidence of men otherwise far removed from him by every barrier of culture, race and language.

Needless to say, it was not for that reason that he welcomed it so enthusiastically. A British protectorate of Ladakh would buttress in the best way possible his do-it-yourself commercial treaty. It would secure for Britain all the commercial, political and strategic advantages which Ladakh possessed from its position at the crossroads of Asia. With Ladakh under its protection, Britain could, Moorcroft believed, control the inland trade of all Asia. Even more, she could end at a stroke all the developing dangers of a Russian flanking movement, whether into India from behind the Himalayas or into China from the west. By which line of argument, Moorcroft arrived at the truly breath-taking conclusion that 'the evils that threaten Europe through the conquest of China may be averted by the Honourable Company accepting the allegiance of Ladakh'.[61] Conversely, of course, calamitous consequences would eventually follow if the company did nothing. The most immediate beneficiary in that case would be Ranjit Singh himself. Moorcroft genuinely feared 'the horrible evils this country [Ladakh] would inevitably experience through falling into the hands of an oppressor whose rapacity and ambition no wealth can satisfy'. This is not mere cant, or whitewash to conceal the undoubtedly expansionist dynamic in much of his arguments. He was an intensely humane man and much of his life was a costly crusade against suffering, whether in animals or in men. Just as in 1812 he had believed that enlightened British rule would bring blessings to the people of Kumaon and Garhwal in place of Gurkha misrule, so now he believed the same about Sikh oppression in the Punjab and, unless he could forestall it, in Ladakh. Besides, if Ranjit Singh became master of Ladakh, that vulnerable backdoor into India would have a politically unreliable doorkeeper. As for trade, 'all the fair hopes now entertained of commercial enterprize being carried to an indefinite extent in this direction must be considered as completely blasted and destroyed' if the Sikhs were given a free hand in Ladakh.

Contemplating all these arguments, and very many more, Moorcroft convinced himself that he should encourage the tightening of Anglo-Ladakhi links by every means in his power. At the end of July he drafted for the raja and khalun (the convoluted style is unmistakably his) a personal letter to the governor-general, offering the allegiance of Ladakh to Britain and enclosing all the evidence of the earlier links with Mughal Delhi. As if that were not sufficient, he also composed an almost laughably amateurish Anglo-Ladakhi treaty for the government's consideration.[62] Then in early August he wrote what, even by Moorcroftian standards, is a massive 124-page despatch to Metcalfe, whom he wrongly believed to be still secretary of the Secret and Political Department, presenting his 'most fervent hopes and expectations' for a British protectorate of Ladakh and anticipating every objection he could think of.[63] If, however, notwithstanding all his arguments, the government decided to reject the proposal, then he begged that it do nothing until he had been given the opportunity to hasten down to Calcutta and argue the case in person. When the nature of the terrain between Leh and the city, a mere 1000 miles (1600 kilometres) away as the eagle flies, is considered, it is not hard to see that Moorcroft regarded the whole matter as very important indeed.

He was also very much aware that he had neither the power nor the expertise to get so deeply involved in high politics but, so far at least, he could claim with some plausibility that he was merely acting as go-between. Now, deliberately and at great personal risk, he stepped right outside that role. He wrote a long, friendly, but dangerously frank, personal letter to Raja Ranjit Singh himself. Among much else on shawl wool, Moorcroft took that ruler to task for the oppressions done by his officials, reminded him that Ladakh was independent but had once been tributary to the emperors at Delhi and, in view of Ranjit's own rumoured designs upon it, warned him that full information had been passed to Calcutta and that he would shortly 'hear from the British Government regarding the state of its intentions and affairs'.[64] Moorcroft knew that this thinly disguised 'keep off' would not, to put it mildly, be very pleasing to Ranjit. Indeed in the letter he said that it was friendship alone which compelled him to be so frank, even if it 'should wound your ear, which it doubtless will much'. Such friendly frankness to an oriental despot, he well knew, 'might introduce me to one of the oubliettes [secret dungeons] of Lahour, if not to a more summary recompense'.[65] On the other hand, as his physician he was on terms of intimacy with Ranjit and had been of consider-able help to him. Besides, Ranjit would scarcely dare to lay violent hands on Moorcroft so long as his initiatives appeared to have the support of the British government. It was really that aspect of things which worried Moorcroft most of all. He knew that he had put himself on very thin ice, but could only hope that Calcutta would share his view of the importance of Ladakh and would therefore see also that the need to buy time for the establishment of a British protectorate would 'extenuate the offence'.

In the middle of August 1821, Moorcroft sealed up his enormous letter to Metcalfe, enclosed copies of all the supporting documents and despatched the whole bulky package on its long journey back across the Baralacha to the plains.

In many ways it represented the high point of his long sojourn in Ladakh, but it carried high risks too. Moorcroft had become enmeshed in a web of intrigue and rivalry which involved, first, international trade, then espionage, and now international diplomacy and politics. Just how high the stakes were, in the game he was playing, began to be apparent a few days after his return to Leh from Nubra. In the early hours of 27 June Trebeck was working late at his desk behind the paper screen covering the window, when a shot was fired into the room from outside. Had he not just left his seat he would probably have been killed.[66]

Trebeck and Moorcroft could discover nothing to explain the assassination attempt, so set off next morning, as planned, on another short expedition. Again, the ostensible reason was to relieve the most useful pain in Moorcroft's shoulder. This time they went south-west from Leh, across the Indus and the ridge beyond it, to some medicinal hot springs at Knarung.[67] They were back in Leh on the morning of 4 July in time to record a noon temperature of $134°F$ ($56°C$). The following night, however, Leh with its average rainfall of 3 inches (7.5 centimetres) a year, unexpectedly experienced nearly as much in a single night.[68] The flat roof of Moorcroft's house, consisting of the usual willow shoots and pressed earth, proved no match for the downpour and collapsed. The khalun thereupon kindly offered Moorcroft and Trebeck temporary accommodation in the upper rooms of a small house standing in a nearby garden.

Scarcely had they moved in, when the would-be assassin tried again. The night was dark but they both distinctly heard cautious movements outside the barred door in the adjacent room. The following night they armed themselves and stayed on watch, but in vain. Shortly afterwards they were compelled to move again, this time into tents in a walled plantation of willows and poplars. Moorcroft and Trebeck, for added security, placed their tents close together but once again their slumbers were disturbed by nocturnal movements nearby. The owner of the garden said it was haunted, but Moorcroft thought that the three men he had seen examining the tents from a distance were the more likely suspects. Next night, he wrote,

> a hand was put into my tent it was grasped but withdrawn instantly and something dropped at the opposite door within the tent as if from alarm or inability to carry it off. I could discover no-one in the neighbourhood under the side walls of the tent in . . . the moonlight. I sprang out of bed and followed the line the stranger had taken but examined some bushes near the tent. When I had gone halfway around it I perceived a figure near the ground entering a belt of trees. Its form was indistinct but I fired upon it from a pistol and pursued it with a sword though without success. The next morning I saw only two of the strangers. They departed that day.[69]

The third man was said to have been suddenly taken ill and was disposed of in the river. It looked as though Moorcroft's pistol had found its mark after all. From that moment he loaded it with shot instead of ball and always kept it either by his head or under the pillow at night. Not long afterwards that pistol was tampered with so as to make Moorcroft 'my own executioner'. Trebeck had borrowed it to drive off some hyenas when it exploded in his hand. The pistol was 'mangled'. His hand, fortunately, was not.[70]

Determined to bring things to a head, Moorcroft deliberately made it known that he was taking up residence 'in a large house greatly distant from my party which I had hired under the hope that my antagonists, tempted by my situation would renew their attack in the night for which I was abundantly prepared'. Perhaps that is why they resorted to poison instead, as Moorcroft learned in a dramatic and rather alarming fashion. Again the incident is best told in his own words.

> Alone one night I was reflecting on the condition of some of my party who appeared to be under the operation of an unusual and little intelligible influence, whilst I myself was assailed by spasms which prevented me from guiding my pen. It was late when my reverie was suddenly broken by a knock on the door of my apartment. . . . Two strangers with their heads muffled up in blankets entered my room. One of them drew from under his coat not a sword but a little butter, a few dried fruits and some other small articles of food and threw a little of each with precipitancy into his mouth. They speedily retired with demonstrations of respect and I readily understood that the object of their visit was to put me on my guard against poison, a subject which engaged my thoughts at the very moment when they disturbed a train of reflections little satisfactory.[71]

Without telling anyone, Moorcroft disposed of some suspect tea – and, sure enough, everyone recovered his health. He never discovered who was responsible for these various attempts nor what lay behind them. Raja Ranjit Singh was certainly a prime suspect. For the remainder of the stay in Ladakh, Moorcroft remained very watchful indeed, especially at night.

19 Setback in Ladakh,

AUGUST 1821–OCTOBER 1822

As the summer of 1821 drew on, and the rippling fields of barley and the slender poplars and willows in the broad valley round Leh began to put on the first tints of autumn, everyone in the party must have been wondering just how much longer their stay in Ladakh would have to be.[1] Guthrie, at least, was still expecting to move on before winter shut them in once more,[2] but that was looking increasingly unlikely as each day passed without news. Moorcroft's immediate financial anxieties had been relieved, for the time being at least, by generous loans from two of his patients, one a Kokandi merchant in the Amritsar-Yarkand trade, the other a man from Nurpur.[3] Yet without the return of Hafiz, of whom there was still not a word, Moorcroft could neither repay his debts nor move on.

In any case, where should he go? From the Chinese authorities at Yarkand, as indeed from his friends and masters in India, he had heard nothing at all for the best part of a year. The looked-for Chinese permission to advance across the Karakoram, and the pack-pony caravan to make it possible, were expected any day.[4] And every day they did not arrive. Eventually Moorcroft decided to send Izzat-Allah to Yarkand, armed with letters and presents, together with a trusty servant of Khoja Shah Nias who would, if all went well, go on to smooth the next step at Kokand. The mir set out on his long and dangerous seven-and-a-half-week journey early in August 1821.[5] At the very best it would be another three months before he could return. Moorcroft once again had to wait.

He decided to fill the interval with another journey across the Ladakh range, this time to the high and barren north-eastern corner of Ladakh in the direction of the shawl-wool pastures of Changthang in Tibet. He had, as usual, many aims. He wanted to capture some examples of the elusive *kiang* or wild horse of Tibet. He also wanted to survey the Ladakh end of the route beyond the Himalayas, which he still hoped the Tibetans would one day allow him to open up from Niti and Josimath as the main British commercial highroad to Central Asia. He also hoped to see at first hand the home of the shawl goat. Finally, he wished to examine the mysterious and secret short-cut to Yarkand, by which he believed Ladakh had been invaded by armies in the past, and hoped Central Asia would be invaded by British goods in the future.

[274]

It was an ambitious programme and August was really far too late in the season for it to be feasible. Then came further delays. In late September, the long-awaited news that Hafiz was in Kashmir and on his way required more letters and additional instructions had to be sent off across the Karakoram after the mir. The khalun too was reluctant to give permission. He was already in trouble with his Tibetan neighbours for his dangerous dalliance with British trade and now they requested that no supplies should be made available to Moorcroft for his trip. He promptly relieved the khalun of all embarrassment on that score by recruiting Tibetan guides, buying 100 sheep to carry the baggage, and ordering sheepskin coats and felt stockings for all his party. 'Our tour,' he told one friend,[6] 'will be one of great privation and discomfort in a line of country destitute of fixed inhabitants for the most part.' It was important that nothing went wrong. As he admitted in his journal, 'had a single individual died his death would have been imputed to my temerity in ignoring every obstacle'. However, 'I made it a point of honor not to be foiled in order to convince the Gov[ernmen]t of this country that when Europeans had determined upon the performance of any task no difficulties whether natural or artificial was sufficient to prevent their accomplishing it,' – not even the sub-zero temperature which froze the ink as he tried to write those words. The mercury was already plummeting in Leh by early October, at the beginning of what was to be an unusually harsh and snowy winter.

Moorcroft with Trebeck and about fourteen servants and the animals laden with supplies did not leave till 21 October. Even in an average year, that was very late for a journey in this direction. For the first few marches they were retracing their steps south-eastwards, back up the young Indus along the route which, over a year before, had first brought them to Leh. This time, however, the hospitality from their new and influential friends was overwhelming, almost literally on one occasion when the Tibetan guides passed out in a drunken stupor.

On 25 October they crossed the Indus and turned north-east towards the Chang-la across the main Ladakh range. In a normal year, the pass is not snowbound in October and they got safely across on the last day of the month. Moorcroft and Trebeck waited two hours on the broad saddle of the summit for the barometer tubes and mercury to arrive. They never came, but Moorcroft's estimate of 17,800 feet (5,423 metres) was only about 500 feet (152.3 metres) too low. On the north face of the ridge, they ran into trouble. The snow there was so deep, up to the horses' necks in places, that the party became dangerously spread out as night came on and the temperature fell below freezing point. Moorcroft and Trebeck spent an anxious, hungry and sleepless night, with the provisions somewhere on ahead and the tents, some of the precious sheepskin coats and three of the servants somewhere out in the darkness, higher up towards the bare summit. Moorcroft was tormented with the thought that they could not survive the night. At first light, leaving Trebeck, who was feverish, behind, he fortified himself with hot tea and then set off up the pass in search of what he feared must be three frozen corpses. All three were alive, although, in the case of the cook, only just. It took some pretty brutal resuscitation before he could walk again, even with assistance. That night they celebrated round a huge fire 'in high spirits feasting on the sheep I had given and the impression of the past danger was effaced'. Well-fed and 'in tolerable comfort' under his layers of clothing, Moorcroft slept soundly that night, despite the intense cold.

They journeyed on for the next few days through high, empty, open valleys and past the occasional remote village. Moorcroft as usual was speculating busily in his journal, not only about the implications of the geological mysteries all round, but about the defensive possibilities of closing this route to an invader from the north. At last they descended to the head of the Pangong Lake, its spectacular fjord-like surface mirroring the empty sky and the bare, steep-walled mountains. The Pangong is the largest lake in Ladakh and the first of a series stretching nearly 90 miles (144 kilometres) to the south and east, at an average width of 3 miles (4.8 kilometres). They had not proceeded very far along the southern shore, before rumours began to reach them that armed Tibetans were waiting ahead to intercept them. On 13 November, and with considerable relief, they met the cause of these stories – three shepherds and a lama. They were, wrote Moorcroft, 'merry good-humoured fellows' and easily appeased. More genuinely alarming was the weather. Moorcroft kept his fears to himself but noticed that the snow on the mountains ahead and behind was creeping inexorably lower as each day passed.[7] They were all suffering from altitude headaches and breathlessness but Moorcroft had a real fright on the evening of 12 November. 'I was seized with vomiting which lasted almost incessantly till 12 and reduced me almost to the brink of death. The most distressing feeling was a sensation of fainting. Hot water drunk freely and the feet put into it as hot as possible relieved me.'[8] Four days later he was in trouble again.

> My pulse gradually became smaller and weaker till the forced expiration took place when it suddenly filled. . . . I never experienced under the greatest fatigue of which I have known such a disposition to sleep so overwhelming and so severely distressing. I should have conceived my dissolution inevitable and immediate if I had not been visited by sensations exactly similar on the Niti Pass from which I relieved myself by opening a vein in my arm and taking about 20 ounces (0.57 litre) of blood.[9]

It was not like Moorcroft to be talking of death not once but twice in four days.

Fortunately perhaps, three horsemen arrived that same day – it was 16 November – with important news. Men had arrived at Leh from Yarkand to check the information about Moorcroft supplied there to the Chinese authorities by Izzat-Allah. It was essential to return as soon as possible if their cause were not to be lost by default. Leaving Trebeck and the main party to capture the *kiangs* and complete the survey up to the Tibetan border, Moorcroft turned back with two of the servants and set out in haste for Leh. Or rather, that was his intention. Somehow he got separated from the others and was compelled to spend a smoky night, after a meal of parched barley and tea, with a Ladakhi family. Moorcroft remained fast asleep until eight in the morning. He makes it sound like midday. We shall, he confided to his diary, have cause to regret this delay. Although the views down the lake were marvellous, it was snowing more heavily than ever on the mountains both in front and behind them.

In fact their only really unpleasant experience on the return trip came, not from snow or ice, but from the edge of a billowing dust-cloud 600 feet (182 metres) high. Had they been engulfed by it, Moorcroft reckoned they and the animals would all have been suffocated.[10] Trebeck, however, was not so lucky. He caught no *kiangs* and he lost a man coming back across the Chang-la a fortnight later. At the end of the day, it was not the difficulties of this bleak winter journey to north-eastern Ladakh that Moorcroft remembered most, but the tens of thousands of sheep he met along the way, carrying wool from Changthang down to Leh in exchange for salt. They seemed to him further evidence of the hitherto unknown, but apparently vast, potential of the trans-Himalayan trade.[11]

When Moorcroft reached Leh he was distressed to learn that the mysterious official visitors from Yarkand had already set out on their long return journey. He had missed them by only three days but the consequences were likely to be serious. Fortunately, however, circumstances gave him a second chance and he seized it with relish.[12]

Mir Izzat-Allah had reached Yarkand on 25 September and presented his credentials and testimonials soon afterwards. The kaleidoscope he gave as one of his presents seems to have been a particular success. He soon discovered why all Moorcroft's applications had come to nothing. Agha Mehdi and the Kashmiri merchants had done their work so well that the Chinese seemed genuinely fearful that Moorcroft was bringing an army with him. Even Khoja Nias's representations had been ignored. The most that the mir was able to achieve, after lengthy negotiations and in face of implacable opposition from the Kashmiri merchants, was the sending of a commission of inquiry to Leh to check their *bona fides* at first hand. This was the party of three men which arrived during Moorcroft's absence and left again before he returned. They carried with them from Leh a letter drafted by the khalun which confirmed Moorcroft's benevolent and mercantile character but, ominously, it was the Kashmiri merchants who had provided the Persian translation and sent other letters of their own as well. Fortunately the mir, homeward bound, encountered the three investigators on the road. Suspecting foul play he persuaded them, 'partly by representations partly by menace', to part with the letters they were carrying and return with him to Leh. They all arrived on 10 December 1821. Smothering his suspicions for the time being, Moorcroft gave a party for the Kashmiri merchants to celebrate the mir's safe return. Then, when they were all off their guard, he struck.

Next morning Moorcroft was in secret session with the khalun and persuaded him to summon the leading Kashmiri merchants before him about a week later. Moorcroft was there too. He confronted each in turn with the unopened letter he had sent to Yarkand and challenged each, as he claimed to be his friend, to state what he had written. The silence was unbroken. Then the khalun, probably by prior arrangement, handed over his own letter to be read. It became obvious at once that there were substantial differences between the

Persian 'translation' and the original draft. Thereupon Moorcroft turned on his Kashmiri opponents and gave them a remarkable dressing-down. He began by appealing to their sense of fair play.

> Ever since my arrival in this country I have endeavoured to do as much good as was in my power and if I have committed injustice to anyone I am ready to make him reparation. If I have been medically useful to any of the Kashmeeree merchants now present the act was its own reward. I looked for no mark of gratitude . . . but I expected not that benefits would be returned by enmity the most malicious as has been the case.

Their agent in Yarkand, Nuckajoo had plotted against him and there had even been attempts on his life. He would now tell them how, by underselling them, he would ruin them.

> The change from comfort to misery will have been brought on by your own fault. I sought not your ruin. I seek it not now but you attack me and I defend myself. I shew to you without concealment the means that may be employed against you . . . whether they shall be employed or not depends upon your conduct. Should you act as friends what is past shall be overlooked.

His terms were as follows:

> By Nuckajoo and others the road of Yarkand has been closed against me. . . . By you the road of Yarkand must be opened to me. Nothing short of this will be considered by me as a satisfaction for the injury I have sustained. Bear this in mind.

Moorcroft seems to have enjoyed himself. New letters were drafted, the three investigators compensated for the delay, and a servant of the khalun, together with Abdul Latif and a Persian in Moorcroft's service, set off with them back to Yarkand. This time, Moorcroft must have thought, Kashmiri treachery was impossible.

Further delay at Leh was now unavoidable. Poor Guthrie, who had been moving his estimated departure dates backward ever since they arrived, must now have scrapped his latest timetable, which was to leave in midwinter 1821–2 and be safely back in India again by the end of 1822.[13] It was depressing, but Moorcroft remained convinced that he was right to persevere so long as there was a chance to push his caravan and his enquiries across the Karakoram range to Chinese Turkestan. If he could reach Yarkand he could consolidate his commercial success in Ladakh, open a two-way channel into the heart of Central Asia for British exports and imports, gain access to valuable raw materials and pre-empt Russian ambitions.[14] He spent a lot of time during this winter wrestling with lengthy and elaborate despatches to Calcutta justifying this further delay and pleading for patience.

This was all the more necessary because some of the private letters Hafiz had carried back with him in November brought rumours of growing official disenchantment at Moorcroft's prolonged absence from the stud, and news that suspension of his salary was in the air. From the government itself there was no word whatsoever. Moorcroft was anxious but, predictably, defiant.

On account of my children I could wish to avoid touching upon my property in the Company's funds. Yet even this shall not be saved if its expenditure be requisite to the completion of my object. . . . I am accused in India of 'pursuing shadows'. It seems not improbable that suspension or loss of service may ensue but a knowledge of either of these facts shall not deter me from pursuing my objects to a decided conclusion. My efforts will lead me to impracticability, success or death.[15]

The other option, surrender, was not even mentioned.

Not all his letters carried bad news. One from dear old George Saunders in Oxford Street, written nearly eighteen months before and crammed on to a single sheet would have been particularly precious.[16] It brought news of the safe arrival in London of little Anne in June 1820, speaking scarcely a word of English at first but in good health and spirits, charming everybody she met, although 'wild as the untamed antelope'[17] and soon setting the staid dame's school at Blackheath by the ears. Moorcroft spent two long days on his reply,[18] gratefully approving all Saunders was doing for the child and conveying, through him, news for other mutual friends in England. From France came two nearly identical letters from the Baroness de Rouvron, telling of Mary's death and enclosing a lock of her hair.[19] It must have been the conjunction of all this private news about his family and the public threat to his salary, which spurred him, at the end of November, to revise his will so as to give John Palmer power of attorney over his estate, in the event of his death on the road.[20]

Yet all this news from Europe must have seemed unutterably remote to Moorcroft in his second, lonely, winter exile in that high, primitive, little town beyond the Himalayas. His London friends would have been appalled if they could have seen him. He was confined to his freezing house for days at a time in that unprecedentedly savage winter of 1821–2. He shared his frugal meals of boiled turnips, buttered tea and unleavened cakes with young George Trebeck without even a table or chairs, let alone a tablecloth. With felts round his feet and legs, saving his one remaining shirt for state occasions and clad in a coat 'made out of a dyed English blanket, my last save one which is sewn into a sack in which with the aid of two or three inclosures of felts of the same form and as many thatchings of breeches . . . I have kept myself from being quite congealed'.[21]

Not that the weather or the primitive conditions seem to have cramped his style unduly. He was still as busy as ever. There were his medicine and surgery; there were the botanical specimens to describe and crate for Dr Wallich at the Calcutta Botanical Gardens; there were long essays on topics like the population, food and grasses of Ladakh; there was the continuing need to keep his options open for the next stage of the journey.[22] Izzat-Allah had returned from Yarkand with the personal physician of the ruler of Kokand. This man soon became the latest of Moorcroft's medical friends and was duly recruited to ease the next stage of the planned journey from Yarkand westwards across the Pamirs to Kokand.

That assumed, of course, that they could get as far as Yarkand. In January 1822 some Chinese officials arrived at Leh, apparently to investigate Moorcroft and his party yet again.[23] When a month had passed without any move, he invited them to his house, explained his business, and exhibited before them some of the contents of his many packages. They were greatly impressed. A few days later Moorcroft organized for them an immense dinner party at which over 100 people, 'enemies as well as friends', were entertained. He seems to have taken great delight in the fact that no European had probably ever before played host to men from so many different religions, races and cultures. Subsequently Moorcroft treated the senior Chinese official for asthma and taught his assistant the technique of vaccination. Then, having done all he could to win their confidence, he asked Trebeck to accompany them as far as the Chang-la, on the opening stages of their long and dangerous winter journey back to Yarkand. The leader never completed it alive. Close to the summit of the pass (where Moorcroft had nearly lost his cook the previous November and Trebeck did lose a man in the December) the Chinaman was blown from his yak in a snowstorm and died in the deep drifts. The rest of the party eventually reached Yarkand, carrying the corpse with them. Fortunately the older man seemed the most suspicious of all, so his death might have been a blessing in disguise.

In truth, Moorcroft's anxieties during this long second winter in Leh seem to have concentrated more on what lay behind him in Calcutta, than on what lay ahead. Half of him was still so convinced of the crucial political, strategic and commercial importance of Ladakh, that he simply could not believe that the government would fail in the end to accept the self-evident validity of his arguments, and the political and commercial initiatives he had founded upon them. Hence the confident spate of requests for further official favours like additional presents and a change of Gurkha escort. On the other hand, and more realistically, the dispiriting rumours of official disapproval, his own lack of authority, the impenetrable silence, his millstone reputation as a shadow-chasing enthusiast, and above all his lack of confidence in his ability to present his arguments with sufficient force – all these sapped even his unquenchable optimism and sometimes brought him close to despair. 'Would to God,' he exclaimed to Palmer,[24]

> that persons more competent to form political conclusion than myself could see this extraordinary country . . . for the purpose of impressing upon our Government its importance to our future relations. The facts break upon me conclusive (in addition to the little influence my experience has had in Stud affairs) that any statement I can adduce will have but little weight.

That is why he went on making them so earnestly and so continuously.

Just before Christmas 1821, he returned to the theme in two despatches to the political department.[25] The first, fairly short, assembled the additional information about Agha Mehdi's activities at Yarkand which Izzat-Allah had acquired there from an unnamed individual. It emphasized the frailty of China's grip upon those remote western outposts and Russia's designs there. The second, at enormous length, fleshed out these bare bones. It forecast the ease by which Russia could acquire both eastern and western Turkestan and, by using the secret road of earlier invasions from Yarkand, approach Leh. Moorcroft painted for Calcutta enthusiastic word-pictures showing how a handful of British officers, in command of 'a band of the hardy natives', could imitate nature by rolling huge boulders down the unstable gravel slopes and cut swathes through the massed grey columns of even the finest army in the world. All that was required was timely and modest preparation now. Closer links with Ladakh and Kabul would, he argued, be sufficient for the time being. At about the same time Moorcroft wrote to Palmer sentiments which, in 1821, would have led many to doubt his sanity and yet, a mere decade later, were commonplace in official correspondence. They amount to a formidably accurate forecast of what was to come.

> Things will not from appearances, remain in an indolent condition much longer in Central Asia and our Government may be called for an early development of energetic measures of precaution against the [Russian] projects of rage for conquest marked by the pretext of extension of commerce.[26]

Whenever opportunity offered during the remainder of that long and bitter winter at Leh, he hammered away at the same simple and alarmist message and he waited with growing anxiety for the government's response to his commercial treaty, the offer of Ladakh's allegiance and the letter to Ranjit Singh.

It came at last, at the end of March 1822, with all the effect of a thunderclap. As soon as Ranjit had received Moorcroft's extraordinary letter, he wisely passed it at once to Sir David Ochterlony at Delhi. He in turn, merely hinting his astonishment at its tone, passed it down the line to Calcutta.[27] There it was received by the governor-general in council with, he now informed Moorcroft,

> considerable surprise and displeasure. . . . Coming from an English gentleman, known to hold employment under the British Government, and to have proceeded out of its territory under sanction, it strikes His Lordship in Council as being the height of indiscretion in you to address any letter to the Maha Raja upon such a subject. . . . The disposition betrayed in the letter in question to interfere and tender unsolicited advice in matters wholly foreign to your situation is the least reprehensible feature of the case.[28]

More serious even than that, was the way Moorcroft had deliberately brought the government into it. His letter 'could only be construed as a threat of the eventual assertion by the British Government of a right to interfere in the affairs of Ludagh on the ground of its having theretofore been subject to Hindoostan'.[29] The government flatly rejected any such intention, 'feeling . . . little desire to extend our influence and political relations into regions beyond the Himmaleyah' or to preempt any ambitions of their ally, Ranjit Singh.[30] Ochterlony was instructed to send Ranjit a soothing official letter and to Moorcroft he privately wrote another. It has not survived but it was written in what Moorcroft called 'a commanding tone'.[31] As for the precious and hard-won commercial engagement, not to speak of the reams of other information which Moorcroft had poured upon Calcutta, they were not even mentioned. For Moorcroft, it could hardly have been a more brutal and contemptuous rejection of twelve months of patriotic effort and achievement.

He was shattered. A crowd of emotions jostled for expression: bitterness at the immensity of the lost opportunities, anger at the injustice of the rebuke and the neglect of all his efforts, concern for the future of the unoffending Ladakhis, and anxiety for the safety of his party. Moorcroft was always a sensitive man yet this was the closest he ever came to self-pity. He sincerely believed it to be the heaviest calamity ever to befall him in the whole of his life and claimed that his feelings were 'harrowed up in a degree not to be expressed by words'.[32] Express them, however, he did – and at great and passionate length.[33] The government, he argued, had completely misunderstood the nature of his doctor–patient relationship with Ranjit and the whole context of his letter. It was not a threat nor could it be since Ranjit had no shred of a claim to Ladakh. Moorcroft recapitulated, even more starkly, the immense commercial, political and strategic advantages for Britain which would have flowed from a protectorate over Ladakh, and the short- and long-term evils which would now follow its rejection. He lamented that the government had not, as he had particularly asked, given him an opportunity to explain his actions before rejecting them so comprehensively. More personally, and with a touch of bitterness, he added:

> It behoves me to offer my thanks for the solicitude the government have been pleased to express for my personal safety of which the continuance is certainly not improved by the communication of their disapprobation of my conduct made to Runjeet Singh. . . . In using a figure nearly allied to the actual fact I may say that hitherto I have had only to contend with the machinations of intrigue and with the dagger of the assassin. Before me I well know stands the poisoned bowl. That misfortune, which if it occur at all, may involve the principal individuals of my party in one common fate.

He was not joking. The same dark, foreboding mood persuaded him to add a long postscript to his March letter to George Saunders. It too talks of death by poison and anticipated that he would never see his friend again, to shake by the hand and thank for all his unwearying kindness towards young Anne.[34] On 7 April he wrote an equally sombre valedictory letter to Palmer.

> If I fall in this expedition it is probable that few of my companions will survive and in that case your property will be lost. This event may take place in consequence of which is imputed to me as an indiscretion but which as a man and as an Englishman I contemplate with no other feelings than those of self-complacency and honest pride . . . therefore I enclose an obligation that I beseech you to accept.

The enclosure was a new set of instructions to his executors, requiring them to refund to Palmer and MacKillop from his estate the full value of the merchandise they had provided. He also gave instructions for the education of young Richard at Eton or Westminster and made Saunders guardian of both children. Moorcroft's letter to Palmer ended 'God bless you. Farewell. Ever your sincerely affectionate friend.'[35]

It is true that these letters were the fruit of a dark mood which soon yielded to the light of his more usual stubborn optimism. Just how real a danger he was in from some act of premeditated violence from Ranjit Singh will never be known, but it was probably just as well for Moorcroft that Ranjit did not believe the government's disavowal of him.[36] Moorcroft realized that, after this crushing rebuke, things could never be quite the same again. Hitherto, he and his party had toiled and journeyed, secure at least in the hope of official approval. Only a month before, Moorcroft had been contemplating a dash to Calcutta for consultation before proceeding. Now, in a very real sense, he was on his own. Three years had passed and the official purpose of the mission was as remote from attainment as ever. Moreover, its substantial unofficial achievements had been either ignored or repudiated. In due course came the suspension of Moorcroft's salary and, later still, his peremptory recall to India. It all begins to seem inevitable. None the less Moorcroft clung on to all his old dreams. Indeed his own belief in them became more consuming, and his expression of them more dogged and defiant, as his confidence in any official endorsement slowly ebbed away.

There is not the slightest reason to doubt the genuineness of his belief in the central importance of Ladakh to British strategic and commercial interests. Nor was it very many years before his countrymen were worrying about Russian penetration and Sikh expansion in this direction and seeking, as avidly as Moorcroft, to introduce British political and commercial influence into Ladakh and across the Karakoram to Yarkand.[37] His vision was usually sound enough; it was the timing that was wrong, but that was badly wrong. In 1822, Russia was still as important a British ally in Europe as Ranjit Singh was in India. The thin British military presence in northern India was very dependent upon Sikh goodwill. In 1822, just at the end of a long period of war and territorial expansion, the Calcutta authorities simply could not contemplate the fresh risks of expansion and commitment in unheard-of lands beyond the Himalayas, on the mere say-so of their itinerant stud superintendent. Even if they had, London would have overruled them.

Moorcroft's unorthodox reputation as an enthusiast and his bizarre and disordered official literary style simply made things worse. Not even the most passionate Moorcroft supporter could really quarrel with the view of the London authorities, when they reviewed this voluminous correspondence three years later. Mr Moorcroft's 'political views are characterised,' they concluded, 'for the most part by zeal, rather than by sound judgement'[38] and, they might have added, by a pinch of unscrupulousness. It is clear, notwithstanding all Moorcroft's anguished huffing and puffing, that he had been engaged in unblushing and quite unauthorized political activity in Ladakh.[39] The letter to Ranjit, as he well knew, was a deliberate threat and it took a calculated risk. The Calcutta authorities could hardly be expected to stomach such unorthodox means, when they disagreed totally with the ends which alone might have justified them.

To Calcutta, Moorcroft wrote in sorrow. It was for the 'very jealous and tender'[40] British resident in Delhi that he reserved his anger. Moorcroft had been seething for months about the difficulties which Ochterlony had placed in Hafiz's way and his aggressive non-cooperation over the financial credits which were so desperately needed. Now, all the pent-up anger flowed out into what must have been the most extraordinary official letter the great hero of the Nepal war had ever received. Moorcroft began with his own letter to Ranjit.

> I was not prepared to expect that a letter called for by Ranjit Singh himself, sanctioned by previous communications, justified by the interests of Ladakh and those of Britain, written in a private form and positively disavowing connection with the Government be treated as a virtual assumption of official character. Still less was it within the range of expectation that the Resident of Delhi would so employ this letter as to break up my private relations with Runjeet Singh; to compromise the safety of my party and probably to frustrate the success of the expedition. . . . The man who with his own hand struck off his mother's head [Ranjit] is likely little to scruple about the means of removing an individual now obnoxious and whom he will consider as cast off by his Government . . . perhaps tomorrow's sun might shine on the lifeless bodies of the principal persons of my party.

Ochterlony, one feels, would not have wept too many tears over that. It was the rest of the letter which must really have galled him. Moorcroft said he had intended to keep quiet about Ochterlony's long and apparently deliberate series of acts, or failures to act, which, in one way or another, had jeopardized his mission. Now he deliberately put the whole matter on the official record.[41] It is a damning indictment and London later (and very properly) wanted to know why Calcutta had taken no action to investigate such serious charges.[42] Wilson cited the less vitriolic parts of this letter in his introduction to the *Travels* but he omitted the section in which Moorcroft, in a crescendo of patriotic indignations summarized the cumulative effect of Ochterlony's attitude.

> Actively you have lent yourself to injure not merely the credit of an individual from causes unknown to himself apparently become odious to you, but to poison the sacred character of British commercial credit, to blast the fair hopes of the vast extension of British commerce. . . . You have attacked not a single insulated individual. Through him you have attacked thousands, by this attack you may have involved the interests of hundreds of thousands, you may have inflicted a deep, a dangerous wound on the reputation . . . on the liberality, on the justice of the British Indian Government.

Moorcroft should have stopped there. But he could rarely leave well alone. His letter went on for several more thoroughly anti-climactic pages, imagining what a hostile native newswriter would make of the whole affair. It was a useful technique to allow himself even more bitter observations on Ochterlony's behaviour. The great man never replied. He probably never got to the end of the letter, for the early pages apparently threw him into such a towering rage that, for the sake of his blood pressure if nothing else, he read no further.[43]

Moorcroft, on the other hand, must have felt very much better once he had unburdened himself so resoundingly. The light begins to filter back into his letters almost at once. Within three weeks of his gloomy farewell to Palmer, he was writing to his friend again, crisply organizing credits for the next stage of his journey in a way that would bypass Ochterlony.[44] By then, spring and early summer had returned to Ladakh, heart-warming and supportive private letters from some of his many friends arrived from India,[45] and soon Moorcroft was on his travels once more.

Not alas on the road to Yarkand as he would have liked. Since any further word from that quarter was unlikely till late summer he and Trebeck decided to put the interval to good use by further separate travels inside Ladakh itself. Trebeck left Leh on 8 June, along with the faithful, forgetful Ghulam Hyder Khan (who was to return to India to collect 15,000 rupees' worth of pearls and corals), and headed south-eastwards on a 200-mile (320-kilometre) journey back to Spiti.[46] The prime aim was to explore and survey a direct route from Ladakh to British territory and, at the same time, escort back with him one of the exploring Gerard brothers from the Subathu garrison. Lieutenant Gerard, it was hoped, could remain at Leh to watch over British interests when Moorcroft's caravan moved on.

Moorcroft himself with Guthrie spent the same three months travelling roughly the same distance in the other direction. They went westwards along the main trade route down the Indus as far as Dras, the last inhabited valley on the Ladakh side of the watershed. Moorcroft, of course, was keen to examine the line to Kashmir taken by the shawl wool. It was also a possible escape route for them from Ladakh, if Yarkand in the end proved impossible. There were other objectives too. Moorcroft was anxious to increase his botanical collection and he wanted to buy a flock of the diminutive sheep of Ladakh. He had already arranged to graze them there until his return or bequeath them to the government for trial in England, in the event of his death. He believed that the fleece of the animal he had seen was as fine, dense and tough as any in the world and the meat had a superlative flavour. Moorcroft wanted some of his wealthy friends in England to put the animals on trial and distribute some of them 'to their tenantry, to industrious cottagers and to farmers of small capital'.[47] Another object of this trip was also connected with sheep and the improvement of British agriculture. Moorcroft wanted to see growing, and get hold of samples and seeds of, the vegetable called 'prango', which apparently grew in quantity on the thin soil round Dras. It needed little cultivation, but when dried into hay appeared to contain a substance fatal to the causes of most common, worm-induced complaints in sheep. Moorcroft had an exciting vision of the empty heaths and downs of Britain (not to speak of South Africa) carrying vast flocks of the tiny, disease-free sheep of Ladakh, as a result of the introduction of this vegetable.[48] Finally, on his return from Dras, he intended to visit the Zanskar district south-west of Leh, thus completing the mission's two-year coverage of Ladakh's principal regions.

The mere planning of a journey like this was a clear sign that Moorcroft was almost his old self once more. Early on the morning of 11 June, his first day out from Leh, he was lying under a tree delightedly listening to the song of the willow wren and dreaming of the nightingales he used to hear on his many journeys out of London to Padnalls, long ago. The early stages of this summer journey were something of a triumphal progress, as one grateful patient after another from his Leh surgery entertained him along the way. His cataract needles were still as busy as ever whenever they halted near a village and his surgical notes are often detailed and sometimes dramatic. On 24 June, a distraught mother brought to him a distressed 2-year-old, with the worst case of protrusion of the rectum he had ever seen.

> The cone of paper recommended as a means to return the gut would wholly have failed, however by no small exertion I succeeded in pressing it up by pinning with the portion most recently protruded and the infant within less than half an hour recovered its tranquility whereas had I not been on the spot within the space of a few hours the gut must have mortified

and the child would have died a painful death. It must have been immensely rewarding, as was another occasion when he entertained thirty red-robed Buddhist monks to breakfast. It was his way of thanking them for allowing him to witness what he called 'divine service' in their 'church', in the great *gompa* of Lamayuru.

The journey was not, however, one of unalloyed delight. Today, in summer, the tourist buses grind past Lamayuru along the new strategic road linking Leh with Dras, completing the journey along the central Indus corridor of Ladakh in a single day. In Moorcroft's time it usually took about a fortnight. Although he was riding most of the way, there are signs that he was finding the journey and the swooping extremes of day and night temperatures unusually exhausting. It was even worse once they turned away south-westwards from the Indus and toiled upwards into the high ridges and steep valleys. Moorcroft reckoned that he had seen more terrific roads than this, but none more dangerous, simply because of the narrowness and the instability of the path and the ferocity of the rivers. It is perhaps significant that it was Guthrie, not Moorcroft, who was more often up on the bare hillsides after game, to vary the dreary diet of 'ill-boiled rice, pulse and an occasional dish of turnip-tops'. For almost the first time, Moorcroft's journal begins to betray an uncharacteristic weariness. On 19 June, after a 'somewhat disastrous day', he confessed with a fierce underlining that 'in such a country as this the *miseries* of travelling are almost constant, the pleasures few and comparatively light'. Just two weeks later, on 3 July, those words were illustrated by the quite unnecessary loss in the mountain torrent of his cherished folding brass bedstead. It was never found. One cannot help feeling that, even three years before, Moorcroft would not have lamented its loss quite so fervently as he did in his journal on this occasion. That volume also betrays signs of a ducking in the river, but that may have happened a few weeks later, for the river gods of western Ladakh had not quite finished with them yet, despite the sacrificial offerings of some of the animals, a powder-horn, Moorcroft's writing desk and now his bed.

They spent about a month in the vicinity of Dras, huddled rather miserably in its narrow, flat-floored valley. Moorcroft completed his purchases of sheep and prangos, did more than fifty cataract operations and learned, the hard way, of the pilfering dishonesty of its demoralized, predominantly Muslim population. Like the occasional monsoon clouds, Islam had spilled over the watershed from the Kashmir side and maintained, as it does today, a precarious grip on the very margin of Buddhist Ladakh. It was probably just such a monsoon incursion somewhere up in the hills above them, which gave them all a very nasty experience on the night of 12 August. They had set up camp on an island in the middle of a quiet and apparently benevolent stream. During the night its level rose sharply, the banks collapsed and they were all woken by a rush of icy water which invaded the tents and drove them all into the trees. There they perched for several miserable hours, until daybreak revealed the extent of the damage. No lives were lost, but one of the many casualties was the precious botanical collection of the past ten weeks.[49] Moorcroft's journal of this period was probably another. At all events it has not survived.

Perhaps fearing further disasters, he halted the party while he wrote his lengthy and minutely detailed report on prangos (and other plants, vegetables and fruit) and despatched it together with seeds and samples to Calcutta and the Board of Agriculture in London.[50] Moorcroft was as enthusiastic as ever about the likely benefits of this wonder vegetable for British agriculture, but then seems to have checked himself, as if recalling his recent mauling by his Calcutta masters and his earlier experiences at the stud. He conceded in his ponderous way that he was now firmly cast as one of those

> enthusiasts who have suffered their judgement to be diverted from a severe examination and from a sound testimony by an attachment to a favoured object little short of infatuation. And the circumstances under which I urged, undertook and continue to prosecute my present journey are not ill-calculated of themselves alone to produce and keep alive the imputation of my being infected by enthusiasm.[51]

Nevertheless, he argued, his belief in the potential of the unlovely prango had not gone one step beyond the facts, whereupon he laboured the arguments all over again, and at even greater length. Here is the authentic tone of all his official despatches in those closing years. His convictions burn as brightly as ever, but his confidence of a fair hearing has gone. The irony is that, in this matter at least, he was vindicated. The seeds he sent failed to germinate but, thanks to Nathaniel Wallich at the Calcutta Botanical Garden, Moorcroft's researches were generously acknowledged. Later the government made unavailing efforts to get more of the seed from Ladakh, long after Moorcroft had left it for ever.

That departure he knew, as he headed back to Leh in late August 1822, could not prudently be delayed much longer. Everything now depended on the Chinese at Yarkand. By this time, there was a new European member of Moorcroft's party and he was almost as anxious as Moorcroft to cross the Karakoram and reach Yarkand. The impoverished ascetic and Hungarian linguist and traveller, Alexander Csoma de Körös, had encountered Moorcroft near Dras on 16 July. That meeting changed his life.[52] He and Moorcroft were very dissimilar in so many ways, but they shared a common desire to unlock the secrets of Tibetan culture. In the next five months of travelling and living together, they became firm friends. The solitary Csoma was grateful for the security and regular meals afforded by Moorcroft's company and the Englishman, in his usual open-handed and enthusiastic way, was glad to encourage and fund the linguistic researches of his new friend. Moorcroft lent

Csoma his precious 1762 Tibetan dictionary and suggested to him that he should embark on the study of Tibetan. Not only that, he gained for Csoma access to the great monastic libraries of Ladakh and, later, successfully won for him a modest stipend and some necessary reference works from the Indian government as well. As Moorcroft reminded his masters, access to the Tibetan language was 'not without a certain commercial or possibly political value' to Britain, even if Csoma himself expressly rejected such a motivation.[53] The outcome of all this, many years later, was a pioneering Tibetan grammar in which the original debt to Moorcroft is generously acknowledged.[54] Csoma proved to be more immediately useful too, for soon after they all returned safely to Leh on 26 August, he was able to translate for Moorcroft the letter in Russian which Agha Mehdi had been carrying to Ranjit Singh. This, rendered into Latin by Csoma in case it should fall into the hands of Ranjit's spies, was speedily despatched to Calcutta. Ironically enough, its first effect was to raise entirely unjustified doubt as to whether Csoma himself was a spy.[55]

Trebeck and his party came in from the south-east on 13 September, bringing, among other things, some welcome letters from friends in London and India. From Saunders came encouraging news of Anne's good health and growing proficiency in English, and at the end was a little note signed in large careful letters by her, which must surely have brought a lump to Moorcroft's throat as he read,

> My dear Papa, I hope you are very well and my dear Mama and my little brother. I hope I shall see my dear Papa soon in England at 252 Oxford Street. Pray give my kind love to my dear Mama and to my brother Richard. I am your dutiful daughter, Anne Moorcroft.[56]

Palmer, writing in Calcutta a mere three months earlier, again cheerfully consigned to the devil horses, 'the monopoly of the most lucrative trade in the world' and his whole investment if only Moorcroft would return alive to Pusa. None of these things, he wrote, was worth 'the life or liberty of a friend'.[57] Moorcroft would have disagreed.

In fact, on the very day that Moorcroft read those words, the dangers both to his life and his liberty were immeasurably increased, far more than he could ever have realized at the time. That same day Abdul Latif also returned to Leh with letters to Moorcroft. These, from the Chinese, finally and irrevocably, closed Yarkand to him as a route to Bokhara. For him, 'this disaster'[58] was the final catastrophe of that *annus horribilis* of 1822. The Kashmiris, the Russians, even in a sense the odious Ochterlony, had all beaten him in the end, although only by the narrowest of margins, or so he thought. In fact Moorcroft seriously underestimated the determination of the Manchus to keep Europeans out of the remote eastern corridors of their sprawling imperial mansion. According to later reports, they responded to the Moorcroft threat by erecting a huge wall-painting of a European in Yarkand so that their subjects would recognise one when they saw one. All his possessions could be seized so long as his head was forwarded to the authorities![59] Perhaps Moorcroft had had a narrow escape, although he could not be expected to see it like that. He confessed that he could not bear even to think of the affair without 'feelings of pain'. He had spent valuable time and money to gain access to new sources of shawl wool, to pre-empt a Russian bid to dominate the trade of inland China and to open a safer, but largely unknown, commercial route to Bokhara along well-beaten caravan trails which avoided the dangerously anarchic Muslim lands beyond the Indus; and all in vain.[60]

At least, after all the weary months of negotiation and waiting, he now knew what he had to do. Ranjit Singh had already granted him permission to return to the Punjab by way of Kashmir. From there he would attempt the direct Khyber route from Peshawar to Kabul. Thence he would cross the mighty Hindu Kush and the Oxus River and approach Bokhara from the south. It was, as he knew from the start, very much third best. Whatever might have been the case under the strong and friendly rulers who had welcomed Moorcroft in 1813, the fierce Muslim lands on both sides of the Hindu Kush were now rapidly becoming the most disturbed and lawless in all Asia. Yet there were always grounds for optimism. After all, the 'wayward and suspicious' emir of Bokhara was said to have an unspecified surgical complaint which his doctors could not alleviate and which, Moorcroft hoped, would gain him access to the royal favour.[61] Moreover, there was always the friendly influence of Khoja Shah Nias and Moorcroft's other highly placed Muslim friends to fall back upon.[62] Why, if all went well they could be back in India inside twenty months.[63]

Soon it was not *if* we return, but *when* we return. Moorcroft was almost his old self again. I am, he once told Parry, 'thoroughly convinced that little is unattainable to man if he will only set himself *doggedly* to make the acquisition, and I am led to think from a retrospect of my past life, that my obstinacy almost equals my enthusiasm'.[64] That was one of his opinions which nobody would deny. The great question for the future was whether those qualities, even in Moorcroftian quantities, would be enough. Once upon a time, his supplies of time, money, energy and official support had appeared to be almost limitless. Now, all were noticeably diminishing. With them slowly drained away the confidence of even the most loyal servants, like Hafiz and, eventually, Izzat-Allah himself. The best days of 'the Himalaya concern' were emphatically over.

To Moorcroft himself (and indeed to many of his contemporaries),[65] his two-year stay in Ladakh hardly seemed worth its cost in time and money. His commercial initiatives had been ignored by the government and frustrated by the Kashmiris, his political activities had been overruled, and the government's confidence in him shaken beyond redemption. Moreover, the volumes of novel and potentially invaluable information about practically every aspect of Ladakh which he had poured upon Calcutta and London, had not even been so much as acknowledged. He noted bitterly that

> reproof is borne to me on the wing of the eagle but approbation if such there be lingers on the pace of the snail. The presence of the former, the absence of the latter impress my mind irresistibly with the conviction of my communications being wholly without value in the eyes of the Government.[66]

He could not even comfort himself any longer with the satisfaction of knowing that he and Trebeck were the first Europeans to visit Leh. They were not even the second.[67] Nor were they the first to use the Kulu and Lahul route to it, as Wilson wrongly believed.[68] In his blacker moments, Moorcroft must have felt that the whole episode was an almost total failure.

And yet, of course, when measured on a longer time-scale, it was nothing of the kind. The young George Trebeck, whose three years on the road with Moorcroft must have given him a closer insight into the man and his schemes than anyone else at the time, saw this very clearly. His opinion bears extended quotation.

> So people say Moorcroft is an enthusiast the completion of whose views will never yield profit to himself or anyone else. . . . You are perhaps not aware that since his arrival in Hindoostan, there has always been a party which has entertained the same notion respecting him as the one that appears now to be very general. I will admit his enthusiasm and I consider it more as an useful stimulus to ability than as a failing. I admire his temper, perseverance and wisdom in effecting what he has. . . . If the suggestions our journey has given rise to fall into the hands of the enterprizing . . . I do not scruple to assert our country will be gainers by at least a million per annum. How? By novel systems of agriculture or more by the introduction of plants and cattle useful to the agriculturist. By the establishment of manufactures not yet practised or only prosecuted on a small scale. And by a commerce with Central Asia hitherto not rendered available. I exclude all political advantages, all improvements in our knowledge of countries, of everything connected with which we are as yet almost ignorant, what will be gained to Geography. . . . The man who led the way is not to be forgotten or spoken of as a visionary enthusiast.[69]

Trebeck could be dismissed simply as Moorcroft's mouthpiece, but time has confirmed much of his judgement. Whatever the scanty record left by earlier visitors, Moorcroft and Trebeck were certainly the first Europeans to visit Ladakh in modern times and the first to reside there. Between them they assembled a corpus of samples, routes, maps and information about the country and its neighbours which, at the time, was entirely new. Its accuracy and value was confirmed again and again by those who followed later.[70] None did follow for many years. As for Moorcroft's neglected and rejected views about the political, strategic and geographical importance of Ladakh, they were all in due course taken up by the British more or less exactly as he had predicted.[71] Many of his other predictions came true as well. Even the Chinese encroachments in north-east Ladakh, which caused the independent Republic of India such anguish in the 1960s, were anticipated by Moorcroft. Indeed his writings were disinterred from the archives and played their part both in the long Sino-Indian paper war which preceded the real thing, and in the *post mortems* which followed.[72]

Even leaving aside all hindsight justifications, there must have been countless men and women in Ladakh who owed their sight or lives to the little *Ma-ka-ra-phad Sahib*, as he is recorded in the *Chronicles of Ladakh*.[73] They at least would not have regarded his visit as unproductive. Nor it seems did his many friends among the Ladakh establishment – the raja, his son, the khalun, the lompa, the banka khalun, and the many others to whom Moorcroft paid his farewell visits in the closing days of September 1822. The regret at his going seems to have been genuine and widespread.

It would not have been shared by many of Moorcroft's party. Among them all was bustle, for they had very little time to get the great caravan and its sixty hired ponies out of Ladakh, across the great snow ridge into Kashmir, before winter closed the passes yet again. The plan was that Moorcroft and the bulk of the party (including Khoja Shah Nias) would push on down the Indus valley towards Dras as fast as possible, leaving Trebeck and Csoma, with twelve horses, to wait a few more weeks for the return from India of Ghulam Hyder Khan, along with the replacement military escort and muskets which, it was hoped, he was bringing with him.

On the last day of September, Moorcroft and the main party, eyes no doubt screwed up against the perpetual glare of that pale land, finally cleared the last of the narrow streets of Leh which had been their home for so long. Many of Moorcroft's friends and well-wishers rode out with them. Some did not turn back, and then with many mutual expressions of goodwill and regret, until the third morning out of Leh. For Moorcroft, this return journey to Dras gave him a welcome opportunity to repair his water-ravaged botanical collection and buy more seeds and samples for transmission to England. It was also a welcome and rare chance to examine again the progress of his recent cataract patients. The results gave him much satisfaction. So too did the contents of the mail-bag which reached him near Lamayuru. There was cheering news and encouragement from friends in India, together with books and magazines. Better still was the belated news that all his lengthy official despatches from 1821 right down to April 1822, which he believed had been totally and deliberately ignored by the government, had in fact crossed half India in mistaken pursuit of Charles Metcalfe, and had not come before the attention of the Political and Secret Department in Calcutta until July 1822.[74] There were other encouraging indications that official support had not been entirely withdrawn. Things were improving.

Unchanged, however, were the hazards of that truly awful road near Dras. On 16 October, not very far from where his bed had disappeared and his camp been engulfed, Moorcroft nearly came to grief once again in the headwaters of that same malignant Dras river. He and his horse

fell from a narrow path glazed with ice and we both pitched sideways upon a large slab of jasper, from the polished surface of which we rolled rapidly down a steep slope covered with snow. A slight check in our progress enabled me to disengage my feet from the stirrups but one leg remained tightly girthed by the rein of the bridle and the horse continuing to slide along the slope dragged me down after him till within a few feet of the edge of the cliff which bordered the river that ran in a glen greatly below us. I was expecting that we should go together over the precipice . . . but when he had reached the very brink of the cliff he was suddenly stopped by a block of stone the only one discoverable on its edge.[75]

Moorcroft was badly bruised and suffered mild frostbite in his left hand but he was lucky to be alive and in one piece. The only serious casualty was his pocket compass.

That night, in a heavy snowstorm and sub-zero temperatures, 800 armed raiders from neighbouring Baltistan descended upon Dras and sacked it. Moorcroft was busy the next day dressing the wounds of the victims and sheltering the shivering, half-naked wretches who sought his protection. It looked as though his party would be attacked next. Before nightfall they had built a defensive stockade in the drifting snow with anything that came to hand (including the luckless replacement botanical collection, which once again suffered extensive damage). Moorcroft's five Tibetan wolfhounds ranged up to 400 yards (365 metres) beyond the encampment and the men stood anxiously on watch all through that freezing night. At daybreak they were all relieved to find that the raiders had vanished. Not that Moorcroft escaped entirely unscathed. For among their booty were sixty-seven of the flock of Ladakhi mini-sheep, which he had left in the care of a local official.[76]

They were delayed ten days at Dras, although Izzat-Allah pushed on across the watershed to make contact with the Kashmiri authorities on the other side. It was not until 30 October that the long column of men, horses and laden sheep trudged up in the bitter cold towards the summit of the Zoji-la. Moorcroft was as busy as ever, noting in immense detail where and how the pass might be defended against a Russian army approaching from the Ladakh side. Soon they were up on the broad back of the pass and a minute or two later, visible on their left, there opened up the spectacular view downwards into the Sindh valley of Kashmir.[77]

The Zoji, like the Niti and the Rohtang, is one of nature's great divides. All three passes mark the outer limits of the great, rain-bearing monsoon winds from the southern oceans, and also of the rich vegetation that goes with them. Moorcroft was astonished at the contrast between the black soil of the hills down below him, clothed with pine, fir and beech to their very summits, and 'the bare sterile surface to which our eyes have been so long accustomed'. First they had to get down in safety before nightfall. The Kashmir side of the Zoji is the steeper of the two and they had a hard struggle in the deep snow. When eventually the first of the party arrived safely among the trees, they celebrated their safe arrival, despite the unaccustomed mildness of the air, by lighting 'such a fire as Tibet never witnessed'. For Moorcroft, however, it was an anxious night, as he sent back horsemen and sat up under the fitful moon and the scudding snow-clouds waiting for the remainder of his exhausted men and animals with their precious cargoes to come in. Some, mindful of the evil reputation of the Zoji-la, began to murmur of disaster. It might well have been, but, in the middle of the night, the rest of the party came safely into the firelight.

It was the last day of October 1822. 'We are now', wrote Moorcroft in his journal with evident relief and delight, 'in Kashmir.'

20 KASHMIR AND THE PUNJAB,
NOVEMBER 1822–DECEMBER 1823

FOR CENTURIES, AND long before the Mughal emperors had adorned its natural beauty with their gardens and pavilions, Kashmir was a land of legendary reputation. The fertile valley, threaded with rivers and lakes and set like a jewel in its green summer frame of alpine valleys, soaring, tree-clad hills and the encircling snowpeaks beyond, has always attracted poets, merchants, conquerors and visitors seeking a refuge from the scorching summer heat of the Indian plains below the Pir Panjal. Kashmir is at its glorious best in late spring and summer. By late autumn, however, the greenery and the sun have gone, the high pastures are parched russet brown and the angled masses of trees below the snowline are black and sinister. As Moorcroft's long caravan threaded its way down from the Zoji-la in November 1822, he confessed his disappointment at the scenery, but he was never much concerned with the purely picturesque. The abundance of the rich and varied vegetation was pure delight to him after the parched moonscape of Ladakh. He seems, in those first few days, to have spent much of his time rushing from one leafless tree or plant to the next, or firing questions about agriculture and rural husbandry at anyone he could find to answer.[1]

The Kashmiris were as curious about the first European they had ever seen as he was about their plant life. At every scruffy timber village, the whole population turned out to stare. They were, Moorcroft thought, dirty and often hideously diseased. They bore all the marks of poverty and the grinding oppression of their Sikh masters. 'The former seat of Asiatic Romance,' he wrote to Lord Harewood,[2] has become 'the present scene of the vilest tyrany and . . . every possible complication of human misery.' It was not very long before he and many of the party were wishing themselves back among the cheerful, healthy Ladakhis and their bare, beautiful land of far distances.[3]

However, the welcome from the Sikh governor and his senior officials seemed friendly enough and the mountainous pilaos of rice, the plentiful roast meat and the cheerful log fires they provided along the way must all have been appreciated by men who had experienced the privations of the road from Leh. The chief of the Sikh cavalry escort which came to lead them in, was a man called Surat Singh. In the next twelve months until they quit Ranjit Singh's kingdom, he was their constant guide, protector and, eventually, friend. On the afternoon of 3 November 1822, accompanied by Surat Singh and an impressive escort of troops, they entered Srinagar, the crazy Asiatic Vienna threaded with water which is Kashmir's capital. Its jumbled, jutting timber houses and filthy lanes were thronged with spectators as they passed. They were led through the town to a timber garden-house, standing at the edge of the water in the so called garden of Dilawar Khan, in the north-east corner of the town. That little house, put at his disposal by Ranjit, became home for Moorcroft and many of his party for the whole of their stay in Srinagar.[4] Other European visitors were housed at the same spot later. It was comfortable enough and especially welcome when the snow arrived on the floor of the valley shortly afterwards and lingered there till mid-March. The winter temperatures in waterlogged Srinagar were nothing like as cold as those of Leh, but the dampness of the air under the grey skies made it much more unpleasant. Kashmir in winter is a long way from paradise. Moorcroft came to believe that the unhealthy atmosphere from the near stagnant water sometimes addled his wits.[5] Certainly his party was far less healthy in Kashmir than it had been in Ladakh and one of the hapless Gurkha sepoys died soon after their arrival in the valley.[6]

Nevertheless, healthy or no, it was imperative that they spend the winter in Srinagar and one of Moorcroft's first jobs was to confirm Ranjit Singh's permission. For one thing, they were badly in need of a refit and time to repair or replace the tents, clothes and equipment ravaged by two years in Ladakh, three since leaving India. For another, they needed time to prepare the ground in Afghanistan, before launching the great caravan into that anarchic land. In any case, Trebeck was still on the wrong side of the Zoji-la awaiting replacements to the sepoy escort, and there was no news of the still missing Ghulam Hyder Khan. Without the pearls, corals and ammunition he was carrying back from the plains, they simply could not move on. In fact, although Trebeck came in safely with Csoma towards the end of November 1822, Ghulam Hyder Khan, after some extraordinary adventures, did not catch up with them until early the following year.[7] There was yet another reason for delay. Moorcroft knew that he and Trebeck were the first Europeans to visit Kashmir for forty years.[8] He wanted time to examine the geography and natural products of the valley and report on what he had already seen. It was therefore fortunate in every way that Ranjit Singh so readily granted permission for them to stay.

That did not mean that he was not extremely suspicious of what Moorcroft was up to and seems to have had him as closely watched and confined as he decently could. It was just as well for Moorcroft that some of the information with which he was beginning to fill his journal and his official despatches in those months at Srinagar did not fall into the hands of Ranjit's spies.

Moorcroft's first political despatch to Calcutta from Kashmir was completed just before Christmas 1822.[9] It was more like a small book. In it he returned once again to his old theme, that India was vulnerable to Russia, not necessarily from Persia and the north-west as the prevailing orthodoxy would have it, but from the extreme north by way of Ladakh and then Kashmir. He provided in immense detail the results of his observations along the route from Leh across the Zoji-la, in places giving an almost yard by yard and blow by blow description of how and where the road could best be defended. At all costs, he argued, the Russians must be kept out of Kashmir. Its mountain walls made it a natural fortress and its fecundity was such that up to half a million men could be fed and provided with every war material. As he summarized it later, if Britain had Kashmir in her possession she

> might mock any possible movement against her Indian possessions . . . but it may be said with truth that from the moment it fall into the possession of any other European power from that moment the safety of British India is endangered.[10]

Even more so if the unreliable Ranjit Singh remained master of the Punjab. Moorcroft even suspected that Ranjit might sell Kashmir to the Russians for cash, and that the French adventurers training his army were former Napoleonic agents secretly in the pay of the Russians.[11]

It was not only as a vital defensive bastion, or even as a potential commercial emporium on the road to Asia, that Moorcroft coveted Kashmir for Britain. The more he and Trebeck saw of the needless poverty, neglect, oppression and disease on every side during that damp winter and chilly, sunless spring of 1822–3, the more angry they both became. As guests of Ranjit Singh they could only vent their feelings in private letters.[12] Trebeck admitted that he felt almost 'savage' at it all. 'We are too fastidious,' he told his Irish friend, Captain Leeson.

> Extension of European power is a general blessing apprehended perchance by a few but prayed for by a million. It has nearly as much justice in it as . . . arresting the blow of a murderer and I wish to Heaven, Leeson, some thousands of your own distressed countrymen and of our emigrants had a footing in the heart of Asia.[13]

Moorcroft felt exactly the same. Only then would the blessings of enlightened rule and ordered government transform Kashmir into the paradise Nature intended it to be – 'the Venice or Palmyra of Upper Asia'. It cried out for improvement. Moorcroft could find only one consolation in the present situation and, perhaps wisely, crossed it out from the draft of one of his official despatches.[14] Venereal disease in Kashmir seemed to be so rife that any advancing Russian army after the 'hardship and privations of a march from Toorkistan' would be speedily incapacitated.

Never in all his life had Moorcroft come across disease on such a scale as he found among the patients who were soon crowding round the door. His laconic list of them is stomach-turning and Trebeck and Guthrie were both seriously shaken.[15] Guthrie was soon busy compounding purgative pills available free of charge to whoever seemed to need them each day.[16] Moorcroft set aside every Friday to examine his patients, a task which he regarded as a duty but which, he admitted, he found 'as laborious as it is appalling to the senses of the sight and smell'.[17] Saturday was surgery day. Moorcroft sometimes treated more than 300 poor wretches in a single day, working from early morning till long after dark.[18] The results were sometimes startling. To Parry, he explained[19] that:

> the performance of operations on the horse has given me a boldness in operating on man which, doubtless bordering on temerity, might startle the regular surgeon. . . . The liberties I take are followed by a success which creates surprise even in one, who during the last twelve years has had no small experience in operating on cases which would be considered incurable by discreet practitioners. . . . I feel that many of my patients if not relieved by me must sink under their complaints.

One of these was a 'poor woman who had for some years been a most disgusting object from a cancerous mass which projected from the right cheek involving both eyelids and the eye itself. The eyelids were taken off, the eye taken out and the woman has got almost entirely well.'[20]

On the basis of this case alone, Moorcroft's fame spread far and wide throughout the valley. In due course it brought before him a labourer, who mutely showed Moorcroft a cancerous growth weighing more than 8 lb 13 oz (4 kilograms)

> which occupied a great portion of the space between the lower end of the breast bone and the navel and adhered to the ribs on one side. Its growth took its rise many years back and the mass was unmovable in any direction. The risks and probabilities were fairly presented to the patient who was prepared to die rather than to submit to the longer continuance of a very painful disorder which disabled him from pursuing the occupations necessary to his maintenance. As was previously apprehended the muscles of the belly in their whole thickness were found to be inextricably involved in the substance of the cancerous mass and were so completely removed with it that a large portion of the stomach and a great extent of the cowl were plainly descried through the transparent membrane that lines the belly and now formed the only obstacle to the escape of the intestines which were so strongly pushed outwards in the action of breathing as to convey to the bystander an apprehension of their bursting through the thin partition. Let it suffice that this man perfectly recovered.

An hour before he wrote those words he had removed a cancer from a man's neck like a second head. The following day he was going to tackle the first male breast cancer he had ever met.[21] And these, of course, were only a tiny fraction of the many thousands who sought his help. Moorcroft had only one major medical disappointment in Kashmir and that was not his fault. He hoped to introduce vaccination into the valley because smallpox was such a disfiguring scourge there but in every case, as had happened in Ladakh, the vaccine he badgered his friends for either miscarried or arrived from India inert. With this exception, it is clear that Moorcroft's medical practice brought him immense personal satisfaction. It was also, as he well knew, something of 'a passport of safety' for him and his party.

All the same, they had to be continuously on their guard. Shortly before they left Srinagar, a Sikh fanatic drew his sword on Izzat-Allah but was seized before he could cut the mir down. At about the same time, a truculent band of armed fakirs had to be driven away from Moorcroft's door and later shouted insults and threatened violence. Perhaps the most curious experience of all happened to Moorcroft. A Sikh who had apparently dreamed the previous night of murdering him

> came to my apartment with the charitable intention of cutting me down and sate along with me for about five hours in the hope of finding a favourable opportunity for accomplishing his purpose. Seeing him frequently in the act of grasping the hilt of his sword my eye was often directed towards him although I was engaged in writing . . . .

This unnerving cat and mouse game was only terminated when Moorcroft's servants arrived with his dinner and the stranger was compelled to leave.[22]

Looking at the almost unbelievable range and quantity of subjects which Moorcroft investigated and wrote about during these months in Kashmir, one can easily see why even a would-be assassin could not be allowed to interrupt the torrent of words. Whatever Moorcroft's weariness along the Dras road, there is no sign of it once he reached Srinagar. Most men half his age would have been well pleased with a quarter of his output. A mere list of some of the topics he tackled is impressive enough, even without the extraordinary detail which make his writings such an underestimated gold mine for the specialist researcher. Wilson's edition inevitably gives only a glimpse of the riches among the papers themselves.[23] Nor was Moorcroft merely concerned with the useful. His researches extended into antiquities, social customs and ancient manuscripts. At his own expense he restored the tomb of a sixteenth-century conqueror of Kashmir, who had invaded by way of Ladakh from eastern Turkestan,[24] and he went to immense trouble, and some expense, to enable Csoma to return to Ladakh and pursue his literary and linguistic researches.[25]

His chief interests, however, were always in anything useful and practical which might prove of benefit in Britain or India. The techniques of rice cultivation and storage, bee-keeping, manuring and viticulture; the extraordinary botany and husbandry of the lakes; walnut, fruit and medical drugs; gun, sword, cotton, chintz, leather and papier-mâché manufacture are but a few. Above all, a sojourn in Kashmir was, for Moorcroft, a unique opportunity to complete the enquiries into the shawl industry, which he had first launched in Tibet in 1812 and pursued avidly ever since. He had inspected the pastures of the shawl goats, had travelled along the high pack-routes along which the wool was carried, had mastered the technique of separating the fine wool from the coarse and now he could examine at first hand the brilliant techniques of the shawl artists and weavers. His writings and samples not only played a key role in the establishment of a British shawl industry, but have become a unique and priceless source of information to textile historians.[26] Moorcroft's information was not simply the result of earnest questioning. Where necessary he took local experts directly on to his payroll and often into his house. There were twelve shawl-pattern artists and 300 pattern embroiderers working for him at different times.[27] A few of the exquisite gouache pattern paintings he commissioned are now in the Metropolitan Museum of Art in New York and are of great importance to scholars.[28] Perhaps even more important – indeed it turned out to be unique – was the ancient Kashmiri-Sanskrit text on which Moorcroft set ten pandits to work preparing a translation.[29] He also employed a bee-keeper, a musician and four craftsmen.[30] Moorcroft rarely did things by halves, and it makes his own output even more remarkable.

'I am writing,' he told one of his aristocratic friends in England,[31] 'in a small room filled with workmen who chatter in several languages with such a never ceasing clack as renders it difficult for me to keep my attention from them.' It all cost much more than merely his comfort and concentration. During his stay in Kashmir, he was depleting his funds roughly twice as fast as his salary was replenishing them.[32] There is nowhere a hint of regret about this in his correspondence. On the contrary, the possibility that his researches would augment what he called 'the stock of public capital' seems to have been reward enough.[33] He took great care, before leaving Kashmir, to assign the whole of his papers to the government in case anything should happen to him. As well as the flood of information, he sent down to Calcutta twenty-five huge consignments of seeds, samples, routes, drawings and maps, for expert examination in Calcutta and London.[34]

'The Himalaya concern' was a formidable international enterprise by any standards and one at which even George Trebeck marvelled. He, of course, played his own valiant part, by concentrating on the geography and natural resources of Kashmir, but his admiration for the older man who was the inspiration of it all grew as the months went by.

> So convinced is he (and in my opinion so justly convinced) of the importance of his mission and so ready to devote himself to the service of the public, that I dare affirm, he would suffer the ban of office and the injury of his property rather than to stop short of its completion. . . . The man who will voluntarily expose himself to hardships, privations, and dangers in the cause of his employers has, at least, a right to expect their concurrence in a patient and impartial trial of his plans. . . . You may contradict . . . any assertion that Moorcroft is acting either for his own emolument or pleasure (in the usual acceptation of the word).[35]

That parenthetical qualification is important for, although Moorcroft derived the greatest satisfaction from what he was doing and trying to do, there was nothing 'usual' about him at all. The point is well illustrated by the journey he chose to make in mid-December 1822.[36] He had not long completed the exhausting journey from Leh, bad weather at that time was usual and imminent, and there was much head-shaking and objecting from officials and others. All were brushed aside by what he called 'a measured obstinacy'. The justification for the journey was, to him at least, self-evident. He had noticed that the timber piles supporting the bridges and houses of Srinagar were untouched by decay even after centuries of immersion in water. The finest deodar trees, he was told, grew on the hills flanking the narrow Lolab valley, just across the ridge to the north-east of the Wular lake. Their introduction into Britain might bring immense benefits. That was sufficient justification.

He would go and collect some seeds. And go he did, first by boat down the Jhelum and across the lake, and then over the hills into the valley. In those days it was a much more wild and untamed place than it is today and when Moorcroft at last arrived, it proved to be sometimes waist-deep in snow. Measured obstinacy was not always enough. He failed to find any worthwhile seeds and turned back disappointed on 22 December, but once again his medical skills came to the rescue. A nameless village headman, who was also a grateful patient, heard about the problem and set some of his people to work. Soon Moorcroft had his precious pound or two of the seeds in good condition for trials in Calcutta and England. He was back in the little house by the lake on Christmas Eve, just in time for a white Christmas. Shortly afterwards, a splendid dinner with some generous gifts was organized for him and the Muslims of the party by the ever generous Khoja Shah Nias.[37]

It was not really until the April of 1823 that the sun returned properly to Kashmir, and they at last began to see the valley in all its famed and iridescent glory of blossom and bird-song, lake and distant snow mountain, alpine meadow and rich forest. This was the traditional time of pleasure and of endless parties among the gardens and islands. 'Nothing but music and song resounds over the waters,' recalled old Ghulam Hyder Khan wistfully.

> Mr. Moorcroft went to three or four parties of pleasure given by the viceroy, Motee Ram Dewan, to the gardens beyond the lakes; most of the trips were performed by water, in those little boats; he had dinner dressed for him, consisting of pillaus and kubabs; and separate sets of dancing women allotted to him for his entertainment.

The dancing-women of Kashmir were particularly accomplished and beautiful, he noted.[38]

Notwithstanding these temptations, Moorcroft was anxious to be on the move again by May in order to give his party the best chance of getting across the high summer passes of the Hindu Kush, before yet another winter shut them off from Bokhara.[39] Besides the Srinagar of 1823, with its insanitary houses, filthy streets and choked canals was no place to linger in. As the sun climbed higher in the sky each day, the servants began to go down with fevers one after another.[40] Unfortunately, much of the humming activity in and around the little summer house by the lake was still so incomplete, that Moorcroft and Trebeck decided to take advantage of the delay to make a short tourist excursion to the source of the Jhelum River, on the first slopes under the snow ridge of Pir Panjal.[41] The gardens there, beautified by the Mughal emperors, have not changed much since Moorcroft and Trebeck's visit. The young and romantic Trebeck was assailed there with bitter-sweet reflections about the passing of greatness and the brevity of human life which were 'almost painful'. Perhaps it was a presentiment. He had less than eighteen months more of his own short life to live by then.

They all knew that once they left Kashmir and the relatively settled territories of Ranjit Singh for the tribal hills, they would be in a very different world where every man was armed, where life was cheap, where plundering rich caravans had been a way of life for centuries, and where no empire in history had ever succeeded in imposing more than a temporary veneer of law and order on the more accessible valleys. Moorcroft and Trebeck both took the opportunity in the early summer of 1823 to write letters of farewell or send presents to everyone they held dear.[42] They also committed as much as possible of their discoveries to paper, before sending all that could be spared down for safekeeping to the British forward post at Ludhiana. The intention was to collect them on their return in the autumn of 1825, but, as Moorcroft informed Calcutta, 'if I should fall, a circumstance the troubled state of Kabool and the exaggerated notions of European wealth render not improbable, the Government it is conceived have a right to whatever information may have been obtained from the labor of their servant'.[43]

The same considerations prompted the considerable attention which Moorcroft, and especially 'Corporal' George Trebeck, devoted to the question of caravan security while they were in Kashmir. The hoped-for replacements for the dwindling little band of Gurkha troops, now down to eleven, never arrived. It was probably Ochterlony's final revenge for that scorching letter.[44] Moorcroft tried instead to raise the number of his escort to about thirty, by enlisting active young Muslims into his private army, smart in their new black uniforms faced with grey.[45] Trebeck picked the brains and library of his friend Captain Leeson for guidance on cavalry drill and sword exercises; a forge was busy at Moorcroft's door from December 1822 onwards, beating out lances and swords; excellent Kashmiri copies of their British guns were made; and, twice a week all through the winter, the open space near their house attracted spectators to witness their exercises.[46] All this military activity apparently caused some alarm but Trebeck was well pleased with the results. The infantry, he believed, were capable of firing 100 rounds a minute[47] and the artillery corps, with its newly arrived brass mini-cannon, was augmented at the last minute by the specialist skills of a ragamuffin European deserter from the Bombay Horse Artillery called John, or James, Lyons.[48]

It is quite clear that 'considerable and vexatious delays and much anxiety' accompanied their departure from Srinagar.[49] In mid-June the tents were first pitched at the halting-place outside the town, but it was not until late afternoon on the last day of July that the polyglot members of the party, now eighty in number, were safely loaded aboard thirty river boats (the horses and much of the baggage proceeding by land), and set off down the Jhelum. They were watched by vast and noisy crowds at every bridge and vantage-point and, in Trebeck's words, were 'not a little troubled by parties of women coming to us in small skiffs and accompanying their application for alms by a song in full chorus'. Moorcroft missed all this. He was paying his final respects to the Sikh governor up in the great fort-palace on the left bank of the river. He may even have been there watching, as his little convoy passed down the river below. At all events he did not rejoin them in camp, just north of the town, till after sunset.

For most of the party those early August days of 1823, as they moved gently downstream towards Baramula were unusually restful, apart from the attention of clouds of mosquitoes. Not, of course, for Moorcroft. He left early in the morning on 2 August to make a two-day botanical excursion to Gulmarg. That most lovely of Kashmir's high alpine valleys, with its green meadows, dark forests and distant views across the valley towards the snow giants, reminded him, as it has reminded countless other of his countrymen down the years, of home. His admiration for the fine cattle and healthy horses he saw there led him, by a natural train of thought, to speculate once more about what would happen to the Punjab and Kashmir when Ranjit was dead.[50] It was a theme which recurred often in his journals and occasionally in his political despatches. His forecasts, at least for the Punjab, were surprisingly precise and accurate. That he longed fiercely for a British takeover, so that all the rich potential of these lands could be achieved, goes without saying.[51]

At Baramula, the Jhelum enters the gorge by which it leaves Kashmir and tumbles down into the Punjab plain. They spent some rather uncomfortable days there 'writing letters, winding up accounts and adjusting other matters'. The wind blew incessantly; there were signs of trouble from the near-rebellious chief of Muzaffarabad, at the other end of the Jhelum gorge; it looked as though their Kashmiri porters would cut and run at the first opportunity; and Moorcroft was unwell.

> For the preceeding four days I had been suffering under continual fever with much headache and pains in the region of the liver and for three nights I was greatly delirious. However convinced of the necessity of leaving Kashmeer and equally satisfied of the propriety of a person in a fever quitting the spot on which it was contracted I stiffened myself as much as possible against the influence of painful feeling and sate on horseback though with some difficulty.

At last, on 10 August, they said goodbye to their mentor and friend, Surat Singh, and set off unescorted down the Jhelum gorge. Ominously, the merchants who had travelled under their protection as far as Baramula, stayed behind. Moorcroft's men were little more than a day's march down that rugged but stiflingly hot river-gorge, when they discovered why. About 100 armed men were drawn up across the path in front to enforce what was an extortionate demand for customs duty. After an anxious night under arms, Moorcroft suppressed his instinct to fight and decided to turn back towards Baramula.[52] There were some uncomfortable moments, for they were expecting to be attacked at any moment. Moorcroft stationed himself at the rear and they set off back the way they had come, soon meeting the good Surat Singh and thirty of his soldiers riding hard towards them. Eventually, in response to his anxious urgings and those of the governor, Moorcroft was persuaded to return to Srinagar for a few weeks. He was not entirely convinced that the whole thing was not a plot, perhaps like many of the earlier delays, to detain them in Kashmir indefinitely for some dark purpose known only to Ranjit Singh. 'All is crooked with the Singhs,' he wrote in his journal. At least a short delay would give time, both for the monsoon on the edge of the plains and the apparently widespread anti-Sikh rebellion there, to abate their fury. So it was that they returned to the little wooden house in the Dilawar Khan Bagh, watched by the same crowds who had seen them on their way just seventeen days before.

Moorcroft and Trebeck were soon immersed in their various researches and activities. The unexpected return to the fleshpots, however, proved too much for the deserter, James Lyons. Taking advantage of the absence of Moorcroft and Trebeck (who were out of town hunting bears on the estate of one of Izzat-Allah's relatives), Lyons took some of the sepoys with him on a liquor-shop crawl. He came back so drunk and violent that he could scarcely be restrained at all. Even when they did manage to lock him up in Guthrie's room, he smashed the door down and attacked one of his guards. It took two attempts and more drunken uproar, before they finally packed him off under escort towards Ludhiana on 28 August.

Moorcroft returned thankfully to his medicine and to more investigations into the botany and rural husbandry of Kashmir. On 20 August he was out with Guthrie in the hills behind the Shalimar gardens examining a medicinal root growing there. On the 29th he was inspecting the beehives of one Russool Shah, a humble painter of papier-mâché pen-cases. And so it goes on. From 7 September, he was so busy reporting all this new information to Calcutta that his journal stops for a month.[53] By the time it started again, he and his party had left Srinagar, this time for good.

There were the usual irritating delays, of course. If it were not the heavy rain, then it was the colourful Muharram festival; but at last, on 23 September, they headed out across the valley, already lovely in its autumn colours. Instead of striking westwards by the direct Jhelum gorge route to the plains as before, they were persuaded to go on a lengthy detour much further to the south-west. This time, Surat Singh and his men had orders to accompany them all the way. Moorcroft once again left the main party briefly, this time to examine saffron cultivation near Srinagar and a novel means of asphyxiating its rodent predators with smoke. They were soon in the hills that ring the valley and at last, on 30 September, passed over the ridge by the old Mughal road across the Pir Panjal pass. From the summit they could only see the hills at their feet. Perhaps it was just as well that the haze hid from them what would have been a tantalizing view of the Jhelum, wriggling its silvery way across the distant plain far below. Had they been able to follow that river's escape route from Kashmir as they had first intended, they would now have been more than two months on their way, but at least they were finally and safely quit of Kashmir.

Their welcome from the raja of the first of the little kingdoms which lay in those broken, jungly hills along the rim of the Punjab was a warm one and he put his humble but picturesque palace at their disposal. It was just as well. Trebeck had fallen victim to one of the fevers, which then raged all along those hills in summertime, and was in no condition to travel further. Moorcroft discovered, in the well-informed raja of Rajaori, a congenial fellow-improver and noted with approval that his little kingdom was well cultivated. They went hawking together; Moorcroft preached the virtues of vaccination and doubtless much more besides; he conducted experiments in the palace garden on the ant-resistant properties of different timbers; and, of course, he launched his 'coarse but energetic' treatment for fever on the many patients who were willing to undergo it.[54] Moreover, he and Guthrie also co-operated in an interesting case of facial tubercular leprosy in a young teenager. By using nitrate of arsenic and powdered milkweed, they seem to have effected in three months what sounds almost like a miracle cure but probably has a more prosaic explanation. Some years later, when English visitors in these hills were more common, the raja recalled his first of the breed with affection, and he was wont to produce the testimonial which Moorcroft had written for him during those four days in September 1824, together with the coloured prints of London left by his visitor. He also showed them, as no doubt he did to Moorcroft, that he had six toes on each foot.[55]

Moorcroft put the interval to good use by composing yet another enormous report to Calcutta, on more of the useful crops and techniques he had examined in Kashmir.[56] He made no mention at all of the most recent rumour that he was to be recalled or dismissed, this time conveyed in a letter from Palmer written only three months before. Palmer added a personal plea of his own.

> As far as I and McKillop are concerned, your return would be hailed with equal vivacity and satisfaction as if you sent us – or even brought us – golden fleeces, capital brood cattle, and all the treasures of the trans-Himalihea regions for verily I fear your falling a victim to your adventurous spirit and patriotic zeal. I beseech you to come back my dear friend and pass the remnant of your eventful [days] in a society you delight, adorn and instruct.[57]

No doubt Palmer would have sighed when he received in reply the defiant but entirely predictable memorandum, which Moorcroft composed for him to present to the governor-general.[58] Resign the stud appointment he would at any time on request, but return voluntarily he would not.

> A voluntary abandonment by me of the enterprise in which I am engaged would, in my own estimation, constitute me guilty of a base cowardly and scandalous forfeiture of my own honor and consistency, of a breach of my convenanted faith to the Honourable Company and of a dereliction, almost traitorous, of my bounden duty to my country. Under such an impression it will not afford ground for surprise if I push the attempt to its accomplishment even though its prosecution involve my fortune, my liberty and my life.

Were he not so transparently sincere, the effect of his ironclad and rumbling sentences would sometimes be almost laughable.

By 8 October 1823, Trebeck was well enough to be carried in a litter,[59] so Moorcroft tore himself away from the open-handed hospitality of Rahim Allah of Rajaori, and the long caravan began once again its laborious traverse through the foothills along the edge of the great plain. With each day's march, the heat rolled up at them and the Punjabi people along the way became noticeably more unfriendly and avaricious. On 16 October they came to the banks of the broad Jhelum once more and, crossing by boat, found themselves compelled to halt beside the unhealthy little town of Jhelum for over a month. With that delay, whatever lingering prospects there might have been of getting safely across the jagged Hindu Kush before the onset of another winter disappeared.

There were two ostensible reasons for their enforced halt. The first was because the attentive, and apparently friendly, Surat Singh received orders to repair to Ranjit Singh in order to report and obtain the necessary passports for crossing and clearing the remainder of the Punjab. Moorcroft could not decide whether this was genuine or part of a continuing plot to detain him as long as possible. He was certainly getting the feeling 'that a mine would spring under my feet before our party could reach Peshaor'.[60] It was at this time, too, that the stout Izzat-Allah began to display those symptoms of loss of nerve which became more and more pronounced with each delay or near disaster during the next twelve months. Surat Singh was back with the necessary permissions on 2 November, but it still took another eight days to procure sufficient camel carriage to carry the baggage to the Indus. That was the other reason for the delay. Even after that, it needed two more days of noisy confusion before the loads were properly repacked and roped. To Moorcroft, some of the studied delays looked downright sinister and the camel drivers began to seem like a fifth column, planted in their midst by Ranjit Singh.[61]

Jhelum was hardly the ideal place in which to spend a month. Moorcroft reckoned that its Muslim inhabitants were even more diseased and unlovely than those of Kashmir, away behind the snow ridge to the north-east. At least this gave him plenty of opportunity to distribute his purges and treat some fearsome cases of leprosy, graphically described in his notebook. Plenty of time too, to write and dream, as he watched the broad Jhelum slide past the town. He imagined the day when steamships would convert the river into a great artery for goods between Bombay and Kashmir, *en route* to Central Asia. He also used the time to write new instructions to Palmer[62], increasing the annuity to his mother and appointing new executors, and he put together yet another epic despatch to the political department, the second in three weeks. It was inspired by belated news of the strained Anglo-Russian relations which followed the 1820 revolutions in Europe. This encouraged Moorcroft to rehearse all over again his fears, of unobserved Russian encroachments in the far north and of the unreliability of Ranjit Singh. To this he added all the information of the military routes and resources of Central Asia which he, and particularly Trebeck, had been able to obtain from local informants. It was, he admitted, partial and incomplete. But it was better than nothing in view of 'the increased probability of disaster befalling my party through the crooked policy of some Rulers and the distracted state of countries which must be traversed'.[63] He was rather unwise to keep harping on the dangers and difficulties like this for it gave the long-suffering authorities in Calcutta the final excuse they needed to recall him. On 9 January 1824 they finally did so, only reserving to him discretion to push on in the unlikely event of his having reached Kabul.[64]

Knowing nothing of all this, of course, but with pressing enough reasons of his own for hurrying on, Moorcroft led his party away from Jhelum on 13 November and into the gravelly defiles which mark the last of the Punjab plain as it approaches the Indus crossing at Attock. This is good ambush country. The watchful escorting troops were all armed to the teeth and Moorcroft was scouting out ahead, ostensibly in search of game, but really on the look-out for the attack which he felt in his bones was coming.

In fact it was all quiet enough for them to visit some of the sites which attract tourists along this route today. They examined the dramatic and lofty bulk of the sixteenth-century fortress at Rohtas. Later Moorcroft was perhaps the first to identify correctly the great stupa of Manikyala as a Buddhist monument.[65] They admired the ruined Mughal gardens at Wah and Hassan Abdal, lovely in their autumn colours, and all the time Moorcroft was doing what he could for the often hideously deformed wretches who beseeched his help along the way.

There was one unhappy and unnecessary incident on 21 November, one day after leaving the then scruffy and ancient town of Rawalpindi. Jemal, Moorcroft's faithful servant, had unwisely grabbed a snake beside the path. He ignored Moorcroft's sharp shout to let it go and the flickering, forked tongue struck at his fingers. Moorcroft was off his horse in a flash and crushed the snake beneath his boot. He lanced and bled the frightened man at once, but Jemal's arm soon swelled alarmingly and he began to vomit and pass blood. Despite everything that Moorcroft could do for him, he died three pain-wracked days later. Moorcroft was distressed by his inability to help his old servant, but the professional in him itched 'to open the body of Jumal' in order to discover more of the action of the snake venom on the body. Only the sensibilities of the other Muslims in the party persuaded him to leave well alone. Instead, he filled his journal with interesting speculations based on his earlier investigations about the possible use of snake serum in cases of lockjaw and hydrophobia. He promised himself that he would take up the whole subject 'as soon as I shall have leisure'. The notion is laughable. Men like Moorcroft, besieged by the multi-faceted riches of this world, never live long enough to have 'leisure'. By that word he simply meant time to go on being busy.

So they moved on in mid-November 1822, across the last of the broken plain, towards those bare, brown hills beyond the Indus which mark the cultural and geographical north-western bounds of Hindustan, and came at last to the river bank. The young Indus, which they had last seen in high Ladakh a year before, grows to manhood in the awesome canyons and gorges at the foot of Nanga Parbat, as it sweeps round the eastern and northern end of Kashmir. Now free at last of the iron grip of the mountains, it flowed serenely past before them, fully 100 yards (91.4 metres) wide. As Trebeck stood at the historic river crossing, under the soaring, castellated walls of the Attock fort on 26 November, and contemplated the river down which Alexander the Great had sailed his fleet, he was moved to one of his bouts of sweet melancholy. How changeless the river and how swift the decay of human empire! The down-to-earth Moorcroft was more concerned about the future of the British Empire. His journal is busy with dreams of the Indus as a great commercial highway, carrying British goods steam-borne from Bombay to numerous depots from which they would penetrate all over inner Asia. On the return journey, the steamers would transport fine Turkestani horses, ice and other commodities down to Bombay. He was not quite the first to argue the river's commercial potential, as Wilson believed[66], but he certainly came closest to foreshadowing the politico-commercial vision which launched Britain's forward policy along the Indus only six years later.

On 27 November, they inspected the Attock fort where Izzat-Allah had been incarcerated while on his 1812 reconnaissance journey. Next day, just downstream of the fort, the men and animals were loaded aboard the ponderous, high-stemmed boats and slowly ferried to the other side. Moorcroft vainly tried to take soundings in the deep water as they went. That evening they set up camp at the foot of some low hills about 500 yards (457 metres) from the river bank, and settled down for a few days to await replies to the letters which Moorcroft had sent on from Jhelum to the Afghan chiefs at Peshawar. The rumours of civil war and anarchy in Afghanistan, and of the limitless gold and jewels said to be stuffed into their camel bags, were alarming enough. Even when warm messages of welcome arrived from Yar Muhammad Khan, the eldest of the Afghan Sadozai brothers at Peshawar, Moorcroft's Muslim servant, who conveyed them, was convinced that a trap was being set for them there. Even before reaching Peshawar, they would have to run the gauntlet of the robber Khattaks, who traditionally preyed on the caravans which passed along that way.

Those few November days beside the Indus must have been an agreeable interval of peace before the unknowable but inevitable troubles to come. Moorcroft seems to have been drawn back, again and again, to the bank of the great river. There he speculated busily about how a hostile (Russian?) general might go about securing the river crossing and silencing the great but vulnerable fort on its hill beyond. He was convinced that mobile columns and river gunboats, not fixed fortifications, were the modern way to meet the threat. The proof that the river was not an insuperable barrier was right before his eyes as he stopped writing on one occasion to watch the leisured progress across its bright surface of a lad on an inflated buffalo skin, sliding slowly ½ mile (0.8 kilometres) downstream in the fifteen minutes it took him to reach the far bank.

On 6 December, with the goods all safely stowed on the backs of a new set of hired camels, they were ready to move on. It was time for Lalla Surat Singh and his ragamuffin Sikh escort to ride forward, one by one, to salute him and then turn back to the comparative security of the great plain across the river. In the Pathan hills beyond the Indus, every Sikh was (and still is) a marked man. Moorcroft watched them go with genuine regret. In the year they had travelled together, he came to like and trust Surat Singh more than any Sikh he had ever met. His presence seemed a sort of talisman against treachery from Ranjit and, indeed, from anyone else. Now they were very much on their own and the air was already heavy with rumours of violence at the hands of the robber Khattak tribesmen of Abbas Khan. As soon as Moorcroft learned that this chief had just come hastening back from a meeting with his hated overlord across the river, Ranjit Singh, he feared the worst. His mistrust of the wily Sikh ruler had grown to almost pathological proportions since their meeting two and a half years before. Now he felt sure that the destruction Ranjit had in store for him was to be accomplished by proxy, so that no blame could be pinned on the Sikh ruler by his powerful British allies and neighbours.[67]

They marched on for the rest of that long day in close order, the vulnerable camels protected by horsemen on the flanks with the guns primed and loaded. There was a spot of trouble from some tribesmen who rolled boulders down upon them in one place, but otherwise the day was without untoward incident. Then, towards evening, they came in sight of the little walled village of Akora on the bank of the Kabul River. In other circumstances the thought of its caravanserai would have been very welcome to dusty, weary men who had been on the road all day, but Akora was the home of Abbas Khan and the headquarters of his robber clan. Wisely, fearing to get entangled in its narrow streets or besieged in the serai, Moorcroft turned aside from the open gateway at the last minute and pitched his camp in the best defensible spot he could find, just to the west of the village and close to the river bank.

They were soon surrounded by the usual curious crowds and by a number of armed horsemen who wheeled their animals round and round in the dust and fired their matchlocks into the air. Moorcroft stood there amidst the confusion quietly assessing the quality of the animals and the horsemanship of their riders. He was not quite sure whether this display was intended to greet or intimidate them. Abbas Khan's representative came into camp soon afterwards. He merely hinted at exorbitant customs duties, but requested them not to move until the chief himself was able to pay them a visit. Moorcroft's courteous but firm refusal to do any such thing was doubtless the reason for all that followed. After a tense but quiet night, they were up as usual well before daybreak but the late arrival of the camels and camelmen delayed the early start they had intended. Moorcroft, Trebeck, Guthrie and Ghulam Hyder Khan have all left detailed accounts of what happened next on that heart-stopping morning[68] but Moorcroft's is the best. As soon as it was light:

> a crowd of armed footmen started up suddenly from behind tombs on the plain where they had passed the night. Both cavalry and infantry were assembling rapidly from every quarter of the country as well as pouring out of the town and by the time our camels were loaded, a messenger from the Naib reported by order of his master that if we dared to move a single pace from our ground before the Khan arrived we should at that instant be attacked. As it was obvious that whether the Khan was in town or not the delay was intended to favor the assemblage of a greater armed force and our situation was becoming more unfavorable every moment, so fast the strength of the adversary acquired accession. Without the slightest delay the messenger was desired to tell his master that we should march instantly and should fire upon any person who might venture to approach within a certain distance

indicated. . . . The river was behind us on one side, our tents were left standing, their ropes crossing to prevent the horsemen getting in upon this flank without cutting them; a deep ravine was on the other side and the armed force of our enemy was in our front, whilst about a thousand of the town people hid in an angle to be in readiness to assist in plundering our baggage as soon as we should be hors de combat, but at present were not nearer than five hundred yards [457.2 metres]. Our Dooranee acquaintances [the envoys from Peshawar] had come in to report that they had employed every argument in their power to bring the Khuttucks to terms but in vain. It was reported that our bales contained the most costly merchandise of Britain, that my medicine chests were filled with rubies and the small ones really containing spare ammunition were stuffed with gold mohurs. They regretted that we had not temporised so as to have admitted of their bringing the Dooranee force to our aid and took somewhat a hasty leave and, in retiring to a distance from the presumed field of action, deemed our destruction inevitable.

At this moment the enemy were in motion as if about to come on to the charge and spears and men's heads were seen just above the edge of the ravine whilst others were levelling their guns at us by resting them on the bank within sixty yards [54.8 metres] of our line. [Moorcroft was an easy target riding out a few yards ahead of his men.] Mr. Trebeck immediately drew off one half of our force with one cannon to a point on the edge of the ravine from which the flank of the whole line of the before half concealed infantry was brought directly in the line of fire of the gun and told them that if they did not instantly retire he would give orders to fire. . . . The tone of Mr. Trebeck's short but emphatic address, the steady countenance of our men and the lighted match of the gunner aimed at the foremost of the assailants who, perceiving the danger of their situation, pressed upon those behind them and the whole retired with so much precipitation as to become clubbed with the horsemen in a dense mass pressing upon the line of tombs in their rear and at the distance of about two hundred yards [182.8 metres] from our fronts. Their condition was tempting. This was the point of time in which our fire by sections along with that of our guns must have produced the utmost confusion but I thought it improper to become the actual assailant and waited for the Khuttuks to advance to the attack. Whilst the mixed horse and foot were wavering first to one flank and then to the other, confused and apparently irresolute, the Naib came forward alone but was soon followed by Runjeet Singh's man the newswriter. The former attempted to disclaim the array of attack saying the people were acting from themselves and without orders on which it was observed that, if so, they were acting as banditti and he had only to avow this fact and disclaim their proceedings when he should see us act also in the manner best suited to the occasion. That as to himself he might do as he thought proper but we should directly commence our march and he alone was answerable for [the] consequences. . . . Runjeet Singh's man entreated that we would not fire and the Naib proposed that we should march 2 kos there to wait the arrival of the Khan and with this compliance we promised on the condition of the Naib accompanying our party alone as a hostage for his troops not infringing the engagement and that they should not hang upon our rear. On these terms we began our march with our armed force and our spare servants dragging the cannon in the rear of the caravan but we had gone scarcely two miles [3.2 kilometres] before many horsemen were perceived filing off by low roads between the line of our course and the river apparently with the design of getting into our front whilst the heights in our rear were crowded by an increased assemblage of armed men. The Naib, reminded of the terms of the engagement which were stated to have been broken by his party, desired to ride back for the purpose of reproving his men which was agreed to. He lost no time but disappeared in one of the numerous ravines by which the road was intersected and we saw no more of him.

The crisis was over.

With immense relief, they marched on for the rest of the morning without seeing so much as a glimpse of an armed Khattak. Those Pathan warriors are not easily beaten and Moorcroft had every reason to be delighted with the steadiness of his little untried force. It alone, he was convinced, had saved them from the destruction masterminded by Ranjit Singh and planned for them ever since they had left Ladakh. In reality, it was probably nothing of the kind. The Khattaks, who are not rich, had been plundering caravans and levying tolls on this section of the Grand Trunk Road for several centuries. Moorcroft, after all, had refused either to pay or to stop. Moreover, Abbas Khan may have had a reason for detaining Moorcroft even more pressing – literally so – than extortion. The comic sequel to this whole affair came shortly afterwards at Peshawar when the fearsome Abbas Khan stood before his erstwhile victim with his baggy trousers down. He had come to be fitted with one of Moorcroft's leather trusses to relieve his painful hernia.[69]

At lunchtime they reached Nowshera, scene of a recent important battle between Sikhs and Afghans[70], and the *de facto* outer limit of Ranjit Singh's kingdom. By evening on that 7 December 1823, they were encamped for the first time on Afghan territory at the little village of Pir Pai. Even after all the excitements of that long, long day and the disturbed night which had preceded it, Moorcroft was soon at work operating on some of the villagers besieging his tent. One can only marvel at him.

21 AFGHANISTAN,

DECEMBER 1823–AUGUST 1824

THE FIRST MARCH in Afghan territory on 8 December across the widening plain of Peshawar, was happily uneventful.[1] Beyond and above the bare hills which ring the plain, they would glimpse, high in the sky, the first snows of winter on the great peaks of the Hindu Kush, spanning the remote horizon in front of them. There could be no crossing of that ancient rampart until the coming of spring.

Next morning a cloud of dust ahead of them indicated the approach of a considerable cavalcade. A double line of cavalry with colours and kettledrums was drawn up and through it Moorcroft advanced to meet Sirdar Pir Muhammad Khan, youngest of the Barakzai brothers ruling Peshawar, resplendent in silver brocade and a green turban. Ghulam Hyder Khan was watching. 'They both dismounted, embraced, and after mutual ceremonies of inquiries after their health, in Persian, they mounted and proceeded together to Peishawur,' he wrote,[2] preceded by a column of infantry, resplendent in orange, green and silver. As they approached the walls of the city, the crowds thickened by the minute. Once inside the narrow streets, the press was such that they had to stop for several minutes at a time, while the outriders struggled to clear a way through the confusion. Moorcroft was the first Feringi to visit Peshawar since the resplendent official mission of Mountstuart Elphinstone fifteen years before. Moreover, according to popular belief, he was so old (more than 150) that his beard no longer grew. Not only did he possess the secret of long life but also that of turning base metals into gold. No wonder every rooftop and window was crammed with people anxious to catch a glimpse of him.

The spacious, two-storey house set aside for their accommodation, once the baggage was all safely stowed inside the walled courtyard below, must have seemed a welcome haven after the noise and confusion outside. Pir Muhammad Khan accompanied Moorcroft to the threshold of the house and soon trays of sweetmeats and, later, a sumptuous dinner were sent over to them, served by well-dressed servants. 'Our first reception among the Dooranees was as favourable as we could have wished,' wrote Trebeck thankfully and he spoke for them all.[3] Indeed it was the very warmth and apparent genuineness of their reception by Pir Muhammad Khan and his older brothers, that chiefly persuaded Moorcroft to halt his party in Peshawar for the winter. As the brothers were quick to point out, with the Hindu Kush routes already closed to caravans for the winter, there was little point in pressing on to Kabul. Besides, events there were brewing up for another power struggle, this time between Dost Muhammad Khan, younger half brother of the Peshawar sirdars, and his nephew Habibullah Khan. Moorcroft probably did not need much persuading. Despite the recent ravages of the hated Sikhs, Peshawar was a congenial place to linger in, its narrow streets and bazaars thronged with colourful objects and lean, weatherbeaten men from every corner of Asia. Sultan Muhammad Khan, the eldest of the brothers, seems to have been particularly attentive. Moorcroft spent many congenial hours with him in the women's quarters, at his house on the western edge of the city. We know from the accounts left by later British visitors just how generous the hospitality of these urbane and cultivated princes could be, and how absorbing the conversations which, after dinner, often went on far into the night. Moorcroft must have been as welcome a conversationalist and as full of stories and experiences as any of the enterprising sahibs who followed him to Peshawar in the next decade. Yet it is a strange fact that his presence at Peshawar in the winter of 1823–4, not to speak of the detailed information he recorded on Afghan history and politics, seems to have been completely unknown to its principal, recent Western historian.[4] This is because his journal for much of the period has not survived and Wilson's account passes over these five months in almost as many pages.

At Peshawar Moorcroft was not, as he had been in Ladakh and Kashmir, the first European visitor in recent times. The sumptuous volume produced by Elphinstone's 1809 mission rendered unnecessary much of the detailed reporting which Moorcroft would otherwise have undertaken, although he was still very active. His medical practice kept him busy and he wrote in detail about recent events since Elphinstone's visit. He investigated aspects of the local industry, such as leather tanning and fruit production,[5] and he paid a lot of attention to the local horseflesh. The absence of disease and the cool winter climate made Peshawar, he thought, the best area he had yet seen in the Indian subcontinent for productive horse-breeding. His first long despatch to the political department after his arrival was chiefly concerned with the navigation, commerce and defence of the Indus.[6] Later, towards the end of his stay, he reported on what he thought were Russian-inspired attempts to spy on him and, once again, he urged Calcutta to take much more active steps to defeat Russian intrigues in Afghanistan and encourage, by influence and support, a pro-British ruler on the throne of Kabul. Apparently the Peshawar chiefs made an explicit request to be taken under British protection but, after his experiences in Ladakh, Moorcroft wisely did no more than report in general terms that there seemed to be 'a strong desire of a large mass of the population to be placed directly under the protection of British Government'.[7] However he did hint, without naming names, that Britain should back Shah Shuja, the enemy of the Peshawar brothers, in the struggle for power at Kabul. It was a subject he returned to more openly later when he reached Kabul.[8] Notwithstanding all this highly-charged political matter in his despatches to Calcutta, he was careful to add a personal disclaimer of any role in Afghan affairs beyond that of observer.

So far as Calcutta was concerned, of course, the only proper role for their stud superintendent concerned horses. It will have been obvious that in all the reams of information which Moorcroft gathered and reported during his long absence from the stud, the subject had scarcely been mentioned. That is one reason why his recall was even then on its way up-country in the early months of 1824. However, just before it reached him in March 1824, he was given a belated opportunity to put horses back on his agenda. The Peshawar chiefs, themselves no mean judges of good horseflesh, had praised the endurance of the Waziri horses above all others. The trouble was that the Waziris were the most feared of all the Pathan tribesmen of the trans-Indus hills and their wild valleys were a virtual *terra incognita*. The presence of an infidel among them would normally lead to speedy plunder or death. No wonder that the Peshawar chiefs were all horrified when Moorcroft calmly proposed to visit Waziristan, practically alone, in search of horses for the stud. A respected and venerable Pathan *pirzada* (holy man) called Qamar ud Din, had come to Moorcroft with that most uncomfortable combination – a bad cough, a bad hernia and a bad truss. From Moorcroft he received not only relative comfort, but some medicine and two flannel shirts as well. In return he offered to be Moorcroft's guide and protector in Waziristan. He was as good as his word. Such is the rigid Pathan code of hospitality to an honoured guest, that Moorcroft and his party were generously welcomed and fiercely protected by those tall, hawk-eyed warriors wherever they went.

On 19 March 1824, Moorcroft, Guthrie and a handful of servants, together with a supply of medicines and presents, rode out from Peshawar with Qamar ud Din and turned south across the plain, in the direction of what is today the metalled road to Kohat. The remarkable journey through the heart of tribal Waziristan which followed filled Moorcroft's extended journal with a mass of detailed information. He was clearly fascinated by the curious social, political and economic organization of the tribes and his notes provide undoubtedly the earliest detailed European eye-witness account of them on record, but, since Wilson barely mentioned his visit, the information is virtually unknown to scholars. The standard history of the Pathans[9] does not even name Moorcroft.

They went first across Khattak country to Kohat, sitting like a child's sandcastle on the ridge above its green plain. Moorcroft was not feeling at all well in these early stages of the journey and was unable to sleep because of severe stomach and bowel pains. He was in this state when, on 22 March, he was overtaken by Trebeck. The young man had, in Moorcroft's absence, effectively been offered Peshawar and its plain on easy terms by some of the chiefs and was clearly of a mind to accept this extraordinary offer.[10] It is obvious from one of his letters to his brother during his great journey with Moorcroft, that he was often intrigued by the various investment opportunities which it seemed to open up.[11] Moorcroft's advice to his naïve young friend was emphatic. He had already declined a similar, although rather less attractive, offer for himself and he begged Trebeck to think very hard before he risked his life and fortune in such a vortex of ambition and treachery as Afghan politics. It was obviously sound advice but whether Trebeck took it or not, when he rode back across the hills to Peshawar early next morning, is not clear. At all events, the scheme in the end came to nothing, although the outcome seems to have strained the already uneasy relationship between the Peshawar chiefs themselves.

Moorcroft was in too much pain to see much of Kohat. After Trebeck left, he seems to have spent the greater part of the day lying in the shade of a tree. He did not catch up the rest of the party, heading south-westwards through the welter of gaunt sandstone hills along the track that is now the Kohat–Bannu road, until late in the afternoon. They all halted for the night at the fortified village of Teri which, then as now, was the headquarters of the western Khattaks. Their friendly welcome could hardly have been a greater contrast to that which they had received from the Khattaks of Akora. Even so the chief, who was a cousin of Abbas Khan of Akora, apologized for being less attentive than he would have liked. He had, after all only been married five days and was being distracted by his 2500 wedding guests! He seemed quite surprised that Moorcroft was only in his fifties and not three or four times that age, as popular rumour had it. Leaving Teri, the little party continued along the lonely track, south-westwards across the empty, folded hills towards Bannu. On 27 March Moorcroft at last got his first glimpse of the black tents of the Waziris and that evening, in camp near Bannu, as he watched the servants at their simple supper, he was suddenly transported across half a century to a day when he was a child on his grandfather's estate near Ormskirk.

Just exactly where Moorcroft went in those bare brown Waziri hills during the next few days, as he zigzagged from the hospitality of one isolated walled village or black-tented camp to another, it is now impossible to say. He certainly crossed the Kurram River and penetrated deep into the Tochi valley, well to the west of Bannu. One thing is sure: the hawk-eyed mullahs and the heavily armed warriors, who squatted round their visitor from another world and struggled to understand his broken Persian (he had no Pashto), would never have met anything remotely like him before. The sanctity of the revered Qamar ud Din was in demand to heal the sick but Moorcroft was amused to notice that the difficult medical cases were always passed over to him. Many of these were the result of savage sword wounds inflicted in the implacable blood feuds which, then as now, stain Pathan society from generation to generation. One of the local doctors apparently made most of his living treating cases of this kind and Moorcroft taught him the latest approved method of wound stitching. He also, of course, preached the gospel of agricultural improvement whenever he got the chance. The merits of oat and potato, grape and prango cultivation, of new strains of sheep, and even of modern veterinary medicine were all paraded before those long-haired warriors. Noticing that a number of the sheep were afflicted with the gid, exactly as the heifer in that Lancashire field back in September 1791, he begged a sheep's head and, using his curved needles, demonstrated how parasites caused the condition. He also explained the medical treatment for other common sheep afflictions like foot rot.

It is perhaps not surprising that the memory of all this was still vivid in Waziristan nearly a quarter of a century later. One of the leading Waziri chiefs, a shaggy giant of a man called Malik Sawan Khan, was Moorcroft's companion and host for several of these days in early April 1824. Years later he recalled his visitor with affection and admiration.

> He was very wise, and wrote down everything; the trees, the crops, the stones, the men and women, their clothes and household furniture, and everything! He also gave medicine to their sheep and horses and cured them all![12]

Who else could it have been but William Moorcroft! In December 1848 two of his testimonials to the hospitality and civility of his Waziri hosts were brought down to Herbert Edwardes and the yellowing scraps of paper, carefully preserved for nearly twenty-five years, proudly unfolded and displayed before him. Edwardes was moved and carefully noted Moorcroft's words. The documents reminded him, he said, 'of those sealed bottles, which have sometimes been found in tombs, and when opened, give up the perfume of a forgotten age'.[13]

For Moorcroft the journey was certainly not unalloyed joy. The incapacitating pain which marred his journey out from Peshawar has already been mentioned. He had scarcely recovered from that when, on 30 March, he had a heavy fall with a borrowed horse in the pebbly bed of the Kurram River. The stock of his favourite gun was split by the impact and so too would Moorcroft's head have been, had he not been wearing a quilted cap. He was speechless for a few seconds, had severe chest pains and bled profusely where the horse stood on his leg while struggling to rise. That night he treated himself with a complicated poultice and a hot stone on his chest. At first he seems to have suffered no further ill effects, but in the cold wind and rain on the journey back to Peshawar, he suffered what he called agonizing rheumatic pains in his bruised side and shoulder. He probably had a few cracked bones after all.

There was not even a string of fine Waziri horses to console him. Moorcroft only saw seven horses on the whole journey and bought two of these.[14] As usual, the quality animals were always somewhere else, in this case in the high summer pastures further west. Undismayed, Moorcroft made provisional arrangements with the Waziri tribesmen, by which the East India Company would send an agent under safe conduct to Waziristan each year. He would have been a brave man! His task would be to buy 250 animals annually and provide large Turki stallions for crossing with Waziri mares, so as to give the offspring bone enough for cavalry use.[15] It is amusing to speculate how the board would have reacted to such a scheme, had it ever heard of it.

Moorcroft returned to Peshawar in the first half of April. He had been given by Qamar ud Din promises of safe conduct to Kabul, along a circuitous northerly route through tribal Mohmand and Yusufzai country. Although it would have avoided the dangerous Khyber pass altogether, the Peshawar chiefs and Izzat-Allah were horrified. Indeed the mir felt its unwisdom so strongly that he raised his voice disrespectfully to Moorcroft at a time when the Englishman was so prostrated with fever that he was too weak even to dress. Izzat-Allah later apologized and the affair was forgotten. Not long afterwards, with typical open-heartedness, Moorcroft was writing to Calcutta advocating his Persian secretary's suitability as British agent at Lahore, once the Bokhara journey was over.[16] The excellent Izzat-Allah was obviously beginning to wonder if it ever would be.

So were the authorities at Calcutta. Their letter of recall was waiting for Moorcroft when he returned to Peshawar. 'Little prospect remains, either of your accomplishing the original and authorised ends of your journey or of your even penetrating into the desired quarter,' he read. Your public spirit and the information you have obtained is greatly valued but you can no longer be spared from your important duties at the stud. Therefore 'close your commercial concerns, and make preparations for returning to the British Provinces as soon as practicable after the receipt of this despatch'. Only in the unlikely event of your having already reached 'as far as Caubul or the vicinity of that place' before these instructions reach you, do you have discretion to continue to Bokhara.[17]

For most men that would be that. Indeed, for most men, an honourable opportunity to escape from five years of wearying travel, ill-health and danger would have been extremely welcome. Moorcroft is of interest precisely because he was not like most men. That he intended to push on, goes without saying. In that case, the letter seemed to give him the bleak choice either of resignation, insubordination or dishonesty. He saw another way. He merely assumed, or pretended to assume, that by reaching Peshawar he had met the government's condition and so could continue. A glance at the map is sufficient to show that only by the most strained interpretation can Peshawar be said to be 'in the vicinity of Kabul'. It is 200 miles (320 kilometres) from it! Yet, if challenged, Moorcroft knew that he could always fall back on the (admittedly rather thin) argument that, even if he were nowhere near the *city* of Kabul, he had at least reached the so-called *kingdom* of Kabul. The officials at Calcutta should have known better. If they were to stop a man like Moorcroft their orders needed to have been categorical, unambiguous and without loopholes of any kind. As it was, his reply[18] simply claimed the latitude he had been offered to proceed serenely on his way to Bokhara, offering neither explanation or justification. It was masterly.

Moorcroft then went on, as he was required to do, to spell out his plans for the remainder of the journey. So far as horses for the stud were concerned, the prospects of obtaining them at Bokhara and returning in safety with them were, he claimed, 'abundantly gratifying'. A renowned Peshawari holy man and Koranic lawyer called Mir Fazl Haq was on his way to Bokhara at the emir's request. Thanks to Khoja Shah Nias who put them in touch, Moorcroft would pay Fazl Haq's travel expenses in return for his powerful influence with the emir and the other chiefs along the way north of the Hindu Kush.[19] South of it, in Afghanistan proper, the friendly influence of the Peshawar chiefs could be relied upon, even if civil war did flare up again at Kabul. After Bokhara, Moorcroft planned to go north-east to Kokand and here he relied upon the khan's former physician, a man called Mirza Jowad who had been travelling with them (also at Moorcroft's expense) ever since they left Ladakh. From Kokand, Moorcroft hoped to return to India with the main party and the horses via Yarkand and Ladakh. Trebeck, travelling light and further west, would explore the Pamirs' approaches to northern India. With normal good fortune, they should all be safely back in India by early 1826 at the latest.

This optimistic programme, as Moorcroft admitted, was designed to enable him to complete his commercial investigations into the prospects for British trade in inner Asia, his geographical enquiries into trade and invasion routes there and his political detective work into the progress of Russian intrigue and trade. If successful it would have done even more than that, although Moorcroft seems to have been unaware of the fact. It would have vindicated all his unfashionable enthusiasm and anticipated European investigation and government intervention in these areas by up to half a century. It would, in other words, have been a personal triumph so striking, that William Moorcroft would not be the forgotten and unappreciated man he is today.

His letter to Calcutta concluded with a simple assertion: 'I feel little apprehension of the ultimate result disappointing the expectations in which I have so long and pertinaciously indulged.' With that the government had to rest content. By the time they received his letter and despatched a reply explaining that he had blatantly misunderstood their instructions, he would, if his forecasts were correct, be well on his way back to India anyway.

His optimism was quite genuine and Trebeck shared it.[20] Moorcroft was not the kind of man who would deliberately carry himself and his party to destruction in obsessive pursuit of an unattainable dream. He and they had already achieved what men had said was impossible. He believed that they could continue to do so, given reasonably good fortune. The dangers were obvious, and Moorcroft at this time sent another batch of papers to his friends in India for safekeeping, but things were certainly looking more promising at the beginning of May 1824, when letters from Habibullah Khan arrived, assuring them of his friendly welcome and protection at Kabul. The fratricidal fighting there had, apparently, ceased.[21] Best of all, Sultan Muhammad and Pir Muhammad decided to take their troops to join their brother Yar Muhammad, who was already at Kabul. This offered not only welcome protection to the caravan in the dangerous Khyber defile, but also some promise of security once it had reached the Afghan capital. Moorcroft abandoned his risky alternative route without regret.

Early on 28 May word was received from Sultan Muhammad that they should be ready to leave at dawn next day. There followed the usual frenzy of chaotic preparation, as the great caravan girded itself for the road once again after six months of immobility. One casualty was Trebeck's last surviving mercury barometer tube. The chaos on departure day was nearly as bad. The camels did not arrive until late in the day and then a fierce sandstorm so delayed the loading that they were not really on the move until sunset. They blundered along in the darkness across the plain, expecting attack or theft at any moment. When they reached Sultan Muhammad's camp, they supped off a cup of water and dozed where they could till daylight. Moorcroft was uneasy. He had no more confidence in his Afghan friend's 1200 wild-looking and badly armed troops than he had in the tribesmen who lived in, and on, the Khyber pass.

They rode into the jaws of that bloodstained, historic corridor on the first day of June 1824. The furnace heat was beating back off its bare, rocky walls and the Afridis up on the crags could be seen gazing hungrily at those swaying bundles and chests, said to be stuffed with solid gold. It was a tense and trying time. Moorcroft became utterly confused as to which day it was and his writing deteriorated dramatically. It is not surprising, for the tribesmen singled him out for particular attention in their endless clamour for baksheesh. The heat was appalling. Moorcroft slept only fitfully at night because of the constant threat of attack and, in consequence, often found himself dangerously asleep in the saddle by day.

Considering all this, the amount of detailed information he managed to record for the government, particularly on the defensibility of the pass against foreign incursion from the west, is quite remarkable. He believed (wrongly) that he was the first Englishman to travel through the pass. He was certainly the first to provide detailed eye-witness information about it.[22] In the end, there were only two casualties in the long pass, although both caused Moorcroft much sorrow. One was his favourite spaniel bitch, Missy. She was a loving friend who had hardly ever left his side since the great journey began.[23] The other was a fine pointer called Sheena, probably the one he had been given recently by a Pathan chief as a fee in return for a surgical truss. Both dogs died of heat-stroke in the furnace wind and Sheena's puppies, in a basket on one of the camels, only just survived. It must have been with immense relief all round that they came at last to the western end of the pass where the hills fall back. That evening they were able to refresh their tired and dusty bodies in the sparkling, blue-green waters of the Kabul River.

The ensuing journey across the tawny bare hills to Jalalabad was uneventful, although thieves were still a hazard after dark. At scruffy, run-down Jalalabad, they rested a day on the river bank. Moorcroft, remembering his nocturnal riverside experience in Ladakh, wisely kept his tents back some distance from the water. Sure enough, fierce thunderstorms and torrential rain brought the river over its banks and set the Afghan camp in disarray. Moorcroft's ailing tent somehow survived the storms and to it flocked a number of the local chiefs and mullahs to seek medical assistance or bewail their poverty and the lawlessness of their misgoverned country. Why, they asked, did the British not come and rule it properly? Moorcroft was flattered but kept his counsel. Yet the question intrigued him. Why not? A month later he drafted from Kabul an astonishing letter to the government,[24] in which he contemplated what then was utterly unthinkable – an active British interference in the affairs of Afghanistan.

Does the objection lie in the distance? . . . It may not impertinently be asked if Kabool be more distant from the British frontier than from that of Russia. . . . It is presumed that external policy is not bound by other laws than the maxims of state necessity guided by honest and manly feeling.

Both maxims led Moorcroft irresistibly to the same conclusion, just as they had in the case of Ladakh. British security, British trade and the well-being of the people themselves all called for British involvement.

It would be easy to dismiss this last argument as cant, the respectable fig-leaf to cover the nakedness of the other two. But no one who understands Moorcroft can take such a simple view. An intensely humane man, he was also a patriot, proud of the record of his countrymen in Asia and convinced that the blessings of enlightened British rule were immeasurably superior to anything else available. The two impulses together inevitably made him an advocate of what were later called 'forward' policies. He can hardly be blamed for not seeing what his successors had to learn so painfully – that self-government can be more precious even than good government, especially to men who have lost it. Nearly everything that was said to him in Afghanistan seemed to suggest quite the contrary.

It is not at all certain that this July letter of Moorcroft ever reached Calcutta. Perhaps that is just as well, for it would assuredly have convinced the members of the governor-general's council that their wandering stud superintendent had finally taken leave of his senses. Read in the late 1830s its words would have seemed remarkably wise; in the 1840s, foolish; and in the 1870s, again wise. Such is timing in the affairs of men. But foolish or wise, it was strangely prophetic. Not only did Moorcroft advocate 'forward' policies (he actually used the word) in Afghanistan, as in the 1830s and later, but, more specifically, he proposed the use of the exiled Sadozai ruler, Shah Shuja. That ploy was attempted in 1833–4 and more whole-heartedly in 1838–9. Even more uncanny, Moorcroft used almost the very words – 'a single British regiment would suffice to establish Shuja-ul-Mulk as sovereign' at Kabul – which, when written by the man who followed Moorcroft to Bokhara and got all the credit for it, finally persuaded a reluctant governor-general to launch the ill-fated invasion of Afghanistan in 1838.[25]

It was just as well that the outwardly urbane and ever-attentive Sultan Muhammad Khan and his brothers were not mind-readers, for Shah-Shuja and his family were their most bitter rivals and enemies. Needless to say, Moorcroft would have kept these dangerous thoughts very much to himself, when he came to talk with the Peshawar brothers in the cool of the evening after the day's march was done. He must have become a familiar sight on his evening stroll round the Afghan camp. The fine horses of the chiefs were of particular interest to him and some of them reminded him vividly of animals he had known in days gone by, in the stables of his titled friends in England. He remembered horses as most of us remember people. Like every other British traveller in the barren upland desert that is most of middle Asia in summer, he also remembered those cool green islands and northern seas which were his home. He knew that he would never see them again, but it is noticeable that the further he penetrated into those unknown heartlands, the more he peppered his letters and journals with references to the familiar and ordered world of his earlier days. Battersea gardens, Bagshot Heath, Hampstead and Highgate, the Temple gardens, Appuldurcombe on the Isle of Wight, the Surrey hills, Furness and the Cheviots, the intimate topography of south-west Lancashire – to a British reader these familiar names and reassuring syllables on the faded, endless pages seem like little lights amid the darkness of cruelty, intrigue and danger with which he was surrounded.

Moorcroft himself had no illusions about the faithlessness of the men he was dealing with and the fragile balance of dynastic politics in Afghanistan, on which the lives of his party depended. All is 'projects, counter-projects and modifications and schemes', he wrote bitterly during an enforced week's delay in scorching heat just outside Jalalabad in mid-June, while the Peshawar chiefs held a great council of war with emissaries from the two contending parties at Kabul. Moorcroft consoled himself with the renowned fruit of the area grown in ancient walled orchards and with earnest conversations with the local greybeards. He also rode out to visit some of the historic sites and commented, in considerable detail, on some of the ancient coins he found and collected there. In a few years those same coins were to yield a rich harvest of evidence about the successive dynasties, invasions and civilizations of northern India and Afghanistan in the then unknown years between the death of Alexander the Great and the Muslim invasions of the twelfth century. It is curious that Wilson, who played an important, and not entirely honourable, role in that process,[26] should not so much as mention Moorcroft's notes. They are practically the earliest which exist.

Eventually it was decided by the Barakzai princes that Pir Muhammad and Yar Muhammad (who had joined them from Kabul) would return to Peshawar, leaving Sultan Muhammad to go on to Kabul alone, in the hope of mediating the simmering fratricidal quarrel there. That at least was a satisfactory outcome for Moorcroft. On 14 June the reduced party set out westwards once more, climbing higher in the cooler air on to the Kabul plateau.

The places along that 70-mile (112-kilometre) track through grim and rocky defiles – Bhutkak, Jagdalak, Tezin, Khurd Kabul and Gandamak – were just names to Moorcroft in midsummer 1824. It was as well that his prophetic insight did not extend to the deep midwinter of 1841–2 and the nightmare outcome of the British forward policies he advocated. Then the snow at these places became a shroud for thousands, as a shattered British army at Kabul tried in vain to reach the comparative safety of Jalalabad. Moorcroft's journey in the other direction was relatively uneventful. On the night of 16 June, just before moonrise, the high winds brought his tent down in a shower of sparks along the frame of his iron bedstead. Trebeck's turn for excitement came the following night. Despite the bright moon and the armed guard, a stealthy brown hand under the wall of his tent deprived him of his helmet, cloak, pistol and, most serious of all, one of the bearing compasses on which his route survey so depended.[27] The two supposed sentries, one of whom was missing and the other asleep, were solemnly court-martialled by Moorcroft as soon as they reached Kabul.

That ancient city, dominated by its great fort-palace of Bala Hissar and wedged in by hills, was clearly visible across the plain next morning. An armed escort, sweltering in green and scarlet velvet, came riding out to meet them and led their caravan under the Lahore gate and into the narrow swarming streets and covered bazaars of the town. They were taken to the peace of a walled garden and house of Sultan Muhammad Khan and, in due course, trays of dinner, desserts and the matchless fruit of Kabul arrived. It was 18 June 1824.

Moorcroft had good reason to be satisfied. It was another milestone, another justification of his own indomitable faith in the feasibility of his mission. He had, as he announced to Calcutta, arrived 'in perfect safety'.[28] He had brought his great caravan unscathed across some of the most unruly and rugged terrain in Asia and pushed his political, commercial and topographical enquiries to the very heart of Afghanistan. From Peshawar, which was the limit of Elphinstone's official journey in 1808–9, Moorcroft believed they were on new ground for Englishmen. It is almost true and, certainly in terms of detailed information gathered, wholly true. The solo journey of George Forster, who preceded Moorcroft to Kashmir and Kabul in 1783–4 (although not beyond), remarkable as it was, simply does not compare in this respect. Not that anyone would know this from Wilson's version. He treats Moorcroft's two-month sojourn at Kabul in a single, misleading paragraph.[29] It gives no inkling, either of the dense and often fascinating detail in Moorcroft's letters and journals, or of the tension in the city in that crucial year when Dost Muhammad, later the great father of modern Afghanistan, ousted his nephew, Habibullah, and first came to supreme power at Kabul.

Moorcroft met Habibullah, a handsome man of about 25, soon after he reached Kabul. The occasion was one of those civilized and colourful set-piece ceremonials which the Afghan chiefs so delighted in. Habibullah was surrounded by his senior officials. He rose as Moorcroft approached, ushered him to a chair on his right and, as soon as the velvet twilight of the summer evening had come, entertained him with illuminations, music, fireworks, dancing-girls and a sumptuous dinner of many courses. Whether Habibullah's generosity also extended to 'one damsel of easy virtue', apparently provided to a resourceful rogue who arrived in Kabul about this time, penniless and nearly naked but claiming to be Moorcroft's brother, is understandably not recorded, but it was an auspicious start.

On another occasion some time later Moorcroft and Trebeck were invited to join Sultan Muhammad and Habibullah in the garden under the plane trees beside the tomb of Emperor Baber. From that terraced hillside one can gaze, as the great emperor himself loved to do, across the plain westwards towards the great snow ridge of the central Hindu Kush and the cherry orchards, tawny, fortified houses and waving corn of the favoured valley of Paghman at its feet. On that occasion Habibullah, who was playing chess with Sultan Muhammad, seemed irresolute and childish. It was perhaps the first warning that things were not likely to remain so outwardly favourable for very long. Moorcroft and his party were about to learn the same lesson as the British and Russian armies which followed them fifteen and 125 years later. Hard as it is to reach Kabul, it is often even harder to leave it again.

The Peshawar brothers had not exaggerated the difficulties Moorcroft had to face at Kabul. It was soon clear that his good relations with the popular Sultan Muhammad were, at the same time, something of a liability. That prince's own relations with his unpopular and jealous nephew rapidly deteriorated and his proffered mediation in Habibullah's dispute with Dost Muhammad, advancing rapidly on the city from the north-west, was angrily rejected. As another military showdown for control of Kabul loomed, the fabulous wealth rumoured to be hidden in that array of sealed packages in Sultan Muhammad's compound, became an increasing temptation to the hard-pressed Habibullah in his own fight for survival. Equally, of course, it was a source of danger to him in the hands of his rivals. He was already beginning to suspect that Sultan Muhammad and Dost Muhammad were in collusion, and that Moorcroft's wealth was underwriting the costs of Sultan Muhammad's force. In the end, that was not so far from the truth.

What is certainly true, is that Moorcroft's presence in Kabul played its own part in the growing and dangerous hostility between Habibullah and Sultan Muhammad. An early sign of trouble was Habibullah's repeated failure to invite Moorcroft and Trebeck to his house, as he had promised. That this was not an oversight was confirmed when he twice ostentatiously ignored them when he encountered them riding in the crowded streets of the city. Moorcroft's attempt to mollify him, by a present of a gun conveyed through Sultan Muhammad Khan, was received with contempt. Scenting trouble, Moorcroft began to prepare in secret for an early departure. It was probably news of this, conveyed to Habibullah by one of his spies, which led to the next development.

On 17 July, one of Habibullah's men arrived at the compound with a peremptory demand for the payment of customs dues. Sultan Muhammad, for whatever reason, was furious. He went at once to remind his nephew, in very harsh language indeed, that Moorcroft and his party were his personal guests and had come to Kabul with written assurances of favourable treatment from Habibullah himself. As soon as Sultan Muhammad was out of the city a few hours later, a second demand for customs was received, this time carried by one of Habibullah's brothers-in-law. There was a heated exchange between him and Moorcroft and, later, Izzat-Allah was subjected to some hostile questioning from the irate ruler himself. Hearing of all this, Sultan Muhammad came galloping back to the city in a great rage and the customs demand was again dropped, at least for the moment. Probably only Habibullah's more immediate preoccupations saved them. Increasingly the city was seething with disaffection and was apparently only waiting for an opportunity to rise up in open insurrection against him.[30]

Even this tense situation did not prevent Moorcroft from pursuing his usual busy enquiries, apparently as tirelessly as ever. On the day he arrived at Kabul, he was fascinated to hear that a caravan from Bokhara had just come in. That same evening he was inspecting the only two horses it had brought for sale. They were disappointing. So were the 500 or so he examined in Habibullah's stables. Moorcroft reckoned that only about half a dozen of them would be suitable for use as stud stallions. As usual, he was always able to rationalize, without difficulty or hypocrisy, the absence of the horses which alone, so far as Calcutta was concerned, justified his journey. In this case, apart from the hazards of the road, it must be Habibullah's unsavoury reputation for extorting from the horse-dealers and merchants every quality horse to arrive from Bokhara that was to blame. Even so, the quality and quantity of horseflesh at Kabul was higher than anything Moorcroft had seen on his journey so far, and he made a close study of the unusual feeding systems used.[31] The rural economy of Kabul and its environs was also a source of unfailing interest to him. The result was a very long report which he began to write in August for the Board of Agriculture in London, on Afghan techniques of ice storage, of crop, fruit and vegetable husbandry, and of animal health.[32] He was not to know that the board had been defunct for two years, even as he struggled to put his ideas into words. He also assembled a camel-load of labelled seeds and samples for transmission down to Calcutta, courtesy of Ranjit Singh.

The anarchic state of Afghan politics did nothing to improve Moorcroft's low estimation of his old adversary, the Sikh ruler. Indeed it was partly because he was so convinced that the British native newswriter in Kabul was being paid by Ranjit Singh to supply deliberately garbled information to Calcutta, that he compiled such a massive political despatch himself.[33] It is, even for him, an exceptionally long and circumlocutory document. He had never found writing easy but his problem in this respect seems to have increased. It must, however, be remembered that he had now been away from native English speakers, other than Trebeck, for over five years and the effect was beginning to show.

> I have been so long accustomed to such a mixture of tongues as to have contracted insensibly the vicious habit of pressing into my service such words as first present themselves to my mind . . . without being sufficiently curious as to their origin so that I much doubt whether my sentiments preserve the idiom of my native speech.[34]

For all its great size and verbosity, Moorcroft's political despatch from Kabul is a document of great interest. Moorcroft's bible, ever since his arrival in Afghanistan, was the splendid illustrated account of that country which Elphinstone wrote after his mission to Peshawar in 1808. One of Moorcroft's aims was to provide a corrected up-dating of the events of recent Afghan history since then. His account represents not only considerable research and industry, but also contains some information which appears to be unrecorded anywhere else. He then turned to the present and the future state of Afghanistan's external relations. Some of what he wrote has already been summarized and quoted. It is a curious mixture. On the one hand there is the accurate prophecy and discerning prognosis, particularly on the subject of

Afghanistan's quite crucial role as a barrier to protect British India from Russian menace. On the other is Moorcroft's breath-taking ability to pile far-fetched speculation upon hypothesis and call it unimpeachable fact. For such a good-natured, optimistic man, he had a remarkable capacity to see almost limitless malevolence, low cunning and treachery in others. His views of Agha Mehdi, the Kashmiri merchants at Leh and Yarkand, and Ranjit Singh are all examples. In this July letter the Russians in general are the bogey men. They are active and hostile in Lahore, in Kabul, everywhere. Yet even in this alarmist nonsense, Moorcroft was anticipating the future. He was a fully-fledged, classic Russophobe before almost any of his countrymen had even discerned the possibility of a Russian threat to British interests in Asia, let alone thought about how to respond to it.

The most pressing dangers facing Moorcroft in July 1824 were those on his very doorstep. The mounting tensions in Kabul suggested the wisdom of leaving the city as quickly as possible, before Habibullah changed his mind about customs duties again or attempted to levy them by force. But where should they go? Both of the main caravan routes to the north and north-west were said to be sealed. The rumour in the bazaar was that Habibullah intended to pounce on their ponderous and slow-moving caravan as soon as it left the confines of the city and Sultan Muhammad's protection. It was all too likely. Even if they somehow evaded that fate, there was good authority for believing that Dost Muhammad Khan (then at Bamian) intended to plunder them when they came within his reach. Moorcroft rather despairingly sent him a placatory gift of a fine double-barrelled shotgun. In due course he received the delphic reply that the Dost would henceforth consider Moorcroft and his party as his nephews. That, noted Moorcroft with grim humour, was 'no complimentary proof of relationship conveying friendship ... when the circumstances of D. M. Khan cannonading his nephew in his own city have been duly weighed'. Supposing that all these dangers from the Afghans were somehow overcome there remained the alarmingly disturbed state of the lands north of the Hindu Kush. Sultan Muhammad Khan, and his amiable brother, Nawab Jubbar Khan, were graphic in their warnings of the anarchy in that region since the death of the late ruler of Balkh. Bokhara was weak, the slavers from Khiva were roaming ever further in their raids from the west and the Hazaras, emboldened by their recent successful raids on the caravans, were waiting 'on the tiptoe of expectation' for the fabulous treasures which Moorcroft's party was believed to be carrying.[35]

Moorcroft's dilemma was that he could never be sure that these dire warnings were all they seemed. Suppose Sultan Muhammad had designs of his own on Moorcroft's baggage, perhaps to assist him in his bid for power at Kabul? Even if he were the true friend he seemed, his friendship was beginning to look as though it might be nearly as costly as his enmity. On 26 July, he tapped Moorcroft for a loan of 12,000 rupees and, not long afterwards, for another of 8000. Moorcroft dared not refuse. His desperate attempts to raise money, not an easy matter in a city on the brink of civil war and with his own resources running down 'far beyond the bounds of common prudence', are evident in his papers.[36] Still, costly as Sultan Muhammad's friendship might be, at least his presence in Kabul offered some sort of guarantee against total disaster. Ominously enough, Habibullah was putting the strongest pressure on his uncle to leave Kabul and return to Peshawar. Worse, Habibullah was insisting that Moorcroft remain in Kabul after Sultan Muhammad's departure 'as a proof of friendship'. That would have been folly. For many of Moorcroft's now demoralized party it would also be folly not to retire with Sultan Muhammad to the relative safety of Peshawar. Moorcroft conceded that the case for retreat was a very strong one, although for him it was as out of the question as ever.

> The mere thought of retreating without completing my commissions . . . smote my mind with a force that, almost inducing temporary confusion whenever entertained for a few moments, if often repeated would have gone near to have overset my reason under their appalling influence. I might indeed be acquitted by the world but I should ever stand convicted at the bar of my own conscience of a scandalous, base and dastardly desertion of the interests of my country through considerations merely personal.[37]

Behind the long-windedness, something of the personal cost of these tense weeks comes over clearly enough. He was struggling to steer a course through what Trebeck called 'this disgusting scene of uproar and heartless nay villainous intrigue and deception'[38] and, like all leaders in a tight corner, trying at the same time to remain outwardly calm and cheerful. Privately he confessed in his journal that the prospects were 'most dark and dangerous'. Trebeck felt the same, although he was also firm in his determination not to retreat, but for the servants it was a different matter. Some of them simply deserted and even the stout Ghulam Muhammad Khan was ready to do so.[39] Izzat-Allah remained loyal but indicated what he felt by sending his son back to India, so as to ensure the continuity of his line, as he put it. Then, as if morale among the sepoys were not already low enough, the deserter and troublemaker James Lyons, whom they had last seen in Kashmir, turned up once again. At Peshawar, Moorcroft had replaced him with another alcoholic deserter, an artilleryman called Thomas Griffiths. He proved a valuable addition to their little army and his behaviour for a time was impeccable, but when Lyons arrived in Kabul, seeking revenge for his own dismissal, Griffiths was soon persuaded to desert, along with four other members of the Gurkha escort. Lyons also helped to spread yet more rumours of the gold and jewels in their baggage.

These worrying developments could hardly have come at a worse moment for Moorcroft and his beleaguered caravan, as they gloomily prepared for a showdown. They were not alone. In the last week of July, Kabul was seething. The streets were full of armed men, the shutters were going up on the shops in the bazaar and the peaceful and more prosperous citizens were moving their women and children out. On 25 July, Moorcroft took Sultan Muhammad's advice and moved to a more easily defended house, eluding what seemed like an attempt by Habibullah's men to seize the baggage in transit. On the 26th the cannons of the great Bala Hissar boomed out at intervals all day under the joint direction of Griffiths and Lyons, who had both joined Habibullah's service. Three days later a breathless messenger arrived at the gate with the news they had been expecting and preparing for all week: Habibullah's troops were on their way to attack them. Luckily they were not. They were moving out to do battle with Dost Muhammad's men. Moorcroft was a valuable eye-witness and chronicler of the confused fighting which followed, but he was more than that. He turned his house into a field hospital and did what he could for the injured. Most of the sometimes fearful sword wounds were in the back, he noted. And 'poor' Griffiths was among the dead. Despite the advantage of numbers and superior equipment, Habibullah's men were defeated in the field and withdrew behind the massive walls of the citadel. For the moment it was stalemate.

It was also, clearly, the moment for Moorcroft to get his party out of Kabul as swiftly as possible, before one side or the other became free to turn its attention to him. Trebeck and some of the other stalwarts agreed, although Sultan Muhammad thought they were mad. However, loyal to the last, he provided an escort of fifteen of his own men and used his influence to obtain more from Dost Muhammad. He also assisted with the carriage arrangements and wrote letters of introduction to some of the chiefs along the road.[40] In retrospect it is plain that Moorcroft was extraordinarily lucky and his 20,000-rupee 'loan' to Sultan Muhammad looks cheap at the price. It is true that he disliked his new *kafilabashi* (caravan supervisor), a weasel of a man, who slept in Trebeck's tent and repaid the kindness by stealing his carpet. It is equally true that they were grossly overcharged for carriage, but at least the caravan was still intact as the final preparations were made to move out of the city on 16 August. There was hassle and haggling and tension right to the very end. Some of the servants flatly refused to go on and it was late in the day, far too late for comfort, before the baggage began to move out across the plain towards the foot of the great range which spanned the north-western horizon. Moorcroft and Trebeck followed the next day.

Almost their last act in the city before the final farewells, was to record a sincere testimony to the one Afghan chief whose friendship and hospitality, whatever his private hopes, had not faltered in all the eight months they had known him.[41] Without Sultan Muhammad Khan, it is hard to see how their two months in troubled Kabul could have ended other than in disaster. Moorcroft's presents to him were suitably generous. Years afterwards, the crystal chandeliers he gave were on show when visitors from India enjoyed Sultan Muhammad's hospitality at Peshawar.[42] The tough little horse he gave Moorcroft in return, later carried his new owner on his life or death flight for 120 miles (192 kilometres) across the desert without respite, and undoubtedly saved his life.[43] All in all the honours were pretty even and the two men parted with genuine regret.

On the evening of 17 August Moorcroft looked back across the plain towards the city and could plainly see the hillside gardens round Baber's tomb where he had first begun to have his doubts about Habibullah. From the great, brooding citadel came the sporadic boom of that chief's cannon, as if to remind them of their good fortune in escaping the confines of the city. Not that there was much sense of danger averted. They were still too close to the city for that. Besides, that first night in camp was bitterly cold – a first taste of the winter breath of the high Hindu Kush. This was apparently the last straw for two more of the Gurkhas, who absconded with their precious swords under cover of darkness. The excellent corporal followed next morning. One can hardly blame them. For more than five years those loyal little fighting men had been separated from their homes and families and the end of this never-ending journey must have seemed to them as far away as when they set out for Tibet, all those long years before. All the same, for Moorcroft it was a serious blow. It took another two days of anxiety in that exposed spot to recruit Afghan replacements and to resolve other distracting problems. Not until 19 August did their journey really begin.

That first evening Moorcroft was hospitably entertained in the fort of one of Dost Muhammad's friends, but the events of the night that followed were a reminder both of the need for vigilance and the ever-present danger of accident. Moorcroft had a burning thirst and slept badly. Hearing a noise in the darkness close by, he called out and shortly afterwards the sentry challenged a shadowy figure in the darkness. Trebeck, whose watch it was, came riding up to investigate and the jittery sentry fired straight at him, hitting his horse in the jaw. Trebeck, to Moorcroft's immense relief, was unharmed but by early morning Moorcroft himself was 'in great distress', shivering and vomiting. He continued like that for most of the day. Nevertheless he extracted the ball and pieces of shattered bone from the jaw of Trebeck's horse as best he could before they moved on once again, westwards and northwards into the foothills of the mighty Hindu Kush.

As the ancient, curving caravan trail climbs higher, the fruit trees and orchards gradually give way to willows and poplars and, eventually, to the utter emptiness and awesome sterility of the high, empty passes across the great watershed between the Oxus and Indus. Moorcroft's track, and most of the intimate landmarks along it which he noted as he passed by, are still virtually as he described them one and a half centuries ago. Up there in August it is still fiercely hot by day and bitterly cold by night and still, as then, the Ghilzai nomads are on the move bringing their black tents and livestock down to milder pastures before the onset of another bitter winter. Some aspects of it, the height and the emptiness in particular, reminded Moorcroft of Ladakh, although it was infinitely more dangerous.

There were no further alarms and on 25 August 1824 they came safely to the peaceful, green-gold valley of Bamian. Their camp-site beside the sparkling river, thanks to the bearings and distances recorded in Moorcroft's journals, can be precisely located. Behind it, to the south, is the turreted and melancholy ruined citadel of Golgola; in front, the now famous curtain of cliff, honeycombed with black caves and dominated by its two huge, faceless sentinel figures, for ever staring out across the fertile valley. Once upon a time, long before European sailing ships rolled up the empty southern oceans, this quiet valley was one of the great and busy crossroads of the world. Now only some of the monuments remain. Moorcroft had chosen to come this way particularly because of what he had heard of them.

In those next two days, which were all he dare allow himself in this last outpost of Afghanistan, he was not disappointed. He rode his horse along the bottom of that soaring cliff, doubtless shading his eyes against the glare as he craned up at the two huge and mysterious figures, and then climbed busily through the echoing warren of chill, dark caves beside and above them, making precise notes and peering carefully at the fading, delicate stucco paintings and the weird, architectural carving of the soft stone. He longed for more time. 'Were not my attention directed to the improvement of a distant country,' he wrote,[44] 'after leaving the service of the Hon. Company I would again visit Bamian to explore its curiosities.' He never did of course, but he did enough in those two days to establish an unassailable, and still largely unacknowledged, claim to priority. He was the first of a stream of European visitors in modern times to visit and describe Bamian. More than that, he was the first to confirm by on-the-spot observation what local tradition had long forgotten and scholars were only beginning to guess at: the great figures and paintings, and the culture from which they came, were Buddhist. Moorcroft's extensive notes on Bamian[45] deserve publication, although one would never guess it from the desultory scraps in Wilson's summary or the use scholars have failed to make of them.[46] It was another eleven years before the bitter loner, James Lewis alias Charles Masson, came to Bamian and published what is generally regarded as the first European eye-witness account of the antiquities there, even though he denied that they were Buddhist.[47] High on the back wall of one of the caves in what is known as Group XII, he pencilled neatly:

> If any fool this high samootch [cave] explore
> Know Charles Masson has been here before.

He at least knew that before Charles Masson had come Moorcroft, Trebeck and Guthrie. Their three names in charcoal are also there as is, in another place, Moorcroft's solitary signature.[48] It was normally his stern rule never to deface ancient monuments in this way.[49] One is somehow glad that on this occasion he did.

Congenial as his contemplation of the remote past high on that great cliff must have been, the reality of the present and the immediate future was, as ever, waiting for Moorcroft when he returned to the dazzling sunshine of the valley floor below. There were extra horses to be hired so that the whole party could be mounted and a guide to be recruited who could pilot them along the next stage of the journey. Once again heads were shaken, this time at the risks from the slaving Hazara raiders who infested the narrow, rocky defiles to the north of Bamian. Moorcroft was determined to push on, but he was much relieved when he heard that the Tajik chief of the Syghan valley to the north would meet them with an escort at the frontier pass. As they left Bamian on 28

August, they were shadowed by a sinister group of slavers on horseback waiting to fall upon any stragglers, so Moorcroft rode along at the rear and doubtless kept a wary eye over his shoulder. Later they passed the rough graves of a party attacked and murdered the previous year. The Afghan *kafilabashi* was a pest to the very last but their final parting from Sultan Muhammad's escort on the crest of the Ak-robat pass was dignified. Each man rode forward in turn to salute Moorcroft and wish him well. Then they all turned and cantered away in a dwindling cloud of dust back the way they had come.

It was another milestone and Moorcroft confessed his relief to be safely clear of Afghanistan. Now they were in Turkestan – at last Bokhara seemed within reach. 'If we arrive safely beyond the Afghan frontier we shall have overcome the difficulties most to be apprehended,' Trebeck had written a few weeks earlier.[50] He could hardly have been more wrong.

22 MURAD BEG OF KUNDUZ,

AUGUST 1824–JANUARY 1825

MOORCROFT WAS PLEASED with his first impressions of his new host, Muhammad Ali Beg, Tajik chief of the fertile Syghan valley.[1] That first evening in Turkestan, with Guthrie and Trebeck in charge, Moorcroft's little force was put through its exercises at speed. The chief was impressed. If these men and his own worked together, they could soon make the roads safe again for caravans. That at least is what he told Moorcroft. He was more frank with Trebeck. Together with the help of some bandits he was in touch with, they would all be able to surprise and sack Tashkurghan, the thriving bazaar town across the hills to the north and now under Uzbek control!

It was a timely, if uncomfortable, reminder that the anarchy and violence north of the Hindu Kush was no whit less dangerous than in Afghanistan to the south. In some ways it was worse. For while no self-respecting Afghan would stoop to man-stealing, in the lands ahead of them they themselves, as well as the swollen caravan, were commodities of value, to be bought and sold like any other. Moorcroft soon realised that he had seriously underestimated the extent of the change which had taken place since the death of the powerful and respected Mir Qalich Ali of Balkh.[2] In the ensuing fratricidal feuds between the various Tajik, Uzbek and Turkmen chiefs of the neighbourhood, one man had proved conspicuously successful. When the name of Murad Beg, chief of Kunduz, had first entered Moorcroft's journal, he had added the dismissive words, 'with him no difficulty was expected'.[3] It was an understandable judgement amidst the encompassing dangers at Kabul but here, on the northern edge of the Hindu Kush, things looked rather different. By a combination of shrewd timing and undeniable skill as a leader of fast-moving, irregular cavalry, Murad Beg had gradually extended his power westwards across the plain and into the northern foothills, so that it now lay in a great swathe of territory right across the major caravan routes from the south to Bokhara.

Moorcroft and his caravan entered it on the last day of August 1824, when they descended from the desolate plateau to the north of Syghan into the steep-walled valley of Kamurd. This is the last of the three parallel, east-west river-valleys which lie to the north of Bamian, like green gashes in the brown side of those empty hills. It is also the most beautiful. The local chief was friendly and the myriad orchard fruits, the sunflowers and the flourishing cotton were all welcome signs that they were approaching warmer latitudes and that the worst of the Hindu Kush was safely behind them. Moorcroft as usual was scribbling busily. In Syghan, it had been the evil-smelling asafoetida which intrigued him, as a possible means of protecting vegetables in England from slug attack. In Kamurd, it was the methods by which productive fruit trees could be grown on apparently unproductive soil. 'Were I a going man,' he wrote, 'I would endeavour to purchase many dells in England and plant them with fruit trees.' It all seemed peaceful and safe enough.

As they pushed on without incident northwards down the Tashkurghan river-valley, through sterile gorges and along open, watered valleys, lovely with grain and laden orchards, Moorcroft's journal becomes almost light-hearted. The good-humoured but curious local people, who pushed into his tent to gaze at their first Feringi, were friendly and begged him to excuse their curiosity. To judge by his journal, the curiosity was mutual. He was recording the shape of their skulls, the prettiness of some of the women and children and much else besides. Even Murad Beg's representative, sent to conduct them into Aibek, was amiable and affected to be airily unconcerned when it was whispered to him that the Feringis were noting down everything. When they came on 5 September to Aibek[4], standing sentinel over its lovely open valley, its chief – the youngest son of the former ruler of Balkh and now tributary to Murad Beg – was kindness itself. He was amusing and witty too, reminding both Moorcroft and Izzat-Allah of their mutual friend, Charles Metcalfe. He conducted Moorcroft personally to some of the remarkable Buddhist antiquities nearby and so careful is Moorcroft's description of the astonishing hill-site known as Rustam's Throne, that one can follow him today every step of the way. Could it be, he wondered excitedly, that he had found one of the famed altars of Alexander the Great?[5]

On 6 September, Mir Fazl Haq and Mir Wazir Ahmad (a friend of Izzat-Allah's who had joined them at Kabul) returned from their courtesy visit to Kunduz. They had carried there Moorcroft's presents and letter of introduction and found Murad Beg troubled by the usual inflated account he had received of Moorcroft's wealth, his great armaments and his apparently assiduous spying activities. The two Muslims did their best to demonstrate the absurdity of these stories and believed they had been successful. At all events, they won from Murad Beg a letter of welcome and assurances of good treatment. Wazir Ahmad felt sure that there would be no problems over agreeing transit duties and, soon afterwards, he and Fazl Haq set off for Bokhara to prepare the way for Moorcroft and his caravan there. It was a serious misjudgement in the case of Wazir Ahmad; perhaps something more sinister in the case of Fazl Haq.[6] From all that happened later, it seems likely that Murad Beg was deliberately enticing Moorcroft's party into his power.

The ferocious nature of the man became more obvious when they moved off again northwards up the Aibek valley on 8 September. They soon saw several empty, ruined, mud villages whose inhabitants had been carried off to Kunduz and slavery. The remaining villages, however, seemed prosperous enough and Moorcroft was very interested to notice the large numbers of cheap, healthy and good-sized horses everywhere. 'Had we possessed such a body as this at the commencement of the Stud the task of the Superintendent would have been a very different matter,' he noted. So it would, but then the long chain of consequential events, which brought him to that remote valley where no European had ever been before, would also have been very different.

Moorcroft would have been in no mood for abstract speculations of that kind. Both he and Trebeck were feverish and suffering from headaches as they rode northwards, although this did not prevent them from leaving the main party in order to examine the weird hill caves at Hazar Sum. Their lack of torches prevented a proper investigation. Besides, 'the tracks of wild animals, leading to the deep and more remote recesses . . . somewhat checked a spirit of enterprise in the dusk which might have been damped also by striking the head against fragments of rock half hanging from the ceiling'. A bigger danger, although they did not realize it till afterwards, came from the robbers who haunted the caves. Moorcroft and Trebeck, innocent of the danger, both fell into a deep sleep just where they lay in the dust. Later they became separated and Moorcroft fell asleep twice more. When he eventually emerged, after being woken by weird and unaccountable noises in the darkness that sent his hand to his sword and his heart to his mouth, Trebeck and the others were searching anxiously for him. Moorcroft knew he had been careless – one of the stragglers from his party was seized by four hovering horsemen that very day – but the sleep had refreshed him and the headache was gone.

The Aibek valley ends, on the north, in a chaos of rocky hills and is finally brought up short by what appears to be a blank wall of rock. At the last possible moment, a narrow gap opens into a dramatic, shadowy gorge and thence the road at last emerges into the open at the walled town of Tash-kurghan. They arrived on 9 September and made their camp on the ridge of rock which lay about ½ mile (0.8 kilometres) to the south of the city gate. It was another milestone. The great mountain rampart was now behind them. Ahead, stretching away just beyond the town to the Oxus River, and beyond it to Bokhara itself, was the endless, desert plain of Turkestan.

Moorcroft had good reason to be pleased with his safe arrival at the thriving little town of Tashkurghan. He liked its colourful bazaars piled high with fruit, the sparkling streams and the shady, walled orchards. He was not so pleased with its high blind walls and its equally anonymous shrouded women. The Hindu merchants of the town gave these visitors from distant Hind a friendly welcome and the curious Uzbeks, crowding among the tents to stare, were also not in any way hostile. Even the customs official sent to count the baggage was courtesy itself. There seemed no hint of menace anywhere.

None, that is, until the Tashkurghan chief, known as Baba Beg, 'a short, squat thickset man of about 35, clothed in an outer coat of flame patterned silk with an under dress of black satin', came striding into their camp. He alas, unlike his amiable brother at Aibek, was not in the least like Charles Metcalfe. His salutation to Moorcroft was cold and perfunctory and he made a gratuitously insulting remark to one of the servants about working for an unbeliever, which brought an unwisely sharp retort from Moorcroft. At least Baba Beg's manners were otherwise good, Moorcroft noted wryly: he spat inside the lining of his coat rather than on the carpet! Once he was convinced, by an examination of Moorcroft's seal, that this was indeed the man who had corresponded with his father years before, he became a little more civil, although never friendly. Then came the bombshell. His orders, he said, were to forward Moorcroft to Murad Beg at Kunduz, and he made it clear that Moorcroft was expected to go 'largely furnished with presents'. The outlook, Moorcroft conceded, was 'gloomy'. Kunduz was 80 dreary miles (128 kilometres) away across the desert and its undrained swamps made it a byword for fever and disease until well into the twentieth century. Murad Beg's own evil reputation as a robber and slaver was just as unhealthy. In the hardly encouraging words of the proverb,

> Whosoe'er may wish to die
> Straight to Qunduz let him hie.

The only encouragement that Moorcroft could see was that Murad Beg's chief minister, a Hindu called Atma Ram,[7] was reputed to be a just man with considerable influence over his master. Taking with him an uneasy and reluctant Izzat-Allah, together with generous presents of cloth and guns, Moorcroft set out with a small escort across the nearly waterless desert on 16 September 1824.

On that featureless plain, the only things that moved were the occasional scattered groups of cows or goats, the swirling dust devils that frequently enveloped them, and fast-moving bands of mounted slave raiders from the Oxus striking at small parties like their own. That their nerves were all on edge is clear from an incident which Moorcroft recorded:

At a considerable distance I descried a line of figures that looked like horses of various colours interspersed with men on foot. . . . All at once the great body was enveloped in a cloud of dust. . . . It was thought that a body of horsemen had suddenly mounted their steeds and gone for the purpose of lying in ambush. . . . It appeared to me that our best plan would be to attack them from the bank or cliff of the defile in which they had taken up their position. I went to reconnoitre their position and my men followed with orders to obey the signal I should make. . . . From a gently rising ground I again got a view of our presumed foe whom I now clearly distinguished and found to be nothing more formidable than a large body of cows.

Their relief would have been shortlived for, that evening, ominous orders came in from Kunduz that part of the escort was to return to Tashkurghan and bring the whole caravan to Kunduz. Moorcroft promptly sent a message back with one of his own men, ordering Trebeck to stay exactly where he was for as long as he could. He was not optimistic. It was beginning to look as though Murad Beg had deliberately encouraged them into his clutches 'for the purpose of subjecting us to extortion and according to the report of his servants of reserving us for ends more grievous than death itself at least to Englishmen'. Even if slavery did lie in store for them, Moorcroft was privately resolved to speak like an Englishman to Murad Beg. In the meantime, he amused himself by writing up from his cards a report about the antiquities at Bamian. Izzat-Allah, it seems, was too gloomy to be very good company.

On 18 September the depleted party forded the Kunduz River and reached the unprepossessing dilapidated town of mud hovels, sitting on its peninsula in the midst of reed and swamp. At the eastern end, surrounded by a once impressive high mud wall, was the fort and inside that, the newly-built moated citadel which served Murad Beg as his winter quarters. There, on the afternoon after they arrived, Moorcroft and Izzat-Allah uneasily prepared for their first audience with Murad Beg.[8] It was in its way an impressive gathering. The chiefs in their huge, floppy turbans and loose coats of chintz or silk were kneeling in total and unnerving silence along the left-hand wall. The court officials, some with white staffs, were standing just as silently, eyes down, on a low raised platform. In the midst of them, clothed in blue silk and with his booted legs arrogantly stretched out before him, was the burly chief himself. Moorcroft and the mir as instructed kept their eyes lowered until a short prayer had been said. Then all stroked their wispy beards, Moorcroft passed his hand self-consciously across his shaven chin and the audience proper began.

First impressions of Murad Beg were not encouraging. The skin of his flat face was stretched tight across his high cheekbones, the teeth in his narrow jaw were crooked and his myopic narrow eyes disappeared completely when he smiled. He seemed satisfied with the presents laid before him and with Moorcroft's answers to his rapid questions. Then the conversation turned to the unhealthiness of Kunduz. For that Moorcroft recommended the drainage of the fens. He was right. Since the drainage schemes of the 1920s, Kunduz has become one of the most fertile and healthy places in all Afghanistan. Altogether, concluded Moorcroft, that first meeting could have been much worse.

In the evening Murad Beg sent over a sheep for their dinner but it was clear, from the long and hostile questioning which Izzat-Allah faced from him next evening, that he was far from satisfied. He still seemed half inclined to believe, not only the hostile rumours about Moorcroft's spying activities, but those regarding the size of the treasure concealed in the chests and baggage of his caravan as well. In the end, however, he reluctantly agreed with the mir's suggestion that Baba Beg's officials could check the accuracy of Moorcroft's inventories by opening any packages they selected at Tashkurghan. Customs duties on the whole caravan would then be levied in the usual way on the strength of the lists provided. Moorcroft and Izzat-Allah left Kunduz on 23 September and rejoined Trebeck and the others at Tashkurghan, after an exhausting ride across the desert next day. The relief of all of them was great.

In fact their ordeal had scarcely begun. Days of delay, argument and negotiation succeeded one another in futile and dreary succession, as

September gave way to October. It was plain that they were virtual prisoners until they paid an extortionate sum for their release. Moorcroft began to write in a way which suggested that even he saw no outcome but death or disaster. When figures were at last mentioned, the astronomical sum of 20,000 rupees was demanded. That sum, by prolonged haggling, was eventually reduced to roughly a fifth of that figure, plus a further 1500 rupees as a sweetener to Atma Ram and the other officials. Bad as it was, Moorcroft settled thankfully.

Yet, on one pretext or another, they were not allowed to leave. Once again, morale among the little party slumped and in nobody more than Izzat-Allah. He had been showing uncharacteristic signs of loss of nerve whenever things went wrong for the last twelve months. The unhealthy reputation of Kunduz had terrified him, all the more when two strangers in the serai, whom Moorcroft tried to relieve with medicine, died of yellow fever. Then, soon after they returned to Tashkurghan, Izzat-Allah's servant succumbed to the same complaint and the mir himself began to exhibit similar symptoms. He could take no more. He begged in tears to be relieved of his post, so that he could return to India and his family while there was still time. It was a bad time to be without him, but his demoralization seemed so total that he would probably have been more of a hindrance than a help in the future. Moorcroft wrote him a typically generous testimonial, paid him his travel expenses[9] and watched him set out with a few of the others for Kabul on 19 October. In the same little party was Izzat-Allah's friend Askar Ali, but he had an important task to perform. Since it was beginning to look as though they might need a return route from Bokhara to India which would avoid both Kabul and Kunduz, Askar Ali was despatched to reconnoitre the old caravan trail across the Dora pass into Chitral, in the mountains further east.

A day or two later the main party was at last cleared for the last leg of the journey to Bokhara. The camels were hired, the baggage roped for loading and all was ready for a departure inside five hours. This time next year, Trebeck jubilantly told his friend Leeson, you will see us all back in India.[10] Then came a second bombshell. Murad Beg required Moorcroft and ten of his soldiers to return to Kunduz, ostensibly to treat two wounded men and put on a military display. The real reason for separating the caravan from its leader and defenders seemed disconcertingly clear and Baba Beg's uncharacteristic levity when relaying these orders, hardened suspicion into near certainty. Short of fighting their way clear of Tashkurghan, Moorcroft could see no alternative but to face the dreary desert ride to Kunduz once again. This time Guthrie and Ghulam Hyder Khan went with him and they left on 24 October.

It was an uneventful trip, apart from a frightening sandstorm which engulfed them in the night and compelled Moorcroft to stand for two exhausting hours holding and calming his frightened horse and waiting for the dawn. When they reached Kunduz after two days and a night, no arrangements for their accommodation had been made. Even when they did find a horizontal surface on which to rest, Moorcroft could not sleep because of the 'unceasing' activities of the fleas in the carpet.

It is hardly surprising, therefore, that he had the greatest difficulty in restraining his tongue when Murad Beg, outwardly amicable, informed him that he had arranged for the whole party to come to Kunduz so that their goods would be safe, while he made enquiries, at Bokhara and elsewhere, into the truth of Moorcroft's claim to be a genuine merchant and horse-dealer. Sure enough Trebeck and the rest of the party came in on 30 October.[11] Next day Izzat-Allah, feverish and depressed, and his intercepted party were also brought in under escort. Whatever Murad Beg had in store for them he did not, it seemed, want any news of it to get back to Afghanistan or British India. They were virtually prisoners, utterly dependent on the whim of the chief. What dependence, asked Trebeck bitterly, 'can be placed upon a wretch who murdered his uncle and brother, prostituted to a robber his sister and daughter and sells into slavery women he has kept for a very considerable time in his seraglio'?[12] There seemed no way out. Their fighting strength might be adequate to overawe caravan robbers, but Moorcroft knew that he could not ask his escort to take on the forces of a warrior chief in his own capital. There was, as he put it, 'no remedy but patience'. They could only hope that the result of Murad Beg's enquiries, and of Moorcroft's own appeals for support to Fazl Haq and Wazir Ahmed at Bokhara and to his other well-wishers elsewhere, would in the end clear them of all suspicion.

Even that might not be enough. Sometimes it was hard to avoid the feeling that, whatever the outcome of these initiatives, Murad Beg would in the end resort to plunder. The way great multitudes of the townspeople came to stare at them in unnerving silence seemed to confirm the worst. At best, they might escape with their freedom and their lives, but the purchase price would probably be so high as to destroy Moorcroft's chances of buying horses at Bokhara. There is the clearest evidence in his papers that the alarming drain on his resources was already causing him serious concern. The previous eighteen months alone had cost him roughly three times his salary in that period. As if all this were not bad enough, his beloved dogs were dying of distemper or rabies.

Moorcroft decided to hurry things along, by trying the effect on Murad Beg of his file of welcoming letters going back more than ten years. Since these were mainly from the late chief of Balkh and the then rulers at Kabul, all of whom had been Murad Beg's enemies, this was not the best tactic to use, but Moorcroft must have felt that anything was worth trying. So, carrying his pile of papers and accompanied by the slippery Atma Ram, he returned once more to that same crowded and silent audience chamber.

Murad Beg seemed to Moorcroft to be drunk. At first he listened in silence as the letters were read but suddenly he burst into a voluble stream of abuse, waving his arms about and becoming almost incoherent. Moorcroft, icily angry but not intimidated, just managed to check his temper. He calmly corrected Murad Beg on a point of fact concerning the age of the letters. He then added very tellingly that, if their age were the objection, he could produce a much more recent letter, one written by Murad Beg himself. 'This reproach on his treachery was conveyed in a tone of some warmth and produced a most irritating effect upon the Chief,' recalled Moorcroft. Murad Beg exploded into a further stream of unintelligible invective and then sprang to his feet and stormed out 'in a paroxysm of rage'. Doubtless pale and trembling a little, Moorcroft gathered up the offending letters before the eyes of the silent, hostile court and returned to his quarters to await the worst.

The violence which erupted soon afterwards came not from Murad Beg at all but from an earthquake. With a great 'racking and crash', it split the long, flat roof of Moorcroft's house completely in two. Murad Beg did nothing. Indeed shortly afterwards he left Kunduz with his feudal cavalry to meet a threat from one of the chiefs to the west and to celebrate the marriage of one of his sons. Moorcroft and Trebeck used the interval as best they could. Trebeck, as discreetly as possible, accumulated valuable information on the caravan routes across the great mountains, which they could see high in the sky away to the east.[13] It was an accurate updating of the hearsay information gathered by Elphinstone at Peshawar fifteen years earlier but, like so many of the fruits of this long journey, it lay neglected and unknown in the East India Company's library and the information had to be rediscovered all over again later on.

Moorcroft took up his medical practice again although without much pleasure. Indeed he grew increasingly appalled and indignant at almost every aspect of Uzbek society: the cruel game of *buzkashi* – he provided the first European eye-witness account of this still popular but now much refined sport – by which young men on horseback were trained to snatch up children and property without leaving the saddle; the slave labour and slave trading; the religious fanaticism of the debauched priesthood; the harsh treatment of new-born babies; the utter contempt for, and cruelty to, women and daughters. Once he gave a scruffy little girl a coral bracelet and slid it on her arm himself. 'The child gave me a look that was worth more than a dozen armlets and ran off to shew the acquisition to her mother.' Only the hardy Uzbek horses, and the methods of feeding and schooling them, seem to have aroused any kind of enthusiasm in Moorcroft. If only, he mused, he had come to Turkestan in 1814, or even in 1816, during the benevolent and peaceful rule of Mir Qalich Ali Khan of Balkh. Then there would have been no trouble from Murad Beg and he could have purchased droves of brood mares suitable for the stud at keen prices. That thought often tantalized him during this trying waiting period at Kunduz, but there was some consolation too. 'It may afford some satisfaction to my friends to know that my views seem as far as horses are concerned to have been not unfounded.'

Moorcroft was badly in need of consolation at this time. His frustration was all the keener because Bokhara, of which he had dreamed so long, was now not much more than a mere 300 miles (480 milometres) away to the north-east. A heartening letter which arrived from one Dr Abel, physician to the new governor-general down in Calcutta, could hardly have come at a better time. Abel told Moorcroft what he had longed to hear for five years – that his voluminous reports and writings were at last properly appreciated. They were, wrote Abel, 'to my mind, so pregnant with matter of the highest value to the public that I am anxious . . . to persuade you to permit of their publication'.

They would be received 'by the learned with gratitude and would be highly prized'. Moorcroft's reply[14] is a long one which, amidst much interesting information about his recent observations, expressed the wish that Horace Wilson should undertake the task, with the prior permission of the government, of editing for publication anything considered of interest. On 7 December 1824 Moorcroft brought his letter to an end with the words, 'from the house of Konad Khan who was poisoned by his wife, who was cut to pieces by her mother-in-law'. It was a neat way of underlining both his low view of Uzbek society and the dangers of what he called his 'present predicament'.

In fact the long deadlock was broken just one week later. The merchants at Kabul, organized by one of Moorcroft's servants left behind as a newswriter there,[15] sent a supporting testimonial, but the decisive intervention was that of Wazir Ahmad. He came hastening back from Bokhara as soon as he heard of their difficulties. Not only did he bring with him the apparently powerful backing of Mir Fazl Haq, but he appealed to Murad Beg directly with all the authority of the one who had negotiated the safe conduct to Kunduz in the first place. The Kunduz chief was at last honest. He admitted that he was still considering murdering the lot of them. When reproached for the shame this would bring to his character he replied, 'The only character I desire is a character for riches obtained in any way I can. Do I not sit here to plunder Moosulmans and shall I hesitate to plunder Infidels?' He did not hesitate. He finally agreed to let them all go, but only after payment of 50,000 rupees. It was, of course, only his opening bid. Wazir Ahmad's tireless diplomacy eventually reduced the sum to 10,000 rupees plus a further bribe of 2000 to Atma Ram. Even at that level, it was daylight robbery. Moorcroft calculated that his three and a half months at Kunduz had cost him, in ransom money alone, the equivalent of eight months' salary. No wonder that, at the final audience of leave on 15 December, Murad Beg was so odiously affable. He quizzed Moorcroft about the benefits of senna for his constipation and had the effrontery to claim that they were now friends. Moorcroft must have choked over the word. 'I doubt whether Christendom ever beheld a miscreant who committed such enormities,' he fumed in a lengthy postscript to his earlier letter to Dr Abel. At least they had escaped death or slavery and were free to go.

Mir Izzat-Allah, very weak from fever and low in spirits, was the first away next day, heading south for Delhi. He never reached it, dying miserably at Peshawar in February 1825. Wazir Ahmad, who had amply demonstrated his courage and negotiating skills, replaced him as Persian secretary.[16] They all set out westwards for Tashkurghan on 17 December. Or rather, nearly all of them did. Missing was Guthrie who, with his servants, had been sent to prescribe medicine for a sick man about 30 miles (48 kilometres) away to the north and had unaccountably not returned. Moorcroft was uneasy but felt that he should get the caravan clear of Kunduz while the going was good. Even that was not plain sailing. It was a cold, windy and wet day and the Kunduz River was so swollen that they were lucky to get safely across without loss of life. When they reached Tashkurghan on 20 December the townsfolk crowding round the city gate to welcome them back were unfeignedly astonished that they had escaped from the clutches of Murad Beg intact.

Moorcroft was not entirely sure that they had. As day followed anxious day, the absence of Guthrie became more and more alarming. Moorcroft and Trebeck were in a dilemma. Common sense told them that they should get the caravan clear of Murad Beg's western boundary as quickly as possible. Yet to do so might compromise the safety of their friend and his servants. They eventually decided, although with great misgivings, to wait until the morning of Christmas Eve. Then, leaving an escort and money at Tashkurghan to speed Guthrie after them, they would cross the desert to Balkh and wait for him there. As soon as he had scribbled a note to Guthrie informing him of this decision,[17] Moorcroft regretted it. 'I was struck with a feeling of disapprobation at my own conduct which seemed like a desertion of individuals who had devotedly performed their duty towards me.' In any case Atma Ram made it plain that they should wait for Guthrie. And so they lingered on through that last anxious Christmas for a few more days, more and more convinced, as Moorcroft put it, that Guthrie's 'protracted detention was an indication of further designs inimical to my interest'. Baba Beg's sudden departure for Kunduz and the ban on any move during his absence also looked ominous. With a heavy heart Moorcroft at last gave orders to prepare for departure immediately after Christmas.

The morning of 27 December dawned cold, wet and stormy. The camels were tethered close to the camp, the loads were roped and already being distributed to the drivers. Then, as Moorcroft recalled much later, 'we were interrupted by the astounding information . . . from Koondooz ordering that my baggage was to be detained and that I should be sent back' alone, to answer new charges of spying. Just in case he was tempted to make a run for it, some 200 armed horsemen came riding hard out of the murk to the east and swiftly surrounded the camp. 'Every one who contemplated the past and present proceedings considered our destruction as certain,' wrote Moorcroft. The merchants, who had been gathering in the hope of travelling with them to Balkh, swiftly melted away.

That evening – it was misty and drizzling with rain, with the Uzbek guard patrolling their tents closely – Moorcroft and Trebeck with their principal servants held an anxious council of war.

> It was acknowledged [wrote Trebeck][18] that there appeared no other mode of saving ourselves from plunder and imprisonment, death or slavery, than by attacking the Oozbuck guard in the night, seizing their horses and making the best of our way across the frontier. . . . This line determined upon I was despatched to prepare for action and arrange our most valuable property in the way least likely to encumber us. Moorcroft went to delay the departure of himself . . . till the 28th when it was hoped we should have burst our net. He succeeded but with difficulty.

Then Moorcroft had second thoughts. For one thing, lives would be lost in the fighting and their reputation as a peaceable mercantile enterprise seriously compromised. For another, Guthrie and his servants who were still at Kunduz would either be jailed, killed or enslaved by the enraged Murad Beg. Yet, if Moorcroft tamely put himself back in Murad Beg's hands again, the same fate would in the end probably come to all of them. What happened next is best described in the words of the only man who can tell the full story, Moorcroft himself.[19]

Meer Wazeer Ahmad observed that if I had strength of body and mind sufficient to undertake and to perform at one stretch in the disguise of an Oozbuk a journey of about a hundred and forty miles [224 kilometres] without being discovered, I might reach the residence of Kasim Jan Khoja in Talikan and through personal application possibly succeed in interesting this individual in my favor.

Kasim Jan Khoja is a Syud . . . united by the ties of a double marriage with Mahommed Morad Begh and exercising over this Chief that influence which belongs to . . . the authority that appertains to the head of the Priesthood.

A retrospect of occurrences convinced me that my recall [to Kunduz] . . . formed part of a pre-meditated plan to extract as much money as possible from me under the pretext of duties previous to the arrival of the moment when it would be thought expedient to drop the mask and to proceed avowedly to the plunder of our property . . . and . . . that bourne from which no traveller returns. . . .

I saw no probable mode of breaking the toils by which I was enveloped without bringing ruin upon the objects of my mission save through an enterprize that could not have been foreseen by my enemy and of course against which he would have adopted no precautions. Doubtful indeed was the result of the application should I escape the dangers of the road, but in desperate emergencies, desperate measures are admissible. . . .

My small tent was pitched upon the bare plain and a considerable body of Oozbuck horse had been stationed round it.

Greatly increased in number towards the evening they retreated in two parties to the distance of thirty and forty yards [27 or 36 metres] in front and rear of the tent but could distinctly see all that passed outside whilst they were partially sheltered from the driving sleet and rain and the cold wind which blew from the desert.

Other horsemen patrolled upon the roads, the gates of the town were shut at an hour unusually early and every avenue to escape was guarded except the road to Kabool. Just at the close of the day I went out of the tent in European attire, which guise till this time I had constantly wore, . . . so . . . that I should be clearly observed by both the squads on guard.

With as much despatch as possible after re-entering my tent I dressed myself in the habilements of an Oozbuck and having concealed the lower part of my face in the last folds of the turband that enveloped my head as is frequently practised here in cold weather I quitted the tent alone unmolested, disregarded, or mistaken for an Oozbuck. . . . It was not a difficult task to affect the heavy waddling gait of the Oozbuck the cumbrous weight of the apparel imposing its emulation as a matter of necessity.

Suddenly dipping into a ravine I followed its course along its bed and by a few windings reached a burying ground where two guides provided by Meer Wuzeer Ahmad also in the dress of the country were waiting for me. The horses were mine but their absence from the garden in which they had been placed had apparently not been noticed as they were not the best and as Oozbuk horsemen were still coming along the road from the fort and guides were probably thought to belong to the guard. A horseman who galloped up to the party just as I was mounting my horse . . .

[339]

when he had come within a few yards of us suddenly turned round and returned towards my tent.

We took the road to Kabool but on reaching the mountains followed a narrow path and joined the desert. My guides displayed their ability in keeping the general direction of the road on a surface now so completely covered with water as to be without obvious vestige of path, a trackless waste without tree or bush or projecting indication of any kind till without the aid of a single star they reached the first Abdan [small covered reservoir]. But their sagacity somewhat failed them in a deep ravine on the pass of Shibaghlee from which we could not extricate ourselves after the loss of an hour till the dawn of morning, a delay then much regretted but altogether fortunate as in the first break of day we descried the fires of a body of banditti lying in wait at the eastern foot of the pass and who plundered a caravan two days afterwards.

Through long detours which at a great distance from frequented paths, skirted the foot of the mountains and through fording rivers to gain unbeaten lines where practicable we sometimes in the second night lost the general direction and made not the progress expected. Yet after having travelled for two nights and until four o'clock in the afternoon of the second day, without giving rest to our horses which had only taken one feed of barley carried on our saddles we reached in safety the house or rather camp of Kasim Jan Khoja. . . .

Every traveller who completes successfully an adventure of this nature is inclined to think that he has had several hair breadth 'scapes in its execution and perhaps the avoiding a *rencontre* with the banditti or with Baba Begh whom we saw on the road to Talikan accompanied by a large cavalcade and the fact of not being discovered by any of the numerous Oozbuks going to meet and conduct the before mentioned personage to the latter place . . . may be ranked amongst circumstances of hazard. However if there be any merit in the journey it belongs to the sagacity and instructions of Meer Wuzeer Ahmad and the obedience of his servants who were guides. . . .

A letter from Meer Wuzeer Ahmad introduced me and my business to the Patriarch of the Kattaghan Oozbuks and probably much contributed to procure for me a kind reception.

Finding the door of a large mud walled court open I entered and sent one of my guides to the Peerzada to whom I was speedily ushered through a crowd of attendants surrounding a circular house or tent made of reeds and mats with a high domed roof of the same materials and altogether resembling a gigantic beehive.

Within the structure I found the Peerzada sitting on a wolf skin placed upon a thin cushion of brocade of crimson satin and gold. As instructed by Meer Wuzeer Ahmad I placed the presented right hand of the Peerzada between mine and slightly bowed over it on which he bade me welcome, enquired after my health and desired me to be seated.

My conductor placed before him a present from me according to the custom of the country and taking hold of the skirt of his robe I stated that I was a merchant from a far distant country who being sorely oppressed and hearing of the reputation of the Khoja for justice had sought his presence for the purpose of soliciting his interposition on my behalf.

Here pausing he desired me to proceed on which I observed that although this was a task indispensably necessary, its performance was both delicate and difficult as it involved a complaint of injustice committed by a personage connected with him both by the ties of blood and of friendship, so that the recital however managed could scarcely fail to be grating to his feelings. He requested me to speak freely and without regard to the connection I had mentioned. I then represented the objects of my journey. . . .

I related the application made by me to Muhammud Morad Begh for permission to pass through his territories, recited the terms of his letter conveying the fullest assurance of safety and of the same treatment experienced by other merchants instead of which I had been compelled twice to visit Koondooz, had been detained above three months, had twice suffered two most unreasonable exactions under the pretext of duties and at this moment was threatened with the loss of property and of life unless I would immediately pay the enormous sum of two laks of rupees as the price of my liberation. That having come into this country through invitation and having committed no crime I had determined that if Mahummud Morad Begh was resolved to take away my life, that at least my blood should stain the floor of his own High Priest. But relying on the respect paid by the Khoja to the just claims of strangers I felt the fullest confidence that he would relieve me from a treatment without precedent and wholly undeserved.

And so, miraculously, he did.

Baba Beg of Tashkurghan turned up at Taliqan next day, probably in a vain effort to avert Murad Beg's wrath. The chief was certainly angry. He would, wrote Moorcroft, 'have cut open the belly of any Oozbuks who had given me assistance'. Baba Beg tried to tempt Moorcroft to take just one step too many outside his sanctuary and had horsemen concealed behind a wall to seize him if he had been silly enough to do so. Next day, the man who had been so effectively spreading rumours at Kunduz that Moorcroft was a spy also arrived at Taliqan. He was a mullah, a priest, and harangued the *pirzada*'s crowded durbar to such good effect that, at the end, most of those present were convinced of Moorcroft's guilt. Hearing the way things were going, Moorcroft insisted that he should be allowed to attend and refute the charges in person.

His accuser, wrote Moorcroft, reminded him 'of a gentleman late an ornament of the English Bar'. Luckily he was without that gentleman's skill in cross-examination. He began rather unpromisingly by asserting that Moorcroft was the commander-in-chief of the Indian army, a general called Metcalfe, who had been away from India for many years. This was one court appearance Moorcroft seems to have relished and he related the details with gusto. It was not difficult to make mincemeat of such absurd accusations and his opponent flew into a violent rage. He eventually left for Kunduz, presumably to press his charges there.

The *pirzada* declared himself convinced of Moorcroft's innocence, but, he admitted, this placed him in an acute dilemma. Moorcroft takes up the story again.

He wished so to conduct himself that I should not be injured and that Mahummud Begh should not be displeased but these conditions seemed little compatible. . . . He said that with me he would have no reserve and stated that if in virtue of the office he held he should command Mahummud Morad Begh to desist from persecuting me, he must obey but that such an exertion of authority would break up the friendship that now subsisted between them. . . . It may suffice that on my paying the further sum of two thousand rupees he would engage for the safety of all my party and of my property to which proposition I assented. Information of this condition was despatched to the Chief who . . . departed immediately for Talikan. . . . There had been a large meeting of the heads of the Kattaghans who deciding that I was a spy had counselled the Chief to insist upon the Peerzada abandoning my cause and leaving me to my fate or that if this point could not be carried that I should be forced to return. The Peerzada greatly disconcerted and mortified at this intelligence waited on the Chief early in the morning . . . where Mahummud Morad Begh repeated the decision of his courtiers and exhorted the Peerzada to abandon my cause as he was thoroughly convinced of my being a spy. Kasim Jan replied with great firmness. . . . The discussion was warmly conducted but at length the chief was obliged to yield a reluctant consent to the proposition of the Peerzada on the further condition that I should remain in the territories of Mahummud Begh until he should have returned from an expedition he was about to undertake, with the option of joining my party at Koondooz or of remaining at Talikan. As I knew that the safety of the party hung on the thread of my life alone and that soldiers had been stationed in the neighbourhood of the house of the Peerzada to seize me if I should come out, I preferred to reside till the return of Mahummud Morad Begh at Talikan.

There, in perfect safety, he remained for the best part of a month. Moorcroft's interesting retrospective account of this period goes on for another 100 sides and generally confirms Wilson's version, which is based on a now missing journal. He had neither pen nor paper (nor indeed razor) and his time in the plainly furnished falconer's room, with its fire in the middle, must often have hung very heavily indeed. The *pirzada* often sent for him or visited him and they conversed about everything under the sun. On one occasion Moorcroft taught him how to prepare saffron. On another he attempted to translate Gibbon into Persian for him. Extraordinary, he mused, 'that an Englishman should . . . have been engaged in an attempt to translate the History of Chinghiz Khan to one of his descendants'. The whole situation was extraordinary.

At last at the end of January 1825, word came that Moorcroft could rejoin the rest of his party. No wonder he gave the man who had saved his life almost the most precious thing in his possession – the folding iron bedstead which had been made to replace the original brass one lost in Ladakh. The two men, the one uncharacteristically bearded like the other, took an affectionate leave of one another at Taliqan on 25 January, and Moorcroft rode off to rejoin Trebeck, Guthrie and the others at Kunduz.

There must have been so much to talk about. Trebeck would have told[20] of the uproar and consternation in the camp at Tashkurghan in torrential rain, when Moorcroft's absence was discovered, of the circumstantial rumours in the town that he had been seized, and of Trebeck's own eventual summons to proceed to Kunduz under escort. The young man it seems had the greatest difficulty in preventing his men from attacking their guards and only the argument that this would have sealed Moorcroft's fate finally restrained them. They had set out across the desert for Kunduz on the last day of 1824. That evening, Trebeck recalled, 'whilst dozing by the side of a fire at midnight after a tedious day's journey a man thrust a note into my hand which I found was from Moorcroft' with the confirmation that his risky flight to sanctuary had been successful. On the first day of 1825, Trebeck, Guthrie and Wazir Ahmad had been joyfully reunited at Kunduz where, in tolerable comfort, they had been waiting for Murad Beg's return and their leader's release ever since.

At the final interview on 26 January, Murad Beg had the effrontery to ask for Moorcroft's folding chair and coolly helped himself to medicines prescribed for someone else. Moorcroft, for all his sufferings and extortion at the hands of this treacherous rogue, had the greatest difficulty not to laugh. To cap it all, when a parting prayer was uttered for Moorcroft's well-being and prosperity, the chief 'joined in the ceremony and clutched and stroked the scanty and straggling crop of hairs that stood him in line of a beard with great solemnity and apparent fervour'.[21] No wonder Moorcroft added hypocrisy to his long and highly uncomplimentary list of the qualities of Murad Beg of Kunduz.

That night Moorcroft rejoined his party, encamped in the snow outside the town. Next day they set off as fast as they could, westwards across that now familiar scene of desolation, for what they all fervently hoped was the very last time. It was. At dawn on 30 January they were on the western edge of Murad Beg's territory out in the bleak plain beyond Tashkurghan and, later that day, left it safely behind. They were on the final lap to Bokhara at last.

23 JOURNEY'S END,
FEBRUARY–AUGUST 1825

WHATEVER PRIVATE RELIEF they may have felt at their eventual escape from Murad Beg, there could have been little else to cheer the members of Moorcroft's lonely little caravan on that bleak late January day in 1825 as, hunched against the bitter wind, they plodded on across the empty snowscape towards the little town of Mazar i Sharif.[1] In those days, the domed houses behind their high walls clustered close around the white tomb which is said to house the bones of Ali, the Prophet's son-in-law. The khan, who was custodian of the tomb, pretended horror at the greed of Murad Beg and gave them a cordial welcome. A few months later he was not quite so charitable. Moorcroft halted the caravan for a few days at Mazar because of the choked condition of the desert road in the melting snow, but this did not stop him riding several miles out to the west to treat the sword wounds of one of the khan's friends.

One more march beyond Mazar brought them to Balkh, once celebrated in history and legend as the rich and beautiful 'mother of cities' but now, in the wind and snow, a crumbling, melancholy ghost town with its massive walls and fine buildings in ruins. Moorcroft shrewdly doubted whether these sprawling ruins really marked the site of the celebrated capital of ancient Bactria and he was right to doubt, as recent archaeology has confirmed. The weather remained vile but the welcome from the governor was warm. At least in February they avoided the midsummer heat which gave Balkh such an evil reputation for fevers. They were detained there five days by heavy rain and did not leave until 8 February. Once clear of the orchards and ruined walls and buildings just outside the city, they turned more to the north, across the last of the plain before the Oxus River. When they reached its banks three days later at the ferry hamlet of Khoja Saleh, all sign of the Hindu Kush had at last disappeared below the southern horizon. Behind them the flat plain was as empty as that beyond the river to the north.

Through this scene of desolation rolled the great brown river. It is at its most serene in midwinter but still, Moorcroft reckoned, was as wide as the Thames opposite Temple gardens in London (before it was confined by the later Victoria Embankment). Contemplating 'this truly noble stream', its broad surface apparently unnavigated except for the crude ferry rafts of lashed tree-trunks which carried the caravans across, Moorcroft was lost in dreams of improvement.[2] In his mind he peopled the empty banks with fine cities and rich cultivation, and furrowed the bright surface of the empty river with steamships. He soon had a rod out but failed to land a fish, although one of the camel-drivers was more successful. They crossed on 12 February – it took most of the daylight hours – and pushed on northwards into the desert next day. Moorcroft was roaming on horseback across the plain pursuing anything of interest: game, the winter settlements of the Kazak nomads, the passing pony caravan of some Turcoman merchants, and on one occasion a vivid mirage of an extensive low building away to the north-west, which suddenly vanished as he galloped towards it.

The awful weather and the dreary, treeless emptiness of the desert must have made the thriving and substantial bazaar town of Karshi, even in midwinter, seem like paradise. It is hard to know who was the more curious, the good-natured crowds from almost every corner of Asia who came to stare, or Moorcroft himself. In the four days they were there, he was out recording prices in the bazaar and noting such diverse matters as how to preserve melons or butter, how to clean wet leather boots or red woollen cloaks and how to clear a head of lice with quicksilver. On the third day they slithered through the muddy streets to pay a state visit to the young prince-governor of the town, Tora Bahadur Khan, second son of the emir of Bokhara. The court ceremonial was appropriately impressive and Moorcroft must have been well schooled beforehand in the mandatory ritual obeisances, arms crossed upon the breast or, during the prayers, kneeling with hands raised and palms inward. To his first British visitors, the prince was friendliness personified although Moorcroft was shrewd enough to prophesy,[3] accurately as usual, that he was quite capable of murdering his elder brother to gain control of the great oasis city, now only three or four marches away across the desert. This in due course he did and later won European notoriety as the murderer of his English prisoners, the hapless Stoddart and Conolly.

They left Karshi on the final leg of their long journey on 21 February and, four days later, caught their first glimpse, above the leafless fruit trees, of the domes, minarets and towering walls of the great city. Moorcroft's journal recording that precious moment is missing but Wilson ends his book with what sounds like an authentic piece of Moorcroftian understatement. 'It was with no slender satisfaction that on the morning of the 25th of February, 1825, we found ourselves at the end of our protracted pilgrimage, at the gates of that city which had for five years [it was nearer six] been the object of our wanderings, privations and perils.' Fortunately Trebeck had left a rather more quotable sentence to mark that magic moment:

After a long and laborious pilgrimage of more than five years we had a right to hail the domes and minarets of Bokhara with as much pleasure, as had the wearied remnant of the first Crusaders the sight of the Christian banners waving triumphantly on the walls of the Holy City.

So they had. If distance is measured by the time taken to cross it, Bokhara was, for Europeans, more remote than the moon is today. It was certainly far more interesting. 'Bokhara the noble', former capital of Transoxiana and queen of the old silk route, is one of the great historic cities of the world. No Englishman had reached it since the reign of Elizabeth I and none from the south. For Moorcroft, it•was the triumphant fulfilment of a fifteen year dream and vindication of a conviction going back almost to the beginning of his time in India. The critics had said it could never be done, at least not with a ponderous caravan, across some of the most lawless lands in the world. Well, he had done it and added greatly to the stock of human and geographical knowledge while doing so. Doubtless dismounting at the Kabul gate, for infidels were not allowed to ride inside the gigantic walls of the great Islamic city, he passed into the teeming streets. They took up their abode in the empty *serai* of the Khivan merchants, under the watchful eye of its custodian, Dalla Bai.

There Moorcroft spent the next, and almost the last, five months of his life. A frosty February and March slowly gave way to a wet and chilly April and then, from early May when all rain stopped, the pitiless sun cartwheeling across the shimmering sky each day, slowly raised the great inland desert to a furnace heat greater than he had ever experienced. It was a pity that Wilson perversely decided to include nothing of this period in his account of the travels because, he claimed, Moorcroft's notes were 'so very desultory and imperfect'.[4] They are nothing of the kind. Admittedly Moorcroft regarded his sojourn in Bokhara, notwithstanding the great but inaccessible beauty of its women, as the dullest five months of his whole journey, but that is not how it seems today.[5] His surviving letters and journals are full of interest.[6] It is true too that, by the time Wilson's account was ready for publication, the scintillating account of the later visit by Alexander 'Bokhara' Burnes was already a reprinted and much translated bestseller, which had turned that ambitious little Scotsman into an international celebrity and made Bokhara almost a household word in Europe.[7] It is also true, as Wilson emphasized more than once, that Moorcroft's rambling writings do not lend themselves to easy editing. Even so, the attempt to write some account of what was the first British visit to Bokhara for two and a half centuries, and the first ever from the south, should surely have been made. The arrival in Bokhara was not, as Wilson would have it, the 'legitimate close' of the great journey.[8] It was both its climax and its supreme test.

Moorcroft's first task at Bokhara after accommodating the caravan, was to announce his arrival to the 'lord of the household' or *khushbegi* and show his credentials. He was led by court officials through the teeming streets, the chidren rudely shouting 'Ooroos, Ooroos' (Russian) as he passed, across the great open registan, which was once the commercial heart of all Asia, and under the twin-turreted gateway of the Ark guarding the 1000-year-old bulk of the royal palace.[9] He was probably apprehensive. It is true that he possessed a welcoming letter from the emir himself, received while he was in faraway Ladakh. Moreover, Wazir Ahmad and Fazl Haq had both visited the city and been assured of a friendly welcome, but then all that had been true of Murad Beg as well. As it turned out, the silver bearded *khushbegi* was amicable enough, although he insisted on a 10 per cent duty on the value of any goods Moorcroft managed to sell during his search for horses. This tax was subsequently levied, firmly but fairly. Some years later, when the diminutive Alexander Burnes was presented to the tall *khushbegi*, he asked whether all Britons were small. It is another tiny confirmation that Moorcroft was not a tall man.[10]

Emir Khan Haydar himself was away from the city at the time but, two days after his return, Moorcroft was summoned to the Ark once again and led with Trebeck through the warren of courts, corridors and rooms to the great hall of public audience. This was a much more daunting occasion altogether. The emir had waded to his shaky throne through the blood of many of his relatives a quarter of a century before. In those days he had been a cruel lecher with a taste for virgins but, since then, had converted himself into a puritanical and tyrannical bigot. He was 'arbitrary gloomy and suspicious' to use Moorcroft's description and with a 'ticklish temper' as well. Indeed, observing the ruler's irrational, high pitched laughter and the bizarre inconsistencies of his behaviour, Moorcroft later wondered about his sanity. Insane or not, his power was absolute and he was clearly an object of the greatest fear to all those about him. Like many unpopular tyrants, he buttressed his rule with an army of secret police, spies and informers. The *khushbegi* had agreed in advance with Moorcroft and Trebeck that they should doff their hats and incline their heads as they were led into the royal presence.

Moorcroft has left a vivid description of what happened next.

> The Ameer or Commander of the Faithful was seated in a small room about fifteen feet [4.5 metres] higher than the area of the court dressed in a plain drab colored coat of broad cloth with a large loosely folded turband of white muslin having a narrow gold border and before him was a large book the leaves of which he frequently turned over with apparent earnestness.
>
> Meer Umeer Haider is about forty eight years of age, of a complexion somewhat olive and rather dark than fair.
>
> His features partake of the Oozbuk character in some degree and the deep lines on his face with the rapid change of expression from lively to serious indicate a mind of great activity in which benevolence and good temper are said to be strongly mixed up with distrust and hauteur. He enquired after our healths, our names, ages, country and occupation and from the long intervals betwixt the questions it appeared probable that a Secretary concealed behind the pier belonging to the window through which we conversed was occupied in committing the details to writing ... Mr. Trebeck and myself had been directed to stop at the distance of about twenty yards [18.2 metres] from the window near which His Majesty was seated but after a time the King beckoned us to approach near and indeed as close as he could see us from the window which we afterwards learned was to be held as an especial mark of condescension favor, confidence and honor.

After further conversation, the emir 'said that we were at liberty to sell our property to whom and in any manner we might think proper and to purchase any articles that might please us'.

It was a good start. Unfortunately the horse brokers refused to sell animals to Moorcroft without specific authority, so he had to go back to petition the king once more. It afforded him a fascinating glimpse of an age-old method of oriental government. He:

> attended on the day when petitions were presented and was placed by the Master of the Ceremonies at the head of the line of a very large body of petitioners and appellants. The King read my note and directed me to be seated in a situation from which I could see the mode of despatching business which was summary and rapid. To the petitions of those individuals whose claims were admitted and approved the King himself affixed a finger seal which a secretary occasionally smeared with ink from a stick of that substance prepared in China.
>
> His Majesty frequently assigned reasons why he refused the suit of the petitioner and in every instance the rejected petition was torn up. At the conclusion of every decision whether favorable or otherwise the Master of the Ceremonies repeated a short prayer in Toorkee for the preservation of His Majesty's impartial administration of justice at the end of which the whole assembly joined in approving by stroking their beards. There was much respectful solemnity in the whole proceeding and the King delivered his commands with great promptness and rapidity.
>
> On observing by my change of position that the posture had been continued so long as to have become inconvenient His Majesty sent me a sealed permission to buy horses and directed the Master of the Ceremonies to inform me that in future the act of taking off the hat would be dispensed with and it would only be expected from me to place my right hand upon my breast and slightly to bow my head as a salutation whenever I should have occasion to come into His Majesty's presence.

Moorcroft had done well. It is true that he did not stint his presents to the emir, as his account book shows.[11] Pride of them all were the two brass cannons which had been so invaluable at Akora. It is also possible that the emir was hoping for some political connection with the East India Company, or at least for financial or military assistance, so as to cope with the enemies which threatened him on every side. Moorcroft also seems to have worked his usual charm, even on this fearsome and unsavoury tyrant.[12] Whatever the reasons, Emir Haydar accorded his first British visitor privileges never before granted to foreign merchants, let alone to infidels, and only rarely to Muslims of high rank. Moorcroft was even allowed to ride his horse in the city to the very gate of the Ark. Most precious of all, he was granted a *firman* forbidding all interference in his efforts to purchase horses and ordering the remission of all duties on his merchandise. To ensure its safety, Dalla Bai, the keeper of the *serai* in which it was housed, was warned by the emir that the loss of a single item would cost him his eyes. Uncomfortable as this must have been for Dalla Bai, for Moorcroft it all amounted to a far more auspicious start than he dared hope for. Perhaps the long journey to the forbidden city was about to be crowned with the successful horse purchases, which were its original and principal justification.

So far as he could see, and Moorcroft was observing every detail of Bokharan horse management very minutely indeed, the desert lands along the Oxus were better fitted by nature than any he had ever seen to raise the finest horses in the world. This was, as he put it, 'the great mine of horses'. Unfortunately it soon became apparent that more than five years of warfare, raiding and anarchy of the kind he had already experienced further south, had fragmented the unity of the Asian heartland and all but dried up the rich channels of the ancient horse trade. The teeming bazaars, which had once made Bokhara the commercial hub of all Asia, were now relatively empty and the caravans which did get through 'might truly be said to fight their way to this city'. In consequence, lamented Moorcroft, 'probably the finest horse markets in the world have been almost wholly broken up'. Another uncomfortable discovery was that most of the goods from Palmer and MacKillop's Calcutta warehouses, which they had been carrying at such trouble and expense for six weary years, proved to be totally unsuitable for the Uzbek market. Commercially 'the Himalaya concern' was a flop and Russian goods retained their dominance unchallenged. Moorcroft was soon driven to augment his dwindling resources by raising yet more cash on the credit market. Part of it he spent on sample Russian goods to take back to Calcutta.

There was still hope of some high-quality breeding-horses, however, even if not in the numbers he had first hoped, for the wealthy men about court still had some remarkably fine animals in their stables. Moorcroft was just embarking on the long process of inspection, negotiation and purchase, when the emir suddenly called together his feudal levies and departed over 100 miles (160 kilometres) to the east. The object of the expedition was to suppress the latest insurrection by the semi-nomadic Kitay-Kipchaks on the road to Samarkand. Moorcroft was present at the grand parade before the army departed. The trouble was that large numbers of horses went with it, including almost all the best animals he had earmarked for purchase.

Still, he consoled himself, the army should not be away long. In the meantime the absence of the prickly emir left him much freer to pursue all his other enquiries in Bokhara. As usual his personal charm, his medical skill and his lively interest in everything under the sun seem very quickly to have won him the friendship of some of the more important men of the city. The influential *khushbegi* soon became a frequently visited friend, as did the good and hospitable Aziz Shah, custodian of one of Bokhara's most prestigious shrines, but the 'worthiest fellow we have met with in this city' was an Armenian Christian from Georgia, named Gregor Zakaria. He proved to be not only immensely learned in all aspects of viticulture and wine production, but a valuable source of political information too.

There is no doubt that politics were an important, though entirely unofficial, reason for Moorcroft's presence at Bokhara. Ever since his astonishing discovery in 1812 that the Russians had already penetrated to Bokhara, every successive piece of evidence of Russian activity on India's borders made him more obsessively determined to see for himself just exactly what game it was they were playing. Was it merely a bid to dominate the trade of inner Asia? Or was it, as Moorcroft was much more inclined to believe, a gigantic and ancient plot to upset the world balance of power by seizing the Asian heartland and making India untenable? Either way, his country's need for accurate political and topographical information was urgent. Significantly, it had been this argument which Moorcroft deployed in April 1824 at Peshawar, when explaining his decision to go on to Bokhara despite the Government's recall.[13] Now that he was in Bokhara, he set about acquiring information with all the enthusiasm of a schoolboy and compiled an alarming dossier of evidence about the most recent Russian embassy to Bokhara, complete with disguised nocturnal visitors and far-reaching plans to link up with Agha Mehdi and open up the north-eastern Ladakh approach into India.

It would be easy to dismiss Moorcroft, as his superiors were inclined to do, as an unbalanced and over-imaginative Russophobe. He certainly fell victim to his own enthusiasm and made the error of all the later alarmists of rolling up the events of half a century into something like a single decade, but timing apart, his forecasts of coming events were disturbingly accurate. The inexorable Russian advance southwards, the destruction of Bokhara and its sister khanates, the pressure on western China, even the danger to Herat after the Russian seizure of Merv, which brought Britain and Russia to the edge of war in the 1880s – they are all there in his feverish writings and speculations. As has been said already, Moorcroft was the first British player of the Great Game in Central Asia. Before he left Bokhara he set up a spy network, complete with secret signs, to watch and report on the developing situation. Whether he realized that he in his turn was also being closely watched, by the Russians, is doubtful but it is so. Almost before he left Bokhara his visit was known about in St Petersburg. Soon it was being seen there as a development of the highest importance which justified the measures that were being taken to strengthen Russian influence in Central Asia.[14] The vicious circle of mutual Anglo-Russian suspicion and counteraction in that great heartland virtually began with William Moorcroft.

Fortunately there were also plenty of less weighty matters to absorb him, even in the searing summer temperatures and burning winds. He decided to protect himself against the heat, Uzbek style, by concealing himself from the sun under a heavy woollen robe and waistcoat and he lived largely on a diet of iced buttermilk and something like fruit ice cream from the bazaars. It is a regime which would have killed a man half his age. Sometime during these five months, Moorcroft passed his fifty-eighth birthday. Yet his energy and his enthusiastic investigations of Bokhara's teeming street life and rural economy seem as unflagging as ever. He composed almost a small book for the defunct Board of Agriculture in London on Bokharan ploughing, threshing, irrigation and manuring techniques, viticulture and wine-making, ass- and poultry-breeding, dairying, silk production, cannabis and fruit cultivation. So keenly interested was he in the production of Bokhara's renowned white crusty bread, and the ability of the bakers to withstand the intense heat of the great clay ovens, that he took careful temperature measurements and eventually entered one of the ovens himself. He emerged very hastily indeed minus his eyebrows and eyelashes, doubtless to general merriment. There were other lighter moments too. Moorcroft purchased a prize fighting-cock and pitted it very successfully for wagers against all comers. Medicine and surgery, however, did not take up much of his time at Bokhara, although he did practise privately on some of his well connected friends, as occasion required.

There was, though, one surgical matter which did absorb him. Bokhara from time immemorial (and until very recently) has been notorious for the existence of a peculiarly unpleasant intestinal worm, afflicting man and animal alike. This rekindled in Moorcroft an interest in parasitic worms going right back to his days at the Liverpool Infirmary. Although Moorcroft dare not pursue his investigations too publicly, he was convinced that the water tanks and channels of Bokhara were to blame. The contrast between the city's cleanly swept streets and stables, and the appalling state of its stinking and insanitary water supply never ceased to amaze him. He was absolutely right. If the *khushbegi* had listened to the hygienic measures which Moorcroft urged upon him, Bokhara would have been rid of a scourge which killed and disabled thousands of its citizens for well over another century. Moorcroft itched to carry out *post mortems* on some of the unlucky ones, but that was out of the question. What he did do instead was spend many hours in the company of Bokhara's most successful barber-surgeon, a man named Mirza Omar and known universally in the city as 'worm killer'. Moorcroft not only watched his superior extraction techniques closely but even suggested ways of improving them still further. He also closely examined the worms, some up to 34 inches (1 metre) long, which came from the bodies of the mirza's patients. For those with strong stomachs, Moorcroft's long illustrated paper on the Bokharan worm is typical of the man, with its ceaseless and lateral search for cause, explanation, reason and connection. Typical too, is the open willingness to recognize skills and knowledge superior to those of contemporary European medicine.

He was certainly not an unqualified admirer of all that he saw in Bokhara. The inhuman treatment of the women, many of them 'amongst the most beautiful in the world', appalled him. He loathed even more the odious traffic in slaves. Moorcroft's suspicion of Russia did not extend to individual Russians. He purchased the freedom of three of them (for less than the price of a good horse) intending to take them back with him to India for eventual repatriation to Russia. Their distress when the emir required him to sell them back into slavery clearly upset him considerably. During their few precious weeks of freedom, he had set these humble men to work looking after the horses which were slowly accumulating in the walled compound he had hired for the purpose.

Horses! It is often easy to forget that these animals were the excuse and justification for this long six-year odyssey. For Moorcroft the problem was intensely frustrating. It was clear to him that Bokhara had positively bulged with fine animals, not only when he had first proposed the journey, but until very recently. Now most of the relatively few good ones left, which he had the emir's permission to purchase, were one hundred miles away across the desert towards Samarkand with the royal army. As late as early June, Moorcroft was still awaiting their return, but his fear of being caught on the wrong side of the Hindu Kush by yet another winter eventually convinced him that he would have to leave.

His plan was to dispose of the remnants of his commercial caravan at whatever prices he could get and to mount his servants for a rapid horseback journey, travelling light, by whatever route to India seemed most feasible. In the end he was able to secure about forty 'moderately good horses', although almost none of them were really good enough to be stud stallions. For quality animals, Moorcroft had decided, once they were safely south of the Oxus, to make one last bid in the sandy deserts somewhere to the west of Balkh in the vicinity of Andkhoi. He had first heard that good horses still existed in this area while detained at Kunduz but more recent evidence confirmed the story. They were it seemed 'of qualities admirably suited for military purposes'. Moorcroft decided, therefore, to 'leave my party and with two or three attendants at all risks make an effort by some means to accomplish less imperfectly than at present the object of my mission'.

By the beginning of July, there seemed nothing to be gained by waiting any longer for the still uncertain return of the emir and his army, so Moorcroft applied to his friend the *khushbegi* for permission to depart. The result after a few days was a summons from the emir to join him in camp, together with an ominously heavy insistence on the numbers, military talents and weapons of the members of his escort who were to accompany him. It must have sounded like Murad Beg all over again, but so long as the emir had no evil designs upon them, then the unwelcome journey at least offered a final chance to secure a few top quality Bokharan stallions.

Moorcroft and his five troopers had an uncomfortable time of it in the desert, once the green orchards of Bokhara had disappeared into the shimmering heat haze behind them. By the time they were escorted into the relative comfort of the Bokharan camp, well beyond the range of the besieged walled town, they were badly blistered on face and hands. The emir's green tent with its silken lining was pitched on a low hillside in the midst of his men and there, in the evening, Moorcroft found the ruler with a few of his officials 'sitting on his knees on a thin silken cushion'. The interview seemed to go well. The emir was pleased with the presents Moorcroft had brought and undertook to write letters to some of the chiefs along the probable routes to the south. Encouraged, Moorcroft raised again the question of horses.

> I represented that I had been led to believe that there were many fine horses in Bokhara but that few had as yet fallen into my hands. I was willing to hope that as His M[ajesty] had called me thus far he would permit me to purchase some horses in the camp where I had found many that would suit my purpose as stallions. He said, 'Purchase, Purchase' – I thanked him and said I should make a point of making known in my country the civilities I had experienced from His Majesty.

Immediately after this meeting, Moorcroft was taken to see and treat men with gunshot wounds and next morning he removed a ball from the neck of one of the emir's officers. Indeed nearly every day in camp, similarly wounded men were brought to him for treatment. Moorcroft noted that, either because they invariably kept their distance from the fort, or because the defenders were running low on gunpowder, the wounds were rarely fatal. Moorcroft began to wonder if he had been called to the camp for his medical skills, but then another reason emerged at his second interview with the emir, the following evening. A breathtakingly magnificent Turcoman horse was put through its paces before him and he was encouraged to believe that it could become his, either by gift or purchase. With considerable fearlessness and skill, Moorcroft steered his way past dangerous questions from the fanatical ruler concerning the divinity of Christ and the eating of pork. Finally Emir Haydar came to the heart of the matter. How skilful were Moorcroft and his men with siege artillery? Moorcroft had been half expecting and half fearing that question, but he knew what he had to say. He boldly replied that, although adequate to repel caravan robbers, he and his men were not equipped for siege warfare nor for regular fighting. Moorcroft could see that it was a decisive turning point. Emir Haydar's face:

> which when I began to speak was bedecked with smiles had its features deformed by a fierce frown which gradually abating left the countenance overspread with a deep gloom. I saw that I had lost my influence and after a short period of silence the King gave a signal [to withdraw].

Next day, as soon as Moorcroft was finished with his patients, he began his search for horses among the wealthier courtiers and chiefs. He was so successful that by evening he believed that, when the formalities were completed next day, he 'should have obtained about a dozen of such horses for stallions as India has seldom seen from any other country save Britain and which might have surprised even those persons accustomed to the sight of the finest horses of the turf'. One of them, a magnificent black stallion, was good enough to send back to England for breeding and there was the prospect of even more the following day. It was not to be. When Moorcroft returned to his tent that evening there was a message waiting for him from the emir that he must return to Bokhara at once and complete no more purchases. Moorcroft hastened at once to the royal tent but failed to gain admission and, when he finally did so next morning, was curtly told that all horses in the camp were now needed in the siege of the Kitay-Kipchak rebels. Even the fine stallion Moorcroft had been led to expect as a parting gift was replaced by an indifferent dress of honour. It was the final bitter disappointment.

On the dreary four day journey back through the burning desert winds to Bokhara, Moorcroft asked himself again and again whether he had been right to sabotage his official mission for the sake of a principle. He was sure he was. For one thing, the Kipchaks were only in rebellion against intolerable oppression and they had already offered reasonable terms. More to the point, some of Moorcroft's men were East India Company troops. They could not be recruited as mercenaries in wars which did not in the least concern either them or the company and in which their lives would have been put at risk. Even if Moorcroft *had* put himself at the head of his men and successfully carried the fort by assault – and he did not think it would have been too difficult – there was no guarantee that the unstable emir would not then dream up further reasons for delay or difficulty. Moorcroft had already been entangled too often in the dangerous politics of Eastern courts. It was already mid-July. If he delayed any longer, his chances of getting across the Hindu Kush before the high passes closed would be jeopardized. Better to go while the going was good and trust to finding some good animals south of the Oxus. 'I have certainly injured my own views', Moorcroft wrote, 'but am consoled by my motives.'

Back in Bokhara, George Trebeck had everything ready for a speedy departure. There only remained the now familiar but still painful formalities of leavetaking of their many new friends. That included the children who no longer jeered at Moorcroft in the street, but instead showed every mark of respect and 'prayed that Allah would make my path white'. Even on that very last full day in the great city, 21 July 1825, Moorcroft still found time to commit to paper some interesting speculations about the possible medical effects of cannabis in the treatment of disease and he purchased a quantity of the drug for trial in Britain.

Trebeck was off next morning at dawn with the horses, leaving Moorcroft to follow with the camels and baggage later. There followed the usual but none the less frustrating delays which continued all through the heat of the day. At dusk Moorcroft and his party were outside the walls, but still not ready to move and with no supper prepared either. So he sent into the town for a large quantity of rice, borrowed a huge cauldron and commissioned a Kashmiri silversmith who had been on his payroll to cook a mountainous mutton pilau to see them through the night. It must have been very good indeed, for Moorcroft made a careful note of the recipe before stretching out to sleep on the warm ground under the stars. At dawn they moved out through the orchards which fringe the city, no doubt looking back occasionally at the domes, walls and minarets fast disappearing into the shimmering haze of another hot day. The faithful Gregor Zakaria was the last to turn back, after presenting Moorcroft with a farewell gift of some of his own delectable wines and brandies.

The combined party headed south-east into the open desert. There were sixty horses, about as many men and a number of hired camels to carry the diminished baggage. For the first time in more than six years they were homeward bound at last. Just what private hopes and dreams each man carried of a world beyond those endless deserts and tumbling mountain ranges we shall never know. For Moorcroft, it was retirement among the limpid, pine-filled air and the rushing mountain streams of Himalayan hills that beckoned most strongly, but, and he spoke for them all, 'much of difficulty and of danger must be encountered before I can enjoy the leisure available to this object'. Trebeck consoled himself with the thought that they were no longer impeded by ponderous baggage, they could move at speed, and they were 'somewhat formidable' if anyone should seek to dispute their passage.[15]

At this stage Moorcroft had no clear idea of the route they would take. Two of the possibilities he had seriously considered earlier, either of going west to Khiva and the Caspian, or striking east into the snow peaks at the head of the Oxus towards Yarkand and thence into Ladakh from the north, were already ruled out. The dangerously disturbed state of Turkestan, the need to try for more quality horses and the lateness of the season probably accounted for that. Southwards, once he had investigated the horse resources west of Balkh, there were really only two viable alternatives. If Sultan Muhammad Khan were still at Kabul and things seemed reasonably peaceful there, then they would cross the Hindu Kush far enough west to escape Murad Beg's long reach and return as they had come via Kabul, the Khyber and Peshawar. Alternatively, there was the more difficult possibility of striking north and east of Kunduz by way of Badakhshan on the Upper Oxus, and then turning south across the mountains along a little used but direct caravan route by way of Chitral and Peshawar. Moorcroft already had introductions from Qamar ud Din to some of the chiefs along this route and while detained at Kunduz the previous winter he had sent Askar Ali back to Peshawar with Izzat Allah, charged with instructions to reconnoitre the route back from there by way of Chitral and the Upper Oxus.[16] If all had gone according to plan he should have been well on his way back to them by this time.

For the moment, Moorcroft's only plan was to retrace his steps to Balkh. Leaving the bulk of the party there, he would make his short reconnaissance further west in a final bid for horses and then together they would make a dash southwards by whatever route seemed best at the time.

He was not feeling very well at the start of the journey. The scorching return from the emir's camp had weakened him and as his riding horse was also injured, he climbed into a swaying camel basket. The awkward motion, not to speak of muscle spasms and the return of some of his old rheumatic pains, gave him little rest. Away to the north-east at dawn, he could still see the great snow range beyond Samarkand. But along their route, as he noted laconically in his diary, there were 'no habitations, no cultivation. Desert no water.' To avoid the pitiless heat they did most of their marches at night. At Karshi, four marches from Bokhara, the welcome from Prince Tora Bahadur was far from friendly this time. Moorcroft felt he was lucky to get away with the virtual extortion of some shawls and one of his precious horses. Considering the young tyrant's usual methods with passing caravans, he noted ruefully, 'it would seem that we actually have been treated with lenity and some appearance of justice'.

As soon as they had purchased enough forage for the next stage across the empty, shimmering desert to the Oxus, they moved on again. Even Moorcroft's busy pen could find little to record except the occasional and not always friendly meetings with nomads encamped near the scattered water holes. On one of these occasions he noticed something about the wooden utensils the women used for camel buttermilk that sent him into a long and fascinating reverie about the early farming experiences of his grandfather Richard far away in Lancashire eighty years before. But the future always interested him more than the past. He wondered about the military potential of these unpromising deserts and he wrote enthusiastically about the possibilities for their improvement if scientifically irrigated.

They reached the Oxus on about 4 or 5 August. Moorcroft was too light headed to be sure of the date but his dream of improvement and future prosperity along the empty river banks was precise enough:

> I have elsewhere touched upon the improvement of which this country is susceptible in good hands and cannot but deeply regret that our unfortunate countrymen, who have suffered so much in Southern Africa had not bent their steps towards the country of Badakhshan which the tyrrany of Murad Beg has almost emptied of its inhabitants . . . I may be accused of fostering schemes of ambition, but here there is abundant room for indulging speculations of this kind . . . A body of European emigrants would speedily have allies in the natives of the neighbouring districts tired of the confusion, oppression and tyranny under which they have long labored –

We shall never know what interrupted him but the long and busy travel journal comes to an abrupt halt at this point. It was never resumed. The mute pages which follow are heavy with disaster, but there is something supremely right about these last words in Moorcroft's journal. After all, compassion, improvement, patriotism, the righting of wrongs, the export of European civilization and breathtaking visions of the future – all these had been Moorcroft's continuing hallmarks since the great journey began. Moreover, both the handwriting and the ideas are as vigorous on the last, interrupted page as they had been on the very first, four and a half years before.

One march after leaving the Oxus they came to the walled town of Akcha, clustering round its lofty citadel. Waiting for them there was Askar Ali, just back from Peshawar via Chitral and Kunduz. He carried mails from India including a letter written as recently as February by Captain Wade at Ludhiana. Less welcome would have been the news of the death of Izzat Allah, careworn and ill, at Peshawar. It looks as though Askar Ali failed to convince Moorcroft, or did not recommend, that the Chitral route was the best way back to India. At all events, after three days at Akcha he returned to Kunduz once again, with secret letters from Moorcroft to the ministers of Murad Beg exploring the possibility of negotiating a genuinely safe passage in that direction.[17] Moorcroft and the rest of the party, meanwhile, moved on to the sprawling ghost town of Balkh where its governor gave them a friendly welcome once more and assembled as many of the local Turcoman horses as he could find for Moorcroft's inspection.

Their wretched quality finally convinced Moorcroft that he would indeed have to go in search of the superior animals said to be reared in the desert towns a few marches further west. A tantalizing mystery hangs over this last lonely journey. Moorcroft knew it would be dangerous. All regular contacts with the area had been cut off in the anarchy of the last few years and Andkhoi in particular had an unsavoury reputation as a nest of robbers.[18] But there is a hint of something else, something more personal and more mysterious in the letter he had sent from Bokhara two months earlier. 'I have', he wrote, 'the strongest hopes that my party will reach Hindoostan and that I shall accompany them but I have one if not two separate duties to perform individually and in their execution I may almost be said to tread upon gunpowder.' What were those individual duties which made him insist on going alone, apart from only two or three personal servants? And, if he anticipated danger, why would he not, or could he not, take an armed escort with him? To another correspondent, in a letter written about the same time but now missing, he was no more specific. He admitted that the experiment is full of hazard, but *le jeu vaut bien la chandelle*.[19]

His plan at least seems clear enough and he sketched on the back of his rough route map the way he intended to go.[20] He would return to Akcha and then make first for the dilapidated mudwalled town of Andkhoi, due west across the plain about 100 miles (160 kilometres) from Balkh. Thence he would head south about the same distance to Maimana before turning back north-westwards via Saripul to rejoin the others at Balkh. He expected to be away about three weeks. On the morning of 18 August 1825, Moorcroft's little party rode away from the sprawling walls of the ruined ancient town, through the green fringe of orchards and out into the tawny desert to the west.

Next day in distant Calcutta, a small group of his fellow countrymen sitting round a large table in the ornate Council chamber came to a decision. None of them was known to Moorcroft personally but each agreed 'that Mr Moorcroft be informed that he will be considered to have vacated his situation of Superintendent of the Stud in the event of his failing to return . . . within a reasonable period' and a letter to that effect was despatched.[21] But Mr Moorcroft never returned – not even to his waiting friends at Balkh.

The last few days are shrouded in mystery. He seems to have reached Andkhoi safely. It was a notoriously unattractive place in summer – a local Persian proverb called it 'a real hell' on account of its 'bitter salt water, scorching sand, venomous flies and scorpions'.[22] 'There,' according to one circumstantial account, 'he felt the symptoms of a fever gaining on him, but he wrote to one of his Indian friends, full of hope that the medicines he had taken to remove them, would be effectual.'[23] The source is dubious but it sounds like Moorcroft's optimism. This time the little *hakimbashi* was wrong. His already weakened body no longer responded even to his iron will, and the fever gained on him remorselessly. Three days later, apparently on 27 August 1825,[24] even his stout heart could take no more and the tortured, feverish body at last lay still. William Moorcroft was dead.

At least that is what everybody thought.

Twenty years later, and 2000 miles (3200 kilometres) away across the ranges to the south-east, two Lazarist priests from the French mission at Pekin reached Lhasa. Their somewhat optimistic hope was to convert the Dalai Lama and his people to Roman Catholicism. As soon as they arrived, Fathers Huc and Gabet faced close and suspicious questioning from the Tibetan authorities on the subject of maps. Why maps they asked? Their interrogator explained.

Maps are feared in this country – extremely feared indeed; especially since the affair of a certain Englishman named Moorcroft who introduced himself into Lha-Ssa, under the pretence of being a Cashmerian. After a sojourn there of twelve years, he departed; but he was murdered on his way to Ladak. Amongst his effects they found a numerous collection of maps and plans which he had drawn during his stay at Lha-Ssa.[25]

Huc and Gabet had never heard of Moorcroft. Shortly afterwards they met and quizzed a Kashmiri called Nisan who said that he had arrived at Lhasa with Moorcroft in 1826 and was his servant during his twelve-year stay at the Tibetan capital. Nisan said he never doubted that his master, who spoke fluent Persian and dressed and behaved as a Muslim, was anything but the Kashmiri he claimed to be. He:

> had purchased a few herds of goats and oxen, which he had confided to the care of some Thibetian shepherds, who dwelt in the gorges of the mountains, about Lha-Ssa. Under the pretext of inspecting his herds, the feigned Mussulman went freely about the country, making drawings and preparing his geographical charts. It is said that never having learnt the Thibetian language, he abstained from holding direct communication with the people of the country.

It was only after his murder that the Tibetan authorities discovered from his maps, charts and papers that the *soi-distant* Kashmiri was an Englishman named Moorcroft. Many other witnesses, some of them of high rank, confirmed the essentials of this story but Nisan added one tantalizing extra piece of information. Before Moorcroft set out on his long journey to Ladakh, he:

> had given him a note, telling him to show it to the inhabitants of Calcutta, if he ever went to that city, and that it would suffice to make his fortune. It was doubtless a letter of recommendation. The seizure of the effects of Moorcroft created such a disturbance in Thibet, that Nisan, afraid of being compromised, destroyed his letter of recommendation. He told us himself that this note was written in characters exactly similar to ours.

There is nothing inherently impossible in this curious story.[26] Indeed there is much superficially to endorse it. The chronology is right, the pasture farming fits Moorcroft's plans for his retirement, he had long been interested in opening a trade link with Lhasa, he was certainly a frequent writer of letters of recommendation and testimonials, and he had friends in Calcutta. Besides, none of Moorcroft's deliberately small entourage at Andkhoi is recorded as having witnessed his death, and the body which was carried in the summer heat back to Balkh after some delay would have been quite unrecognizable. In any case, Trebeck by then was too ill himself to face the unpleasant task of examining it.[27] It could have been anybody. Moreover if Moorcroft were planning to fake his own death and slip away into oblivion, then this might explain the cryptic reference to the individual duties he had to perform and the puzzling insistence on only a handful of servants to accompany him into the desert on what he admitted to be a dangerous journey.

Why then would he plan such a thing? He was certainly a sensitive man. Perhaps the ultimate realization at Andkhoi that there were no fine horses to be had, and that his great journey had failed to open either the markets of Central Asia or the eyes of his masters at Calcutta, persuaded him that he simply could not face the I-told-you-so's of his many carping critics in Calcutta and the near certainty of professional disgrace. It is even possible that he was so unnerved by the dangers facing his party at the hands of Murad Beg, or the other robbers along the way, that he decided to cut and run for it, in disguise and alone. After such a gross betrayal there would indeed be little choice but a self-imposed exile in some remote spot beyond the reach of his compatriots. Where better to hide than on the far side of the Himalayas in a country closed to Europeans?

So far, so good, but the doubts are already beginning to clamour for attention. The notion that Moorcroft, dogged and courageous to a fault, would run away from anything is preposterous. He had already come to terms with the possibility of the ostensible failure of his mission and, in any case, his sense of obligation to his employers, not to speak of that to his friends, servants and young family, was far too sharp to consider abandoning them all and stealing away like a thief in the night. Besides, as he had often stated, the mission had not failed. He had acquired some good horses and was still hopeful of getting more. Even without any horses at all, Moorcroft believed he had gained priceless and unique information which he intended to make available to his government and his countrymen, before resigning his post at the stud and embarking on his great rural improvement project in the Himalayas. For that too he needed resources and approvals only available in Calcutta. Only temporary insanity, perhaps under the influence of high fever, could account for actions so utterly inconsistent with Moorcroft's character, his record, and everything he stood for.

It is unlikely, but even if one allows for a moment the possibility, some formidable difficulties still remain. A faked death and a substitute body would require the collusion of others; secrets like that, in a small desert community in northern Afghanistan, would have been almost impossible to keep. There was never any doubt among those who were close to events, either then or later, that Moorcroft had become ill of fever and died. The confident allegations of murder or violence came later and from more distant and unreliable sources. Even if, against all probability, Moorcroft had succeeded in faking his own death and buying total silence from those who helped him to do it, he still had to cross nearly 2000 miles (3200 kilometres) of difficult terrain, in much of which he was well known, without detection. It would not have been easy. In any case, the man believed to be Moorcroft at Lhasa is not so much like Moorcroft as appears at first sight. There is clear evidence that Moorcroft did not speak Persian fluently as this man did,[28] and he certainly did not speak it well enough to persuade other Kashmiris that he was one of them. Any Kashmiri would be familiar with one of the other local languages besides Persian. Moorcroft was not. Nor did he have any cartographical or artistic skill, always leaving that work to others like Hearsey or Trebeck. Finally, all the evidence of his long life suggests that he would have been constitutionally incapable of keeping aloof from the Tibetans at Lhasa and of not acquiring some knowledge of their language, as the mysterious figure is said to have done for twelve years. Whoever it was, it can hardly have been William Moorcroft.

Why then were the Tibetans so convinced that it was? Not presumably because of the paper evidence since, as Huc and Gabet make clear, nobody in Lhasa could read English or even distinguish between a printed and a manuscript map.[29] The evidence was never shown to the two missionaries. As for the alleged letter of recommendation which Nisan destroyed but could not read, the only positive assertion about it was that it seemed to be in Roman script. The Tibetans, in other words, could only assume the identity of the mysterious owner of the indecipherable maps and papers. Moorcroft was the most likely candidate simply because he was well known by reputation, both to the Tibetan authorities and to the Kashmiri traders at Lhasa. He had entered Tibet illegally in 1812 and threatened or tried to do so in 1819, 1820, 1821 and 1822. If the maps and papers were indisputably his, as the Tibetans believed and as is certainly possible, then the most likely explanation is that the mysterious stranger was one of Moorcroft's Kashmiri servants (and he had several), who survived the death of his master and escaped with some of his papers and maps and even perhaps with a letter of recommendation. After all, the extraordinary traveller and freebooter Alexander Gardiner met just such a man in 1830, somewhere north of Kunduz.[30]

The haunting possibility that Moorcroft himself may, somehow, have cheated the fate which befell the rest of his party in northern Afghanistan, and lived out a lonely old age in the forbidden city of Lhasa until, a septuagenarian and presumably homeward bound at last, he was robbed and murdered somewhere near the empty sacred lake of Manasarowar, must be abandoned. The great weight of evidence and of probability is against it.[31]

On 6 September 1825 Trebeck wrote on a scrap of paper, 'Mr. M died August 27'.[32] Trebeck was a very sick man himself by then but he saw no reason to doubt the truth of what he wrote. Nor need we.

24 EPILOGUE AND CONCLUSION

WHILE MOORCROFT RESTED at last in his lonely grave at Balkh, his death set in motion 'a strange succession of casualties',[1] betrayals and disappointments which overwhelmed the remainder of his party and did much to obscure his own achievements as well. The speed with which the rest of his caravan fell into demoralized disarray speaks volumes for Moorcroft's qualities as a leader. His body, the servants, his nine horses and the other goods with him when he died were all immediately impounded at Andkhoi. It was only with considerable difficulty that Mir Wazir Ahmad was able to negotiate for their release and return, with the now almost unrecognizable corpse of Moorcroft on a camel, to Balkh. The Jews there refused him burial in their sepulchre, the Muslims denied him a marked grave anywhere else. In the end he was buried unceremoniously beneath a dilapidated wall, beside a watercourse, some-where outside the crumbling walls of the ancient city.[2]

By then both Trebeck and Guthrie were already seriously ill – either from fever, slow poison, or both. On 6 September, however, Trebeck managed to write a letter to Captain Wade, the nearest British representative, 700 miles (1120 kilometres) away at Ludhiana, announcing Moorcroft's death.[3] On the same day he noted on a scrap of paper the date of that death.[4] Guthrie was the next to go and was buried beside his master. In the meantime Askar Ali, having failed to get anything at Kunduz except the sternest warnings from Atma Ram of what would happen to them if they dared to re-enter Murad Beg's territories, himself fell ill at Mazar and lay there helpless for nearly a fortnight. When Trebeck heard this, he sent a man to bring Askar Ali back to Balkh on horseback. There the two sick men wept together over the loss of their companions and debated what they should do next. Trebeck was determined to remove the whole party from Balkh, before its notorious summer fevers destroyed them all. Against the advice of a number of people, including Askar Ali himself, they moved a few miles across the desert to Mazar, under a promise of good treatment from its chief. That was accomplished without mishap but they got no further. Trebeck's declining health and the inability of Wazir Ahmad, Askar Ali and Ghulam Hyder Khan to agree on a feasible course of action, kept them helplessly pinned at that desolate spot for the next three or four months.

Trebeck's optimism about a speedy return to Kabul soon evaporated. Later British visitors vied with one another to invest his unhappy final weeks with the sort of romantic melancholy Trebeck himself had been rather inclined to adopt in happier days.[5] A more authentic guide to his mood is probably to be found in the journal of the first of his countrymen to follow him to that desolate spot. Only three years later, and at the same time of the year, Edward Stirling was writing as follows:[6]

> I am now become subject to the most grievous and preying anxiety . . . surrounded by a race whose only motive of action is to cheat and deceive . . . in a country which is without a government, unsettled and subject to revolution . . . removed from the sea coast and navigable rivers more than a thousand miles [1600 kilometres], near in the centre of Asia.

Under the influence of thoughts like these, Trebeck seems to have become completely demoralized. Apparently he even virtually gave away the precious pearls which alone might have purchased their freedom.[7] Then, just before his death, he assigned the remaining property under oath to Wazir Ahmad, for onward transmission to Calcutta.

No sooner was Trebeck dead, probably in early December, than the chief of Mazar reneged on his promise of safe conduct.[8] He seized not only all the goods and the 100 or so horses, but some of the men too. Ghulam Hyder Khan was one of those imprisoned for a time at Mazar. Just how and when they all finally made their escape is not clear, but their troubles had scarcely begun. Ghulam Hyder Khan, and those with him at the back of the caravan, were robbed by Hazaras and taken back to Maimana to be sold into slavery. Only renewed efforts by Askar Ali secured their release and they eventually reached Kabul by the roundabout road through Herat and Kandahar. It was not until 1827, after an absence of nearly eight years, that grizzled old Ghulam returned, destitute and alone, to his family at Bareilly and told his remarkable story to his old master, Hearsey.[9] Wazir Ahmad was luckier. He reached Kabul in safety with a portion of the money and some of the horses in mid-December 1825. Then he was robbed twice before reaching Peshawar.

The first rumours of these multiple disasters to reach India were inspired by the earlier death of Izzat-Allah and soon denied.[10] Then, in late October, more circumstantial reports of Moorcroft's death reached his friend Metcalfe at Delhi and hard on their heels came confirmatory stories by way of Amritsar.[11] However, it was not until Trebeck's letter reached Wade at Ludhiana on about 11 December, that the story was confirmed beyond all doubt.[12] Later news of the deaths of Guthrie and Trebeck and the fate of the rest of the party reached Wade in a letter written on 19 December, just after Wazir Ahmad's safe arrival at Kabul. The writer was Guru Das Singh, a Punjabi banker who was doing his anxious best to round up the scattered party and prevent further robbery by the authorities at Kabul. Please, he pleaded, send somebody to help at once.[13]

The Indian government seems to have been more interested in recovering the property than the people.[14] It neither washed its hands of the whole affair, as one writer has it, nor did it make continued efforts over the ensuing years to solve the mystery, as stated by another.[15] Although no action was taken on the crazy suggestion of one Moorcroft well-wisher to send the innocent Csoma de Körös into Afghanistan, a Muslim agent was sent by the authorities to Kabul and returned in March 1827 with some horses and other goods.[16] At Moorcroft's request, and doubtless with Metcalfe's active support, a pension was paid to the faithful Izzat-Allah's eldest son and, after his death, to his son.[17] Whether any of the other servants were treated as generously seems unlikely.

The really determined efforts seem to have come from Moorcroft's friends, and from none more than John Palmer in Calcutta. He personally broke the news to Trebeck's nearly impoverished father and then set about salvaging what he could from the wreckage for him, for Purree Khanum, and for the children. He feared at first that they might be in considerable distress.[18] Despite the care with which Moorcroft had made his will and the insurance policy he had taken out on Purree Khanum's life,[19] he had lost a great deal of money earlier, through faulty investments and the dishonesty of his agent.[20] Most of the rest of his savings had been consumed by the great journey. There remained about 150,000 rupees in company stock, but about a third of this was owed to Palmer for services rendered (not including the 60,000 rupees which had been invested in Moorcroft's caravan and certain other claims against the estate).[21] To make things worse, it looked for a time as though the government did not intend to pay the arrears of Moorcroft's suspended salary.[22] Most alarming of all, Moorcroft's executor and former friend, John Laing up at Allahabad, persistently refused to answer Palmer's letters. His behaviour became so suspicious that Palmer and his friends were eventually driven to threaten legal action.[23] Eventually Laing swore the executor's oath and was granted probate in October 1826.[24] Early the following year he came down to Calcutta and met Palmer over dinner to discuss the accounts.[25] By then things were looking more hopeful. The government had belatedly agreed to pay 139,000 rupees arrears of salary and, when this was eventually done two years later, the estate had a healthy balance of at least 240,000 rupees.[26] It looked at last as though Moorcroft's dependents would be adequately provided for.

Anne, of course, was already in London in the care of George Saunders. She was soon entirely English, as though her Hindi and her French had never been.[27] Richard was still with his mother at Pusa.[28] While in the toils of Murad Beg at Kunduz, Moorcroft had sent back instructions that, in the event of his death, the little boy was to be sent to join his sister.[29] He had earlier directed that Richard was to be educated at Harrow or Westminster and then apprenticed as a surgeon.[30] So, in the autumn of 1826, de l'Étang brought the little 6-year-old lad down to Calcutta where he seems to have charmed the Palmer household as much as his father had done earlier. He was shipped home in a vessel commanded by de l'Étang's son-in-law and, in due course, was reunited with his sister in Saunders' bachelor house in Oxford Street.[31]

It was fortunate that Moorcroft had added a codicil to his will, making

Saunders not only guardian of his children but also a joint executor of his will.[32] Despite this, and endless private and legal letters to the slippery Laing, Saunders was forced to bring the children up entirely at his own expense, until he discovered that Moorcroft still owned property in London which he was able to sell for their benefit.[33] There was no question of Richard attending one of the great public schools. He went instead to a humbler academy in Sloane Square after which, as his father had wished, he was apprenticed to a surgeon. The experiment was not a success. In June 1835 Saunders therefore obtained for him a cadetship in the Madras army.[34] A month later they were both in All Souls, Langham Place, for the wedding of Anne to one Captain George St Barbe Brown of the Bombay Native Infantry.[35] The faithful Saunders was by then in his mid-seventies and must have felt strangely bereft when, later that year, his two charges left England to return to the land of their birth. He died four years later. To the end he received not a penny from Laing.

Early in 1836, as soon as Captain Brown reached India with his young bride, he got in touch with Laing, who was by then collector of customs at Agra. He was also, incidentally, spending large sums of money on his collection of antique coins.[36] Brown's letter was not very polite. He told Laing to settle his debts at once and threatened to come to Agra to ensure that he did so. Laing sent a polite acknowledgement in return, but otherwise appears to have said and done nothing. When Brown found it impossible after all to get up to Agra, he caused Laing the maximum possible embarrassment by placing the whole complaint on the official record.[37] It seems to have goaded Laing into action at last. Rather ominously perhaps, he promptly resigned from government service.[38] He also eventually submitted some rather unsatisfactory accounts to explain, or explain away, his administration of Moorcroft's estate.[39] In the end the children probably got at least some of their money. Richard served with distinction in the first Afghan war and afterwards had embarked on a promising career in the Madras army when ill health forced him to take a series of extended leaves. He died, homeward bound, at Alexandria in the spring of 1855.[40] Although he was only 35, he apparently had substantial sums of money invested.[41] One hopes that Anne too had financial security, for she was by then already a widow. George Brown died just a few weeks before her 31st birthday, in December 1847.[42]

Flotsam from the shipwreck of Moorcroft's great caravan continued, for many years, to bob up all across that great inner Asian sea of mountain and desert. The sportsman-traveller, Godfrey Vigne, met one of Moorcroft's servants at Ghazni in 1836; the explorer, Captain Alexander Cunningham, retrieved some interesting correspondence concerning his death from another at Lucknow; and the buccaneering Alexander Gardiner (as has already been mentioned) came across yet a third, carrying a map and compass belonging to Moorcroft, somewhere north of Kunduz, in July 1836.[43] The Bengal civil servant, Edward Stirling, was the first Englishman after Moorcroft's death to pass through northern Afghanistan, in the winter of 1828. Alone and fearful, he had Moorcroft's death very much on his mind. Beyond noting that some of Moorcroft's horses were still at Mazar, he learned nothing. At Kabul, however, he encountered Askar Ali and obtained from him a most valuable and authentic account of the final weeks before and after Moorcroft's death, which has only recently been rediscovered in London.[44]

Next on the scene, in 1831, was the splendidly eccentric Revd Joseph Wolff. He so closely resembled Moorcroft that in Bokhara and elsewhere it was firmly believed, notwithstanding his emphatic denials, that he was a relative come to discover what had happened. Wolff confirmed that some of Moorcroft's property was at Balkh, but that the bulk of it was in the hands of the governor of Mazar, who had sworn in consequence to kill any European who came within his reach. Later, at Kabul, Wolff met Lieutenant Alexander Burnes, surgeon James Gerard and Mohan Lal all heading north on their own journey to Bokhara.[45] At Mazar Mohan Lal actually stayed in the house in which Trebeck died and met the man who attended him at the end.[46] A week or so later, under a bright moon just before midnight on 12 June 1832, Burnes and Gerard were the first and the only European travellers to see the rough graves in which Moorcroft and Guthrie lay buried side by side.[47] Like all the others, they were too concerned to avoid the same fate themselves to enquire very closely into the question of the sequestered property.

However, five years later when Burnes went to Afghanistan as an official envoy of the Indian government, it was a very different story. While he and his fellow officers were at Kabul in the winter of 1837, word was received from Murad Beg requesting the help of a doctor to treat his brother's blindness. After promises of safe conduct, Dr Percival Lord and Lieutenant John Wood set out together across the Hindu Kush, and reached Kunduz in December 1837. By then, the once fearsome Murad Beg was thirteen years older and thirteen years mellower than when Moorcroft had crossed his path. Lord thought him 'quite a plain, good old man'.[48] He certainly seems to have lost his suspicion of Feringis. Although Lord was unable to do anything for his blind brother, Murad Beg gave Wood permission to make his epic solo midwinter exploration to the sources of the Oxus.[49] He also ordered the chief at Mazar to part with all of Moorcroft's papers still in his possession. The result was an interesting haul of what was left of Moorcroft's extensive library of books, together with some important maps, accounts and loose papers dating from the time of his death. In due course all of this material found its way to the Asiatic Society in Calcutta.[50] It all seems to have disappeared but at least one of the printed books, heavily annotated by Moorcroft, has turned up in Tokyo.[51]

Perhaps the most telling evidence of Murad Beg's new benevolence was the ready permission he granted both Lord and Wood to visit Taliqan to pay their respects to the *pirzada* who had saved Moorcroft's life. Lord has left an amusing tongue-in-cheek account of his interview with the old man which ends:

Before going away he again expressed his astonishment at our being acquainted with what he had done for Moorcroft. 'Is it really a fact,' said he, 'that this is known in Firingestan?' 'Wulla bella', said I, 'the very children take the name of Syud

Mahomed Kusim, the friend of the Firingees'. He did not attempt to conceal his satisfaction. 'God is great!', said he; 'Feel my pulse' . . . said I, 'what strength and firmness! If it please God, one half your life is not yet passed.' We stroked our beards, said a 'fatha', and the old man departed.[52]

In the years that followed, other travellers beyond the frontiers encountered fugitive echoes of the great journey and were shown Moorcroft's fading testimonials. In 1835 the eccentric Scotsman, Dr Henderson, travelling alone in disguise and practically penniless, arrived in Ladakh by the same route as Moorcroft, and at the same time as the Sikh invasion which Moorcroft had foreseen and striven so hard to avert. The Ladakhis believed at first that he had come just in time to save them with the ratification of Moorcroft's treaty of protection. Convinced by Henderson's genuine astonishment when shown the document, they nevertheless used his visit in a way Moorcroft would thoroughly have approved. They pretended that Henderson was an official British representative and thereby brought the Sikh invasion to a halt for three months. Exactly as in the Moorcroft case, the Sikhs made anxious enquiries of the British and the bubble was only pricked when the Indian government was forced to disavow Henderson.[53] At Leh he discovered that Moorcroft's garden was still being lovingly tended and he heard that a flock of his sheep was still being grazed for him, until he should return to reclaim them.[54] In Kashmir, at about the same time, Vigne discovered the stone that Moorcroft had erected over the tomb of Mirza Haidar.[55] Far away in northern Afghanistan the Hungarian traveller, Arminius Vambéry, met a man at Andkhoi in 1863 who plainly remembered Moorcroft's death in his uncle's house, nearly half a century before.[56] Practically all of these later travellers reported the very high regard for Moorcroft which still existed among the people whose paths he crossed.

Whether his memory would be preserved so freshly among his own people and beyond the lifetime of those who knew him, would depend very largely on the fate of his surviving papers and the use that would be made of them. Moorcroft was always punctiliously insistent that, if anything happened to him, the government would have a prior 'right to whatever information may have been obtained from the labor of their servant'. To this he added the hope 'that a plain record may be given of what I have done for the benefit of the public.'[57]

There was certainly no lack of people willing to attempt the task. Dr Abel, physician to the governor-general, was badgering for permission to publish while Moorcroft was still alive.[58] A stronger claimant was the Sanskritist Henry Colebrooke, who had published the 1816 account of Moorcroft's Tibetan journey in association with his young protégé at the Asiatic Society, Horace Wilson.[59] As soon as he heard of Moorcroft's death, he wrote to Wilson from England, asking for the papers to be sent home so that he could prepare an edition. Eighteen months later he repeated the request, this time more forcefully.[60] Wilson would have received that letter in the spring of 1828. By then, the government had agreed to pay Moorcroft's suspended salary up to the date of his death, so the accumulated travel papers were technically government property.

Ever since the beginning of the journey, Moorcroft had been sending batches of his letterbooks and journals back to his friend Captain Murray for safekeeping. The last consignment was sent from Peshawar in the spring of 1824. It was this collection of some twenty volumes, together with Trebeck's fieldbooks, which passed into the ownership of the government and, after a period of neglect, was deposited by them with the Asiatic Society in the 1830s. It covered, however, only the journey up to the departure from Kashmir in the late summer of 1823. Efforts to recover the rest, as has been seen, were put in hand by Palmer and the Indian government, through Claude Wade at Ludhiana and William Fraser at Delhi, as soon as Moorcroft's death was confirmed. Moorcroft had been making considerable efforts to preserve these later papers in the event of his own death at Kunduz. Many of them seem to have escaped the clutches of the authorities at Mazar and were probably among the property salvaged by Guru Das Singh at Kabul and brought back to India in the spring of 1827. Fraser certainly seems to have had the bulk of the later material in his possession at Delhi by 1828 or 1829. There, for some years, it remained.[61]

Interest in the Moorcroft papers in the early 1830s did not abate.[62] In 1830, the Royal Geographical Society was encouraged by a few of its members to obtain some of Moorcroft's official papers from the East India Company in London. The very first number of its new journal began to publish some of them, edited by Mountstuart Elphinstone.[63] That was something, but it was no substitute for a proper account of the great journey and erroneous ideas about it were already rife.[64] In India, Trebeck's younger brother, Charles, began to make copies of some of the material in Fraser's possession[65] and, early in 1835, Fraser himself offered it all to the Asiatic Society, provided only that the material was published for the sole benefit of Moorcroft's surviving family.[66] Shortly afterwards he was assassinated.

By then the earlier papers, together with papers and drawings by Trebeck, were already back in England and in the hands of the lately retired secretary of the Asiatic Society of Bengal, Horace Wilson.[67] He had returned to Britain in 1833 to become Professor of Sanskrit at Oxford and the papers followed him to England shortly afterwards. Wilson's reputation for scholarship and probity has had a mauling recently at the hands of two American scholars. They believe that he sat on Moorcroft's papers, seeing the opportunity they offered for yet another book on the cheap to swell his growing reputation, and that he deliberately denied them to other would-be editors like Colebrooke.[68] Wilson has plenty to answer for but this accusation at least does not stick. As soon as the papers were in his possession, he approached the doyen of travel publishers, John Murray. That was in January 1834. The Asiatic Society in Calcutta was willing to underwrite the costs of publication in return for a guaranteed forty copies of the published work. Wilson would act as editor. No agreement was signed and Wilson nagged Murray more than once during the ensuing year,[69] but without waiting for a formal contract, he pressed on with the work. After what he called 'considerable labour', he had a manuscript ready by the end of 1835.[70] That first version, presumably, must have ended rather unsatisfactorily with Moorcroft's arrival in Peshawar.

The seven missing journals and miscellaneous papers covering the remaining two years of his journey, which had been in Fraser's possession, were eventually sent home by his executors and reached Wilson at the end of 1836. Among them, Wilson was gratified to find a letter written by Moorcroft at Kunduz which actually named him as the man Moorcroft wished to be his posthumous editor.[71] Using this new material, he added five more chapters taking the story up to the arrival at Bokhara, completed his introduction in September 1837, and 750 copies of the two volumes were printed almost at once.[72] The only copy of this unpublished edition known to have survived is dated 1838,[73] although it must have been ready before the end of 1837 because a review of it appeared in January 1838, and dated it 1837.[74] Yet another notice dated it 1839.[75] Whatever the date, several copies of this pre-publication edition were in circulation at that time or soon afterwards.[76] Up to this point at least, Wilson cannot really be faulted.

And yet the book, complete with a new title-page and a fine map by John Arrowsmith, did not go on public sale for another three years. During the interval, Wilson urged haste on the publishers and, he in turn, was being pressed by Charles Trebeck and others.[77] The only reason ever given for the delay was a hold-up in the production of the map.[78] Yet it finally destroyed whatever lingering hopes there still were that the book would do belated justice to Moorcroft's memory and achievement. The fact is that, by 1841, his journey was old hat. Not only had it taken place nearly twenty years before, but others had done it since and rushed successfully into print. Joseph Wolff was the first to follow Moorcroft to Bokhara, but it was Alexander 'Bokhara' Burnes who got all the credit and publicity for the journey. The English edition of his much translated three volume travelogue sold out on publication day early in 1834, and turned its young author into an international celebrity overnight.[79] Most of the still remaining novelties in Moorcroft's journey were pre-empted by other authors in the 1830s like Conolly, Jacquemont and Vigne. Then, in the three years that Wilson's edition lay in Murray's warehouse, gathering dust and waiting for its map, the British invasion of Afghanistan led to a host of works to meet public curiosity about the campaign and the still novel country in which it took place.

When Moorcroft's *Travels* finally made their belated appearance in 1841 they had been well and truly scooped. Several of the reviewers were quick to point this out[80] and, not surprisingly, sales were disappointing. It took many years to dispose of 700 copies, which is fewer than the account of Burnes' much less remarkable journey sold on its first day. To cap everything, no sooner had Moorcroft's book appeared, than the horror stories which accompanied the Afghan disasters in the winter of 1841–2 diverted all attention. Burnes became an assiduously promoted martyr,[81] and the man who truly deserved the nickname 'Bokhara' was swept into obscurity. Even the Asiatic Society of

Bengal only received eight of the forty copies it had been promised by Wilson, although he kept twelve for himself.[82]

Wilson cannot be blamed for the tardy appearance of the Moorcroft *Travels*, but for the content of the book he certainly can. He as good as admitted, in his introduction, that the book was uninteresting and many of the reviewers thought so too. Wilson blamed Moorcroft.[83] Yet it is hard to avoid the feeling that the frenetic Wilson – Oxford professor, examiner at Haileybury, librarian of the East India Company, successful author, scholar and linguist, 'the most fully occupied man in London'[84] – very quickly became bored with the 'considerable labour' Moorcroft's verbose and disordered papers set him. Instead of doing the job properly, and making use of the often lively private letters and the official correspondence, he confined himself almost exclusively to the more accessible, but often less revealing, journals. Even from them he rigorously pruned the personal, the political, the humorous and the salacious, and he made some other damaging decisions, such as that of omitting all the interesting material covering the stay in Bokhara. The only credible explanation is that he wanted to bring the whole time-consuming task to a close as quickly as possible. It is not easy to make Moorcroft dull, but Wilson managed it. His approach was always that of the scholar, less concerned with the entertaining travelogue, which he admitted that public taste demanded,[85] than with the accumulation of accurate information.

At least that is how it has always looked until recently. However, as soon as modern scholars began to penetrate behind Wilson's fact-laden text to the Moorcroftian originals, the real nature of Wilson's failure became horrifyingly apparent. His text was revealed as a slipshod and inaccurate paraphrase, often introducing entirely unnecessary alterations to the sense of the originals and with serious and misleading omissions.[86] The charge is not that he departed from Moorcroft's own language. Moorcroft had left emphatic instructions on that point, insisting with a fierce underlining '*that my own language may not scrupulously be preserved*'.[87] What is unforgivable is that Wilson has so often not scrupulously preserved the sense either. He explicitly asserted quite the contrary. Indeed he also asserted that if he had not done Moorcroft's editing, it would not have been done at all.[88] Both assertions are demonstrably untrue. The fact is that Wilson, like Laing, was unworthy of the trust that Moorcroft gave him. His edition, to use the words of one hostile reviewer in 1844,[89] is 'a thing of shreds and patches', quite unworthy as a memorial to one of the most remarkable extended travel journeys of modern history. A handful of men, at the time and since, who knew at first hand the terrain and the obstacles Moorcroft and his unwieldy caravan had surmounted, recognized the accuracy of his observations, marvelled, and saluted the uniqueness of the achievement. He was indeed the father of modern exploration in the great area he covered and yet few have ever heard of him today. Wilson more than once laments the neglect.[90] He must carry some share of the blame for it although not, of course, for all.

Wilson is certainly not to blame for the quite inexplicable errors of fact which have accumulated round Moorcroft since then. He is repeatedly said to have gone where he never went and to have gone where he did go, but at the wrong time.[91] Even his names are changed.[92] With unconscious humour, one modern author asserts that 'one of the great names of early nineteenth-century trans-Himalayan exploration is Thomas Moorcroft' and goes on to state seven more errors about him on the next page.[93] Even more remarkable, another makes eleven errors of fact about him on one page and, on the next, reproduces as an illustration of Moorcroft's journal, one of Charles Trebeck's transcripts from his brother's notebook.[94] Here too the contrast with the much more modest achievements of 'Bokhara' Burnes is striking.

That contrast also suggests other reasons for Moorcroft's obscurity as a traveller. Burnes was a brilliant self-publicist with an easy and eminently readable prose style which made him an instant best seller. Moorcroft was the world's worst on paper, painfully hammering out his ponderous prose, draft upon draft. Burnes lived long enough to exploit his own success. Moorcroft died obscurely on his travels, and with nobody to turn his magnificent failure into a legend, as in the case of Scott or Livingstone. Burnes and Moorcroft were both tough and hyperactive but Burnes focused his energies like a lens on the single-minded advancement of his own career and rose dizzily within the official machine to a knighthood and high office at a tender age. In contrast, one of the things about Moorcroft as a traveller is his great age.[95] Unlike that of Burnes, his genius was a multi-faceted prism, scattering light in all directions. He was too restless and too much of a lateral thinker to confine his activities very long to the compartments required for more orthodox success. The world tends to value specialist achievement. Moorcroft was a brilliant generalist with a startling number of 'firsts' in a surprising range of fields. Yet, paradoxically, his papers are a treasure-trove for specialists – although a nightmare for a biographer. Even the 'retirement' he lovingly planned, and never attained, would have been simply the latest of his broad-fronted assaults on the unknown in the cause of improvement. No wonder his more cautious and conventional colleagues, even his wondering friends,[96] confronting the unknown in him, tended to regard him as an 'enthusiast' – a wild and over-ardent chaser after shadows. This impression was strengthened because Moorcroft was a man well in advance of his time. So often he glimpsed and elaborated the possibilities of the future before his contemporaries, or events, were ready for them. Hindsight normally enables the historian to be condescending. In Moorcroft's case it is his vindication. The judgements of Alexander Burnes, on the other hand, have not worn well although, to his envious peers, his high-flying timing must have seemed well-nigh faultless.

All this provides clues to explain, not only the undeserved shadow which fell upon Moorcroft's record as traveller and explorer, but the wider neglect of his life and achievements. In his native Lancashire he has been almost totally forgotten.[97] Elsewhere, only the barest outline has remained on record. Wilson once described himself as Moorcroft's biographer, but he was nothing of the sort.[98] His editorial introduction to the *Travels* contains no more than some sketchy, though invaluable, biographical clues. These, compressed in a number of international biographical dictionaries,[99] and later usefully amplified in the 1894 *Dictionary of National Biography*, contained practically all that was known about Moorcroft until well into the twentieth century.[100] As has been seen, the various efforts of his contemporaries, in England and India, to give him the memorial they felt he deserved, all foundered.[101] Those few who came later, and who knew or discovered something of the man, usually acknowledged his importance, lamented the general ignorance, and passed on. There was no biography, no portrait and no public monument, beyond the little marble plaque erected later by an unknown admirer at Lahore. The great mass of Moorcroft's personal documents which survived the *débâcle* in Afghanistan, together with his voluminous official correspondence, slumbered undisturbed in the measureless archives of the old India Office in Whitehall.

In the 1920s, Professor H. W. C. Davis made a lightning raid upon the private papers while researching his brilliant Raleigh Lecture of 1926. He concluded that Moorcroft was really the earliest British player of the Great Game, which Britain and Russia played for supremacy in Central Asia in the nineteenth century and beyond.[102] At about the same time, the veteran and veterinary historian, Sir Frederick Smith, examined them and some of the official records in support of his equally uncontestable contention that Moorcroft was one of the most important pioneers of modern scientific veterinary medicine. He was, Smith came to believe, 'our only gigantic genius'. Indeed Smith became so excited by what he found, that he began feverishly accumulating material and looking forward 'to the day when I can throw myself into his life and work'.[103] That was in October 1928. Nine months later he was dead. Nevertheless Smith's great survey of early British veterinary literature undoubtedly began the restoration of Moorcroft to his rightful place as one of the three 'great pioneers of the 19th century to whom the veterinary profession will ever be indebted'. Those words Smith caused to be set upon a brass plate which he presented to the Royal College of Veterinary Surgeons. There is a certain ironic and perhaps symbolic significance in the fact that Moorcroft's dates are given wrongly and that the plate is placed where nobody can see it. Error and neglect are precisely the two most striking features of his treatment at the hands of posterity in the century and a half since his lonely death. Only very recently have there been signs of wider recognition that the record should at last be set right.[104]

What then by way of a conclusion? Plainly he was not a genius, not a man capable of imposing himself upon an age and changing its direction. He was neither single-minded enough, nor lucky enough, to carve for himself the kind of immortality achieved by his great contemporaries, Pitt, Wellington and Nelson (although like them he served his country and in some ways died for it). Nevertheless, it is impossible to make molehills of his mountains as the modern fashion in biography would seem to require. The heroic quality of the man and his stubborn achievements will not – cannot – be diminished. Perhaps his best epitaph was written by an unknown friend a year after he died.

The enterprising indefatigable Moorcroft is dead. He was the very best man that could have gone upon such exploratory and perilous errands as his were. He was, in his way, eminently gifted. Physician, artizan, horse-doctor, he knew a little of everything and most of what was most useful. Moreover, he was liberal, frank, open and courageous, just the man, in short, for the tribes amongst whom he travelled, and better suited than probably one individual in a thousand to raise our character for general intelligence and fellow feeling.[105]

At the India Office Library in London there is a letter bearing the breathtaking address 'W. Moorcroft Esq, Samarkand or Elsewhere'.[106] That any one should despatch a letter with such an address is remarkable enough. But it arrived, over 1000 rugged miles (1600 kilometres) away and beyond the greatest mountain range in the world. That ageing piece of paper is somehow a symbol, mute testimony to a paradox. The little man, whether at 'Samarkand or Elsewhere', was a giant.

Notes

The following summary references, used in conjunction with the list of sources, should be sufficient to locate the document or page from which the information has come. The prefix *IOL* followed by the call reference is used for all manuscript material at the India Office Library and Records, London, except in the following two cases:

1 References beginning with the letters A to G are to series in the *Moorcroft Collection* in the European Manuscripts and are followed by the volume number and the folio number or date of the document. There is a comprehensive guide to the collection in Kaye 881–962.

2 References beginning with the letter M are to the *Bengal Military Consultations* and are followed by the date of the consultation and number of the document. Information in this form will provide access to the *India Military Proceedings* at the National Archives of India, New Delhi. In both cases the handlists must be used to obtain a correct call reference to the volume concerned.

Introduction (pages ix–xiii)

1 Thompson vi.
2 G28/361.
3 Clemens I 2.
4 D238/74–6.

5 Enclosed in F37/53.
6 D246/50.
7 G28/141–5.

1 Lancashire Child, Liverpool Surgeon, 1767–88 (pages 1–13)

1 Variously from Bagley; E. Baines IV 235–82; Collins; Fishwick and Ditchfield II 23–43; Freeman, Rodgers and Kinvig 18–73; Padfield 1–63; Millward 13–52; Victoria III 261–85.
2 F. Baines LXXXIV 9 and 101; idem LXXXV 209.

3 Victoria IV 275.
4 *Lancs.* PR2886/5, 6, 12 and 13.
5 Ibid. PR2886/5.
6 D254/343–44.
7 *Lancs.* PR2886/6–7, 22–3.
8 Berry and Schofield.
9 Lawton.
10 Holt(1795) 180.

11   D254/343.
12   *Lancs.* DDLm Box 7, Bundle 3.
13   D250/100.
14   e.g. F38/21.5.1820/48; G28/105; D261/1; D266/19.
15   See n.1 above.
16   Holt(1794) 8–9.
17   *Lancs.* WCW/will 9.10.1790; D250/240.
18   Banks to Townely 15.8.1792, *Scarisbrick* DDSc 9/42.
19   *Scarisbrick* DDSc 19/41; Holt(1794) *passim*; *Transactions of the Society for the Encouragement of Arts, Manufactures and Commerce* XVII(1790) 230 and XIX(1801) 165.
20   Holt(1795) 167n; *Scarisbrick* DDSc 9/42.
21   G28/344.
22   Eccleston; Rollinson.
23   G28/334.
24   G28/344; C45/110–11.
25   G28/344 and 434; D262/16–17; D254/95.
26   G28/434 and 314; *Scarisbrick* DDSc 19/41 and 42/16–17; Add. MS 36,901/106, 176, 184, 187, 190 and 194.
27   *Lancs.* WCW/will 9.10.1790.
28   Paine, Moorcroft's stepfather, became Assist. Sec. to the Navigation Board at Dublin Castle on a salary of £450 a year, *Accounts and Papers* (1821) 234. There are letters from him in Add. MS 40,227/348 and 40,247/11; and F36/139.
29   *IOL* L/AG/34/29/43, 301 of Pt. 3; D262/44.
30   Bickerton and MacKenna 35–7.
31   *Ibid.* 45; *Liverpool* 614 INF 5/2.
32   D263/109; D250/93; *Hearsey* 34 and 86; Moorcroft (1816) 455 and 502.

33   The Liverpool material comes from Brooke; Chalkin; Corry; E. Baines IV 144–87; Hyde; Moss(1784) and (1797); Parkinson; Picton I; Anon(3); Taylor; Wallace; and Young(1770) III.
34   Parkinson 136.
35   Corry 173.
36   Enfield 54.
37   Bickerton and MacKenna 13.
38   *Liverpool* 614 INF 1/1, 2/1, 9/1, 10/4, 5/2; *Bickerton* 942 BIC 1/2, 7, and 8. The following information also comes from Bickerton and MacKenna 1–78; D'Arcy Power; and Murray.
39   Enfield 54.
40   J. Currie 6–7 and 238–9.
41   *Bickerton* 942 BIC 2/67; Boardman, entry under 'Baths'; W. Currie 217–19.
42   Williams.
43   Cartwright; Williams.
44   E113/53.
45   D254/120.
46   E113/53; D251/156.
47   Moorcroft's memories of him are G28/344–6 and G31/72.
48   Alanson 43.
49   Based on Bickerton and MacKenna 78.
50   *Bickerton* 942 BIC 8/174.
51   *Lancs.* WCW/will 9.10.1790.
52   Eccleston 75.
53   The following account comes from Moorcroft(1789).
54   Youatt(1857) 324.
55   D261/21.
56   Eccleston 73–5.
57   G28/314/52, cited Moorcroft and Trebeck I xx.
58   Blaine(1802) viii.
59   To Saunders 20.3.1822 D262/44.

2 VETERINARY STUDENT, LONDON AND FRANCE, 1788–92 (pages 14–24)

1   See Smithcors(1958) chaps. 6–8; F. Smith(1919–33) II and III.
2   Anon(1) 8.
3   G31/72.
4   On Hunter, see Palmer; Gray; Kobler; Pasmore (1976–8); Dobson.
5   Moorcroft and Trebeck xx–xxi cited from G28/314. Cf. Gray(1952) 115–16.
6   Anon(1) 5. See Pugh 19–25 and 39;

Veterinary Record 57 (1945) 612.

7   Eccleston 75–6.
8   Pugh 13–14.
9   Hours 42.
10 Prosser(1st 1790) 50. Cf. 125–6. The wording was corrected in the 2nd of 1790.
11 *RSA* Minutes 35, 28.10.1789; Greater London Council 489.
12 *RSA* Subscription Book 4.11.1789. In neither place was he a ratepayer, *Westminster*.
13 *Lancs.* DDSc 19/50, 27.12.1789. Moorcroft is not mentioned.
14 Anon(2); Maxwell; Young(1794) I; Rigby; Gifford.
15 Young(1794) I 2.
16 Andrews 11.
17 Remark in F37/53; G28/314/29.
18 M/13.11.1810/193 note 1.
19 Young(1794) *passim*.
20 Ibid. I 2.
21 D254/32–3.
22 The Lyons material is based on Garden; Charlety (1898) and (1903); Trénard; and Cobb(1975) Pt. 3 and (1972) chap. 2.
23 Cited Trénard 94.
24 Young(1794) I 275.
25 The veterinary school material comes from Arloing; Boitel; Hours.
26 Arloing 56.

27 Ibid. 60.
28 Young(1794) I 291.
29 *Lyons* Register 1790/46 no. 497.
30 Ibid.
31 D254/143, 149 and 151.
32 *Lyons* Register 1790/46 no. 497.
33 *Lyons Réglements pour les Écoles Royales Vétérinaires de France par C. Bourgelat* Titre IX Art. III.
34 Ibid. Titre IV Art. II.
35 Cobb(1975) 88–9.
36 *Lyons* Register 1790/46 no. 497.
37 C45/111.
38 G28/314/33 and see Valli.
39 *Palmer* C97/233; D262/44; D256/132.
40 D254/32–3; D265/18.
41 A. Smith II 295.
42 Described in Moorcroft(1792).
43 Boardman, entry under 'Hydatids'.
44 Moorcroft(1792) 27.
45 Ibid. 28.
46 F. Smith(1919–33) I 133 and 296. See also *Veterinary History* II(1981) 40–1.
47 Moorcroft(1792) 28.
48 M/13.11.1810/193 n. 1.
49 *Lancs.* DDSc 19/41.
50 M/13.11.1810/193 n.1; D253/2; D250/123; D/254/34ff.
51 Moorcroft(1792) 28.
52 Ibid. 33.

3 PRIVATE PRACTICE AND THE VETERINARY COLLEGE, 1792–1800 (pages 25–41)

1   The information on London comes variously from B. Adams; Allen II; Bebbington; Besant(1902) and (1911); Darlington and Howgego; Emsley; Goss; Greater London Council; Horwood; Lockie; Olsen; Rowlandson and Pugin; Rudé; T. Smith; Summerson; Walford; and Wheatley.
2   Malton 107.
3   *Crace* Sheet 46.
4   Cited R. Thompson 30–1.
5   See Taplin I, entry under 'Horse'; F. Thompson(1970) and (1976); Besant(1902) 111.

6   Hall 37.
7   Freeman 97.
8   Taplin I 424.
9   Ibid.
10 Moorcroft(1792).
11 Valli.
12 Valli 15.
13 Ibid. 16.
14 Pugh chaps. 2–4; Simonds.
15 *RVC* Minute Book 1790–3/153; ibid. 1793–1804/12; Pugh 52–3.
16 J. Adams 115.
17 Pugh 53.
18 Blaine(1816) 14.

19 *Marylebone* Ratebook Oxford St. 1793.
20 see p. 42.
21 Horwood.
22 Estimate based on *RVC* Minute Book 1790–3/23.
23 Wakefield.
24 Northouck 733.
25 Pennant 126.
26 Sheppard 94.
27 Malton 103.
28 Sheppard *passim*.
29 Cited Wheatley II 249.
30 *RVC* Minute Book 1793–1804/19.
31 Cited Barber-Lomax(1966) and Pugh 80. The letter itself seems to have disappeared.
32 The information on the joint professorship comes from *RVC* Minute Book 1793–1804/21–37.
33 Ibid. 42.
34 *Veterinarian* VIII 221.
35 *RVC* Minute Book 1793–1804/40.
36 Ibid. 46.
37 Pugh 84–5; F. Smith(1919–33) III 15.
38 Ibid. 24; Coleman II 5.
39 G28/20.5.1823/314/53.
40 The exception is Cotchin.
41 F. Smith(1919–33) II 192 and III 15; idem. (1927) 30.
42 e.g. Blaine(1816) 14–15; B. Clark(1824) 53. See Pattison 6ff.
43 *Veterinarian* XXI(1848) 273.
44 Ibid. 72; *RVC* Minute Book 1793–1804/179.
45 *Veterinarian* VI(1833) 395.
46 Moorcroft(1795).

47 Idem 38.
48 Idem 28.
49 Idem 50.
50 Field 35.
51 Moorcroft(1819) 330ff.
52 Taplin II 133.
53 *IOL* L/Mil/5/388(112) 46ff.
54 Blaine(1841) 10, 13 and 543; B. Clark(1838) 35.
55 Moorcroft(1795) 40.
56 Moorcroft(1819/1) and (1819/2), repr. *Farrier and Naturalist* II(1829) 81 and 97; and commented on by Youatt in *Veterinarian* IX (1836) 362.
57 B. Clark(1838) 35; cf. Barber-Lomax(1963).
58 B. Clark(1838) 32–3.
59 Blaine(1802) 751.
60 M/21.6.1816/90; M/11.4.1817/94. It involved the use of mercuric chloride M/8.3.1816/65.
61 See n. 56; *Veterinarian* XXI(1848) 72.
62 Blaine(1841) 559.
63 The following details are from Moorcroft(1819/2).
64 Freeman 31n.
65 Powis 6.
66 Fleming 500.
67 *Calcutta Journal [of Politics and General Literature]* III(27 Apr. 1819) 283; *Veterinarian* I(1828) 178 and II(1829) 53 and 80.
68 *Veterinarian* IX(1836) 363 and 368.
69 B. Clark(1838) 56; cf. *Sporting Magazine* 12 Oct. 1818; G28/no. 8.
70 Ackermann; Colles and Hickman; Larsen.

4 FAILURE AND SUCCESS – HORSESHOES AND THE INDIA CONNECTION, 1796–1808 (pages 42–52)

1 Smithcors 283–4.
2 J. Clark 65.
3 Moorcroft(1846) 447; idem (1800) 15.
4 B. Clark(1817) 13; Moorcroft(1800) 19.
5 Moorcroft(1800) ix.
6 *Lancs*. WCW/will 9.10.1790.
7 *Patent* 2104 16.4.1796.

8 Explained in Gomme.
9 *Patent* 2104 16.4.1796.
10 Moorcroft(1800) x and 16n.
11 Idem(1846) 446.
12 Idem (1800) viii–ix.
13 Idem (1846) 447.
14 Ibid.
15 Moorcroft(1800) ix.
16 The following material is derived

from *Patent* 2398 3.5.1800. See Plate VIII.

17 Moorcroft(1800) ix–x. It was translated into German, Neumann 254–5.
18 Blaine(1800) II 736–8.
19 Ibid. 738.
20 J. Watson 332–5.
21 Moorcroft(1800) 19n actually defends them.
22 Lane 74–5.
23 J. Clark 63; cf. Hunting 79 and Fleming 544.
24 J. Clark 59.
25 Ibid. 69.
26 Blaine(1802) I 99.
27 Coleman II 5–6.
28 Ibid. 204.
29 Cherry 55–6; cf. Blaine(1802) I 746–7 with idem(1816) 15 and 587; *Veterinarian* XIII(1840) 457.
30 Fleming 516; Blaine(1832) 542.
31 Hickman 84 and 195.
32 Ibid. 97.
33 Moorcroft(1800) 51–60.
34 *Farrier and Naturalist* I(1828) 408; *Veterinarian* IX(1836) 43; *Veterinary Record* XXIII(1910–11) 269; idem LXVI(1954) 90.
35 *RCVS.*
36 Barber-Lomax(1966) 7.
37 Lawrence II 244.
38 Rowlandson and Pugin III 170; Taplin I 424.
39 *Westminster* Ratebook C598 Brook St. Ward 1805.
40 Pasmore(1979); Sandby 48 and 111; Mulvany 187 and 39.

41 *Marylebone* Ratebook Oxford St. 1806.
42 Barber-Lomax(1966) 4; idem (1964) 28. Schrader and Hering say 90 horses.
43 Eby 53. The source of this information has not been traced.
44 To Saunders 20.3.1822 D262/44.
45 G28/314/52.
46 e.g. D265/193.
47 Alder(1979) gives the evidence for what follows.
48 Philips 154.
49 Parry to Moorcroft 24.2.1801 *IOL* L/Mil/5/462.
50 The information in this para. is ibid.
51 Parry to directors 24.3.1801 *IOL* L/Mil/5/461.
52 Recorded in ibid.
53 Moorcroft to Parry 4.4.1803 *IOL* L/Mil/5/462.
54 Rowlandson and Pugin III 170–2; V. Orchard *passim.*
55 On 4.4.1803 *IOL* L/Mil/5/462.
56 Meeting 13.4.1803 *IOL* L/Mil/5/461.
57 In letter 3.11.1823 D265/209.
58 The evidence is *IOL* L/Mil/5/461 and 462.
59 G28/314/41.
60 Parry to Coggan 1.1.1805 *IOL* L/Mil/5/462.
61 Meeting 8.4.1807 *IOL* L/Mil/5/461.
62 Letter 19.2.1814 Add. MS 29,189/34.

5 PRIVATE WORLD AND THE INDIA DECISION, 1792–1808 (pages 53–69)

1 See also Alder(1980/2).
2 Young(1794) I 335–6 and 613–14.
3 Sebag-Montefiore 390–1.
4 Information from ibid.; Barnes; Cousins; White and Martin; and Western.
5 The minute books of the WVC down to 1803 are missing but notes from them are in *Ogilby.*
6 Ibid.; *WVC* Treasurer's Accounts

1797–1817 and Minute Book 1803–9 *passim.*
7 *WVC* Minute Book 1803–9/5.
8 Idem. 23.7.1803.
9 *WVC* Treasurer's Accounts 1797–1817.
10 *WVC* Col. Elliot's Circular Letter; Particular Regulations; and General Regulations, all 1803.
11 *WVC* Minute Book 1803–9/37.

12 Ibid. 96.
13 Collyer and Pocock *passim*.
14 *WVC* Muster Roll 1803–16 lists Moorcroft's attendances.
15 *WVC* General Regulations 24. See p. 53.
16 Anon(5) 12.
17 Anglesey I 95.
18 *WVC* Orderly Book 1804–17/ 10.2.1804.
19 *WVC* Minute Book 1803–9/77; Orderly Book 1804–17/June 1807.
20 *WVC* Minute Book 1803–9/83, 126, 224, 246, 266 and 286; Treasurer's Accounts 1797–1817/20.3.1806.
21 *WVC* Minute Book 1803–9/301.
22 *WVC* Orderly Book 1804–17/ 29.4.1805. Cf. Cambridge.
23 G. Young 25n.
24 To Saunders 20.3.1822 D262/44.
25 Lawrence II 244.
26 C45/33; D254/127; F40/26½.
27 F37/51 and 67.
28 Ibid. On Saunders, see Colvin; Crook 68–70 and figs. 21–4; DNB L 324.
29 *Scarisbrick* DDSc 19/49 *passim*; Banks to Townely 15.8.1792 DDSc 9/42.
30 D263/47; D262/44.
31 Add. MS 29,173/401.
32 Parry letter 24.3.1801 *IOL* L/Mil/ 5/461.
33 M/8.10.1811/92; M/13.2.1813/156; Moorcroft(1819/2).
34 Freeman 31n.
35 *Scarisbrick* DDSc 19/41/6.3.1801.
36 F37/30.
37 F. Smith(1927) 36.
38 G28/314/3.
39 To Coggan 23.10.1804 *IOL* L/Mil/ 5/462; D256/124.
40 The evidence for what follows is all in the Moorcroft Collection at the *IOL*.
41 G28/344.
42 F37/1.
43 G28/314/55; D256/132.
44 D262/48; *Scarisbrick* DDSc 19/49/24 and 29.5.1801.
45 G28/314/53.
46 J. White(1802) went into eleven

47 D265/131.
48 D262/16; G28/344 unnumbered page of draft; D265/224 and 156; to Coggan 3.6.1805 *IOL* L/Mil/5/462.
49 Wilson xxi.
50 G28/346/70.
51 Taplin II 67 and 66.
52 G28/314/53.
53 Ibid.
54 Enclosed with Mary's will in F37/53.
55 Below pp. 246–7.
56 *Smith-Bullock* 12 and 26.8.1923.
57 *Smith-Bullock* 19.8.1924.
58 Steel I 322.
59 Below p. 205.
60 *Westminster* Ratebook C605–6 Brook St. Ward 1811 and 1812.
61 Alder(1979) *passim*.
62 Paras. 259–66 of Milt. Desp. 8.4.1807 *IOL* L/Mil/3/2171.
63 Ibid.
64 Hodgson 20.11.1823 *IOL* L/Mil/5/ 388(112)/82.
65 G28/314/56.
66 Moorcroft(1846) 451–2.
67 On 26.4.1818 *Palmer* C86 congratulated him on his 'matchless temperance'.
68 F40/4–5½.
69 Wilson xxi.
70 F40/5½.
71 G28/314/2.
72 F40/5½.
73 Described in Alder(1979) 20–2.
74 *IOL* L/Mil/5/461 Meeting 11.3.1808.
75 S. Watson 335–6; Parkinson(1937) 34; Schwarz.
76 Milt. letter 8.4.1808 *IOL* L/Mil/3/ 2171.
77 *WVC* Minute Book 1803–9/321.
78 *Scarisbrick* DDSc 19/49,24 and 29.5.1801; 9, 15, 16, 17 and 21.6.1801.
79 Add. MS 36, 901/194.
80 *Bickerton* 942 BIC 2/203.
81 *IOL* L/Mil/5/462.
82 *IOLO*/1/237/2303.
83 *Marylebone* Ratebook Oxford St. 1808.

6 INTERLUDE – THE VOYAGE TO INDIA, MAY–NOVEMBER 1808 (pages 70–81)

1 The prime source for this chapter is the log of the *Indus IOL* L/Mar/B/225C. General background is taken from Anon(4); Bellasis; Chatterton; Cotton; Johnson; Milburn; Parkinson(1937); Valentia; and Wathen.
2 To India 14.1.1807 and 26.2.1808 *IOL* L/P&S/5/541.
3 This para. is based on *IOL* L/Mar/C/529 and 534, ff.3267 and 3283.
4 M/13.2.1813/164.

5 Valentia I 50.
6 Hardy 99.
7 D236/69.
8 D256/49.
9 Moorcroft and Trebeck I xxi.
10 *IOL* G/32/72/16.7.1808.
11 Milburn I 2.
12 Valentia I 4 and 11.
13 D258/32; C45/104.
14 *IOL* L/Mar/B/275K.
15 Blechynden; Burford; Harrold.

7 DISILLUSIONMENT – CALCUTTA AND PUSA, NOVEMBER–DECEMBER 1808 (pages 82–93)

1 Bellew I 106.
2 Hickey *passim* esp. IV; also Kincaid 93–118; Blechynden; Burford; and Harrold.
3 Kopf *passim*.
4 G28/314/39.
5 Cited Howe 33.
6 F40/4.
7 Moorcroft(1814) 2.
8 As he recalled in 1817 F40/4–5.
9 Ibid. 4.
10 M/30.6.1821/79.
11 M/26.12.1808/59.
12 M/12.9.1808/81.
13 M/14.11.1808/73; M/21.11.1808/86.
14 Burton 251.
15 Bute I 106 and 111.
16 M/30.1.1809/64.
17 Moorcroft(1814) 8.
18 M/15.10.1811/80.
19 Moorcroft(1814) 4.
20 M/26.12.1808/56.
21 See *IOL* Map C ix 8.
22 *Veterinarian* I(1828) 195.
23 Alder(1979) 12–13.
24 M/16.7.1811/90. The description

which follows comes from M/2.1.1809/46 and Alder (1979) 15–16.
25 M/22.11.1804/29.
26 M/5.2.1807/32 cited *IOL* L/Mil/5/461 meeting of 11.3.1808.
27 M/30.10.1810/109; M/30.4.1814/88.
28 M/19.12.1809/18.
29 M/15.10.1811/80.
30 M/26.12.1808/56; M/8.9.1810/128.
31 M/15.8.1809/114.
32 M/26.12.1809/90.
33 M/28.5.1810/194.
34 M/27.2.1809/51–4.
35 M/28.5.1810/198.
36 M/30.10.1810/109.
37 M/19.12.1809/16.
38 Moorcroft(1814) 3.
39 M/26.9.1809/93.
40 Moorcroft(1814) 3.
41 Ibid. 1; F40/18.
42 Letter 6.10.1815 F36/1.
43 e.g. Gall minute in M/27.3.1809/75.
44 *NLS* MS 11,331/68.
45 M/21.11.1809/117; M/13.2.1813/156.

8 REFORMS AT PUSA, 1809–10 (pages 94–105)

1 Alder(1979) *passim*.
2 M/15.12.1810/136.

3 M/26.12.1808/61.
4 M/15.10.1811/80.

5   M/13.11.1810/193.
6   M/28.5.1810/199.
7   M/19.12.1809/16.
8   *IOL* L/Mil/5/388(112a)/95 para.18;
    M/30.12.1809/67.
9   M/13.11.1810/193 note 1.
10 Wyatt agreed M/3.10.1809/76.
11 M/30.12.1809/67.
12 M/13.11.1810/193.
13 M/15.11.1811/80.
14 M/28.5.1810/199.
15 Ibid. 198.
16 Moorcroft(1814) 32; M/27.3.1809/
    75.
17 M/28.5.1810/198.
18 M/26.6.1809/90.
19 M/7.11.1809/67.
20 M/28.5.1810/198.
21 M/21.11.1809/117.
22 M/28.5.1810/194.
23 To India 8.4.1807 paras. 259–66
    IOL L/Mil/3/2171.
24 M/30.10.1810/109.
25 D265/209.
26 M/22.5.1813/115.
27 M/13.1.1812/157.
28 M/26.12.1808/56.
29 M/26.6.1809/90; M/28.5.1810/196;
    M/13.1.1812/159; M/6.2.1810/7.
30 M/26.6.1809/90.
31 Moorcroft(1829/1) 91.
32 M/21.11.1809/117.
33 G28/314/56.
34 G28/314/14.
35 M/27.3.1797/29; Watt I no. 1640.
36 M/25.9.1819/114;   G28/314/5;
    D245/142;   D261/42;   Moorcroft
    (1819).
37 M/20.2.1809/6.
38 M/19.12.1809/16.
39 To Minto 29.9.1810 *NLS* MS 11,331/
    68.
40 M/30.10.1810/109.
41 M/19.12.1809/16;   M/21.12.1810/
    20.
42 M/28.5.1810/194; M/19.3.1811/83.
43 M/8.10.1811/95.
44 M/12.9.1809/121;   M/15.10.1811/
    80.
45 M/21.12.1810/20; M/23.4.1811/87.
46 M/28.5.1810/204;   M/13.1.1812/
    163.
47 M/26.9.1809/93.
48 M/30.12.1820/117.
49 D259/16.
50 D262/3.
51 G28/314/55.
52 M/15.1.1811/160.
53 M/28.5.1810/199.
54 M/15.1.1811/160.
55 The following account is taken from
    M/15.1.1811/160, 172–81; *NLS* MS
    11,287/32,   11,299/5.3.1809   and
    11,331/87.
56 M/15.1.1811/172.
57 M/16.7.1811/89–90; M/13.1.1812/
    163.
58 M/15.1.1811/172. Or Ghazipur *NLS*
    MS 11,331/68.
59 M/13.11.1810/193; M/21.12.1810/
    20.
60 Alder(1979) 17.
61 M/23.1.1809/55.
62 M/19.12.1809/135.
63 M/15.1.1811/177.
64 There is evidence that Moorcroft
    came to India fluent in French and
    Italian and familiar with Greek and
    Latin. After 1808 he mastered Hindi,
    could converse in Farsi, Turki and
    Tibetan and had a smattering of
    Punjabi. He had no Pashto. Chiodi
    490 says he spoke all the languages of
    India!
65 M/13.11.1810/193.
66 M/21.12.1810/20.
67 M/19.12.1809/17, 19 and 21.
68 M/21.12.1810/19.
69 M/15.10.1811/80.
70 Alder (1972) 27–36.
71 M/30.4.1814/88.
72 M/28.5.1810/202 and   210;   M/
    16.6.1810/89.
73 M/30.10.1810/109. The rest of the
    chapter is derived from this docu-
    ment.
74 He also approached the governor-
    general privately *NLS* MS 11,331/
    68.
75 M/30.10.1810/108.

9 THE FIRST JOURNEY, 1811 (pages 107–119)

1 The prime source is Moorcroft's letter to the board M/15.10.1811/80. All quotations are from it unless otherwise stated.
2 See map 1.
3 Moorcroft(1814) 11.
4 See Plate IX.
5 M/10.2.1812/192.
6 The expense accounts are M/27.3.1813/84.
7 M/21.1.1812/122; M/11.6.1814/106.
8 M/22.10.1811/72.
9 M/15.1.1811/174 and 177.
10 Pemble(1971) chap. 2.
11 M/21.12.1810/96.
12 M/6.7.1812/148.
13 Enclos. in *IOL* P/119/53, 64, of 2.4.1813.
14 See above p. 107. The detail comes from Pemble(1977); Sharar; Valentia I 135; Nugent 306–12.
15 Pemble(1977) 26.
16 See below p. 261.
17 D263/111.
18 H. Hearsey 118–19.
19 *Moorcroft.*
20 For background see Spear.
21 D251/45.
22 Nugent 354.
23 D260/30.
24 M/16.7.1811/93.
25 M/27.8.1811/70.
26 M/24.9.1811/84.
27 M15.10.1811/78.
28 *NLS* MS 11,319/143 and 145.
29 Ibid. 129; M/4.4.1812/91.
30 M/22.10.1811/72.
31 M/24.12.1811/112a.
32 M/15.10.1811/82.
33 M/10.2.1812/190. Cf. his revealing private letter to Minto *NLS* MS 11,319/129.

10 RETURN TO THE NORTH-WEST, JANUARY–MAY 1812 (pages 120–133)

1 M/15.10.1811/86; M/16.5.1812/65.
2 M/10.2.1812/190.
3 Ibid. 188.
4 M/24.12.1811/112a.
5 F41/1; M/15.10.1811/81; M/27.1.1812/98; M/27.3.1813/84.
6 M/26.11.1811/23 and 110.
7 M/21.1.1812/122; M/13.1.1812/159 and 163.
8 M/4.4.1812/93.
9 M/3.3.1812/70.
10 *IOL* Eur. MS D514/1; Sanders 100–7.
11 To Elphinstone *IOL* Eur. MS F88 Box 131; Elphinstone 142, 296–7, 535–6n.
12 M/6.7.1812/148; M/13.2.1813/156.
13 Moorcroft's are in F38.
14 M/6.7.1812/148.
15 Moorcroft(1814) 12. For his background, Datta(1973) 94.
16 M/6.7.1812/148.
17 As Moorcroft was uneasily aware M/13.2.1813/156. With justice as it transpired C44/154.
18 M/6.7.1812/148.
19 Enclosed in ibid.
20 M/6.7.1812/148.
21 Dainelli 18n; Wilson(1825) and (1843); *Asiatic Journal* XXII(1826) 168; Henderson.
22 M/6.7.1812/148; F38/17.11.1812.
23 M/6.7.1812/150.
24 Ibid.148; F38/29.4.1812.
25 M/6.7.1812/148.
26 Ibid.
27 Mason(1955).
28 Thorn 437.
29 Raper; C. Allen(1980); idem (1982) chap. 3.
30 Pearse(1905); A Hearsey; L. Hearsey; Phillimore II 404–5.
31 See n. 29.
32 Nugent 70.
33 *IOL* P/247, 62 of 19.3.1813.
34 F38/29.4.1812.
35 On 25.4.1812 M/6.7. 1812/148.
36 F38/17.11.1812.
37 Baird 39; Lamb chap. 3;

	Datta(1970); Pemble(1971) chap. 3;	55	*IOL* P/119/46, 60–2 of 25.6.1812.
	Irwin.	56	63 of ibid.
38	M/15.1.1814/63.	57	Pearse(1905/1) 69ff.
39	F38/1.12.1812.	58	*Hearsey* 5.
40	See above n.37 and M/6.7.1812/148.	59	The aliases come from Phillimore II
41	*IOL* E/4/669/433.		430.
42	Crawford I 237–8.	60	*Hearsey* 8.
43	M/6.7.1812/148.	61	Ibid. 1.
44	*Asiatick Researches* XI(1812) 541.	62	M/6.7.1812/148.
45	F38/8.4.1812.	63	There are many secondary accounts
46	M/6.7.1812/148; M/13.2.1813/156.		of varying reliability based on
47	*IOL* P/119/49, 30 of 18.12.1812.		Moorcroft (1816), such as Eyriès;
48	M/13.2.1813/156.		Hedin(1910–13) III chap. 18; idem
49	Ibid.		(1917–23) II chap. 7; H. Murray
50	See below p. 154 n 17.		II 404; Barber-Lomax (1959);
51	M/13.2.1813/156.		Phillimore II 430; Sandberg 112;
52	M/6.7.1812/148; F38/8 and		Snelling 55; Styles 41. Those which
	29.4.1812.		also use *Hearsey* are the brief Pearse
53	M/6.7.1812/148.		(1905/2) and Allen(1982) chap. 4,
54	Ibid.		certainly the best to date.

11 JOURNEY TO TIBET, MAY–AUGUST 1812 (pages 135–156)

1	*Hearsey.* The other prime source for	12	Cf. F36/57 with Moorcroft(1816)
	this and chapter 12 is the published		114.
	version of Moorcroft's journal,	13	M/13.2.1813/156.
	Moorcroft(1816). References are	14	Wessels *passim.*
	given only to other sources.	15	E.g. Survey of India Map Hind 5000,
2	Raper 519.		NH–44, 4th edn. 1945.
3	Published with Moorcroft(1816).	16	*IOL* WD 350. See Plate XVIII. Re-
4	*IOL* WD 348. Reproduced in F. Wat-		produced in F. Watson (1959–60)
	son (1959–60) 205 and M. Archer II		and idem (1960) cover; M. Archer II
	plate 100.		plate 97; Allen (1982) 8 wrongly cap-
5	Atkinson III 641.		tioned; Cameron 67.
6	M/13.2.1813/156.	17	Hedin(1917–23) II. 30. Cf. ibid. 32.
7	D260/85. Cf. the 1812 version	18	Allen(1982) chap. 1. For a Buddhist
	in *IOL* P/119/49, 29 of 18.12.		view Snelling *passim*; Govinda II 108;
	1812.		and Pranavananda 163.
8	M/6.7.1812/148.	19	Useful guides to the literature are
9	F38/1.12.1812.		*Longstaff* and Hedin(1917–23) II
10	*IOL* P/119/49, 29 of 18.12.1812.		esp. 131ff.
11	M/13.2.1813/156.	20	Ibid. II 36.

12 PRISONER OF THE GURKHAS AND RELEASE, AUGUST–DECEMBER 1812 (pages 157–178)

1	See previous chapter note 1.	5	*Calcutta Review* XVIII(Jul.–Dec.
2	*Quarterly Review* XVII (1817) 422.		1852) 95.
3	The text is given Black(1891) 152;	6	*IOL* P/119/49, 29 of 18.12.1812;
	Anon(6).		Chowdhuri.
4	eg. Mason(1923) 429–30.		

7 Enclosure in *IOL* P/119/49, 29 of 25.11.1812.
8 *IOL* P/119/53, 52 of 12.3.1813.
9 F38/5.10.1812.
10 G28/110 printed as Moorcroft (1831) esp. 243n.
11 Moorcroft(1816) 523–4. Cf.F40/9½.
12 Reproduced Allen(1982) 94. (See above p. 157.)
13 It is commonly believed that they were treated with great brutality e.g. Newby 157.
14 *NLS* MS 11,319/165.
15 Ibid. 163.
16 India to London 15.6.1813, para. 31 *IOL* F/4/421. The reply and other correspondence on the subject are *NLS* MS 11,593/112–17; *IOL* P/119/53, 52 of 12.3.1813 and 36 of 15.4.1813.
17 *IOL* P/119/49, 28–30 of 25.11.1812; M/5.12.1812/106–7.
18 F38/1.1.1812.
19 *NLS* MS 11,319/126.
20 F38/1.1.1812.
21 M/9.1.1813/82. On de l'Étang see Boyd App. B.
22 M/13.2.1813/156.
23 M/27.3.1813/83.
24 M/30.6.1821/79.
25 *NLS* MS 11,319/126.
26 Above p. 130.
27 M/13.2.1813/156.
28 *IOL* P/119/49, 31 of 18.12.1812.
29 *NLS* MS 11,319/126.
30 Add. MS 29,189/33.
31 F36/1 and 5.
32 MacCulloch.
33 F39/221; D245/165.
34 *IOL* P/119/53, 64 of 2.4.1813; M/23.12.1814/145.
35 G28/74; D239/19.
36 Irwin 6 and 43.
37 Burkill 30; Stewart(1982) 108 and 131. For Moorcroft as botanical collector, Desmond; Dallman and Wood. The only genus Moorcroftia was not upheld. Among the species which bear, or bore, his name are Achyranthus, Aquilegia, Artemisia, Astragalus, Axyris, Campanula, Caragana, Carex, Corydalis, Elæagnus, Fraxinus, Gagea, Gentiana, Iris, Macromitrium, Ornus, Potentilla, Primula, Rheum, Rosa, Salsola, Salvia, Saxifraga, Sedum, Silene, Sophora, Stachys (taken from Atkinson I; Hooker VII, Pampanini 5–6; Wallich List of Dried Plants *IOL* Eur. MS G32).
38 *IOL* P/119/53, 64 of 2.4.1813 and enclos.
39 Ibid.
40 Alder(1980/1) 209 and n. See also Kaushik 234–5. Morgan(1973) 65 unwittingly added to the confusion but cf. idem (1981) 135–6 and 141.
41 To the governor-general, *NLS* MS 11,319/165.
42 See below p. 189.
43 Bute I 251.
44 Pemble(1971) chap. 3 esp. 85–9.
45 East India Company 551, 673 and 761.
46 F36/114.
47 Lamb 62–3; *IOL* F/4/552/coll.13,384 and F/4/730/coll.19,778.
48 Alder(1972).
49 *IOL* P/119/49, 29 of 18.12.1812.
50 *IOL* P/247, 62 of 19.3.1813. Cf. Henderson 84.
51 Add. MS 39,871/118; *IOL* P/247, 63 of 19.3.1813.
52 Moorcroft(1814) 14.
53 *IOL* E/4/683, 123–5.
54 Argued at length in Alder(1980/1).
55 M/19.1.1816/144; G31/107.
56 e.g. *Palmer* C84/567. An inaccurate account appeared in *Quarterly Review* XIV(1815–16) 184.
57 The evidence that Colebrooke did it is D236/26; Colebrooke I 357; and Moorcroft(1816) 376. But cf. D251/154.
58 D251/154.
59 Anon(7) 414–15; F. Watson (1959–60) 207 and 212.
60 D236/25–6; G28/103; or Add. MS 33,837/60.
61 Phillimore III 286; Hedin(1917–23) II 3.
62 *Calcutta Journal* 31.8.1820, 741; ibid.

26.11.1820, 306; Hedin(1910–13) III 217 and 221; Strachey 6 and 14.

63 Burrard and Hayden 181–2.
64 Above pp. 155–6.

65 Hedin(1917–23) II 27–8.
66 F38/17.11.1812.
67 M/7.8.1813/117.
68 Phillimore II 405.

13 FRUSTRATION AT THE STUD, 1813–14 (pages 179–191)

1 M/13.1.1812/163.
2 F37/53.
3 To judge from his concern for her financial well-being F41/29; *Palmer* C99, to de l'Étang 15.11.1823; *IOL* L/AG/34/29/39.
4 M/5.12.1812/107.
5 M/13.2.1813/156.
6 Ibid. 155.
7 M/30.4.1814/90.
8 M/28.3.1812/97.
9 M/25.3.1815/51.
10 M/5.3.1813/6.
11 Anglesey I 110; Sandhu 78.
12 M/5.3.1813/5.
13 *NLS* MS 11,319/147.
14 M/22.5.1813/116.
15 Ibid.
16 Ibid. 115.
17 M/14.5.1813/114; M/22.5.1813/119.
18 Nugent 186.
19 M/16.4.1814/119.
20 M/7.8.1813/116 and 117.
21 *NLS* MS 11,319/147 and 159.
22 Moorcroft(1814) 48n.
23 D261/21ff.
24 M/15.1.1814/63.
25 M/13.2.1813/164; M/24.4.1813/71.
26 By Dr. S. C. Datta, later director of the Imperial Institute of Veterinary Research, Mukteswar, according to Prof. M. Abdussalam (letters 24.5. and 22.11.1983 to the author and Abdussalam 22). There is no mention of Moorcroft in S. Datta or Edwards.
27 M/15.4.1815/85; M/5.12.1815/199; M/9.2.1816/132; Moorcroft(1819/ 2); D254/320ff.; G28/314/4; Twining 351 and 360; Molyneux; Smith(1919–33) III 10.
28 D258/30 and 60; D265/15 and 115; E113/71 and 75.

29 D256/86; Moorcroft and Trebeck I 49n.
30 D262/44.
31 *Veterinarian* III(1830) 253; M/ 2.2.1816/90; D264/231.
32 M/14.8.1813/74.
33 M/27.11.1813/109 and 110.
34 Ibid. 107.
35 M/7.2.1814/138. The accounts and statistics are ibid. 139 and 140.
36 Ibid. 137 and 145.
37 F40/7; Bute I 212, 218 and 221–2.
38 *NLS* MS 11,319/147.
39 M/30.4.1814/86 printed as Moorcroft(1814). The quotations which follow are pp. 54 and 21.
40 F40/7.
41 M/16.4.1814/119; M/30.4.1814/90.
42 M/30.4.1814/85.
43 Ibid. 86; Nugent 261.
44 *Palmer* C84/525.
45 M/14.10.1814/101; M/23.12.1814/ 121.
46 M/11.6.1814/108.
47 F40/7; M/22.5.1813/119.
48 M/30.4.1814/90.
49 M/14.10.1814/101; M/23.12.1814/ 121 and 122.
50 F40/7; M/14.10.1814/101; D236/ 69–70; F38/21.5.1820.
51 M/14.10.1814/101.
52 Not found but alluded to M/ 19.11.1814/174.
53 M/23.12.1814/117–19 and 125.
54 Ibid. 118.
55 M/14.10.1814/41.
56 M/23.12.1814/117.
57 Ibid. 134–6 and 138.
58 On 23.12.1814 *IOL* E/40/90 paras. 340–1.
59 Referred to M/25.3.1815/62.
60 *Palmer* C84/525 and 567.
61 Pemble(1971) for details of the war.

14 WAR IN NEPAL AND VICTORY AT THE STUD, OCTOBER 1814–MAY 1819
(pages 192–208)

1 M/23.12.1814/132; M/19.11.1814/ 175 and 177.
2 *IOL* H/Misc/645, 39, 59, 71, 80, 91 and 135; ibid. 646, 37, 623 and 635; ibid. 647, 107; ibid. 651, 37.
3 Ibid. 649, 643.
4 Ibid. 643 and 651; ibid. 654, 461, 479 and 493.
5 M/25.3.1815/62.
6 Ibid. 59.
7 Ibid. 50 and 64.
8 *Palmer* C86/26.4.1818.
9 They are M/25.3.1815/56, 57, 62 and 63.
10 M/1.4.1815/7.
11 See esp. M/5.12.1815/197 and 199.
12 Bute I 82–5.
13 F36/22.
14 M/5.12.1815/47.
15 *IOL* L/Mil/5/431.
16 The papers are *IOL* F/4/552/coll. 13,385 and E/4/695, 730.
17 M/27.10.1815/129.
18 M/5.12.1815/198; referred to G28/ 314/1.
19 M/17.10.1815/132.
20 M/29.12.1815/128.
21 Ibid. 133 and 129.
22 M/12.12.1815/129; M/29.12.1815/ 128; M/9.2.1816/133.
23 M/5.12.1815/201.
24 M/19.1.1816/1; M/29.12.1815 129.
25 M/9.2.1816/141. He became president of the board in 1820 when Moorcroft's opponent, Wood, resigned.
26 M/1.3.1816/225.
27 *IOL* F/4/552/colls. 13,385 and 13,386.
28 M/31.5.1816/59 and 60; M/ 21.6.1816/90.
29 F36/1.
30 Ibid 9 and 16; G28/2–3; G31/ 89–90.
31 M/21.6.1816/91.
32 Ibid. 94.
33 M/31.5.1816/60.
34 M/8.11.1816/133.
35 M/10.6.1816/160–1; M/2.8.1816/ 124–5; M/30.8.1816/131.
36 F36/5.
37 F40/76.
38 His enthusiasm is best conveyed in M/20.1.1821/145.
39 Ibid. 139–41.
40 Ibid. 145.
41 M/11.11.1817/87–8; M/14.7.1818/ 91–7.
42 M/13.1.1818/91–9.
43 *IOL* L/Mil/5/388(112a), 95.
44 M/4.11.1817/76.
45 F40/4.
46 G28/5.
47 To Palmer D261/113.
48 M/27.2.1819/102.
49 M/10.2.1818/77.
50 M/30.6.1818/101.
51 e.g. M/21.4.1818/109 and 110.
52 Of 26.4.1818 *Palmer* C86.
53 M/20.1.1821/145.
54 M/19.9.1818/74–6; *Palmer* C87/ 9.10.1818; F37/35.
55 M/26.12.1818/180.
56 F37/53; D261/65.
57 *Palmer* C91/141; *IOL* L/AG/34/29/ 39.
58 Enc. in F37/53.
59 Palmer's reply of 9.10.1818 is *Palmer* C87.
60 F37/51.
61 M/26.12.1818/179.
62 Ibid. 179–83.
63 *Calcutta Journal* 5.2.1819, 333; F36/ 122; Thackeray 182.
64 G28/71, 74 and 91.
65 Moorcroft called him 'my friend' in D240/51 and G28/314/35.
66 D238/obverse of 112–105 and 84.
67 D254/135–9.
68 *Calcutta Journal* 21.2.1819, 495.
69 M/14.5.1819/142; M/20.1.1821/ 143; M/16.5.1823/110.
70 M/16.5.1823/116.
71 M/6.3.1819/123–4; M/25.9.1819/

113–16; M/27.2.1819/113; M/
20.1.1821/145.

72 M/7.5.1819/119.
73 M/30.6.1821/78.
74 M/20.5.1824/98.
75 *IOL* L/Mil/5/467 and L/Mil/7/
9626–7 *passim*; *Veterinarian* XXIII
(1850) 503; Hallen; Gilbey; West 8
and 15–16.

76 M/7.5.1819/134; M/14.2.1820/68–
70.
77 *IOL* E/4/694, 719 despatch of
14.10.1818.
78 *IOL* L/Mil/3/2176, 401 despatch of
17.2.1819; F36/59, 63 and 81.
79 M/30.6.1821/79.
80 F36/104.

15 THE GREAT JOURNEY BEGINS AND IS CHECKED, 1819 (pages 209–223)

1   *IOL* P/121/52, 101 of 14.5.1819.
2   G28/314/3.
3   D260/44.
4   G28/314/1.
5   D256/9; G28/47; G28/314/2.
6   *IOL* P/121/52, 97–100; F37/210.
7   Moorcroft(1814) 14; M/14.10.1814/
101.
8   D258/60.
9   F38/27.12.1819 cited at length
Moorcroft and Trebeck I xxviii–
xxxv. See esp. xxxii.
10 F38/21.5.1820; G28/47.
11 F36/132.
12 Moorcroft and Trebeck I xxix.
13 Ibid.
14 G28/210.
15 D264/184.
16 Ingram 60; Kessler esp. 19; Druhe
93–5; Solov'yev.
17 Alder(1980/1).
18 G28/314/52.
19 F37/41.
20 D262/44.
21 Moorcroft(1819/1 and 2).
22 M/17.7.1819/138.
23 *IOL* P/121/52, 99 of 14.5.1819.
24 The detail which follows comes from
D256/1; D238/63; F37/12,41 and
162; F36/132; D267; *Accounts and
Papers*(1859) 239–40; G30/3; G31/
150; D261/107; F41 *passim*.
25 F41/66.
26 Moorcroft and Trebeck I, 3 and 40.
27 H. Hearsey 108 and 109; F37/105.
28 D267 *passim*; D256/15; D266/18.
29 D236/17.
30 G28/47; D236/17.
31 D250/214; D246/170; D251/176.

32 D257/97;   G28/89;   D262/44;
Sandberg 122.
33 D261/65; M/26.6.1819/142; F36/
120.
34 D249/54; *IOL* P/121/52, 99 of
14.5.1819.
35 H. Hearsey 106.
36 G31/83; D267.
37 Below p. 225.
38 H. Hearsey 108; *Accounts and
Papers*(1859) 237.
39 D257/79.
40 F37/16.
41 Above p. 172; Khalfin 390; Kessler
6; I.O. 197.
42 G31/83; *IOL* P/121/52, 97–9 of
14.5.1819; G28/47.
43 M/24.4.1819/107; M/7.5.1819/115,
119 and 135; G28/10.
44 *IOL* L/AG/34/29/39.
45 F36/139.
46 M/25.9.1819/114 and 115.
47 D267.
48 M/14.8.1819/143.
49 G28/51 and 54; F37/32; F36/132.
50 F37/12 and 37; D256/1 and 36.
51 H. Hearsey 107.
52 Route in ibid. 108.
53 Ibid. 115. See above p. 209.
54 F36/124.
55 D261/10.
56 H. Hearsey 108; F36/114 and 124.
57 G28/47.
58 F36/142.
59 F39/234; F36/124.
60 F37/1 and referred to in 51.
61 D256/3.
62 D243.
63 D236/16.

64 H. Hearsey 108–9.
65 D256/25.
66 Ibid. 9.
67 Moorcroft and Trebeck I xxiv.
68 D256/36.
69 D257/64.
70 D267.
71 *Calcutta Journal* 15.1.1820, 106; *Calcutta Review* XIII(1822) 363.
72 D236/49; F36/142 and 165.
73 D257/90.
74 H. Hearsey 109.

75 D236/13.
76 D262/44.
77 G28/314/56.
78 D258/60 but omitted from Moorcroft(1836) 132.
79 The material which follows comes from ibid. and D265/209 contd. 221; D256/63; D258/30; D250/175.
80 D257/56.
81 D256/3 and 15.
82 As Traill pointed out F36/154.
83 D256/20.

16 An Encounter with Ranjit Singh, January–June 1820 (pages 224–241)

1 The prime source for this chapter is Moorcroft's journal D236–9 and part D240, paraphrased in Moorcroft and Trebeck I 5–120. References are given only to other sources.
2 D257/56.
3 F36/142.
4 Explained in letters D257/53; F37/10; D257/79, 84, 90 and 93.
5 H. Hearsey 109.
6 Moorcroft(1836) 132.
7 Phillimore II 404–5.
8 F37/19. See also the next two letters and D237/1–4.
9 F41/46.
10 D264/168. Crowe and Haywood cite Moorcroft extensively on the gardens he visited.
11 D257/97.
12 D257/79ff.
13 Keay 17–18.
14 Also D256/49.
15 F37/142.
16 G28/58; D256/86.
17 G28/93; F37/45; D261/1; Guthrie 157.
18 See G28/314/49 and D264/211.

19 Moorcroft and Trebeck I 84.
20 D267.
21 Blake 314–15.
22 See Plates XV and XVI.
23 Hasrat 255–6.
24 H. Hearsey 113.
25 F38 21.5.1820. Hasrat 183 discusses Ranjit's impotence.
26 F38/21.5.1820.
27 Its value was not properly appreciated Alder (1980/1) 199 and n.
28 G28/58.
29 F38/21.5.1820.
30 G28/74.
31 F38/48.
32 To Palmer D261/65.
33 D256/86.
34 See Plate I and below p. 243.
35 In a letter to Parry D256/86.
36 He did so G28/58.
37 F38/24 and 49; G30/45.
38 Described in G28/79.
39 Interesting accounts of this second visit to Ranjit are F38/50 and D256/86.
40 D256/86.
41 H. Hearsey 171; G28/93.
42 D257/100.

17 Kangra, Kulu, Lahul and Arrival in Ladakh, June–September 1820 (pages 242–255)

1 The prime source for this chapter is Moorcroft's journal D240/47ff., D241–3, and part D244, paraphrased in Moorcroft and Trebeck I

120–246. Extended extracts are given verbatim in W. Archer(1973) I 250ff. References are given only to other sources.

2 H. Hearsey 172.

3 D237/78; Grey and Garrett 59.

4 H. Hearsey 173.

5 Randhawa(1961) 23.

6 D257/103.

7 Ibid.

8 *Calcutta Journal* 29.9.1820, 342.

9 It still survives and is illustrated Randhawa(1970) no. 25.

10 D262/44.

11 W. Archer(1973) I 262. See also idem (1975).

12 At least one has survived and is at the V & A Museum, London I.S. 173–1950. See above p. 242.

13 This was the view of Vogel(1909) 13; idem (1947) 206; and Gupta 127. Others like the late W. Archer and Aijazuddin 90–1 and 111 regard the picture as a later Sikh work painted after Moorcroft's death.

14 F37/45; G28/93.

15 Described in D262/44 and G31/142.

16 H. Hearsey 172.

17 F36/122.

18 F37/65.

19 Seen later by Vigne(1842) I 109.

20 D261/1.

21 Illustrated Chetwode after 46.

22 From Saunders 6.12.1819. It has not survived.

23 F37/61.

24 *Palmer* C103/210.

25 e.g. F37/51 and 67.

26 Ibid. 53.

27 Attestation of Mary's will dated 1.6.1821 enc. in ibid.

28 *IOL* L/AG/34/29/39.

29 F37/1.

30 Ibid. 67.

31 H. Hearsey 173.

32 G28/102.

33 G28/98.

34 D257/100.

35 Chetwode 180 and 184.

36 F37/142.

37 D261/1.

38 Alder(1980/1) 201 n.121.

39 H. Hearsey 173.

40 D261/1.

41 G28/103.

42 D261/1; D262/39; D263/111; F37/184.

43 See Plate XVII.

44 D264/180; Francke 125.

45 From Traill F37/108; D256/73.

46 D261/1.

47 D245/115.

48 In postscript to letter D256/86.

49 D261/65.

50 D260/54.

18 TRIUMPH IN LADAKH, SEPTEMBER 1820–AUGUST 1821 (pages 256–273)

1 The prime source for this chapter is Moorcroft's journal D244/38ff. taking the story to mid-Oct. 1820, paraphrased in Moorcroft and Trebeck I 246–57 and 383–421. There are also the long letters D261/1 and D258/60, the latter partially reprinted Moorcroft(1836). References are given only to other sources.

2 More accurately, Tsé-dban-don-grub according to Petech 135n.

3 D259/34.

4 D268 *passim*.

5 D256/73; G28/426.

6 Alder(1963) 22–3; *National Geo-*

graphic Magazine CLIII(Mar. 1978) 332.

7 D260/42.

8 D256/68, 73, 83 and 85.

9 D256/73.

10 Moorcroft and Trebeck I 257.

11 D262/44; G28/314/55.

12 D259/16.

13 D259/99; D261/65.

14 D261/65; D258/51.

15 G28/314/50; D262/64; G28/231 and 232; F37/192.

16 G28/314/27.

17 D264/180; D262/44 and 64.

18 D260/42.

19 D262/9; D265/230; D249/110; G31/133.

20 D262/44; D261/65.

21 D255/19.

22 e.g. D246/42.

23 D261/65.

24 Jacquemont 235.

25 D258/51. He was right Alder(1980/1) 208 n.157.

26 G28/242.

27 D245/165.

28 G28/151.

29 D259/5.

30 Some of this material is paraphrased in Moorcroft and Trebeck I chaps. 2 and 3 of Pt II.

31 D244/84 contd. D259/1; Royle I 39. His information was said to be the best available nearly a century later, Stewart (1917) 575.

32 *IOL* Per IO 4546; G28/297.

33 e.g. D259/6, 78 and 96; D260/23 and 35.

34 D256/63 and 86.

35 D256/67; D261/65.

36 D260/42.

37 D260/74.

38 G28/141 reprinted Datta (1973) App. C. The information in the remainder of the para. comes from D260/54 and 74.

39 D245/84; D258/72; D260/87. There is additional information in Datta(1973) 96 and Solov'yev.

40 *IOL* P/123/50, 23 of 10.10.1823; D260/26.

41 To Parry D260/54.

42 The letter to Ranjit (reprinted in Datta(1973) App. A) was sent to Calcutta in May *IOL* P/123/50, 24 of 10.10.1823.

43 25 of ibid.; D260/29.

44 D246/91.

45 G28/130 reprinted Moorcroft(1831)

243n describes the 1812 discovery. D245 for the 1821 exploration. Cf. R. Davies 28.

46 *IOL* P123/13, 56 of 26.7.1822 and P/123/18, 63 and 66–8 of 20.9.1822.

47 D266/48; D258/51; D260/42.

48 *IOL* P/123/18, 76 of 20.9.1822.

49 D262/75 part reprinted Moorcroft and Trebeck I xl.

50 D258/45–8; G28/145–6.

51 D260/42 and 74; D262/21.

52 M/30.6.1821/78.

53 D258/51; D260/42.

54 D260/54. Other info. from G28/314/17; F37/102, 157 and 165; D260/42; D262/25. Neither arms nor men were sent by Ochterlony, Sinha and Dasgupta 186.

55 Described Moorcroft and Trebeck I 395–402 from a journal now missing, Kaye 960.

56 D262/39.

57 Anon(8) 96.

58 F37/85.

59 D256/73. The episode which follows has been described by *inter alia* Ahluwalia; Alder(1963) 16; Datta(1973) 99; Woodman 24.

60 F37/83.

61 This and all the other quotations in this para. from *IOL* P/123/18, 63 of 20.9.1822.

62 64 of ibid.; Datta(1973) App. B.

63 *IOL* P/123/18, 63 of 20.9.1822.

64 *IOL* P/122/66, 90 of 27.10.1821.

65 D256/86.

66 G28/314/19.

67 Described Moorcroft and Trebeck I 413–17 from a journal now missing, Kaye 960.

68 The details which follow are D245/6.

69 G31/4a.

70 D245/134.

71 G28/314/19.

19 SETBACK IN LADAKH, AUGUST 1821–OCTOBER 1822 (pages 274–292)

1 The journals, covering only a small part of this period, are D245/1–71; D246; D247 and part D248, paraphrased Moorcroft and Trebeck

I 422–33 and II 1–44 and 83–96. References are given only to other sources.

2 Guthrie 159.

3   Moorcroft(1836) 133–4; D261/1.
4   D260/42.
5   *IOL* P/123/18, 70 of 20.9.1822; G28/201.
6   J. Hodgson, surveyor-general D258/51.
7   C39/55.
8   C39/68.
9   C39/76.
10 D245/100.
11 D261/65.
12 Described in *IOL* P/123/18, 67 and 70 of 20.9.1822.
13 Guthrie 159.
14 D262/35.
15 D261/65.
16 F37/51.
17 D261/65.
18 D262/44.
19 F37/53.
20 G28/224.
21 D262/44.
22 D245/159; D262/1; D265/27; D263/105.
23 The information which follows comes from *IOL* P/123/18, 69 of 20.9.1822 and F37/142.
24 D261/65.
25 D245/84 and 86.
26 D261/65.
27 Sinha and Dasgupta 185.
28 *IOL* P/122/66, 92 of 27.10.1821.
29 Ibid. 93.
30 India to London 9.1.1824 *IOL* L/P&S/6/34.
31 *IOL* P/123/18, 72 of 20.9.1822.
32 71 of ibid.
33 71 and 76 of ibid.
34 D262/44.
35 D263.
36 Singh 135.
37 Alder(1963) chap. 2.
38 To India 6.4.1825 *IOL* E/4/714.
39 This is clear from G28/82.
40 Fraser to Moorcroft F37/184.
41 *IOL* P/123/18, 72 of 20.9.1822, part cited Moorcroft and Trebeck I xl and in full in Chopra.
42 To India 6.4.1825 *IOL* E/4/714.

43 F37/184.
44 D246/59.
45 Especially F37/108 and 124.
46 Described Moorcroft and Trebeck II 45 from D255.
47 D246/49. Also Moorcroft(1836) 145 and (1827).
48 *Asiatic Observer* II(1824) 91; Lindley; Wallich(1832) 7 and see n.50 below.
49 D266/19.
50 G27; G28/380; Moorcroft and Trebeck I 258ff.
51 G27.
52 See *inter alia* Duka; Hetenyi; H. Hyde chap. 4; Rawlinson; G28/297ff.
53 G28/312.
54 Csoma vii and viii.
55 D265/31; G28/237; Rawlinson 17.
56 F37/67.
57 F37/136.
58 G28/228.
59 Keay 95.
60 G28/244.
61 G28/230.
62 D246/91.
63 G28/234.
64 G28/314/15.
65 e.g. Barrow 113.
66 *IOL* P/123/18, 71 of 20.9.1822.
67 As stated Francke II 69. Cf. *Geographical Journal* LXVII(1926) 576.
68 Moorcroft and Trebeck I xxxv.
69 *Trebeck* no. 4.
70 e.g. Cunningham 7; Strachey iii, 6 and 14; Hedin(1917–23) VIII 126; Petech 4; Stewart(1917) 575 and (1967) 352; Burrard 278–9; Snellgrove and Skorupski I bibliog.; Francke II 69. Holdich 444ff. is critical.
71 Alder(1963) chap. 2.
72 See works cited in idem(1980/1) 215 n.182.
73 Francke II 125 and 146.
74 F37/166; *IOL* P/123/18, 59 of 20.9.1822.
75 G28/314/20.
76 D266/19; D265/221.
77 See above p. 274.

20 KASHMIR AND THE PUNJAB, NOVEMBER 1822–DECEMBER 1823 (pages 293–309)

1 Moorcroft's journals cover only parts of this period and are scattered amid other material in D248/59ff and D249/25–192, paraphrased in Moorcroft and Trebeck II 96–105 and 274–334. References are given only to other sources.
2 D264/180.
3 F37/197; *Trebeck* no. 2.
4 H. Hearsey 181.
5 D264/220.
6 G28/246.
7 D263/120; H. Hearsey 180–1.
8 Forster(1798).
9 G28/249.
10 D265/169.
11 D266/75.
12 D264/299.
13 *Trebeck* nos. 4 and 2.
14 G28/286.
15 G28/284; *Trebeck* no. 1; Guthrie 159.
16 H. Hearsey 282.
17 G28/314/25.
18 D263/105 and 111.
19 G28/314/26.
20 D263/111.
21 G28/314/26–7.
22 Ibid. 20.
23 Moorcroft and Trebeck II 106–217. Some was published Moorcroft (1832). The references to the material in the MS are too extensive to list. See Kaye 88 1ff.
24 D264/229; G28/371; Vigne(1842) II 79.
25 See above chap. 19 n.52.
26 Moorcroft and Trebeck II 165n; Irwin.
27 G28/349; D264/99.
28 Karpinsky.
29 G28/358; D264/257; Mirsky 23, 36 and 42; Stein vii.
30 D265/234; G28/314/45 and 349.
31 Lord Harewood D264/219.
32 G28/375.
33 D264/300.
34 G28/361 and 378.
35 *Trebeck* no. 2.
36 Described Moorcroft and Trebeck II 218 from a missing journal of Trebeck's and by Moorcroft in D265/1 and D249/1.
37 D263/111; D264/234.
38 H. Hearsey 280 and 282.
39 D246/91.
40 F37/197.
41 Described Moorcroft and Trebeck II 239 from a missing journal of Trebeck's, extracts of which are in C44/1.
42 e.g. D264/231.
43 G28/361.
44 F37/165; Sinha and Dasgupta 186.
45 D263/105.
46 *Trebeck* no. 1; D263/109; G28/351; H. Hearsey 282.
47 *Trebeck* no. 2.
48 D249/73; C44/15; *Trebeck* no. 3.
49 Trebeck in C44/15ff. is the source for this paragraph.
50 G28/371.
51 Alder(1980/2) 199–201.
52 Guthrie 159.
53 D265 *passim*, mostly given *IOL* P/123/56, 31ff. of 9.1.1824.
54 D265/207.
55 Vigne(1842) I 225ff; D265/168.
56 D265/129; *IOL* P/123/56, 32 of 9.1.1824.
57 *Palmer* C97/236.
58 D265/166.
59 He recommended his journal C44/98, on which the rest of this chapter is also partly based without further reference.
60 G28/400.
61 G28/402.
62 D265/245.
63 D265/195; *IOL* P/123/56, 33 of 9.1.1824.
64 35 of ibid.
65 D265/248 or the fuller version G28/392. Cf. Prinsep (1835) esp. 192–4.
66 Moorcroft and Trebeck II 339n. Cf. Alder(1980/2) 205 n.139.

67 D266/36.
68 G28/403; *Trebeck* no. 10; Guthrie 160; H. Hearsey 36.
69 D250/47.
70 Moorcroft's important and nearly

contemporary account D250/18 and 29 was sent to Calcutta. An extract is *IOL* H/Misc/664, 303 and P/325, 9 of 29.10.1824. It was used Singh 151 but cf. Caroe 294.

21 AFGHANISTAN, DECEMBER 1823–AUGUST 1824 (pages 310–328)

1 The prime sources for this chapter are Moorcroft's journal D249/182ff., D250 and part D251 and extracts from Trebeck's journal C44/170, all paraphrased in Moorcroft and Trebeck II 334–95. References are given only to other sources.
2 H. Hearsey 37.
3 Cf. Guthrie 161.
4 Caroe e.g. 308.
5 D266/40.
6 Of 28.12.1823, D265/248 and G28/392.
7 D250/133. Cf. Moorcroft and Trebeck II 340.
8 See below pp. 317–18.
9 Caroe.
10 H. Hearsey 38.
11 e.g. F37/197.
12 Edwardes I 52.
13 Idem 51.
14 *Trebeck* no. 6.
15 G31/15; D250/149.
16 D250/133.
17 *IOL* P/123/56, 35 of 9.1.1824.
18 Of 22.4.1824 D266/45.
19 Burnes(1834) I 106 cast doubts on his loyalty to Moorcroft.
20 *Trebeck* no. 6.
21 Ibid.
22 Given D266/49. He was preceded by George Forster in 1783–84.
23 She was remembered years afterwards, Vigne(1842) I 228.
24 D266/49. See also below p. 322.
25 Alder(1980/1) 206n.

26 Idem(1975) I xiv. Cf. III 97.
27 *Trebeck* no. 7.
28 D266/49.
29 Moorcroft and Trebeck II 376.
30 In addition to the sources listed above n.1, there is some interesting fragmentary evidence of this Kabul period in G31/135.
31 C45/14.
32 C45 *passim*; D266/87.
33 D266/49.
34 D264/219.
35 *IOL* P/124/29, 27 of 14.10.1825.
36 Ibid.; D266/83, 85 and 95.
37 *IOL* P/124/29, 27 of 14.10.1825.
38 *Trebeck* no. 7.
39 D251/100.
40 *IOL* P/124/29, 27 of 14.10.1825.
41 D266/96; Wolff(1835) 249.
42 Mohan Lal 325.
43 Lunt 75 and 109.
44 A21/28.
45 D251/12; A21/11.
46 Moorcroft and Trebeck II 387–92. Vigne(1840) 189 and Godard and Hackin 8 give Moorcroft some credit. Dupree, Gaulier, Hackin and Carl do not.
47 Masson.
48 Their position can be precisely located from Masson 710 and his papers *IOL* Eur. MS. E167/116 and F65 drawing 203.
49 D250/240.
50 *Trebeck* no. 7.

22 MURAD BEG OF KUNDUZ, AUGUST 1824–JANUARY 1825 (pages 329–343)

1 The prime source for this chapter is Moorcroft's sporadic journal D251/10ff. and the fragment D252, paraphrased in Moorcroft and Trebeck

II 394–488. References are given only to other sources.
2 *IOL* P/124/29, 27 of 10.6.1825.
3 D250/350.

4 The name is still in use locally but the official name is Samangan.
5 D251/166; A22/32.
6 Burnes(1834) I 106.
7 See drawing above p. 329.
8 This para. is also partly derived from the fragment A20.
9 D266/98.
10 *Trebeck* no. 8.
11 Trebeck's journal of the journey is F35.
12 *Trebeck* no. 9.

13 In C43.
14 D251/150.
15 Cunningham 8; D254/159.
16 D250/423; *Trebeck* no. 11.
17 D251/186.
18 *Trebeck* no. 11.
19 *IOL* P/124/29, 27 of 14.10.1825. An inexact version was published as Moorcroft(1826).
20 As he did in *Trebeck* no. 11.
21 *IOL* P/124/29, 27 of 14.10.1825.

23 Journey's End, February–August 1825 (pages 344–360)

1 The prime source for the remainder of the journey to Bokhara is Moorcroft's journal D253. The paraphrase in Moorcroft and Trebeck II 488–508 is based on material now missing. *Trebeck* no. 11 has valuable corroborative information.
2 D254/386.
3 D254/317.
4 Moorcroft and Trebeck I xlvi.
5 *IOL* P/124/29, 27 of 14.10.1825; D254/311.
6 The remainder of this chap. is based on Moorcroft's journal D254, parts of which are more legible in C68–9; his long letter to govt. as above chap. 22 n.19; and that to Wade 17.8.1825 *IOL* P/124/37, 11 of 20.1.1826. References are given only to other sources.
7 Burnes(1834); Alder(1980/1) 173.
8 Moorcroft and Trebeck I liii.
9 See above p. 344.
10 Burnes(1834) I 315. The other is D263/109.
11 *Accounts and Papers*(1859) 238.

12 Ibid.
13 D266/45.
14 I.O. 97.
15 *Trebeck* no. 11.
16 *Stirling* 2.
17 Ibid.
18 Moorcroft and Trebeck I xlvii; Vambéry 238.
19 Vambéry 238.
20 *Accounts and Papers*(1859) 238; *IOL* P/194/69, 10 and 12 of 11.7.1838.
21 *IOL* P/124/24, 1 of 19.8.1825.
22 Vambéry 239.
23 Hügel 9. Cf. Prinsep(1897) 100.
24 *Accounts and Papers*(1859) 238.
25 Huc II 178. What follows is idem 202–4.
26 Although there appears to be no other evidence of it. It is not in *PRO* FO 17/123/no. 22.
27 Burnes(1834) I 244.
28 D249/189.
29 Huc 182.
30 Edgeworth 289.
31 This is also the conclusion of Fazy.
32 *Accounts and Papers*(1859) 238.

24 Epilogue and Conclusion (pages 361–372)

1 Anon(9) 240. The following account of the break-up of the party is based on the letter of Guru Das Singh *IOL* P/124/41, 13 of 7.4.1826 published *Asiatic Journal* XXII (Nov. 1826) 596; Askar Ali's account in *Stirling* 2; and Burnes(1834) I 233–44. References are given only to other sources.
2 Wolff(1835) 211.
3 Referred to but not given in *IOL* P/124/37, 20 of 6.1.1826.

4 *Accounts and Papers*(1859) 238.

5 e.g. Dr Lord in ibid.; Burnes(1834) I 233–4; Stirling 69.

6 *Stirling* 1/entry of 19.9.1828.

7 *Accounts and Papers*(1859) 238.

8 Stirling 45.

9 H. Hearsey 106–7.

10 *Bengal Hurkaru* 19.1.1826/2.

11 *IOL* P/124/37, 19 of 6.1.1826; *Asiatic Journal* XXI(May 1826) 609.

12 *IOL* P/124/37, 20 of 6.1.1826.

13 See above n.1. A different version is F37/205.

14 *IOL* P/124/41, 14 of 7.4.1826.

15 Keay 43; Harlan 7.

16 *IOL* P/124/48, 11 of 30.6.1826; P/125/21, 17 of 1.6.1827.

17 *IOL* P/124/39, 14–15 of 3.3.1826.

18 *Palmer* C103/139, 146, 190 and 210.

19 *Palmer* C99/to de l'Étang 15.11.1823.

20 G28/314/55.

21 *Palmer* C103/7.

22 Ibid. 146.

23 Ibid. 210; *Palmer* C104/14.

24 *IOL* L/AG/34/29/39.

25 *Palmer* C105/195.

26 M/1.8.1845/122; *IOL* P/13/18, 5 of 22.6.1836; *IOL* L/AG/34/29/43, 301 of Pt.3.

27 F37/67.

28 F37/196.

29 D251/169½.

30 To Parry 13.12.1820 D256/86.

31 *Palmer* C104/14.

32 *IOL* L/AG/34/29/43, 301 of Pt.3.

33 *IOL* P/13/18, 5 of 22.6.1836.

34 *IOL* L/Mil/9/182/181.

35 *IOL* P/13/18, 5 of 22.6.1836.

36 *IOL* Eur. MS D636.

37 *IOL* P/13/18, 5 of 22.6.1836.

38 Ibid. 234 of 1.6.1836; from India 18.1.1837 para. 15 *IOL* L/PJ/3/28.

39 *IOL* P/13/18, 5 of 22.6.1836.

40 *IOL* L/Mil/11/45/255, 50/230, 57/230, 59/230 and 60/230.

41 L/F/197/coll. 49.

42 *IOL* L/AG/34/29/350, 45 of 1849 Pt.1.

43 Vigne(1840) 128; Cunningham 8ff.; Edgeworth 289.

44 By Keay. See *Stirling* 1 and 2 and Stirling 45 and 69.

45 Wolff(1835) 180–3 and 211–12; idem(1845) I 77; idem(1861) 331, 348 and 353.

46 Mohan Lal 94.

47 Burnes(1834) I 243; Gerard 18–19.

48 Burnes(1842) 134.

49 Wood(1872).

50 *Accounts and Papers*(1859) 237–40; *IOL* P/194/69, 12 of 11.7.1838.

51 Enoki 26.

52 *Accounts and Papers*(1859) 146.

53 Hügel 101–2.

54 Vigne(1842) II 342.

55 Ibid. 79; cf. Hügel 119.

56 Vambéry 240.

57 G28/361.

58 Above p. 336.

59 Above p. 175.

60 Colebrooke I 354 and 357.

61 Moorcroft and Trebeck I l–liii; Kaye 882–5; Anon(9) 241.

62 *IOL* Eur. MS E301/2 Thornton letter 14.10.1834.

63 Moorcroft(1831) and idem(1832).

64 Esp. the idea that Moorcroft died at Bokhara, Mohan Lal 128; Wolff(1845) I 77.

65 C40–3; Kaye 883. Prinsep(1835) is based on a now missing Trebeck journal.

66 *Journal of the Asiatic Society of Bengal* IV(1835) 177. The suspicions of Keay 44 are probably unjustified.

67 Trebeck 5.6.1833 *IOL* Eur. MS E301/2.

68 Sirkin(1965) and (1968).

69 *Murray* Wilson's letters of 16.1 and 15 and 19.7.1834; Torrens to Wilson 8.6.1841 *IOL* Eur. MS E301/4.

70 *Murray* Wilson letter 27.11.1835.

71 D251/150; Moorcroft and Trebeck I liii–iv.

72 *Murray* sales ledger 1837; letter from John Murray to author 21.6.1979.

73 It is in the National Library of

Australia, Canberra. Marshall 82
no. 664.

74 Barrow. See too *Bibliothèque Universelle de Génève* XX(1839) 122.

75 *Journal Asiatique* VIII(Aug. 1839)
96.

76 Vigne(1840) 187 and 189; Hügel 4.

77 *Murray* Wilson 23.7.1839; Trebeck
6.7.1840 and Low Nov. 1840 *IOL*
Eur. MS E301/3.

78 Moorcroft and Trebeck II end
advertising p. 2.

79 *Murray* sales ledger; *Bombay Times*
1.1.1842/4.

80 Anon(9) 241; Barrow 107 and 119;
Anon(10) 147.

81 Alder(1972/2) 229ff.

82 *IOL* Eur. MS E301/4.

83 Moorcroft and Trebeck I liv.

84 *IOL* Eur. MS E301/4 Elphinstone
18.11.1841.

85 Moorcroft and Trebeck I lv.

86 Archer(1973) I 224, 247 and 261;
Irwin 43.

87 G28/361.

88 Moorcroft and Trebeck I liii and lii.

89 *Calcutta Review* I(1844) 457.

90 Moorcroft and Trebeck I xix and
xxxvi.

91 e.g. Delpar 112; Terway 159 and

161; Macgregor 252; Dallman and
Wood; Rawling 4.

92 Sandberg 111; Lunt(1964) 666;
Hopkirk 22.

93 Macgregor 251. There are seven
factual errors on the following page.

94 Woodman 22–3.

95 Keay 19.

96 e.g. *Palmer* C97/233. Expert analysis of Moorcroft's handwriting has
independently confirmed the character sketch given in this para.

97 Espinasse; B. Orchard; Sutton. The
exception is Dallman and Wood.

98 Moorcroft and Trebeck I xxi.

99 e.g. Baron; Buckland; Chiodi; Firmin-Didot; Hyamson; Neumann;
Schrader and Hering; Thomas.

100 *DNB* 337–8; B.B.; Barber-
Lomax(1964) and (1966).

101 F37/81, 157 and 184; F38/41; *Veterinarian* XVI(1843) 641; ibid.
XXI(1848) 338.

102 Davis 244–7.

103 *Smith-Bullock* letters of 4.3. and
30.10.1928.

104 Above p. ix.

105 *Oriental Herald and Journal of General
Literature* IX(Apr.–June 1826) 570.

106 F37/81.

LIST OF SOURCES REFERRED TO IN THE NOTES

The place of publication of all books is London unless otherwise stated.

Abdussalam, M. 'William Moorcroft, the first European Veterinarian to visit Lahore', *Veterinary History.* 7(1976), 20.

Accounts and Papers (1821); Accounts ... relating to the increase and diminution of salaries ... in the public offices of Ireland ..., *Accounts and Papers* 1821, XIII (287).

Accounts and Papers (1859), Copies of the correspondence of Sir Alex. Burnes with the Governor General of India, during his Mission to Cabul ..., *Accounts and Papers* 1859, 2nd session XXV 1.

Ackermann, N. *et al.* 'Navicular disease in the horse: risk factors, radiographic changes, and response to therapy', *Journal of the American Veterinary Medical Association* 170 (1977), 183.

Adams, B. *London Illustrated 1604–1851* (1982).

Adams, J. *Memoirs of the Life and Doctrines of the late John Hunter Esq.* (1817).

Add. MS, Additional Manuscripts series at the British Library, London, Those cited are in the collections of: Warren Hastings (29,189 and 29,210); Arthur Young (35,126 and 35,128); Henry Aston (36,901); Charles Grenville (42,072); and Sir Robert Peel (40,227 and 40,247).

Ahluwalia, M. 'Ladakh's Relations with India – an historical study', *Proceedings of the Indian Historical Records Commission* XXXIII 2, 1.

Aijazuddin, F. *Pahari Paintings and Sikh Portraits in the Lahore Museum* (1977).

Alanson, E. *Practical Observations on Amputation and the after-treatment* (2nd edn., 1782).

Alder, G. (1963) *British India's Northern Frontier 1865–95* (1963).

Alder, G. (1972/1) 'Britain and the defence of India – the origins of the problem 1798–1815', *Journal of Asian History* 6(1972), 14.

Alder, G (1972/2) 'The "garbled" Blue Books of 1839: myth or reality?', *Historical Journal* 15(1972), 229.

Alder, G. (1975) Introduction to C. Masson, *Narrative of Various Journeys* (3 vols, repr. Graz, 1975).

Alder, G. (1979) 'The origins of "the Pusa Experiment": the East India Company and horse-breeding in Bengal 1793–1808', *Bengal Past and Present* 98(1979), 10.

Alder, G. (1980/1) 'Standing Alone: William Moorcroft plays the Great Game 1808–25', *International History Review* 2(1980), 172.

Alder, G. (1980/2) 'Moorcroft's life in England – some new evidence', *Veterinary History* n.s. 1(1979–81), 78.

Allen, C. (1980) 'A forgotten pioneer of Himalayan exploration', *Asian Affairs* n.s. 11 (1980), 169.

Allen, C. (1982) *A Mountain in Tibet* (1982).

Allen, T. *The History and Antiquities of London* (5 vols, 1827–37).

Andrews, J. *Letters to a young gentleman on his setting out for France* (1784).

Anglesey, Marquess of. *A History of the British Cavalry 1816–19* (vol. I 1973).

Anon. (1) *An account of the Veterinary College from its Institution in 1791* (1793).

Anon. (2) *A Practical Guide during a Journey from London to Paris* (1802).

Anon. (3) *The Picture of Liverpool; or Stranger's Guide* (Liverpool, 1805).

Anon. (4) 'Outward Bound', *Asiatic Journal* n.s. 18(1835), 195.

Anon. (5) *The Light Horse Drill: describing the several evolutions etc. designed for the use of . . . the volunteer corps* (by 'a Private of the London & Westminster Light Horse Volunteers', 2nd edn, 1800).

Anon. (6) 'Moorcroft and Hearsey in Tibet', *Geographical Journal* 27(1906), 502.

Anon. (7) 'Himalaya Mountains and Lake Manasawara', *Quarterly Review* 17(1817), 403.

Anon. (8) *Confidential Gazeteer of Kashmir and Ladakh* (Calcutta, 1890).

Anon. (9) 'Moorcroft's Travels', *Asiatic Journal* n.s. 34(1841), 240.

Anon. (10) Review of Moorcroft and Trebeck, *The Athenaeum* (20 Feb. 1841), 147.

Archer, M. *British Drawings in the India Office Library* (2 vols, 1969).

Archer, W. (1973) *Indian Paintings from the Punjab Hills: a survey and history of Pahari miniature painting* (2 vols, 1973).

Archer, W. (1975) *Pahari Miniatures: a concise history* (Bombay, 1975).

Arloing, S. *Le berceau de l'enseignement vétérinaire: création et évolution de l'École Nationale de Lyon* (Lyons, 1889).

Atkinson, E. *The Himalayan Districts of the North-Western Provinces of India* (3 vols, Allahabad, 1882–6).

Bagley, J. *A History of Lancashire* (Henley-on-Thames, 1972).

Baines, E. *The History of the County Palatine and Duchy of Lancashire* (4 vols, 1836).

Baines, F. *The Visitation of the County Palatine of Lancaster made in the year 1664–65* (Chetham Society vols 84–5, Manchester, 1872).

Baird, T. *General View of the Agriculture of the County of Middlesex* (1793).

Bamzai, P. *A History of Kashmir . . . from the earliest times to the present day* (Delhi, 1962).

Barber-Lomax, J. (1959) 'Moorcroft's Journey into Hiundes', *Veterinary Record* 71(1959), 451.

Barber-Lomax, J. (1963) 'Equine Ovariectomy', *Veterinary Record* 75(1963), 662.

Barber-Lomax, J. (1964) 'William Moorcroft', unpubl. paper read before Liverpool University Veterinary Society, summarized *Rumen* (1965), 27.

Barber-Lomax, J. (1966) 'Moorcroft's Life in England', unpubl. paper read before Veterinary History Society, London, 23 Apr. 1966.

Barnes, R. *The Soldiers of London* (1963).

Baron, A. *Biographie Universelle* (vol. 13, Brussels, 1845).

Barrow, J. Review of Moorcroft and Trebeck, *Quarterly Review* 61(1838), 96.

B. B., (Beryl M. Bailey) 'William Moorcroft', *The Incisor* 3(1961), 13, 26.

Bebbington, G. *London Street Names* (1972).

Bellasis, M. *Honourable Company* (1952).

Bellew, F. *Memoirs of a Griffin* (2 vols, 1843).

Berry, B. and Schofield, R. 'Age at Baptism in pre-industrial England', *Population Studies* 25(1971), 453.

Besant, W. (1902) *London in the Eighteenth Century* (1902).

Besant, W. (1911) *London North of the Thames* (1911).

Bickerton, The Bickerton Collection in the Local History Collection, Liverpool Record Office.

Bickerton, T. *A Medical History of Liverpool from the Earliest Days to the Year 1920* (1936).

Black, C. *Memoir on Indian Surveys* (1891).

Blaine, D. (1802, 1816, 1832 and 1841) *The Outlines of the Veterinary Art* (1st, 2nd, 4th and 5th edns).

Blake, B. 'Description of the royal gardens of Lahore', *Quarterly Journal of Literature Science and the Arts* 9(1820), 311.

Blechynden, K. *Calcutta Past and Present* (1905).

Boardman, T. *A Dictionary of the Veterinary Art* (1805).

Boitel, L. 'École Vétérinaire', *Lyon ancien et moderne* (vol. 2, Lyons, 1843), 17.

Boyd, E. *Bloomsbury Heritage*, (1976).

Brooke, R. *Liverpool as it was during the last quarter of the eighteenth century* (1853).

Buckland, C. *Dictionary of Indian Biography* (1910).

Burford, R. *Description of a view of the city of Calcutta* (1831).

Burkill, I. *Chapters on the History of Botany in India* (Delhi, 1965).

Burnes, A. (1834) *Travels into Bokhara* (3 vols., 1834).

Burnes, A. (1842) *Cabool* (1842).

Burrard, S. 'The Mountains of Karakoram: a defence of the existing nomenclature', *Geographical Journal* 74(1929), 277.

Burrard, S. and Hayden, H. *A Sketch of the Geography and Geology of the Himalaya Mountains and Tibet* (Delhi, 1933–4).

Burton, R. *Goa and the Blue Mountains* (1857).

Bute, Marchioness of, *The Private Journal of the Marquess of Hastings* (2 vols, 1858).

Cambridge, Marquess of, 'The volunteer reviews in Hyde Park in 1799, 1800 and 1803', *Society for Army Historical Research* 40(1962), 117.

Cameron, I. Mountains of the Gods (1984).

Caroe, O. *The Pathans, 550 BC–AD 1957* (1964).

Cartwright, F. *The Development of Modern Surgery* (New York, 1968).

Chalklin, C. *The Provincial Towns of Georgian England* (1974).

Charlety, S. (1898) *Lyon en 1789* (Lyons, 1898).

Charlety, S. (1903) *Histoire de Lyon depuis les Origines jusqu' à nos Jours* (Lyons, 1903).

Chatterton, E. *The Old East Indiamen* (1933).

Cherry, F. *The Art of Shoeing Horses by the Sieur de Solleysel to which are added notes on his practice by F.C.C.* (1842).

Chetwode, P. *Kulu: the end of the habitable world* (1972).

Chiodi, V. *Storia della Veterinaria* (Milan, 1957).

Chopra, G. 'An autograph letter addressed by William Moorcroft to Major General Sir David Ochterlony, Bart., KCGB', *Journal of the Panjab Historical Society* 2(1933), 85.

Chowdhuri, R. 'Anglo-Russian Commerical Rivalry in 1812', *Journal of Indian History* 29(1951), 15.

Clark, B. (1817) *Stereoplea: or the artificial defence of the horse's hoof considered* (1817).

Clark, B. (1824) *A Short History of the Horse and Progress of Horse Knowledge* (1824).

Clark, B. (1838) *Hippiatria: or the surgery and medicine of horses* (1838).

Clark, J. *Observations upon the Shoeing of Horses together with a new inquiry into the causes of diseases in the feet of horses* (Edinburgh, 1782).

Clarke, E. 'The Board of Agriculture, 1793–1822', *Journal of the Royal Agricultural Society of England* 3rd ser. 9(1898), 1.

Clemens, S. L. *Mark Twain's Autobiography* (2 vols, New York, 1924).

Cobb, R. (1972) *Reactions to the French Revolution* (1972).

Cobb, R. (1975) *A Sense of Place* (1975).

Colebrooke, T. *Miscellaneous Essays I The Life of H. T. Colebrooke* (3 vols, 1873).

Coleman, E. *Observations on the structure . . . of the foot of the Horse* (2 vols, 1798–1802).

Colles, C. and Hickman, J. 'The Arterial Supply of the Navicular Bone and its variations in navicular disease', *Equine Veterinary Journal* 9(1977), 150.

Collins, H. *Lancashire Plain and Seaboard* (1953).

Collyer J. and Pocock, J. *An Historical Record of the Light Horse Volunteers of London and Westminster* (1843).

Colvin, H. *A Biographical Dictionary of British Architects 1600–1840* (1978).

Conolly, A. *Journey to the North of India, overland from England* (2 vols, 1838).

Corry, J. *The History of Liverpool* (Liverpool, 1810).

Cotchin, E. 'Edward Coleman – a tentative reappraisal', unpubl. paper given before Veterinary History Society, London, 23 Apr. 1966.

Cotton, H. *East Indiamen – the East India Company's maritime service* (1949).

Cousins, G. *The Defenders: a history of the British volunteer* (1968).

Crace, Collection by F. C. Crace of views of London in the Prints and Drawings Department of the British Library, London.

Crawford, D. *A History of the Indian Medical Service 1600–1913* (2 vols, 1914).

Crook, J. *The British Museum* (1972).

Crowe, S. and Haywood, S. *The Gardens of Mughal India: a history and a guide* (1972).

Csoma, A. de Körös, *Essay towards a Dictionary of Tibetan and English* (Calcutta, 1834).

Cunningham, A. *Ladak, Physical, Statistical and Historical* (1854).

Currie, J. *Medical Reports on the effects of water . . . as a remedy in fever* (Liverpool, 1797).

Currie, W. *Memoir of the Life, Writings and Correspondence of James Currie* (2 vols, 1831).

Dainelli, G. *La Esplorazione della regione fra l'Himalaja occidentale e il Caracorum* (Bologna, 1934).

Dallman, A. and Wood, M. 'A Biographical List of Deceased Lancashire Botanists', *Transactions of the Liverpool Botanical Society* 1(1909), 54.

Darlington, I. and Howgego, J. *Printed Maps of London circa 1553–1850* (1964).

Datta, C. (1970) 'Significance of the shawl-wool trade in western Himalayan politics', *Bengal Past and Present* 84(1970), 16.

Datta, C. (1973) *Ladakh and Western Himalayan Politics 1819–48* (Delhi, 1973).

Datta, S. 'The Etiology of Bursati', *Indian Journal of Veterinary Science and Animal Husbandry* 3(1933), 217.

Davies, R. *Report on the trade and resources of the countries on the north-western boundary of British India* (2 vols, Lahore, 1862).

Davis, H. 'The Great Game in Asia, 1800–44', *Proceedings of the British Academy* 12(1926), 227.

Delpar, H. *The Discoverers: an encyclopaedia of explorers and exploration* (1980).

Desmond, R. *Dictionary of British and Irish Botanists and Horticulturists* (1977).

DNB, Dictionary of National Biography (vol. 13, 1917).

Dobson, J. *John Hunter* (Edinburgh, 1969).

Druhe, D. *Russo-Indian Relations, 1466–1917* (New York, 1970).

Duka, T. *Life and Works of Alexander Csoma de Körös* (1885).

Dupree, N. *The Valley of Bamiyan* (Kabul, 1967).

East India Company, *Papers respecting the Nepaul War* (1824).

Eby, C. 'William Moorcroft 1767–1825', *Modern Veterinary Practice* 40(1959), 52.

Eccleston, T. 'The improvement of Martin Meer', *Transactions of the Society of Arts* 7(1789), 50.

Edgeworth, M. 'Abstract of a Journal kept by Mr. Gardiner during his travels in Central Asia', *Journal of the Asiatic Society of Bengal* 22(1853), 283.

Edwardes, H. *A Year on the Punjab Frontier in 1848–49* (2 vols, 1851).

Edwards, J. 'The Chemotherapy of Surra of Horses and Cattle in India', *Therapeutics* 39(1926), 83 and 169.

Elphinstone, M. *An Account of the Kingdom of Caubul* (1815).

Emsley, E. *British Society and the French Wars 1793–1815* (1979).

Enfield, W. *An Essay towards the history of Liverpool* (1774).

Enoki, K. 'Dr. G. E. Morrison and the Toyo Bunko', *East Asian Cultural Studies* 7(1968), 1.

Espinasse, F. *Lancashire Worthies* (2nd series, 1874–7).

Eyriès, J. 'Voyage au Lac Manasarovar, situé dans l'Oundes, Province due Petit Tibet, fait en 1812 par MM. Moorcroft et Hearsey', *Nouvelles Annales des Voyages* 1(1819), 239.

Fazy, R. 'Le Cas Moorcroft: un problème de l'exploration Tibetaine', *T'oung Pao* 35(1940), 155.

Field, W. *Posthumous Extracts from the Veterinary Records of the late John Field* (1843).

Firmin-Didot frères, *Nouvelle Biographie Générale* (vol. 36, Paris, 1865).

Fishwick, H. and Ditchfield, P. *Memorials of Old Lancashire* (2 vols, 1909).

Fleming, G. *Horse-shoes and Horse-shoeing: their origin, history, uses and abuses* (1869).

Forster, G. *A Journey from Bengal to England* (2 vols, 1798).

Francke, A. *Antiquities of Indian Tibet – II The Chronicles of Ladakh and Minor Chronicles* (Calcutta, 1926).

Freeman, S. *Observations on the Mechanism of the Horse's Foot* (1796).

Freeman, T., Rodgers, H. and Kinvig, R. *Lancashire, Cheshire and the Isle of Man* (1966).

Garden, M. *Lyon et les Lyonnais au xviii*ᵉᵐᵉ *Siècle* (Paris, n.d.).

Gaulier, S. *et al. Buddhism in Afghanistan and Central Asia* (Leiden, 1976).

Gerard, J. 'Continuation of the route of Lieut. A. Burnes and Dr. Gerard from Peshawar to Bokhara', *Journal of the Asiatic Society of Bengal* 2(1833), 1.

Gifford, J. *A residence in France during the years 1792, 1793 and 1795* (2 vols, 1797).

Gilbey, W. *Horse-Breeding in England and India and Army Horses abroad* (1901).

Godard, A. and Y. and Hackin, J. *Les antiquités bouddhistiques de Bamiyan* (Paris, 1928).

Gomme, A. *Patent of Invention: origin and growth of the patent system* (1948).

Goss, C. *The London Directories 1677–1855* (1932).

Govinda, Li Gotami, *Tibet in Pictures* (vol. 2, California, 1979).

Gray, E. (1952) *Portrait of a Surgeon* (1952).

Gray, E. (1957) 'John Hunter and Veterinary Medicine', *Medical History* 1(1957), 38.

Greater London Council, *Survey of London – XXX The Parish of St. James Westminster* (1960).

Grey, C. and Garrett, H. *European Adventurers of Northern India, 1785–1849* (Lahore, 1929).

Gupta, S. 'The Sikh school of painting', *Rupam* 3(1922), 125.

Guthrie, G. 'The late Mr. Moorcroft', *Asiatic journal* (1828), 157.

Hackin, J. and Carl, J. *Nouvelles recherches archéologiques à Bamiyan* (Paris, 1933).

Hall, S. 'Coughing in Horses – an historical aspect', *Equine Veterinary Journal* 9(1977), 37.

Hallen, J. 'Government Horse-Breeding in India; past, present and future', paper read before United Services Institution of India, 6 May 1887.

Hamilton, B. 'The Medical Profession in the eighteenth century', *Economic History Review* 2nd ser. 4(1951), 141.

Hamilton, W. *A Geographical, Statistical and Historical description of Hindoostan and the adjacent countries* (2 vols, 1820).

Hancock, R. 'Odd Shoes', *Veterinary Record* 66(1954), 90.

List of Sources

Hardy, C. *A Register of Ships employed in the service of the Honourable United East India Company from the year 1760–1812* (1813).

Harlan, J. *Central Asia: personal narrative of . . . Harlan, 1823–41* (1939).

Harrold, P. 'The India Office Library's Prints of Calcutta', *Report of the India Office Library and Records* (1972–3), 7.

Hasrat, B. *Life and Times of Ranjit Singh: a saga of benevolent despotism* (Hathikana, 1977).

Hearsey, Manuscript Journal of Hyder Y. Hearsey entitled 'A Tour to Eastern Tatary performed in 1812' in the possession of John Hearsey, Angmering, Sussex.

Hearsey, A. *Military and other services of the Hearsey family 1745–1821* (privately printed – n.d.).

Hearsey, H. 'Mr. Moorcroft's Journey to Balkh and Bokhara', *Asiatic Journal* 18(1835), 106, 171 and 278 and idem 19(1836), 35 and 95.

Hearsey, L. *Military and other services of the Hearsey family brought up to 1954 by J. Stephens* (privately printed – n.d.).

Hedin, S. (1910–13) *Trans-Himalaya* (3 vols, 1910–13).

Hedin, S. (1917–23) *Southern Tibet* (9 vols, Stockholm 1917–23).

Henderson, P. *Travels in Central Asia by Meer Izzut-Oollah in the years 1812–13* (Calcutta 1872).

Hetenyi, E. 'Alexander Csoma de Koros', *Bulletin of Tibetology* 9(1972), 36.

Hickey, W. *Memoirs of William Hickey* (4 vols, 1913–25).

Hickman, J. *Farriery: a complete illustrated guide*, (1977).

Holdich, T. *The Gates of India* (1910).

Holt, J. (1794) *General View of the Agriculture of the County of Lancaster* (1794).

Holt, J. (1795) *General View of the Agriculture of the County of Lancaster* (1795).

Hooker, J. *Flora of British India* (7 vols., 1875–97).

Hopkirk, P. *Trespassers on the Roof of the World: the race for Lhasa* (1982).

Horwood, R. *Plan of the Cities of London and Westminster . . . showing every House* (8 sheets 1792–9).

Hours, H. 'La lutte contre les Épizooties' and 'L'École Vétérinaire de Lyon au xviiie siècle', *Collection des Cahiers d'Histoire publiés par les Universités de Clermont, Lyon, Grenoble* (Paris, 1957).

Howe, S. *Novels of Empire* (1971).

Huc, E. *Travels in Tartary, Thibet and China during the years 1844–46* (2 vols, 1851).

Hügel, C. von, *Travels in Kashmir and the Panjab* (1845).

Hunting, W. *The art of horseshoeing* (1905).

Hyamson, A. *Dictionary of Universal Biography* (1916).

Hyde, F. *Liverpool and the Mersey: an economic history of a port 1700–1970* (Newton Abbot, 1971).

Hyde, H. *Simla and the Simla Hill States under British Protection 1815–35* (Lahore, 1961).

Ingram, E. *The Beginning of the Great Game in Asia 1828–34* (1979).

I.O., 'Ekspeditsiia general'nago shtaba polkovnika Berga na Ust-Urt 1825–26gg', *Voennyj Sbornik* 12(1879), 195.

IOL, Manuscript official correspondence at the India Office Library and Records, London.

Irwin, J. *The Kashmir Shawl* (1973).

Jacquemont, V. *Letters from India 1829–32* (1936).

Johnson, J. *An account of a voyage to India . . . in H. M. ship Caroline . . . in 1803–4–5* (1806).

Karpinsky, C. 'Kashmir to Paisley', *Bulletin of the Metropolitan Museum of Art* (22 Nov. 1963), 116.

Kaushik, D. 'British Designs in Central Asia in the nineteenth century', *Proceedings of the Indian Historical Congress* 29(1967), 233.

Kaye, G. *India Office Library: Catalogue of Manuscripts in European Languages* (vol. 2, Pt. 2, Section 1,1937), 881.

Keay, J. *When Men and Mountains Meet* (1977).

Kelly, C. *The R.G.S. Archives: a handlist* (repr. from *Geographical Journal* 141(Mar. 1975).

Kessler, M. 'Ivan Viktovich Vitevich 1806–39: a Tsarist Agent in Central Asia', ed. R. Lowenthal, *Central Asia Collectanea* 4(Washington D.C., 1960).

Khalfin, N. 'British expansion in Central Asia in the thirties and forties of the nineteenth century', transl. *Central Asian Review* 6(1958), 386.

Kincaid, D. *British Social Life in India 1608–1937* (1973).

Kobler, J. *The Reluctant Surgeon* (New York, 1960).

Kopf, D. *British Orientalism and the Bengal Renaissance* (Berkeley, 1969).

Lamb, A. *Britain and Chinese Central Asia: the road to Lhasa 1767 to 1905* (1960).

Lancs., Various wills, parish registers, estate and personal papers in the Lancashire Record Office, Preston.

Lane, J. *The Principles of English Farriery Vindicated* (1800).

Larsen, L. 'Navicular Disease – its diagnosis and treatment', *Victorian Veterinary Proceedings* 28(1969–70), 58.

Lawrence, J. *A philosophical and practical treatise on horses* (2 vols, 1796).

Lawton, R. 'Population Trends in Lancashire and Cheshire from 1801', *Transactions of the Historical Society of Lancs. and Cheshire* (1962), 114 and (1963), 189.

Lewis, Lady T. *Extracts of the Journal and Correspondence of Miss Berry* (3 vols, 1865).

Lindley, J. 'Some account of the prangos hay plant of Northern India', *Quarterly Journal of Science and the Arts* 19(1825), 1.

Liverpool, Records of the Liverpool Royal Infirmary in the Local History Collection, Liverpool Record Office.

Lloyd, W. *Narrative of a Journey from Caunpoor to the Boorendo Pass* (2 vols, 1840).

Lockie, J. *Lockie's Topography of London* (1810).

Longstaff, T. Typescript (1908?) by T. Longstaff entitled 'The Manasarowar–Sutlej Problem' in the archives of the Royal Geographical Society, London.

Lunt, J. (1964) '"Bokhara" Burnes', *History Today* 14(1964), 665.

Lunt, J. (1969) *Bokhara Burnes* (1969).

Lyons, First pupil register in the library of the École Vétérinaire de Lyon.

MacCulloch, J. 'On the attempts recently made to introduce the shawl goat into Britain', *Quarterly Journal of Science, Literature and the Arts* 9(1820), 330.

MacGregor, J. *Tibet: a chronicle of exploration* (1970).

Malton, T. *A Picturesque Tour through the Cities of London and Westminster* (1792).

Marshall, J. *Britain and Tibet 1765–1947* (Bundoora, 1977).

Marylebone, Ratebooks of St. Marylebone on microfilm in the Archives Department of Marylebone Library, London.

Mason, K. (1923) 'Kishen Singh and the Indian Explorers', *Geographical Journal* 62(1923), 429.

Mason, K. (1955) *Abode of Snow* (1955).

Masson, C. 'Notes on the antiquities of Bamian', *Journal of the Asiatic Society of Bengal* 5(1836), 707.

Maxwell, C. *The English Traveller in France 1698–1815* (1932).

Milburn, W. *Oriental Commerce, containing a geographical description of the principal places in the East Indies etc.* (2 vols, 1813).

Millward, R. *Lancashire: an illustrated essay on the history of the landscape* (1955).

Mirsky, J. *Sir Aurel Stein: archaeological explorer* (Chicago, 1977).

Mohan Lal, *Journal of a Tour through the Panjab, Afghanistan, Turkistan etc.* (Calcutta, 1834).

Molyneux, R. 'On the Kumree', *Veterinarian* 3(1830), 253.

Moorcroft, Manuscript letter of 9 May 1811 from Moorcroft to Colonel MacGregor entitled 'Reports on Farcy' in the library of the Royal Veterinary College, London.

Moorcroft, W. (1789) 'History of the Disorder Among the Horned Cattle at Standish', *Transactions of Society of Arts* 7(1789), 78.

Moorcroft, W. (1792) 'Case of a Cyst containing Hydatids, extracted from the right anterior Ventricle of the Brain of a Cow', *Medical Facts and Observations* 3(1792), 17.

Moorcroft, W. (1795) *Directions for using the Contents of the Portable Horse Medicine Chest adapted for India* (1795).

Moorcroft, W. (1800) *Cursory Account of the Various Methods of Shoeing Horses hitherto Practised with Incidental Observations* (1800).

Moorcroft, W. (1814) *Observations on the Breeding of Horses within the provinces under the Bengal Establishment* (unpubl. 1814 repr. Calcutta, 1862 and Simla, 1886).

Moorcroft, W. (1816) 'A Journey to Lake Manasarowara in Undes, a province of Little Tibet', *Asiatic Researches* 12(1816), 375.

Moorcroft, W. (1819/1) 'Veterinary Practice' (letter by W.M., Calcutta 26 Mar. 1819), *Calcutta Journal* 2(1819), 883.

Moorcroft, W. (1819/2) 'Reply to the strictures of C.D. on Veterinary Practice' (letter by W.M., Calcutta 28 Apr. 1819), *Calcutta Journal* 3(1819), 330.

Moorcroft, W. (1826) 'Mr. Moorcroft', *Asiatic Journal* 21(1826), 609 and 709.

Moorcroft, W. (1827) 'On the purik sheep of Ladakh etc.', *Transactions of the Royal Asiatic Society* 1(1827), 49.

Moorcroft, W. (1829/1) 'On the fruit trees of Kashmeer and the neighbouring countries', *Transactions of the Agricultural and Horticultural Society of India* 1(1829), 78.

Moorcroft, W. (1829/2) 'Account of Prangos, a plant used at Droz for making hay', *Transactions of the Agricultural and Horticultural Society of India* 1(1829), 94.

Moorcroft, W. (1831) 'Notice on Khoten dated Leh 15 Apr. 1812 [sic]', *Journal of the Royal Geographical Society* 1(1831), 235.

Moorcroft, W. (1832) 'Notices of the Natural Productions and Agriculture of Cashmere', *Journal of the Royal Geographical Society* 2(1832), 253.

Moorcroft, W. (1836) 'Letters of the late Mr. Moorcroft', *Asiatic Journal* n.s. 21(1836), 132 and 217.

Moorcroft, W. (1846) 'Manuscript Papers of the late Mr. Moorcroft', *Veterinarian* 14(1846), 445.

Moorcroft, W. and Trebeck, G. *Travels in the Himalayan Provinces of Hindustan and the Panjab etc.* (2 vols, 1841 reprinted Delhi, 1971 and, with an introduction by G. Alder, Karachi, 1979).

Morgan, G. (1973) 'Myth and Reality in the Great Game', *Asian Affairs* 60(1973), 55.

Morgan, G. (1981) *Anglo-Russian Rivalry in Central Asia 1810–1895* (1981).

Moss, W. (1784) *A familiar medical survey of Liverpool* (Liverpool, 1784).

Moss, W. (1797) *The Liverpool Guide* (Liverpool, 1797).

Mulvany, T. *The Life of J. Gandon* (1846).

Murray, Correspondence with H. Wilson and sales ledgers in the custody of John Murray (Publishers) Ltd, 50 Albemarle Street, London.

Murray, H. *Historical Account of Discoveries and Travels in Asia* (3 vols, Edinburgh, 1820).

Murray, R. *Edward Alanson and his times* (Liverpool, 1914).

Neumann, L. *Biographes Vétérinaires* (Paris, 1896).

Newby, E. *The Mitchell Beazley World Atlas of Exploration* (1975).

NLS, Papers of the First Earl of Minto in the National Library of Scotland, Edinburgh.

Northouck, J. *A New History of London* (1773).

Nugent, Lady Maria, *A Journal from the year 1811 till the year 1815* (1839)

Ogilby, Benson Freeman Collection, Westminster Volunteer Cavalry file at the Ogilby
Trust, Army Museum, London.
Olsen, D. *Town Planning in London: The Eighteenth and Nineteenth Centuries* (New Haven,
1964).
Orchard, B. *Liverpool's Legion of Honour* (Birkenhead, 1893).
Orchard, V. *Tattersall's – 200 Years of Sporting History* (1953).
Padfield, H. 'The Story of Ormskirk' (typescript Ormskirk, 1963).
Palmer, Letters and account-books of John Palmer at the Bodleian, Oxford.
Palmer, J. *The Works of John Hunter F.R.S.* (4 vols, 1835–37).
Pampanini, R. *La Flore del Caracorum* (Bologna, 1930).
Parkinson, C. (1937) *Trade in the Eastern Seas 1793–1813* (Cambridge, 1937).
Parkinson, C. (1952) *The Rise of the Port of Liverpool* (Liverpool, 1952).
Pasmore, S. (1976–78) 'John Hunter in Kensington', *Transactions of the Hunterian Society*
35–6 (1976–8), 69.
Pasmore, S. (1979) 'Rural scenes of Bayswater: the London of Paul Sandby (1725–
1809)', *Country Life* 165(1979), 586.
Patent, Original patent specifications held at the Patent Office Library, London.
Pattison, I. *The British Veterinary Profession 1791–1948* (1983).
Pearse, H. (1905/1) *The Hearseys: five generations of an Anglo-Indian family* (1905).
Pearse, H. (1905/2) 'Moorcroft and Hearsey's visit to Lake Manasarowar in 1812',
Geographical Journal 26(1905), 180.
Pemble, J. (1971) *The Invasion of Nepal: John Company at War 1814–16* (Oxford, 1971).
Pemble, J. (1977) *The Raj, the Indian Mutiny and the Kingdom of Oudh 1801–59* (Hassocks,
1977).
Pennant, T. *Some Account of London* (1793).
Petech, L. *The Kingdom of Ladakh c.950–1842 A.D.* (Rome, 1977).
Philips, C. *The East India Company 1784–1834* (Manchester, 1940).
Phillimore, R. H. *Historical Records of the Survey of India* (4 vols, Dehra Dun 1945–54).
Picton, J. *Memorials of Liverpool* (2 vols, 1875).
Power, D'Arcy. 'Two Liverpool Surgeons – I Henry Park II Edward Alanson', *British
Journal of Surgery* 24(1936–7), 205 and 421.
Powis, R. *A concise dissertation on the anatomy, physiology . . . of the foot of the horse* (1823).
Pranavananda, Swami *Kailas – Manasarovar* (Calcutta, 1950).
Prinsep, H. (1835) 'Remarks on the Topes of Manikyala', *Asiatic Journal* 18(1835), 190.
Prinsep, H. (1897) *Origin of the Sikh Power in the Punjab and Political Life of Maharaja Ranjit
Singh* (Lahore, 1897).
PRO, Records and private papers held at the Public Record Office, Kew.
Prosser, T. *Treatise on Strangles and Fevers of Horses* (1790).
Pugh, L. *From Farriery to Veterinary Medicine 1785–95* (Cambridge, 1962).
Randhawa, M. (1961) 'Maharaja Sansar Chand – the patron of Kangra Painting',
Roopa Lekha 32(1961), 2, 1.
Randhawa, M. (1970) *Maharaja Sansar Chand the Patron of Kangra Painting* (Delhi, 1970).
Raper, F. 'Narrative of a survey for the purpose of discovering the source of the
Ganges', *Asiatic Researches* 11(1810), 446.
Rawlinson, H. 'Csoma de Körös', *Indian Art and Letters* n.s. 19(1945), 15.
RCVS, Manuscript H.682.1. '18' by B. Clark (1853) entitled 'The Twisted Shoe' in the
library of the Royal College of Veterinary Surgeons, London.
Reymann, F. L'Ecole Vétérinaire de Lyon au xviiie siècle (unpubl. thesis Lyons 1980,
no. 102).
Rigby, E. *Dr. Rigby's letters from France . . . in 1789* (1790).
Robertson, A. *Handbook of Animal Diseases in the Tropics* (1976).

Rollinson, W. 'Schemes for the reclamation of land from the sea in North Lancashire during the eighteenth and nineteenth centuries', *Transactions of the Historical Society of Lancs. and Cheshire* 115(1963), 133.

Rowlandson, T. *The illuminated school of Mars, or Review of the Loyal Volunteer Corps of London and its Vicinity* (1799).

Rowlandson, T. and Pugin, A. *The Microcosm of London* (3 vols., 1808).

Royle, J. *Illustrations of the Botany of the Himalayan Mountains* (2 vols, 1839).

RSA, Subscription Books 1773–1802 and Committee Minutes 35(1789–90) at the library of the Royal Society of Arts, London.

Rudé, G. *Hanoverian London 1714–1808* (1971).

RVC, Minute Books in the library of the Royal Veterinary College, London.

Sandberg, G. *Exploration of Tibet: its history and particulars from 1623 to 1904* (Calcutta, 1904).

Sandby, W. *Thomas and Paul Sandby, Royal Academicians: some account of their lives and works* (1892).

Sanders, C. *The Strachey Family 1588–1932* (Durham N.C., 1953).

Sandhu, G. *The Indian Cavalry* (New Delhi, 1981).

Scarisbrick, Papers of the Scarisbrick estate and family at the Lancashire Record Office, Preston.

Schrader, G. and Hering, E. *Biographisch–literarisches Lexicon der Thierärzte aller Zeiten und Länder* (Stuttgart, 1863).

Schwarz, L. 'Income distribution and social structure in London in the late eighteenth century', *Economic History Review* 2nd ser. 32(1979), 250.

Scott, H. 'Some account of the method of operating for the cataract practised in India, with observations', *Journal of Science and the Arts* 2(1817), 67.

Searight, S. 'Ladakh – Barrier or Entrepot?', *History Today* 26(1976), 256.

Sebag-Montefiore, C. *A History of the Volunteer Forces* (1908).

Severin, T. *The Oriental Adventure – explorers of the East* (1976).

Sharar, S. *Lucknow: the last phase of an Oriental Culture* (1974).

Sheppard, F. *Local Government in St. Marylebone 1688–1835* (1958).

Simonds, J. *The Foundation of the Royal Veterinary College* (1897).

Singh, D. 'Moorcroft: the first modern eye-surgeon in Punjab', *Indian Journal of Ophthalmology* 27(1979), 53.

Singh, K. *Ranjit Singh: Maharaja of the Punjab* (1962).

Sinha, N. and Dasgupta, A. *Selections from the Ochterlony Papers (1818–25) in the National Archives of India* (Calcutta, 1964).

Sirkin, G. and N. (1965) 'Horace Hayman Wilson and Gamesmanship in Indology', *Asian Studies* 3(1965), 301.

Sirkin, G. and N. (1968) 'Of raising myths for fun and profit', *Columbia Forum* 11(3), (1968).

Smith, A. *An Inquiry into the nature and causes of the Wealth of Nations* (repr. 1961).

Smith, F. (1927) *A History of the Royal Army Veterinary Corps 1796–1919* (1927).

Smith, F. (1919–33) *The Early History of Veterinary Literature and its British Development* (4 vols, 1919–33).

Smith, T. *A Topographical and Historical Account of the Parish of St. Marylebone* (1833).

Smith-Bullock, Correspondence between Major-General Sir Frederick Smith and Frederick Bullock, Secretary of the Royal College of Veterinary Surgeons, in the library of the RCVS, London.

Smithcors, J. *Evolution of the Veterinary Art* (Kansas City, 1957).

Snellgrove, D. and Skorupski, T. *The Cultural Heritage of Ladakh* (2 vols, Warminster 1977–80).

Snelling, J. *The Sacred Mountain: travellers and pilgrims at Mount Kailas in Western Tibet* (1983).

Solov'yev, O. 'Russia's relations with India (1800–1917)', *Central Asian Review* (1958), 448.

Spear, P. *Twilight of the Mughuls: studies in late Mughul Delhi* (Cambridge, 1951).

Steel, D. *National Index of Parish Registers* (vol. 1, 1976).

Stein, M. *Kalhana's Rajatarangini: a Chronicle of the Kings of Kashmir* (2 vols., 1900).

Stewart, R. (1917) *The Flora of Ladak, Western Tibet* (Int. Scholarly Book Service, Forest Grove, repr. 1978 of 1917).

Stewart, R. (1967) 'Plant Collectors in West Pakistan and Kashmir', *Pakistan Journal of Forestry* (July 1967), 337.

Stewart, R. (1982) *History and Exploration of Plants in Pakistan and adjoining areas* (Islamabad, 1982).

Stirling, Manuscript Journal (387F) and 'An account of the accidents which befell Mr. Moorcroft and the Party with him in Turkestan as given by Laskaree Khan one of his servants', from the papers of Edward Stirling in the archives of the Royal Geographical Society, London.

Stirling, E. *Some Considerations on the Political State of the intermediate Countries between Persia and India with reference to the project of Russia marching an army through them* (1835).

Strachey, H. *Physical Geography of Western Tibet* (1854).

Styles, S. *The Forbidden Frontiers. The Survey of India from 1765 to 1949* (1970).

Summerson, J. *Georgian London* (1970).

Sutton, C. *List of Lancashire Authors* (Manchester, 1876).

Tallis, J. *London Street Views* (1839).

Taplin, W. *The Sporting Dictionary and Rural Repository* (2 vols., 1803).

Taylor, I. 'The court and cellar dwelling: the eighteenth century origin of the Liverpool slum', *Transactions of the Historical Society of Lancs. and Cheshire* 122(1970), 67.

Terway, V. *East India Company and Russia 1800–57* (Delhi, 1977).

Thackeray, W. *Roundabout Papers* (1911).

Thomas, J. *Lippincott's Universal Pronouncing Dictionary of Biography and Mythology* (vol. 2, 1911).

Thompson, E. *The Making of the Indian Princes* (1943).

Thompson, F. (1970) 'Victorian England: the horse drawn society', Inaugural Lecture, Bedford College London, 1970.

Thompson, F. (1976) 'Nineteenth Century Horse Sense', *Economic History Review* 2nd ser. 29(1976), 60.

Thompson, R. d'Arcy. *The Remarkable Gamgees* (Edinburgh, 1974).

Thorn, W. *Memoir of the War in India conducted by General Lord Lake . . . 1803–06* (1818).

Trebeck, Copy letters of George Trebeck to Captain Joseph Leeson, in the archives of the Royal Geographical Society, London.

Trénard, L. 'The social crisis in Lyons on the eve of the French Revolution', in ed. J. Kaplow, *New Perspectives on the French Revolution* (New York, 1965).

Twining, W. 'On worm in the eye of the horse', *Transactions of the Medical and Physical Society of Calcutta* 1(1825), 345.

Valentia, G. *Voyages and Travels to India, Ceylon, the Red Sea . . . 1802–06* (3 vols, 1809).

Valli, E. *Experiments on Animal Electricity, with their Application to Physiology* (1793).

Vambéry, A. *Travels in Central Asia* (1864).

Victoria. History of the Counties of England: Lancashire (8 vols, 1906–14).

Vigne, G. (1840) *A Personal Narrative of a visit to Ghuzni, Kabul and Afghanistan* (1840).

Vigne, G. (1842) *Travels in Kashmir, Ladak, Iskardo* (2 vols, 1842).

Vogel, J. (1909) *Catalogue of the Bhuri Singh Museum at Chamba* (Calcutta, 1909).

Vogel, J. (1947) 'Portrait Paintings in Kangra and Chamba', *Artibus Asiae* 10(1947), 200.

Voisard, P. *Histoire de l'École vétérinaire de Lyon pendant la periode révolutionnaire 1792–99* (Lyons, 1932).

Wade, C. *A Narrative of the Services, military and political, of Lt. Colonel Sir C. M. Wade 1809–44* (Ryde, IOW, 1847).

Wakefield, T. *Merchant and Tradesman's General Directory* (1794).

Walford, E. *Old and New London* (vol. 4, 1794).

Wallace, J. *General and Descriptive History of Liverpool* (Liverpool, 1795).

Wallich, N. (1828) *Catalogue of Indian Plants: a numerical list of dried specimens of Plants of the East India Company's Museum* (1828).

Wallich, N. (1832) *Plantae Asiaticae Rariores* (3 vols, 1830–2).

Wathen, J. *Journal of a voyage in 1811 and 1812 to Madras and China* (1814).

Watson, F. (1959–60) 'A pioneer in the Himalayas: William Moorcroft', *Geographical Magazine* 32(1959–60), 204.

Watson, F. (1960) 'The Passion of William Moorcroft', *The Listener* 11 Feb. 1960, 260.

Watson, J. Steven *The Reign of George III, 1760–1815* (Oxford, 1960).

Watt, G. *Dictionary of Economic Products* (6 vols, Calcutta 1889–96).

Wessels, C. *Early Jesuit Travellers in Central Asia, 1603–1721* (The Hague, 1924).

West, G. *A History of the Overseas Veterinary Services* (2 vols, 1961–73).

Western, J. 'The Volunteer Movement as an anti-revolutionary force, 1793–1801', *English Historical Review* 71(1956), 603.

Westminster, Ratebooks of the City of Westminster at the Westminster Public Library, London.

Wheatley, H. *London Past and Present* (vol. 2; 1891).

White, A. and Martin, E. 'A Bibliography of Volunteering', *Society for Army Historical Research* 23(1945), 2.

White, J. (1802) *A Compendium of the Veterinary Art* (Canterbury, 1802).

White, J. (1815) *A Treatise on Veterinary Medicine* (4 vols, 1815).

Williams, G. *The Age of Agony . . . 1700–1800* (1975).

Wilson, H. (1825) 'Travels beyond the Himalaya', *Quarterly Oriental Magazine* 3(1825), 103 and 285 and 4(1825), 126 and 285.

Wilson, H. (1843) 'Travels beyond the Himalaya by Mir Izzet Ullah', *Journal of the Royal Asiatic Society* 7(1843), 283.

Wolff, J. (1835) *Researches and Missionary Labours among the Jews, Mohammedans and other sects* (1835).

Wolff, J. (1845) *Narrative of a Mission to Bokhara in the years 1843–45* (2 vols, 1845).

Wolff, J. (1861) *Travels and Adventures of the Rev. Joseph Wolff* (1861).

Wood, J. *A Personal Narrative of a Journey to the Source of the River Oxus* (1872).

Woodman, D. *Himalayan Frontiers: a political review of British, Chinese, Indian and Russian rivalries* (1969).

WVC Archives of the Westminster Volunteer Cavalry in the custody of the Royal Green Jackets Territorial and Volunteer Trust, London.

Yates, W. *Map of the County of Lancashire, 1786* (facsimile reprint, Liverpool, 1968).

Youatt, W. *The Horse, its breeds, management and diseases* (1857).

Young, A. (1770) *A six months tour through the north of England* (4 vols, 1770).

Young, A. (1794) *Travels during the years 1787, 1788 and 1789 [in] . . . France* (2 vols, 1794).

SOURCES AND ACKNOWLEDGEMENTS FOR ILLUSTRATIONS

(where abbreviated references are given, see List of Sources)

Plates (between pages 242–3)   *Plate*

Sikh or Kangra painting inscribed in Nagari characters 'Morkraft'; by permission of the Director, Lahore Museum.   I

Church Street, Ormskirk by an unknown artist; by permission of the Editor, *Ormskirk Advertiser.*   II

John Hunter by J. Jackson after Reynolds (NPG 77); by permission of the Trustees, National Portrait Gallery, London.   III

Lime Street, Liverpool in 1797, from W. G. Herdman *Pictorial Relics of Ancient Liverpool* (II 1878); by permission of the Liverpool City Libraries.   IV

Edward Coleman by an unknown artist from F. Smith (1919–33) III; by permission of Bailliere, Tindall.   V

George Saunders by Sir Francis Chantrey (NPG 316a [106]); by permission of the Trustees, National Portrait Gallery, London.   VI

Francis Augustus, 2nd Baron Heathfield, by J-L Agasse in the Royal Collection; by permission of the Lord Chamberlain, St James's Palace, London.   VII

Moorcroft's Horseshoe Machine redrawn from *Patent* 2398 of 3.5.1800; by permission of the Controller, Her Majesty's Stationery Office.   VIII

A party of horse merchants from Afghanistan and Persia, Company School, circa 1850 (1966, 10-10, 08, Location LXVIII, Dept. of Oriental Antiquities); by permission of the Trustees, British Library, London.   IX

The Hur Hur Chittur Fair at Hajipur, 1809, a Company Drawing (*IOL* Add Or 15); by permission of the Trustees, British Library, London.   X

Gilbert Elliot, 1st Earl of Minto by J. Atkinson (NPG 836); by permission of the Trustees, National Portrait Gallery, London.   XI

Francis Rawdon-Hastings, 1st Marquess of Hastings by an unknown artist, circa 1800 (NPG 2696); by permission of the Trustees, National Portrait Gallery, London.   XII

Horace Hayman Wilson by an unknown artist (NPG 2748); by permission of the Trustees, National Portrait Gallery, London.   XIII

The Abbé Huc from S. Hedin (1910–13) II; by permission of the Macmillan Press Ltd.   XIV

The pavilion and plaque in the Shalimar Gardens, Lahore; photographed by the author.   XV, XVI

Acknowledgements

	Plate
Lithograph from Trebeck's drawing of Leh from Moorcroft and Trebeck II; by permission of John Murray (Publishers) Ltd.	XVII
Moorcroft and Hearsey in Tibet in 1812 by Hyder Hearsey (*IOL* WD350); by permission of the Trustees, British Library, London.	XVIII

Line Drawings — Page

	Page
North front of Liverpool Infirmary in 1786; based on Enfield.	1
West wing of Lyons Veterinary School in 1790; based on drawing in the Bibliothèque Nationale copied by Reymann.	14
London Veterinary College in the 1790s; based on F. Smith (1919–33) III.	25
Moorcroft's Oxford Street house and horse-practice in the 1830s; based on Tallis.	42
Private soldier of the Westminster Volunteer Cavalry; based on Rowlandson.	53
East Indiaman like the *Indus*; based on the *Lady Kennaway*, National Maritime Museum, London.	70
English cavalry charger; based on J. Walsh, *The Horse in the Stable and the Field* (1862).	82
Bleeding a horse; based on J. Lupton, *Mayhew's Illustrated Horse Management* (1896).	94
The British Residency at Lucknow before 1857; based on C. Ball, *History of the Indian Mutiny* (n.d.).	107
Shawl goat; based on 1779 painting by Zayn ul Din (I.S. 51–1963) in the Victoria and Albert Museum, London.	120
Lake Manasowara and Mount Kailas; based on S. Hedin (1917–23) IV.	135
Hearsey's sketch of Moorcroft and himself bound by the Gurkhas; based on Hearsey.	157
Examining a horse for lameness; based on J. Lupton, *Mayhew's Illustrated Horse Management* (1896).	179
Equine neurotomy; based on E. Mayhew, *The Illustrated Horse Doctor* (1861).	192
View from the summit of the Gogger Pahar; based on H. Bellew, *Views in India* (1833).	209
Maharaja Ranjit Singh in the 1830s; based on Mohan Lal, *Life of the Amir Dost Mohammed* (2 vols, 1846).	224
Raja Sansar Chand and his son in 1796; based on a painting given to Moorcroft and now in the Victoria and Albert Museum, London (I.S. 173–1950).	242
Tikse, a typical monastery-village in Ladakh; based on S. Hedin (1910–13) I.	256
Sindh valley, Kashmir, from near the summit of the Zoji-la; based on W. Conway, *Climbing in the Karakoram Himalayas* (1894).	274
Srinagar, capital of Kashmir; ditto.	293
Great Buddhas and cliff caves at Bamian, Afghanistan; based on A. Burnes (1834) II.	310
Atma Ram, chief minister of Murad Beg; based on J. Rattray, *The costumes of the various tribes . . . of Afghanistan* (1848).	329
Entrance to the Ark, Bokhara; based on G. Curzon, *Russia in Central Asia* (1889).	344
Andkhoi, Afghanistan, in 1886; based on a wash drawing by Sir Edward Durand (WD462) in the India Office Library, London.	361

INDEX

Every entry in this selective index may be read as if followed by 'Moorcroft and'. Only personal characteristics appear under the entry Moorcroft, William. Place-names are excluded throughout. Entries in italic indicate an illustration.